D0944099

THE UNIVERSAL
STANDARD
ENCYCLOPEDIA

BASKETS AND POTTERY OF THE AMERICAN INDIAN

1, trinket basket, Tulare Indian Reservation, California; 2, 3, and 6, pottery from ancient Arkansas mounds; 4, basket of Louisiana Indians; 5, Pueblo water jar.

THE UNIVERSAL STANDARD ENCYCLOPEDIA

VOLUME 12

HANUKKAH—IDAHO

An abridgment of The New Funk & Wagnalls Encyclopedia
prepared under the editorial direction of
JOSEPH LAFFAN MORSE, Sc.B., LL.B.
Editor in Chief

UNICORN PUBLISHERS, INC., NEW YORK

THE UNIVERSAL
STANDARD
ENCYCLOPEDIA

LIST OF ABBREVIATIONS USED

abbr., abbreviated
A.D., Anno Domini
alt., altitude
A.M., ante meridiem
anc., ancient
approx., approximately
Ar., Arabic
AS., Anglo-Saxon
A.S.S.R., Autonomous Soviet Socialist Republic
at.no., atomic number
at.wt., atomic weight
b., born
B.C., before Christ
b.p., boiling point
B.T.U., British Thermal Unit
Bulg., Bulgarian
C., centigrade, syn. Celsius
cent., century
Chin., Chinese
cm., centimeter
Co., County
colloq., colloquial
cu., cubic
Czech., Czechoslovakian
d., died
Dan., Danish
Du., Dutch
E., east, easterly, eastern
ed., edition
e.g., for example
Egypt., Egyptian
Eng., English
est., estimated
et seq., and following
F., Fahrenheit
fl., flourished
fr., from
Fr., French
ft., foot

Gael., Gaelic
Gen., General
Ger., German
Gr., Greek
Heb., Hebrew
Hind., Hindustani
Hon., Honorable
h.p., horsepower
hr., hour
Hung., Hungarian
I., Island
i.e., that is
in., inch
Ind., Indian
Ir., Irish
It., Italian
Jr., junior
kg., kilogram
km., kilometer
lat., latitude
Lat., Latin
lb., pound
lit., literally
long., longitude
m., mile
M., Middle
min., minute
M.L., Medieval Latin
mm., millimeter
mod., modern
m.p., melting point
M.P., Member of Parliament
m.p.h., miles per hour
Mt., Mount, Mountain
N., north, northerly, northern
N.T., New Testament
OE., Old English
OF., Old French
OHG., Old High German
ON., Old Norse

ONF., Old Norman French
O.T., Old Testament
oz., ounce
Phil., Philippine
P.M., post meridiem
Pol., Polish
pop., population
Port., Portuguese
prelim., preliminary
pron., pronounced
q.v., which see
R., River
rev., revised, revision
Rev., Reverend
Rom., Romanian
Russ., Russian
S., south, southerly, southern
sec., second
Skr., Sanskrit
Sp., Spanish
sp.gr., specific gravity
sq., square
S.S.R., Soviet Socialist Republic
Sum., Sumerian
Sw., Swedish
syn., synonym
temp., temperature
trans., translation, translated
Turk., Turkish
U.K., United Kingdom
U.N., United Nations
U.S., United States
U.S.A., United States of America
U.S.S.R., Union of Soviet Socialist Republics
var., variety
W., west, westerly, western
yd., yard

Note.—The official abbreviations for the States of the Union are used throughout. For academic degrees, see article DEGREE, ACADEMIC. Other abbreviations or contractions are self-explanatory.

HANUKKAH (Heb., "dedication"), an annual Jewish festival celebrated on eight successive days beginning on the 25th day of Kislev, the third month of the Jewish calendar, corresponding, approximately, to December in the Gregorian calendar. Also known as the Festival of Lights, Feast of Dedication, and Feast of the Maccabees, Hanukkah commemorates the rededication to Yahweh (q.v.) of the Temple of Jerusalem by Judas Maccabæus in 165 B.C., after the Temple had been profaned by Antiochus VI Epiphanes,

An 18th-century Polish Hanukkah candelabrum

King of Syria and overlord of Palestine. A principal feature of the celebration is the lighting of candles, one being added each night until a special, eight-branched candelabrum is completely filled and lit.

In 168 B.C., on a date corresponding to Dec. 25 in the Gregorian calendar, the Temple was dedicated to the worship of Zeus Olympius by order of Antiochus. An altar to Zeus was set up on the high altar of burnt offerings. When Judas Maccabæus recaptured Jerusalem three years later, he had the Temple purged and a new altar put up in place of the desecrated one. The Temple was then rededicated to Yahweh with festivities that lasted eight days. According to Talmudic tradition, only one cruse of pure olive oil, blessed by the high priest and necessary for the ritual, could be found, but that small quantity burned miraculously for eight days. The succession of eight candles commemorates the miracle. Modern historical opinion holds that both the profanation and rededication took place in Dec. 25, of 168 B.C. and 165 B.C. respectively, a day on which Syrians and Jews may have celebrated the winter solstice by kindling lights. The legend of Hanukkah is told in the Apocryphal books of the Old Testament entitled Maccabees. See MACCABEES.

HANUMAN (Skr. *Hanumant,* "having large jaws"), a monkey god, celebrated in Hindu mythology and the legends of the epic period of India, and still a favorite divinity in Hindustan. Hanuman, the friend of the legendary hero Rama, is the subject of many stories in the Sanskrit epic, the *Ramayana.* His mother was a celestial nymph, forced by a magic spell to assume a simian shape; his father was the god of the wind, and hence Hanuman is sometimes called Marut, a child of the wind. Hanuman's monkey jaw is explained by the following legend. Angered at his youthful prowess, the god Indra tried to slay him with a thunderbolt, but was able only to break his jaw. Thereafter he was known as Hanuman, from the monkey-like aspect of his dislocated jaw.

HANYANG, a city of Hupeh Province, China, situated at the junction of the Yangtze and Han rivers, opposite Hankow and Wuchang (see WUHAN). Hanyang has extensive iron and steel works, and ranks among the leading textile-manufacturing centers of China. Because of its strategic site, the town became an important military post in early times and subsequently figured in numerous wars and revolutions. During the Taiping Rebellion (1852–64), most of Hanyang was destroyed. Recovery and reconstruction began in 1889, when the city was selected as the site of a modern iron and steel plant and other industrial enterprises. Pop., about 450,000.

HAPHTARAH (Heb. *haphtārāh*, "conclusion"), one of the fifty-four sections from the Prophets (Nebiim), recited in the Jewish synagogue on Sabbaths, after the reading of the *parashoth*, or lessons from the Torah (q.v.).

HAPSBURG, or (Ger.) HABSBURG, the name of a noble and royal German family which, at various periods in European history, was the ruling house of Germany, as a separate kingdom as well as a part of the Holy Roman Empire, and of Austria, Bohemia, Hungary, Spain, and many small or independent European realms.

The founder of the family, as far as can be ascertained, was Guntram the Rich (d. 950), a German count; the family name derived from its ancestral seat, the Castle of Habsburg, or Habichtsburg (Eng., "Hawk's Castle"), situated on the Aar R. in Aargau, now a canton of N. Switzerland. The castle was built in 1028 by Guntram's descendant, Werner, Bishop of Strasbourg, whose nephew, Werner I (d. 1096), was the first to call himself Count of Hapsburg. The countship descended in a direct line to Werner I's great-grandson, Albert the Rich (d. 1199), who greatly increased the family estates in Alsace by the addition of extensive domains in Switzerland. Albert's son, Rudolph the Old (d. 1232), added to the Hapsburg riches by acquiring the countships of Laufenburg and Aargau. On Rudolph's death, his sons, Albert the Wise and Rudolph the Younger, divided the family possessions. Rudolph, who received Laufenburg, founded the house of Hapsburg-Laufenburg, which became extinct in the direct male line in 1415; most of the family possessions reverted to the elder branch, known as the Hapsburg-Hapsburg line. This branch, comprising the descendants of Albert the Wise, gave the House of Hapsburg its historical fame, beginning with Albert's son, Rudolf I (1218–91), who was elected king of Germany and Holy Roman emperor in 1273. (For data concerning most of the Hapsburg rulers, from and including Rudolph I, see articles under their names; see also, below, the countries which they ruled.) The direct male Hapsburg line became extinct in 1740 with the death of Holy Roman Emperor Charles VI; the family thenceforth descended in the female line, beginning with Charles's daughter, Archduchess Maria Theresa of Austria, who, by her marriage to Francis Stephen, Duke of Lorraine (Francis

I of the Holy Roman Empire), founded the House of Hapsburg-Lorraine, the imperial house of Austria-Hungary. Among the more famous members of the Hapsburg-Lorraine line, other than Austrian rulers, are Marie Antoinette, wife of Louis XVI of France, and Maria Luisa, wife of Napoleon I, both daughters of Francis I and Maria Theresa; and Maximilian I, Emperor of Mexico.

GERMANY. Rudolph I, King of Germany and Holy Roman Emperor (reigned 1273–91); Albert I, King of Germany (reigned 1298–1308) and Duke of Austria (1282–1308); Albert II, King of Germany and Holy Roman Emperor (reigned 1438–39). Beginning with Albert II, all the Holy Roman emperors (except Charles VII and Francis I) were Hapsburgs, those ruling from 1765 to the end of the Empire in 1806 being of the House of Hapsburg-Lorraine. See HOLY ROMAN EMPIRE.

BOHEMIA AND HUNGARY. In 1526 Holy Roman Emperor Ferdinand I was elected king of Bohemia and Hungary, which he claimed by right of his marriage to Anna, the daughter of Ladislas II, King of Bohemia and Hungary. From 1526 the thrones of these two countries became hereditary possessions of the Hapsburg archduchy of Austria, which later (1804) became the empire of Austria-Hungary (q.v.).

AUSTRIA. During the first centuries the duchy of Austria existed as an entity; it was nominally at the disposal of the Holy Roman Empire. Emperor Rudolf I dispossessed Duke Ottokar II in 1278 and, five years later, invested his sons, Albert and Rudolf, with princely titles and the duchy, jointly. Under Frederick III the domain became an archduchy (1453), and the succession was made hereditary in the Hapsburg line, and, from 1740, in the Hapsburg-Lorraine dynasty, the last monarch of which was Charles I (1916–18).

SPAIN. Philip I, son of Holy Roman Emperor Maximilian I, married Juana, daughter and heiress of Ferdinand and Isabella, joint rulers of Spain; on their death in 1504, he became king. The Spanish Hapsburgs included Charles I (Charles V as Holy Roman Emperor), Philip II, Philip III, Philip IV, and Charles II. The death of Charles II in 1700 gave the throne to Philip V, first of the Bourbon kings of Spain.

OTHER POSSESSIONS. Hapsburg dominions, either as part of large monarchies or as independent territories, have included Naples, Sicily, Sardinia, Milan, Mantua, Parma, and

Piacenza, in Italy; Franche-Comté and Burgundy, in France; and the Netherlands.

HAPTOTROPISM. See TROPISM.

HARA, TAKASHI (1854–1921), Japanese statesman, born in Morioka. He studied law and was a journalist before he entered the Japanese diplomatic service in 1886 as chargé d'affaires in Paris. Between 1886 and 1906 he held important diplomatic and political posts and was also editor in chief successively of two Osaka newspapers; he was minister to Korea in 1896–97 and minister of communications in 1900–01. In 1900 he became the principal organizer of the Seiyukai or liberal party, which soon became strong in Japan. After 1906 Hara gave up journalism entirely. He served as minister for home affairs in a number of cabinets and in 1918 became prime minister of Japan, the first commoner to hold this office. Although he was the leader of a liberal party, his administration was on the whole conservative in policy. His cabinet was formed on the model of cabinets of Western Europe, being drawn from members of his own party, which had won the general election of 1917 and had a majority in parliament; however, the Hara ministry opposed universal suffrage for Japan and other Western political ideas. Hara was assassinated by an insane youth; his murder is believed to have been without political significance.

HARA-KIRI (Jap., "stomach-cutting"), the Japanese practice of ceremonious suicide by disembowelment, a method originally restricted by custom to noblemen and later adopted by all classes. The practice originated in the Middle Ages, when it was used by warrior noblemen (see SAMURAI) to avoid capture by their enemies. It later developed into a formal method of execution in which a noble, on receiving a message from the emperor that his death was essential to imperial welfare, performed hara-kiri, following a rigidly prescribed ceremony.

In most cases, a richly ornamented dagger accompanied the imperial message, and was used as the suicide weapon. A specified number of days was allotted to the offender for his preparations for the ceremony. A red-carpeted dais was constructed in the offending noble's home or in a temple. At the beginning of the ceremony the nobleman, dressed in ceremonial costume and attended by a group of friends and officials, took his place on the dais. Assuming a kneeling position, he prayed, took the dagger from the representative of the emperor, and publicly avowed his guilt; then, stripping to the waist, he plunged the dagger into the left side of his abdomen, drawing it slowly across to the right side and making a slight upward cut. At the final moment a friend or kinsman severed the suicide's head with a sword. The bloodstained dagger was then usually sent to the emperor as proof of the offender's death by hara-kiri. If the offender committed voluntary hara-kiri, that is, because of his own guilty conscience rather than by order of the emperor, his honor was considered restored and his entire estate went to his family; if hara-kiri had been ordered by the emperor, half of the suicide's property was confiscated by the state. Hara-kiri as an obligatory form of execution for members of the nobility was officially abolished about the middle of the 19th century.

As practiced by persons of all classes, hara-kiri frequently served as a manifestation of devotion to a superior who had died, or as a form of protest against some act or policy of the government. Eventually, the practice became so widespread that in recent years an estimated annual total of 1500 deaths occurred by this method. See BUSHIDO.

HARALD, Kings of Norway. See HAROLD.

HARANOBU, SUZUKI (1718–80), Japanese figure painter and designer of wood-block prints. He was the pupil of Shighenega. One of Haranobu's major contributions to Jap-

"Lovers in the Snow," by Suzuki Haranobu

anese art was his invention of polychrome block printing, the method of using separate blocks for each color in a picture. He also made new and beautiful use of the tall, narrow Kakemonoye scroll, surpassing all his predecessors in his handling of this type of design. Single-figure and group studies of graceful women were his typical subjects. There are prints by him at the Metropolitan Museum of Art, New York, the Boston Museum of Fine Arts, and in many museums in Europe and in the Far East.

HARAR or **HARRAR,** the easternmost province of Ethiopia, bounded on the N. and E. by French Somaliland and British Somaliland, and on the S.E. and S. by former Italian Somaliland and British East Africa. The capital is also called Harar (q.v.). The province comprises a broad, fertile plateau, having an average elevation of about 5000 ft. above sea level. It is renowned for the cultivation of fine coffee. The population is of mixed Hamitic and Semitic descent; Mohammedanism is the prevailing religion. The region is believed to have been settled by Arab immigrants in the 7th century A.D. In 1875 it was occupied by the Egyptians who maintained their control until 1885, when the uprising of the Mahdi (q.v.) in the Sudan forced them to retire. Harar was next ruled by a native emir, or military commander, from whom the area was captured, in 1887, by Menelik, King of Shoa (subsequently Emperor of Ethiopia as Menelik II). In 1891 Harar was taken by the Italians, but again came under Ethiopian control in 1897, following the Italian defeat at Aduwa. See ETHIOPIA.

HARAR, capital of Harar Province, Ethiopia, 184 m. by rail S. of the port of Djibouti, French Somaliland. Harar, a major city of Ethiopia, is surrounded by a high wall, and contains the governor's palace, foreign consulates, an Abyssinian church, and a number of mosques. The city lies in a fertile district, the chief agricultural product of which is coffee; other products of the area are cotton, fruit, and gum. The city also has a flourishing trade in camels, cattle, and mules. Harar was founded by the Arabs in the 7th century A.D. Pop. (1948 est.) 40,000.

HARATIN, or HARRATIN, a Berber people, living in oases of the Sahara Desert and on the southern slopes of the Atlas Mountains. They are known as "black" Berbers, their dark complexions probably being due to intermarriage with Negroes, but they are physically of the Berber (q.v.) type. Their social organization is tribal and patriarchal.

HARBIN, a city of Kirin Province, China, on the Sungari R., about 250 miles N.W. of Vladivostok and about 220 miles N.N.E. of Mukden. The second-largest city (after Mukden) of the North-Eastern Provinces (Manchuria), Harbin is a flourishing commercial center, situated in the heart of a rich agricultural region. The city is served by five railway lines, which provide direct connections with all major points in N.E. Asia, and by inland water carriers operating on the Sungari and its affluents. Besides an extensive trade in grain, soybeans, sugar, tobacco, lumber, furs, leather, and woolen goods, Harbin contains large railway repair shops and numerous manufacturing industries, notably flour-milling and other food-processing enterprises. The commercial importance of Harbin dates from the completion (1901) of the Chinese Eastern Railway, an extension of the Trans-Siberian Railway. Following the subjugation (1931–32) of Manchuria by the Japanese and the establishment of the puppet state of Manchukuo, Harbin became the capital of the newly organized province of Pinkiang. The city remained under the control of Japan until the end of World War II. In April, 1946, during the civil war between the Chinese Nationalists and Communists, Harbin was captured by Communist forces. Pop. (1947 est.) 760,000.

HARBOR, a naturally or artificially protected basin on an ocean, lake, or river in which ships may be anchored or docked without danger from waves or high winds. In the strictest sense the term harbor is confined to the water area of a port, but in general usage it includes the protective breakwaters and jetties and the piers and docks which surround the harbor proper; see BREAKWATER; DOCK. According to their use, harbors may be divided into three types: harbors of refuge, commercial harbors, and naval harbors. A harbor of refuge is a harbor created solely as a temporary haven for ships in storms. Commercial harbors are equipped with docking or other facilities for the loading and unloading of cargo and, usually, with installations for the refueling and repair of ships. Naval harbors contain, in addition to the facilities of the commercial harbor, buildings and equipment for the storage and handling of munitions. A number of large and important harbors such as those of San Francisco and New York in the U.S. and

Southampton in England are both commercial and naval harbors.

Harbors can also be classified in three types according to the ways in which they are protected. Natural harbors are those which have the protection of natural bays, peninsulas, headlands, or offshore islands. Improved harbors are those in which the natural features which afford shelter have been augmented with breakwaters and other works. Artificial harbors are those which are entirely protected by man-made structures.

Natural Harbors. Most of the important natural harbors have been improved to some extent by dredging channels which permit ships of deep draft to use them. Such is the case in New York Harbor, one of the finest natural harbors in the world. Before 1885 the 24-foot-deep natural channel through the sandbanks at the harbor's mouth was entirely adequate for the vessels that used the port. Then, as larger vessels were constructed, it became necessary to deepen the channel and ultimately to cut an artificial channel, the Ambrose channel, to the northeast of the natural one. Both channels now are maintained at a depth of 40 feet by regular dredging. Among the other important natural harbors of the world are those of San Francisco and Boston in the U.S., Southampton and Falmouth in England, Rio de Janiero in Brazil, Kingston in Jamaica, Sydney in Australia, Hong Kong in China, and Bombay in India. During World War II the U.S. Navy made extensive use of the natural harbor facilities afforded by such large Pacific atolls as Kwajalein; see ATOLL.

Improved Harbors. Improved harbors have been constructed in all parts of the world, and are designed to suit the natural topography of the locations. One type of improved harbor has been made by providing a channel entrance to an inland bay or lagoon by means of jetties. The harbors of Charleston, S.C. and Galveston, Texas, are of this type, as are those of Venice in Italy and Durban in South Africa. Many bay and lagoon harbors suffer from the sanding or silting of the entrance channel between the jetties, so that constant dredging becomes a necessity. In some cases the natural building up of a sandbar at the entrance to the harbor has necessitated the complete abandonment of the harbor.

In open bays, or in bays in which the mouth is directly open to prevailing winds and storms, protection can often be given by constructing a single breakwater to guard the harbor mouth. The harbor of Los Angeles is of this type, with single breakwater stretching out from the land to protect the opening to the inner harbor.

Artificial Harbors. On coastlines having no natural shelter, harbors are made by surrounding an area of water with a series of breakwaters to form an artificial bay. The plans of such harbors vary widely but all have at least two breakwaters with the harbor entrance between them. One of the largest completely artificial harbors is that of Buffalo, N.Y., on Lake Erie. Other important harbors of this type include Marseille in France, Port Said in Egypt, Casablanca in North Africa, Naples in Italy, and Trieste on the Adriatic Sea.

History. The earliest artificial harbor works known are those built by the Cretans in about 2000 B.C.; archeologists do not entirely agree on this date. In the 13th century B.C. the Phenicians created the harbors of Tyre and Sidon by building moles or breakwaters. Under Roman rule a large number of harbors were constructed around the Mediterranean Sea, some of which, such as Taranto and Brindisi, are still used.

In the centuries following the fall of the Roman Empire no harbors were made, but the art of harbor engineering was revived in the Middle Ages when sea commerce had become an important source of revenue to the Italian republics. The harbors of Venice and Genoa were begun in this period and in both ports some of the original works still survive. France followed the example of Italy, embanking, protecting, and deepening the mouths of rivers to make such harbors as those of Le Havre, Dieppe, and Dunkirk. The first harbors in England were those built at Hartepool in 1250 and at Arbroath in 1394. In the 16th and 17th centuries a number of harbors were protected with piers and jetties.

In America little was done to improve natural anchorages until the 18th century, when the colonial government made improvements to the more important northeastern harbors such as Boston, New York, and Philadelphia. Under the U.S. Constitution all harbor rights are vested in the Federal Government, and the design, construction, and maintenance of harbors is the responsibility of the U.S. Army Engineers. In many cases cities and States pay for harbor improvements with their own funds, but the work is supervised by the Federal Government.

Federal funds for harbor work are appropriated by Congress in an annual or biennial

River and Harbor Bill. The first regular appropriation made for harbor improvement was $30,000 voted by Congress in 1892 for building public piers in Philadelphia. In a recent year the appropriation for river and harbor work amounted to almost $142,-000,000.

HARBORD, JAMES GUTHRIE (1866–1947), American army officer and business executive, born in Bloomington, Ill., and educated at Kansas State Agricultural College. He enlisted in the U.S. Army in 1889 and was commissioned in 1891. In the Spanish-American War he held the temporary rank of major in the cavalry, and from 1903 to 1914 served in the Philippine Constabulary with the temporary rank of colonel. He served under General John J. Pershing on the Mexican border, and was Pershing's chief of staff in Europe from 1917 to 1918. Later in 1918 he commanded a brigade at Château-Thierry and then an entire division in the Soissons offensive. He was promoted to major general in 1919, and from 1921 to 1922 was deputy chief of staff of the U.S. Army. He left active duty in 1922, and retired with the rank of lieutenant general in 1942. He was president of the Radio Corporation of America from 1923 to 1930, and thereafter chairman of the board until a month before his death.

HARBORING, in criminal law, the act of receiving and retaining a person in violation of the rights of another or of the public. One who knowingly harbors a felon becomes at common law an accessory to the crime; the intentional harboring of one who has committed a misdemeanor is punishable as a conspiracy to defeat justice.

HARBURG-WILHELMSBURG, commune of Hamburg, Germany, situated on the Elbe R., 6 m. by rail s. of the city of Hamburg. The commune was formed by the union in 1927 of the former seaport town of Harburg and the city of Wilhelmsburg. Harburg was originally part of the bishopric of Bremen and in 1297 received a charter as a town. It was annexed by Hanover in 1705 and by Prussia in 1866. Wilhelmsburg was founded in 1333. Products manufactured or processed in the commune are machinery, iron, linseed and palm oils, rubber, chemicals, and jute. After World War II Harburg-Wilhelmsburg was included within the British Zone of Occupation. Pop. (1933) 112,593.

HARCOURT, the name of a noted English Yorkshire family, the principal members of which were the following. **1.** EDWARD (1757–1847), ecclesiastic whose original family name

was Vernon, and who took that of Harcourt in 1831. He was archbishop of York from 1807 to 1847. **2.** SIR WILLIAM GEORGE GRANVILLE VENABLES VERNON (1827–1904), statesman, grandson of the preceding, born in York, and educated at Cambridge University. He was called to the bar in 1854 and became professor of international law at Cambridge in 1869. During the American Civil War he opposed recognition by Great Britain of the Southern States as a belligerent nation. Sir William Harcourt was a member of Parliament from 1868 to 1898; he held many high political offices, and was one of the outstanding leaders of the Liberal Party. He was solicitor general in 1873–74, home secretary from 1880 to 1885, and chancellor of the exchequer in 1886, and again from 1892 to 1895. He was knighted in 1873.

HARDANGER FIORD, a fiord of the Hardanger Fjeld region, Hordaland County, s.w. Norway, extending 114 m. from the sea (70 m. from the fringe of islands at its mouth), and attaining a maximum depth of about 350 fathoms. Many smaller fiords branch off the main inlet, which is itself separated into numerous parts, each having a different name. Waterfalls cascade from the slopes of the mountains which line the fiord. In the areas bordering the Hardanger Fiord are fertile valleys and many small villages. The Hardanger inhabitants preserve traditional customs, dress, and dialect. The Hardanger Fiord and Fjeld are popular with vacationists and tourists.

HARDECANUTE, HARDICANUTE, or HARTHACNUT (1019?–42), King of Denmark (1035–42) and of England (1040–42), the last of the Danish kings of England. The son of Canute II and Emma of Normandy, Hardecanute was in Denmark at the time of his father's death in 1035. His half brother, Harold Harefoot, who was then in England, took control of that country and was acknowledged as King Harold I by the English witan in 1037. The ensuing struggle between the two brothers was ended by Harold's death in 1040. Hardecanute, officially chosen as king by the witan, was unpopular with his subjects and left the control of his realm to his mother and the powerful Earl Godwin. Hardecanute was succeeded by his English half brother, Edward the Confessor.

HARDEN, SIR ARTHUR (1865–1940), English chemist, born in Manchester, and educated in England and Germany. Harden was professor of biochemistry at London University and head of the biochemical department of the Lister Institute. He was known for his researches in enzymes, particularly in alcoholic fermentation (q.v.), and shared the Nobel Prize for chemistry with Hans von Euler-Chelpin (q.v.) in 1929. He was editor of the *Biochemical Journal* after 1912 and was the author of *Alcoholic Fermentation* and *Inorganic Chemistry for Advanced Studies.*

HARDENBERG, BARON FRIEDRICH VON (1772–1801), German poet and novelist, born in Oberwiederstedt (now in Prussian Saxony), and educated at Jena, where he studied philosophy, and at Leipzig and Wittenberg, where he studied law. He wrote under the pen name of Novalis (Lat., "fallow land"), and was one of the founders of the Romantic movement in German literature (see GERMAN LITERATURE: *The Classical and Romantic Period*). He is particularly noted for his lyric poetry and prose, which are characterized by deep religious mysticism (see MYSTICS AND MYSTICISM). His best-known work is his book of poetic prose *Hymnen an die Nacht,* which expresses his sense of bereavement at the death in 1797 of his betrothed, Sophie von Kühn. Among his other poems are *Geistliche Lieder.* Novalis was also the author of two novels, *Heinrich von Ofterdingen* (unfinished) and *Die Lehrlinge zu Sais.*

HARDENBERG, PRINCE KARL AUGUST VON (1750–1822), Prussian statesman, born in Essenroda, Hanover, and educated at the universities of Leipzig and Göttingen. He was at first in the Hanoverian civil service (1779–82) and then in that of Brunswick (1787–90). Subsequently Hardenberg was administrator of the principalities of Ansbach and Bayreuth (1790–91); when these states were annexed by the kingdom of Prussia (1791), he became a Prussian minister of state. In 1795 he was the Prussian plenipotentiary at Basel, Switzerland, where he negotiated the Treaty of Basel between Prussia and France; by this treaty Prussia withdrew from the war it had been waging in alliance with other German states and with Austria against France (War of the First Coalition, 1792–97). Hardenberg was foreign minister of Prussia from 1804 to 1806, and chancellor from 1810 to 1817. In the latter office he gave effect to liberal social, economic, and educational policies, and played a prominent part in the War of Liberation (1813–14) fought by most of Germany against Napoleon (see GERMANY: *History*); his war efforts earned him the title of prince. He was Prussia's chief representative at the Congress of Vienna (1814–15) and the

Norwegian Official Photo
Hardanger Fiord at the town of Ulvik, Norway

conferences in Paris at the end of the Napoleonic wars; both at Vienna and Paris he was diplomatically outmaneuvered by the Austrian statesman Prince Metternich, who in the general postwar settlement in Europe secured for Austria a more advantageous position in German affairs than Hardenberg could obtain for Prussia. In his later years Hardenberg became reactionary in politics and took an active part in the Holy Alliance (q.v.), by means of which Russia, Austria, and Prussia banded together to oppose the rise of political democracy in Europe.

HARDING, CHESTER (1792–1866), American portrait painter, born in Conway, Mass. Originally a cabinet maker, then successively a soldier in the War of 1812, a house painter, a tavern keeper, and a sign painter, he became a self-taught portrait painter. In 1832

President Warren G. Harding

he went to London, where his art proved very popular. After his return to the U.S. he worked in St. Louis, Philadelphia, and Boston, painting portraits of such notables as Daniel Webster, Daniel Boone, General William Tecumseh Sherman, Henry Clay, and Presidents Madison, Monroe, and John Quincy Adams. Some of his pictures are in the Corcoran Gallery, Washington, D.C. An *Autobiography of Chester Harding,* edited by his daughter Margaret White, was published at Boston in 1890.

HARDING, SAINT STEPHEN (about 1048–1134), Christian prelate and cofounder of the Cistercian Order, born in Sherborne, near Dorchester, England. He joined the Benedictine Order at Molesmes, near Dijon, France, and in 1098 he left the Molesmes monastery in company with its abbot St. Robert de Molesmes and twenty other monks. They founded the abbey of Cîteaux (Lat. *Cistercium*), south of Dijon, and adopted, as the rule of the new (Cistercian) order, the Benedictine rule in its original severity. Stephen was elected abbot of Cîteaux in 1110, and founded a number of other monasteries, including that at Clairvaux. He wrote the *Carta Caritatis* (1119), or "Charter of Charity", which remains essentially unchanged as the rule of the Cistercian Order.

HARDING, WARREN GAMALIEL (1865–1923), twenty-ninth President of the United States, born on a farm near Corsica (Blooming Grove), Morrow County, Ohio, and educated at Ohio Central College. He was editor of the college paper and, on leaving school in 1882, taught for a year and then entered the printing trade, becoming first compositor and then pressman. He later became a reporter and editorial writer on the Marion (Ohio) *Star,* and in 1884 purchased this newspaper. He acted as its editor and increased its circulation, and after it had developed into a profitable business, transferred ownership of it to the Harding Publishing Company. He himself became president of this company, but gave many shares of stock to his employees.

Harding was elected Ohio State senator in 1900 and re-elected in 1902, and was elected lieutenant governor in 1904; he was defeated as candidate for governor in 1910. In 1914 Harding ran against his political patron Joseph B. Foraker in the Republican primaries for U.S. senator, and having won the nomination was elected with a plurality of more than 100,000 votes over his Democratic opponent. In the Senate Harding favored protective tariffs and the arming of American merchant ships during World War I; after the war he opposed the entry of the United States into the League of Nations, and advocated reduction of excess-profits taxes. In the National Convention of the Republican Party in 1920, Harding was nominated for the Presidency of the United States on the tenth ballot. He did little traveling, conducting a "front-porch" campaign from his own home. His platform consisted largely of two planks: U.S. isolation from European politics, and specifically from the League of Nations; and a quick return to peacetime economic and political conditions, epitomized as "back to normalcy". His opponent, James M. Cox, advocated continuance of Woodrow Wilson's policies and U.S. entry into the League of Nations. Harding was elected by an enormous majority: more than sixteen million popular votes to nine million, and 404 electoral votes to 127.

The principal international events of Harding's administration were the establishment of peace with Germany, rejection of membership by the United States in the League of Nations (though Harding advocated American participation in the World Court), and the calling of an international conference at Washington to discuss limitation of naval armaments; see WASHINGTON CONFERENCE. In domestic affairs the administration was marked by corruption in office of many Presidential appointees, notably the secretary of the treasury, Albert Bacon Fall (q.v.), who was accused and convicted of having accepted a $100,000 bribe in connection with the leasing of the Teapot Dome and Elk Hills naval oil reserves.

In July, 1923, President Harding undertook a tour of the western States and Alaska. On the return trip he was taken ill at Grant's Pass, Oregon; he was removed to San Francisco where he died August 2.

HARD LABOR, in criminal law, a statutory penalty imposed on convicted offenders as a punishment in addition to the penalty of imprisonment. The type and amount of work comprising hard labor ranges from heavy manual labor, such as the construction of roads, to clerical duties, such as the filing of prison records.

Hard labor as a legally defined penalty was unknown in ancient times and at common law. It was introduced in England in 1706 and, about the same time, in the American colonies. It was conceived as a degrading form of punishment, and was so intended when subsequently included in the United States criminal code and in the criminal codes of the States. Today it is imposed, for the most part, as a punishment for felonies, but also, in some States, for misdemeanors, as, in New York State, for vagrancy and disorderly conduct. Hard labor, however, no longer connotes a shameful punishment; widespread penological reforms, originating in the latter part of the 19th century, have stressed the importance of labor as a means of rehabilitating prisoners, and numerous enactments provide some form of labor for virtually all convicts.

HARDNESS, the ability of a solid substance to resist surface deformation or abrasion. Various interpretations, depending on the usage, are applied to the term. In mineralogy, hardness is defined as the resistance of the smooth surface of a mineral to scratching. A soft surface is scratched more easily than a hard surface; thus a hard mineral, such as diamond, will scratch a soft mineral, such as graphite, and the hard mineral will not be scratched by the soft. The relative hardness of minerals is determined according to the Mohs' scale of hardness. In the Mohs' scale ten common minerals are arranged in order of increasing hardness and are assigned numbers: 1, Talc; 2, Gypsum; 3, Calcite; 4, Fluorite; 5, Apatite; 6, Orthoclase (feldspar); 7, Quartz; 8, Topaz; 9, Corundum; and 10, Diamond. The hardness of a mineral specimen is obtained by determining which mineral in the Mohs' scale will scratch the specimen. Thus, galena, which has a hardness of 2.5, can scratch gypsum and can be scratched by calcite. Although hardness is not synonymous with durability, the hardness of a mineral determines to a great extent its durability; precious gems are harder than quartz and are not scratched and dulled by the finely divided particles of quartz present in dust.

In metallurgy and engineering, hardness is determined by impressing a small ball or cone of a hard material on the surface to be tested, and measuring the size of the indentation. Hard metals are indented less than soft metals. See BRINELL TEST.

Hardness is related to the strength, durability, and toughness of solid substances, and in common usage the term is often extended to include those properties.

HARDWAR UNION (formerly KAPILA), a city of the Saharanpur district, United Provinces of Agra and Oudh, India, situated on the Ganges R. The city, one of the most ancient in India, is the site of the Hari-Ka-Charan, a bathing ghat sacred to Hindus. Thousands of religious pilgrims visit the ghat annually for the purpose of ablution. Pop., about 33,000.

HARDWICKE, EARLS OF. See YORKE, family.

HARDY, THOMAS (1840–1928), English novelist and poet, born in Dorsetshire, and educated in the local schools and later pri-

Thomas Hardy

vately. His father, a builder, apprenticed him early to a local ecclesiastical architect engaged in restoring old churches, and after 1862 he worked for an architect in London. In 1859 he had begun writing verse and essays, and in London, despite his success as an architect, he gave increasing time to his writing. His first short story was published in a London journal in 1865.

He then wrote several novels, and achieved his first popular success with the publication of *Far from the Madding Crowd* (1874); printed anonymously in the *Cornhill Magazine*, this novel was thought by some to be the work of George Eliot, an established literary figure. In the first creative period of his career Hardy wrote the *Return of the Native* (1878), generally regarded as his most powerful and characteristic novel, drawn in somber colors. Among his other works emphasizing character and environment were *The Mayor of Casterbridge* (1886); *Tess of the D'Urbervilles* (1891), possibly his most widely-read novel, and *Jude the Obscure* (1895). At this time also Hardy wrote a group of lesser works which he characterized as romances and fantasies, including *Two on a Tower* (1882) and a *Group of Noble Dames* (1891).

During his second creative period Hardy concentrated on poetry, notably *The Dynasts* (1904–08), an epic poem in three parts. Originally intended to treat of England's role in the Napoleonic Wars, *The Dynasts* developed into a vehicle for Hardy's philosophical views of human nature. Following the publication of two volumes of poems he had written earlier, *Wessex Poems* (1898) and *Poems of the Past and Present* (1901), Hardy, in 1909, as he was entering his seventieth year, turned from fiction to lyrical poetry. His poems, written in unusual and often unpoetic diction and employing unconventional techniques, revealed the same skill, understanding of human nature, and glorification of the commonplace which distinguish his many novels.

Both as a novelist and poet, Hardy devised human situations compounded of irony and tragedy. His reputation as a fatalist rests on his recurring use of the theme of fate as a power before which human beings are helpless; this overpowering fate, personifying nature to a great degree, was for Hardy not only cruel and inexorable, but also indifferent. His feminine characters symbolize the irresponsible and capricious elements in nature, working in various subtle ways toward man's destruction. Hardy's sensitive descriptions of the heath, the village, the fields, the seasons, and even the local changes of weather, are indicative of his concept of man's conflict with nature. His works display little passion except in the portrayal of the villagers of his native Dorsetshire and Wessex, whom he represents as being close to the earth and a source of rustic humor and innate wisdom.

Hardy was the last of the great Victorians (see ENGLISH LITERATURE). Among his works, in addition to those already mentioned, are the novels *Desperate Remedies* (1871), *Under the Greenwood Tree* (1872), *A Pair of Blue Eyes* (1873), and *The Trumpet-Major* (1880); the volumes of short stories *Wessex Tales* (1888) and *Life's Little Ironies* (1894); and several volumes of poetry, including *Time's Laughing Stock* (1909), *Satires of Circumstance* (1914), *Moments of Vision* (1917), *Late Lyrics and Earlier* (1922), *Human Shows, Far Fantasies* (1925), and the posthumous volume *Winter Words* (1928). The latter contains some of his most powerful and original lyrics.

HARE. See RABBIT.

HARE, ROBERT (1781–1858), American chemist, born in Philadelphia. Hare studied privately, acquiring a considerable knowledge of physics and chemistry while he was employed in his father's brewery. In 1801 he invented the oxyhydrogen blowpipe, for which he was awarded the Rumford medal by the American Academy of Arts and Sciences. Hare became professor of chemistry at William and Mary College in 1818 and held the same post at the University of Pennsylvania until 1847. He was the first honorary member of the Smithsonian Institution, where his collection of chemical and physical apparatus is still kept. In addition to his chemical researches, he conducted electrical investigations and constructed the first electric furnace. He wrote *Chemical Apparatus and Manipulations* (1836).

HAREBELL, the common bluebell. See CAMPANULA.

HARELIP, SPLIT LIP, or **CLEFT LIP,** a deformity of the upper or lower lip of a human being, so called because it resembles the notched upper lip of a hare or rabbit. Harelip is caused by failure in the embryological development of the lips (see TERATOLOGY) and is often associated with other deformities, especially cleft palate. Harelip of the upper lip rarely occurs in the center of the lip but usually appears on the left or right side, or both (unilateral or bilateral harelip). Harelip of the lower lip usually appears in the center of the lip. For treatment of harelip, see PLASTIC SURGERY.

HAREM (Ar. *harīm*, "forbidden", "sacred"), in Mohammedan countries, the apartments or portions of a house set aside for the female members of the household, including the wives, concubines, and female relatives and servants of the master of the house. The presence of more than one wife in a harem is comparatively rare, however; although the Koran permits the taking of as many as four wives, the costliness of such a ménage has prevented all but the wealthiest Mohammedans from having large harems. In certain lavish harems, such as that formerly maintained by the Sultan of Turkey, the harem involved a complex organization which included a corps of eunuchs entrusted with the guarding of the women.

About the middle of the 19th century, the influence of European social attitudes on the Mohammedan countries led to a decline in the harem system. By the early 20th century, monogamy had become the rule and harems had almost disappeared. In 1926, the Turkish government ordered the abolition of polygamy and the harem.

HARES, an Indian tribe native to the regions of N.W. Canada which stretch from the Great Bear Lake westward to the Eskimo country. Their language is of the Athapascan linguistic stock.

HARGREAVES, JAMES (?–1778), English inventor and industrialist, born in Standhill, Lancashire. In 1760 he invented, or aided in inventing, a carding machine. The spinning jenny, which Hargreaves is said to have invented in 1764, made possible the automatic production of cotton thread. A spinning mill was erected by Hargreaves in Nottingham in 1768, but he did not patent his machine until 1770. The patent was declared invalidated by the courts because he had sold some of the machines before patenting them. However, Hargreaves achieved moderate success as a yarn manufacturer in competition with other users of the jenny. In spite of opposition by hand workers, spinning became a factory industry and an important part of the factory system in England. See FACTORIES; SPINNING.

HARICOT. See KIDNEY BEAN.

HARI-KARI. See HARA-KIRI.

HARI RUD (anc. *Arius*), river of N. central Afghanistan, rising in the Koh-i-Baba range west of Kabul and flowing west to the Iranian border, thence north, forming successively the border between Afghanistan and Iran and that between Russia and Iran, and finally disappearing in the steppe region south of the Kara Kum desert. In Afghanistan, between Obeh and Kuhsan, the waters of the river are used to irrigate the Herat region, noted for its fertility. While coursing through Russian territory, the river is known as the Tejend or Tedzhen. The total length of the Hari Rud is about 650 m.

HARIVANSHA, the title of a Sanskrit narrative poem, comprising an epilogue to the *Mahabharata* (q.v.). The *Harivansha* is almost entirely an account of the life of the Hindu deity Krishna (q.v.).

HARKNESS, EDWARD STEPHEN (1874–1940), American banker and philanthropist, born in Cleveland, O., and educated at Harvard University. During his business career he acted as a director of many important railroads, but he was best known as a philanthropist. He made donations to many educational institutions and organizations, for social and charitable work, in both America and Europe. Among the institutions to which he contributed were the Metropolitan Museum of Art and the New York Public Library, for which he also acted as trustee; Harvard and Yale universities, at which he was largely responsible for the current systems of houses and dormitories; and Columbia University, at which he founded the Eye Institute at the Medical Center.

Harkness made his most memorable donations in the field of medicine for research, treatment, and education. In 1918, when his mother, Mrs. Anna M. Harkness (1838?–1926), established a foundation known as the Commonwealth Fund, his liberal contribution formed the major part of the endowment. The foundation's assets, which have risen from an original endowment of $10,000,000 to over $50,000,000 at the present time, are used for medical research and education, medical and public health services in rural areas, and mental health services. It also publishes books relating to its supported activities, and grants fellowships to British students for postgraduate work in the U.S. See FOUNDATION.

HARLAN, JOHN MARSHALL (1833–1911), American jurist, born in Boyle County, Ky., and educated at Centre College and Transylvania University, where he studied law. From 1861 to 1863 he served as a colonel in the Union Army. In 1863 he was elected attorney general of Kentucky, a position he held for four years. He took an active part in politics

Collection of Irwin Untermyer

18th-century Dresden china harlequin

and was a Republican candidate for the governorship in 1871 and 1875, but was defeated both times. In 1877 he was appointed to the U.S. Supreme Court by Rutherford B. Hayes. He held office for thirty-four years, and became known as a justice of marked independence and an upholder of popular rights.

HARLEIAN COLLECTION, a valuable collection of manuscripts in the British Museum, consisting of 7639 volumes and 14,236 original rolls, charters, deeds, and other legal documents. The original collection, made by Robert Harley (q.v.), 1st Earl of Oxford, and his son Edward Harley, also contained a large library of books which were sold after the death of Edward Harley. In 1753 the British government purchased the manuscript collection for £10,000, and deposited it in the British Museum. A selection of the rarer tracts and manuscripts in the collection was made by William Oldys (1696–1761) and published, with a preface by Dr. Samuel Johnson, under the title *Harleian Miscellany* (8 vols., 1744–46).

HARLEM, a former village, now a residential and business district of the borough of Manhattan, New York City. The name is generally applied to that part of the borough lying between the East and Harlem rivers and Eighth Avenue north of 106th Street. The section is known as the unofficial capital of the Negro population of the U.S., although there are large Latin-American and Italian population groups residing in the area. The latter groups live E. and N.E. of Central Park, extending to the East R.; the Negro district occupies the remainder of the area. The principal business thoroughfare of Harlem is One Hundred and Twenty-fifth Street, running E. and W., and its widest street is Seventh Avenue, which cuts through the district from N. to S. Housing conditions in most parts of Harlem are notoriously bad, and the community contains extensive slum areas. In recent years a number of housing developments have been erected for low-income residents of Harlem.

The first settlement of Harlem was in 1636, on the site of the present-day Mount Morris Park. In 1658 the village was named New Haarlem by Peter Stuyvesant, the Dutch colonial administrator, after Haarlem, Holland. It retained its character as a Dutch village and a pastoral community for almost two centuries, while the other early Dutch settlement of New Amsterdam became, as New York City, the country's most important commercial center. About 1830 Harlem commenced to develop as a suburb of New York City, and with the arrival of the elevated rapid transit lines in 1880 it reached its peak as a fashionable residential area. The district commenced its development as a great Negro population center during World War I, when many thousands of Negroes came to New York City from the South and the West Indies in search of industrial employment.

The old village of Harlem was described by Washington Irving in his *Knickerbocker's History of New York.*

HARLEQUIN, ARLECCHINO, or ARLEQUIN (Old Fr. *harlekin*, "demon" or "goblin"), a conventional character in the Italian commedia dell' arte (q.v.) of the 16th to 18th centuries and of modern pantomime (q.v.). Harlequin first appeared in 12th-century French folk literature as an invisible, prankish goblin and, as Alichino, was one of the demons mentioned in Dante's *Inferno* (14th century). In the commedia dell' arte he was a clownish, black-masked servant who courted Columbine and who was intended to ridicule the supposedly clownish citizens of Bergamo, Italy. From this original character two characters of modern pantomime have arisen:

Pierrot, the blundering, pathetic figure of French pantomime; and Harlequin, the shaven-headed, motley-dressed clown, represented in pantomime throughout the world. Harlequin's original demonlike character is preserved in the wooden sword he always carries, which, like a wand, enables him to perform miraculous feats. The word "harlequin" has become practically synonymous, in modern usage, with clown or with a motley combination of colors.

HARLEQUIN BUG. See CABBAGE BUG.

HARLEQUIN SNAKE. See CORAL SNAKE.

HARLEY, ROBERT, 1st EARL OF OXFORD (1661–1724), English statesman, born in London. He entered Parliament as a Whig member in 1689, and remained in the House of Commons until his elevation to the nobility in 1711. In 1701 he became speaker of the House, and three years later, through the influence of John Churchill (q.v.), Duke of Marlborough, was made a secretary of state for the northern part of the country. Although Harley was at this time ostensibly a supporter of the Whig ministry, he began to influence Queen Anne against two of her principal ministers, Sidney Godolphin and Marlborough; in 1707 they became suspicious of his activities, and early the next year forced him out of the government.

As a moderate Tory and a critic of the ministry for the costliness of the war with France, Harley gained great popularity. He was successful in influencing public opinion by employing the writers Daniel Defoe and, later, Jonathan Swift as political propagandists. In 1710, when Marlborough and his party lost favor with the Queen, Harley was appointed chancellor of the exchequer. He tried unsuccessfully to form a coalition ministry of both parties, but in 1711 his popularity was entirely restored after a refugee from France attempted to assassinate him. Harley was created Earl of Oxford and Mortimer, and appointed lord treasurer.

He reformed the finances of the country, and in 1713 forced the treaty of Utrecht (see UTRECHT, PEACE OF) through the House of Lords by the creation of twelve new peers. He soon lost his influence with the Queen, and the next year was replaced in office by his former friend Viscount Bolingbroke (q.v.). Harley retired from public life, but in 1715 George I imprisoned him in the Tower of London on suspicion of plotting for the return of the Stuart dynasty. He was released in 1717, and the charges against him were dismissed. Harley, assisted by his son Edward

(1689–1741), spent his last years collecting books and manuscripts. The collection, later named the *Bibliotheca Harleiana,* was purchased by the government in 1753 and given to the British Museum; see HARLEIAN COLLECTION.

HARLINGEN, a city of Cameron Co., Tex., situated 25 miles N.W. of Brownsville, in the lower Rio Grande Valley. The surrounding irrigated agricultural area is noted for the production of citrus fruits, vegetables, cotton, dairy products, and poultry. Harlingen is served by two railroads, and is a shipping point and important wholesale and retail trading center. Among the industrial establishments in the city are cotton gins, cotton compresses, cottonseed-oil mills, fruit and vegetable canneries, packing plants, a frozen-food plant, and factories manufacturing machinery and furniture. Harlingen was founded about 1900 and incorporated as a city in 1910. Pop. (1950) 23,229.

HARMACHIS, in ancient Egyptian mythology, a god of the rising sun. He is one of the many forms of the sun deity Ra (q.v.). He was worshiped at Heliopolis, and represented by the great Sphinx at Gizeh.

HARMATTAN, a dry desert wind that blows along the coast of Upper Guinea, Africa, at times between November and March. The wind blows westward from the interior of northern Africa and is felt over the Atlantic Ocean at a considerable distance from the coast. The wind lowers the humidity of the atmosphere 25 to 50 per cent below normal. All vegetation dries, and the natives use oil to keep their skins from cracking. Clouds of penetrating dust are carried along with the wind, forming a dense haze. The harmattan lasts for several days and, in extreme cases, several weeks. It is called "the doctor" by the natives, because, despite its disadvantages, it brings relief from the damp heat of the previous season. See WIND.

HARMENSEN, JACOB. See ARMINIUS, JACOBUS.

HARMHAB, HOREMHAB, or **HOREMHEB** (d. 1315 B.C.), Pharaoh of Egypt, first ruler of the XIXth Dynasty. Harmhab was an efficient monarch and a noted military leader. He reorganized the administration of Egypt when he came to the throne, and devoted himself to restoring fully the Amen worship which his predecessors, Ikhnaton and Tutankhamen (qq.v.), had attempted to replace with monotheistic sun worship (see EGYPTIAN RELIGION).

HARMODIUS and **ARISTOGITON**, two Athenian citizens, renowned for their great friendship. Hipparchus, the younger brother of the tyrant Hippias, attempted to separate the two friends, and to supplant Aristogiton in the affections of Harmodius. Failing of his purpose, he avenged himself by publicly insulting the sister of Harmodius. Thereupon the two friends formed a plot to murder both Hipparchus and Hippias on the day of the Panathenæa, the most important festival of ancient Athens. The plot proved abortive, however, because Harmodius and Aristogiton prematurely attacked and slew Hipparchus. Harmodius was at once killed by the tyrant's guards; Aristogiton made good his escape, but was later taken and executed. Not long afterward, Hippias was expelled by the Athenians, who thenceforth honored Harmodius and Aristogiton as martyrs to the cause of liberty.

HARMONICA, name of two musical instruments. **1.** The GLASS HARMONICA, invented by Benjamin Franklin in 1763, a series of graduated glass basins fixed on a horizontal spindle which is made to revolve by means of a treadle. The spindle is arranged in a trough of water so that the glasses are kept wet. The sound is produced by touching the fingers to the wet edges. This instrument, popular in the late 18th and the early 19th century, had several pieces composed especially for it by such notables as Mozart (*Adagio in C Major, K. 356,* and *Quintet, K. 617,* for harmonica, flute, oboe, viola, and cello) and Beethoven (in his melodrama *Leonora Prohoska,* 1814). **2.** The MOUTH ORGAN, probably invented in 1871, a small oblong box fitted with a row of air channels, each leading to a small metal reed. Alternating tones of the scale are produced by blowing or suction. This instrument is popular particularly in the U.S., where it is played frequently on the radio.

HARMONICS, a series of subsidiary vibrations which accompany a primary or fundamental vibration, as in the vibrations of a stringed instrument or the oscillations of a tuned electrical circuit. The frequencies of harmonic vibrations are integral multiples of the frequency of the fundamental vibration: if the fundamental has a frequency of 100 cycles per second, the second harmonic has a frequency of 200, the third of 300, and the fourth of 400. Harmonics in music are a class of overtones which bear simple mathematical relationships (such as 1:2, 1:3, or 1:4) to the fundamental.

A stretched string when plucked with a pick or set into vibration with a violin bow will vibrate in several ways. Its fundamental vibration will be that of the whole length of the string vibrating as a unit, but the string will also vibrate in halves, thirds, quarters, and so on, producing the various harmonics, most of which are beyond the range of hearing of the human ear.

Most musical tones and electrical oscillations consist not of one fundamental frequency alone, but of a combination of the fundamental with varying amounts of the harmonics related to the fundamental. The presence and amplitude of the various harmonics determine the quality of the sound and the wave form of the electrical oscillation. A number of devices such as the phonodeik and the cathode ray oscilloscope (q.v.) can be used to obtain a graphic picture of such complex vibrations or oscillations, and their components can be calculated mathematically by means of Fourier's series. See FREQUENCY; PITCH; SOUND; VIBRATION.

HARMONISTS, a 19th-century Protestant religious sect, founded in Germany by George Rapp; its members moved to the United States in 1803 and established the town of Harmony, Pennsylvania. The Harmonists, also called Harmonites and Economites, practiced a cult derived from quietism (q.v.), which included severe asceticism, celibacy, and community ownership of property. The original colony consisted of about 600 members, who called themselves the Harmony Society. Rapp sold the Pennsylvania holdings in 1814 and moved to Indiana, founding the village of New Harmony (q.v.). Although the colonists were industrious and frugal and soon became prosperous, factional disputes arose; the community became divided into several branches, and adventurers took advantage of the Harmonists' credulity to abscond with some of their funds. In 1825 those of the Harmonists who had remained attached to their founder, Rapp, moved back to Pennsylvania, selling their holdings to Robert Owen (q.v.) and establishing a new community at Economy, in Beaver County, near Pittsburgh. The Economy settlement accumulated a fortune of about two million dollars by 1868, but litigation depleted the funds. The Harmonists' practice of celibacy inevitably led to their gradual extinction, only four members of the community surviving in 1903, when the property was sold to a land company. The Harmony Society was formally dissolved in 1906.

HARMONIUM. See ORGAN.

HARMONY, one of the most important branches of musical science, dealing with the structure, relationship, and progression of chords, i.e., two or more tones of different pitch sounded simultaneously.

Evolution of Harmony. The ancient Greeks, who accompanied a melody with its octave above, were probably the first people to make a conscious use of combined tones of different pitch. This phenomenon came as a result of combining boys' voices with men's; the former, unable to sing in the low registers of the men, adjusted their pitch to an octave above. The practice of combining such tones was known as *magadizing,* a term derived from the harplike instrument the *magadis,* which, by means of frets, was capable of producing octaves.

The theoretical writings of the Greeks disclose that they considered the octave, fifth, and fourth as being concordant; and the thirds and sixths as discordant. The use of fifths and fourths did not, however, become a common practice until the 10th century. The manner in which they were used was similar to the way the ancient Greeks used the octave; the melody and its fifth or fourth were used together in parallel motion. This style was known as *organum.*

Greater freedom in the use of octaves, fifths, and fourths came during the 11th century, when two voices were allowed to progress not only in parallel motion, but in contrary motion as well. This practice was a milestone in the evolution of harmony because it made possible, while the voice parts progressed from one concord to another, the use of other intervals (thirds, sixths, seconds, and sevenths).

The next important step in the history of harmony came during the 12th century with the advent of the *fauxbourdon,* the addition of a third voice part to the two-voiced organum which resulted in what is now known as sixth chords. The development of these three-voiced chords continued during the next three centuries, with many variations upon the structure of the three parts, inevitably leading into the use of triads (see TRIAD).

The triad was known as the "perfect chord", and by the end of the 17th century, triad harmony was the basis of common practice, with emergence of the tonic, dominant, and subdominant as the central chords of a composition.

The classical concept of harmony came into being in the 18th century, with the publi-cation of *Traité de l'Harmonie,* by Jean Philippe Rameau (q.v.). This work not only forms the theoretical basis of classical harmony, but is the foundation of harmonic analysis at the present time.

Chord Structure. The triad consists of three types, all based on the various degrees of the major mode (q.v.): major triads, based on the I, IV, and V degrees (tonic, subdominant, and dominant); minor triads, based on the II, III, and VI degrees (supertonic, mediant, and submediant); and the diminished triad, formed on the VII degree, and having a flatted fifth, or tritone (q.v.). In actual practice, other types of triads can be formed by raising or lowering any of the three tones.

The triads can be expanded by the superimposition of thirds, so as to make such combinations as seventh and ninth chords; for example, the major triad C-E-G, by the addition of B♭ or B, becomes a seventh (C-E-G-B♭ or B), and by the addition of D♭ (or D) becomes a ninth chord (C-E-G-B♭-D♭).

Chord Relations and Progressions. All chords within a given mode, having one or more tones in common, are said to be directly related, i.e., C-E-G and G-B-D; and those chords having no common tones are said to be indirectly related, i.e., C-E-G and D-F-A. Progressions from one chord to another are considered logical when they are in direct relation to each other. A chord may therefore move a third or a fifth up or down; i.e., C-E-G may move to E-G-B, to G-B-D, to A-C-E, or to F-A-C. Chord progressions may move in indirect relations, but when there are no tones in common between two connecting chords, smooth movement within the voice parts is much more difficult.

Cadence. A close in a section of music is called a cadence, of which the two most common types are the *authentic* and the *plagal.* A close is considered authentic when the final chord is preceded by its dominant chord; the cadence is plagal when the final chord is preceded by its subdominant.

Modulation. One of the means of obtaining variety in a musical composition is to use different tonalities (see TONALITY) within a composition. In order to make the change smoothly from one key (tonality) to another, a sequence of directly related chords is used. This sequence is called *modulation.* The modulatory factor within the sequence is the *pivot chord,* a chord which is common to the two connecting keys. In modulating from C to B♭, the pivot chord could be F-A-C, which is the IV chord in the key of C and the V chord in the key of B♭. The use of a cadence at the close of a modulating sequence is a very important part of the technique because it emphasizes the entrance into the new key.

HARMONY OF THE SPHERES, or MUSIC OF THE SPHERES, the belief of the Greek philosopher Pythagoras that the distance of the various planets from the earth conformed to the ratio of numbers found in a musical progression, thus producing a harmony in the heavens. See PYTHAGORAS.

HARMSWORTH, ALFRED CHARLES WILLIAM, VISCOUNT NORTHCLIFFE (1865–1922), born in County Dublin, Ireland. From 1882 to 1886 he did freelance work for various publications, and in 1887 he established a general publishing house in London, in association with his brother Harold (1868–1940). Their first successful venture, founded in 1888, was *Answers to Correspondents,* a weekly periodical which later gained wide popularity under the name *Answers.* The profits realized from this and other enterprises enabled the brothers to organize the Amalgamated Press, later the largest periodical-publishing enterprise in the world.

In 1894 Harmsworth purchased the London *Evening News,* organ of the Conservative Party, and within one year carried out a reorganization which converted it from a financial liability into a profitable investment. Two years later he founded *The Daily Mail,* a halfpenny newspaper which introduced a number of journalistic innovations, and which attained a circulation in excess of 1,000,000 by 1900. Another Harmsworth newspaper venture, *The Daily Mirror,* launched in 1903 as a penny paper for women, was at first a financial failure; Harmsworth converted it into a halfpenny illustrated paper, and it quickly became a success. In 1904 he was made a baronet, and in the following year was elevated to the peerage, with the title of Baron Northcliffe. He acquired control of *The Times* in 1908, reorganized and enlarged it, and in 1914 lowered its price to one penny, thereby bringing about a tremendous rise in its circulation. He introduced a number of reforms into newspaper management, notably a five-day week and higher salaries for editorial employees, and a profit-sharing system for key members of his staff.

During World War I Baron Northcliffe conducted several notable press campaigns for the vigorous prosecution of the war. His attacks on the Asquith government played an important role in bringing about the formation of the Lloyd George (q.v.) coalition government during the crisis of 1916. In 1917 he was offered the ambassadorship to the United States, but declined that office, accepting the post of chairman of the British War Mission to the United States. Returning to England in November, 1917, he was created Viscount Northcliffe of St. Peter-in-Thanet. In the following year he served as director of propaganda in enemy countries, and was instrumental in bringing about the agreement between the government of Italy and the Yugoslav authorities which ensured the defeat of the Austrian armies.

In the postwar period, his chief efforts were devoted to the maintenance of amicable relations between England and France, and to a settlement of the Irish problem.

HARNACK, ADOLF VON (1851–1930), German Protestant theologian, born in Dorpat, Russia (now Yurev, U.S.S.R.), and educated at the universities of Dorpat and Leipzig. He was appointed professor extraordinary of church history at the University of Leipzig in 1876, and later held professorships at the universities of Giessen, Marburg, and Berlin. He served as president of the Evangelical Congress from 1902 to 1912, and as director of the Prussian National Library from 1905 to 1921. In 1914 he was elevated to the nobility. Harnack exerted a profound influence on modern Protestant theology; he advocated free criticism of church dogma, and sought to dissociate Christianity from early Greek philosophical influences. His writings include *Lehrbuch der Dogmengeschichte* (4 vols., 1886–90), *Das Wesen des Christentums* (1900), *Marcion* (1921), and *Briefsammlung des Apostel Paulus* (1926).

HARNESSED ANTELOPE. See BOSCHBOK.

HARNETT, WILLIAM MICHAEL (1848–92), American still-life painter, born in County Cork, Ireland, and brought to America as an infant. He engraved silverware for a living until 1875, when he began to devote his entire time to painting. Harnett is known chiefly for his remarkably realistic or *trompe d'oeil* still lifes. Though celebrated in his lifetime, his name faded into obscurity after his death; he has recently been exhibited as a "rediscovery". In his work Harnett combined a meticulous realism with an arbitrary juxtaposition of unrelated objects, producing an effect similar to that obtained by certain modern Surrealist painters. His work is now represented in a number of American museums.

HAROËRIS. See HORUS.

HAROLD I, known as HAROLD HAREFOOT (?–1040), King of England from 1037 to 1040, illegitimate son of Canute II (q.v.). At the death of his father he claimed the English crown, despite Canute's designation of Hardecanute (q.v.), Harold's legitimate half brother, as the successor. In 1037 the English witan decided to compromise the rival claims by giving Mercia and Northumbria to Harold and Wessex to Hardecanute. Wessex, however, surrendered to Harold and he was crowned king of all England. His reign was oppressive and marked by continual struggle with Hardecanute.

HAROLD II (1022?–66), King of England (Jan. 6–Oct. 14, 1066), last of the Saxon rulers. The second son of Godwin, Earl of Wessex, Harold was made earl of East Anglia through his father's influence in 1045. In 1051, when Godwin lost the favor of King Edward the Confessor, and was exiled with his sons, Harold took refuge in Ireland, where he raised an army and harried the English coast. William, Duke of Normandy, visited England in 1052, and the witenagemot, uneasy because William was known to covet the English throne, restored the family of Godwin to its lands and titles in order to strengthen the security of the country. A year later, Harold succeeded his father as earl of Wessex, becoming chief minister to the king and the most powerful man in the realm. Through his efforts, the warlike Welsh were subdued in 1063 and several of the discontented English earls, who threatened the power of the monarchy, were conciliated. However, a revolt of the Northumbrians against Harold's brother Tostig, earl of that domain, caused Harold to banish Tostig, keeping the peace but making a bitter enemy.

In 1063, while sailing in the English Channel, Harold was shipwrecked on the coast of Normandy and captured by Duke William. In order to secure his release, the English lord was forced by William to swear on a chest of holy relics (Harold later claimed he was ignorant of their nature) that he would aid William to obtain the crown of England. On the strength of his oath, Harold was permitted to return to England. When King Edward was dying, in 1066, he recommended that the throne be awarded to Harold, whom the witenagemot elected and crowned. William immediately asserted his claim, which was supported by the dispossessed Tostig and Harold III of Norway, who had become Tostig's ally. Tostig and the Norwegian king invaded Yorkshire and, after several military

successes, were routed by the English forces at Stamford Bridge (Sept. 25, 1066). About the same time William landed in England with his army and engaged the English in battle at Senlac (see HASTINGS, BATTLE OF). The defeat and death of Harold II in the battle made the Duke of Normandy undisputed ruler of England.

HAROLD or **HARALD,** the name of three kings of Norway.

1. HAROLD I, called THE FAIRHAIRED (850?–933), king from 860 to 930, the first ruler to unite all Norway into a single dominion. He succeeded his father, Halfden the Swarthy, as ruler of several small kingdoms in southern Norway. According to a Norse saga, Harold's beloved, Gyda, the daughter of a neighboring king, refused to wed him unless he should become king of all Norway. He therefore waged continual war against the other petty rulers until, in 872, he defeated a general confederacy of Norwegian chieftains in a naval battle at Hafrsfjord and became lord of the entire kingdom. As a result of his conquest, many of the lesser kings left Norway and founded Viking colonies on the heretofore uninhabited islands of the Orkneys, Hebrides, Shetlands, and Faeroes. These Vikings harried the Norwegian coast so effectively that Harold was forced to send an expedition against them. The success of the expedition caused a second large migration; many Vikings fled to Iceland, which became an independent Viking commonwealth, and others founded Normandy on the coast of France. Harold established a strong kingdom, but his later reign was disturbed by strife between his sons. When he became old, the king abdicated in favor of his favorite son, Eric Bloodaxe, who ruled from 930 to 934, when he was deposed by his half-brother Haakon (q.v.).

2. HAROLD II, called GRAYFELL, king from 961 to 970, the son of Eric Bloodaxe. Harold and his brothers ruled Norway until 970, when Earl Haakon, a feudal vassal, killed Harold and seized control of the kingdom.

3. HAROLD III, called HARD RULER, king from 1047 to 1066, a descendant of Harold I. He took part in the battle of Stiklestad (1030), fighting with his half brother, King Olaf of Norway, against Norwegian rebels aided by Denmark. When his brother was killed, Harold was forced to flee. During the course of his travels, in the next fourteen years, he visited several Russian cities and, in 1033, entered the service of the Empress Zoë of Byzantium, becoming head of the Varangian guards. His exploits in the Medi-

Metronome

Harpist playing a modern harp

terranean are described in many Norse sagas. Harold returned to Norway in 1046 and his nephew, Magnus the Good, then king, gave him half the kingdom in return for half the treasure Harold had amassed in the East. At the death of Magnus, a year later, Harold became sole ruler. He warred against the Danes until 1064. In 1066 he joined Tostig, Earl of Northumbria, in warfare against Tostig's brother, Harold II of England. However, in the battle of Stamford Bridge, in England, the Norwegian king was killed.

HAROUN-AL-RASCHID. See HARUN-AL-RASHID.

HARP, a stringed musical instrument triangular in shape played by plucking the strings with the fingers of both hands. The strings are stretched between two sides of the frame; one of these sides contains a sounding board and the other has the wrest pins by which the strings are tuned.

The harp is among the oldest of musical instruments; harps were in use in Mesopotamia at least as early as 3000 B.C. A large standing harp was in use in Egypt at least as early as 1200 B.C., and was depicted on the tomb of Ramses III. Harps were little used in classical times, the Greeks and Romans

preferring such related instruments as the lyre. The harp of medieval Europe came from Ireland. Harps which were perhaps developed indigenously were in use in Ireland at least as early as the 8th century A.D. A type of harp called the *crot* or *cruit* is pictured on Irish stone crosses of the 8th and 9th centuries, and was in use in both Ireland and England; the harp has since been considered the national instrument of Ireland. In continental Europe the medieval harp was known as the *rotta*. The rotta was very popular during the Middle Ages and was of various dimensions, ranging from the small, seven-string rotta that could be suspended from the player's neck, to the large rotta of seventeen strings.

The modern harp was originated in 1720 by the Bavarian musician Christian Hochbrucker, who developed foot pedals which "stopped" (i.e., tuned) the strings by semitones. This device left the player's hands free to pluck the strings while playing accidentals (i.e., sharped or flatted notes), which originally were produced by retuning the strings or by stopping them by hand during a performance. In 1810 the French manufacturer Sébastien Érard (1752–1831) developed a double-action harp in which the foot pedal can be depressed one or two notches, thus raising the pitch of each string one or two semitones.

The typical modern harp is a double-action instrument with 46 strings (6½ octaves, 7 strings to the octave), the bass strings being made of covered wire and the treble strings usually of gut. The strings are vertical, stretching from a straight *body* containing the sounding board upward to a curved *neck*. The third side of the triangle forms the *pillar*, which is vertical and rests on the *pedal box*. The harpist sits with the body between his legs and tilts the harp toward himself so as to be able to pluck the strings. Each of the seven pedals in the pedal box controls one string in each octave; when the C pedal, for example, is in its normal position, each C string sounds C flat; when the pedal is depressed one notch, the string sounds C natural; and when the pedal is depressed two notches, the string sounds C sharp. The harp, therefore, like the violin but unlike the piano, can play the appreciable difference between C sharp and D flat.

The harp can play any note or combination of notes on the diatonic scale; combinations are usually played in the form of an arpeggio (q.v.) rather than a chord. Because of the unusual effects which can be gained by plucking a number of strings at one time, or by playing extended arpeggios over several octaves, and because of its fine tone, the harp came into use as an orchestral instrument during the 19th century. Much chamber music has been written for small instrumental groups including the harp, and it is today an important component of all symphony orchestras.

HARPAGUS (fl. 6th cent. B.C.), Median general. According to a legend recounted by the Greek historian Herodotus, Astyages, king of Media, ordered Harpagus to expose the king's infant grandson Cyrus, later Cyrus the Great (q.v.) of Persia, on a hillside to die. The general, however, gave Cyrus to a shepherd, who substituted a still-born infant for the royal babe and raised Cyrus himself. When Astyages became aware of this, he punished Harpagus by giving a banquet at which the general was served with the flesh of his own son. According to historical fact, in 553 B.C. Cyrus, then king of Anshan and a vassal of Media, rebelled against Astyages. Harpagus and his army joined the rebellion in 550 B.C., and Cyrus was able to conquer Media. Later, Harpagus became one of the most trusted Persian leaders during the establishment of the Persian Empire.

HARPER, WILLIAM RAINEY (1856–1906), American educator, born in New Concord, Ohio, and educated at Muskingum College and Yale University. He was appointed professor of Hebrew in the Baptist Union Theological Seminary, Chicago, in 1879, and in 1886 he became professor of Semitic languages at Yale. In 1891 he became the first president of the newly formed University of Chicago, and made great contributions to the growth and development of that university. He was the author of many books on Hebrew and education, including, *Hebrew Method and Manual* (1885), *Elements of Hebrew Syntax* (1888), *The Prospects of the Small College* (1900), and *The Trend of Higher Education* (1905).

HARPERS FERRY, a town of Jefferson Co., W.Va., located at the confluence of the Potomac and Shenandoah rivers, 55 m. by rail N.W. of Washington, D.C. Maryland, Virginia, and West Virginia are separated at this point by the two rivers. The town, in the Blue Ridge Mountains, overlooks a picturesque gorge of the Potomac. It is the site of Storer College, established in 1867, one of the earliest Negro colleges in the U.S. Harpers Ferry was first settled about 1747 by Robert Harper, who established a ferry across the Potomac at that point. In 1796 a U.S. arsenal and armory were established there, and many of the rifles used in the War of 1812 were manufactured at Harpers Ferry. The town became famous after the raid of John Brown (q.v.), who seized the arsenal on Oct. 16, 1859. A museum and a monument in Harpers Ferry commemorate the event.

The town became famous after the raid of considerable importance during the Civil War, because of its strategic situation at the lower end of the Shenandoah Valley. On April 18, 1861, the day after the secession of Virginia, the small Federal garrison of 45 men under Lt. Roger Jones abandoned the post and fired the arsenal upon learning of the approach of a superior force of Virginians under Gen. Kenton Harper. It was held by Confederate troops until June 15 when, on the withdrawal of the Confederates, it was again occupied by a Federal garrison. Gen. Robert E. Lee, advancing northward, found his lines of communication in the Shenandoah Valley obstructed by the garrison at Harpers Ferry, and sent General "Stonewall" Jackson to capture the Federal force. After a bombardment of two days, Harpers Ferry was surrendered on Sept. 15, 1862. Col. Dixon S. Miles, in command of the garrison, was mortally wounded during the attack, and the total Federal loss in killed and wounded was 217, with 12,250 being taken prisoner. The Confederate loss in killed and wounded was 288. After being abandoned alternately by the Confederate and Federal armies, Harpers Ferry was permanently occupied by Federal troops following the battle of Gettysburg. In Oct., 1878, the town was considerably damaged by a flood of the Shenandoah R. Pop. (1950) 822.

HARPOCRATES. See HORUS.

HARP SEAL or GREENLAND SEAL, common name of a hair seal, *Phoca groenlandica*, found in huge herds on the coasts of Greenland, in the islands between Greenland and North America, and over most of the completely frozen arctic regions. The adult female is about 4½ ft. long; the adult male about 6 ft. long. Both are yellowish white but the adult male has a black face and a huge black mark, resembling a harp or saddle, on each side of its body. This mark has earned the species its common name and has earned the male the names of "saddleback" or "saddler". When newborn the harp seal is completely white and is known as a "whitecoat";

Metropolitan Museum of Art

Flemish harpsichord of the 17th century

when older, though still immature, it assumes a bluish tinge and is commonly known as "bluesides" or "bedlamer".

Harp seals are widely hunted by seal fishermen and Eskimos who value their skin, from which excellent leather can be prepared, and their oil.

HARP SHELL, common name for any marine snail in the genus *Harpa* and order Stenoglossa of gastropods (q.v.). Harp shells are so called because their shells have smooth, elevated ridges reminiscent of the strings of a harp. About nine species are known, all living on the bottoms of warm seas. The best-known species, *H. articularis,* is about 2 inches in shell length and is brilliantly colored.

HARPSICHORD (English variant of the original Italian name, *arpicordo*), a keyboard instrument similar to the modern grand piano, having two keyboards instead of one, and differing in tone production in that the strings are mechanically plucked by a plectrum, instead of being struck with hammers. The harpsichord was a very important instrument from the 16th to the 18th century, occupying the place in music that the piano holds today. The literature written for the instrument is extensive, and compositions for the harpsichord written by such famous composers as Bach, Domenico Scarlatti, and François Couperin are still played in recitals at the present time; contemporary composers, such as the Spaniard Manuel de Falla, have also written for the instrument.

HARPY (Gr. *harpazein,* "to snatch"), in Greek mythology, a personification of the swift, destructive windstorm; hence, by extension, a symbol of death, a power carrying mortals off to sudden death. In this char-

acter, harpies are depicted on graves and monuments in Lycia, s. Asia Minor. The harpies are the daughters of Thaumas, personification of the wonders of the sea, and of Electra, the daughter of Agamemnon. Homer mentions but one Harpy, *Podarge* (Swift-footed), who by Zephyrus, god of the west wind, became mother of the horses of Achilles. In Hesiod's *Theogony* the Harpies are two in number, namely Aëllo (Storm-swift) and Ocypete (Swift-flyer). They are represented as winged goddesses, swifter than birds or winds. Later writers give other names, such as Celæno (the black one), who, in Virgil's *Æneid,* is the leader of the Harpies. The later writers also make them loathsome and filthy, defiling all that they approach. The Harpies appear in the legend of the Argonauts (q.v.) as sent by the gods to punish Phineus, the blind king of Thrace, whose food they snatch away and pollute. They were pursued by Zetes and Calais, winged sons of Boreas, god of the north wind, as far as the Strophades Islands in the Ægean Sea, where they were either killed or, in the usual version, forced to promise that they would cease harassing Phineus. In earlier Greek art the Harpies are depicted as winged human beings. Later, however, they appear with the head, breasts, and arms of a woman, and the claws, wings, and tail of a bird.

HARRATIN. See HARATIN.

HARRIER, a breed of sporting dog that hunts by scent. It is generally believed to be descended from the English foxhound, which it resembles in most respects except size, the harrier being the smaller dog. The harrier is used for hunting the hare, a sport which is particularly favored in Great Britain. The dog has a medium-sized head and a bold forehead; a deep chest; a level and muscular back; straight legs; and catlike feet. Its coat is dense, short, and hard, and its color is generally tan, black, and white, or any combination of these colors. The dog is from 19 to 21 in. high at the shoulders.

HARRIER, any of several birds in the Hawk family, especially those in the genus *Circus,* so-called because of the erroneous assumption that they harry or despoil poultry. Harriers subsist on small rodents, reptiles, and insects, and are found throughout the world. Unlike other hawks they place their large, circular nests, which are built of dried grass, on the ground, usually amid high grass.

The marsh hawk, *C. hudsonius,* is the only species of harrier in North America, found in open, swampy regions from N. Canada to N.

United States in the summer, and as far south as Central America in winter. It averages 19 in. in length. The male is ash-blue above and white streaked with red below. The female is brown above and yellowish below. Both sexes have large, white markings on their tails and are therefore occasionally called "white-rumped hawks". Marsh hawks feed chiefly on field mice. The female lays as many as eight or nine eggs in a clutch.

The hen harrier, *C. cyaneus,* is the commonest harrier in the Old World, and frequents N. Europe and Asia. It resembles the marsh hawk in size and coloring.

HARRIMAN, EDWARD HENRY (1848–1909), American railroad magnate, born in Hempstead, N.Y., and educated in Jersey City and New York City public schools. At the age of fourteen he became a brokerage clerk in Wall Street and seven years later became a member of the N.Y. Stock Exchange. In 1883 he became a director of the Illinois Central Railroad, and in 1898 formed a syndicate which acquired the bankrupt Union Pacific Railroad. He rejuvenated the railroad and proceeded to extend it and to eliminate competition by gaining control of many other lines, including the Central and Southern Pacific railroads. His unsuccessful attempt to wrest control of the Northern Pacific from James J. Hill in 1901 resulted in a panic on the N.Y. Stock Exchange. Harriman's railroads were investigated by the Interstate Commerce Commission in 1906, but the only practical results of the investigation were to demonstrate Harriman's enormous power in the railroad world and to arouse the indignation of the public. At the time of his death Harriman controlled over 60,000 miles of railroad track, and estimates of the value of his estate ranged between two and three hundred million dollars.

HARRIMAN, W(ILLIAM) AVERELL (1891–), American financier and government official, son of Edward Henry Harriman (q.v.), born in New York City, and educated at Yale University. After 1917 he was the head of various railroad, shipping, and banking enterprises. He entered government service in 1934 and was thereafter closely associated with the "New Deal" and the Democratic Party. During World War II he was Lend-Lease administrator from 1941 to 1943, when he became U.S. ambassador to the Soviet Union. After the War he served as ambassador to Great Britain (March-September, 1946), U.S. secretary of commerce (1946–48), overseas administrator (1948–50) of the European Recovery Program (q.v.), and director (1951–53) of the Mutual Security Agency. In November, 1954, he was elected governor of New York State on the Democratic ticket.

HARRIS, FRANK (1854–1931), British-American author and editor, born in Galway, Ireland. He left school at the age of fifteen and went to the United States, where he later became a citizen. For some years he studied law at the University of Kansas, and in 1875 was admitted to the Kansas bar. He later returned to England; there, at various times, he edited the London *Evening News* and the periodicals *Fortnightly Review* and *Saturday Review.* In 1913 he again journeyed to the United States, and during World War I was editor of Pearson's *Magazine.* Shortly after the end of the war he went to Nice, France, where he resided until his death. His fictional writings include *The Bomb* (1908), a novel based on the Chicago Haymarket Square Riot (q.v.); and the short-story collections *Elder Conklin* (1894), *Montes the Matador* (1900), and *The Yellow Ticket and Other Stories* (1914). In *Contemporary Portraits* (4 series; 1914, 1919, 1921, 1923) and *Latest Contemporary Portraits* (1927), he presented short, vivid sketches of the many political and literary figures whom he knew personally. His full-length biographies, including *Oscar Wilde, His Life and Confessions* (1916) and *The Life of George Bernard Shaw* (1931), and his autobiography *My Life and Loves* (1923), are marked by outspoken frankness.

Ancient Greek relief carving of a harpy

HARRIS, GEORGE WASHINGTON (1814–69), American humorist, born in Allegheny Co., Pa. After working as a steamboat captain on the Tennessee River for some years, he became a writer, contributing humorous sketches to various newspapers and periodicals. *Sut Lovingood Yarns* (1867), a collection of his stories relating the ribald adventures and tall tales of an uncouth Tennessee mountaineer, ranks among the finest examples of American humorous literature.

HARRIS, JOEL CHANDLER (1848–1908), American writer, famous as the creator of the "Uncle Remus" tales, born in Eatonton, Ga. He joined the staff of the Atlanta *Constitution* in 1876, and became its editor in 1890. His whimsical, imaginative stories, based on Negro legends and centering about the figure of Uncle Remus, an aged, philosophical, Negro storyteller, were among the first and remain the greatest writings in the school of American Negro folk literature (see FOLK TALES). The collections containing these stories include *Uncle Remus, His Songs and Sayings* (1880), *Nights with Uncle Remus* (1883), *Uncle Remus and His Friends* (1892), and *Uncle Remus and Brer Rabbit* (1906). Harris also wrote a number of works depicting Southern life in realistic, humorous terms. Among these are the short-story collections *Mingo, and Other Sketches in Black and White* (1884) and *Tales of the Home Folks in Peace and War* (1898), and the novels *Sister Jane: Her Friends and Acquaintances* (1896) and *Gabriel Tolliver: A Story of Reconstruction* (1902). The 100th anniversary of Harris' birth, Dec. 9, 1948, was declared a statewide holiday and celebrated with gala festivities in Georgia; to commemorate the occasion, a special Joel Chandler Harris postage stamp was issued by the Federal government.

HARRIS, ROY (1898–), American composer and educator, born in Lincoln Co., Okla. After studying composition with Arthur Bliss, Arthur Farwell, Modest Altschuler, and Scalero, in 1926 he went to Paris to study with Nadia Boulanger. He returned in 1929 to begin an extended teaching career, including posts at Westminster Choir School (1933–38), at Cornell University (1941–42), at Colorado College, Colorado Springs (1942–48), and at Utah State Agricultural College (after 1948). Harris is considered one of the foremost contemporary American composers. He wrote many instrumental works, including *When Johnny Comes Marching Home* and *Folk-Song Symphony*.

HARRIS, TOWNSEND (1804–78), American diplomat, born in Sandy Hill, N.Y. He had little formal education, but was a member of the Board of Education of New York City, and served as its president from 1846 to 1847. He was instrumental in establishing the New York Free Academy, now the College of the City of New York, and one of the buildings of that college was named Townsend Harris Hall in his honor. He also played a prominent role in establishing Townsend Harris High School, which was in existence from 1847 to 1942.

Harris was appointed the first U.S. consul general to Japan in 1855 and the first U.S. minister to Japan in 1859. He won the confidence of the Japanese and arranged a commercial treaty in 1858 which secured for Americans the rights of trade, residence, missionary operations, and teaching in Japan.

HARRIS, WILLIAM TORREY (1835–1909), American educator and philosopher, born near North Killingly, Conn., and educated at Philips Andover Academy and Yale College. He was superintendent of the public-school system of St. Louis, Mo., from 1868 to 1880, and from 1889 to 1906 was U.S. Commissioner of Education. Harris was intensely interested in the doctrines of 19th-century German philosophers, and was a leading exponent in the U.S. of Hegelian thinking. He founded the *Journal of Speculative Philosophy* in 1867 and from 1867 to 1893 edited the magazine, which had a strong influence on philosophy in America. He wrote many influential books, including *Introduction to the Study of Philosophy* (1889), *Hegel's Logic* (1890), *The Psychologic Foundations of Education* (1898), and *Elementary Education* (1900). He was editor in chief of the first edition of *Webster's New International Dictionary* (1909).

HARRISBURG, capital of the State of Pennsylvania, and county seat of Dauphin Co., situated on the Susquehanna R., 105 miles N.W. of Philadelphia. It is served by two railroads, and by major air lines. Four bridges span the river, which is a mile wide at Harrisburg. The city is a political, commercial, and industrial center. It is surrounded by a mining and agricultural area producing coal, iron ore, livestock, poultry. general farm crops, and dairy products. Harrisburg contains extensive railroad shops, employing about 8000 persons. Among other industrial establishments in the city are printing and publishing plants, meat-packing plants, and plants producing steel, iron, foodstuffs, lumber products, boilers and engines, machinery, textiles, knit goods, leather and leather goods, clothing, chemicals, candy, and tobacco and cigars. Coal, extracted from the river bed by the river coal fleet, furnishes power for the industrial plants of the city. The national, State, and municipal governmental agencies at Harrisburg employ many of the inhabitants of Harrisburg. In addition, the city has a large volume of wholesale and retail trade. As the present eastern terminus of the Pennsylvania Turnpike, the 160-mile-long super-highway to Pittsburgh, the city, is a headquarters for tourists and conventions.

Capitol Park, in the heart of the city, contains the principal State buildings, including the Pennsylvania State Capitol, the dome of which, rising to 272 ft., was designed after that of St. Peter's Cathedral in Rome. The marble staircase in the Capitol was modeled after that of the Paris Grand Opera House, and the building is noted also for its bronze doors, mural decorations, and stained-glass windows. The other structures in the park are the North Office Building, the South Office Building, the Finance Building, the Education Building, housing the State Library and the Law Library, and the State Museum, containing among its historical and scientific exhibits the original Penn Charter and the original manuscripts of famous Pennsylvania composers and authors. The Pennsylvania Farm Show Building, site of the annual Pennsylvania Farm Products Show, is in the N. of the city, and covers an area of 13 acres under one roof. Harrisburg has a total park area of 1100 acres. The municipal bathing beach and baseball park occupy an island, reached by two bridges, in the middle of the Susquehanna R. Handsome residences, including the governor's mansion, are situated on Front St., bordering River Park, which extends for 5 m. along the bank of the river.

Harrisburg was first settled about 1715 by John Harris, who established a trading post on the site and operated a ferry across the river. The settlement was known as Harris's Ferry until 1785, when his son and namesake, John Harris, laid out a town and named it Harrisburg. It became the county seat of the newly created Dauphin Co. in the same year. In 1791 Harrisburg was incorporated as a borough, and in 1812 it was made the capital of the State. The city of Harrisburg was chartered in 1860. Pop. (1950) 89,544.

HARRISON, Benjamin (1726?–91), American statesman, born in Charles City County, Va. He was a member of the Virginia legisla-

President Benjamin Harrison

ture from 1749 to 1775, from 1777 to 1782, and from 1784 to 1791. As representative from Virginia in the Continental Congress from 1774 to 1778, he worked on many important committees and presided over the debates preceding the adoption of the Declaration of Independence. He was one of the signers of the Declaration of Independence. From 1782 to 1784 he served as governor of Virginia. In 1788 he was a member of the Virginia convention which ratified the Federal Constitution. He was the father of William Henry Harrison, ninth President of the United States, and the great grandfather of Benjamin Harrison, twenty-third President of the United States.

HARRISON, Benjamin (1833–1901), American statesman and twenty-third President of the United States, grandson of William Henry Harrison (q.v.), the ninth President. Benjamin Harrison was born in North Bend, Ohio, and educated at Miami University, Oxford, Ohio. He was admitted to the bar in Cincinnati, in 1853, and was elected reporter of the Supreme Court of Indiana in 1860. He entered the Union Army in 1862, and served as colonel of a brigade which saw action at Kennesaw Mountain, Peachtree Creek, and Nashville. He was brevetted brigadier general of volunteers in 1865, and returned to his Supreme Court post in Indianapolis. Harrison was defeated, in 1876, as Republican candidate for Governor of Indi-

Metropolitan Museum of Art
President William Henry Harrison

ana. In 1878 he was appointed a member of the Mississippi River Commission. He was elected United States senator from Indiana in 1880 and declined a post in the cabinet of President James A. Garfield (q.v.), preferring to serve in the Senate. He served as senator from 1881 to 1887, but was defeated for re-election.

The Republican convention held in Chicago in 1888 nominated Harrison for the presidency. He defeated Grover Cleveland (q.v.), the Democratic candidate, in the bitterly fought 1888 election, obtaining a majority of the electoral college vote although losing the popular vote. During Harrison's administration the public debt was reduced and American industry expanded. The outstanding national events during his term of office were: the first meeting of the Pan-American Congress, passage of the McKinley Tariff Act, passage of the Sherman Silver Bill, civil service reform, abolition of the Louisiana Lottery, and expansion of the Army and Navy. He was nominated for re-election by the Republican convention in 1892, but was defeated by his predecessor, Grover Cleveland. After leaving office he returned to the practice of law. In 1899 he appeared as counsel for Venezuela before the international commission appointed to arbitrate the British Guiana-Venezuela boundary dispute, and was the principal representative of the United States at the Hague Conference (q.v.), held

in 1899. Harrison wrote *This Country of Ours* (1897), and a collection of essays, *Views of an Ex-President* (1901).

HARRISON, JOHN (1693–1776), English inventor and clockmaker, born in Foulby, near Pontefract. Harrison produced such improvements in clockmaking as the "gridiron pendulum", which permits exact operation during variations of temperature, and the "going ratchet", which prevents loss of time during rewinding. In 1761 Harrison produced an extremely accurate chronometer, in response to an appeal by the British Government for accurate timepieces to improve the science of navigation. The government paid Harrison a prize of £20,000 for this invention, which he described in *A Description Concerning Such Mechanism as Will Afford a Nice or True Mensuration of Time* (1767).

HARRISON, MARY ST. LEGER. See KINGSLEY, family.

HARRISON, WILLIAM HENRY (1773–1841), American soldier and statesman, ninth President of the United States, son of Benjamin Harrison (q.v.), a signer of the Declaration of Independence, and grandfather of Benjamin Harrison (q.v.), twenty-third President of the United States. William Harrison was born in Berkeley, Charles City Co., Va., and attended Hampden-Sidney College in Va. and the College of Physicians and Surgeons in Philadelphia. He served in the U.S. Army from 1791 to 1798, when President John Adams appointed him secretary of the Northwest Territory. He became the delegate in Congress of the Territory in 1799, and was the first Territorial delegate ever to sit in Congress; in the following year he was appointed governor of the then newly created territory of Indiana. Presidents Jefferson and Madison subsequently reappointed him and he served until 1812; his tenure of office was marked by conciliatory policies toward the Indians, with whom he negotiated about thirteen treaties providing land for their use. When hostilities with Indians led by the Shawnee chief Tecumseh (q.v.) broke out in 1811, Harrison won a decisive victory at the battle of Tippecanoe (q.v.).

During the War of 1812 Harrison was in command of the American forces of the Northwest and was promoted to the rank of major general. In September, 1813, he won a signal victory over the British forces and their Indian allies in the battle of the Thames in Canada.

After the war he was a representative of Ohio in the U.S. House of Representatives from 1816 to 1819 and in the U.S. Senate from 1825 to 1828; in the next year he served as the first U.S. minister to Colombia. Thereafter he lived in retirement but emerged in 1835 to become the Presidential nominee of the Whigs. He was defeated in the election but was renominated in 1839; John Tyler of Virginia was his running mate. The election campaign of that year was made notable by the innovation of political mass meetings and processions, theretofore unknown in Presidential election contests. Harrison's simple life, his associations with the democratic life of the frontiersmen, and his military exploits were emphasized during the campaign in a number of effective slogans, among which "Tippecanoe and Tyler too" was the most popular. Harrison won an overwhelming victory. Thirty-one days after his inauguration he died of pneumonia; he was the first President to die in office.

HARRISSE, HENRY (1830–1910), American scholar and historian, born in Paris, France. In 1847 he settled in the United States, where he became a naturalized citizen and practiced law for several years in New York City. His major interest was the collecting of documents pertaining to the early history of the New World. Among his chief works is *Bibliotheca Americana Vetustissima* (1866), a bibliography of about 300 works published between the discovery of America and 1551. Harrisse was also the author of the biographies *John and Sebastian Cabot* (1882) and *Christopher Columbus* (1884–85), and of *The Discovery of North America* (1892) and *The Discovery of Newfoundland* (1900).

HARROGATE, municipal borough in the West Riding of Yorkshire, England. It is located 18 miles N. of Leeds and is composed of two townships, Low Harrogate and High Harrogate, which are connected by a series of villas built in the area between them. High Harrogate is situated in the uplands, where the climate is bracing; Low Harrogate, however, lies in a protected position, and has a mild winter climate. Over eighty mineral springs, some of which were discovered as early as the 16th century, attract tourists to Harrogate, which is the chief inland vacation and health resort of N. England. The borough was incorporated in 1884. Pop. (1951 prelim.) 50,454.

HARROW ON THE HILL, urban district and residential community of Middlesex County, England, 12 m. by rail W.N.W. of London. The town is built on a hill, on the summit of which stands the Church of St. Mary, reputedly founded in the 11th century by Lanfranc (q.v.), Archbishop of Canterbury under William the Conqueror. Lord Byron is supposed to have spent many hours daydreaming on a stone on the grounds of the church. The famous Harrow School (q.v.) is also located in Harrow on the Hill. Pop. (1951 prelim.) 219,463.

HARROW SCHOOL, an English institution of secondary and higher education, situated at Harrow on the Hill, Middlesex. It was founded in 1571 by John Lyon, a prosperous yeoman, under a charter granted by Queen Elizabeth. In 1590 Lyon drew up the statutes of the institution, providing for the education of thirty poor boys of Harrow parish, and left two thirds of his fortune to the school when he died two years later. In 1611, pupils were admitted to the first completed building, which is still in use today. Some fifty years later, when the school was in financial difficulties, a clause in the statutes permitting the enrollment of "foreign" (or nonparish), paying scholars was invoked; Harrow's rise to its present eminent academic position dates from this enlargement of the institution.

The governing body of the school, under the Public Schools Act of 1868, consists of six members, selected respectively by the assistant masters of the school, the lord chancellor of Great Britain, the universities of Cambridge, London, and Oxford, and the Royal Society of London for Improving Natural Knowledge. The course of instruction was originally exclusively classical, but the study of mathematics was introduced in 1837 and of modern languages in 1851, and other branches of a modern education have since been added. Harrow now offers a liberal education and preparation for the universities. Among the distinguished graduates of the school are the statesmen Sir Robert Peel, Lord Palmerston, and Sir Winston Churchill, and the authors Lord Byron, Anthony Trollope, and Richard Brinsley Sheridan.

HART. See DEER.

HART, ALBERT BUSHNELL (1854–1943), American historian and educator, born in Clarksville, Pa., and educated at Harvard University and the University of Freiburg. He taught history and government at Harvard from 1883 until 1926, when he retired. As an educator he stressed studying history from original sources, and as one of the leading historians of his day edited several important series of historical works, notably *The American Nation* (28 vols., 1903–18), for which he wrote many volumes, and *Epochs of American History* (4 vols., 1891–1926). His writings include *Formation of the Union* (1892), *Essentials of American History* (1905), *New American History* (1917), and *We and Our History* (1923).

HART, GEORGE OVERBURY, known as POP HART (1868–1933), American artist, born in Cairo, Ill., and mainly self-taught. He was noted for his free, colorful watercolors and etchings done during his extensive travels in Italy, Egypt, Tahiti, Iceland, the West Indies, and Mexico. His paintings were included in the exhibit of 19 Living Americans at the Museum of Modern Art, New York City, in 1929. He was twice president of the Brooklyn Society of Etchers. His work is represented in a number of American museums, including the Museum of Modern Art, New York, the Chicago Art Institute, the Cleveland Museum of Art, and the National Museum in Mexico.

HART, JOHN (1711?–99), American statesman, born in Mercer County, N.J. He was a member of the New Jersey provisional assembly from 1761 to 1771, and served in the Continental Congress from 1774 to 1776. Hart was one of the signers of the Declaration of Independence. In 1777 and 1778 he was chairman of the New Jersey Council of Safety.

HART, Moss (1904–   ), American playwright and motion-picture scenarist, born in New York City. His first play, *The Hold-Up Man,* was produced at the National Theatre, Chicago, when he was twenty-one. He later became known for his collaboration with George S. Kaufman (q.v.) in the writing of a number of comedies notable for their witty dialogue and deftly-drawn, if somewhat exaggerated, characters. Among the plays they wrote together are *Once in a Lifetime* (1930); *You Can't Take It with You* (1936), for which the co-authors were awarded the Pulitzer Prize; *I'd Rather Be Right* (1937), a musical comedy poking affectionate fun at President Franklin D. Roosevelt; *The Man Who Came to Dinner* (1939), a thinly-veiled caricature of the author and raconteur Alexander Woollcott (q.v.); and *George Washington Slept Here* (1940), a satire on suburban life. Hart was the sole author of the librettos of several widely acclaimed musical comedies, including *Face the Music* (1932), *As Thousands Cheer* (1933), *Lady in the Dark* (1941), and *Winged Victory* (1943). He ultimately turned to the writing of serious drama; among his plays in that field are *Christopher Blake* (1946), the story of a young boy faced with the problem of a parental divorce; and *Light Up the Sky* (1948), a satirical study of a group of temperamental actors and actresses.

Many of Hart's plays were made into successful motion pictures. He also wrote the screen plays *Gentleman's Agreement* (1947) and *A Star Is Born* (1954).

HART, SIR ROBERT (1835–1911), British administrator in the Chinese imperial service, born in Portadown, Armagh County, Ireland, and educated at Queen's College, Belfast. He joined the British consular service in 1854, and was sent to China, where he served for five years. In 1859 he entered the Chinese imperial service as a local customs inspector at Canton. He was appointed inspector general of customs in the Chinese service in 1863. In this post, which he held until his death, Hart virtually created the system of customs regulations which opened China to orderly foreign trade relations.

Hart's organization of customs collections was so efficient that these revenues became the most stable element of the imperial finances, and his statistics on customs are the most reliable information available on Chinese affairs during his administration. In connection with his supervision of customs, Hart instituted many modern reforms, including a public health service which developed from his network of port physicians; a postal service, of which he was appointed inspector general; a system of convention markings of channels and ports by buoys and lights; and a school of European languages which later became a national university.

His influence, based on his amicable relations with both Chinese and foreign authorities, was instrumental in establishing Chinese consulates and legations abroad. Although Hart was appointed British minister to China in 1885, he declined the post and continued in the imperial service. In 1893 the British government recognized Hart's services in opening China to international commerce by creating him a baronet.

HART, WILLIAM S. (1872–1946), American actor, born in Newburgh, N.Y. He began his acting career at the age of nineteen, and subsequently starred in *Ben Hur, The Squaw Man,* and *The Trail of the Lonesome Pine;* from 1914 he acted in motion pictures. Hart was one of the earliest and most popular stars of silent motion pictures, achieving his greatest fame as a cowboy hero in scenes of Western life. From 1917 to 1924 he was the star of twenty-seven pictures, each of which brought in gross returns of over one-half million dollars. Among the pictures in which he played were *Wagon Tracks, Travelin' On, O'Malley of the Mounted,* and *Tumbleweeds.* His writings include the autobiography *My Life East and West* (1929) and *And All Points West* (1940).

HARTE, FRANCIS BRETT, known as BRET HARTE (1836–1902), American author and poet, born in Albany, N.Y. He went to California in 1854, and during the ensuing three years was successively a schoolteacher and gold miner. In 1857 he became a typesetter on the *Golden Era,* a San Francisco newspaper, and four years later began to contribute poems and short fictional sketches to that journal. He was subsequently appointed staff member of the *Californian,* San Francisco, to which he contributed a series of parodies satirizing the works of various popular authors of the time. In 1868 he helped establish and became editor of the *Overland Monthly.* Many of his most successful stories, including *The Luck of Roaring Camp, The Outcasts of Poker Flat, Miggles,* and *Brown of Calaveras,* were published in the *Monthly,* as was his comic poem *Plain Language from Truthful James* (also known as *The Heathen Chinese*).

These works, which have come to be regarded as classics of American folk literature, are notable for their descriptions of the lusty, humorous, and sometimes tragic life of the mining camps and towns of California in the second half of the 19th century. A collection of his stories, published in 1870 under the title *The Luck of Roaring Camp and Other Sketches,* was greeted with acclaim throughout the United States.

Harte subsequently went to New York City, where he was commissioned to write for the *Atlantic Monthly,* but the quality of his contributions was far below the standard of his earlier writings. The ensuing decline in his popularity, coupled with his extravagant mode of living, soon left him almost penniless. Friends obtained for him an appointment as U.S. consul at Crefeld, Prussia, Germany, in 1878; two years later he was transferred to Glasgow, Scotland, where he remained until 1885. Although he continued to write while serving in these positions, he did not produce any works comparable to his early stories; from 1885 until his death he was a hack writer in London. Additional collections of his stories include *Mrs. Skaggs's Husbands* (1873) and *Tales of the Argonauts* (1875).

HARTEBEEST, common name for any of several antelope in the genus *Alcelaphus* (or *Bubalis*), characterized by a long, narrow head, shoulders higher than the hindquarters, and a cowlike tail. The ringed horns, curved like the arm of a lyre, which are present in

Bret Harte

both sexes, do not grow directly out of the sides of the head but arise from a short central horn. Most species are about 4 ft. high at the shoulder, and are brownish gray in color, with black markings on the face, and a white or yellow patch on the rump. Hartebeests are keen-sighted, fleet-footed beasts which can outdistance greyhounds and the fastest horses. They feed on grass and inhabit open plains or dry desert regions, being capable of going without water for several weeks at a time. Their flesh is good to eat. Nine species are known, all found only in Africa except for the bubalis, which is also found in Arabia and Syria.

The best-known hartebeest is *A. caama,* the Cape hartebeest, to which the name hartebeest was originally applied. It was once common from Cape of Good Hope to Mashonaland in Southern Rhodesia, but is now almost extinct. Other hartebeests include Lichtenstein's hartebeest, *A. lichtensteini,* found in E. Africa from Mozambique to Tanganyika Territory, the western hartebeest, *A. major,* of W. Africa, Coke's hartebeest, *A. cokei,* of E. Africa, the lelwel, *A. lelwel,* of W. and E. Africa, and the tora, *A. tora,* of E. Africa.

Several species of antelope in the genus *Damaliscus,* including the blesbok (q.v.) and bontebok, resemble the true hartebeests and are often called "bastard hartebeests". Antelopes in this genus are generally purplish brown in color. They are not as high at the shoulders as true hartebeests, and have horns

N.Y. Zoological Society

The Cape hartebeest

arising directly from the head rather than from a projection from the head. The hirola, or Hunter's hartebeest, *D. hunteri,* is found in E. Africa and is characterized by white, V-shaped markings on its forehead. The sassaby, or tsessebe, *D. lunatus,* is common over the greater portion of S.E. Africa, and is black above, with a black face. *D. corrigum,* known as the "tiang" in N.E. Africa and "topi" in E. central Africa, is characterized by a silky, purplish coat.

HARTFORD, capital of Connecticut, county seat of Hartford Co., and port of entry, situated at the head of navigation on the Connecticut R., 38 m. from Long Island Sound, 100 miles N.E. of New York City, and 120 miles S.W. of Boston. It is served by rail and by major air lines. The city is an important commercial and manufacturing center, and is especially famous as the greatest insurance center in the U.S. The buildings housing the home offices of more than forty insurance companies are an important feature in the city's architecture. The principal products of the numerous industrial establishments in Hartford are typewriters, precision machines, sewing machines, presses, airplane motors, gears, valves, radiators, firearms, hardware, nails, wire fencing, brushes, tools, vacuum cleaners, rubber goods, chemicals, plastics, and leather, lumber and paper products. The city has an extensive wholesale and retail trade, with a trading area embracing about half of the State. It is also an important market for agricultural products, particularly tobacco.

The principal building in Hartford is the State Capitol situated on Capitol Hill over-looking Bushnell Park. It was completed in 1878 at a cost ($2,642,524) within the original appropriation and is constructed of Connecticut marble. The building contains several historical relics, including the tombstone of the American Revolutionary general Israel Putnam, and the battle flags of Connecticut regiments in several wars. Facing the Capitol on the south are the State Office Building, and the State Library and Supreme Court Building. Memorial Hall in the latter building contains a portrait of George Washington by Gilbert Stuart, and the original royal charter of 1662. Other governmental buildings in the city include the federal, county, and municipal buildings, and the State armory. The Old State House, designed by Charles Bulfinch, one of the architects of the National Capitol in Washington, and completed in 1796, is now a historic shrine. The cultural collections of Hartford are centered in a group of buildings including the Wadsworth Atheneum, housing the public library and Connecticut Historical Society; the Colt Memorial Museum, with a collection of early firearms; and the Avery and Morgan Memorials, museums of art. The most interesting of the city's many churches is the First Church of Christ (Congregational), known as Center Church, which was organized in 1632. The present structure dates from 1807 but its burying ground contains graves of settlers buried there in 1640. Opposite the church is the highest structure in New England, the building of the Travelers Insurance Company, with a tower rising to 527 ft.

The municipal park system covers nearly 3000 acres and provides facilities for a wide variety of recreational activities. Elizabeth Park contains famous rose gardens, and is the site of an annual rose festival. Among the educational institutions in the city are Trinity College, founded in 1823, the Hartford Seminary Foundation, the Hartford College of Law, and the Hartford College of Insurance.

Hartford was once an important literary and publishing center. One of the oldest newspapers in the country, the Hartford *Courant,* founded in 1764, is still published. Noah Webster, the lexicographer and author, who was born in Hartford in 1758, published his *Grammatical Institute of the English Language* there in 1783–85. In the 1790's Hartford was the home of the "Hartford Wits", a group of Federalist writers who published a series of political parodies and satires. Among other prominent Americans born in Hartford were Henry Barnard, Frederick Law Olmsted, John Fiske, and J. Pierpont Morgan (qq.v.) ; and the city was the residence of Harriet Beecher Stowe and Samuel Langhorne Clemens (Mark Twain).

In 1633, within the limits of the present city, the Dutch built a fort which they called Good Hope; the site is still known as Dutch Point. In 1635-36 the first English settlers came from New Town, Massachusetts, to the locality. They were led by Rev. Thomas Hooker and Rev. Samuel Stone, and the settlement, called New Towne at first, was named Hartford in 1637 from Hertford, the English home of Rev. Stone. On Jan. 14, 1639, the freemen of the settlements of Windsor, Hartford, and Wethersfield met at Hartford and adopted the Fundamental Orders of Connecticut, the first written constitution in Connecticut. Peter Stuyvesant, the Dutch administrator in America, and commissioners from the English settlements signed a treaty at Hartford on Sept. 19, 1650, by which boundary disputes were adjusted and the Dutch confirmed in possession of the fort at Hartford. In 1654, however, the fort was seized by the English and the Dutch expelled from Connecticut. In 1662 a royal charter was granted the Connecticut colony, and Hartford became the capital. In 1687 Sir Edmund Andros, governor of the New England colonies, came to Hartford to demand the surrender of the royal charter, but was thwarted in his purpose (see CHARTER OAK). From 1701 to 1873 Hartford and New Haven were joint capitals of Connecticut. Hartford was incorporated as a city in 1784. Its industrial development was marked by the building of the first woolen mill in New England there in 1788, the writing of the first insurance policies there in 1794. In 1814 the city was the site of the important Hartford Convention (q.v.). Pop. (1950) 177,397.

HARTFORD CONVENTION, in the history of the United States, the political assembly representing the Federalist Party (q.v.) of the New England States, which met at Hartford, Connecticut, on December 15, 1814, and adjourned on January 5, 1815. Its members numbered twenty-six, of whom twelve came from Massachusetts, seven from Connecticut, four from Rhode Island (all appointed by the legislatures of their respective States), two from counties in New Hampshire, and one from Windham County, Vermont. The convention was called in consequence of the opposition of the New England Federalists to the War of 1812 (q.v.) between the United States and Great Britain. The New Englanders were unsympathetic to the war because of its crippling effect upon their fishing industry and foreign commerce. The object of the convention was to devise means of security and defense against foreign nations, and also to safeguard the privileges of the individual States against the alleged encroachments of the Federal government. Because the meetings of the convention took place behind closed doors, and because the members were pledged to absolute secrecy, a rumor spread to the effect that the New England States were contemplating secession from the Union. Subsequent investigation failed to disclose any basis for the report, which nevertheless irreparably damaged the reputation of the Federalist Party, already in disfavor because of its pro-British, aristocratic tendencies.

The recommendations of the convention, stated in the form of amendments to the Federal Constitution, were that taxation and representation in each State should be proportionate to the number of its free inhabitants; that no new State should be admitted to the Union except upon a two-thirds vote in both houses of Congress; that Congress should not have the power to impose more than a sixty-day embargo on ships owned by citizens of the United States; that Congress should not prohibit foreign commerce or declare offensive war except by a two-thirds vote; that no person thereafter naturalized should be entitled to sit in Congress or to hold any civil office in the Federal government; that the Presidency should not exceed one term; and that the President should never be chosen twice successively from the same State. The delegates further resolved that if their recommendations should not be heeded, and if the defense of their respective States should still be neglected, a further convention should be held, vested "with such powers and instructions as the exigency of a crisis so momentous may require". The legislatures of Massachusetts and Connecticut approved the proposed Constitutional amendments and dispatched commissioners to Washington, D.C., to urge their adoption. The war, however, was practically over before the convention finished its business, and American military successes increased the popularity of the government and hastened the downfall of the Federalist Party, which did not survive the Presidential election of 1816.

HARTFORD FERN. See CLIMBING FERN.

HARTHACNUT. See HARDECANUTE.

HARTLEY, DAVID (1705-57), English philosopher, born in Armley, Yorkshire, and educated at Jesus College, Cambridge University. He studied at first for the Church, but dissented from some points in the Thirty-nine Articles (the official creed of the Anglican Church), and took up the study of medicine. He practiced as a physician successively in Newark, Bury St. Edmunds, London, and Bath, where he died.

Hartley's major work, the *Observations on Man* (1749), which occupied him for sixteen years, was the first attempt to explain all the phenomena of the mind by a theory of association. Though thinkers before him, among them John Locke and David Hume (qq.v.), had used the principle of association to explain many of the more developed mental contents and processes, Hartley carried their ideas to a new point of comprehensiveness. Like them he considered the mind to be a *tabula rasa* (i.e., a blank) before sensation, but he extended the laws of mental growth through contiguous associations to include not only such phenomena as memory (which others had done) but also imagination, reason, and finally the emotions. He classified the emotions under six heads, and argued that developed or adult emotions were the products of elementary feelings uniting, passing into new connections, and giving rise to complex emotions, under the general law of contiguity.

Another of Hartley's major theories had to do with the physical nature of sensation, and was drawn from Newton's *Principia*. Hartley argued that any sensation of the external world sets up a vibratory motion in the nerve affected, producing corresponding vibrations in the cerebral substance; he assumed that impulses from the brain to the muscles proceed in the same manner. He extended this doctrine of vibrations to include other tissues.

In addition to the work mentioned above, Hartley's writings include *Conjecturæ Quædam de Motu, Sensus et Idearum Generatione* (1746). See also ASSOCIATION OF IDEAS; PSYCHOLOGY.

HARTLEY, DAVID (1732-1813), English political leader and diplomat, the son of the philosopher David Hartley. As a member of the House of Commons from 1774 to 1780, he attained prominence as a stanch opponent of the war against the American colonists. He set forth his views on this subject in vigorous terms in *Letters on the American War* (1778). For many years he was a friend and correspondent of Benjamin Franklin; in 1783 Hartley and Franklin collaborated in drawing up the peace treaty which ended the Revolutionary War.

HARTLEY, MARSDEN (1877-1943), American painter, born in Lewiston, Maine. He first attracted attention in 1909 by his exhibit of dark landscapes at the Photo Secession Gallery directed by Alfred Stieglitz (q.v.). In 1912 Hartley went to Europe, where he experimented with Cubist and Expressionist painting techniques for some years. Hartley's late paintings, particularly his New England landscapes done at Gloucester and Maine from 1931 to 1943, emphasize stark and elemental qualities in nature. A large retrospective exhibition of his work was held at the Museum of Modern Art, New York City, in 1944. His paintings are in many American museums.

HARTMANN VON AUE (d. between 1210 and 1220), Middle High German poet (see GERMAN LITERATURE: *Middle High German Period*). He was a member of the lesser nobility of Swabia and entered the service of a nobleman who ruled the domain of Aue (present-day Obernau on the Neckar). Hartmann took part in the Crusade of 1196-97 and a number of his religious poems deal with the Crusades. He is best known for his four narrative poems. Two of these, *Erek* and *Inwein,* are based on works of the French 13th-century poet Chrétien de Troyes (q.v.), and are the earliest German poems based on legends of the Arthurian cycle (q.v.). Of the other two narrative poems, *Gregorius* is a romance, and *Der Arme Heinrich* is the tale of a leper cured by the devotion of a young girl.

HARTSHORN. See AMMONIA.

HART'S-TONGUE FERN, common name of a fern, *Phyllites scolopendrium,* belonging to the family Polypodiaceae. The hart's-tongue, unlike typical ferns, has long, dark-green, strap-shaped leaves, dotted with parallel rows of sporangium clusters. It is common in temperate regions of Eurasia, and is found in Mexico and a few isolated localities in E. United States, in ravines and under limestone cliffs.

HARUN-AL-RASHID (Ar., "Aaron the Upright"), fifth of the Abbasside caliphs of Bagdad (see ABBAS), who reigned from 786 to 809 A.D. He was born at Rages, and succeeded to the throne upon the death of his brother, Musa al-Hadi. The administrative power during a considerable part of Harun's reign was entrusted to Yahya, the Grand Vizier, or councilor of state, and head of the illustrious family of the Barmecides. Baghdad, the capital of Harun's realm, became the most flourishing city of the period. Tribute was paid to the caliph from all quarters, and splendid edifices were erected in his honor at enormous cost. He is said to have exchanged gifts with the Frankish ruler Charlemagne. Harun was a generous patron of learning, poetry, and music, and his court was visited by the most eminent Mohammedans of the age. He was celebrated in countless songs and stories, and is perhaps best known to the West as the caliph around whom center the fabulous tales of the *Arabian Nights*. Disguised, and accompanied by Ja'far, his court favorite, Harun delighted in taking nocturnal rambles through the streets of Baghdad, observing the activities of his subjects, frequently joining their revels.

From 791 to 809 Harun was at war with the Eastern Roman emperor Nicephorus I, whom he defeated at Heraclea Pontica (Eregli) and Tyana, in Asia Minor. Toward the end of his reign Harun conceived a hatred for the Barmecides, due, perhaps, to envy of their growing influence and power. At length he caused the Grand Vizier, his four sons, and all their descendants, one only excepted, to be killed. Nor did he spare Ja'far, also a Barmecide. Harun died of apoplexy at Tus while on his way to put down an insurrection in the E. part of his empire.

HARVARD, JOHN (1607–38), English clergyman, born in London, and educated at Cambridge University. In 1637 he emigrated to New England, and settled in Charlestown, Massachusetts, where he was active as a minister for a short time. Upon his death he left the college at New Towne (later Cambridge) half his fortune (about £780) and his library of 400 books. The Massachusetts General Court named the institution Harvard College in his honor in 1639. See HARVARD UNIVERSITY.

HARVARD COLLEGE OBSERVATORY, an astronomical observatory originally founded in Cambridge, Mass., in 1839, and re-established from 1843 to 1847 by public subscription. It is affiliated with Harvard University. Its most notable telescopes are a 61-inch reflector, a 24-inch reflector, and a 16-inch refractor telescope. The Observatory also maintains a radio-telescope, which detects radiation from interstellar hydrogen; it has a movable 25-ft. reflector and operates over a frequency range of 300 to 1600 megacycles. Much of the equipment used in the Northern Hemisphere is kept at the Oak Ridge station in Harvard, Mass.; in the Southern Hemisphere,

a branch station has been maintained in Bloemfontein, South Africa, since 1891.

HARVARD UNIVERSITY, the oldest institution of higher learning in the United States, founded in 1636 at New Towne (now Cambridge), Mass., by a decree of the General Court of the Massachusetts Bay Colony, and currently situated in both Cambridge and Boston, Mass., In 1638 the college was endowed by the nonconformist clergyman, John Harvard (q.v.), and in March, 1639, was named Harvard College in his honor.

The aim of its founders was to provide for the sons of the highly placed colonial families an education modeled on that offered by the best European educational institutions. Beginning with the administration of the first president, Henry Dunster, in 1640, and for a century and a half thereafter, Harvard's curriculum, teaching methods, and standards followed the lead of its European counterparts. Courses leading to the B.A. degree stressed the traditional medieval training in the "Seven Liberal Arts" and the "Three Philosophies", though even at this time the curriculum began to expand with the introduction of courses in Hebrew, Syriac, and Aramaic. Although, during this early period, many graduates entered the ministry, the college was not primarily a divinity school; its graduates took a standard course and were expected to be schooled in all branches of available knowledge. During the first eighty years of its history, Harvard's instruction was conducted by the president together with three or four tutors. In 1721 the first professorship was established, but no major additions were made to the faculty until the first half of the 19th century, when chairs of law, chemistry, philosophy, French, history, and zoology were created. In 1817 the Law School was founded and the Divinity School followed two years later. A new emphasis on the teaching and development of scientific research was expressed in the establishment in the 1840's of the Harvard Astronomical Observatory and the Lawrence Scientific School. During this period, due to the impact of German university teaching, the old classical curriculum was relaxed, the study of modern foreign literature was introduced, and some recognition was provided for postgraduate students.

Originally the members of the university's board of overseers were clergymen appointed by the Massachusetts legislature. In 1823, when the State ceased its financial support of the university, the composition of the

Harvard U. News Office

Statue of John Harvard in front of University Hall, on the campus of Harvard University

board began to change until, by the mid-19th century, no clergymen were members. Today the board members are elected by the alumni, and the university is entirely self-supporting.

When, in 1869, Charles William Eliot (q.v.) became president, the curriculum was drastically altered. The elective system, under which students could freely choose their courses, was extended and graduate study was organized in a Graduate School of Arts and Sciences and in the graduate schools of education, architecture, business administration, and public health.

Under the presidency of Eliot's successor, A. Lawrence Lowell (q.v.), which lasted from 1909 until 1933, the elective system was modified by the requirement that each student select a specific field of concentration, thus acquiring a professional knowledge in one restricted field, and in addition meet certain minimal distribution requirements by taking courses in other specified fields. Lowell also introduced the system of individual tutorial conferences to supplement conventional course study. He greatly expanded the physical plant of the university and utilized a grant of Edward S. Harkness (q.v.) to found the House System, whereby the majority of upperclassmen live in seven separate "houses"; each house is a cultural and economic cross-section of the undergraduate body, and in-

cludes such facilities as a library, dining room, common room, and dormitories.

James Bryant Conant (q.v.), who became president in 1933, introduced the system of general education, beginning in 1946. Under this system each student takes a survey course in each of the three main areas of study (natural sciences, social sciences, and humanities); this plan was devised to offset the tendency toward overconcentration in one field. Conant has also been responsible for the system of national scholarships, the Nieman fellowships (whereby outstanding journalists are afforded a free year of unsupervised study at the university), and the Littauer School of Public Administration.

Harvard is the wealthiest university in the world, with an endowment (1953) of over $215,000,000. In the years before World War II, Harvard had an enrollment of about 8300 students, of whom about 3500 were undergraduates. During the war enrollment increased about 50 percent; in 1953–54 a total of 9988 full-time students was enrolled. Ten separate faculties serve 18 schools and departments and include 3000 members of the teaching staff. The university maintains 77 libraries, of which the most important is the Harry Elkins Widener Memorial Library. The Harvard library system comprises the largest university library in the world, and is one of the largest libraries of any type in the U.S., with about 5,700,000 books and pamphlets (in 1953).

Other well-known institutions of Harvard University located in Cambridge and Boston are the Peabody Museum of Archeology and Ethnology, the William Hayes Fogg Art Museum, the Asa Gray Herbarium (see HERBARIUM), the Arnold Arboretum, and the Harvard-Yenching Institute for the study of Oriental languages and Oriental culture, which is affiliated with Yenching University in Peiping, China. Harvard also operates a 2300-acre forest in Petersham, Mass., a meteorological observatory in Blue Hill, Mass., and the Marine Biological Laboratory in Woods Hole, Mass. See also BROOKHAVEN NATIONAL LABORATORY; DUMBARTON OAKS; HARVARD COLLEGE OBSERVATORY. Radcliffe College (q.v.) has administrative affiliations with Harvard, and many classes comprise students from both institutions.

For the past century Harvard's faculty has at all times included many outstanding scholars. Thousands of notable persons are numbered among Harvard's alumni, including four Presidents of the U.S., and numerous world-famous scholars, writers, statesmen, scientists, and industrialists.

HARVEST FISH, common name of several marine acanthopterygian fishes in the family Stromateidae, especially *Peprilus paru* and the butterfish (q.v.). Both fish are short, *P. paru* averaging six inches in length, and the butterfish ten. Their bodies are flattened from side to side and are deep from top to bottom. Jellyfishes constitute their chief food. Harvest fishes are found in the Atlantic Ocean from Cape Cod to Brazil and are valued as food. *P. paru* is most common off the shores of Virginia where it is known as "whiting"; another of its common names is "poppyfish". The butterfish is known under many other names, including "dollarfish", "lafayette", "sheepshead", and "starfish".

HARVEST FLY. See CICADA.

HARVESTMEN or **HARVEST SPIDERS.** See DADDY LONGLEGS.

HARVEST MITE, HARVEST LOUSE, or HARVEST BUG, common name for the chigger (q.v.).

HARVEST MOON, the full moon at harvest time in the north temperate zone, or more exactly, the full moon occurring nearest to the autumnal equinox, September 23. At this season the moon rises at a point opposite to the sun, or close to the exact eastern point of the horizon. Moreover the moon rises at this season only a few minutes later each night, affording on several successive nights an attractive moonrise close to sunset time and strong moonlight almost all night. The continuance of its light after sunset is useful to farmers in northern latitudes, who are then harvesting their crops. The full moon following the harvest moon, which exhibits the same phenomenon in lesser degree, is called the hunter's moon. See MOON.

HARVEST MOUSE, common name for any of several field mice, so called because they inhabit grain fields. Their characteristic, globular nests are constructed of grass in any convenient sheltered place, such as an abandoned bird's nest or a hollow log. Three to seven young are born in one litter. The English harvest mouse, *Micromys minutus,* is the smallest mouse in England and is common throughout Europe. In the U.S. about twenty-two species of harvest mice, all in the genus *Reithrodontomys,* are found in the open grassy regions of the South. They are among the smallest of American mice and average about 5 inches in total length, half of which is the tail. The best-known species is *R. humulis,* found in the coastal regions of

S.E. United States. It is yellowish chestnut above, ashy below.

HARVEY, a city of Cook Co., Ill., situated on the Little Calumet R., 20 m. by rail s. of the center of Chicago, of which it is a residential and manufacturing suburb. The principal industries in the city are the manufacture of railroad cars, stoves, cement, automobiles, aluminum ware, foundry equipment, Diesel engines, and road, mining, and oil-well machinery. Harvey was founded in 1890 by Turlington W. Harvey, a Chicago industrialist, for whom the city is named. It was incorporated as a village in 1891 and as a city in 1895. Pop. (1950) 20,683.

HARVEY, GEORGE BRINTON McCLELLAN (1864–1928), American journalist and publisher, born in Peacham, Vt., and educated at Peacham Academy. After working as a reporter for various newspapers, he became managing editor of the New York *World* in 1891. From 1893 to 1898 he was engaged in the construction and administration of electric railways and succeeded in accumulating a substantial fortune. In 1899 he purchased the *North American Review,* a monthly periodical which he edited until 1926. He was president of the publishing firm of Harper & Bros. from 1900 to 1915, and editor of *Harper's Weekly* from 1901 to 1913. Harvey was one of leading supporters of Woodrow Wilson in the Presidential campaign of 1912; later, when Wilson requested that Harvey withdraw his support because his publications were popularly suspected of propagating the views of certain financial interests, he turned against Wilson. In 1918 he founded the *North American Review's War Weekly* (later called *Harvey's Weekly*), in which he expressed bitter criticisms of Wilson's second administration and of the proposal for American entry into the League of Nations. In 1920 Harvey supported the Presidential candidacy of Warren Harding, and in the following year was appointed ambassador to Great Britain. He resigned from that post in 1923.

HARVEY, WILLIAM (1578–1657), English physician and anatomist, celebrated as the discoverer of the circulation of the blood. Born in Folkestone, Kent, Harvey first attended Caius College, Cambridge. He later studied medicine in Italy, at Padua, under Fabricius ab Aquapendente. In 1602 Harvey obtained his degree and returned to London to practice. He was admitted as a fellow of the Royal College of Physicians in 1607. In 1609 he became physician of St. Bartholomew's Hospital, and in 1615 he was

William Harvey explaining his theory of the circulation of the blood through the heart

made professor of anatomy and surgery there. Harvey perfected his theory of the circulation of the blood in 1616, publishing his findings under the title of *Essay on the Motion of the Heart and the Blood* (1628). In this work Harvey explained his discovery of the work of the heart in receiving blood from the veins and propelling it through the arteries. His reasoning prepared the way for Malpighi (q.v.) to demonstrate the existence of the capillaries, the final link in the circulation of the blood between the arteries and the veins.

Harvey was a Royalist and was appointed physician to James I and Charles I. Under the sponsorship of Charles, who furnished him with female deer for his studies, he conducted researches on embryology (q.v.), publishing his results in his book *Essays on Generation of Animals* (1651). In this work Harvey discussed his investigations concerning the formation of the embryo and disproved the old idea of spontaneous generation (q.v.). Harvey stated the dictum, *omne vivum ex ovo*, "all life comes from the egg", a finding on which much of the modern science of embryology is based. Harvey carefully observed and described the development of the fetuses of many animal species.

HARVEYIZED STEEL. See ARMOR PLATE.

HARZ MOUNTAINS, northernmost mountain range of Germany, extending over an area of 784 sq.m. between the Elbe and Weser rivers. The N.W. part of the system is called the Upper Harz (aver. elev. 2100 ft. above sea level) and the S.E. part, the Lower Harz (aver. elev. 1000 ft. above sea level); the loftiest peak in the range is the Brocken, rising to a height of 3745 ft. above sea level in the Upper Harz. Abundant forests and pasture lands cover the slopes of both parts of the range, and in the Lower Harz are found fertile plateaus. Since the 10th century mining has been carried on in the Harz Mountains, which contain veins of silver, lead, gold, copper, iron, sulfur, alum, and arsenic. The quarrying of marble, granite, and alabaster, the manufacture of coarse lace, and the breeding of native songbirds, chiefly canaries, are also important occupations. Pagan traditions have survived in the Harz region longer than in any other part of Germany, and have given rise to a number of weird and romantic legends, many of which have been incorporated into German literature. The Walpurgis Night legend, centering about the Brocken, forms a part of Goethe's *Faust*.

HASDRUBAL, the name of two Carthaginian generals. **1.** HASDRUBAL (d. 221 B.C.), son-in-law of Hamilcar Barca (q.v.). Upon the death of Hamilcar in 228, he became commander of the Carthaginian forces in Spain. He founded the city of New Carthage (now Cartagena) as the capital of the Carthaginian domains in Spain, and negotiated a treaty with Rome defining the Spanish areas to be governed by each of the two powers. He was killed by an assassin. **2.** HASDRUBAL (d. 207 B.C.), son of Hamilcar Barca, and brother of Hannibal (q.v.). In 218, when Hannibal left Spain for his campaign in Italy, he named Hasdrubal commander of the Carthaginian armies in Spain. Hasdrubal fought against the Roman generals Gnæus Cornelius Scipio and Publius Cornelius Scipio for six years, and in 212 routed their army, killing the generals. Hasdrubal was defeated in 209 by Scipio Africanus, who captured New Carthage. Two years later Hasdrubal led his troops across the Alps in an attempt to bring reinforcements to Hannibal, but encountered a Roman army on the Metaurus River in central Italy, and was defeated. He was slain in the battle, and by order of the Roman commander his head was cast into the camp of Hannibal.

HASHIMITE, the name of two Arabian dynasties. **1.** The descendants of Hashim, of the tribe of Koreish, traditionally the custodians of the sacred Mohammedan shrine, the

Kaaba, at Mecca. The Hashimites included the founders of Mohammedanism, notably the Prophet Mohammed (q.v.); Mohammed's uncle, Abbas (q.v.), progenitor of the Abbaside dynasty; and Mohammed's son-in-law, the Caliph Ali. **2.** A contemporary Arabian dynasty, by tradition the descendants of Mohammed, founded by Husein ibn-Ali, King of the Hejaz. The sons of Husein were Abdullah ibn-Husein, Emir of Trans-Jordan; Faisal, King of Iraq (qq.v.); and Ali, King of the Hejaz.

HASHISH or **HASHEESH.** See CANNABIS.

HASMANÆAN. See MACCABEES.

HASSAM, CHILDE (1859–1935), American painter and etcher, born in Dorchester, Mass. He studied in Paris in 1899 and returned to America, where he became the chief American exponent of Impressionism (q.v.). Hassam won a great many awards for his brilliantly sunlit landscapes. In 1933 he held an exhibition in New York City of over 350 etchings, including figure studies and landscapes. His works are in the Pennsylvania Academy of Fine Arts, the Carnegie Institute, Pittsburgh, the Buffalo Fine Arts Academy, the Corcoran Gallery, Washington, D.C., the Metropolitan Museum, New York City, the Detroit Museum, the City Art Museum, St. Louis, and other galleries.

HASSELT, capital of the province of Limburg, Belgium, situated on the King Albert Canal, 18 miles N.W. of Maastricht. A famous fete, the Feast of the Assumption of the Virgin, is held there septennially on August 15. In 1831, during the Belgian Revolution, the Dutch gained an important victory over the Belgians at Hasselt. The city is served by several railways. Among its industries are brewing and distilling. Pop. (1952 est.) 31,097.

HASTINGS, county seat of Adams Co., Nebr., situated 100 miles W.S.W. of Lincoln. It is served by four railroads, and maintains a municipal airport. The city is the shipping point and trading center of an extensive agricultural area including portions of s. Nebraska and N. Kansas. Grain and livestock are the principal products shipped. The chief industries in Hastings are meat packing and the manufacture of creamery products, flour, agricultural implements, air-conditioning equipment, foundry products, caskets, brick and tile, grain bins and tanks, millwork products, automotive specialties, irrigation pumps, plastic articles, trailers, canvas hose, and mattresses. Hastings is the site of Hastings College (Presbyterian), established in 1882, and the State Hospital, the largest State-owned institution in Nebraska. The municipal museum, called the House of Yesterday, contains an extensive collection of historical exhibits. In the vicinity of the city is a U.S. Naval Ammunition Depot, covering 48,000 acres and containing about 1900 permanent buildings. Hastings was settled in 1872 and incorporated as a city in 1874. Pop. (1950) 20,211.

HASTINGS, a municipal, county, and parliamentary borough of Sussex, England, situated on the English Channel, about 62 miles S.E. of London. The town is a popular summer resort, with excellent bathing facilities and a boulevard, 3 m. in length, fronting the English Channel. Other features of Hastings are the Marina promenade, a number of public parks and gardens, and the ruins of an 11th-century Norman castle. Hastings was a flourishing community during the Anglo-Saxon period of English history and received mention in 928, during the reign of Athelstan, as the site of a royal mint. In the reign (1042–66) of Edward the Confessor, the town was enfranchised as one of the Cinque Ports (q.v.). William, Duke of Normandy, led his invading army ashore in the vicinity of Hastings on September 28, 1066. The subsequent battle, in which William conquered Harold II, occurred about 6½ m. inland from the town (see HASTINGS, BATTLE OF). After 1377, when it was raided and burned by the French, Hastings declined in importance as a seaport. The town was extensively damaged by German air raids during World War II. Pop. (1953 est.) 64,510.

HASTINGS, name of a famous English family. Among its more important members were the following. **1.** HENRY (1535–95), 3rd Earl of Huntingdon. On the death of his father in 1561, he succeeded to the title of earl. He opposed the projected marriage of Mary, Queen of Scots to the Duke of Norfolk (see HOWARD, family), and was commissioner at the trial of Mary in 1569 and that of Norfolk in 1573. He had a prominent part in the preparations of 1588 for defense against the Spanish invasion; see ARMADA. **2.** SELINA (1707–91), Countess of Huntingdon, wife of the 9th earl. She joined the Methodists in 1739, and, after her husband's death in 1746, became associated with John Wesley and George Whitefield in promoting the great revival of religious fervor in England (see METHODISTS). She founded a sect known as "The Countess of Huntingdon's Connexion", built sixty-four chapels in various parts of the country, and in 1768 established a seminary to train ministers for the Connexion. During her lifetime she maintained a close personal superintendence over her establishments, and on her death bequeathed them to a trust composed of four trustees.

HASTINGS, THOMAS (1860–1929), American architect, born in New York City. He graduated from the École des Beaux-Arts in Paris in 1884, and shortly afterward went into partnership with John M. Carrère (q.v.). The firm of Carrère and Hastings won several municipal and Federal commissions for public buildings, among them the New York Public Library, and Senate Office Building, Washington, D.C.

HASTINGS, WARREN (1732–1818), British statesman and colonial administrator, born in Churchill, Oxfordshire, and educated at Saint Peter's College, Westminster, known as the Westminster School. At the age of eighteen Hastings went to India as a clerk in the service of the English East India Company (q.v.) and by 1761 had been promoted by the company to the position of member of the Calcutta council. In 1764 he resigned and returned to England, living there in retirement until 1768 on the modest fortune he had acquired in India. In 1768 he was appointed by the East India Company to the second most important post in the government of the presidency of Madras, India; and in 1772 Hastings became governor and president of the council of Bengal. In the latter post he initiated the reforms in the civil service which he later realized throughout the East India Company's administration in India.

In 1773, when Parliament passed the Regulating Act, changing the constitution of the Bengal government and limiting the administrative authority of the East India Company, the British government appointed Hastings the first governor-general of Bengal and India. In that post, Hastings was the presiding member of the four-member Bengal council, and also exercised a limited control over the Madras and Bombay presidencies. The other three members of the Bengal council were inimical to Hastings, both personally and politically, and found pretexts for attacking him in the issues involved in the controversy for authority in India then being waged by Parliament and the East India Company. From 1780 to 1784 Hastings led the British in a successful war against the Nizam of the Deccan and Haidar Ali, ruler of Mysore, and he deposed the Zamindar of Benares, Chait Singh, in 1781. While thus extending British power in India by force of arms, Hastings initiated judicial reforms, and put the finances of his administration on an orderly basis.

He resigned as governor-general in 1784, after the passage of the India Bill by Parliament had abolished the political authority of the East India Company. On his return to England Hastings was at first received with favor, but in 1788 a group consisting in part of personal enemies, headed by Sir Philip Francis (q.v.), instituted impeachment proceedings against him in Parliament, charging him, among other things, with cruelty and corruption in office. His trial lasted seven years; in 1795 Hastings was completely exonerated, but his fortune was so depleted by the cost of his defense that he was forced to appeal to the East India Company for an annuity, and to live on this bounty until his death.

HASTINGS, BATTLE OF, in English history, a decisive military engagement fought on October 14, 1066, between a national army led by Harold II (q.v.) and an invasion force under the command of William, Duke of Normandy (see WILLIAM I). A claimant of the English throne, which had been promised to him by his cousin Edward the Confessor, William challenged Harold's election as king on the death in 1066 of Edward and, with the blessings of Pope Alexander II, made preparations for an expedition against England. The invasion army, which included infantry armed with crossbows and contingents of heavily armed cavalry, landed on the English coast near Hastings on September 28, 1066. After a forced march from Yorkshire, where Harold had recently defeated his rebellious brother Tostig in the battle of Stamford Springs, the English army occupied a height (later called Senlac) on the Hastings-London highway about 6½ m. from Hastings. The royal force was composed exclusively of infantry, armed with spears, swords, and axes.

The initial Norman attack, launched at 9:00 A.M. on October 14, failed to dislodge the English, who met the barrage of enemy arrows with interlocked shields. Harold's axmen turned back a Norman cavalry charge, whereupon a section of William's infantry turned and fled. At this juncture, several units of the English army broke ranks, contrary to Harold's orders, and pursued the retreating Normans. Other Norman troops quickly surrounded and annihilated these units. Taking advantage of the lack of discipline among Harold's soldiers, William ordered a feigned retreat. The stratagem led to the entrapment of another large body of English troops. Severely weakened by these reverses and demoralized by the mortal wounding of Harold by an ar-

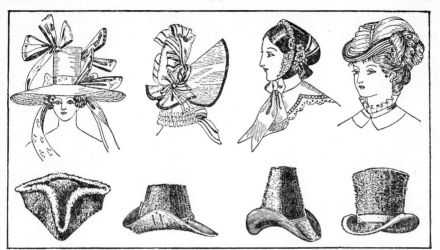

Top: Hats worn by women of 19th century. From left to right, 1828; 1829; 1854; 1880.
Bottom: Early men's hats. Left to right, the "Continental," cocked hat of 1776; clerical,
18th century; "Paris Beau," the style in 1815; "D'Orsay," fashionable in 1820.

row, the English were forced to abandon their strategic position on the crest of Senlac. Only small remnants of the defending army survived the subsequent onslaughts of the Norman cavalry. William's victory at Hastings paved the way for Norman subjugation of all England. See ENGLAND: *History*.

HAT, in general, a headdress or covering for the head, of a particular shape or design, and especially such a covering having a crown and a brim. A *cap* is a close-fitting head covering resembling a hat but differing from it usually by not having a brim, or by having a brim which only partially circumvents the crown. The hat, like all types of headdress, may serve several purposes, sometimes more than one simultaneously. It may be used chiefly as an ornament, or to protect the head against climate, or to indicate the office, rank, or political or religious affiliation of the wearer.

No hats of ancient times are extant, but knowledge of them can be derived from ancient sculpture and painting. In ancient Assyria the hat was a badge of office: musicians wore hats resembling the lower half of the body of a fish, the crown being shaped like the tail; harpers wore close-fitting caps decorated with a circle of beads; and cooks wore tiaralike caps. The men of ancient Greece and Rome wore three principal types of hat: the *causia*, a felt hat with a high crown and broad brim slightly rolled; the *petasus*, worn chiefly by travelers, a broad-brimmed hat of felt,

with a low crown, and tied under the chin or behind the ears; and the *pileus*, a simple cap of felt, often resembling a skullcap. The use of hats was far less extensive in classic times than it is in modern days. Greek and Roman women generally wore no hats, covering the hair with a veil; this they supplemented in cold or wet weather with a square-shaped hood, of linen in the summer and of wool in the winter. Anglo-Saxon men wore close-fitting, conical-shaped caps made of animal skins; hair was left on the hide and the shaggy side was turned outward; the caps of members of the wealthy classes were ornamented. Anglo-Saxon women wore a long veil, which was sometimes kept in place by a gold circlet or headband.

In Europe, including England, in early medieval times caps or hoods of a simple design were in vogue for head covering, but during the late Middle Ages hats were extravagant and eccentric in shape and proportions. Thus, the ordinary cap of the 11th century, which had a folded brim and a crown that fell to one side, in the 14th century had loose folds that reached to the shoulder; by the 15th century it had developed folds that fell to the knee, ending in a long, thin point. In like manner, the close-fitting, helmet-shaped cap of the 12th century was succeeded in the 13th by a hat with a high crown, peaked front, and turned-up back, and in the 15th by a high hat that was often brimless. Toward the end of the

15th century, flat hats with low crowns and turned-up brims, sometimes with a bunch of plumes placed in front and curving backward, came into vogue. They were usually worn over a scarlet skullcap and tilted to one side. Women's hats of the 15th century were particularly extravagant. They were elaborate, towering structures ending in such objects as cornucopias and baskets; an especially eccentric piece of millinery was a creation with a high receding crown which was flanked by huge horns. In the 16th century the fashion changed to flatter headgear. Women wore caps of velvet or gold brocade; men in general wore hats with broad, serrated brims; the upper classes had hats shaped like the tam-o-shanter, which were decorated with feathers and worn tilted. In Queen Elizabeth's time, men's hats in England were narrow, with a turned-down, curved brim and a full crown encircled with a gold band or with a feather worn on the right. Also in vogue for men were small, tight-fitting, round hats with rolled brims and with feathers in front. Women wore hats that had a brim curved in over the brow, hats with full-gathered crowns, and tall hats with feathers at the side.

In the reign of James I of England, men wore hats with a broad brim and a high crown ornamented at the back and sides with feathers; the brim was often fastened up on the right side with a jewel. In the time of Charles I, men's hats had slightly lower crowns, and curved brims with feathers falling over them to side or back. Political and religious differences were marked by hats in 17th-century England; the Puritans wore the steeple hat, which was high and narrow and devoid of ornament, whereas the Cavaliers wore a hat that had a low and broad crown and a feather stuck to one side. The Quaker hat, a plain hat with a round, low crown and a broad brim, dates from the origin of the Quaker sect in the middle of the 17th century. After the Restoration (1660) in England, the fashion for men was for hats with a high crown that had a band and a bow in front, with a flat, waved, or curved brim, and with feathers on either side or all around. The three-cornered hat, made by turning up the brim at both sides and in front, came into vogue in the second half of the 17th century and remained in style until the beginning of the 19th century, when it was replaced by the top hat.

The principal types of men's hats which originated or came into general use in the 19th century, and which are still in vogue today, are the modern felt hat, the silk hat, and the straw hat and other varieties of hat for summer wear. Felt hats are made principally of animal fur; some are made of a mixture of fur and wool, and others of wool alone. Two principal types exist: the soft felt hat, and the stiff or hard felt hat, known as the "derby" in the United States and the "bowler" in Great Britain; the latter has a dome-shaped crown and a narrow brim. The soft felt hat, which was introduced into the United States in 1851 by the Hungarian patriot Lajos Kossuth (q.v.), who visited the country in that year, was for a time known as the "Kossuth". The silk hat, worn on formal occasions, has a high, straight crown which is made of calico covered by a glossy plush of silk. It was developed in Florence about the middle of the 18th century, but did not come into general use until the first half of the 19th century. Straw hats are made from straw braids which come from Italy, China, and Japan. Italian straw braid, which consists of two principal types, leghorn and Milan braid, is particularly valued. The principal type of light hat for summer wear in the United States in addition to the straw hat in the Panama hat, which is made chiefly in Ecuador and Colombia from shreds of the immature leaf of the tree *Carludovica Palmata,* or "screw pine".

The manufacture of hats is an important industry in the United States today. Some men's hats are imported, notably from Italy and Belgium, but the United States is today a hat-exporting country. The principal hat-manufacturing centers are New York City; Philadelphia; Danbury, Bethel, and Norwalk, in Connecticut; Reading, Pa.; and Orange and Newark, N.J. In a recent year the United States had 254 establishments making men's and boys' hats of all types, and the value of their product exceeded 101 million dollars.

Modern hats for women are made of a variety of materials, including felt, straw, velvet, and other fabrics, and are often decorated with ribbons, veiling, feathers, artificial flowers, and other ornaments. Bright colors are frequently used, matching or contrasting with a particular garment. Women's hats vary in size and shape according to current styles in costume and according to the taste of the individual wearer. In a recent year the United States had nearly 1100 establishments manufacturing women's hats, and the value of their product exceeded 96 million dollars.

HATASU. See HATSHEPSUT.

HATAY, the southernmost il of Turkey, until 1939 a part of Syria. It borders on the Gulf of Alexandretta (İskenderon). The administrative center is Antakiya (pop., about 28,000). İskenderon (Alexandretta) is the largest city and chief seaport. Pop. (1950) 296,297.

HATCH ACT, the popular designation of the Political Activity Act, passed by Congress in 1939 and amended in 1940, forbidding Federal employees to engage in certain types of political activity. See ELECTORAL REFORM.

HATCHING. See INCUBATION.

HATHAWAY, ANNE (1557?–1623), wife of William Shakespeare (q.v.).

HATHOR. See EGYPTIAN RELIGION.

HATSHEPSUT, HATSHEPSET, or **HA-TASU,** Egyptian queen of the XVIIIth dynasty (see EGYPT: *History, Ancient*), who flourished about 1500 B.C. She was the daughter of Thutmose I, and was associated with him in the last years of his reign. Hatshepsut became the concubine of her half-brother Thutmose III, with whom she ruled after the deposition (about 1501) of their father. During their reign, which lasted until her death (except for the years between 1496 and 1493 B.C.) she was supreme in Egypt. She built the sumptuous temple of Der el-Bahri near Thebes, approached by a lane of sphinxes and surrounded by obelisks. The temple contains many evidences of the queen's reign, notably, a vivid mural representation of the Egyptian expedition to Punt, an ancient district in E. central Africa. The evidence of recent archeological excavation strongly suggests that Hatshepsut was the princess of Scripture who discovered the infant Moses in the bulrushes.

HATTERAS, CAPE. See CAPE HATTERAS.

HATTIESBURG, county seat of Forrest Co., Miss., situated at the confluence of the Leaf and Bowie rivers, 70 miles N. of Gulfport and about 90 miles S.E. of Jackson. It is served by four railroads, and maintains a municipal airport. Hattiesburg lies in a fertile agricultural area, and is one of the principal cities of Mississippi, of particular importance as a commercial and manufacturing center. The city contains more than sixty-five industrial establishments producing a variety of products, including clothing, lumber, naval stores, fertilizers, boilers, castings, piping, roofing, ventilators, mattresses, and explosives. A shrub nursery at Hattiesburg is one of the largest in the South. The city is the site of Mississippi Southern College, a State teachers college established in 1912. In the vicinity of Hattiesburg is Camp Shelby, an important U.S. Army training center during World War II. Hattiesburg was founded in 1881 and commenced its industrial growth as a lumbering center. It

Metropolitan Museum of Art

Ancient Egyptian sculpture of Hatshepsut

was incorporated as a town in 1884 and as a city in 1899. Pop. (1950) 29,474.

HAUPT, PAUL (1858–1926), German-English Assyriologist and Semitic scholar, born in Görlitz, Germany, and educated at the universities of Leipzig and Berlin. He became professor of Assyriology at the University of Göttingen in 1883. In the autumn of that year he came to the United States, where he was appointed professor of Semitic languages at Johns Hopkins University. He continued to lecture at Göttingen during the summers of the ensuing six years. He edited the *Polychrome Bible,* a critical edition of the Hebrew text of the Old Testament with an annotated English translation. A unique feature of this work is the use of different colors to distinguish the various sources and component parts of the several books of the Old Testament. His other writings include *Prolegomena to a Comparative Assyrian Grammar* (1888), *The Aryan Ancestry of Jesus* (1909), and *Golgotha* (1920).

HAUPTMANN, GERHART (1862–1946), German writer, notable as one of the greatest playwrights in German literature and a founder of the naturalist drama; see DRAMA: *German Drama;* GERMAN LITERATURE; NATURALISM. He was born in Obersalzbrunn, Silesia, and after attending school locally and in Breslau, took up farming, which he shortly

Gerhart Hauptmann

afterward abandoned for artistic pursuits. He studied sculpture in Breslau in 1880–81, attended the University of Jena for a year, and then went abroad and settled in Rome to study and practice sculpture. Ill health compelled him to return to Germany, where he married an heiress and began his writing career. In 1912 he was awarded the Nobel Prize for literature, and, in 1922, was honored for his literary achievements by the German republican government. He remained in Germany following Hitler's rise to power and during World War II; throughout the period of Hitler's dictatorship, Hauptmann's plays continued to be among the most popular in the German theater.

After experimenting with epics, ballads, and other literary forms early in his literary career, Hauptmann turned to the drama. His first plays revealed the influence of Henrik Ibsen, the Norwegian writer, of plays on the social evils of the time. However, Hauptmann was already developing his technique of naturalism, and his play *Before Dawn* (1889), written during this period, is regarded by some critics as marking the birth of naturalistic drama. In a play of social protest, *The Weavers* (1892), perhaps his greatest work, Hauptmann created a new dramatic form; discarding the traditional method of creating drama through the conflict of individuals, he counterposed social groups in *The Weavers,*

and consequently had no need for individual central characters or heroes. The Silesian weavers depicted in the five parts or tableaux comprising the play, as a group, are the heroes of the drama. The same dramatic form was used by Hauptmann in the comedy *The Beaver Coat* (1893) and the tragedy *Florian Geyer* (1895); the latter was based on the Peasants' War (q.v.) of the 16th century. In 1893 Hauptmann gave expression to a vein of romanticism in the imaginative play *Hannele,* the first drama in world literature in which the heroine is a child; in *The Sunken Bell* (1897), one of his most popular plays, he gave even fuller expression to his romantic spirit.

Following *The Sunken Bell,* Hauptmann wrote both naturalist dramas and romantic plays. Among the former are the tragedies *Drayman Henschel* (1899) and *Rose Bernd* (1903); the romantic plays include the verse drama *Henry of Auë* (1902), *And Pippa Dances* (1907), and a study of nymphomania, *Charlemagne's Hostage* (1908).

Prior to World War I Hauptmann developed an antipathy to Christianity which he compared unfavorably with pagan attitudes toward life, particularly those of ancient Greece. After the outbreak of the war, he wrote a number of dramas embodying his views. Included among these plays are *The Bow of Odysseus* (1917); the verse drama *The White Savior* (1920), scorning the Christian conquistadors and extolling the Aztec Indian ruler Montezuma; and *Indipohdi* (1921), devoted to a favorable presentation of Buddhistic ideas. Two later dramas were *Iphigenie in Delphi* (1941) and *Iphigenie in Aulis* (1944).

Other works by Hauptmann include the novels *The Fool in Christ, Emanuel Quint* (1910) and *Atlantis* (1912); the latter is esteemed as one of the greatest novels in German literature. An epic *Till Eulenspiegel* (1928) was regarded by Hauptmann as his greatest work. *The Adventure of My Youth* (1937) is an autobiography of the first 26 years of his life.

HAUSA, a group of African Negro peoples, with admixtures of other races such as the Tuareg, Berber, and Fulah, living in N.W. Nigeria. The *Hausa Land* or *Hausa States,* a territory now defined in ethnographic rather than geographical terms, is supposed to have been an empire of considerable power about the middle of the 15th century. It was conquered by the Fulahs (q.v.) in the early part of the 19th century and incorporated into

Nigeria in 1900. It now lies in the region north of the Benue and Niger rivers, and embraces two kingdoms or emirates. The total area is estimated at 150,000 sq.m., with about 4,000,000 inhabitants.

The Hausa peoples are among the most civilized of Central Africa, engaging in agriculture, cattle raising, and widespread commerce. They are skillful artisans and craftsmen, and maintain a high level of literary and cultural activities. The religion is Mohammedan (adopted from their conquerors, the Fulahs), with many animistic and totemistic survivals. Social organization is essentially feudal and locally centralized, with local chiefs and councils, but within this structure the Mohammedan laws of inheritance are followed.

The *Hausa language* is now a *Lingua Franca;* it is used as the language of trade and intertribal communication far beyond the boundaries of the Hausa Land, spread by trade and the exportation of slaves over a large region to the west, and northward to the Barbary states. It is an isolated branch of the Hamitic languages (q.v.), but the Hausa peoples are only distantly related to the Hamites (q.v.); their Hamitic language was not originally native to the Hausa tribes, but was brought to them by northern immigrants and adopted some time before their recorded history began. The Hausa language shares certain characteristics, such as the lack of definite and indefinite articles and the method of formation of the genitive, with the Bantu languages (q.v.), which are not Hamitic. Hausa is unique among the Hamitic languages in expressing differences of meaning by changes in tone.

An extensive literature exists in Hausa, consisting largely of folk tales, religious poems, and proverbs, much of which has been recorded in a variety of Arabic script called by the Hausa Ajami. The status of the language as a *Lingua Franca* for Central Africa, its inherent linguistic interest, and the body of literature extant in it have made it the subject of intensive study since the 19th century. An association for the study of Hausa was formed in London in 1892, and a professorship in the language has been established at Cambridge University.

HAUTBOY, an Anglicization of the French word for oboe, *hautbois* (literally, "high wood"). See Oboe.

HAUTE-GARONNE, a department of s.w. France, bounded on the s. by Spain. From the foothills in its N. portion it rises gradually in the s., reaching a height of more than 10,000 ft. above sea level in the Pyrenees on the Spanish border. It is watered by the Garonne R. and six of its tributaries. The Garonne is navigable for part of its course through the department, and the Canal du Midi, connecting the Mediterranean Sea with the Atlantic Ocean, passes through Haute-Garonne for 32 m. The soil in the fertile basin of the Garonne is productive, yielding wheat, corn, garden truck, grapes, peaches, apples, melons, tobacco, and chestnuts. Stock raising and dairying are other important agricultural industries in the department. Extensive areas of Haute-Garonne are covered with forests of fir, pine, and oak, and the department contains deposits of marble, zinc, lead, and salt. Among the principal industries are lumbering, mining, quarrying, shipbuilding, and the manufacture of leather, paper, and shoes, cotton, woolen, and linen goods, and tobacco, copper, and iron products. Several of the towns in the department contain mineral springs. The capital of Haute-Garonne is Toulouse (q.v.), and other leading towns are Saint Gaudens (pop. in 1946, 6916), Bagnères-de-Luchon (3480), and Montréjeau (2574). The department of Haute-Garonne was formed in 1790 from parts of the old provinces of Languedoc and Gascony. Area, 2458 sq.m.; pop. (1953 est.) 518,000.

HAUTE-LOIRE, a department of s. central France, formed mainly of portions of the former provinces of Auvergne and Languedoc. The surface is mountainous, with the Boutières, Mégal, Velay, and Margeride mountain ranges crossing the department from N. to s. The highest peak is Mont Mézenc, rising 5755 ft. above sea level. Haute-Loire is watered by the Loire, Allier, Borne, and Lignon rivers. The forested areas of the department contain stands of oak, beech, fir, and pine, and lumbering is an important industry. Other leading industries are agriculture, quarrying, the mining of coal and antimony, and the manufacture of silk, rubber, lace, paper, glass, and lumber products. The principal agricultural products are cattle, goats, rye, wheat, oats, barley, lentils, peas, potatoes, forage crops, and aromatic plants. Le Puy (pop. in 1946, 18,347) is the capital of the department. At various localities in Haute-Loire are old churches and the ruins of ancient castles. Area, 1931 sq.m.; pop. (1953 est.) 222,000.

HAUTE-MARNE, a department of N.E. France, composed chiefly of part of the old province of Champagne. The plateau of Langres, covering a large part of Haute-Marne, attains a maximum elevation of 1693 ft. above sea level. The N. part of the department contains extensive forests. Haute-Marne is watered principally by the Marne and the Aube rivers, and their tributaries; and the Meuse R. flows through the department for a distance of 31 m. The leading agricultural pursuits are the raising of horses and cattle, and the cultivation of wheat, oats, alfalfa, potatoes, and grapes. Iron mining and stone quarrying are other important industries. Among the manufacturing establishments in the department are flour mills, tanneries, wineries, foundries, blast furnaces, forges, metalworking shops, and factories manufacturing nails, cutlery, gloves, and baskets. The capital of Haute-Marne is Chaumont (pop. in 1946, 15,068); other important towns are Saint-Dizier (pop. in 1946, 15,936), Langres (5624), and Wassy (2524). In 1562, during the French religious wars, a number of Protestants were massacred at Wassy. Area, 2416 sq.m.; pop. (1953 est.) 195,000.

HAUTES-ALPES, a department of S.E. France, formerly part of the old provinces of Dauphiné and Provence. It is bounded on the E. by Italy. The surface of the department is mountainous, with the Cottian Alps traversing the E. section, and the Pelvoux Mountains of the Dauphiné Alps rising to a height of over 13,000 ft. above sea level in the Pic des Ecrins, in the N. portion. The principal rivers draining the department are the Durance, noted for its picturesque scenery, the Drac, and the Buech. The rockiness of the soil and the severity of the winters limit the agricultural development of the region, and the department contains few large industrial establishments. Some coal and lead are mined, and marble is quarried. The capital of the department is Gap (pop. in 1946, 11,086); other towns are Embrun (pop. in 1946, 2166) and Briançon (q.v.). Next to Basses-Alpes, it is the least populous department of France. Area, 2179 sq.m.; pop. (1953 est.) 86,000.

HAUTE-SAÔNE, a department of E. France, comprising part of the old province of Franche Comté. The Vosges mountain chain traverses the department in the N.E. The greater part of Haute-Saône lies within the valley of the Saône R., which flows through the department from N. to S. Wheat, oats, rye, potatoes, tobacco, cherries, plums, apples, and grapes are the principal crops, and horses and cattle are raised. Haute-Saône is well timbered, with forests of oak, fir, beech, and aspen covering a considerable area. The department contains

several stone quarries, coal mines, and salt mines. Among the industrial establishments are machine shops, ironworking shops, steel and copper foundries, glassworks, starchworks, sugar refineries, distilleries, tanneries, vegetable-oil mills, flour mills, brick and tile works, paper mills, sawmills, printing and dyeing plants, chemical plants, and factories manufacturing machinery, agricultural implements, tools, nails, pottery, hosiery, cotton textiles, and straw hats. The capital of the department of Haute-Saône is Vesoul (pop. in 1946, 10,744). Other towns are Lure (pop. in 1946, 5486), Gray (5310), Héricourt (5025), and Luxeuil-les-Bains (5264), a thermal spa. Area, 2075 sq.m.; pop. (1953 est.) 208,000.

HAUTE-SAVOIE, a frontier department of E. France, at one time part of the old duchy of Savoy. It borders on Switzerland and Italy, and is bounded on the N. by Lake Geneva. The highest point in the department is Mont Blanc (q.v.), rising to a height of 15,782 ft. above sea level in the Alpine chain which traverses the department in the S. and S.E. The chief rivers are the Arve, the Fier, and the Rhone. Cheeses, honey, poultry, and cattle are the principal agricultural products of Haute-Savoie, and coal and building stone are the most important mineral products. Other industries are the manufacture of clocks, bells, and cotton textiles. The department is chiefly noted for its tourist industry. The best known of the many winter resorts in Haute-Savoie is Chamonix (q.v.), lying in a valley of the same name in the midst of the Alps. In addition, the department contains several mineral springs. Lake Annecy, formed by the Fier R., is situated near the town of Annecy (q.v.), capital of the department. Other important towns are Thonon-les-Bains (pop. in 1946, 11,267) and Cluses (2646). Area, 1775 sq.m.; pop. (1953 est.) 294,000.

HAUTES-PYRÉNÉES, a department of S.W. France, bordered on the S. by Spain. Approximately two thirds of the department is mountainous, traversed by the Pyrenees Mts. Several of the peaks in the department exceed 10,000 ft.; the Vignemale, 10,820 ft. above sea level, is the highest peak in the French Pyrenees. Among the mountains are many cirques, containing scenic glaciers. The most famous of these deep recesses is the Cirque de Gavarnie, noted for its waterfall, and the source of two of the rivers draining the department, the Gave de Pau and the Neste. The other principal river in the department is the Adour. The highlands are forested and also contain extensive pastures; the lowlands in the N. of the department contain fertile farming areas. Wheat, corn, rye, barley, oats, fruits, grapes, and chestnuts are grown in Hautes-Pyrénées, and cattle, sheep, goats, horses, pigs, and poultry are raised. Other leading industries are tanning, the quarrying of marble and slate, the mining of zinc, lead, lignite, and manganese, and the manufacture of flour, lumber, paper, looms, woolen textiles, agricultural implements, slate products, and marble products. Hautes-Pyrénées is noted for its numerous mineral and thermal springs, the most famous of which are those at the villages of Barèges, Capvern, Cauterets, and Luz-Saint-Sauveur. In addition to the capital, Tarbes (pop. in 1946, 42,778), the principal towns are Lourdes (q.v.) and Bagnères-de-Bigorre (pop. in 1946, 8499). Hautes-Pyrénées was formed in 1790 of districts from the old province of Gascony. Area, 1751 sq.m.; pop. (1953 est.) 207,000.

HAUTE-VIENNE, a department of w. central France, formed mainly from portions of the old Limousin, Marche, and Poitou provinces. It is traversed in the S. by the Limousin Mountains. The highest elevation, 2549 ft. above sea level, is in the plateau of Millevaches, in the extreme S.E. The department is drained chiefly by the Vienne R., which crosses it from E. to w., and the Isle R., in the s.w. Rye, oats, wheat, buckwheat, apples, potatoes, chestnuts, and walnuts are the most important crops grown in the department, and horses, cattle, and sheep are raised. Granite and kaolin are quarried and the manufacture of porcelain is the principal industry. Other leading industries are brewing, tanning, dyeing, printing, liqueur distilling, and the manufacture of iron foundings, agricultural implements, and hats. Limoges (q.v.), the capital of the department, is a famous center of the porcelain industry. Other important towns in Haute-Vienne are Saint-Junien (pop. in 1946, 8103), Saint-Yrieix (3707), and Bellac (3455). Area of department, 2145 sq.m.; pop. (1953 est.) 340,000.

HAUT-RHIN, a department of E. France, bounded on the E. by Germany and on the s. by Switzerland. It lies in the fertile basin of the Rhine R., and is traversed in the w. by the Vosges Mountains. One other important river in the department is the Ill. Extensive forests of oak, fir, and beech cover the mountainous areas. The principal crops produced are corn, flax, potatoes, grapes, and fruits. Clays, potash, and lime are the chief mineral products. Among the leading industries are

French Embassy, Information Division
Scenic gorge in Hautes-Pyrénées, France

the manufacture of pottery, bricks, tiles, paint, chemicals, paper, wine, machinery, cotton textiles, and silk and woolen goods. The Rhine-Rhone canal provides water transportation. Colmar (q.v.) is the capital, and Mulhouse (q.v.), Guebwiller (pop. in 1946, 9695), and Altkirch (3565) are other important towns. Haut-Rhin, formerly a part of Alsace, was annexed to Germany in 1871, returned to France by the Treaty of Versailles after World War I, and occupied again by the Germans during World War II. Area, 1354 sq.m.; pop. (1953 est.) 504,000.

HAVANA, a province of Cuba, situated between Matanzas and Pinar del Río provinces, in the w. portion of the island, and extending from the Gulf of Mexico on the N. to the Caribbean Sea on the s. The province is a rich agricultural region, yielding sugar cane, tobacco, corn, vegetables, and fruit, and also containing valuable stands of timber. Among its industrial enterprises are sugar refineries, tanneries, sawmills, and distilleries. Havana (q.v.) is the provincial administrative center. Area, 3173 sq.m.; pop. (1943) 1,235,939.

Pan American World Airways

IN HAVANA, CUBA

Above: An old church and a typical suburban house, both built of white coral limestone, on the outskirts of the city.
Left: The national Capitol of Cuba, in the heart of the business district of Havana.

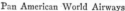

HAVANA (Sp. *La Habana*), capital and chief seaport of Cuba and the largest city of the West Indies, situated on the N. coast of the island approximately 90 miles s. of Key West, Florida. The city is situated on the w. side of the Bay of Havana, one of the safest harbors in the world. A strait about 250 yards wide and 1400 yards long affords entrance to the bay, which is navigable by ocean-going vessels. The E. side of the outer entrance is dominated by Morro Castle, a 16th-century fortress. Castillo de la Punta,

another old fortress, is on the w. side of the strait. Numerous docks, warehouses, and other facilities for the receipt and discharge of waterborne freight occupy considerable frontage along the inner harbor. Havana, a regular port of call for passenger vessels plying between the United States and Central and South American points, is serviced by steamship and air-transport lines operating to all parts of the world. Railway connections are maintained between the city and all important points on the island.

Havana is constructed largely of white coral limestone, and is one of the oldest and most picturesque cities of the western hemisphere. The original portion of the city, located near the inner entrance of the harbor, contains narrow, crooked streets, old houses with overhanging balconies, and various historic landmarks. Beyond the older section, Havana is essentially modern, with numerous magnificent residences, imposing public buildings and ecclesiastical edifices, beautiful parks and plazas, and broad, tree-lined boulevards. Among the boulevards are the Paseo de Martí, better known as the Prado, and the Avenida del Puerto, the Malecón, the Alameda de Paula, and the Avenida de las Misiones. Several of the drives, notably the Avenida del Puerto, extend along the edge of the bay. Noteworthy edifices include the national Capitol, a white limestone structure similar in design to the Capitol of the United States, the Capitanía, administrative headquarters of the captain of the port, the presidential palace, and the University of Havana (see HAVANA, UNIVERSITY OF). Besides Morro Castle, the outstanding historic landmarks are the former convent of Santa Clara, constructed in 1644; El Castillo de la Real Fuerza (called La Fuerza), a fortress built between 1565 and 1583 and once the headquarters of the Spanish colonial governors; the Cathedral (La Catedral de la Immaculada Concepción de la Virgen María), dating from 1656; the city post office, originally the church of San Francisco, which dates from 1575; the Castillo del Principe, another old fortress, currently employed as the city jail; and the City Hall, a former palace of the colonial governors, completed in 1792. The last named structure is generally regarded as the best example of Spanish colonial architecture in Cuba. Among the principal public parks of Havana are the Plaza de la Fraternidad, the Parque Central, and the Parque de Colón. The city contains a number of notable educational and cultural institutions, including, besides the University of Havana, the College of American Augustinian Fathers, the St. Alexander Fine Arts School, the Municipal Conservatory of Music, the National Museum, and the National Library.

Approximately two thirds of the import trade of Cuba is handled at Havana, and a substantial part of the country's exports pass through the port. Cigar making is the major manufacturing activity of the city. Rum, cigarets, beer, confections, and perfumes are other important products. Because of its proximity to the United States, an equable tropical climate, and an abundance of recreational facilities, Havana is a very popular winter resort, visited annually by tens of thousands of tourists and vacationists.

Founded in 1515 on the site of the modern town of Batabaño by the Spanish administrator Diego de Velásquez, Havana was established in its present location four years later. The settlement was sacked by pirates on a number of occasions during the next fifty years, but the Spanish authorities gradually transformed it into the chief naval station of Spain in the New World. During the 17th century Dutch fleets frequently attacked and blockaded the port. British naval forces harassed it during the next century. Morro Castle was captured in August, 1762, after a sanguinary siege, by the British, who occupied the city until the following July. The commercial importance of Havana dates from 1766, when the Spanish government began to remove various restrictions on Cuban trade. On February 15, 1898, the U.S.S. *Maine* was blown up in Havana harbor, and during the ensuing war between Spain and the United States the port was blockaded by the American fleet. The American military administration, which assumed control of the city after the defeat of Spain, eradicated various unsanitary conditions (see GORGAS, W.C.) and otherwise began the modernization of the municipality. Population (1943) 673,376.

HAVANA, UNIVERSITY OF, an institution of higher education founded at Havana, Cuba, in 1721. The university grants bachelors' degrees in letters, philosophy, pedagogy, science, engineering, agriculture, architecture, electricity, medicine and pharmacy, dental and veterinary surgery, and law. The faculties of law, medicine, and philosophy also offer postgraduate courses leading to masters' and doctors' degrees. In a recent year the student body numbered 14,000 and the university libraries contained over 100,000 volumes.

HAVASUPI, an Indian tribe of northwestern Arizona, of the Yuman linguistic stock. They are essentially a nomadic tribe, spending the spring and summer months in the Cataract Canyon, a branch of the Grand Canyon, and the fall and winter on the plateau above it. Though they hunt deer and mountain sheep during their stay on the plateau, their main sources of food supply are agricultural; Cataract Canyon has a plentiful supply of water and a fertile soil which, strengthened by a primitive system of irrigation, permit the Havasupi to practice more intensive farming than neighboring tribes. The native crops of corn, beans, and squash have been supplemented in modern times by peaches and figs, and a part of the harvest is regularly stored in granaries in the mountain walls.

Though a small tribe (a recent census gives their number as only 174), the Havasupi are interesting to anthropologists because of their singular freedom from culture contacts.

Living at the bottom of a canyon isolated from the outside world by barriers of rock, and almost entirely self-supporting, they have preserved their indigenous culture to a greater degree than any other tribe in the Southwest, and their basketweaving, language, and customs have been the objects of considerable study.

HAVERFORD COLLEGE, an institution of higher education for men, founded as Haverford School in 1833 at Haverford, Pa., under the auspices of the Society of Friends, and established as a college in 1856. From the date of the organization of the school until 1849 the student body was restricted to sons of members of the Society. The college grants degrees of B.A., B.S., and M.A., and awards five thousand-dollar fellowships, established in 1947, for graduate study in the history, sociology, religion, and philosophy of the Society of Friends. The institution has an endowment of over $4,500,000. In a recent year the college had 70 faculty members, and a student body of about 525.

HAVERHILL, a city of Essex Co., Mass., situated at the head of navigation on the Merrimack R., 3 miles S. of the New Hampshire boundary and 33 miles N. of Boston. It is served by a railroad, and is an important manufacturing center and the shipping point and trading center of an extensive area embracing part of N. Massachusetts and S. New Hampshire. Dairy products and garden truck are the principal agricultural products of the surrounding region. Haverhill, one of the oldest industrial centers in the country, has been noted for the manufacture of leather and shoes since the middle of the 17th century. The first tannery was built there in 1643, and the manufacture of shoes, which supplanted tanning in importance, developed shortly afterward.

Haverhill is still a leading shoe-manufacturing center, containing more than a hundred factories producing shoes and shoe accessories. Other important industries are the manufacture of textiles, hats, leather goods, boxboard, communication equipment, vending machines, industrial machinery, refrigerators, and beverages. The city is situated among rolling hills on both banks of the river, and contains five lakes within its limits. It is the site of Bradford Junior College (founded as Bradford Academy in 1803), the oldest institution in New England for the higher education of women. Among the points of interest in Haverhill is the birthplace of "the Quaker Poet", John Greenleaf

Whittier, which is maintained as a public shrine. The house, built in 1688, was described by Whittier in his famous poem *Snow-Bound*. The Haverhill public library contains an extensive collection of Whittier first editions and material pertaining to the poet. The Haverhill Historical Society is housed in "The Buttonwoods", erected about 1800, on the grounds of which is the John Ward House (1641). The most valuable article in the Society's collection is the original deed to the site of the present city, bought from the Indians in 1642.

Prior to the arrival from Ipswich in 1640 of the first colonists, an Indian village known as Pentucket, "The Place by the Winding River", stood on the site of Haverhill. In 1642 the land was purchased from the Indians for three pounds ten shillings, and permission of incorporation was granted the settlers in 1645. The name was then changed to Haverhill, for Haverhill, England, birthplace of the settlement's first preacher, John Ward. As a frontier town Haverhill was long harassed by Indian raids. Hannah Dustin was captured during one such attack in 1697, and she later escaped after scalping several of her captors. A monument to her memory now stands opposite the city hall. In 1708 a force of French and Indians attacked the town, burning many of the buildings and killing about forty of the inhabitants. Haverhill was incorporated as a city in 1870. In 1897 the township of Bradford became part of the city. Pop. (1950) 47,280.

HAVRE, LE, a city and seaport of the department of Seine-Inférieure, France, situated on the N. bank of the estuary of the Seine R., about 55 miles W. of Rouen and about 143 miles N.W. of Paris. Le Havre is the chief seaport on the W. coast of France and second in importance only to Marseille among French ports; it has extensive facilities, including more than 8 m. of side wharfage, for the receipt and discharge of waterborne freight. Le Havre harbor, completely enclosed by two long breakwaters, except for a narrow entrance, contains fourteen basins. Passenger and freight vessels in the transatlantic trade service the port on regular schedules, and steamship connections are maintained with all parts of the world. The port is also a terminal of inland-water carriers operating on the Seine. Coffee, cotton, and petroleum comprise the chief bulk cargoes received at Le Havre. Other important imports are metals, wool, dyewoods, and foodstuffs. The manufactured products

Hawaiian Pineapple Co.

SCENES IN HAWAII. *Above: Netting fish. Right: A palm-lined lagoon. Below, right: Riding surfboard.*

of N. and central France are the principal exports. Among the basic manufactures of Le Havre are cordage, wire cables, chemicals, lumber, machinery, firearms, toys, dyes, textiles, glass, earthenware, lace, starch, paper, refined sugar, flour, and beer. Shipbuilding is a leading industry, and there are extensive ship-repair facilities. Le Havre contains a number of noteworthy points of interest, including the 16th-century Church of Notre Dame, the Palais de Justice, the City Hall, and the municipal museum.

Originally a small fishing village, Le Havre began to figure in the maritime affairs of France after 1516, when Francis I authorized a number of harbor improvements. In 1562, during the religious strife in France, the Huguenots turned the town over to the control of the English. The English were driven out in the following year. Modernization of the port, begun during the administration of Cardinal Richelieu, was substantially advanced by Napoleon I. In World War I, the American and British expeditionary forces used Le Havre as a disembarkation and supply base. The city was badly damaged by Allied air raids after the capitulation of France in World War II. German occupation forces were expelled from Le Havre shortly after the Anglo-American invasion of Normandy on June 6, 1944. For the duration of the war in Europe, the port was a major Allied supply base. Hundreds of thousands of American

troops embarked for the United States from Le Havre after the surrender of Germany. Pop. (1946)· 106,934.

HAWAII, the largest of the Hawaiian Islands and a county of the Territory of Hawaii (see HAWAII, TERRITORY OF), situated in the North Pacific Ocean about 2150 miles s.w. of San Francisco, Calif. The island is the southernmost and most easterly of the Hawaiian archipelago and is separated from Maui and Kahoolawe islands by Alenuihaha Channel, a strait about 30 m. in width. The island is triangular in shape and has a coastline of about 300 m. Hawaii, like the other islands of the Hawaiian chain, was formed by volcanic action and is extremely mountainous. The dominant feature of the terrain is a series

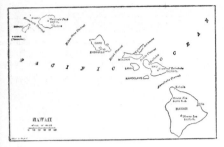

of volcanoes, linked by lava ridges which range from 3000 to 7000 feet in height. The highest of the volcanoes is Mauna Kea (q.v.), 13,823 feet above sea level, which is now inactive. South of Mauna Kea is Mauna Loa (q.v.), the most massive mountain in the world. Its height is 13,684 feet. Kilauea (q.v.), a volcano projecting from the side of Mauna Loa, has one of the most active craters known to man. The last explosive eruption of Kilauea, which is included with Mauna Loa in the Hawaii National Park (q.v.), occurred in 1924. Earthquake tremors are frequently felt in Hawaii. The island has considerable scenic beauty, an equable climate, excellent transportation facilities, including a railway along the N.E. coast and good motor highways, and numerous vacation resorts. Coffee is the leading product. Hilo (q.v.) is the administrative center, largest town, and principal seaport of the island. Area, 4030 sq.m.; Pop. (1950) 68,350.

HAWAII NATIONAL PARK, a national park in the Territory of Hawaii, established in 1916. Its area of 343 sq.m. includes the summits of three famous volcanoes, Haleakala, on the Island of Maui, and Mauna Loa and Kilauea, on the Island of Hawaii. The crater on the summit of Haleakala (10,032 ft. above sea level) is the largest extinct crater in the world; it is 2720 ft. deep, covers 19 sq.m., and contains cinder cones rising as high as 900 ft. Within the crater grows the rare silversword plant (*Argyroxiphium Sandwicense*), a large herb with narrow, silvery leaves. Mauna Loa and Kilauea are active volcanoes. The first, rising 13,684 ft. above sea level, is the largest volcano in mass in the world. Its summit crater, Mokuaweoweo, is more than 3 sq.m. in extent, with walls rising to 600 ft. This crater is no longer active, and during the frequent eruptions of Mauna Loa, the lava flows from newer craters on the sides of the mountain. A recent eruption was that of Jan. 9, 1949. Kilauea (4090 ft. above sea level) projects from the slopes of Mauna

Loa; its crater is the largest active volcanic crater in the world, covering 4.14 sq.m. Within its 500-foot walls is the vast inner pit, Halemaumau, sometimes called the "House of Everlasting Fire". Kilauea's activity is confined to this inner pit. Of the total park area, the Mauna Loa and Kilauea sections and the land connecting them comprise 317 sq.m., and the Haleakala section, on Maui, comprises 26 sq.m.

HAWAII, TERRITORY OF, a semiautonomous Territory of the United States, consisting primarily of the Hawaiian Islands, an archipelago of the North Pacific Ocean, and including Palmyra Island (q.v.) and several other islets unrelated geographically to the archipelago. Situated near the geographic center of the North Pacific Ocean, the Hawaiian Islands lie within the area bounded by 28° 25′ north latitude on the N., by 154° 48′ west longitude on the E., by 18° 55′ north latitude on the S., and by 178° 25′ west longitude on the W. The archipelago is composed of some 20 islets and islands, of which 8 are inhabited. In the order of size, the inhabited islands are Hawaii, Maui, Oahu, Kauai, Molokai, Lanai, Niihau, and Kahoolawe. Midway Island (q.v.), the westernmost of the chain, which extends from N.W. to S.E., is about 1500 m. from S. Oahu, a central point of the main group. From S. Oahu to San Francisco, Calif., the distance is about 2090 m. Other distances are 2228 m. to Los Angeles, Calif.; 3394 m. to Yokohama, Japan; 4685 m. to the Panama Canal; and 6472 m. to Cape Horn. The distance between the outermost islands of the main group is about 390 m. Honolulu (q.v.), situated in S. Oahu, is the capital, only metropolis, and chief seaport of the Territory. The total area of the Territory of Hawaii is 6441 sq.m.; the population (1950) is 499,794.

All of the larger islands of the archipelago are mountainous and of volcanic origin. Many of the smaller islets to the W. of the main group are lava formations, while the outlying islets and atolls consist of coral. Among the outstanding physiographical features of the main group are Haleakala (q.v.), with the largest extinct crater known to man; Mauna Kea (q.v.), an extinct volcano and the highest peak (13,823 ft. above sea level) in the Territory; Mauna Loa (q.v.), an active volcano; and Kilauea (q.v.), which has the largest active crater in the world. Both Haleakala and Mauna Loa form part of Hawaii National Park (q.v.), an extensive area which, together with more than one million acres

Hawaiian Pineapple Co.

HAWAIIAN PINEAPPLES

Above: Pineapples growing on a plantation. Furrows follow contours of the land, which is terraced for proper irrigation. Right: Laying mulch paper on soil to prevent weed growth and to keep soil warm.

Below: Processing fruit.

Hawaiian Pineapple Co.

Bishop Street in Honolulu, capital of the Territory of Hawaii, on Oahu Island

of national forests, preserves much of the natural beauty of the islands.

The inhabited islands lie within the tropical zone, but the climate is tempered by the prevailing N.E. trade winds. The mean annual temperature in the vicinity of Honolulu is 74.9° F., with extremes of about 71.5° F. in January and about 78.3° F. in August. Temperatures as high as 98° F. and as low as 25° F. are frequently recorded in the islands, the lower temperatures occurring at extreme elevations. Wide variations of climatic conditions, especially rainfall, result from the mountainous terrain. Maximum precipitation occurs on the windward slopes of the islands. Rainfalls totaling 200 inches annually are common in these regions, and the mean annual rainfall near the summit of Mount Waialeale (5170 ft.), on Kauai Island, is 444 inches, one of the highest recorded averages in the world. Precipitation on the leeward

sides of the mountains is generally low. In the vicinity of Honolulu, for example, the mean annual rainfall is about 28.5 inches.

The Hawaiian Islands have an extremely luxuriant flora, including more than 900 species of flowering plants, numerous types of tropical trees, about 140 species of ferns, and many other indigenous varieties of plant life. Imported species, highly cultivated for food or industrial plants, include sugar cane, pineapple, taro, banana, yam, breadfruit, coconut, papaya, olona, tobacco, sisal, candlenut, mango, citrus fruits, and coffee. The only mammal indigenous to the islands is a species of bat, but bird life is abundant. Several species of lizards comprise the reptilian fauna of the islands. Land and fresh-water gastropods are exceptionally varied and numerous. The coastal waters teem with fish, of which there are more than 600 species.

The Territory has a predominantly agrarian

economy, marked by large-scale agricultural enterprises. About 81% of all Hawaiian farm lands, which total more than 2,432,000 acres, are distributed among large holdings operated by managers. The remainder are small holdings operated by owners or tenants. Sugar cane is the leading crop of the islands. In 1952 the yield totaled about 1,020,000 tons. Pineapples rank next in importance among the crops of the Territory. More than 24,-875,000 cases of canned juice and fruit are produced from the pineapple harvest in 1951–52. The sugar crop and the pineapple pack are almost entirely exported, chiefly to the United States. Other important agricultural products are coffee, bananas, fresh flowers, rice, taro, potatoes, and macadamia nuts. Various other fruits and vegetables are cultivated for domestic consumption, and hogs, cattle, sheep, and poultry are raised for the home market. The fishing industry is another significant source of domestic foodstuffs. Mineral deposits are rare, consisting chiefly of salt, lime, and building stone. Canning, sugar refining, and related enterprises are the principal manufacturing industries of the Territory. Fertilizer, sugar-processing machinery, musical instruments, boats, clothing, furniture, shoes, poi, macaroni, confections, and various other commodities are produced for the domestic market. The tourist business of the Territory is highly lucrative, with tens of thousands of vacationists, mainly from the United States and Canada, visiting the islands annually.

Freight and passenger steamship service is maintained between the Territory and all parts of the world, and inter-island steamship and airplane services provide connections between the principal islands. Six commercial air lines connect Hawaii with other islands of the Pacific and with North America and the Orient. Communications facilities within the Territory include about 2200 m. of highways, about 60 m. of public railway lines (used mostly for freight-handling), and a telephone system linking the islands of Oahu, Maui, Kauai, Hawaii, and Molokai. The Territory figures prominently in the Pacific defense system of the United States, which maintains a number of military installations on the islands. Pearl Harbor (q.v.), a major American naval base on Oahu Island, was the target of the Japanese air attack (December 7, 1941) which brought the United States into World War II.

Largely because of intermarriage with other races, and because of the high native mortality due to disease immediately following the first contact with Europeans, pure-blooded

At a Hawaiian luau, a feast at which a wide variety of native delicacies is served

Polynesians (q.v.), the native racial stock of the Hawaiian Islands, comprise a very small segment of the population of the Territory. In the order of size, the other most important ethnic groups are Caucasians, Japanese, Filipinos, part-Polynesians, Chinese, Puerto Ricans, and Koreans. Christianity is the religion of the overwhelming majority of the Hawaiians, and English is the official language.

Education in the Territory is free and compulsory between the ages of 6 and 16. In 1952–53 there were 194 public schools from kindergarten through the twelfth grade, with an enrollment of 101,321; private schools numbered 125, with an enrollment of 25,864. The chief institution of higher learning in the islands is the University of Hawaii, a Territorial university founded in 1907. Enrolled students at the university in 1952–53 numbered 6025, and the faculty numbered 235.

Under the laws of the United States, the executive authority of the Territory of Hawaii is vested in a governor and secretary, both appointees (subject to the approval of the U.S. Senate) of the President of the United States, and in certain other officials, including an attorney general and a treasurer, who are appointed by the governor. Legislative power is lodged in a bicameral legislature, consisting of a senate of 15 members elected for four-year terms and a house of representatives of 30 members elected for two-year terms. The legislature meets biennially. The Territory is represented in the Congress of the United States by an elected delegate, who has a voice in congressional deliberations but no vote. Judicial power in the Territory is vested in a supreme court, a circuit court, a United States district court, and various minor courts. The judges of these courts are appointed by the President of the United States.

History. Hawaii was originally settled by Polynesians who probably migrated from S.E. Asia around the 6th century A.D. in large sea-going canoes. In later centuries a feudal system of land ownership akin to that of medieval Europe arose, according to which lands on the islands as well as fishing rights in the coastal waters were owned by chiefs who allotted smaller portions of the land to the commoners who tilled it for them, and supplied part of the produce to the ruling family. A system of taboos (see TABOO) served to regulate relations between commoners and chiefs. Interisland warfare was common.

The English explorer James Cook was the first European of whom there is record to visit the archipelago. Cook, who landed at Kauai on January 18, 1778, named the group the Sandwich Islands, in honor of the Earl of Sandwich. At that time, political sovereignty in the islands was divided among four native monarchs. Between 1782 and 1810, Kamehameha, the king of the island of Hawaii, extended his rule over the other islands. The dynasty established by Kamehameha, a wise, capable ruler, endured until 1872. In the interim, the Hawaiian kingdom came increasingly under the influence of western civilization, particularly after the arrival, beginning in 1820, of a large body of missionaries from New England. Among other things, the missionaries devised a written form for the Polynesian language, taught many of the islanders to read and write, and converted large numbers of them to Christianity. Constitutional rule was adopted in the kingdom in 1840, and twelve years later the royal government was liberalized. For more than two decades after the death (1872) of Kamehameha V, the last of the dynasty, the kingdom was torn by political strife, a result of royalist attempts to usurp constitutional rule. The constitutional movement, supported mainly by foreigners who favored annexation of the kingdom by the United States, effected the deposition of Queen Liliuokalani on January 17, 1893, and the organization of a provisional government. Failing to secure President Grover Cleveland's approval of the annexation project, the constitutionalists, led by Sanford Ballard Dole (q.v.), proclaimed, on July 4, 1894, establishment of the Hawaiian Republic. The movement for annexation continued, and on July 6, 1898, the Congress of the United States approved the necessary legislation. On June 14, 1900, the islands were formally constituted as the Territory of Hawaii. A protracted movement for admission of the Territory as a State of the Union was endorsed by the Hawaiian electorate by a vote of 46,174 to 22,428 in the elections of 1940. Subsequently, a bill authorizing the admission of the Territories of Alaska and Hawaii as the 49th and 50th States of the United States, respectively, was introduced into the U.S. Congress. The bill received the approval of the House of Representatives in 1947 and again in 1950, but the Senate failed to take action. Delegates from the various islands convened (April, 1950) in a Statehood convention and drafted a State constitution. This document was approved later in 1950 by the Territorial legislature and electorate. Statehood for the Territory was endorsed in 1952 by the Republican and Democratic national conventions.

The U.S. Senate combined the Hawaiian and Alaskan Statehood bills in March, 1954, and approved the combined bill on April 1. On July 26 the House Rules Committee tabled a resolution for a joint conference on the measure. The 83rd Congress took no further action on the bill.

HAWK, common name for any of the smaller birds of prey in the family Accipitridae, the larger birds being known as eagles, and the birds of intermediate size as hawk eagles. Hawks have strong, curved beaks, long legs with large, powerful claws, and long tails. Contrary to popular belief, not all hawks feed on poultry; although a few hawks regularly eat birds, most species subsist chiefly on small rodents, reptiles, and insects. Hawks are keen-sighted and have a loud, piercing cry. They build bulky, loosely constructed nests of twigs and bark at the top of a high tree or on a rocky ledge. Two to six eggs are laid in a clutch.

Hawks were formerly grouped in the same family as the falcons (q.v.), from which they differ in having short, broad, rounded wings. In falconry (q.v.), or hawking, falcons are known as "noble" hawks and true hawks as "ignoble" or "short-winged" hawks. Many American falcons are today popularly called hawks because of past confusion between members of the Hawk and Falcon families. Fifteen genera in the Hawk family are found in North America, including buzzards and eagles, and the goshawk, harrier, kite, and osprey (qq.v.).

Two well-known American hawks are the sharp-shinned hawk or bird hawk, *Accipter velox,* and Cooper's hawk, *A. cooperi,* both found throughout North America. These two hawks are unusual in that their diet consists chiefly of birds. The sharp-shinned hawk is about 1 ft. long. Above it is leaden gray; below, white, streaked with gray, black, and light orange. Its tail is square tipped. Cooper's hawk, *A. cooperi,* also known as the quail or swift hawk, is similar in coloring when young to the sharp-shinned hawk; when adult it differs in having a black crown. It is from 15 to 18 in. long and has a rounded tail. Cooper's hawk eats chickens, grouse, ducks, and pigeons. The Mexican black hawk, *Urubitinga anthracina,* is found from s. Arizona and Texas to N. South America. It is about 22½ in. long and is grayish black.

The common European hawk is the sparrow hawk, *Accipter nisus,* which is about 14 in.

American Museum of Natural History
Adult male Cooper's hawk

long and resembles the sharped-shinned hawk in coloring. The American sparrow hawk, *Falco sparverius,* also known as the kitty hawk or grasshopper hawk, is not a hawk but a falcon. It is the commonest falcon in the U.S. It is about 10 in. long, and is chestnut above and tan below. Its crown is red; the sides of its head are bluish. Its wings are bluish gray streaked with white. Another American falcon is the duck hawk or great-footed hawk, *F. peregrinus anatum,* a subspecies of the European peregrine falcon. It is about 17 in. long, and is leaden blue above and tan below. The pigeon hawk, *F. columbarius,* is widely distributed in the U.S. It is about 11 in. long, and is bluish above and brown below.

HAWK EAGLE. See EAGLE; HAWK.

HAWKING. See FALCONRY.

HAWKINS, SIR ANTHONY HOPE (1863–1933), English novelist and playwright, who wrote under the pen name of Anthony Hope, born in London, and educated at Oxford University. He was called to the bar in 1887 and practiced as an attorney until 1894. In that year he wrote his most famous novel, *The Prisoner of Zenda,* a tale of adventure, intrigue, and romance laid in a mythical European kingdom, Ruritania; it was enormously popular and became the model for a whole school of novels, sometimes known as "Ruritanian romances", which dealt with similar adventures in mythical European kingdoms. The story was also widely popular in its dramatized form by Edward Everley Rose, and it was several times made into a motion picture. Its sequel, *Rupert of Hentzau* (1898), was also widely read and dramatized also by Rose. Among Hope's other writings were the works of fiction *The Dolly Dialogues* (1894, a series of witty scenes from the life of the British upper classes), *Quisante* (1900), *The Intrusions of Peggy* (1902), and *Little*

Tiger (1925); and a number of plays. He was knighted in 1918.

HAWKINS or **HAWKYNS**, SIR JOHN (1532–95), English admiral and privateer, born in Plymouth of a family of Devon shipowners and captains. Hawkins' career started in the Guinea slave trade; he stole slaves from their Portuguese captors and sold them himself to the Spanish colonies. In 1567, on a privateering venture, Hawkins was attacked by a Spanish force in the harbor of Vera Cruz and, although defeated, managed to escape to England. Hawkins did not go to sea for several years thereafter; however, he financed several privateering voyages. He became treasurer of the Navy (1573) and then comptroller. In 1588 he was rear admiral in the battle with the Spanish Armada and was knighted for this service. In 1595 Hawkins accompanied Sir Francis Drake on a treasure-hunting expedition to the West Indies and died at sea, off Puerto Rico. See PRIVATEERING; DRAKE, SIR FRANCIS.

HAWKINS or **HAWKYNS**, SIR RICHARD (1562?–1622), English naval hero, only son of Sir John Hawkins (q.v.). He became a captain in 1585, commanded a queen's ship against the Spanish Armada in 1588, and, in 1593, bought a ship, the *Dainty,* which he used to prey on the overseas possessions of the king of Spain. In 1594, after a journey for plunder around the coast of South America, he was attacked in the Bay of San Mateo (California) by two Spanish ships, captured, and sent to prison first at Seville in 1597 and then at Madrid. He was released in 1602 and returned to England, where he was knighted in 1603. In 1604 he was elected to Parliament, and in the same year he became a vice-admiral. From 1620 to 1621 he served under Sir Robert Mansell in his unsuccessful expedition against the Algerian pirates in the Mediterranean.

HAWK-MOTH or **SPHINX MOTH**, common name for any of the large moths of the family Sphingidae, which are world-wide in distribution. They have thick bodies, pointed at the hind end; their forewings are long, narrow, and pointed, and their hind wings are short. They average about 1½ inches in length and 4 to 5 inches in wingspread. They are powerful and graceful flyers, and usually fly at twilight. The larvae, 3 to 4 inches in length when fully grown, are hairless and usually have a horny projection on the last abdominal segment. They habitually assume a sphinxlike position when at rest by raising the anterior segments of their body. The larvae pupate on the ground or a few inches underground; the cocoon often has a hollow extension to accommodate the developing tongue. The larvae of several species are capable of producing squeaking sounds. The digger wasp (q.v.) uses hawk-moth larvae in the genus *Sphinx* to provision its young.

A common and typical species of American hawk-moth is the white-lined or purslane sphinx, *Celerio lineata,* which has a body length of almost 2 in. and a wing span of 3 in. Its forewings are greenish brown, longitudinally striped with tan, and crossed by a network of white lines. Its hind wings are dark brown with a central orange patch in each. The larva, which reaches a length of 3 in., feeds on the leaves of purslane, apple trees, grapevines, and cotton plants. Also well known are the tobacco and tomato hawk-moths, *Phlegethontius sexta* and *P. quinquemaculata,* so called because of their larvae, the tobacco and tomato hornworms which destroy tobacco and tomato plants and also ravage eggplant and potato crops. The larvae are about 4 in. long. They are pale green, obliquely striped with white, and have a prominent orange horn. The adult moths have a body length of about 2½ in. and a wingspread of about 5½ in. Their wings are grayish brown, spotted with black and white. *Phlegethontius sexta* has six oblong, orange markings on each side of its body; *P. quinquemaculata* has five such markings similarly located.

Other common hawk-moths are the death's-head moth and the hummingbird moth (qq.v.).

HAWK OWL, or DAY OWL, common name for a large owl, *Surnia ulula,* which flies in the daytime, and which has a hawk-shaped head, long, powerful wings, and a long tail. The hawk owl is found in N. North America as far south as Montana, in N. Europe, and in Asia. It is about 16 in. long. Above it is dusky brown spotted with white; below, white streaked with brown. The large circular region (facial disc) under its eyes is white, margined with black, and its tail has about seven thin, white, transverse stripes. While in flight the hawk owl utters a cry similar to that of the osprey.

The name hawk owl is also given to various owls in the genus *Ninox,* found in Madagascar, India, the East Indies, and Australia. Their small heads, long tails, and compact plumage give them a hawklike appearance. Birds in this genus reach a length of 2 ft. See OWL.

HAWKS, Frank Monroe (1897–1938), American aviator, born in Marshalltown, Iowa, and educated at the University of California and the U.S. School of Military Aeronautics. Hawks entered the U.S. Army Air Force in 1917, and served as an instructor until 1919. He was made a lieutenant commander in the U.S. Navy Reserve Air Force in 1933. Hawks made dozens of record-breaking flights. He established a transcontinental speed record for a flight of 12 hours, 25 minutes, and 3 seconds, west to east, and an east-to-west record of 14 hours, 50 minutes, and 43 seconds, both in 1930. He also flew nonstop across the country in 13 hours, 27 minutes, and 15 seconds in 1933. Hawks was an advisory member of the board of the Guggenheim School of Aeronautics of New York University, and the author of *Speed* (1931) and *Once to Every Pilot.*

HAWKSBILL TURTLE or **TORTOISE-SHELL TURTLE,** common name for a small, carnivorous sea turtle, *Eretmochelys imbricata,* the most valuable of all the turtles. It is characterized by a hooked, beaklike upper jaw and by thirteen smooth, clear, imbricated (overlapping) shields on the back of its shell. Natural, commercial tortoise shell is obtained only from these shields, which are black or dark brown in color, richly splashed with yellow. The shields are removed from the turtle's back by the application of heat, often while the animal is still alive. The turtle usually survives such treatment and regenerates new shields which, however, are of low quality and are unfit for commercial use. Tortoiseshell turtles reach a maximum length of about 2½ ft. and subsist on fish, mollusks, and crustaceans. They are found in all warm seas, and in the southwestern Pacific are called "carets".

HAWKWEED, common name of plants of the genus *Hieracium,* belonging to the Chicory family. The genus comprises about seventeen species of perennial herbs, most of which are native to North America and Eurasia. The orange hawkweed, *H. aurantiacum,* has long, hairy, basal leaves, and small, orange-red flowers borne on long, hairy, leafless stems. It is a common weed in fields of N.E. United States. The king devil, *H. pratense,* is a yellow-flowered hawkweed, having bristly basal leaves and smooth upper leaves, which grows in the same area as the orange hawkweed. The rattlesnake weed, *H. venosum,* is a yellow-flowered species of eastern U.S. having thin, often purple-veined leaves. Plants belonging to other genera of the Chicory family, such as

The hawk owl

Picris hieracioides and *Erechtites hieracifolia,* are sometimes called hawkweeds.

HAWKYNS. See Hawkins.

HAWORTH, Sir Walter Norman (1883–1950), English chemist, born in Lancashire, and educated at the universities of Manchester and Göttingen. He was a lecturer and reader in chemistry at the University of St. Andrews from 1912 to 1920, professor of chemistry at the University of Durham from 1920 to 1925, and after 1925 professor of chemistry at the University of Birmingham, of which he was made vice principal in 1947. Haworth did outstanding research in carbohydrates and vitamins. He was awarded many honors, including half the 1937 Nobel Prize in chemistry. He was knighted in 1947.

HAWTHORN. See Crataegus.

HAWTHORNE, Charles Webster (1872–1930), American painter and teacher, born in Maine. He studied with William Chase, in New York City, and later with teachers in Holland and Italy. After winning a number of prizes in National Academy exhibits, he was elected a member of the Academy in 1911. He founded (1899) and for many years conducted the Cape Cod School of Art, which was attended by students from the entire country. Among his works are many paintings of New England fishermen and their wives. "The Trousseau", in the Metropolitan Museum of Art, New York City, is considered one of his finest paintings. He is represented in other permanent American collections.

HAWTHORNE, NATHANIEL (1804–64), American author, born in Salem, Mass., and educated at Bowdoin College. He made lasting friendships at college with his fellow classmates Henry Wadsworth Longfellow, Franklin Pierce (qq.v.), and Horatio Bridge, all of whom were subsequently of great aid to his career. For many years after his graduation his writings received no public recognition; during this period he wrote *Fanshawe* (1828), an unsuccessful novel, and contributed articles and a large number of short stories to magazines. Several of the short stories were published in the volume *Twice-Told Tales* (1837), but the book was not well received by the public even though it included such now-famous stories as *The Minister's Black Veil.*

As he could not earn a living by literary work, he took the job of weigher in the Boston customhouse in 1839; two years later he returned to writing, and produced a series of sketches of New England history for children, *Grandfather's Chair* (1841). The same year he invested in and joined the co-operative community at Brook Farm (q.v.) near Boston, but his taste for solitude was incompatible with the communal demands of the co-operative; he withdrew, and in 1842 married Sophia Amelia Peabody, an abolitionist and transcendentalist, with whom he went to live

Nathaniel Hawthorne

at Concord, Mass. Through his wife he became intimate with his distinguished literary neighbors Bronson Alcott, Ellery Channing, Ralph Waldo Emerson, and Henry David Thoreau. At this time he wrote for the *Democratic Review* a number of sketches and stories which were later collected and published as *Mosses from an Old Manse* (1846); included in this volume were *Roger Malvin's Burial, Rappaccini's Daughter,* and *Young Goodman Brown,* stories which represented his mature genius.

Despite the merit of his work Hawthorne was still unable to earn a living from his writing, and in 1846 he returned to civil service as surveyor of the Salem customhouse. After three years he was dismissed because of political change in the administration, but he had already begun writing *The Scarlet Letter* (1850), a novel which was to bring him international fame and insure his future literary career. This work, considered his masterpiece, has become one of the classics of American literature.

In 1850 Hawthorne moved to Lenox, Mass., where his life, except for the friendship of Herman Melville, was even more secluded than previously. At Lenox he wrote his celebrated novel *The House of the Seven Gables* (1851) and *The Wonder Book* (1851), a recast of classical legends for children; during a short stay in West Newton, Mass., he produced *The Snow-Image and Other Twice-Told Tales* (1852) and *The Blithedale Romance,* which was inspired by the Brook Farm episode.

In 1852 he restlessly returned to Concord, where he wrote the *Life of Franklin Pierce;* for this work Pierce, after becoming U.S. President, rewarded Hawthorne with the consulship at Liverpool, England. He spent seven years in Europe, and during a stay in Italy collected material for his popular romance *The Marble Faun* (1860).

In 1860 he returned to the United States on the eve of the Civil War; his isolation from current partisan politics is indicated in his dedication of his last book, *Our Old Home* (1863), to the then unpopular ex-President Pierce. While traveling with Pierce in 1864, Hawthorne died, and was buried at Concord, near the graves of Emerson and Thoreau.

Hawthorne, romancer of a grim New England past, was a moralist whose conscience-ridden Puritan mind was concerned always with ethical problems. In his preoccupation with sin he followed the tradition of his Puritan ancestors, but in his concept of the consequences of sin, as either punishment or regen-

Stockton C. of C.

Modern machinery greatly reduces the amount of time and labor required to harvest a hay crop. Above: Machine which compresses and ties the hay into bales.

eration, he deviated radically from the views held by his forebears. His special genius lay in his ability to evoke a shadowy and unworldly atmosphere peopled by characters struggling with emotional conflicts.

Among Hawthorne's other works are the unfinished novels *Septimius Felton* (1872), edited by his daughter Una and the poet Robert Browning, and *Dr. Grimshawe's Secret* (1883), edited by his son Julian; and his *American Notebooks* (1868), *English Notebooks* (1870), and *French and Italian Notebooks* (1871), edited by his widow.

HAY, term applied to forage plants, such as certain grasses and legumes, used to make cured fodder for livestock. Curing may be done in the field, or by "barn finishing" or dehydration.

Hay which is to be field cured is cut in the morning as soon as the dew has evaporated. The hay is piled in rows, called windrows, as soon as the leaves begin to wilt. Windrows are turned with pitchforks the following day to allow the hay to dry uniformly. When the weather is favorable, field-cured hay is ready for storage in the afternoon of the day following cutting. The hay is then stored indoors in a haymow, or piled in a large outdoor heap, called a haycock. Properly cured field hay con-

tains between 20 and 25 percent of moisture.

Barn-finished hay is incompletely dried in the field and then placed in a mow, where drying is completed by forcing natural or heated air through the hay.

In artificial dehydration, hay is taken from the field as soon as it is cut, or after it has wilted. The hay is then chopped to a suitable size and passed through a hot-air chamber which rapidly evaporates the moisture.

Proper curing is necessary for efficient preservation of hay. When hay is not dried soon after harvesting, fermentation processes reduce the quantity of carbohydrates and carotene. Excessive drying, on the other hand, results in loss of protein.

Over 75,000,000 acres of hay are harvested in the U.S. each year, yielding over 100,000,-000 tons of hay. For information on hay grasses and legumes see GRASS; LEGUME.

HAY, JOHN MILTON (1838–1905), American statesman and author, born in Salem, Indiana, and educated at Brown University. He studied law in the office of Abraham Lincoln, and was admitted to the Illinois bar in 1861. Upon Lincoln's inauguration, the President made Hay one of his private secretaries, and the latter served in that capacity until Lincoln's death in 1865; during that period he also saw sev-

Joseph Haydn

eral months' active field service in the Civil War, from which he retired with the brevet rank of colonel.

Hay was appointed secretary of the U.S. legation in Paris in 1865, and in Madrid in 1868. He returned to the United States in 1870 and devoted himself to writing for the next twenty years, except for a short period in 1879–80 when he was first assistant secretary of state. He was an editorial writer on the New York *Tribune* from 1870 to 1875, and during that period wrote a book of his travels, *Castilian Days* (1871) ; a book of poems in the dialect of the Illinois frontier, *Pike County Ballads* (1871) ; and an anonymous novel, *The Bread-Winners* (1884). With John Nicolay, another one of Lincoln's secretaries, he wrote the authoritative work *Abraham Lincoln: A History* (10 vols., 1890).

In 1897 Hay was appointed ambassador to Great Britain, and in 1898 he became U.S. secretary of state, serving until his death in the cabinets of Presidents William McKinley and Theodore Roosevelt. As secretary of state he directed the peace negotiations after the Spanish-American War, was influential in protecting American interests in China during the Boxer rising, initiated the Open Door (q.v.) policy in China and worked for the preservation of the administrative entity of the Chinese Empire, and arranged for arbitration of the dispute over the boundaries of Alaska between the United States and Great Britain. His most important achievement was securing the abrogation of the Clayton-Bulwer Treaty

by means of the Hay-Pauncefote Treaty (qq.v.), which opened the way to American construction and management of the Panama Canal.

Hay was also a notable orator; among his best-known speeches were *On the Unveiling of the Bust of Sir Walter Scott in Westminster Abbey,* May 21, 1897, and his memorial address on President McKinley. In 1910 the John Hay Library, a memorial contributed by Andrew Carnegie and others of Hay's friends, was dedicated in his honor at Brown University.

HAY ASTHMA. See HAY FEVER.

HAYDN, JOSEPH, in full FRANZ JOSEPH (1732–1809), Austrian composer, born in the village of Rohrau. At the age of eight he became a chorister at St. Stephen's, in Vienna, where he studied singing, the clavier, and the violin. In 1749, when his voice began to break, he was dismissed from St. Stephen's and turned adrift, penniless, in Vienna. He acquired a few pupils and became an accompanist at the singing lessons of the Italian composer Niccolo Antonio Porpora, who corrected Haydn's composition exercises; this was the closest contact Haydn ever had with regular musical training in composition. In 1751 he composed his first Mass (No. 11, Novello edition), in which was revealed his lack of training; to overcome this weakness, Haydn studied the theoretical works of Johann Joseph Fux, Johann Mattheson, and Johann Peter Kellner.

Haydn's prestige as a composer and teacher mounted steadily during the next ten years, and in 1761 one of the wealthiest men in Hungary, Prince Paul Anton Esterházy, engaged him as assistant kapellmeister at Eisenstadt. In 1766, under his second employer, Prince Miklós Esterházy, Haydn was raised to the position of kapellmeister at the sumptuous palace of Esterház. There he had an orchestra of his own and by writing constantly for it he was enabled to develop an extraordinary technique; during his stay at Esterház he composed 5 masses, 11 operas, 60 symphonies, 40 string quartets, 30 piano sonatas, and other works. In 1781 Haydn met Mozart and the respect and admiration of each master for the other resulted in mutual benefit to their subsequent creative output.

After the death of Prince Miklós, Haydn accepted the frequently proffered invitation of the concert manager Johann Peter Salomon, and on New Year's day, 1791, he arrived in England. He was well received in London, and although he stayed only six months he returned in 1794 to stay another year. Haydn's visits to England are well marked by the twelve celebrated *London* symphonies written at the request of Salomon; and he received an honorary degree of Doctor of Music from Oxford University, for which he presented a symphony (*Oxford*), written three years previously. Having been asked by Salomon to write music for a poem based on Milton's *Paradise Lost*, in 1798 Haydn used the poem for his famous oratorio *The Creation*. About this time Haydn, who had admired greatly the English anthem *God Save the King*, presented Austria with the anthem *Gott erhalte Franz den Kaiser*. In 1808 Haydn made his last public appearance. He died a year later, and memorial services were held for him in all the principal cities of Europe.

Haydn has been called the "father of orchestral music"; he enlarged the symphony orchestra, and contributed greatly toward perfecting the quartet and symphonic forms. His compositions number approximately 104 symphonies, 85 string quartets, and many other works, including operas, concertos, overtures, and sonatas.

HAYES, CARLTON JOSEPH HUNTLEY (1882–), American historian, born in Afton, N.Y., and educated at Columbia University. He was appointed lecturer in history at Columbia in 1907 and was advanced to a professorship in 1919. He became Seth Low professor in 1935 and professor emeritus in 1950. From 1942 to 1944 he was U.S. ambassador to Spain. He is well known for his textbooks and studies in history. Among his numerous works are *Essays on Nationalism* (1926), *The Historical Evolution of Modern Nationalism* (1931), *Political and Cultural History of Modern Europe* (1936), *Generation of Materialism, 1870–1900* (1941), *Wartime Mission in Spain* (1945), *The United States and Spain* (1951), *Modern Europe to 1870* (1953), and *Contemporary Europe Since 1870* (1953).

HAYES, HELEN (1900–), American actress, born Helen Hayes Brown, in Washington, D.C., and educated at the Sacred Heart Academy in that city. She made her debut at the age of six at the National Theatre, Washington, in the role of Prince Charles in *The Royal Family*. She subsequently gained considerable popularity as a child star, performing in *Little Lord Fauntleroy*, *The Prince and the Pauper*, *The Babes in the Wood*, and *Old Dutch*. She made her first appearance in an adult role as Elsie Beebe in *To the Ladies*

(1922–24). In 1928 she married the American playwright Charles MacArthur. Her best-known role was that of Queen Victoria in *Victoria Regina* (1935–38), in which she portrayed the vigorous personality of the celebrated queen from youth through old age. In 1936 she won the annual award of the Drama League of New York.

Among the many notable plays in which she appeared are *She Stoops to Conquer* (1924), *Caesar and Cleopatra* (1925), *What Every Woman Knows* (1926), *The Good Fairy* (1931), *Mary of Scotland* (1933), *Candle in the Wind* (1941), *Harriet* (1943–44), *Happy Birthday* (1946), and *Mrs. McThing* (1952). She appeared in the motion pictures *Arrowsmith* (1931) and *A Farewell to Arms* (1932), and received the Motion Picture Academy Award for 1931–32 for her performance in *The Sin of Madelon Claudet*. She made her television debut in 1950, and in 1952 received the award of the Academy of Television Arts and Sciences as best actress of the year. She wrote *Star on Her Forehead* (with Mary Kennedy, 1949).

HAYES, PATRICK JOSEPH, CARDINAL (1867–1938), American Roman Catholic prelate, born in New York City, and educated at Manhattan College in New York City, St. Joseph's Seminary in Troy, N.Y., and the Catholic University of America in Washing-

N.B.C.

Helen Hayes

ton, D.C. He was ordained to the priesthood in 1892. In 1903 he became chancellor of the archdiocese of New York, and from 1903 to 1914 was first president of Cathedral College, New York. In 1907 he was appointed domestic prelate by Pope Pius X. He was consecrated auxiliary bishop of New York in 1914 and the following year became rector of St. Stephen's Church in that city. In 1917 he was appointed Roman Catholic chaplain bishop for the United States Army and Navy; in 1919 he became archbishop of New York, and in 1924 he was created a cardinal. Cardinal Hayes was the personal representative of Pope Pius XI at the Eucharistic Conference at Cleveland, Ohio, in 1935.

HAYES, ROLAND (1887–), American Negro tenor, born in Curryville, Ga. He received his general education at Fisk University and through an extension course at Harvard University. He subsequently studied music both in America and in Europe. Hayes made concert tours in the U.S. and Europe from 1916 on, and gave command performances before George V of England (1921) and the Queen Mother Maria Christina of Spain (1925). He achieved special recognition as an interpreter of Negro melodies. In 1925 he was awarded the Spingarn medal for "most outstanding achievement among colored people".

HAYES, RUTHERFORD BIRCHARD (1822–93), nineteenth President of the United States, born in Delaware, Ohio, and educated at Kenyon College and Harvard Law School. He was admitted to the Ohio bar in 1845. After practicing law for several years at Lower Sandusky (now Fremont), he moved in 1850 to Cincinnati, where he became a prominent lawyer. He was active in 1856 in the first Presidential campaign conducted by the Republican Party. From 1858 until 1861 he served as city solicitor of Cincinnati. Following the outbreak of the Civil War, he was commissioned a major in the Union Army. He served with distinction throughout the war, rising to the rank of colonel in 1862 and brigadier general in 1864. In 1865 he was brevetted a major general. His distinguished war record gave him a popular reputation in his home State; and in 1864, while still in the army, he was nominated and elected a U.S. representative from Ohio, on the Republican ticket. Re-elected in 1866, he remained in Congress until November, 1867, when he was elected governor of Ohio. In 1876, while serving his third term as governor, Hayes was nominated by the Repub-

lican Party as its candidate for President of the U.S. Samuel J. Tilden received the nomination of the Democratic Party. The election was closely contested and the electoral votes of several States were challenged in Congress, which established a commission to adjudge the contested returns (see ELECTORAL COMMISSION OF 1877). The commission rejected Tilden's claims and Hayes won by a majority of one electoral vote, the count being 185 to 184.

New York Historical Society
President Rutherford B. Hayes

The Hayes administration pursued a conciliatory policy toward the defeated Confederate States (see RECONSTRUCTION); because Hayes withdrew the Federal occupation troops from the South, he incurred the hostility of many Republicans. His advocacy of civil-service reform also antagonized various Republican politicians. In fiscal affairs, he endorsed the resumption of specie payments by the government, and recommended that government bonds be paid in gold; see GREENBACKS. After his term expired, Hayes retired to private life.

HAYES-TILDEN DISPUTE, THE. See ELECTORAL COMMISSION OF 1877; ELECTORAL COLLEGE; HAYES, RUTHERFORD B.; TILDEN, SAMUEL J.

HAY FEVER, a seasonal ailment, having symptoms similar to those of a severe head cold, which affects the mucous membranes of the nose, pharynx, and eyes. The ailment has many other common names, such as hay asthma, rose fever, and summer catarrh. Hay fever usually occurs in late spring or early fall as an allergic reaction to specific types of windborne pollen which are inhaled into the respiratory tract. Individuals affected by hay fever develop symptoms during every season in which pollen to which they are sensitive is released. At least one hundred different species of plants produce pollen which causes hay fever in specific individuals. The most widely recognized irritant is ragweed pollen, which causes a large minority of hay fever cases. Goldenrod pollen, formerly thought to be the most common irritant, is insect-distributed and rarely enters the human respiratory tract. The reaction of individuals who have hay fever may be due to a single type of pollen or to any of a large number of types. Methods of diagnosis of the causative pollen are similar to those used to diagnose other allergies; see ALLERGY. Relief may be obtained most effectively by administration of antihistaminic drugs; see HISTAMINE.

HAYMARKET SQUARE RIOT, a riot which took place on May 4, 1886, in the Haymarket, a square in Randolph Street, Chicago. At the time, a strike was taking place at the McCormick reaper works in Chicago, and on the previous day several men had been killed by the police during a riot at the plant. The May 4th meeting was called at the Haymarket by a group of international anarchists (see ANARCHISM) living in Chicago, and had as its object a protest against police violence. The police attempted to disperse the Haymarket meeting, and in the ensuing riot a bomb was thrown which killed seven policemen and wounded twenty-seven. Eight anarchists attending the meeting were arrested and charged with being accessories to the crime, as they had publicly and on frequent occasions advocated such violence. The eight were tried and found guilty of the bomb throwing; seven were sentenced to death and one to imprisonment. Eventually four were hanged; one committed suicide; the death sentence of two was commuted to life imprisonment; and one was sentenced to a fifteen-year term. In 1893 the three who were in prison were pardoned by the governor of Illinois, John Peter Altgeld (q.v.), on several grounds, of which the most important was that no evidence had been presented at the trial actually connecting the defendants with the throwing of the bomb.

HAYNE, ROBERT YOUNG (1791–1839), American politician, born in St. Paul's Parish,

Colleton District, S.C., and educated privately at Charleston. After studying law he was admitted to the Charleston bar in 1812. In 1814 he was elected to the State legislature, becoming speaker in 1818. He also served as attorney general of South Carolina from 1818 until 1822. In 1823 he was elected to the U.S. Senate, where he became known as a vigorous supporter of States' rights and of the institution of slavery. He participated in 1830 in a noted debate with Daniel Webster (q.v.) on the relation of the States to the Federal government, contending that the States could, at their discretion, nullify or refuse to enforce a Federal law. In 1828, and again in 1832, he opposed the Federal protective tariffs, and in November of the latter year was active in the Nullification Convention which nullified "certain [Federal] acts . . . purporting to be laws". Soon after, Hayne resigned from the Senate.

In December, 1832, he was elected governor of South Carolina; at his inaugural address he pledged himself to maintain the principle of nullification, thus setting himself up in opposition to President Andrew Jackson, who had issued a proclamation upholding the Federal laws; see NULLIFICATION. He was mayor of Charleston from 1835 to 1837, and president of the Louisville, Cincinnati, and Charleston Railroad from 1836 until his death.

HAYNES, ELWOOD (1857–1925), American inventor, born in Portland, Ind., and educated at the Worcester Polytechnic Institute and Johns Hopkins University. In 1894 he built one of the first successful American "horseless carriages"; this automobile is now on exhibition at the Smithsonian Institution. From 1898 to 1925 Haynes was at the head of a company which manufactured passenger automobiles bearing his name. He also developed a number of alloys, such as tungsten chrome steel, used in automobile manufacture, and alloys of cobalt, chromium, and molybdenum. In 1919 he patented a type of stainless steel.

HAYNES, JOHN (1594–1654), English colonial administrator in America, born in Essex. He was a Puritan, and in 1633, with other members of his sect, he emigrated to America, settling in Newe Towne (now Cambridge), Mass. He served as governor of Massachusetts in 1635–36, and in 1637 moved to Hartford, Conn. After helping to frame the constitution of Connecticut, he was chosen governor of that colony in 1639, and served in that capacity until his death.

HAY-PAUNCEFOTE TREATY, an agreement negotiated in 1901 between the United States and Great Britain, providing for the construction and regulation of a canal across the Isthmus of Panama; it was signed by John Hay, then secretary of state of the U.S., and Lord Julian Pauncefote, then British ambassador to the U.S. The treaty superseded the Clayton-Bulwer Treaty (q.v.) of 1850 as the definitive statement of Anglo-American policy concerning an Atlantic-Pacific canal.

Following the Spanish-American War of 1898, with a resultant American interest in South and Central America, American public opinion began to demand abrogation of the 1850 treaty, which permitted neither the U.S. nor Great Britain to act alone in regard to the canal. Though several attempts had been made by European companies to construct the canal, the U.S., cognizant of defense problems in an area so near its boundaries, felt that such an enterprise should be wholly American. Great Britain was amenable, provided that the neutrality of a canal zone would be maintained.

Conversations between Hay and Pauncefote, in 1900, resulted in a treaty draft giving the U.S. complete direction of the construction project, establishing permanent neutrality of the zone and a ban on fortifications, and inviting other nations to join in guarantees of neutrality. The U.S. Senate, refusing to ratify the original draft, amended it to permit the U.S. to take any measures for its own defense in the canal zone, and deleted the clause concerning other nations. Great Britain opposed these amendments, and conversations were resumed. A revised draft was presented to the Senate in 1901 and ratified shortly after its presentation. By the terms of the ratified treaty, the U.S. was given full control of the construction and management of the canal; the U.S. was named sole guarantor of canal neutrality and permitted to build fortifications; and the canal was opened to ships of any nation under equal terms, though the U.S. could forbid passage in time of war. In 1911 Great Britain claimed that the U.S. had contravened the last clause by passing the Panama Canal Act, exempting American coastwise shipping from paying canal tolls; President Woodrow Wilson, agreeing with the British view, persuaded Congress to repeal the Act in 1914. See PANAMA CANAL.

HAY RIVER, a river of Canada, rising in the Rocky Mountains in N.E. British Columbia, and flowing N.E. through Alberta, emptying into Great Slave Lake in Mackenzie District,

Northwest Territories. It has a total course of about 360 m., and is navigable for 140 m. from its mouth. In its upper course, the flow of the river is swift, forming falls and rapids, the most notable of which are the Alexandra Falls, which have a drop of about 250 ft.

HAYS, WILL H. (1879–1954), American politician and administrator in the motion-picture industry, born in Sullivan, Ind., and educated at Wabash College. He became an active member of the Republican Party in his youth, and after serving on the Indiana Republican State Central Committee was elected chairman of the Republican National Committee in 1920. As a reward for his support in the Presidential election campaign of 1920, President Harding appointed him postmaster general in the following year. Hays resigned from that office in 1922 to become president of the Motion Picture Producers and Distributors of America, Inc. He brought about the establishment, by the producers themselves, of a code of motion-picture censorship, and became widely known for his stringent enforcement of the code. He retired in 1945.

HAYTER, STANLEY WILLIAM (1901–), English painter and etcher, born in London. His works, characterized by an abstract pattern of interwoven lines, were exhibited extensively in England and Paris before he came to New York City, where he organized a graphic workshop chiefly concerned with experimental techniques. He also formulated a theory on "automatism" in drawing, which, in his own words, is "the unconscious activity of the mind . . . exhibited by the uncontrolled movement of the hand". Among his works are the paintings "Jeux d'Enfant" (owned by the French government) and "Victim" (St. Louis City Museum), and the etchings "Laocoön" and "Tarantelle" (National Gallery, Washington, D.C.) and "Lucrèce" (Museum of Modern Art, New York City). He wrote *New Ways of Gravure* (1949).

HAYWOOD, WILLIAM DUDLEY (1869–1928), American labor leader, born in Salt Lake City. He began working as a miner at the age of fifteen. In 1896 he joined the newly formed Western Federation of Miners, and first received national attention through his leadership, in 1904, of a strike in Cripple Creek, Colo. In the following year he became one of the founders of the Industrial Workers of the World (q.v.). In 1905 also, he was accused, along with others, of having taken a part in the murder of Frank R. Steunenberg, the former governor of Idaho. However, after a trial that attracted nationwide attention, Haywood was acquitted in 1907. He led the textile strikes in Lawrence, Mass., in 1912 and in Paterson, N.J., in 1913. When the United States entered World War I, Haywood was arrested on charges of sedition for his antimilitarist activities and was tried in 1918. Later he was released on bail while awaiting a new trial, and fled to the Soviet Union, where he remained until his death. He was co-author, with Frank Bohn, of *Industrial Socialism* (1911). His autobiography, *Bill Haywood's Book,* was posthumously published (1929).

HAY WORM, the clover hay worm. See CLOVER: *Diseases and Injurious Insects.*

HAZARA, a district of the North-West Frontier Province, Pakistan, situated between the Indus R. on the w., and the Indian state of Kashmir on the E. The district consists chiefly of the valley of the Kunhar R. and is enclosed by towering ranges and spurs of the Himalayas. Among the seminomadic tribes inhabiting Hazara are the Akazais, Chargarzais, and Umarzais. Area, about 3000 sq.m.; pop. (1951) 846,000.

HAZARD, a game played with two dice, which originated at least 700 years ago, and was very popular in England, particularly from the 16th to the 18th centuries. It is the game from which craps or dice (q.v.) is derived; the rules varied widely, but were in all cases more or less like craps. *Grand hazard,* or simply *hazard,* as it is called today, is a popular banking game played with three dice. The players place their bets on various spaces of a layout, as in roulette (q.v.). The betting is on any total for the three dice, on even, odd, high, or low throws, and on "raffles", the same number on each of the three dice. The various bets are paid off at different odds. The three dice are thrown by the banker, either from a hazard cup or through a hazard chute which may contain a series of steps down which the dice roll.

HAZELNUT, common name applied to trees and shrubs of the genus *Corylus,* belonging to the Birch family. Hazelnut trees are found throughout the temperate regions of North America and Eurasia. Each plant has separate male flowers borne in catkins and female flowers borne in clusters. The fruit, called the filbert or hazelnut, is an ovoid nut. Two species of hazelnut, *C. americana,* the common hazelnut, and *C. rostrata,* the beaked hazelnut, are native to the U.S. Nuts of these native species are small, and so the plants are not cultivated. The European filbert, *C. avel-*

European filbert, or hazelnut

lana pontica, the cobnut, *C. avellana grandis,* the giant filbert, *C. maxima,* and several hybrids among them furnish the bulk of commercially grown filberts, and are raised extensively in Europe and the U.S. The thick-shelled nut is highly prized for the sweet flavor of its meat. When pressed, filberts yield a bland fixed oil equivalent in quantity to approximately half their weight.

HAZLETON, a city of Luzerne Co., Pa., situated 30 miles s. of Wilkes-Barre. It is served by two railroads. Hazleton, lying at an altitude of 1800 ft. above sea level, is the highest city in the State. It is in the heart of the anthracite coal region, and is an important coal-mining center. Other industries in the city are the manufacture of iron, steel, pumps, chemical filters, brushes, caskets, silk, knit goods, shirts, and clothing. Hazleton is the site of a State Hospital. Coal was first discovered in the region in 1818, and Hazleton was founded in 1820. It was incorporated as a borough in 1856 and as a city in 1891. Pop. (1950) 35,491.

HAZLITT, WILLIAM (1778–1830), English essayist and critic, born in Maidstone, Kent, and educated in private schools. He was sent by his father to Unitarian College, Hackney, to prepare for the ministry, but he left in 1795 and spent the next few years studying metaphysics and painting. In 1812 Hazlitt became dramatic critic for the London *Morning Chronicle*. He was a frequent contributor to the newspaper *Examiner*, which was owned by his friend Leigh Hunt (q.v.). After 1814 he also contributed to the influential *Edinburgh Review*. He also lectured widely on the English drama, particularly on the plays of Shakespeare, for which he created a new appreciation in England. In this period Hazlitt wrote the essays which chiefly established his reputation. They include the volume of literary sketches *The Round Table* (1817), originally printed in the *Examiner; Characters of Shakespeare's Plays* (1817) ; *Lectures on the English Poets* (1818), *Lectures on the English Comic Writers* (1819), and *Lectures on the Dramatic Literature of the Reign of Queen Elizabeth* (1821). Among his other important works are *The Spirit of the Age* (1825) ; *Life of Napoleon Buonaparte* (4 vols., 1828–30), which he considered his major work; and *Sketches and Essays* (1829). Hazlitt belonged to the Romantic school of criticism, which stressed the effect of a work of art on the emotions of the critic and did not seek to apply intellectual standards of criticism. His work is distinguished by acuity, subtlety, and a smooth, colorful style, and was of great influence on both his contemporaries and subsequent writers.

H.D., pseudonym of Hilda Doolittle Aldington (see DOOLITTLE, HILDA).

HEADACHE, or CEPHALALGIA, deep-seated pain in any part of the head except the face. Headaches may occur as a result of mental disturbances, direct pressure within the skull, or physical disturbances in other parts of the body. Headaches of brief duration are usually of minor significance, but persistent, severe headaches are usually an indication of major disturbances.

Headaches due to pressure on the brain are caused by swellings, such as abscesses, tumors, or cysts, or by circulatory disorders, such as hemorrhages. Headaches are frequently present in organic diseases, such as those caused by bacteria, in disturbances of the circulatory or gastrointestinal system, and in disorders of the endocrine system. Headaches may also result from mental disturbances, such as mental fatigue, anger, or frustration. Mild headaches may be caused by almost any disturbance in body function, such as eyestrain, excessive motion, excessive noise, fatigue, or insomnia.

Headaches are named according to the region of the skull in which they occur. *Occipital headaches,* occurring at the back of the head,

may result from meningitis, maxillary sinus disorders, or diseases of the cerebellum. *Parietal headaches,* occurring beneath the anterior portion of the crown, may be caused by sunstroke or constipation. *Frontal headaches,* occurring beneath the brow, may result from catarrh, gastric hyperacidity, or eye infections. *Temporal headaches,* occurring in the region beneath the temples, may be caused by sinusitis or eyestrain. *General headaches,* occurring throughout the head, may be caused by bacterial infection, toxemia, or high blood pressure. *Unilateral headaches,* occurring on only one side of the head, may be caused by brain tumors or abscesses, and are also typical of migraine (q.v.).

Headaches can be relieved by administration of analgesic drugs, such as aspirin, but can be cured only by removal of the organic or functional conditions which cause them.

HEAD-HUNTING, the practice, formerly common among Malay and Melanesian tribes, of decapitating enemies and preserving their heads for trophies or for use in tribal ceremonies. Among some tribes special houses were constructed for the heads taken by the tribe, and in others the heads were kept in the house of the warrior; customs of the Kiwai in British New Guinea required a youth to take an enemy's head to earn manhood and the right to marry. Head-hunting is still practiced in remote sections of Borneo and, to a limited extent, among the Dyaks (q.v.) of Sarawak. The Jivaro Indians of Ecuador also practice head-hunting; their trophies are treated so as to shrink the head to about the size of the fist, and are ornamented in various ways.

HEAD TAX, in the United States, a tax imposed by the Federal government on the owner of a vessel or other medium of transportation, for every alien transported to and legally admitted to the country. When collection from such owner is impracticable, the tax must be paid by the alien. The tax was originally imposed in 1882 on owners of steamships and sailing vessels. Since 1917 the tax has been eight dollars per person; children under sixteen years of age, when accompanying a parent, are exempt from the tax.

HEALD. See LOOM.

HEALTH, term applied to the condition of a living body which is functioning normally. The precise meaning of the term depends on the context in which it is used. In common usage, health is a state in which there is absence of pain or related malfunctions such as dizziness, nausea, or weakness, and in which all readily observable body functions, such as growth, respiration, digestion, and excretion, are being carried on regularly and painlessly. In this sense health is often considered to be a state of absence of disease. In the technical sense used by pathologists, however, health is an ideal state in which all parts of the body are performing with optimum efficiency at all times; such a state of efficiency has never been observed in any organism, but is used as a standard for diagnosis and treatment of structural, functional, or mental disturbances in living bodies. See DISEASE, FUNCTION (in biology); MEDICINE; PATHOLOGY.

HEALTH, BOARDS OF. See PUBLIC HEALTH.

HEALTH, EDUCATION, AND WELFARE, DEPARTMENT OF, one of the ten executive departments of the Federal government of the United States, created by Congressional enactment in 1953. The department is administered by a secretary, who is appointed by the President with the approval of the Senate, and who is a member of the cabinet. Under the provisions of the Congressional enactment, all functions of the Federal Security Agency (q.v.) were transferred to the department. The purpose of the department is the promotion of the general welfare in the fields of health, education, and economic security. The secretary is assisted by an under secretary and two assistant secretaries. Administrative responsibility within the headquarters organization is divided among six staff offices, namely the Office of Administration, which is responsible for planning and co-ordinating all management functions; Office of General Counsel, which is responsible for legal activities; Office of Field Services, which supervises field activities; Office of Publications and Reports, which directs the information program; Office of International Relations, which co-ordinates policies relating to international and other Federal agencies; and Office of Federal-State Relations, which co-ordinates activities in conjunction with the States. Ten regional offices of the department are responsible for the implementation of its policies on the regional level.

The major agencies of the department include the Public Health Service, the Social Security Administration, the Food and Drug Administration (qq.v.), the Office of Education (see EDUCATION, OFFICE OF), and the Office of Vocational Rehabilitation. The last-named agency co-operates with the States in providing vocational rehabilitation and guid-

ance for those who are vocationally handicapped.

Also under the supervision of the department are Saint Elizabeth's Hospital, an institution for the treatment of qualified mentally ill persons, the American Printing House for the Blind, which distributes educational materials for the blind without cost to public institutions, Columbia Institution for the Deaf, which provides free instruction for the deaf of the District of Columbia, and Howard University (q.v.).

HEALTH INSURANCE. See INSURANCE, HEALTH.

HEALTH, NATIONAL INSTITUTE OF. See PUBLIC HEALTH SERVICE, U.S.

HEALTHS, DRINKING OF. See TOASTS.

HEALY, GEORGE PETER ALEXANDER (1813–94), American portrait painter, born in Boston. He studied art in Paris, and in 1858 settled in Chicago, where he painted a number of portraits. In 1869 he went to Europe with his family and remained for a long period in Rome. He painted portraits of the French statesman François Guizot and Pope Pius IX in 1871, and also executed portraits for King Louis Philippe. On his return to America he was given many important portrait commissions. His portraits of General Grant, Henry Clay, and John Calhoun are in the Smithsonian Institution, Washington, D.C. His well-known portraits of Presidents John Quincy Adams, Andrew Jackson, Van Buren, and Lincoln are in the Corcoran Art Gallery, Washington, D.C.

HEALY, TIMOTHY MICHAEL (1855–1931), Irish nationalist leader and first governor general of the Irish Free State, born in Bantry, County Cork. He went to London in 1878, and wrote articles, dealing chiefly with the question of Irish independence, for the *Nation,* an American periodical. In 1880 Healy was elected a member of the House of Commons. He immediately distinguished himself by his vitriolic attacks on the policy of the British government with regard to Ireland. In 1900, when nationalist factions formed the United Irish League, Healy became a member of the league, but was expelled two years later for his disruptive influence. He thereupon became one of the sharpest critics of the Irish nationalists in the House of Commons, and gradually adopted a political position which accorded in many respects with that of the Sinn Fein (q.v.) party. Shortly after the proclamation of the Irish Free State in 1922, he was appointed its first governor general. During the five years of his

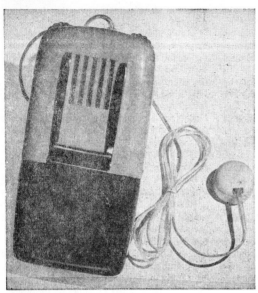 

Western Electric Co., Inc.

THE MODERN HEARING AID. *Left: Exterior of vest-pocket size electronic amplifier and receiver. Right: Interior of amplifier showing batteries, tubes, and other parts of the mechanism.*

tenure in that office he fostered good relations between the Irish Catholics and Protestants, and did much to assist the Irish government in establishing itself on a sound basis. He resigned in 1927, and wrote his memoirs, published under the title *Letters and Leaders of My Day* (1928).

HEARING. See AUDITION; EAR.

HEARING AIDS, a term sometimes applied to any instruments designed to assist the partially deaf to hear, but generally confined to compact electronic amplifiers used for this purpose. A modern hearing aid is usually a three- or four-tube amplifier with an associated microphone, telephone receiver, and batteries. The amplifier is sometimes so designed that it gives a maximum of amplification in the frequency range in which its wearer's hearing loss is greatest. By the use of small electron tubes and dry cells, and such techniques as printed circuits (q.v.), hearing-aid amplifiers, complete with their batteries, can be made small enough to fit in a man's vest pocket. The receivers used are also of miniature size and are either fitted into the wearer's ear or are clamped against the bone back of the ear by means of a headband so that sound is conducted to the inner ear through the bones of the head. Hearing aids using transistors as substitutes for vacuum tubes are in the experimental stage of development.

The chief present-day advantage of these electronic devices is the greatly reduced operating costs, as transistors require only one battery and no heater current; see TRANSISTOR.

HEARN, LAFCADIO, full name PATRICIO LAFCADIO TESSIMA CARLOS HEARN (1850–1904), writer, born on the Greek island of Santa Maura, the son of an Irish father and a Greek mother. He was educated at Ushaw Roman Catholic College, Durham, England. Hearn came to the United States at the age of nineteen, and for some years worked as a newspaperman in Cincinnati and New Orleans. In 1887 he was sent to the West Indian island of Martinique as correspondent for *Harper's Weekly;* the record of his experiences there is contained in *Two Years in the French West Indies* (1890). He went to Japan in 1890, and taught English at the University of Tokyo until 1902, when his health began to fail. So ideal did the life and customs of the Japanese seem to him that he married a Japanese woman and became a Japanese citizen under the name of Yakumo Koizumi; he also adopted the Buddhist religion. He was the author of a number of works in which he sought to interpret the Japanese to the Occident. These writings include *Glimpses of Unfamiliar Japan* (1894), *Gleanings in Buddha Fields* (1897), *A Japanese Miscellany* (1901), and *Japan, an Attempt at Interpretation* (1904).

HEARSAY EVIDENCE. See EVIDENCE.

HEARST, WILLIAM RANDOLPH (1863–1952), American newspaper and magazine publisher, notable in the history of United States journalism for the vast extent and influence of his enterprises. He was born in San Francisco, the son of George Hearst (1820–91), a wealthy lead-mining entrepreneur and politician. The younger Hearst attended Harvard University from 1883 to 1885; in 1887 his father made him owner and editor of the San Francisco *Examiner*. Hearst adopted the sensational journalistic methods of the newspaper publisher Joseph Pulitzer (q.v.), featuring large banner headlines, a profusion of pictures and other illustrative material, colored comic and magazine sections, and detailed news accounts of crimes. The paper prospered, and Hearst, an active member of the Democratic Party, became an influential figure in local, State, and national politics.

In 1895 he purchased the New York City *Morning Journal* for $7,500,000. Under Hearst's direction, the *Morning Journal* became the chief competitor of Pulitzer's New York *World,* from whose staff Hearst recruited such outstanding journalistic figures as the editorial writer Arthur Brisbane, the author Stephen Crane, and the cartoonist Richard Outcault (qq.v.). In 1896 Hearst began publication of the *Evening Journal*. By the middle of that year, the combined daily circulation of these two newspapers had reached the then unprecedented figure of 1,500,000.

For some years prior to 1898 Hearst insistently advocated war with Spain. Following the war the Hearst papers attacked President William McKinley in such violent language that when McKinley was assassinated in 1901, a large number of persons boycotted the Hearst papers. Hearst changed the name of the *Morning Journal* to the *American;* it was this paper which, in 1937, was merged with the *Evening Journal* to become the New York *Journal-American.*

Hearst was elected a Democratic member of the U.S. House of Representatives in 1903 and again in 1905, but was defeated in his campaigns for the mayoralty of New York City in 1905 and 1909, and for the governorship of New York in 1906. In ensuing years he twice attempted to win the Democratic nomination for the New York governorship and on one occasion the nomination for the Presidency; he was unsuccessful in these endeavors.

During the years of his political activities

Hearst steadily expanded his journalistic properties; by 1925 he controlled a chain of twenty-five newspapers, published in most of the major cities of the United States. In the same period he developed and controlled the International News Service, a press agency which supplied his papers with news from all parts of the world. In the management of his journalistic enterprises he employed the method of syndication, previously developed by a rival publisher, Edward Wyllis Scripps (q.v.), whereby feature articles were distributed to all papers of his chain for simultaneous publication.

As Hearst acquired newspapers he also entered the field of magazine publishing. In 1905 he purchased *Cosmopolitan Magazine,* the name of which he later changed to *Hearst's International-Cosmopolitan.* Eventually, his magazine properties in the United States included also *Good Housekeeping Magazine, Harper's Bazaar, Town and Country,* and several other periodicals. He also acquired the ownership of several magazines published in England, including *Nash's Magazine, Pall Mall Magazine,* and the British editions of his American periodicals.

During the economic depression of the 1930's, a general decline in newspaper circulation in the United States caused Hearst to reduce the number of his newspaper holdings. At the conclusion of these operations, his chain comprised seventeen daily newspapers. Those with the largest circulation were the New York *Daily Mirror,* the New York *Journal-American,* the Chicago *Herald-American,* the Los Angeles *Examiner,* and the Boston *Sunday Advertiser.* In a recent year, the combined circulation of the Hearst daily newspapers was in excess of 5,500,000, and that of the Sunday editions was almost 9,000,000. The combined circulation of Hearst's eight American magazines was approximately 6,260,000. In addition, he published a Sunday supplement, the *American Weekly,* which was distributed to all of the Hearst Sunday papers and to several others as well, and had a total circulation exceeding 9,410,000.

Hearst's newspaper and magazine properties comprised only a portion of his enterprises. He was also one of the first American businessmen to recognize the uses and value of the motion picture, and began the production of newsreels about 1911. He later formed the Hearst Cosmopolitan Film Corporation, and in association with the Metro-Goldwyn-Mayer Corporation, became the owner of Hearst-Metrotone News, one of the largest

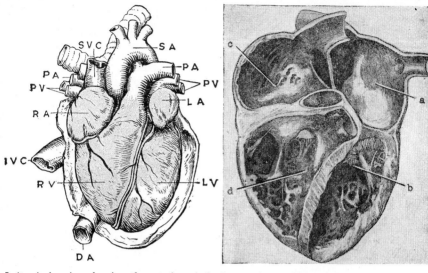

Left: A drawing showing the exterior of the human heart. SVC, superior vena cava; PA, pulmonary arteries; PV, pulmonary veins; RA, right auricle; IVC, inferior vena cava; RV, right ventricle; DA, dorsal aorta; LV, left ventricle; LA, left auricle; SA, systemic arch leading to the aorta. Right: Drawing showing the interior of the human heart. (a) left auricle; (b) left ventricle; (c) right auricle; (d) right ventricle.

newsreel companies in the United States. He also made large investments in a variety of other business fields in the United States, South America, and Africa.

The nature of the policies advocated by Hearst's publications made him one of the most controversial figures of his time. He was denounced by many for his isolationist policy and for his extreme nationalism. He was praised by others as an ardent patriot, who was devoted to what he considered the best interests of his country. In his later years, Hearst retired to the comparative seclusion of his estate at San Simeon, Calif., and gradually entrusted to his son, William Randolph Hearst, Jr., an increasing measure of active control of his enterprises.

HEART, in anatomy, the hollow muscular organ which receives blood from the veins and propels it into and through the arteries. In man the heart of an individual is about the size of his closed fist, and from ⅝ to ⅔ of 1 percent of his total weight. It is situated behind the lower part of the breastbone, extending more to the left of the midline than to the right. It is roughly conical in shape, with the base directed upward and to the right and slightly backward; the apex touches the chest wall between the fifth and sixth ribs. The heart is held in place principally by its attach-

ment to the great arteries and veins, and by its confinement in the pericardium, a double-walled sac with one layer investing the heart and the other attached to the breastbone, the diaphragm, and the membranes of the thorax.

Within the adult heart are two parallel, independent systems, each consisting of an auricle, or *atrium,* and a ventricle; from their anatomical positions these systems are often designated the right heart and the left heart respectively.

Blood from the various veins in the body passes into the superior and inferior venae cavae; blood which has supplied the muscles of the heart itself passes into the coronary vein. These large veins empty into the right auricle; contraction of the auricle forces the blood through the tricuspid (q.v.) valve into the right ventricle which, in turn, contracts, forcing the blood through the pulmonary arteries into the lungs. Blood from the lungs passes through the pulmonary veins into the left auricle; upon contraction of the left auricle, which occurs simultaneously with that of the right auricle, blood is forced through the bicuspid or mitral valve into the left ventricle, which then contracts, forcing the blood through the aorta to all parts of the body, and through the coronary arteries.

The blood forced from the ventricles during contraction, or *systole,* is prevented from returning during *diastole,* or relaxation, by valves at the openings of the aortic and pulmonary arteries. The valves of the heart consist of semilunar (half-moon shaped) flaps of membrane: two flaps in the case of the bicuspid valve, and three flaps in all others. They are curved in the direction of blood flow, so that they open readily on pressure in that direction, but are closed by back pressure, forcing the edges of the flaps together when the original pressure subsides. The tricuspid and bicuspid valves, having to bear the full pressure of systole, are reinforced and prevented from inverting by the *chordae tendinae,* tendinous cords attached to the valve flaps and to the muscles of the heart wall. The muscle fibers of the heart interlace in an irregular, basketlike arrangement; the only muscular connection between the auricles and the ventricles, however, is the atrioventricular bundle, or *bundle of His,* which transmits the impulse of contraction from the auricles to the ventricles, thereby controlling the sequence of contraction in the heart cycle. The rate of heart beat is controlled by the autonomic nervous system (q.v.), being accelerated by the sympathetic system and depressed by the bulbosacral. Although the nerves and certain drugs influence the rate of the heartbeat, heart muscle is inherently contractile and will continue contracting at a regular rate even when all connection with the nervous system is severed. Tissue for a chicken's heart has been kept alive and beating in a flask for many years; see LINDBERGH, CHARLES.

In the embryo the heart develops from the fusion of the two ventral aortas, forming a single pulsating organ. Separation into right and left hearts takes place later with the formation of an interauricular and an interventricular septum (partition). The separation is not completed, however, until the lungs begin their function at birth. Before birth the blood is oxygenated in the placenta and returns to the right auricle through the inferior vena cava; it is then directed by the Eustachian valve through the *foramen ovale,* a persistent opening in the interauricular septum. After birth the Eustachian valve degenerates to a rudiment and the foramen ovale normally closes, but the opening may persist in varying degree even in the adult in about one fifth of the population. See HEART, DISEASES OF THE.

The heart produces two sounds in each cycle of the beat. The first is rather dull, and is caused by vibration of the auriculoventricular valves and by the contraction of the ven-

tricular muscle fibers; the second is sharp and is caused by the sudden closure of the aortic and pulmonary valves. In disease these sounds may be replaced or accompanied by murmurs caused by blood rushing through abnormal openings; their detection is of great importance in diagnosis. Other important diagnostic methods include use of the electrocardiograph, a device which records the currents produced by the heart, and the examination of conditions inside the heart by introducing a fine catheter into a vein and passing it through the venous system into the chambers of the heart. See also CIRCULATION OF THE BLOOD.

HEART, DISEASES OF THE. Disorders of the heart arise from congenital defects, structural or functional changes, infection of the heart tissues, and from the effects of infections elsewhere in the body, high blood pressure, drugs, and prolonged overexertion.

The most important congenital defects include persistence of fetal connections between the arterial and venous circulations, such as the *foramen ovale* (see HEART) and the *ductus arteriosus,* an embryonic vessel connecting the pulmonary artery and the aorta. Such defects, together with insufficient development of the blood vessels leading to the lungs, are the common cause of "blue babies", new born infants whose skin is blue because insufficient blood reaches their lungs. Formerly the expectation of life of such infants was extremely limited; modern surgical developments, however, give blue babies a much better chance of survival; see CYANOSIS.

Rheumatic heart disease is one of the most serious forms of heart disease of childhood and adolescence. It is often secondary to focal infections of such structures as the tonsils or sinuses, and follows attacks of rheumatic fever (q.v.). The damage to the heart generally involves the entire heart and its membranes; in mild cases inflammation of the pericardium and heart muscle causes only temporary damage, but generally the damage to the lining of the heart and to the valves persists, especially after recurrent attacks.

Myocarditis (q.v.) is inflammation or degeneration of the heart muscle. Although it may appear at any age from various diseases such as syphilis, goiter, endocarditis (qq.v.), or hypertension (see ARTERIES, DISEASES OF THE; BLOOD PRESSURE), myocarditis is usually a degenerative disease of old age. It may be due to dilation (enlargement due to weakness of the heart muscle) or to hypertrophy (overgrowth of the muscle tissue).

Minor variations in the heart rhythm usually have little pathological significance. The heart rate responds to the demands of the body over such a wide range that such variations are generally within normal limits. Respiratory arrhythmia (variation of the heart beat with inspiration and expiration) is a normal phenomenon, and extra systoles (occasional irregularities in the heart rhythm) may have no significance. Paroxysmal tachycardia (recurrent periods of extremely fast heart beat) causes no damage in a normal heart, but if the heart is diseased, further weakening of the heart muscle may result. Auricular fibrillation (complete irregularity of the heart beat) is a serious symptom, occurring usually in a heart damaged by rheumatic infection, a toxic heart of exophthalmic goiter, or in chronic myocarditis.

Other diseases of the heart include angina pectoris, pericarditis (qq.v.), and disease of the coronary arteries.

Although in recent years great advances have been made in the early recognition of heart disease through the use of the electrocardiograph and through bacteriological examination of the blood, and the life expectancy of patients with heart disease has been lengthened materially, diseases of the heart lead all other causes of death in the United States, being responsible for more than 30% of all deaths. In a recent year they caused almost 430,000 deaths. See VITAL STATISTICS.

HEARTS, a game of cards, usually played by three or four players, in which each player attempts to lose as many tricks as possible in order to lose all his cards in the heart suit. The game is played with a complete 52-card deck; all the cards are dealt in succession, one to each of the players. The first player to the left of the dealer plays any card he likes, the rest of the players following suit. The highest card of the suit led wins the trick (ace is high), and the winner leads the next trick. If a player cannot follow suit he may play any card he pleases, and thus has an opportunity to get rid of his hearts. When all the tricks are played each player counts the number of hearts he has taken in and, in the usual method of scoring, scores one point for each heart; after several hands have been played the person who scored the lowest number of points wins the game.

There are many variations of the game. In one variation the queen of spades is given the value of thirteen in the settling of the score. In another popular variation a player may attempt to take in all of the thirteen hearts in the deck. If he succeeds he gains a bonus by

losing points; if he takes in less than thirteen hearts the game is scored as usual.

HEARTSEASE, common name applied to several unrelated plants, referring to their supposed healing properties. The wild pansy, *Viola tricolor,* is the plant most commonly called heartsease, but the term is applied to other violets, such as *V. ocellata;* see VIOLET. Selfheal (q.v.), a mint, and lady's thumb, a knotweed (q.v.), are called heartsease in North America. In Australia, members of the genus *Gratiola* (q.v.), the hedge hyssops, are called heartsease. The term was formerly applied to the wallflower (q.v.).

HEAT, the term applied to that form of energy which causes rises in temperature and other related phenomena such as the fusion or melting of solids. For many centuries heat was regarded as an invisible and imponderable fluid, sometimes called *caloric,* but experiments made by 19th-century physicists clearly proved that other forms of energy, such as mechanical and electrical energy, can be converted into heat energy and also that heat energy can be converted into energy of other forms. According to the well-established kinetic theory (q.v.), the phenomena of heat are caused by the agitation or movement of the molecules and atoms of which matter is constructed. The greater the motion of the atomic particles of a given object, the hotter it is; and similarly the less the activity, the colder the object is. At the point where there is no activity whatever, there is no heat whatever, and the object reaches *absolute zero* (q.v.), about $-273.16°$ C. $(-459.69°$ F.). In actual practice absolute zero has never been attained, but researchers in the field of cryogenics (q.v.) have produced temperatures less than one-hundredth of a degree Centigrade above absolute zero.

A distinction is made between heat and temperature. Heat is a form of energy. Temperature is the measure of the intensity of the heat of a body. Two bodies at the same temperature may contain different amounts of heat because of differences of mass or of specific heat (q.v.). Heat never flows naturally from an object to another object at higher temperature. Heat has been called the "lowest form of energy"; other forms, such as electrical, mechanical, or chemical, can be readily transformed into heat, but heat energy can be transformed into work only when it is available in the form of two heat reservoirs at different temperatures, and even then only a fixed percentage of the heat which flows from the high-temperature to the low-temperature reservoir can be so transformed. See THERMO-DYNAMICS.

Temperature Scales. In the study of heat, scientists have found it convenient to adopt scales to admeasure degrees of heat in the same way that distances are measured, by reference to a convenient arbitrary unit. Two such temperature scales are in general use: the Fahrenheit and Centigrade scales. In the former scale (which originally defined as its zero point the lowest temperature obtainable with a mixture of ice and common salt) the temperature of freezing water is 32° and that of boiling water 212°. In the Centigrade scale the temperature of freezing water is taken as 0° and that of boiling water as 100°. Temperatures given in Fahrenheit can be converted to Centigrade by subtracting 32, dividing by 9, and multiplying by 5. Centigrade temperatures can be converted to Fahrenheit by dividing by 5, multiplying by 9, and adding 32. The Centigrade scale has been generally adopted by scientists all over the world and is also used by the general population in most countries. The Fahrenheit scale, which because of its smaller divisions is somewhat more convenient for describing atmospheric temperatures, is used in the English-speaking world. A third scale, the *absolute* or *Kelvin* scale, is also sometimes used in scientific work; see ABSOLUTE TEMPERATURE. For instruments used in the measurement of heat see CALORIMETRY; THERMOMETRY.

Heat Energy. Heat energy is measured in terms of the *calorie,* defined as the amount of heat necessary to raise the temperature of one gram of water from 15° to 16° C. This unit is sometimes called the "small calorie" to distinguish it from the *Calorie* or "large Calorie", equal to 1000 calories, which is used in nutrition studies. See also BRITISH THERMAL UNIT. Mechanical energy is converted into heat energy by friction, and the mechanical work necessary to produce one calorie is known as the *mechanical equivalent of heat.* It is equal to 41,800,000 ergs (99.3 foot-pounds) per calorie. According to the law of the conservation of energy, all the mechanical energy expended to produce heat by friction appears as heat energy in the objects on which the work is performed. This fact was first conclusively proved in a classic experiment performed by the English physicist James Prescott Joule, who heated water in a closed vessel by means of rotating paddle wheels and found that the rise in water temperature is always proportional to the work expended in turning the wheels.

When heat energy is converted into mechanical energy, as in an internal-combustion engine, the law of energy conservation also applies, and the heat loss is equivalent to the mechanical energy produced. In any engine, however, some energy is always lost or dissipated in the form of heat because no engine is perfectly efficient.

Latent Heat. A number of physical changes are associated with the change of temperature of a substance. Almost all substances expand when heated and contract when cooled. The behavior of water between 0° and 4° C. (32° and 39° F.) constitutes an important exception to this rule. Even more important are the so-called *changes of state:* the change of a solid to a liquid and the change of a liquid to a gas as the temperature of the substance is raised. Associated with these changes of state is the phenomenon of latent heat. When water is boiled in an open vessel the temperature does not rise above 100° C. (212° F.) no matter how much heat is applied to the outside of the vessel. The heat which is absorbed without changing the temperature of the water is the latent heat and is not lost but is expended in changing the water to steam and is then stored as potential energy in the steam; it is again released when the steam is condensed to form water. Similarly a mixture of water and ice in a glass will not change its temperature when heated until all of the ice is melted. The latent heat absorbed is used up in overcoming the forces holding the particles of ice together and is stored as potential energy in the water. To melt one gram of ice 79.7 calories are needed, and to convert one gram of water to steam at 100° C. requires 540 calories.

Transfer of Heat. Heat is transferred from one point to another and from one object to another by three methods: *convection, conduction,* and *radiation* (q.v.). A liquid or gas expands when heated and becomes lighter. Thus when a body of fluid is heated the warmer portions rise and the colder portions sink. This motion, known as convection, distributes the heat throughout the body of the fluid. When one end of a metal rod is heated, heat "flows" along the rod and can presently be felt at the other end, remote from the heat source. The mechanism of this phenomenon, called conduction, is not entirely understood but is probably analogous to electrical conduction in that it results from the transmission of the molecular agitation of heat to adjacent molecules. In general, substances which are good conductors of heat are also good conductors of electricity. Radiant heat, like

Nature Magazine

Long-leaved heath (Erica longifolia)

light and radio waves, has the ability to propagate itself through empty space; the warmth of the sun, for example, traverses millions of miles of space before it reaches the earth. All substances which are not at absolute zero radiate heat but also absorb heat radiated from other objects. Thus, although a piece of ice placed near a steam radiator loses heat by radiation, it simultaneously receives more radiant heat than it gives up, and hence melts. On the other hand, a piece of ice in a cold storage plant loses at least as much heat as it receives and thus remains frozen.

Dull surfaces radiate and absorb more heat than do bright surfaces, and rough surfaces radiate and absorb more than smooth ones. In measuring heat radiation, physicists make use of the concept of the *absolutely black body,* a body which absorbs the total amount of radiation that strikes it and which radiates more heat than any other body at the same temperature. The number of ergs per second radiated by such a body per sq. cm. is equal to the fourth power of the absolute temperature of the body times the constant .0000572. Other substances which are less perfect radiators follow the same general law but with proportionally smaller constants. Industrial furnaces are almost ideal black bodies and their temperatures may be calculated by measuring the heat radiated and applying the formula stated above.

HEATH, common name applied to the plant family Ericaceae (q.v.) and to two ericaceous genera, *Calluna* and *Erica,* which are also called heather. The common heath or heather, also called broom or ling, is *C. vulgaris,* a native of northern and western Europe and of New England and the maritime provinces of Canada. It is the principal vegetation of low waste areas near seacoasts of both continents. This plant is a small, evergreen shrub which usually grows only a few inches tall but may exceed three feet in height when growing in sheltered places. It has purple stems bearing small, crowded leaves and feathery spikes or racemes of small, white or rose, bell-shaped flowers. The stems are used in making brooms, baskets, and brushes. The flowers, which have a cool, pleasant odor, are often dried and made into sachets.

The genus *Erica* contains about 500 species, the majority of which are native to the western portions of South Africa, although many species grow in the Mediterranean region, and a few extend into northern Europe. Two species, *E. cinerea* and *E. tetralix,* are naturalized on Nantucket Island, Massachusetts, but no members of the genus are native to the United States. The Scotch or purple heath, *E. cinerea,* is an abundant N.W. European species which produces large amounts of honey in its nectaries. Its capsular fruits are eaten by grouse and other moorland birds. Other common species of the British Isles are *E. tetralix,* the cross-leaved heath, and *E. vagans,* the Cornish heath. The white heath or bruyère, *E. arborea,* which grows in the w. Mediterranean region, has thick, heavy underground roots which yield brierwood, used in making brier pipes. The Irish heath, *Daboecia cantabrica,* is a close relative of the true heaths. Several heaths are cultivated in gardens of the U.S. The most popular and hardy form for northern gardens is *C. vulgaris,* but many of the more attractive South African species of *Erica* are grown in California.

HEATH COCK. See BLACKCOCK.

HEATHER, a popular name for plants of the genera *Calluna* and *Erica,* also called heath (q.v.).

HEATHFIELD, BARON. See ELIOTT, GEORGE AUGUSTUS.

HEATH HEN, common name for either the female black grouse (q.v.) or for an extinct subspecies of prairie chicken (q.v.), *Tympanuchus cupido cupido.* The latter bird, which closely resembled the common prairie chicken, was formerly abundant from New Hampshire to Pennsylvania. It was so widely hunted as a game bird that about 1800 it began to diminish in number, and by 1896 could be found only on the island of Martha's Vineyard, Massachusetts, where it was protected by law. First fire and then disease overtook the remaining specimens, and in 1932 the last heath hen died and the variety became extinct.

HEATING, VENTILATION, AND AIR CONDITIONING, the allied processes of warming the interiors of buildings and of circulating, humidifying, dehumidifying, cleansing. and cooling the air within them. The purpose of these processes are twofold: to make buildings comfortable for the people who live and work in them, and to control the temperature, humidity, and cleanliness of the atmosphere in factories where atmospheric conditions affect the quality of the products made.

Heating. Two basic methods are employed for the heating of buildings: direct heating by radiation, and indirect heating in which air is warmed and then circulated through the building. The earliest forms of househeating were all direct. They included the open fires with which primitive men warmed their dwellings, and stoves and braziers of various types, adopted by the Romans and still employed in various parts of the world. In the colder portions of Europe, the fireplace was developed as a method for heating rooms by means of an open fire. The first fireplaces were hearths, recessed into the walls of buildings, with short flues that communicated with the open air. Fireplaces with high chimneys, which rose above the roof of the building and which provided adequate draft to keep the fires on the hearth burning brightly, were introduced during the 12th century. Modern types of direct heating include gas fires, the radiators of hot water and steam systems, and various types of "radiant heating" devices in which a panel or an entire floor, wall, or ceiling surface is used to radiate heat.

The most common form of indirect heating system is a centralized hot-air system in which air is warmed in a central furnace and distributed by means of pipes to the various rooms of a building. Hot-air furnaces were developed in the 19th century and were the first type of centralized heating units. This type of heating was later supplanted by steam and hot-water furnaces, but in recent years has once more become important as a part of integrated heating and air-conditioning systems.

Fireplaces. Ordinary fireplaces consist of a hearth enclosed on three sides with brick and surmounted by a completely enclosed chimney or flue which carries away the smoke and combustion products of the fire. On the hearth is a metal grate raised on legs or a pair of metal supports called *firedogs* or *andirons* (q.v.). Grates are used when coal, coke, or cannel coal is used for fuel, and andirons when wood is used. The purpose of these devices is to permit the circulation of air under the fuel for combustion. Another type of fireplace has a circular hearth in the center of the room over which hangs a metal hood shaped like an inverted funnel which leads to the chimney.

The useful heat given off by a fireplace consists of the heat radiated directly by the burning fuel and that which is absorbed and reradiated by the side and back walls. From 85 to 90 percent of the heat of the burning fuel is lost in the combustion gases and smoke which go up the chimney. The inclusion of fireplaces in modern houses is for their esthetic value rather than their thermal efficiency. In an effort to improve the heating efficiency of fireplaces, some modern fireplaces are built with an arrangement of interior ducts in which cold air from the room is warmed and then recirculated through the room.

Stoves. The stove, an enclosure of metal or ceramic materials in which fuel is burned, is an improvement over the fireplace because its radiating surface is relatively larger and also because it is in contact with the air of the room and gives a certain amount of heat by air convection. An efficient modern stove utilizes about 75 percent of the heat of the fuel burned in it. In rural areas of the U.S. and in many other parts of the world stoves are still employed extensively for the heating of houses. The fuels burned in stoves include wood, coal, coke, peat, illuminating gas, and kerosene.

Centralized Heating. In the early 19th century a number of attempts were made to develop a practical system whereby one centralized heating unit could be used to warm several rooms or an entire house. The hot-water system of centralized heating was first used to a limited extent in England about 1816, but the first wholly succesful centralized system was not constructed until 1835. This system, which was of the hot-air type, became popular in the U.S. Steam heating was developed about 1850.

In England the term central heating is applied to the heating of a single dwelling or other building by an individual furnace. In the U.S. the term is applied to the distribution of heat, usually in the form of steam, to a group of buildings. Such a central-heating

When bin transmits heat, cool air from room is fanned into bin. This makes salt solidify, releasing warmth from cans and sending it into rooms. Cooled air is then sent up to collectors for reheating. ↓

Winter sunbeams → strike heat collector, become warm air, flow to storage bins below.

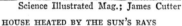
↑ When bin stores heat, cans of Glauber's salt absorb warmth from air, become liquid, send cooled air to collector in attic to pick up more heat from sunlight.

Science Illustrated Mag.; James Cutter

HOUSE HEATED BY THE SUN'S RAYS

Above: Cutaway drawing of a section of the experimental house built in 1948 which utilizes the thermal properties of Glauber's salt to hold and distribute solar heat.

Left: A diagram of this house in summer, when sun's angle is high. Due to the high angle, the sun's most intense rays do not strike the heat collector, and the well-insulated house remains cool all summer.

system may be private, as in the case of the heating systems of schools and institutions, or may be conducted as a public utility. In New York City thousands of buildings are heated with steam provided from central boiler rooms operated by a public-utility company. Central heating is only practical where buildings are grouped closely together, and most heated buildings are provided with their own systems.

Hot-Air System. In its simplest form a hot-air heating system consists of a firebox and flue set within a sheet-metal casing and located below the first floor of the house. Cold air either from within the house or from outdoors is admitted between the firebox and the casing and is heated by its contact with the walls of the firebox. As the air is heated it rises and passes through a grill or *register* in the floor above the furnace to circulate through the building. A hot-air furnace of this kind, having only one hot-air outlet, is usually called a *pipeless furnace*. More complicated hot-air furnaces are connected by means of large, sheet-metal ducts to individual registers, usually one in each room, which can be opened or closed to control the temperature of the rooms. Frequently the furnace in such a system is so arranged that the warm air passes over a water pan in the furnace for humidification before circulating through the house.

The simple hot-air furnace which circulates air by convection has a number of drawbacks, the most important of which is the difficulty of obtaining an adequate circulation of air by convection alone. Unless the warm air ducts are comparatively large in size, are slanted upward from the furnace, and are properly insulated to prevent heat losses, such a system will not heat a house adequately in cold weather. The addition of a fan or blower in the furnace hood provides a forced draft and allows a large amount of air to be circulated even under unfavorable conditions. With forced draft it is also possible to include dust filters in the system to insure the cleanliness of the air. When combined with cooling and humidifying and dehumidifying units, hot-air systems represent one of the most efficient methods of air conditioning (see below).

Hot-Water Systems. The first hot-water heating systems are said to have used the waters of natural hot springs as a source of heat. In general, however, systems of this type employ a boiler in which water is heated to a temperature of from 140° to 180° F. by means of a coal or coke fire or an oil or gas flame. The water is then circulated by means of pipes to *radiators* or other heat-transfer units located in the individual rooms. Circulation of the hot water can be accomplished either by convection or by means of a pump. For small buildings convective circulation is adequate, but in large installations pumps are normally employed.

Hot-water systems can be classified in two ways according to the method used to return the water to the furnace for reheating. In the one-pipe system, water is admitted to each individual radiator from the upper side of the main supply pipe, flowing back into the underside of the pipe farther along the system. The disadvantage of this arrangement is that the water becomes increasingly cool the farther it flows from the furnace and the radiators farthest from the furnace must be larger than the nearer ones in order to deliver the same amount of heat. In the two-pipe system, all radiators are supplied with hot water from a single supply pipe and the water from all the radiators flows back to the furnace through a common return pipe. The two-pipe system is somewhat more expensive to install than the one-pipe system but is more efficient. In both systems a partially empty expansion tank is included to compensate for variations in the volume of water in the system as it is heated and cooled.

Steam Systems. Steam-heating systems in general resemble hot-water systems except that steam rather than hot water is circulated through the pipes to the radiators. The steam is generated in a boiler similar to that used for water heating in the latter system. Both one-pipe and two-pipe arrangements are employed for circulating the steam and for returning the water formed by condensation back to the boiler. One of the chief advantages of steam systems is that comparatively small radiators can be used, since steam gives off a large amount of latent heat (see HEAT) in condensing, whereas the water in a hot-water system never gives off all its heat in the radiator. Steam systems are sometimes operated at pressures above atmospheric pressure, in which case each radiator is fitted with a valve to permit air (but not steam) to escape into the room. Other systems, called *vapor systems,* have a thermostatic valve at each radiator which permits water and air, but not steam, to pass into the return pipe. In such systems the air is allowed to escape through a single valve in the return pipe. *Vacuum systems,* which are sometimes installed in large buildings, employ vacuum pumps in the return pipe to suck the condensate back to the boiler. With the use of such a system radiators can be installed at a point lower than the boiler.

Radiators. The devices generally employed to transfer heat from the heating system to the area to be warmed are commonly known as radiators, although actually they transfer heat by convection as well as by radiation. Ordinary radiators consist of a series of metal grids or coils, having comparatively large surface area, through which the hot water or steam circulates. The surface of such radiators is dull in color to promote radiation. In many modern heating systems, radiators are replaced by heat-transfer units which consist of a network of finned copper tubes, which present an extremely large surface area in comparison to their volume. These units are frequently placed in enclosures with provision for air circulation so that they heat largely by convection rather than by radiation. In stores, warehouses, and factories *heat diffusers* are often employed, in which an electric fan or blower is used to force a blast of air through the heated coils of the unit.

Radiant Heating. Although all the forms of direct heating described above are forms of radiant heating, this term has come to be popularly applied to systems in which floors, walls, or ceilings are used as the radiating units. In steam or hot-water systems, pipes are placed in the wall or floor when the building is built. If electricity is used for heating, panels containing heating elements are mounted on the wall or ceiling of the room. "Radiant heating" has several advantages: it provides uniform heat and has a comparatively low cost of installation and operation. Efficiency is high because little heat is wasted in warming the air of the room.

Types of Furnaces. The furnaces used in hot-air heating systems are described above. Furnaces for steam and hot-water systems consist of a boiler (q.v.), usually of the fire-tube type, with a firebox below it. If the furnace uses coal as a fuel and is hand-fired, the firebox contains a grate. Furnaces fired by automatic stokers contain chain grates, feed screws, or other devices for conveying the coal to the fire and removing ashes. When oil or gas are used as fuels, special burners are placed in the firebox. Such burners operate intermittently and are turned on and off automatically by means of a remote thermostatic control. In most modern furnaces, the entire unit, both firebox and boiler, is enclosed in an insulated casing.

Special Heating Systems. In recent years a number of attempts have been made to devise new forms of heating systems which would require less fuel or possess other advantages over conventional systems. The most important of these experimental systems are *solar heating* and *heat pumps*.

On the average about 94.6 kilowatt hours of energy fall on each square yard of the earth's surface each hour of the year in the form of solar radiation. This energy has been harnessed both experimentally and practically for such purposes as heating domestic hot water, particularly in tropical regions. The amount of available energy from the sun is more than sufficient to heat buildings, but the chief problem in designing a solar-heating system, particularly for areas with severe winters, is to store the sun's heat so that there is an adequate reserve for nights and cloudy days. Several methods of heat storage have been suggested, and one of the most successful was incorporated in an experimental house built in 1948. In this house a series of metal plates, protected by glass, were arranged at the top of the house so that they were perpendicular to the sun's rays during the winter months. Air is warmed by circulating around these plates and is then drawn into "storage bins" where it is used to heat a number of containers filled with Glauber's salt, which melts at approximately 90° F. (32° C.). The warm air melts the chemical, storing heat in the form of latent heat of fusion. In the nighttime or on stormy days, cool air circulating in the storage bins is warmed as the chemical solidifies, giving off its latent heat, and the warmed air is circulated through the house. The only power used in this heating system is the comparatively small amount used to operate the electric blowers that circulate the air. Tests showed that this solar system was entirely adequate to heat the house during winter months in New England and that the heat storage capacity was sufficient to keep the house warm during ten successive sunless days.

The principle of the heat pump is that of an ordinary refrigerating system in reverse. Outside air, or underground water, is pumped into the system and cooled, and the heat removed from the air or water is used to warm the air within the house. One great advantage of the heat-pump system is that during the summer months the cycle may be reversed and the system may be used for cooling. The power requirements of such a system are only those of the pump, compressor, and blower. No "fuel" is used. In the years after World War II a number of successful heat-pump installations were made in large and small buildings, and systems were made available commercially.

Portable Heating Units. In houses without centralized heating systems and in houses with antiquated or unreliable heating apparatus, various types of portable and semiportable heating devices are frequently employed. The

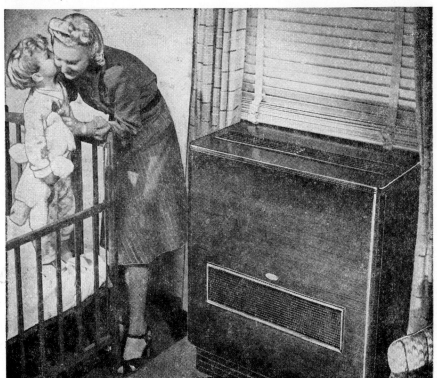

Carrier Corp.; York Corp.

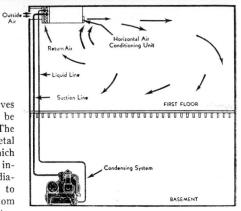

AIR CONDITIONING

Above: A modern air-cooling unit serving only the room in which it is situated. Right: Diagram showing basic plan of the centralized air-conditioning system.

two most common types are kerosene stoves and electric heaters, both of which may be moved from room to room as needed. The usual kerosene stove is made of sheet metal and contains one or more wick burners which heat metal chimneys within the stoves to incandescence. Such stoves heat both by radiation and by convection, being designed to draw in cool air through vents in the bottom of the stove and emit heated air from top vents. Large stoves of this general pattern can provide adequate heat for several rooms and are sometimes known as *space heaters*.

Electric heaters are of several types. The simplest are radiant heaters having a resistance heating unit in front of a reflector which concentrates the radiant heat in a narrow beam. Some devices of this kind include a fan which circulates air around the heating unit, and

thus warm by convection as well as radiation. Another modern type of electric heater consists of a plate of heat-resistant glass in which resistance wires are imbedded. The entire plate is warmed by the wires and gives off radiant heat. As the heater has no incandescent wires, it is safer than the older type. Electric steam radiators are also manufactured and are used to supplement other heating systems. These radiators are miniature steam-heating systems in which an electrical heating unit generates enough steam to warm a small conventional radiator. No piping connections are necessary and the units can be moved from place to place and plugged into any light socket.

Formerly portable radiant gas heaters were used extensively for domestic heating. These heaters, although efficient, have largely been abandoned since gas has been abandoned for illuminating purposes and is no longer piped throughout modern buildings.

Ventilation. Buildings in which people live and work must be ventilated for several reasons: to replenish oxygen and remove carbon dioxide and water vapor; to remove unpleasant odors, such as cooking odors; and to provide a movement of air for the comfort of the occupants of the buildings. In all ordinary buildings a certain amount of air movement or ventilation is provided by convection and by air leakage through small crevices in the building's walls, such as the cracks around windows and doors. A wind blowing against the side of a house creates an excess of pressure on the windward side and a low pressure area on the leeward side which produces natural forced ventilation through the cracks. The flues of chimneys also promote ventilation by drawing off warm air from the interior of the building. Such natural methods of ventilation are, however, usually not sufficient for adequate circulation of air, particularly in buildings such as stores and theaters where large numbers of people are gathered. Engineers estimate that for proper ventilation the air in a room should be completely changed 1½ times each hour or that about 10 cu. ft. of fresh air per minute should be supplied for each occupant. To afford this much ventilation mechanical devices must usually be employed to augment the natural flow of air. Simple ventilation devices usually consist of fans or blowers which are arranged either to exhaust the stale air from the building or to force fresh air into the building. In some more complicated installations both supply and exhaust fans are provided. Ventilating systems are frequently combined with heaters, dust filters, humidifying and dehumidifying devices, and cooling devices. Frequently in an installation of this type outside air is mixed with a certain amount of recirculated air from within the building, particularly when the air has been heated or cooled.

Air Conditioning. True air conditioning consists of a system, usually centralized, which performs all the functions outlined above and provides an atmosphere of controlled temperature, humidity, and purity at all times regardless of weather conditions. In popular language, however, the term "air conditioning" is often improperly applied to air cooling. Many so-called "air-conditioning units" consist of refrigerating units with blowers which simply provide a flow of cool air, filtered or unfiltered.

A number of manufacturing processes demand air conditioning for the control of the products manufactured, such as paper, textiles, and printed books. Such air conditioning is usually based on adjusting the humidity of the circulated air. When dry air is required, it is usually dehumidified by cooling (see REFRIGERATION) or by passing through chambers containing such adsorptive mediums as silica gel. Air is humidified by circulation through water baths or sprays. When air must be completely free of dust, as is necessary in the manufacture of certain drugs and medical supplies, the air-conditioning system is designed to include some type of filter. Some such filters operate by passing the air through water or through a labyrinth of oil-covered plates, but in a number of installations the Cottrell precipitator (q.v.), which removes dust electrostatically, is employed.

Centralized air-conditioning systems are widely employed in theaters, stores, restaurants, and other public buildings. Such installations are usually complex to install and generally must be put in when the building is constructed. In older buildings, single apartments or suites of offices are frequently air-conditioned by installing a refrigerating unit, blowers, air ducts, and a plenum chamber in which air from the interior of the building is mixed with outside air. Such installations are used for cooling (and dehumidification of the air by cooling) during the summer months, and the regular heating system is used during the winter. Smaller units for cooling single rooms consist of refrigerating unit and blowers in compact cabinets which can be mounted in windows.

The design of an air-conditioning system depends upon a number of factors: the amount of space to be cooled, the structure in which the system is placed, the number of people in the space, and the nature of their activity. A room or building with large windows which are heated by the sun, or an indoor office space which has many heat-producing lights, will require a larger cooling capacity than an almost windowless room in which cool fluorescent lighting is used. The circulation of air must be greater in a theater or cocktail lounge where there is much smoking than in an office having the same volume and used by the same number of people. In certain air-conditioning installations, as for example in apartments, most of the cooled or heated air can be recirculated without discomfort to the occupants; but in laboratories or factories employing processes which generate noxious fumes, no air must be recirculated and a constant supply of cooled or heated fresh air must be supplied.

Air-conditioning systems are rated in two ways: the amount of air per minute that the system can circulate, and the amount of cooling or heating of which the system is capable. The smaller units which provide only ventilation, filtering, and air cooling are commonly rated in "tons" of cooling capacity. One ton is equivalent to a cooling capacity of 12,000 B.T.U. per hour.

HEAT TREATMENT. See TEMPERING.

HEAVEN, in Christian theology, that place where the Deity, although present throughout infinite space, gives a more immediate manifestation of His glory to the souls of just men, who, being made perfect, enjoy there the bliss of intuitive contemplation of the Godhead, the beatific vision. Heaven is the abode of the blessed angels who minister to the Most High in perpetual praise and adoration.

Among primitive peoples the concept of life after death was substantially a shadowy continuation of life on earth. Even in that concept, however, the principle of the necessity for vindication of divine justice was manifested. This principle is illustrated in the distinction between Elysium and Tartarus (qq.v.) in the Greek and Roman religions, and the various depths of Sheol (see HELL) of the Jewish Scriptures. Later Jewish mystics regarded the heavens as contained in the seven spheres of the firmament, and found in the Persian doctrine of resurrection a hope of release from Sheol to a new life on earth or in the heavens.

The Greek philosopher Aristotle declared that all (polytheistic) religions united in placing the abode of the gods in the most elevated place in the universe. Such regions were, in classical times, considered as closed to ordinary mortals. The Islands of the Blessed were reached only by heroes, demigods, and favorites of the gods. The heaven of later polytheistic religions was conceived as a place where mortals might continue the pleasures of earthly life, as in the Valhalla

(q.v.) of the Germans and Scandinavians, and the happy hunting ground of the American Indians.

The general belief of Christians is that, since the resurrection of Christ, the souls of the just who are free from sin are admitted immediately after death into heaven, where their chief joy consists in an unclouded vision of God. Their bliss is eternal, but at the general resurrection the souls are to be reunited to their perfected bodies to enjoy an existence like that of the angels of light (Luke 20:36). See also MILLENNIUM.

Mohammedanism, in the Koran, adopts the concept of the seven heavens of the firmament, differing in degrees of glory from the seventh, the abode of the Most High, downward to the first, or most earthy, paradise (q.v.). Although the Koran portrays the happiness of heaven as the unrestricted and inexhaustible partaking of the joys of physical sense, many writers consider this portrayal to be purely allegorical.

Nirvana, the heaven of Buddhism (q.v.), is a state of extinction of all desire, and union with Brahma, achieved by perfecting the soul in the course of its successive transmigrations.

HEAVES, a chronic disease of horses, often called *asthma* or *broken wind,* characterized by difficult breathing and a dry, wheezing cough, and resulting in its final stage in emphysema. Various chronic inflammatory conditions of the lungs, chiefly bronchitis, act as a predisposing cause, and the feeding of dusty or moldy roughage as an immediate cause. Inhalation of dust from such roughage aggravates any respiratory disorder which may be present. The disease is also aggravated by overwork or overfeeding of roughage. Treatment is based upon the administration of arsenic and other tonics and feeding with a restricted diet of sound hay. In advanced cases, however, no permanent remedy is known, and the characteristic symptoms, which include redness of the eyes, deformation of the chest, and abscesses of the neck, are invariably followed by pulmonary emphysema.

HEAVISIDE LAYER. See IONOSPHERE.

HEAVY HYDROGEN. See DEUTERIUM; TRITIUM.

HEAVY WATER, term applied to water in which the hydrogen of the water molecule consists entirely of deuterium, the heavy hydrogen isotope of mass number 2. Heavy water, known also as deuterium oxide, is designated by the symbol D_2O. For the properties and the uses of heavy water, see DEUTERIUM.

The term "heavy water" might also be extended to include tritium oxide, i.e., water in which the hydrogen consists of the heavy hydrogen isotope of mass number 3, called tritium (q.v.).

HEBBEL, FRIEDRICH (1813–63), German poet and playwright, born in Wesselburen, Schleswig-Holstein (then a Danish province). He was largely self-educated, and also attended lectures on law, literature, and philosophy at Heidelberg University. Until 1845 his life was one of poverty; he won no success as a playwright in spite of the literary merit of his dramas. These included the drama in prose *Judith* (1840), the play in verse *Genoveva* (1841), and the prose tragedy *Maria Magdalena* (1844), which in realism was the forerunner of the problem plays of Henrik Ibsen (q.v.). In 1845 Hebbel began a liaison with a noted Viennese actress, Christine Enghaus, whom he married in 1849 and who helped him to gain success as a playwright. His fame depends for the most part on the dramas he wrote after 1845, including the blank-verse tragedy *Herodes und Mariamne* (1848), the prose tragedy *Agnes Bernauer* (1851), the tragedy in verse *Gyges und sein Ring* (1854), and the trilogy *Die Nibelungen* (1862).

HEBE, one of the planetoids (q.v.), the sixth to be discovered, first observed by the German amateur astronomer Karl Ludwig Hencke (1793–1866) in 1847. It revolves about the sun in 1380 days.

HEBE (Gr. *hēbē,* "youth"), in ancient Greek mythology, the goddess of youth, the daughter of Zeus and Hera, and the wife of Heracles after he had been deified. Hebe was the cupbearer of the gods on Mount Olympus before Zeus conferred that office upon the beautiful boy Ganymede. She had the power of restoring the bloom of youth and beauty to the aged. Statues of Hebe are rare, although she is depicted on vases and reliefs. In Rome she was worshiped under the name of Juventas.

HEBER, REGINALD (1783–1826), English prelate and hymn writer, born in Malpas, Cheshire, and educated at Oxford University. In 1804 he became a fellow of All Souls', Oxford, and three years later was ordained to the Anglican ministry. In 1815 he was appointed lecturer at Oxford and in 1822 preacher at Lincoln's Inn. In the latter year he became bishop of Calcutta, India. His writings include *Poetical Works* (1812) and the prose works *A Life of Jeremy Taylor* (1822), *Journey Through India* (1828), and

Sermons (1829, 1830). He is chiefly known for his hymns, including *From Greenland's Icy Mountains; Brightest and Best; God, that Madest Earth and Heaven;* and *Holy, Holy, Holy, Lord God Almighty.*

HEBERT, JACQUES RENÉ, known as PÈRE DUCHESNE (1775–94), French journalist and Revolutionary politician, born in Alençon, and educated at the local college. He lived in poverty in Paris from 1780 to 1790, and then became editor and writer of pamphlets for *Le Journal du Soir,* a journal advocating the most extreme revolutionary measures (see FRENCH REVOLUTION). Later he became editor of the journal *Le Père Duchesne,* for which he wrote violently phrased and highly popular articles in favor of republicanism. From 1792, when he became a member of the Revolutionary Commune, to 1794, he led a revolutionary group so extreme in its policies and in its manner of declaring them that its members were called *les enragés* ("the mad ones"). In particular Hébert and his followers sought to overthrow the Girondists (q.v.), a party with moderate republican principles. The National Convention, which then governed France, became alarmed at the violence of the Hébertist party and had Hébert arrested, but popular demand caused his release. In 1794 he came into conflict with the Committee of Public Safety, which, under Maximilien Robespierre, then exercised a dictatorship over France. Robespierre had Hébert and his followers arrested; after a summary trial Hébert and many of his group were guillotined.

HEBREW LANGUAGE. See SEMITIC LANGUAGES.

HEBREW MUSIC. See JEWISH MUSIC.

HEBREWS, the name given to a group of tribes of Semitic stock which migrated from Mesopotamia into Palestine, and then into Egypt where they were enslaved. They escaped from bondage in Egypt and conquered and settled Palestine. The term was first applied in the Bible to Abraham (Gen. 14:13), in reference to his ancestor Eber or Heber (Gen. 10:21). It is now generally assumed by scholars that the Hebrews are the peoples called Habiri in the Tell el-Amarna (q.v.) tablets (about 1400 B.C.). This assumption coincides with Biblical tradition, although the Amarna correspondence makes no reference to the origin or ethnic character of the Habiri. In Genesis 40:15 Joseph explains to the Egyptians that he had been kidnapped from the land of the Hebrews; in Exodus 2:6 Pharaoh's daughter recognizes Moses as "one of the Hebrews' children". The implication of these sources is that the Israelites were known to foreigners as Hebrews. Etymologically *Hebrews* may mean "those who pass from place to place" or "nomads", and may have been a designation given them by the Amorites. In later times the name was applied to the Jews, not only by foreigners, but also by themselves. See ISRAEL: *History;* JEWS; PALESTINE: *History;* SEMITES; SEMITIC LANGUAGES.

HEBREWS, EPISTLE TO THE, the nineteenth book of the New Testament. The authorship of the epistle has been a subject of controversy since earliest Christian times. Tertullian ascribes it to Barnabas; Origen, to an unknown scribe who organized and set down the oral teachings of St. Paul. In Alexandria and the Eastern Church, it was regarded as the work of St. Paul, either directly or through a translator; this opinion was adopted by St. Augustine and, later, by the Roman Church. Modern scholars are almost unanimous in believing that the epistle was not written directly by St. Paul. This view is based entirely on internal evidence. The language is a purer form of Greek than any other New Testament writing; the style is rhetorical and rhythmic; and the form is carefully planned and systematic, having none of the abruptness and sudden transitions characteristic of the Pauline writings. The writer quotes always from the Septuagint, rather than the Hebrew Scripture, and bases his reasoning on its renderings, even when it deviates from the Hebrew.

The epistle was addressed to a church, such as that at Jerusalem, whose members were largely converts from Judaism, exhorting them to persevere in the faith. It consists of a dogmatic part and a moral part. In the former, the dignity of Christ as the Son of God is contrasted with that of the angels and Moses, through whom the Old Law was given (1 to 4:13), and the priesthood of Christ is compared with that of Aaron, and the sacrifice of Christ with those of bulls and goats under the Old Law (4:14 to 10:18); in the latter part (10:19 to 13:17), the faithful are exhorted to persevere in the faith and in Christian life.

In language, the epistle is the most artistic and literary book of the New Testament; in content, it is necessary to an understanding of the dogma of the early Church, and shares with the Epistle to the Romans (see ROMANS, EPISTLE TO THE) the designation of the first treatise on Christian theology.

HEBRIDES or **WESTERN ISLANDS,** an archipelago off the w. coast of Scotland, generally identified as the Outer Hebrides (or the Long Island) and the Inner Hebrides. The Hebrides total more than 500 islands and islets distributed for administrative purposes among Ross and Cromarty, Inverness, and Argyll counties. The chief islands of the Outer Hebrides, which are separated from the Inner Hebrides by North Minch, Little Minch, and the Gulf of Hebrides, are Lewis with Harris, North Uist, South Uist, and Barra. From the N. to the s. extremity of the Outer Hebrides the distance is about 130 m. The largest of the Inner Hebrides is Skye (q.v.), which is separated from the mainland by narrow Inner Sound. Among the other important islands of the Inner Hebrides are Mull, Islay, and Jura. The group also includes Tyree, Coll, Rum, Eigg, Lismore, Ulva, Kerrera, Staffa, Oronsay, Colonsay, Scarba, Gigha, the Small Isles, and the Slate Islands. Approximately 100 of the islands of the Hebrides are populated, with considerably more than half of the inhabitants living on Lewis with Harris, Skye, and Islay. The language of nearly a tenth of the populace is Gaelic, while the remainder speak either English or both English and Gaelic.

Under the influence of branch currents from the Gulf Stream, the climate of the Hebrides is generally mild. The outstanding physiographical feature of the archipelago is the rocky terrain, which is broken by numerous bogs, moors, lakes, and valleys. The only forests of importance are confined to the islands of Lewis with Harris, Skye, Mull, and Jura. Less than 250,000 acres of the total area are cultivable. Fishing and the raising of livestock are the principal year-round industries; during the summer season catering to tourists and vacationists occupies many of the residents. Other industries on the islands are the growing of oats, potatoes, barley, and turnips, the manufacture of woolen textiles, distilling, and quarrying. Regular steamboat connections are maintained between the mainland and the larger islands.

In the writings of the Roman scholar Pliny, the archipelago is referred to as the *Hebudæ.* The Greek scholar Ptolemy later called the islands the *Ebudæ.* To the Norsemen, who invaded the islands in the 6th century, the group was known as *Sudreyjar* ("Southern Islands"). The early Norse invaders were assimilated in time by the native Celts. A second Scandinavian invasion occurred about

British Information Services

A lake in the moors on the island of Skye, largest of the Inner Hebrides Islands

the end of the 9th century. Norway retained control of the Hebrides until 1266, when the archipelago was transferred to Scotland. During the next few centuries, various Scottish chieftains, chiefly the leaders of the clans MacDougall and MacDonald, ruled the islands. The royal house of Scotland gradually extended its authority over the Hebrides during the 16th century. Beginning with Sir Walter Scott, whose *Lord of the Isles* (1815) dealt with the Hebrides, various Scottish authors have written vivid portrayals of the islands. Total area, 2900 sq.m.

HEBRIDES, NEW. See NEW HEBRIDES.

HEBRON, city of Palestine (since 1950 included in the Kingdom of Jordan) and, according to some authorities, one of the oldest communities in the world, situated in a mountainous region, about 20 miles s.w. of Jerusalem. Among the interesting features of Hebron are the narrow winding streets, the flat-roofed stone houses, the native bazaars, and the mosque of El-Haram. The mosque is built around the supposed sepulcher of Abraham, Isaac, Jacob, Sarah, and other Biblical personages. Known as the cave of Machpelah, the sepulcher has been closed to non-Mohammedans for more than 600 years. Hebron has a number of small-scale industrial establishments, which produce cotton goods, leather water containers, and glass bracelets, rings, and lamps.

Frequently mentioned in the Bible and reputedly founded nearly a decade before the city of Zoan, Hebron was closely identified with the career of Abraham. The town was captured by Joshua, who granted it to Caleb. In later years David made Hebron his seat of government, Joab murdered Abner thereabouts, and Absalom there began his revolt against David. Hebron was later destroyed by the Romans, restored by the Moslems, and captured by the Christians during the Crusades. In 1187 the town again became a Moslem possession. British troops occupied Hebron in December, 1917, during World War I. By the provisions of the United Nations Palestine partition plan in 1947, Hebron was included in the Palestinian territory awarded to the Arabs. Pop. (1946 est.) 26,390.

HECATÆUS OF MILETUS, an early Greek historian and geographer. He strove in vain to dissuade the Ionians from revolting against Persian rule in 500 B.C., and after their defeat in the war with Persia, he went as an ambassador to Artaphernes, the Persian satrap, or provincial governor, and induced him to treat the Ionians kindly. The works of Hecatæus include the *Travels around the Earth* (the authenticity of which, however, has been called into question) and the *Genealogies,* a prose version of the poetic legends of the ancient Greeks.

HECATE (Gr. *Ekate,* "she who works from afar"), an ancient Greek divinity, originally a goddess of the moon. She is first mentioned in Hesiod's *Theogony* as the only daughter of the Titan Perses, and of Asteria, or night. Hecate is praised by Hesiod as a mighty goddess ruling earth, heaven, and sea, the friend of hunters and fishermen, and the bestower of victory in battle. Like other moon divinities, she appears as the helper of women in their confinement, the guardian of children, and the patroness of marriage; she also possesses the power of purifying from sin. Mysteries were celebrated in her honor at Ægina and Samothrace. Another function associated with Hecate was the guardianship of doors and roads, and her sanctuaries seem for the most part to have been little more than wayside shrines. The crossroads were under her special protection, and at them sacrifices, especially of dogs, were offered. In later times, Hecate came to be identified with the lower world, and as such had control of the spirits of the dead and of specters; her coming was greeted by the howling of dogs, and she was invoked with dark incantations by magicians and witches. In art, Hecate was at first depicted as a maiden with a torch, in allusion to her search for Persephone, the daughter of the earth goddess Demeter, whom Hades, king of the underworld, had abducted. Subsequently, however, she assumed the more familiar form of the three-headed and six-armed divinity, variously interpreted as representing the new, the full, and the waning moon, or as the tutelary spirit of the meeting place. A statue of the triple Hecate stood near the entrance to the Acropolis at Athens.

HECHT, BEN (1894–), American writer, born in New York City. He began his writing career at the age of sixteen as a reporter for the Chicago *Journal.* From 1914 to 1923 he was on the staff of the Chicago *Daily News,* heading the Berlin office of that paper in 1919. Hecht founded in 1923 the periodical the *Chicago Literary Times,* which for the next two years expressed the iconoclastic views of a group of artists and writers who had gathered in Chicago after World War I.

Hecht's work is known for its original dramatic qualities, and for the wit and brilliance of its style. His first published novel was *Erik Dorn* (1921), and the short stories he wrote for his column in the *Daily News* were published in 1923 as *1001 Afternoons in Chicago.* His play *The Egotist* (1923) met with some success but was outshone by the brilliance of *The Front Page* (1928), which he wrote in collaboration with Charles MacArthur. With MacArthur he also wrote *Twentieth Century* (1933), *Jumbo* (1935), and *Ladies and Gentlemen* (1939).

Several of the plays on which they collaborated were made into motion pictures, and Hecht wrote the scenarios for a number of outstanding films, including *Scarface* (1932), *Nothing Sacred* (1937), *Wuthering Heights* (1939), and *Kiss of Death* (1947). In 1934 Hecht and MacArthur formed a company to produce the motion pictures they wrote, and their two films completed that year, *Crime Without Passion* and *The Scoundrel,* were acclaimed as masterpieces by the critics. Among Hecht's other works are the collections of short stories *Broken Necks* (1924) and *A Book of Miracles* (1939); the novels *The Florentine Dagger* (1923), *Count Bruga* (1926), and *A Jew in Love* (1930); and the plays *The Great Magoo* (1933, with Gene Fowler), *To Quito and Back* (1937), and *A Flag Is Born* (1946); the musical comedy *Hazel Flagg* (1953); and the autobiography *A Child of the Century* (1954).

HECKELPHONE. See OBOE.

HECKER, ISAAC THOMAS (1819–88), American Roman Catholic priest, born in New York City, and brought up as a Protestant. In 1843 he was a member of the socialistic community at Brook Farm (q.v.), Mass., and also lived for a time at Walden with the writer Henry David Thoreau. In 1844 he was converted to the Roman Catholic faith, and was ordained a priest of the Redemptorist order in 1849. From 1851 until 1857 he worked as a missionary. In 1858, with several colleagues, Hecker founded the Congregation of the Missionary Priests of St. Paul the Apostle, known as Paulist Fathers, or Paulists (q.v.). He became the Congregation's first superior, serving until his death. In 1865 he founded the periodical *Catholic World,* and in 1866 the Catholic Publication Society. His writings include *Questions of the Soul* (1855), *Aspirations of Nature* (1857), and *Catholicity in the United States* (1879).

HECKSCHER, AUGUST (1848–1941), American industrialist and philanthropist, born in Hamburg, Germany, and educated at Weinheim, Germany, and at Neuchâtel, Switzerland. After spending three years in the employ of the importing house of Nolting & Co., in Hamburg, he came to the U.S. in 1868 and entered the coal business, in which he was engaged until 1884. In 1881 Heckscher was one of the organizers of the Lehigh Zinc and Iron Company, and after its subsequent consolidation with the New Jersey Zinc Company he was general manager of the latter concern until 1904. He was a director of several financial and industrial corporations, and the chairman of the Heckscher Foundation for Children (q.v.), which he founded in 1921.

HECKSCHER FOUNDATION FOR CHILDREN, THE, an organization founded by August Heckscher (q.v.) to promote the welfare of children. The Foundation was incorporated on March 15, 1921, and occupies headquarters at 480 Lexington Ave., New York City. The Foundation serves as a distribution center for free new clothing supplied to children recommended by other agencies, such as the Juvenile Aid Bureau, hospitals, schools, and recreation centers. Both money and gifts of equipment are given to agencies for the benefit and welfare of children in New York and other parts of the U.S. The Foundation also grants musical and educational scholarships to deserving students

HECTOR, in Homer's *Iliad* (q.v.), the mightiest of the Trojan warriors. He is the eldest son of Priam and Hecuba, the husband of Andromache, and the father of Astyanax. During a battle of the Trojan war (q.v.), Patroclus, a Greek warrior, dons the armor of his friend and compatriot, the hero Achilles (q.v.). Hector slays Patroclus in the belief that the latter is Achilles. The Greek hero thereupon pursues Hector three times around the walls of Troy, kills him, and, tying the body to his chariot, drags it into the Greek camp. Later the aged Priam, with pathetic supplication, prevails upon Achilles to yield the body of Hector, which is then given an honorable interment at Troy.

HECUBA, in Greek legend, the wife of Priam, king of Troy, and the mother of Paris, Hector, Cassandra (qq.v.), and Helenus, among others. In Homer's *Iliad* (q.v.), she is taken prisoner by the Greeks following the capture of Troy and the death of Priam. In the tragedy *Hecuba,* by Euripides (q.v.), the queen's youngest son Polydorus has been placed, during the siege of Troy, in the care of the Thracian king Polymestor. En route to Greece, where she is being taken by her captors, Hecuba sees the body of her son being washed ashore. To avenge his murder she tears out Polymestor's eyes and kills his two sons.

HEDDLE. See LOOM.

HEDGEHOG, HEDGEPIG, or URCHIN, common name for any spiny, Old World mammal in the genus *Erinaceus* of the family Erinaceidae. Though superficially similar in appearance to the porcupines, it is more closely related to the moles and shrews; see INSECTIVORA. The hedgehog, which is found in Europe, Asia, and Africa, is characterized by a coat of long, stiff, pointed spines on its back. The fur on its underside is soft. Hedgehogs average 10 inches in length and are somber hued, varying in color from light tan in some species to black in others. They have pointed

A family of common European hedgehogs

snouts, small eyes, short legs, and vestigial tails. When endangered, the hedgehog rolls itself into a ball by the action of several powerful, superficial (integumentary) muscles which arise from the head and neck on each side and loop around the rump. In this position its spines project in all directions. Hedgehogs conceal themselves in hedgerows during the daytime and emerge at night to hunt the insects which constitute their chief food; they also eat worms, frogs, snakes, mice, and birds' eggs. Hedgehogs hibernate during the wintertime but their torpor is not deep and they occasionally awaken and emerge from their nest of dry leaves to hunt food. In July or August the female hedgehog gives birth to four to eight white young, which are blind and covered with soft hair at birth. The hair on their backs hardens into spines by the following March.

The common European species of hedgehog is *Erinaceus europaeus,* which is black and white when adult. Other spiny mammals, such as the porcupine and some tenrecs, are occasionally erroneously called hedgehogs.

HEDGE HYSSOP. See GRATIOLA.

HEDGE NETTLE. See STACHYS.

HEDGE SPARROW, common name for an Old World warbler, *Prunella modularis,* so called because it is often found in hedges. The bird is chestnut brown in color and has a slate-gray head and neck. It is about 4½ inches long. The hedge sparrow has a sweet, often repeated note which has earned it the name "hedge accentor"; other common names are "hedge warbler" and (in England) "dunnock". The bird is common in Europe and has been introduced into Australia; a related bird, *P. montanella,* which shows a number of similar characteristics, is found in Siberia where it is known as the "mountain accentor."

HEDGING, in commodity transactions, a means used by agricultural producers, manufacturers, dealers, and importers to prevent or minimize losses resulting from unexpected price fluctuations in commodities they buy or sell for future delivery. For example, a flour miller makes a contract in June to deliver 1000 barrels of flour in November at a stipulated price. He does not need the wheat to fill this contract until shortly before delivery, and to protect himself against a rise in the price of wheat during the ensuing months, he immediately places an order, through an exchange on which grain is traded, for 5000 bushels of wheat (the amount needed to mill 1000 barrels of flour) for November delivery. If the miller does not place this order, and wheat rises three cents a bushel in price between the time of the flour sale and the actual wheat purchase, his expected profit on the flour contract will be decreased; by placing the order he makes an approximately equal profit on his purchase of wheat for future delivery, and thus protects his normal business profit. See EXCHANGES.

HEDIN, SIR SVEN ANDERS (1865–1952), Swedish explorer and geographer, born in Stockholm, and educated at the universities of Stockholm, Uppsala, Berlin, and Halle. Hedin's extensive explorations in Asia from 1885 to 1923 placed him among the foremost of Asiatic explorers. His travels took him into India, the Gobi Desert, parts of China, Persia, and the Middle East. From 1926 to 1935 Hedin and a large staff of scientists were engaged in scientific work in Central Asia. Among the many honors he received were membership in the Swedish Academy, in which he was one of eighteen members, and in the Paris Academy of Sciences. He was knighted by the Indian government in 1909 and was raised to Swedish nobility in 1912. Hedin is the author of 75 volumes on travel,

explorations, and politics; in the last-named field is *Germany and World Peace* (1937), in which he displayed his sympathies for Hitler and Nazi Germany.

HEDONISM (Gr. *hēdonē,* "pleasure"), in philosophy, the doctrine that pleasure is the sole or chief good in life and that its pursuit is the ideal aim of conduct. Two important hedonistic theories were expounded in antiquity. Some philosophic schools of ancient Greece, notably that of the Cyrenaics, or *egoistic hedonists,* espoused a doctrine in which gratification of one's immediate personal desires, without regard for other persons, was considered the supreme end of man's existence. The Cyrenaics maintained that knowledge is rooted in the fleeting sensations of the moment, and that consequently it is futile to attempt the formulation of a system of moral values in which the desirability of present pleasures are weighed against the pain they may cause in the future. The Epicureans (see EPICURUS) also considered pleasure the supreme good, but their conception of pleasure differed substantially from that of the Cyrenaics. Unlike the egoistic hedonists, the Epicureans, or *rational hedonists,* contended that true pleasure is attainable only by reason. Therefore, they stressed the virtues of self-control and prudence in all things.

The doctrines of hedonism as expounded and developed in classical times survived practically without change until modern times. In the 18th and 19th centuries such philosophers as David Hume and Jeremy Bentham (qq.v.) propounded the doctrine of *universalistic hedonism,* better known as utilitarianism (q.v.). According to this theory, the ultimate criterion of human behavior is the good of society, and the guiding principle of individual moral conduct is held to be allegiance to that which procures and promotes the welfare of the greatest number of people.

HEDWIG. See JADWIGA.

HEDWIG, SAINT (1174–1243), Duchess of Silesia, born in Andechs castle, Bavaria, the daughter of Duke Berthold IV of Croatia. In 1186 she married Duke Henry I of Silesia. She founded and endowed many monasteries and convents, of which the most famous is the Cistercian convent at Trebnitz. When her husband died in 1238 she retired to the convent at Trebnitz, where she lived her remaining years in great austerity, although she did not become a nun. She was canonized in 1267, and became the patron saint of Silesia; her feast is celebrated on October 17.

HEEL FLY. See OX BOT.

Georg Hegel

HEERLEN, city of Limburg Province, the Netherlands, located 15 miles E.N.E. of Maastricht and about 5 miles W. of the German border. The city is an industrial center in the coal-mining region of the S.E. Netherlands. Pop. (1953 est.) 63,197.

HEFNER CANDLE. See PHOTOMETRY.

HEGAN, ALICE CALDWELL. See RICE, ALICE CALDWELL HEGAN.

HEGEL, GEORG WILHELM FRIEDRICH (1770–1831), German philosopher, born in Stuttgart. He was educated at home and in the grammar school of Stuttgart until he was eighteen years old. He then matriculated at the University of Tübingen as a student of theology, graduating in 1793. His university career was unremarkable, and his teachers regarded him as being particularly deficient in knowledge of philosophy. For several years after leaving the university he held positions as a tutor, during which time he studied questions of economics and government and also attempted to fathom the true meaning of Christianity. In 1801, after receiving a small legacy from his father, he obtained a position as Privatdocent at the University of Jena. He had at this time already outlined the general framework of his system of philosophy, but had published no works of importance. His first important treatise, *The Phenomenology of the Spirit,* was published in 1807. In 1808 he became director of the gymnasium of Nuremberg, a post which he held until

1816. He married in 1811, and his greatest work, his treatise on *Logic,* began to appear in 1812 and was completed in 1816. From 1816 to 1818 Hegel was professor of philosophy at the University of Heidelberg, and from 1818 to his death he held a chair of philosophy at the University of Berlin.

Hegel's philosophy is based on the belief that the fundamental reality, the "Absolute", is spiritual rather than physical in nature. This all-embracing reality, according to Hegel, is rational, and only what is rational is real. According to his system, the only approach to reality is by means of logic. Anything that can be proved by logical means to be self-consistent is rational and real. Hegel also adopted an individual logical method known as the *dialectic* in his search for the Absolute. This method consists of contrasting a statement or *thesis* with its opposite or *antithesis* and uniting them to form a *synthesis,* a statement containing the essence of both the thesis and antithesis. By this type of reasoning he believed that the natural error of all finite statements can be ultimately eliminated and the Absolute Idea realized. This Absolute Idea to Hegel consists of pure thought thinking about pure thought—"This unity is consequently the absolute and all truth, the Idea which thinks itself".

Hegel regarded the progress of world history as a close parallel to the process of dialectic reasoning. He described history as a progress from Pure Being (which he identified with China) to the Absolute Idea (which he tended to identify with the Prussian State). "The history of the world is the discipline of the uncontrolled natural will, bringing it into obedience to a universal principle and conferring subjective freedom. The East knew, and to the present day knows, that *one* is free; the Greek and Roman world, that *some* are free; the German world knows that *all* are free". Nevertheless Hegel felt that America was the land of the future and that the Absolute would reveal itself "perhaps in a contest between North and South America". The idea of contrast, of strife between opposites, colored all Hegel's thinking and led him to believe in the necessity for war and even the necessity for clearly defined classes within a state. In his view the state was the worldly organization which most closely approached reality, and the individual citizens of the state approached reality only through their participation in the state.

Pure Hegelianism had a profound, although short-lived, influence on European philosophers, and its influence was still felt in England until about the beginning of the 20th century. Indirectly Hegel's works have had an even more far-reaching effect, since they served as the philosophical groundwork of Marxian "dialectical materialism" and of the state worship of the Communists and Fascists of the 20th century.

HEGESIPPUS, Saint (d. 180), early Christian historian, born in Jerusalem, and probably a convert to Christianity from Judaism. During the religious conflicts aroused by the Gnostic heresy (see GNOSTICISM), Hegesippus composed masterly refutations of these theories, basing part of his arguments on a list of the bishops of Rome (or popes) which proved the continuity of the tradition of orthodox Apostolic teaching. Hegesippus also catalogued the heresies which had occurred in the Christian religion up to his day, and wrote a five-volume treatise on Christianity, of which only fragments exist, in the *Historia Ecclesiastica* of Eusebius of Cæsarea (q.v.). His feast is celebrated on April 7.

HEIBERG, GUNNAR (1857–1929), Norwegian playwright and critic, born in Christiania (now Oslo), and educated at the universities of Christiania, Copenhagen, and Paris. His first works showed him to be an exponent of the liberty of the individual and free human spirit. After the success of his first play, *Tante Ulrikke* (1883), he became the artistic director of the National Theater in Bergen from 1884 to 1888; he was forced to resign because of the unpopularity of the contemporary plays he produced. In 1890 his play *Kong Midas* aroused considerable discussion because of its ridicule of the eminent playwright Björnstjerne Björnson (q.v.). His critical works expounded his belief in the essential value of the individual and the individual's right to liberty in all fields of endeavor. Among his other plays are *Balkonen* (1894); *Folkeraadet* (1897); *Harald Svans Mor* (1899); *Kjaelighedens Tragedie* (1904), which was translated into English as *The Tragedy of Love* (1921) and is considered his masterpiece; and *Parade-Sengen* (1913).

HEIBERG, JOHAN LUDVIG (1791–1860), Danish man of letters, born in Copenhagen, and educated at the University of Copenhagen. He was editor of the weekly *Flyvende Post* from 1827 to 1830, of *Interimsblade* from 1834 to 1837, and of the *Intelligensblade* in 1842–43; to these journals he contributed critical articles denouncing the sentimental extravagances of the Danish Romantic school of literature and drama. Heiberg also wrote

a number of articles on the philosophy of Georg Wilhelm Friedrich Hegel (q.v.), and was the author of many vaudevilles (see DRAMA), a form of entertainment which he introduced to the Danish stage. Among his dramatic works are comedies, including *The Elves* (1835) and *The Newly Wedded Pair* (1841), and dramas such as *Nina* (1822), *Elverhöi* (1828), and *The Nut Crackers* (1845). From 1847 to 1854 he was director of the National Theater in Copenhagen.

HEIDELBERG, a city of the state of Württemberg-Baden, West Germany, on the Neckar River, 11 miles E.S.E. of Mannheim. The city occupies a long narrow site between the river and a parallel range of thickly wooded hills. On the summit of Jettenbühl (330 ft.), which dominates the E. portion of the city, is Heidelberg castle, one of the most impressive historic landmarks of Germany. Dating from the 13th century, the structure, now largely in ruins, preserves numerous examples of medieval and later German architecture. One wing, an addition in the Renaissance style, called the Friedrichsbau, was restored

Staats-Herold Corp.

"Knight's House," old building in Heidelberg

early in the 20th century. Of particular interest are the four granite columns located in the castle courtyard, which were once part of a castle belonging to the Frankish emperor Charlemagne. The cellar of Heidelberg castle contains the famed Heidelberg Tun, a wine vat with a capacity of 49,000 gallons. Noteworthy ecclesiastical edifices of Heidelberg are the 15th-century church of St. Peter, on the door of which the Bohemian theologian and martyr Jerome of Prague nailed his celebrated theses in criticism of the papacy; and the church of the Holy Ghost, also dating from the 15th century. To a considerable extent, the world renown of the city derives from Heidelberg University (q.v.), founded in 1385. Heidelberg contains a number of manufacturing industries, and is an important railway junction. Among the local manufactures are beer, cigars, metal products, and pianos. The chief source of income, however, is the tourist trade.

The community developed around Heidelberg castle and was, until early in the 18th century, the capital of the Palatinate. During the Protestant Reformation, Heidelberg was one of the chief strongholds of German Protestantism. French troops sacked the town during the Thirty Years' War. In 1689 and 1693, Heidelberg was further damaged by invading French troops. Following World War II Heidelberg was assigned to the U.S. zone of occupation. Pop. (1950) 116,488.

HEIDELBERG MAN. See MAN, ANCIENT.

HEIDELBERG, UNIVERSITY OF, the oldest and one of the most famous of German universities. It was founded in the town of Heidelberg, then in the Palatinate, in 1385, by Rupert I, Elector of the Palatinate. The real work of organization was done by the university's first rector, the German religious scholar Marsilius von Inghen, who established it as a Catholic institution. In the middle of the 16th century, during the Reformation, a reorganization in which the great Protestant scholar Melanchthon played a prominent part made Heidelberg into a Protestant university. The institution prospered until the Thirty Years' War (1618–48) between Catholics and Protestants; in 1622 the Catholic commander in chief, the Count of Tilly, captured the town and took possession of the university; he sent its noted collection of manuscripts, the Bibliotheca Palatina, to the Vatican, Rome. In 1626 the university suspended operation and in 1652 it was reorganized as a secular institution. During the next century and a half its work went on under great difficulties, mainly caused by the wars in which the Palatinate engaged with France. Its importance was not restored until 1803, when the Palatinate ceded the town of Heidelberg to the Grand Duchy of Baden, and the Grand Duke of Baden took the university under his patronage.

In the 19th and 20th centuries the University of Heidelberg was one of the most renowned of modern German centers of learning, attracting many foreign students, including Americans. Its student life was the subject of the operetta *The Student Prince* (1924) by Sigmund Romberg. Before World War II, the university had faculties of theology, law, medicine, and philosophy. Its teaching staff numbered over 200, its student body over 3000, and its library contained more than a half million volumes and nearly 5000 manuscripts.

HEIDENSTAM, VERNER VON (1859–1940), Swedish poet and novelist, born in Olshammar. He planned to become a painter, but ill health forced him to interrupt his study of art, and he traveled in southern Europe and the Orient from the age of seventeen to twenty-seven. His first book of poetry, *Vallfart och Vandringsar,* appeared in 1888. He was noted for his colorful style and for the lyricism of his language, and was an important member of the group that revolted against the realism in Swedish literature during the 1880's. He was the author of the epic poem *Hans Alienus* (1892), describing a search for beauty through various countries and periods of time, and of *Dikter* (1895) and *Nya Dikter* (1915), verse in which he revealed a naturalistic (see NATURALISM) point of view. Heidenstam is considered one of the most important Swedish poets of his time.

In his novels, Heidenstam made use of Swedish historical backgrounds supporting his theory that the then current renaissance of Swedish literature should be based on the national culture. Among his outstanding works of this type are *Karolinerna* (1897–98), *Heliga Birgittas Pilgrimsfärd* (1901), and *Folkungaträdet* (1905–07). In 1916 he was awarded the Nobel Prize for literature.

HEIFETZ, JASCHA (1901–), Russian-American concert violinist, born in Vilna, Lithuania. He entered the Vilna music school at the age of four and graduated four years later, entering the St. Petersburg Conservatory, where he studied violin with Leopold Auer. Heifetz made his debut at the age of seven, in Kovno. His first appearance in America was in 1917, when he was hailed by the critics as one of the most important violinists of all time. In 1925 he became an American citizen, and in the same year he gave a concert hall to Tel-Aviv, Palestine. Heifetz made many world tours, receiving high acclaim everywhere; he was noted particularly for his technique and for the lyrical quality of his tone.

HEIJERMANS, HERMAN (1864–1924), Dutch editor, novelist, and playwright, born in Rotterdam. In 1897 he began editing *De Jonge Gids* of Amsterdam, a literary journal with socialist principles, and in 1899 became one of the editors of the socialist newspaper *De Nieuwe Tijd*. He was the author of a number of works of fiction, including *Trinette* (1893), *Diamantstad* (2 vols., 1903), and *Droomkoninkje* (1924); under the pen name of Samuel Falkland he wrote *Schetsen* (13 vols., 1896–1909), realistic sketches of Dutch small-town life. His best-known fictional work was *Kamertjeszonde* (1897), a novel dealing realistically with Jewish family life in the Netherlands, which he wrote under the pen name Koos Habbema. Using the same pseudonym he wrote a number of plays, the most noteworthy of which was the drama *Op Hoop van Zegen* (1900), subsequently performed in London and New York City as *The Good Hope*. Other plays were *Ghetto* (1899), *De Groote Vlucht* (1908), *Eva Bonheur* (1919), and *De Dageraad* (1921).

HEILUNGKIANG, a province of the Northeastern Provinces (Manchuria) of China, occupying the northernmost portion of the country and bordering the Amur R., which separates it from the U.S.S.R. Heilungkiang is well watered by tributaries of the Amur, and is one of the most productive wheatgrowing regions of N. China. Other leading crops are millet, corn, barley, and sorghum; livestock farming is important. The province is traversed by the Chinese Eastern Railway, a component of the Sino-Soviet-operated Chinese Changchun Railway. Pehan (pop., 14,-000), formerly known as Lungchen, is the provincial administrative center. Heilungkiang, formerly the largest province of Manchuria, was occupied by the Japanese shortly after the outbreak (1937) of the Sino-Japanese War. In the territorial and administrative changes carried through in Manchuria following World War II, the Chinese government considerably reduced the size of the province. The Chinese Communists seized Heilungkiang during the early stages of the subsequent civil war. Area, 70,969 sq.m.; pop. (1950) 5,522,000.

Columbia Concerts

Jascha Heifetz

HEIMDALL, in Norse mythology, the watchman of Asgard, home of the gods, and of Bifrost, the rainbow bridge which spans from heaven to earth. Heimdall is gifted with extraordinary powers, having ears so acute that he can hear the growth of grass and sheep's wool, and eyes so sharp that he can see a hundred leagues by day or night, and requiring no more sleep than a bird. At the time of Ragnarok, the doomsday of the world, he will blow the Gjallarhorn to warn the gods of the approaching giants, and will engage Loki, god of mischief, in mortal combat.

HEIMSKRINGLA, an early masterpiece of Scandinavian literature, written in the first part of the 13th century by the Icelandic historian Snorri Sturluson (see SNORRI). The work is part mythological, part historical. It narrates the history of the royal family of Norway from the time of the reputed descent of the Ynglings from the Norse gods, until 1177 A.D.

HEINE, HEINRICH (1797–1856), German lyric poet, literary critic, and essayist, born in Düsseldorf, of Jewish parents. He attended private and public schools in Düsseldorf until 1815; in 1819, after failing in a business venture in which he was subsidized by his uncle Solomon Heine, a banker of Hamburg, young Heine studied law at the University of Bonn and the following year at the University of Göttingen. However, he was more interested in literature than in law. He had already written some poetry as a child, and at Bonn, under the influence of the poets of the German Romantic school (see GERMAN LITERATURE: *The Classical and Romantic Period*), he wrote a number of lyrics and the beginning of a poetic tragedy. Finding student

Heinrich Heine

life at Göttingen dull, in 1821 he went to Berlin, where he became acquainted with eminent members of the German Romantic school such as Adelbert von Chamisso, Friedrich La Motte-Fouqué, and Karl Varnhagen von Ense.

Heine remained in Berlin three years, doing journalistic work and writing poetry. In 1822 his first volume of verse, *Gedichte,* was published and attracted attention because of the delicacy and lyrical beauty of the poem. From 1824 to 1825 he again studied law at Göttingen, and in 1825, since the profession of law was prohibited to Jews in Germany at this time, became a Christian in order that he might obtain a law degree; however, once he qualified, Heine never actually practiced law. In 1826 appeared the book which established his literary reputation, *Die Harzreise,* a prose account of a trip he had taken to the Harz Mountains (1824). The work, with its wit, gayety, and flexible, graceful style, was an immediate success. Three years later (1827) the work by which he is best known was published, *Buch der Lieder,* a volume of lyrics of a verbal flexibility and originality of imagery hitherto unknown in German literature. From 1827 to 1831 he lived in England, Munich, Italy, Hamburg, and Helgoland, and wrote the three volumes of travel sketches which, with *Die Harzreise,* make up the four volumes of his *Reisebilder* (1826–31). He also wrote a number of prose works in which he displayed sympathy with the democratic ideas of the French Revolution and bitterly satirized the conservative and despotic regimes of the various kingdoms and duchies of Germany. Heine became the foremost of a literary group known as "Young Germany" (see GERMAN LITERATURE: *From 1832 to 1871*) which attacked the German Romantic school, which had come under monarchical and ecclesiastical domination. He hoped to obtain a professorship of German literature in Munich or elsewhere in Germany, but his political ideas brought him into the disfavor of the established German governments; Prussia banned both Heine and the third volume of *Reisebilder*. Seeking a more congenial political and literary atmosphere, and filled with enthusiasm for the revolution of 1830 in France, which overthrew the Bourbon dynasty, in 1831 Heine went to Paris; there, except for two brief visits to his native land, he spent the rest of his life.

In Paris Heine was at first financially successful, acting as correspondent for several German newspapers, and he also enjoyed the friendship of such writers and composers as Balzac, George Sand, Berlioz, and Chopin. But in 1835 the publication of writings by members of the "Young Germany" group was prohibited in most of Germany and Heine's income was considerably reduced. Subsequently he lived chiefly on an income from his uncle and for a time on a pension from the French government. Heine quarreled with other German liberal writers in Paris, married an extravagant and vain Frenchwoman whom he loved deeply, and, beginning with 1845, became ill of a spinal disease which slowly paralyzed him. From 1848 to his death he was bedridden and in constant pain. Nevertheless some of his most notable works date from the last years of his life. Among the works he wrote after 1831 are the prose volumes *Geschichte der Neuren Schönen Literatur in Deutschland* (2 vols., 1833), *Die Romantische Schule* (1836), *Der Salon* (4 vols. 1835–40), *Deutschland, ein Wintermärchen* (1844), and *Vermischte Schriften* (3 vols., 1854); and the books of verse *Neue Gedichte* (1844), *Romanzero* (1851), and *Neueste Gedichte* (1853–54). Among his lyrics are some of the best known in the German language, including *Du Bist Wie Eine Blume, Die Lorelei,* and *Die Zwei Grenadier.*

There were several conflicting elements in Heine's intellectual and emotional make-up:

a pagan joy of life opposed to an Hebraic feeling of the importance of ethical values; a love of romanticism opposed by hatred of the German romantic writers of his time because of their subservience to reactionary political and religious forces; and a love for Germany opposing a humanitarianism which embraced the entire world. These inner contradictions created in Heine the spirit of disillusionment, of mockery, and of sharp satire that characterizes so much of his work. He has an important place in German and in world literature. He is considered, second only to Goethe, the greatest of German lyric poets, and his prose was the best written in German in his time.

HEINTZELMAN, ARTHUR WILLIAM (1891–), American etcher, born in Newark, N.J. He studied at the Rhode Island School of Design, in Providence, and first exhibited his work in Boston in 1917. Four years later he went to Paris, where his drawings and etchings became widely known for their lively and intimate glimpses of picturesque Parisian characters. His etchings, rich in tonal values and varied in technique, are represented in the Luxembourg, Paris, the British Museum, London, and the Metropolitan Museum of Art, New York City.

HEIR, in common law, one who succeeds to real property by intestacy and not by will (q.v.). In the statutory law of many States of the United States, the word "heir" still has this meaning. In most States it is generally construed to mean a successor by intestacy to both real and personal property; the various State statutes specify in detail the person or persons who will succeed to a decedent's estate in case of intestacy; see DESCENT. In common usage the term "heir" signifies any person succeeding to a decedent's estate by will as well as by intestacy. In England the term "heir apparent" is applied to a child who will be heir on the death of his parent; the term "heir presumptive" is applied to a person who will be heir barring the birth of a closer relative of the person from whom he expects to inherit.

HEISENBERG, WERNER (CARL) (1901–), German physicist, born in Würzburg, and educated at the universities of Munich and Göttingen. He was appointed professor of theoretical physics at the University of Leipzig, and while he held this position taught for brief periods in the United States, at the University of Chicago in 1929 and at Michigan University in 1932. In 1942 he was appointed professor of theoretical physics at the University of Berlin and director of the Kaiser Wilhelm Institute for Physics in Berlin.

Heisenberg was in charge of scientific research in connection with the atomic-bomb project in Germany during World War II. Under his leadership attempts were made to construct a pile in which the chain reaction would proceed so rapidly that it would produce an explosion, but these attempts were never realized; see ATOMIC ENERGY AND ATOMIC BOMB. He was interned in England at the end of the war; following his return to Germany, he became director of the Max Planck Institute of Physics in Göttingen.

Heisenberg, one of the foremost theoretical physicists in the world, made his great contributions in the theory of atomic structure. Starting in 1925 he developed a new theory of quantum mechanics, in which the mathematical formulation was based on the frequencies and amplitudes of the radiations absorbed and emitted by the atom and on the energy levels of the atomic system; see QUANTUM MECHANICS. The uncertainty principle (q.v.) formulated by Heisenberg played an important role in the development of quantum mechanics and also in the trend of modern philosophical thinking. Heisenberg was awarded the 1932 Nobel Prize for physics. He is the author of *The Physical Principles of the Quantum Theory* (1930), *Physik der Atomkerne* (1943), *Vorträge über Kosmische Strahlung* (1943), *Wandlungen in den Grundlagen der Naturwissenschaft* (6th ed., 1945), and *Philosophic Problems of Nuclear Science* (1953).

HEJAZ or **HEDJAZ**. See ARABIA; SAUDI ARABIA.

HEJIRA or **HEGIRA** (Ar. *hijrah*, "flight"), specifically, the designation applied to the flight, in 622 A.D., of Mohammed from Mecca to Yahrib (now Medina). By extension, the term is sometimes applied to similar flights or emigrations. The Caliph Omar I selected the year of the Hejira as the first year of the Mohammedan era. Hence, 622 A.D. became 1 A.H. (*anno hegiræ*) according to the Mohammedan calendar, which Omar systematized in 639.

HEKLA, volcano of s.w. Iceland, located about 20 m. from the coast. It has a circumference at the base of 12 m. and is surmounted by three snow-covered peaks, the tallest of which is 5110 ft. above sea level. Records show that the volcano has erupted over fo y times since the 10th century.

HEL, in Norse mythology, the goddess of the dead. She dwelt beneath one of the three roots of the sacred ash tree, Yggdrasill, and was the daughter of Loki, god of mischief, by the giantess Angerbotha. Odin, the All-Father, hurled Hel into Niflheim, the realm of cold and darkness, over which he gave her sovereign authority.

HELDENBUCH, DAS. See GERMAN LITERATURE: *Middle High German Period.*

HELDER, DEN, a seaport and fortified town in the province of North Holland, the Netherlands. The town is situated on the Marsdiep, the channel linking the Zuider Zee and the North Sea, and is the terminus of the North Holland Canal, which runs S.S.E. from Den Helder to Amsterdam, 51 m. distant. A dike about 5 m. long runs from the outlet of the canal, called Nieuwe Diep, to Fort Erfprins, and the entire province can be flooded from this point. Den Helder, because of its strategic position, is one of the strongest fortresses in the Netherlands, having first been fortified by Napoleon I in 1811. It contains several naval establishments, including an arsenal and a naval cadet school. The harbor facilities of the port are located on the E. side of the town, and include dry docks, wharves, and warehouses. Pop. (1953 est.) 41,199.

HELENA, capital of Montana and county seat of Lewis and Clark Co., situated at the E. foot of the Continental Divide, 66 miles N.E. of Butte. It is served by two railroads, and maintains a municipal airport. The city lies at an altitude of approximately 4000 ft. above sea level, overlooking an irrigated agricultural area known as the Prickly Pear, or Helena, Valley, and surrounded by a productive mining region. The numerous mines in the vicinity yield gold, silver, lead, and zinc. Since 1935 gold has been obtained also from formerly unworkable gravel deposits by the use of huge modern dredges. In addition to mining and smelting, the principal industries in the city are brewing and the manufacture of paint, brick and tile, cement blocks, fabricated steel, machine-shop products, and foundry products. The most prominent buildings in Helena are the State Capitol, erected in 1899, which contains the collection of the Historical Society of Montana; and the St. Helena Cathedral (Roman Catholic), opened in 1924, a partial replica of the famous cathedral of Milan. The city is the site of the State Vocational School for Girls, a U.S. Veterans Hospital, and Carroll College (Roman Catholic), established in 1910.

Helena was founded in Oct., 1864, following the discovery of gold in Last Chance Gulch, now the main street of the present city. By 1868 an estimated amount of $16,000-000 in gold had been obtained from Last Chance Gulch, and the town which had developed around it had a population of 7500. Helena became the capital of the Territory in 1874, and was incorporated as a city in 1881. From 1870 to 1883, when the Northern Pacific railroad reached Helena, the city's development was slowed by the exhaustion of the early mines; but the arrival of the railroad and the growth of the silver-mining industry gave it renewed prosperity. Earthquakes damaged the city in 1935, but the damaged areas were rebuilt and the city's buildings improved and strengthened against future occurrences of the kind. Pop. (1950) 17,581.

HELENA, SAINT (d. about 330), wife of the Roman emperor Constantius I and mother of the emperor Constantine the Great, born probably in Drepanum, later called Helenopolis in her honor, in the ancient Roman province of Bithynia. Constantius divorced her, because of her nonpatrician origin, when he was named Cæsar or successor to the throne of the Roman Empire in 292. She devoted the rest of her life to religious pilgrimages, visiting Jerusalem about 325 and founding there the Church of the Holy Sepulcher and the Church of the Nativity. According to some legends she was the discoverer of the True Cross in Palestine. Her feast is celebrated on August 18th.

HELEN OF TROY, in Greek mythology, a romantic figure noted for her beauty. She was the daughter of Zeus, father of the gods, and Leda, wife of Tyndareus, King of Sparta. According to the epic poem *Cypria,* however, Helen was the issue of Zeus and Nemesis, the goddess of retributive justice. Zeus, in the form of a swan, pursued Nemesis, who brought forth an egg which was found by Leda. On the birth of Helen from the egg, Leda reared her as her foster child. Helen was so beautiful that at the age of ten she was carried off by Theseus and Pirithoüs, but subsequently was recovered by her brothers, Castor and Pollux. Tyndareus then bound her suitors, who numbered about thirty, in solemn oath to unite in support of the husband whom Helen should choose, in the event that any attempts were again made to abduct her. Thus, when Helen was carried off by Paris, son of the Trojan king Priam, her husband Menelaus, King of Sparta, summoned all the princes of Greece to avenge the insult he had received. The Trojan War (q.v.) resulted.

Helen of Troy and Paris (painting by Jacques Louis David)

One version of the legend states that after the death of Paris, Helen voluntarily married his brother Deiphobus, and that on the capture of Troy by the Greeks, she betrayed Deiphobus into the hands of Menelaus in order to regain the favor of her first husband. According to another version, Helen fled to the temple of Aphrodite, whither she was pursued by the vengeful Menelaus; but such was the power of her beauty that his anger was allayed and he took her once more as his wife. Their voyage home was protracted, as they were driven off their course to Egypt. At length, however, they came in safety to Sparta, where Homer's *Odyssey* shows them living in happiness. By her husband Menelaus, Helen had one daughter, Hermione, but some writers state that by Theseus she was the mother of Iphigenia. Various accounts have also been written of Helen's death. Her grave is said to have existed at Therapne, near Sparta, where she and Menelaus were worshiped. The people of Rhodes, however, told how she was driven out of Sparta after the death of Menelaus, and came to her friend Polyxo in Rhodes. Polyxo, however, having lost her husband in

the Trojan War, forced Helen to hang herself from a tree. Hence, Helen was worshiped by the Rhodians as a tree divinity. In still another account, Helen was translated by the gods to the Islands of the Blessed, where she was wedded to Achilles. She received divine honors at many places, and was believed by sailors in ancient times to appear in the single flame of St. Elmo's Fire (q.v.), which was regarded as a sign of disaster, the double flame of Castor and Pollux being thought to insure safety.

Almost all the episodes of Helen's eventful life have been represented in both ancient and modern art. According to Stesichorus, a Greek lyric poet of the 7th century B.C., Helen remained in Egypt (whither she had come with Paris on her way to Troy), detained by the Egyptian king Proteus, who later restored her to her husband. Paris, said Stesichorus, took to Troy only a phantom, for whom the Greeks and Trojans fought. Many elements in the legends about Helen, and many characteristics of her worship, seem to indicate that she was originally a moon goddess who had been superseded by Selene and Artemis (qq.v.).

HELGOLAND or **HELIGOLAND,** an island of Germany and formerly the site of a powerful German fortress, situated in the North Sea about 40 miles N.W. of Cuxhaven. It is approximately a mile in length and less than a third of a mile in width, and comprises a rocky eminence, known as the Oberland, with a maximum elevation of about 200 feet. Steep cliffs surround the Oberland on all sides. A narrow spit of sand, called the Unterland, extends along the S.E. base of the uplift. The major portion of the island community, a fishing and resort village, is located on the Oberland. Dünen-Insel, a small sandy islet situated about a quarter of a mile to the east of Helgoland, is a popular bathing area.

A former possession of Denmark, Helgoland was seized by Great Britain in 1807. The British ceded the island to Germany in 1890, whereupon it became a part of the Prussian province of Schleswig-Holstein (q.v.). In the period preceding World War I, the German government established on the island a comprehensive system of fortifications, including gun emplacements and submarine pens. British and German naval units fought a sharp naval engagement, known in history as the Battle of Helgoland Bight, off Helgoland on August 28, 1914, shortly after the outbreak of World War I (see HELGOLAND BIGHT, BATTLE OF). As provided by the terms of the Treaty of Versailles, the fortifications on Helgoland were demolished following World War I. The island was subsequently refortified by the Third Reich, and served as a major German submarine base during World War II.

In May, 1945, after the collapse of the Third Reich, the fortress was surrendered to the armed forces of Great Britain. British naval personnel razed the fortifications on Helgoland on April 18, 1947, by the detonation of 3500 tons of explosives.

HELGOLAND BIGHT, BATTLE OF, a naval engagement of World War I, fought between British and German naval forces on August 28, 1914. Confined to Helgoland Bight, an arm of the North Sea to the E. and S. of the island of Helgoland, the action began as a raiding operation by British submarines and destroyers, supported by a flotilla of light cruisers, against German patrol vessels. The fighting during the initial phase of the battle was attended by considerable confusion of both sides, mainly because of a low-hanging fog. After suffering several early reverses, including the loss of a destroyer, the Germans concentrated six light cruisers in the battle area. By 11:00 A.M., the German cruiser force had secured tactical superiority over the British raiders. The British, at this juncture, directed an appeal for help to Rear Admiral Sir David Beatty, commander of four heavy battle cruisers in reserve positions about 50 miles N.W. of Helgoland. Although the British succeeded in destroying the German cruiser *Mainz* before Beatty's arrival, the Germans retained their tactical advantage, threatening the isolated British force with annihilation. Beatty's detachment reached the battle area at 12:30 P.M., and two German cruisers, the *Cöln* and *Ariadne,* were sunk in quick succession. The remnants of the German force escaped. Besides the destruction of four vessels, German losses included serious damage to other fleet units and more than 1200 casualties. Through their victory, accomplished at the cost of damage to 4 vessels and 75 casualties, the British substantially advanced the Allied naval strategy of blockading the German coast.

HELIACAL RISING, the rising of certain stars at approximately the time of sunrise. Every star rises four minutes earlier each night, so that if a star rises at sunset on a certain night, it will rise at sunrise six months later. A star which is near the ecliptic (the sun's path through the heavens) is invisible when near the sun; as it rises earlier each day, there comes a morning when it rises in the half light of early dawn, and is clearly visible for a few minutes. This first visible rising is called the heliacal rising. The heliacal risings of several bright stars, such as Sirius (q.v.), were used in ancient astronomy to mark definite dates in the year, and are still the distinctive features of certain seasons, such as the dog days (see CANIS MAJOR and CANIS MINOR).

HELIAND (Old Saxon, "Saviour") a religious epic poem in Saxon, written in the 9th century. It describes the life of Christ as told by the four Evangelists, and is an attempted correlation of these versions. The *Heliand* was written by an anonymous poet at the order of the Holy Roman emperor Louis I the Pious; it represents Christ in the guise of a German prince, and the Apostles as his thanes, and has a contemporary Germanic background. Except for fragments of a Saxon paraphrase of Genesis, believed to be by the same author, the *Heliand* is the only Saxon manuscript of any importance which has survived until modern times. See GERMAN LITERATURE.

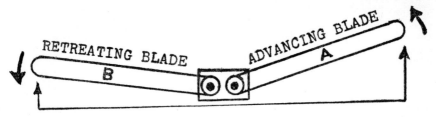

Fig. 1

HELIANTHUS. See Artichoke, Jerusalem; Sunflower.

HELICON, in music, a form of the tuba (q.v.). It is constructed in two pitches, E, and B; its brass tubing forms a circle large enough to be carried around the body, and the instrument, being thus supported, is therefore useful for parades. An American variety of this instrument, with a larger bell, is the Sousaphone, named after the bandmaster John Philip Sousa (q.v.).

HELICOPTER, a heavier-than-air craft which derives its lift not from fixed wings like those of conventional airplanes, but from power-driven rotating airfoils which permit the craft to climb and descend vertically. The helicopter is the only type of heavier-than-air craft that can climb and descend in this way and that can hover motionless. The helicopter differs from the autogiro (q.v.) in that its rotor gives both lift and propulsion.

The rotor of a helicopter usually has two, three, or four blades radiating symmetrically from a central hub which is placed vertically on the top of the fuselage. The rotor is driven by an engine (placed in the fuselage) through a train of gears which reduce the speed of rotation to a tenth or less of the speed of the engine. The reduction in speed results in a corresponding increase in the torque exerted by the rotor, so that an important feature of helicopter design is the development of devices to counteract the torque which would otherwise turn the fuselage of the craft in a direction opposite to the rotation of

the rotor. The most common form of anti-torque device is a small vertical propeller, similar to an airplane propeller, mounted at the tail of the helicopter in such a position as to push the tail to one side. Other types of helicopter use paired rotors turning in opposite directions which automatically neutralize each other's torque. In some helicopters the paired rotors are mounted one above the other on a single axle, while in others they are placed on struts on either side of the fuselage or at the front and back of the fuselage.

When a helicopter is rising vertically from the ground or descending vertically the lift on all the rotor blades is the same, since they are all moving through the air at the same speed. However, when the craft is moving forward (or in any horizontal direction) the lift on some blades is greater than that on others. This is shown in Figure 1. Blade A has a speed through the air that is equal to the speed of rotation *plus* the speed of the helicopter's forward flight but blade B is moving through the air at the speed of rotation *minus* the forward speed. If the blades were fixed, blade A would give more lift than B and the helicopter would tilt to the left. To avoid this instability, most single-rotored helicopters have flapping blades that are hinged close to the hub. As shown in Figure 2, the advancing blade A rises and the retreating blade B drops during rotation. The effect of this flapping is to reduce the lift on the advancing blade and increase the lift on

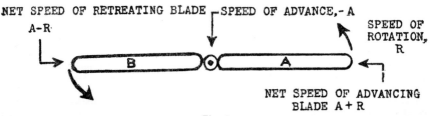

Fig. 2

Aviation Week

The Piasecki XHJP–1 helicopter, with a top speed of 131 m.p.h., carries 2,300 pounds.

the retreating blade, thus nullifying the effect of rotation.

A helicopter can be flown in any direction, forward, backward, or sidewise, by tilting the rotor in the desired direction. Tilting the rotor changes its lift from purely vertical to a combination of vertical and horizontal. To turn a helicopter the rotor is first tilted in the direction of the turn and then the thrust of the tail propeller is altered to turn the fuselage in the desired direction. Ascent and descent in helicopters are controlled by increasing or decreasing the speed of the rotor. In the event of a power failure, the rotor of a helicopter is disengaged and will "autorotate" like the rotor of an autogiro, giving enough lift to permit the craft to descend slowly to a safe landing.

Uses. The helicopter has two principal advantages: the ability to fly slowly or to hover; and the ability to land and take off in a restricted space. One of the most important nonmilitary uses of the helicopter is in searching for and rescuing lost persons, particularly in the sea and in mountainous regions. A helicopter can pick up a man from a life raft or a small forest clearing without even alighting, hauling him aboard the craft with a rope ladder or a winch and cable. Helicopters can also operate from the decks of small vessels at sea and can land and take off in small areas or even from a rooftop in the center of

a congested city. The slow flight of a helicopter makes it the ideal type of aircraft for the inspection of pipelines and power lines from the air, and many machines are employed in this capacity. In addition, the helicopter can be flown safely in storms and other conditions of bad visibility which ground conventional aircraft, because of the speed with which the helicopter can be stopped in the air or turned abruptly to avoid obstacles. Helicopters have also been used successfully for fire patrols in forest areas, for dusting crops with insecticides, for aerial prospecting, for aerial planting of seed for reforestation and erosion control, and for postal service in large cities. "Family-sized" helicopters became available in 1954. Easy to operate, this type of helicopter has a cruising speed of 90 m.p.h. and a range of 300 m. on 22 gallons of gasoline.

History. So far as is known, the first man to envisage the possibility of a helicopter was the Italian artist and inventor Leonardo da Vinci, who produced drawings showing a craft driven by a pair of coaxial wings. Leonardo, however, had no means of powering his invention and so was not able even to build a model of it. A number of later experimenters attempted to produce practical helicopters, among them the Frenchmen Maurice Leger and Paul Cornu, the Hungarian-American Theodor von Kármán, and others in Spain,

Holland, and France. The invention of the hinged, flapping rotor blade, first used in the autogiro by its inventor, the Spaniard Juan de la Cierva, made possible the development of practical helicopters. The first truly successful helicopter was a twin-rotor machine designed by the German engineer Heinrich Focke, which was flown in 1936. In the following year the Russian-American aeronautical engineer Igor Sikorski developed a practical single-rotor craft with an anti-torque propeller at the tail.

HELIODORUS (3rd cent. A.D.), Greek writer, born in Emesa (now Homs), Syria. He was the author of the *Æthiopica*, a Greek romance which influenced works of Cervantes, Tasso, and Racine.

HELIOGABALUS (204–22), Emperor of Rome from 218 to 222. He was born in Emesa (Homs), Syria. His real name was Varius Avitus Bassianus but, when still a child, having been appointed high priest of the Syrian sun god Elagabal, he assumed the Latinized name of that deity. Soon after the death of his cousin, the emperor Caracalla (q.v.), Heliogabalus was proclaimed emperor by the Roman legions in opposition to the legitimate sovereign, Marcus Opelius Macrinus, who had given offense to the troops by his harsh discipline. The rivals met in battle at Antioch, Syria, in 218. Macrinus was defeated and Heliogabalus ascended the throne as Marcus Aurelius Antoninus. His reign, lasting somewhat longer than three years and nine months, was notorious for the wild debaucheries in which he indulged. He was murdered by the Prætorian guard on March 11, 222, and was succeeded by his cousin and adopted son, Marcus Alexander Severus.

HELIOGRAVURE. See PHOTOGRAVURE.

HELIOPOLIS (Lat., fr. Ger. *Hēliou polis,* "city of the Sun"), a city of ancient Egypt, the center of sun worship during the pre-Christian Egyptian civilization. Its ruins are situated 5 miles E. of the Nile R. at the apex of the Nile delta, and about 6 miles N.E. of Cairo. Heliopolis was originally the center of worship of the god Tem, deity of the setting sun, later regarded as a form of the sun god Ra. In Egyptian theological literature, it was known as Per-Ra ("City of Ra"), of which the Greek name is a translation. In the Bible, the city is referred to as On. Though Heliopolis was in existence as far back in Egyptian history as the Second Dynasty, about 2900 B.C., it reached its greatest development during the New Kingdom, beginning about 1580

B.C., when Ra, later called Amon-Ra, came to be regarded as the chief god of the Egyptian pantheon (see EGYPTIAN RELIGION). Under Ramses II (1292–1225 B.C.), the temple of Heliopolis reached the height of its influence, with almost 13,000 priests and slaves serving in it. Most of the religious literature of ancient Egypt was written there, and the temple was the repository for royal records. The city declined under later dynasties and the Ptolemies almost disregarded it. When Rome occupied Egypt, the obelisks of Heliopolis were removed (see CLEOPATRA'S NEEDLES), and the walls of its buildings were used as construction materials for other cities, among them Cairo.

HELIOPOLIS, a city in Syria. See BAALBEK.

HELIOS, in Greek mythology, the name of the sun god. According to Hesiod's *Theogony,* Helios was a son of the Titan Hyperion by Euryphæssa. He is described as giving light to both gods and men. He rises in the east from the marshy borders of Oceanus, into whose dark abysses in the west he sinks once more at evening. Later poets furnished the sun god with a splendid palace in the east, somewhere beyond Colchis, and represented him as being conveyed thither at sunset in a winged boat of gold. In the earlier poets, Helios is a distinct personality; subsequently, however, much of his personality is obscured, and the real sun god becomes Apollo.

The worship of Helios was widely spread. He had temples in Corinth, Argos, Trœzen, Argolis, and many other cities; but the principal seat was at Rhodes, where four white horses were sacrificed annually to him. A similar sacrifice was offered in his honor on the summit of Mount Taygetus (Hagios Elias) in Laconia. In art, Helios was depicted as a young man in the prime of his strength and beauty, with flowing hair and a crown of rays. He was also frequently represented in his four-horse chariot, as in a celebrated statuary group by the Greek sculptor Lysippus, at Rhodes.

HELIOTROPE, or TURNSOLE, common name of plants of the genus *Heliotropium,* belonging to the Borage family. The genus contains over two hundred species which grow in the temperate zones of both hemispheres. Heliotropes are annual herbs with smooth-edged, alternate leaves. The flower has a five-parted calyx, a salver-shaped, five-lobed corolla bearing five stamens, and a deeply four-lobed ovary. The fruits are nutlets. Common heliotrope, *H. europaeum,* is a native of Europe, naturalized in waste areas of E. United States.

Peruvian heliotrope

It has a hairy stem, bearing oval leaves. The white flowers are borne on spikes which are coiled in the bud. Seaside heliotrope, *H. curassivicum,* is a smooth-stemmed plant native to waste places in N.E. United States. It has lance-shaped leaves and white or pale-blue flowers. Peruvian heliotrope, *H. peruvianum,* is the common cultivated heliotrope, grown in gardens all over the United States. The white to deep-purple flowers have a heavy, vanillalike scent. Essential oils from the petals of this species are used in making perfumes. The Peruvian heliotrope has a somewhat woody base and can be trained to a treelike shape by continued pruning of side branches.

Several plants which are not related to *Heliotropium* are called heliotropes; garden heliotrope is the common valerian (q.v.), and winter heliotrope is a butter bur.

HELIOTROPE or **BLOODSTONE,** a gem mineral composed of dark-green chalcedony with scattered red spots of jasper resembling blood. Heliotrope is used as a gem stone in signet rings. It is found in India, Siberia, and the Hebrides. See GEM.

HELIOTROPISM. See TROPISM.

HELIOZOA. See SUN ANIMALCULE.

HELIUM (Gr. *helios,* "the sun"), an element, symbol He, at. no. *2,* at. wt. 4.003, m.p. —272.2° C. (—458° F.) at 26 atmospheres pressure, b.p. —268.9° C. (—451.7° F.), valance 0. It is a chemically inert, monatomic gas, colorless and odorless, and the lightest of all gases other than hydrogen. Helium was discovered in the sun a quarter of a century before it was found on the earth. The French astronomer Pierre Janssen discovered its characteristic line in the spectrum of the atmosphere of the sun during an eclipse in 1868. Shortly afterward it was identified as an element and named by Sir Edward Frankland and Sir Joseph Lockyer. The gas was first isolated from terrestrial sources by Sir William Ramsay in 1895. In 1907 Sir Ernest Rutherford connected helium with the emanations of radioactive elements, and later investigators confirmed the fact that the alpha emanation of radioactive disintegration consists of helium atoms, each with a double positive charge.

Helium is the most difficult of all gases to liquefy, condensing at a temperature more than 16° C. lower than hydrogen. It is also impossible to solidify at normal atmospheric pressures. These properties make liquid helium extremely useful as a refrigerant in producing temperatures close to absolute zero (q.v.; see also CRYOGENICS). When liquid helium is cooled at normal pressures, it is transformed into helium II, a liquid with unique physical properties. It has no freezing point. Its viscosity is apparently zero; it passes readily through minute cracks and pores and even creeps up the sides and over the lips of containers. Its heat conductivity is nearly a million times that of ordinary liquids, so that, when heated strongly, it does not boil, but evaporates quietly from an undisturbed surface. The rare helium isotope of atomic weight 3 shows markedly different properties when liquefied.

The principal use of helium is for inflating airships and balloons. Although it is almost twice as heavy as hydrogen, the lifting power of helium is 92 percent as great, and its chemical inertia eliminates the danger of fire or explosion from sparks or incendiary bullets. Helium is also used to replace the nitrogen of the atmosphere for deep-sea divers, caisson workers, and aviators, because its comparative insolubility in the blood reduces liability to the bends (q.v.). This synthetic atmosphere is also used in medicine for diseases involving difficulty in respiration, such as asthma, because helium is lighter than nitrogen and more easily penetrates the constricted passages.

Helium occurs in the earth's atmosphere, comprising about 5.4 parts per million parts of air at sea level, and slightly more at high altitudes. It also occurs in microscopic interstices within all radioactive minerals. The principal commercial source, however, is from natural gas in Texas, which, in some cases, contains as much as 7 percent helium. During World War II the production of helium in the U.S. reached a peak of about 135,000,000 cu. ft. annually; after the war it receded to about half that amount.

Atmospheric helium contains about one part per million of the atomic-weight-3 isotope, whereas natural-gas helium only contains one part in ten million, and helium from radioactive minerals probably contains even less. It is generally believed (1954) that the majority of these helium isotopes originated from the decay of tritium (q.v.) in the earth's atmosphere.

HELL, in theology, any place of punishment and privation for the souls of men after death. More strictly, the term is applied to the place of eternal punishment of the damned, whether angels or men. The doctrine of the existence of hell is derived from the principle of the necessity for vindication of divine justice, combined with the human experience that evildoers are not always punished adequately during life.

Among the early Teutons the term "hell" signified a place under the earth where the souls of all mortals, good or bad, were consigned after death, and consequently denoted a conception similar to that of the Hebrew *Sheol*. Among the early Jews, as in other Semitic nations, existence in Sheol was a shadowy continuation of earthly life where "the wicked ceased from troubling and the weary were at rest". Later the dictum of Isaiah (chap. 14) that the king of Babylon "shall be brought down . . . to the uttermost depths of Sheol" gave rise to the concept of various depths of Sheol, with corresponding degrees of reward and punishment.

Early Christian writers used the term "hell" to designate: (1) the limbo of infants, where the unbaptized enjoy a natural bliss, but are denied the supernatural bliss of the vision of God (see HEAVEN); (2) the limbo of the fathers, in which the souls of the just who died before Christ awaited their redemption, and which is mentioned in the Apostles' Creed, "He [Christ] descended into hell"; (3) a place of purgation from minor offenses leading inevitably to heaven (see PURGATORY); and (4) the generally accepted modern sense of the term, the place of punishment of Satan and the other fallen angels, and of all mortals who die unrepentant of serious sin.

The duration of the punishments of hell has been a subject of controversy since early Christian times. Origen and his school taught that it was purgatorial in its purpose, and proportionate to the guilt of the individual. They held that, in time, the purifying effect would be accomplished in all, even devils, that punishment would ultimately cease, and that all in hell would eventually be restored to happiness. This doctrine was condemned by the second Council of Constantinople, in 553, and a belief in the eternity of the punishments in hell became characteristic of both the Orthodox and the Roman churches. It also passed into the creeds of the churches of the Reformation, although the doctrine of hell was rejected by many of the more radical thinkers of the Renaissance, especially in the Baptist and Unitarian churches.

In modern times the belief in physical punishment after death has been abandoned by certain Protestants, and the endless duration of this punishment has been rejected by many more. The question as to the nature of the punishments of hell is equally controversial. Opinions range from that holding the pains of hell to be no more than the remorse of conscience, to the orthodox belief that the "pain of loss" (the consciousness of having forfeited the vision of God and the happiness of heaven) is combined with the "pain of sense" (actual physical torment). See JUDGMENT, FINAL.

HELLAS (Gr., "land of the Hellenes"), the name which came to be applied to ancient Greece, together with the Greek islands and colonies, after the great migrations of Hellenic peoples, beginning about 1100 B.C. Modern Greece, in accordance with the classical tradition, is also known as Hellas. See GREECE: *History.*

HELLBENDER, or GIANT SALAMANDER, a large amphibian, *Cryptobranchus alleganiensis,* in the order Urodela. It is sometimes called "alligator", "water dog", or "mud puppy". Unlike the true mud puppy (q.v.), which it resembles, its gills are internal and the skin on the sides of its body is wrinkled. The hellbender reaches a length of two feet and is dark brown in color. Its head, body, and tail are flattened to facilitate swimming. Hellbenders are common in the Ohio River and its tributaries. They live on the gravelly bottom of the river and subsist on worms, insects, and small crustaceans. They are often caught by fishermen. The female hellbender lays about four hundred eggs under a stone in August or September and eats many of them in the six-week period before they hatch. The male often guards the eggs but is also occasionally cannibalistic.

The closest relative to the hellbender is the giant salamander, *C. maximus,* of China and Japan, which reaches a length of five feet, and which is eaten in the Orient. See SALAMANDER.

HELL-DIVER. See GREBE.

HELLEBORE, common name of the perennial herbs in the genus *Helleborus,* belonging to the Buttercup family. Hellebore flowers have five petal-like sepals, eight to ten small tubular petals, many stamens, and three to ten pistils. The fruit is a many-seeded pod. Hellebores are native to Eurasia. Green hellebore or Christmas flower, *H. viridis,* is naturalized in E. United States. It blooms in late winter or early spring, producing yellow-green flowers which resemble buttercups in form. *H. niger,* the Christmas rose, bears white or pale purple flowers in winter.

The false hellebores are plants of the Lily family belonging to the genus *Veratrum.* Flowers of this genus have a six-parted perianth, six stamens, and three pistils. The fruit is a follicle which produces three winged seeds. The commonest false hellebore of the U.S. is *V. viride,* the American white hellebore or Indian poke. It produces yellow-green flowers in pyramidal panicles or spikelike racemes. The American white hellebore grows in low or swampy ground throughout the temperate regions of North America. The European white hellebore, *V. album,* bears green or purple flowers. Rootstocks of both species of false hellebore contain the alkaloid poison *veratrine.* An insecticide called hellebore, which is a powder made from the dried rootstocks of false hellebore, was formerly used extensively but is now used to control only a few insect pests, such as the currant worm.

The Christmas rose, a hellebore

HELLEN, in Greek mythology, the eponymous ancestor of the Hellenes, or Greeks. He was reputed to be a son of Deucalion and Pyrrha, respectively king and queen of Thessaly, and the father of Æolus, Dorus, and Xuthus. From Æolus were descended the Æolian Greeks, from Dorus the Dorians, and from the two sons of Xuthus, Ion and Achæus, came the Ionians and Achæans.

HELLENES (Gr. *Hellēnes,* "the Greeks"), the name applied collectively to the four great Greek tribes, the Achæans, the Æolians, the Dorians, and the Ionians (qq.v.), as opposed to the Pelasgians, the Greek designation for the inhabitants of Greece before the invasions by these northern tribes (see GREECE: *History of Ancient Greece*). The term became popular as a national appellation about the 7th century B.C. Modern Greeks also called themselves *Hellenes.*

HELLENISM. See GREECE: *History of Ancient Greece: Hellenistic Period.*

HELLENIST (Gr. *Hellenistes;* fr. *hellenizein,* "to speak or make Greek"), a term designating a person, not of Greek blood, who adopts or imitates the Greek way of life. The term was especially applied to the Jewish people who adopted the Greek culture and language following the Macedonian conquest of the Near East in 338 B.C.; see GREECE: *History of Ancient Greece: Hellenistic Period.* In countries outside Palestine, especially Egypt, Cyrene, and Syria, the Jewish people came into close contact with Greek thought and literature, and eventually came to speak Greek as their native tongue, using it even in the synagogues. Within Palestine itself the Hellenistic influences were strong, particularly during the rule of Antiochus IV (see ANTIOCHUS), with the result that the Jews revolted (see MACCABEES) and established an independent Jewish state relatively free of Hellenism. The apostle Paul contrasts the "Hellenists" with the "Hebrews", that is, the orthodox Jews who resisted Hellenistic influences.

HELLESPONT or **HELLESPONTUS.** See DARDANELLES.

HELL GATE, a narrow part of the East R., between Long Island and the upper portion of Manhattan Island, New York City; it encloses Ward's Island on the E. and W. The channel separating Ward's and Randall's islands is called Little Hell Gate. Until 1885 Hell Gate was a notorious danger to navigation because of its tortuous course, powerful tidal currents, and jagged rocks. As early as

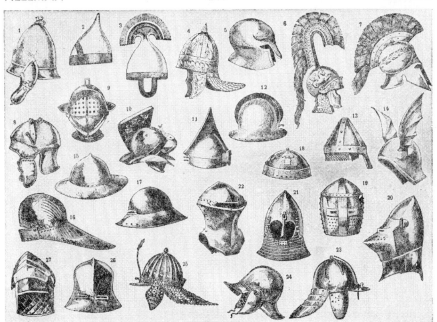

EARLY HELMETS. *1, Italo-Greek; 2 and 3, Assyrian; 4, Dacian; 5, Bœotian; 6 and 7, Dorian; 8, Roman; 9 and 10, Roman gladiator; 11 and 12, Gallic; 13, Norman; 14, Scandinavian, 800; 15, French, 1250; 16, a salade of 1470; 17, a salade of 1430; 18, "cervelière," 1300; 19, heaume, 1220; 20, a large basinet, 1380; 21, small basinet, 1360; 22, 16th-century heaume; 23, "capeline," 16th century; 24, burgonet of 1480; 25, early Polish; 26, 15th-century German salade; 27, Milanese, 1500.*

1851 an attempt was made to clear away the obstructions. On Oct. 10, 1885, the channel was finally freed by blasting operations. The channel derives its name from the Dutch *Helle Gat* ("Beautiful Pass"). It is spanned by the Hell Gate Bridge, completed in 1917.

HELLMAN, LILLIAN (1905–), American playwright, born in New Orleans, and educated at New York University and Columbia University. She was a press representative, a book reviewer, and a play reader before her career as a playwright began. Her plays are distinguished for serious subject matter, character development, and expert construction. Among them are *The Children's Hour* (1934), in which a child wrecks the lives of the heads of her school by maliciously accusing them of lesbianism; *The Little Foxes* (1939), in which the members of a Southern family struggle unscrupulously with one another for the family wealth; and *The Watch on the Rhine* (1941), in which an opponent of Nazism, who has come to the United States to live peacefully, is forced back into the struggle

by his enemies and commits murder to preserve his ideals. Other plays are *The Searching Wind* (1944), *Another Part of the Forest* (1946), and *The Autumn Garden* (1951). She wrote, among others, the scenarios for the motion-picture version of several of her plays.

HELMAND (anc. *Etymander*), river of Afghanistan, rising in Koh-i-Baba, w. of Kabul, and flowing generally s.w. until it enters Seistan, the border district between Afghanistan and Iran, there turning N. and forming the boundary between the two countries until it disappears in the swamps of Seistan. In its early course the river is a mountain stream, used for watering grazing herds. About 40 m. above Girish the Helmand descends to level terrain, where it is used for irrigation purposes. Below its junction with the Arghandab R., the Helmand has a width of 300 to 400 yds. and a maximum depth of 12 ft. The length of the river is about 650 m.

HELMET, a protective covering for the head, usually made of metal or leather, used in warfare and in certain occupations and sports. Military helmets have been used from the earliest times, and have been made in many different forms. The simplest form, a close-fitting skullcap, apparently made of iron, leather, and bronze, appears on Assyrian monumental reliefs. The oldest known elaborations of this form occurred under classical peoples, such as the Greeks, Etruscans, and late Romans, and included protective devices for the neck and face, and plumes or carved figures which surmounted the crown.

During the Dark Ages and the early feudal period, the helmet was a simple casque, usually of plated metal or of leather covered with chain mail or plate, and sometimes bearing additional safeguards for the nape of the neck, the ears, and the nose. In the 11th century this casque, terminating in a conical steel or iron cap, was the typical helmet used by all armored men. From this point it evolved in two divergent directions: the light *basinet,* a pointed iron skullcap worn by ordinary men-at-arms; and the *heaume* (or "helmet"), a large cylindrical iron pot covering the head and part of the neck, worn by knights in armor. The latter was so heavy that it was put on just before engaging in combat, and only when the knight fought on horseback; it was an effective defense against a cut from medieval weapons, but no protection against bruises. Both types, moreover, continued to grow in size and strength, and by the 14th century the basinet, in a variety of forms reinforced by neck guards and vizors, had become the battle helmet of nobles, knights, and sergeants, while the heaume, in increasingly heavy and elaborate forms, had become a special headdress for ceremonies and tournaments.

From the beginning of the 15th century until their eventual decline around 1650, types of helmets proliferated throughout Europe. Some important types, diverse in size and shape and more or less elaborately decorated, were called the *salade,* the *armet,* the *burgonet,* and the *morion* (see ARMOR). As the use of firearms in warfare became more general, helmets lost their utility, especially as protections for the face. Modern military helmets, such as those worn in World Wars I and II, afford no protection for the face; they are usually basinlike, steel or plastic coverings designed for maximum protection against shrapnel and ricocheted bullets.

A number of protective head coverings are today designated as helmets, though their connection with the headpieces described

above is etymological rather than historical. A typical example is the leather and brass helmet which firemen wear as a protection against heat and falling brands and cinders, or the domed hat with a visor and neckguard worn by policemen in some parts of the world. The large headpieces, containing glass windows or lenses, which are worn by divers, and the somewhat similar coverings, open at the bottom, worn by welders, are also called helmets. Other types are the familiar leather helmets worn by football players, aviators, and racing drivers.

Representations of medieval and Renaissance helmets play an important role in heraldry (q.v.).

HELMET BIRD. See TOURACO.

HELMET CRAB. See KING CRAB.

HELMET QUAIL, common name for any of the western-American, galliform birds in the genus *Lophortyx* of the Quail family. They are characterized by a crowning crest of feathers which they can raise or lower by means of special scalp muscles. Helmet quail are hunted by American sportsmen and make excellent eating. Female helmet quail lay an average of eleven eggs in a clutch. These birds subsist on insects, especially grasshoppers, and on berries and grains.

The best-known species is the California helmet quail, *L. californica,* which is found on the Pacific coast from California to Oregon. It is about ten inches long, and has a black crest. Above, it is brownish gray, marked with dark brown at the sides; below, it is black and white on the throat, slate gray on the breast, and black, brown, and white on the abdomen. Another well-known species is Gambel's quail, *L. gambeli,* found in the valleys of the lower Colorado and Gila rivers. Its size and crest are similar to the California helmet quail. Above, Gambel's quail is slate gray; below it is gray, tan, and black.

HELMET SHELL. See QUEEN CONCH.

HELMHOLTZ, HERMANN LUDWIG FERDINAND VON (1821–94), German scientist, born in Potsdam. He studied medicine and natural science in Berlin and served as a surgeon in the Prussian army from 1843 to 1848. From 1849 to 1871 he was professor of physiology successively at the universities of Königsberg, Bonn, and Heidelberg, and from 1871 until his death he was professor of physics at the University of Berlin, also serving as director of the physicotechnical institute at Charlottenburg after 1888.

Helmholtz was one of the great scientists of the nineteenth century. His reputation was securely established in 1847 when he wrote *Über die Erhaltung der Kraft,* in which he gave the earliest general account of the principle of the conservation of energy. From then on he made important contributions, both of a theoretical and practical nature, in many diversified fields of science, including physiology, optics, acoustics, chemistry, mathematics, magnetism, electricity, and mechanics.

His investigations in the field of physiological optics led to his invention of the ophthalmoscope (q.v.), the clarification of the mechanisms of sight, and the development of a theory of color vision, based on the work of Thomas Young (q.v.). His *Physiological Optics* (1856–66) was the definitive study of the physiology and physics of vision. He studied the physiology of hearing, explaining accurately the mechanism of the ear. Helmholtz' work with musical sounds resulted in the first realization that the tonal quality of a musical sound is created by the overtones or harmonics (q.v.) associated with the tone, and his *Sensations of Tone* (1862) formed the basis of the scientific study of acoustics.

In the field of electricity and magnetism Helmholtz contributed to the understanding of electrodynamics, investigated the motion of electricity in conductors, and developed the theory of the electromagnetic properties of light. His last researches were of a purely theoretical nature, and were concerned with the relation of matter to the "ether" and the distribution of energy in mechanical systems. In 1883 the German emperor conferred a title of nobility upon him.

HELMINTH (Gr. *helmins,* "worm"), a worm, especially any parasitic flatworm or threadworm (qq.v.). See also PARASITE; WORMS.

HELMONT, JAN BAPTISTA VAN (1557?–1664?), Flemish physician and chemist, born in Brussels, and educated at the University of Louvain. He was a curious admixture of mystic, alchemist, careful observer of nature, and experimenter. Helmont was the first to realize that there are gases distinct from air; he claimed the word "gas" as his own invention. He believed that the prime elements of the universe are air and water, proving to his satisfaction that plants are composed only of water by planting a willow of known weight in soil of known weight and weighing the willow and the soil five years later. The willow had gained 169 pounds and the soil had lost practically no weight, and he ascribed the gain in weight of the willow to its having taken up water (for the modern explanation

of this experiment, see PHOTOSYNTHESIS). He constructed a mystic system of supernatural bodies which he believed controlled the body, but which had no scientific validity; on the other hand, he applied accurate chemical principles to physiology in his belief that nutrition was due to the action of ferments that converted dead food to living tissue, and in his suggestion that alkalies be used to correct excess acidity of the digestive juices. His works were published posthumously in 1648 as *Ortus Medicinæ vel Opera et Opuscula Omnia.*

HELODERMA. See BEADED LIZARD; GILA MONSTER.

HÉLOISE. See ABÉLARD, PIERRE.

HELOTISM. See SYMBIOSIS.

HELOTS, in ancient Greece, the bondsmen or serfs of the Spartans. They were probably the original population of Sparta who were enslaved by the Dorian conquerors (see DORIANS) of that territory. The Helots represented the lowest of the four classes of Spartans, and had virtually no civil or political rights. They were entirely the property of the state, which assigned them to work on the land of individual Spartans. For their masters the Helots were required to provide a certain fixed amount of produce each year; they were permitted to retain whatever they produced over the amount due their masters. The Helots could be freed or sold only by the state. In wartime they were used as soldiers, or as oarsmen in the navy. Because they were a large and discontented class, the Helots were viewed by the ruling Spartans with suspicion and fear. During the Peloponnesian War about 2000 Helots who had been freed for services to the state were secretly murdered, to forestall plotting against their rulers.

HELPER, HINTON ROWAN (1829–1909), American abolitionist, born in Rowan (now Davie) Co., N.C., and educated at Mocksville Academy, N.C. At the age of twenty-one, Helper went to California, where he lived for three years. Although he was a member of the wealthy class of a Southern slaveholding State, Helper found life in the free State of California superior; he stated this opinion in *The Land of Gold* (1855). In 1857 he published, at his own expense, *The Impending Crisis in the South: How to Meet It.* In this work he expressed carefully documented conclusions that the institution of slavery was economically unsound, and that it had contributed to the moral and intellectual degeneration of the slaveholders of the South. His book sold 100,000 copies in its first year

Philip Gendreau. N. Y.

Aerial view of south harbor in Helsinki, Finland.   St. Nicholas church is in background.

of publication, and during the campaign of 1860 the Republicans distributed millions of copies of a pamphlet of it in digest form. Southern State legislatures forbade the possession or sale of the volume, and men were mobbed and even hanged for owning copies of it. Its immense popularity in the North is said to have contributed, even more than the influence of Harriet Beecher Stowe's novel *Uncle Tom's Cabin,* to hastening the outbreak of the Civil War. Helper was U.S. consul at Buenos Aires from 1861 to 1866, and on his return to the United States he spent the proceeds of his book on the promotion of a scheme for a railroad running from the Bering Strait to the Strait of Magellan. His last years were spent in poverty in Washington, D.C., where he died by his own hand.

HELSINGÖR, or ELSINORE, seaport of Frederiksborg County, Zealand, Denmark, situated on the E. coast of the island, 28 miles N. of Copenhagen. The town is famous as the Elsinore of Shakespeare's *Hamlet.* It was accorded the privileges of a town in 1452. The castle of Kronborg, located E. of the town, was built by King Frederick II during the 16th century and is now used chiefly as a maritime museum. Among the principal in-

dustries of the town are the weaving of fishing nets and coarse cloth, shipbuilding, marine engineering, and iron founding. Helsingör has a fine harbor, equipped with dry docks for the repair of ships. Pop. (1950) 21,010.

HELSINKI (Sw. *Helsingfors*), the capital, largest city, and chief seaport of Finland, and the capital of the Finnish department of Uusimaa, situated on a small peninsula extending into the Gulf of Finland. Small islands fringe the peninsula, and the entrance to Helsinki harbor is protected by the fortifications of Suomenlinna (Sw. *Sveaborg*), covering seven of the islands. Helsinki is 180 m. by rail W.N.W. of Leningrad, U.S.S.R.

The city is laid out with spacious streets interspersed with many gardens and parks. Architecturally, Helsinki is a mixture of old and modern styles, with the senate house and the Lutheran church of St. Nicholas representing the older buildings, and the railway station, designed in 1904 by Gottlieb Eliel Saarinen, a notable example of modern architecture. The capital is the cultural and commercial, as well as the political, center of Finland. About seventy newspapers and periodicals, forty in Finnish and about thirty in Swedish, are published there. The University of Helsinki has been situated in the city since 1827, when it was moved from Turku, where it was founded in 1640. The National Museum of Finland, the opera, and several theaters, playing in both Swedish and Finnish, are located in the capital. The principal manufactures of Helsinki include paper, textiles, liquors, sugar, and metal goods; agricultural and dairy products and lumber and wood products are exported in considerable quantity. A major part of the commercial activity is centered around the harbor, in which separate facilities are maintained for passengers and small shipments, for bulk shipments of lumber and wood products, and for handling large incoming cargoes of coal and grain. The port can accommodate any vessel, but it is icebound from January to May, except for a channel which is kept clear by an icebreaker.

Helsinki was founded by Gustavus I of Sweden in 1550 on a site some miles inland from its present location, to which it was removed in 1640. In 1713, during the Northern War (1700–21) between Russia and Sweden, the city was destroyed by a Russian force; its present fortifications were begun in 1729. Finland was incorporated into the Russian Empire in 1809 and Helsinki was made the administrative capital of the Grand Duchy of Finland in 1821; since 1917 the city has been the capital of the Finnish republic (see FINLAND). Pop. (1953) 394,511.

HELVETIA, the ancient Latin name for Switzerland, meaning "the territory of the Helvetii", and still used poetically for that country.

HELVETIC REPUBLIC, the Swiss republic established by France in 1798 and which endured until 1814. See SWITZERLAND: *History.*

HELVETII, the Latin designation for an ancient Celtic people who, at the time of the Gallic wars of Julius Cæsar, inhabited what is now the western portion of Switzerland. Specifically, the territory of the Helvetii was bounded by the Jura mountain range on the w., the Rhone R. on the s., and the Rhine R. on the N. and E. The Helvetii had their own completely democratic political administration, their chief town being Aventicum (modern Avenches). According to Cæsar's *De Bello Gallico,* they were the bravest of the Gallic peoples.

In 107 B.C., influenced by reports of gold and plunder available in s. Gaul and Rome, the Helvetii crossed the Jura Mts. and defeated a Roman army. Five years later they joined the Cimbri (q.v.) in an attempted invasion of Italy, but were repulsed. In 58 B.C., under the pressure of German invasions, all the Helvetii, numbering almost 370,000, began a mass emigration to what is now s. France. Cæsar, then proconsul in Gaul, pursued them with an army and inflicted such overwhelming defeat that more than two thirds of the Helvetii were annihilated. The remainder returned to their homeland, becoming subject to the rule of the Roman Republic. See GAUL; SWITZERLAND.

HELVÉTIUS, CLAUDE ADRIEN (1715–71), French philosopher, born in Paris. He was appointed farmer general, a post which involved the collection of the royal income, in 1738, but subsequently resigned because of the corruption of his colleagues in office, and purchased the office of *maître d'hôtel* to the Queen. He then devoted his time to literary efforts, and his most famous work, *De l'Esprit,* was published in 1758. In this work Helvétius carried the theory of hedonism (q.v.) to its extreme of selfish sensuality, declaring that all human faculties, including judgment, the power of comparison, and even memory, are mere attributes of physical sensation; that the only motive of human activity is self-interest; and that there exists no choice between good and evil or right and wrong, since even self-sacrifice is a mere choice between competitive pleasures. Helvétius' work was condemned as against public morals by the theological faculty of the Sorbonne, Paris, and was publicly burned in 1759. In 1764 Helvétius visited England, and the following year he was invited to Germany by Frederick II, and received with honor. He then retired to his country estate in France.

HEMATIN. See HEMOGLOBIN.

HEMATITE, a common mineral and the most abundant ore of iron, composed of ferric oxide, Fe_2O_3. It is widely distributed over the world, occurring in rocks of all ages. In the United States hematite comprises more than nine tenths of all the iron ore mined. The chief iron-ore districts in the United States, and probably the most important hematite regions in the world, are located along the shores of Lake Superior in Michigan, Wisconsin, and Minnesota. Extensive deposits are also found in the Appalachian region extending from New York to Alabama, with particularly noteworthy deposits in eastern Tennessee and northern Alabama.

Hematite occurs in rhombohedral crystals, called *specular iron* in massive formations, and in earthy forms, called *red ocher.* The crystals are translucent, range in color from dark gray to black, and have a brilliant metallic luster; the earthy varieties are lusterless and red. The hardness ranges from 5.5 to 6.5 and the specific gravity from 4.2 to 5.25.

In addition to being the principal ore of iron, hematite is a constituent of a number of abrasives and pigments. See OCHER; ROUGE.

HEMEROBAPTISTS (Gr. *hēmera,* "day"; *baptistēs,* "baptizer"), in religious history, sects which practice daily or frequent baptism as part of their ritual. The best known of these Hemerobaptist sects (in Heb., *Tobele-Shaharith*) are a group of Essenes (q.v.) who practiced daily ablution. The term is also applied to certain semi-Christian Oriental sects, notably the Mandæans and the Elkesaites, a group of Sabians who used baptism as a rite of purification rather than one of initiation.

HEMEROCALLIS. See DAY LILY.

HEMICHORDATA or **HEMICHORDA,** a subphylum of the animal phylum Chordata, containing several species of wormlike marine creatures, characterized by a stiff notochord in their head regions. The hemichordates have no common names because they are not popularly known; they are important in biological study because they represent the closest link between invertebrates and vertebrates. Besides the notochord these animals show such typical vertebrate characteristics as a dorsal anterior nerve ganglion and gill clefts in all species, at least embryologically. Unlike vertebrates, hemichordates have no tail in either their adult or their embryological stages. Externally their bodies are divided into three segments, a head or proboscis segment, a collar segment, and a comparatively long trunk segment.

The subphylum Hemichordata contains two orders, Enteropneusta and Pterobranchia. Enteropneusta (q.v.) contains several species which burrow in sand and mud of beaches, ingesting the mud into the mouth, which is situated near the junction of the head and collar segments, and straining minute forms of life from it. Sexes are separate in this order. The larvae are free-swimming at first, but later sink to the mud and gradually become transformed into adults. A common species on the Atlantic coast of the U.S. is *Dolichoglossus kowalevskii,* which reaches a length of 8 in. Other common species in this order belong to the genus *Balanoglossus* (q.v.). Pterobranchia is an order of minute, deep-sea, sessile hemichordates which contains two genera, *Cephalodiscus* and *Rhabdopleura.* These animals live in cylinders which are secreted by cells of the head region; they are unusual in having cilia-bearing arms on the collar which gather food. They breed by budding; the buds of *Cephalodiscus* leave the parent and form new individuals while those of *Rhabdopleura* remain with the parent and form colonies. Compare ASCIDIANS.

HEMICRANIA. See MIGRAINE.

HEMIMORPHITE. See CALAMINE.

HEMINGWAY, ERNEST (1898–   ), American author, born in Oak Park, Ill., and educated at Oak Park High School. In World War I he served in an American volunteer ambulance unit attached to the French army, and later served in Italy; after the war he was European correspondent for the Toronto *Star* and then Paris correspondent for the Syndicated News Service. In 1937–38 he was in Spain, reporting on the Spanish Civil War; he was war correspondent also on the Western Front in World War II during 1944–45.

Hemingway is one of the foremost American authors of the period after World War I. In his early works he is concerned principally with depicting the life of two types of people. One type consisted of men and women whom World War I had deprived of faith in the moral values in which they had hitherto believed, and who now lived with a cynical disregard of anything but their own emotional needs. The other type comprised men of simple character and primitive emotions, such as prizefighters and bullfighters; he wrote of their courageous and usually futile battles against circumstances. His works of this period include the volumes of short stories *Three Stories and Ten Poems* (1923), *In Our Time* (1924), *Men Without Women* (1927), and *Winner Take Nothing* (1933); and the two novels upon which his reputation was founded: the first, *The Sun Also Rises* (1926), is the story of a group of morally irresponsible Americans and Englishmen living in France and Spain, members of the so-called "lost generation" of post-World War I; the other, *A Farewell to Arms* (1929), is the story of the unconventional and deeply moving love affair in wartime Italy between an American officer in the Italian ambulance service and an English nurse, which is terminated by her death in childbirth.

In 1937 the literature of helplessness and defeat which Hemingway had been writing gave way to works which stated a positive attitude toward life. His novel *To Have and Have Not* and his play *The Fifth Column,* published in *The Fifth Column and the First Forty-Nine Stories* (1938), are a strong condemnation of economic and political injustices; and in his novel *For Whom the Bell Tolls* (1940), concerned with the Spanish Civil War, he makes the point that the loss of liberty anywhere in the world is a warning that liberty is endangered everywhere. Among works of his not already mentioned are the satiric novel *The Torrents of Spring* (1926); *Death in the Afternoon* (1933), an account of bullfighting; *Green Hills of Africa* (1935), concerned with big-game hunting; *Across the River and into the Trees* (1950); and *The Old Man and the Sea* (1952), which won the 1953 Pulitzer Prize for fiction. In 1954 he was awarded the Nobel Prize for literature. Hemingway's style is characterized by crispness, laconic dialogue, and emotional understatement. His writings exerted a profound influence on the American writers of his time, who not only adopted his "hardboiled" type of character but imitated his stylistic technique.

HEMIPTERA. See BUG.

HEMLOCK, common name of several poisonous herbs belonging to the Parsley family. The poison hemlock, *Conium maculatum,* is native to Eurasia and grows as a weed in the New World. The plant has compound leaves, spotted stems, and small white flowers which are borne in umbels. The fruit is a five-ridged schizocarp. Hemlock has an unpleasant odor, especially when bruised. All parts of the poison hemlock contain a poisonous alkaloid called *coniine.* Members of the related genus *Cicuta* are called water hemlock; see COWBANE. The American yew (q.v.), a shrub which often grows prostrate, is also called ground hemlock. Fool's parsley (q.v.), a relative of *Conium,* is sometimes called ground hemlock because of its resemblance to yew.

HEMLOCK, common name of coniferous trees of the genus *Tsuga* belonging to the Pine family. The genus includes about ten species, four of which are native to Alaska, Canada, and the United States, and the remainder to E. Asia. They are tall, straight evergreens with slender branches bearing scattered, two-ranked leaves and pendulous cones.

The eastern or Canada hemlock, *T. canadensis,* grows in hilly forests in N.E. United States and E. Canada. It is a tall tree, usually 60 to 100 feet in height, with light, spreading, delicate foliage. The leaves are dark green with longitudinal white lines on the lower surfaces. Wood of eastern hemlock is used extensively as construction lumber, and tannins produced by the bark are used for tanning leather. Canada pitch is a hard,

Ernest Hemingway

dark-red, resinous exudate of the eastern hemlock. The Carolina hemlock, *T. caroliniana,* is a somewhat smaller tree, rarely as tall as 70 feet, which grows in the mountains of Virginia, the Carolinas, and Georgia. The mountain hemlock, *T. mertensiana,* is another relatively small species, 20 to 90 feet tall, which grows along the Pacific coast from Alaska to California. The western hemlock, *T. heterophylla,* is the tallest species in the genus, sometimes reaching a height of 200 feet. It grows along the Pacific coast from S.E. Alaska to central California.

Eastern and western hemlock are important softwood timber trees. The average annual cut of hemlock timber in the U.S. during the 1940's exceeded 1,000,000,000 board feet. Almost three fourths of hemlock used for lumber is western hemlock, and most of the remainder is eastern hemlock.

Small specimens of eastern and Carolina hemlock are used extensively as ornamental trees. Two Asiatic species, the Japanese hemlock, *T. diversifolia,* and Siebold's hemlock, *T. sieboldi,* are cultivated in northern United States. The American yew (q.v.), which belongs to an unrelated coniferous genus, is sometimes called ground hemlock.

HEMOGLOBIN, the bluish-red coloring substance contained within the red blood cells of vertebrates, and within the blood plasma of invertebrates such as the earthworm. Hemoglobin is a "respiratory pigment", i.e., a chemical which picks up oxygen in the lungs and skin to be transported to and given up to the body tissues. When saturated with oxygen, hemoglobin becomes *oxy-hemoglobin*, a bright-red substance.

Hemoglobin is made up of a protein, *globin*, and of an organometallic compound, *hematin*, which is closely related to the chlorophyll of plants. Hematin is a stable, brownish, powdery substance, $C_{34}H_{33}FeN_4O_5$, obtained from oxy-hemoglobin by treatment with acid or alkali; it melts at over 200° C (392° F.), and is soluble in hot alcohol and in alkalis. When blood is treated with hydrochloric acid, or with glacial acetic acid and salt, reddish crystals of hematin chloride, or hemin, separate out from the blood and impart a color to the blood-acid solution; the intensity of this color is proportional to the amount of hemoglobin present, and is utilized in modern colorimetric techniques of determining the concentration of hemoglobin in the blood.

Oxygen forms an unstable linkage with the iron in hematin in a ratio of two atoms of oxygen to one of iron. One oz. (28 grams) of hemoglobin can carry 38 c.c. of oxygen. The normal adult human being has about 3 oz. of hemoglobin per pint of blood. Hemoglobin also forms an unstable compound with carbon dioxide, and relatively stable compounds with such gases as carbon monoxide and hydrocyanic acid. These stable compounds make it impossible for hemoglobin to pick up oxygen and consequently, when formed, result in the death of the individual. Oxidizing drugs such as potassium chlorate change the structure of hemoglobin, producing a substance known as *methemoglobin* which has poor oxygen-carrying power.

Waste hemoglobin, liberated from dead blood cells, is converted by the body into the two bile pigments bilirubin and biliverdin. When body tissues are damaged, hemoglobin often breaks down into a greenish-yellow substance, known as hematoidin, which produces the characteristic color of bruises.

Hemoglobinuria is a condition in which hemoglobin occurs in the urine, giving the urine a cloudy, dark-red to black appearance. It results from systemic poisoning, or from diseases such as typhoid fever and malaria. Syphilis causes *paroxysmal hemoglobinuria*, a condition in which bloody urine is passed whenever the patient is exposed to cold.

HEMOPHILIA, blood disease, usually hereditary, characterized by an abnormal tendency to bleed profusely from even the slightest wounds. Hemophiliac bleeding is usually uncontrollable because of failure of the blood to coagulate. Blood *platelets,* which are broken down in coagulation, are abnormally stable in hemophiliac blood. This stability prevents the activation of *prothrombin,* which is essential to normal clotting; see BLOOD. The disease is almost entirely limited to males, and is a sex-linked trait which is transmitted, but never expressed, by the mother; see HEREDITY: *Sex-Linkage.*

HEMORRHAGE. See BLEEDING.

HEMORRHOIDS. See PILES.

HEMP, common name of an Asiatic annual herb, *Cannabis sativa,* which produces strong, pliable fibers, or of the fibers themselves. This plant is often called true hemp or Indian hemp. It is cultivated in Eurasia, the United States, and Chile. The height of a hemp plant may be as little as 3 or as much as 15 feet, depending on the climate and the kind of soil in which it grows. "Male" plants bear flowers in axillary racemes, and die soon after pollination has taken place. "Female" plants bear flowers in short, crowded spikes, and die after the seed matures. Plants of both sexes are used as sources for fiber.

Hemp stems are hollow and have a fibrous inner bark. The fibers from this bark are used to make a great variety of textile products, including coarse fabrics, ropes, sailcloth, and packing cloth. Soft fibers, used for making clothing fabrics in Asia, are obtained from hemp harvested at the time of pollination; strong, coarse fibers are obtained from mature plants. The fibers are removed and processed by methods similar to those used in processing flax. The stalks are allowed to decompose partially, in order to make the separation of fibers easy. The stalks are then dried, broken, and subjected to a shaking process, which separates the woody parts from the fibers; see FLAX.

Seed of hemp is commonly used as birdseed. Hempseed also yields a fixed oil, called *oil of hemp,* used in manufacture of perfumes and oil plants. A resin, called *charas,* produced by female flower heads and seeds of hemp, is used as a constituent of narcotic smoking mixtures in India. Flowers and leaves of hemp are used by the Arabs to produce the narcotics *bhang* and *hashish* (known in North America as marijuana); these substances are used as narcotics under the name *Cannabis* (q.v.).

Unrelated plants which are commonly called hemp include bowstring hemp, henequen, manila hemp, and sisal (qq.v.). Sunn hemp is obtained from *Crotalaria* (q.v.), an

herb native to India. A palm which grows in
E. Asia, *Chaemerops excelsa,* is called the hemp
palm because fibers obtained from its leaves
are used for cordage. See FIBER.

HEMP NETTLE. See GALEOPSIS.

HEMPSTEAD, a village of Nassau Co., N.Y.,
situated about 20 m. by rail E. of New York
City, of which it is a residential suburb. It is
a center of retail trade in Nassau County, and
is the site of Hofstra College, established in
1935.

In the vicinity of the village are several
large airplane factories, and Mitchell Field, a
U.S. Air Force base. The Presbyterian Society
of Hempstead, organized in 1644, is the oldest
Presbyterian society in the U.S. Hempstead
was settled in 1643 and incorporated in 1853.
Pop. (1950) 29,135.

HEN. See FOWL; POULTRY.

HENBANE, common name applied to herbs
of the genus *Hyoscyamus,* belonging to the
Nightshade family. The genus is native to
temperate regions of the Old World. The
flower has a five-toothed calyx, an irregular,
funnel-shaped, five-lobed corolla, five stamens, and a solitary pistil. The fruit is a cir-
cumscissile capsule. Henbane leaves and seeds
contain two poisonous alkaloids: (1) *hyoscyamine,* $C_{17}H_{23}NO_3$, a colorless, crystalline
substance, and (2) *scopolamine* (q.v.), also
called *hyoscine.* Hyoscyamine is used in medicine as a sedative and mydriatic.

Common or black henbane, *H. niger,* is a
biennial or annual plant, bearing purple-
streaked, dull-yellow flowers. Its stems and
leaves are covered with oily hairs and have
a disagreeable odor. Common henbane is naturalized in waste places of E. North America
and in the vicinities of ports of W. North
America. Yellow henbane, *Physalis viscosa,*
is an unrelated member of the Nightshade
family; see PHYSALIS.

HENCH, PHILIP SHOWALTER (1896–   ),
American physician, born in Pittsburgh, Pa.,
and educated at Lafayette College and at the
universities of Pittsburgh and Minnesota. He
was associated after 1923 with the Mayo
Clinic in Rochester, Minn., and became a
specialist in the treatment of rheumatic diseases. For his outstanding research on the
adrenal cortex hormones Hench shared the
1950 Nobel Prize in medicine and physiology
with the American biochemist Edward C.
Kendall and the Swiss biochemist Tadeusz
Reichstein.

HENDERSON, ARTHUR (1863–1935), British labor leader and statesman, born in Glasgow, and early apprenticed to an ironmolder

The hemp plant. A, "male"; B, "female."

in Newcastle. He joined the trade union
movement and held official positions in several unions. In 1903 he was elected mayor of
Darlington and member of Parliament from
that city. He was chairman of the Labor
Party from 1908 to 1910 and from 1914 to
1917. In the coalition ministries during World
War I, Henderson was president of the board
of education from 1915 to 1916, and pay-
master general from 1916 to 1917. After the
outbreak of the Russian revolution in the
spring of 1917, the British Government sent
Henderson to St. Petersburg (now Leningrad), as its representative to the new Russian
government. Under the Labor Party government of Great Britain of 1924 Henderson
was home secretary. In 1929–31 he was foreign secretary. He was chairman of the League
of Nations International Disarmament Conference in 1932 and in 1934 he was awarded
the Nobel Peace Prize.

HENDERSON, JOHN BROOKS (1826–1913),
American lawyer and politician, born in Dan-
ville, Va. After being admitted to the bar in
1844, Henderson practiced in Louisiana, and
later in Missouri. He was a member of the
Missouri legislature in 1848 and in 1856–57,
and took part in the Missouri Convention
called in 1861 to consider the secession of the
State from the Union. Henderson opposed
secession and was influential in keeping Missouri within the Union. He was elected a U.S.

senator in 1862, supported President Lincoln's policies, and in 1864 he introduced in the Senate the 13th Amendment to the U.S. Constitution, prohibiting slavery. He was an opponent of President Andrew Johnson (q.v.), but voted in the Senate in 1868 to acquit him of the charges on which he was impeached.

HENDERSON, LEON (1895–   ), American economist and government official, born in Millville, N.J., and educated at Swarthmore College and the University of Pennsylvania. He was director of consumer-credit research at the Russell Sage Foundation, New York City, from 1925 to 1934, and in the latter year was appointed a member of the National Industrial Recovery Board. From 1936 to 1938 he was consulting economist with the Works Progress Administration, and from 1939 to 1941 he served on the Securities and Exchange Commission. He was head of the Office of Price Administration in 1941–42, and subsequently was chief economist of the Research Institute of America. In 1947 he helped to found the political organization Americans for Democratic Action, and served for a time as its chairman.

HENDRICKS, THOMAS ANDREWS (1819–85), American statesman, born near Zanesville, Ohio, and educated at South Hanover College, Indiana. He was admitted to the Indiana bar in 1843, and in 1845 was elected to the State legislature. From 1851 to 1855 he was a member (Democratic) of the U.S. House of Representatives, and from 1863 to 1869 of the U.S. Senate. In 1872 he was elected governor of Indiana. Hendricks was candidate for the Vice-Presidency on the unsuccessful Democratic ticket headed by Samuel J. Tilden in 1876. In 1884 he was elected Vice-President on the ticket headed by Grover Cleveland.

HENDRIX COLLEGE, a coeducational institution of higher learning at Conway, Ark. It was founded in 1876 as Central Collegiate Institute, purchased in 1884 by the Methodist Church, and given its present name in 1889. The college offers courses leading to a bachelor's degree in the liberal arts, and music. In 1952–53 enrollment was 454 (440 full-time students); the faculty numbered 40.

HENEQUEN, common name applied to *Agave fourcroydes,* and to the fibers produced by its leaves; see AGAVE. Henequen fiber, which is the chief material for manufacturing binder twine, is grown primarily in Cuba and Yucatan. Henequen has spiny, sword-shaped leaves. In harvesting, mature leaves are severed at the base and spines are removed with large knives. The leaves are "cleaned" by scraping machines which separate the pulpy tissues from the fiber. The fiber is finished by brushing and drying, and is then baled for market. The finished yellow-white fibers, sometimes called Mexican sisal, are strong and flexible; see SISAL.

HENGELO, commune of Overijssel Province, the Netherlands, situated in the Twente manufacturing district, 5 m. by rail N.W. of Enschede. Among its principal industrial establishments are textile factories, dye works, machine shops, and breweries. Pop. (1953 est.) 52,474.

HENGIST ("horse") and **HORSA** ("mare"), two brothers who are said to have led the first Germanic band of invaders to Britain. They are mentioned in the *Historia Britonum* (History of the Britons) by the Welsh historian Nennius, and in the *Anglo-Saxon Chronicle,* attributed to Alfred the Great. According to the tradition, Hengist and Horsa came about the year 449 A.D. at the solicitation of Vortigern, ruler of Britain, to help him in his war against the Picts. For their services, the brothers received the Isle of Thanet, N.E. of Kent. They later turned against Vortigern, and Horsa was slain in the ensuing battle. Hengist is said to have conquered Kent.

HENLEY, WILLIAM ERNEST (1849–1903), English man of letters, born in Gloucester. He attended grammar school in Gloucester, where the poet Thomas E. Brown was for a time his headmaster. As a result of tuberculosis, Henley was crippled from childhood, and it was while he was undergoing treatment at a hospital in 1874 that he began to write poignantly realistic verses describing his experiences. These poems, later known as *Hospital Rimes,* were published in the *Cornhill Magazine,* and led to his meeting with Robert Louis Stevenson, of whom he was afterward a life-long friend. In 1877 Henley went to London and became editor of the weekly periodical *London.* In 1882 he became editor of the *Magazine of Art,* and later edited other magazines. His first volume of poetry, *Book of Verses,* including the poems he wrote in the hospital, appeared in 1880. Among other volumes of poetry he wrote are *The Song of the Sword* (1892), *London Voluntaries* (1893), and *Hawthorne and Lavender* (1899); his best-known poems are *Invictus, The Song of the Sword,* and *England, my England.* With Robert Louis Stevenson he collaborated in writing four plays, *Decon Brodie, Beau Austin, Admiral Guinea* (all published in 1892), and *Macaire* (1895).

Henley was one of the compilers of *A Dictionary of Slang and its Analogues* (1894–1904).

HENLEY REGATTA, an annual program of rowing races at Henley-on-Thames, called in full the Henley Royal Regatta, and usually held in July. It was first staged in 1839 and has been held annually ever since, except when interrupted by wars. It has become the major amateur rowing event in England and perhaps the best known in the world. Most of the events cover a distance of 2310 yards (about 1 1/3 miles), and every event is open to amateur rowers from any country. Boats ranging from eight-oared sculls to single sculls are included in the contests. The first American victory in the regatta was won by a Harvard College team in 1914. See Rowing.

HENNA, common name of a small shrub, *Lawsonia inermis,* belonging to the Loosestrife family, and of the dye obtained from its leaves. The shrub, which is also called alkanna, grows in moist places in northern Africa and southern Asia. It bears small, fragrant, white or rose flowers in clusters. The orange-red dye produced by its leaves is used extensively in the U.S. as a rinse to impart a reddish color to hair. Women of Mohammedan countries use the dye to stain the nails and tips of their fingers and parts of their feet; men of these countries use the dye to color their beards. The dye is also used to stain leather and hides and to color the hoofs and manes of horses.

HENNEPIN, Louis (1640?–1701), Roman Catholic monk and explorer in America, born in Ath, Flanders. He entered the Franciscan order at an early age. After serving as chaplain in the army of the Prince of Condé, he went to Quebec, Canada, in 1675. In 1676 and 1677 he worked as a missionary among the Iroquois Indians, and in 1678 he accompanied the French explorer Robert La Salle on an expedition through the Great Lakes to the Illinois R., on the banks of which they built Fort Crève-Cœur, near the site of the present Peoria. From there Father Hennepin was sent by La Salle on a voyage to explore the upper Mississippi R., which he did by canoe, ascending the river as far as the Falls of St. Anthony, now the site of Minneapolis. He reached the falls in July, 1680, and after giving them their name, proceeded further through the present State of Minnesota and was captured by Sioux Indians, with whom he lived until his rescue in June, 1681, by Daniel Greysolon Duluth, leader of a French exploring party from the Lake Superior region. Father Hennepin then returned to Quebec, from which he sailed for France. There, in 1683, he published *Description de la Louisiane,* an account of his travels. He later wrote *Nouveau Voyage* (1696) and *Nouvelle Découverte d'un Très Grand Pays Situé dans L'Amérique* (1697). The last-named, in which he claimed to have preceded La Salle to the mouth of the Mississippi, was later discredited.

HENOTHEISM (Gr. *heis,* "one"; *theos,* "god"), in the science of comparative religion, a term designating the characteristic of the Vedic and other ancient pantheistic faiths, whereby different gods are worshiped in turn as the supreme deity. See Veda. It is also used to describe the ancient Hebrew religion in which one god was worshiped as the supreme divinity, but in which the existence of other gods was acknowledged, especially those of other religions and those regarded as governing other peoples. Henotheistic faiths are regarded by students of comparative religion as a stage in the development toward monotheism. See God.

HENRI, Robert (1865–1929), American painter, born in Cincinnati, Ohio. He studied at the Academy of Fine Arts, Philadelphia, and at the Academie Julien, Paris. He traveled for years in France, Spain, and Italy, studying particularly the work of the Dutch painter Frans Hals. On his return to America he became a member of "The Eight", a group of important painters who broke with the conventional standards in art, painting more vivid and realistic subject matter and becoming noted for their uncompromising portrayals of everyday life. Henri became known principally for his colorful portraits of gypsies. He was also one of the most prominent and influential teachers of his time, and wrote notes on art published as *The Art Spirit.* His paintings are in the Metropolitan Museum, New York City, the Carnegie Institute, Pittsburgh, the Chicago Art Institute, the Columbus Fine Arts Gallery, the San Francisco Institute, and many other museums.

HENRIETTA MARIA (1609–69), queen consort of King Charles I (q.v.) of England from 1625 until 1649, daughter of Henry IV of France and sister of Louis XIII. When Louis XIII consented in 1624 to her marriage to Charles, then Prince of Wales, he did so on condition that the penal laws for the English Catholics would be revised. Henrietta Maria was married in 1625 but was unable to secure favorable treatment for her coreligionists until after 1636, when she began to engage in political intrigue to aid the Roman Catholic cause. In 1640 she urged Charles I to oppose the Short Parliament, and two years later, after the outbreak of the Civil War, she went to the Continent to secure money and troops to assist the Royalists. The following year she returned with money and, gathering a force of Loyalist troops, led them to Oxford, where she joined her husband. However, the situation grew worse for the Royalists, and in 1644 Henrietta Maria was persuaded to seek refuge in France. She continued to solicit aid for Charles until his execution in 1649. After the Restoration in 1660 she was awarded a Parliamentary grant and permission to live in England, where she resided until 1665. She died in France.

HENRY II (1333–79), Count of Trastamara, King of Castile and León from 1369 until 1379, natural son of Alfonso XI. On the accession to the throne of Alfonso's legitimate son Pedro the Cruel in 1356, Henry fled to France. With an army of mercenaries and supported by money from the English and French kings, Henry set out in 1366 to dethrone Pedro. His expedition was successful until the English Black Prince, Edward, intervened for Pedro and defeated Henry at Nájera in 1367 Subsequently Henry gathered another army of French mercenaries and, aided by Bertrand Du Guesclin (q.v.), defeated and killed Pedro in 1369; Henry then became king. During his reign he continued his alliance with the French king in the wars against the English. In order to retain the domestic support of nobles and cities, he made large grants and agreed to many concessions, earning for himself the title *El de las Mercedes,* or "He of the largesse".

HENRY I (1068–1135), called HENRY BEAUCLERC (Fr., "Henry the Scholar") because of his great learning, King of England from 1100 until 1135, fourth son of William the Conqueror. Having been left money but no land when his father died in 1087, he made several unsuccessful attempts in his early career to gain territories on the Continent. When King William II died in 1100, Henry took advantage of his older brother Robert's absence and obtained his own election to the English kingship by the witan, or council. He subsequently secured his position with the nobles and with the Church by issuing a Charter of Liberties, the basis for the later Magna Carta (q.v.), by reinstating Anselm (see ANSELM OF CANTERBURY, SAINT) to the archbishopric of Canterbury, and by marrying

an Anglo-Scottish princess, Matilda, or Maud, daughter of King Malcolm III of Scotland. In 1101 he defeated his brother Robert, who had invaded England in protest of Henry's kingship, and in the following year put down a revolt of nobles led by Robert of Belesmes. The defeated nobles took refuge in Normandy, where they were aided by the king's brother. By defeating Robert at Tinchebrai, France, in 1106, Henry won Normandy. However, during the rest of his reign he was constantly involved in putting down uprisings that threatened his rule in Normandy. The conflict (1103–06) between Henry and Anselm, caused by the refusal of the latter to invest prelates appointed by the king, was settled in 1107 by a compromise which left the king's prerogative substantially intact.

In 1114 Henry arranged a marriage between his daughter Matilda and Emperor Henry V. Because of the death of his only son, and his failure to secure a male heir by a second marriage after the death of his first wife, Henry was forced to designate his daughter Matilda as his heiress. In the latter part of his life he was concerned with securing the succession of his daughter, who had been widowed and married next to Geoffrey of Anjou. He was unsuccessful in this attempt, for after his death a civil war between Matilda and Stephen of Blois ensued, with Stephen gaining the victory. Henry's reign was generally peaceful and progressive. He made reforms in the administration of justice, established an unofficial law code, called the *Leges Henrici,* and created the department of the exchequer for the collection and management of the royal revenue.

HENRY II (1133–89), King of England from 1154 until 1189, first monarch of the house of Anjou or Plantagenet, son of Geoffrey Plantagenet, Count of Anjou, and of Matilda, daughter of King Henry I of England. He was sometimes called CURTMANTLE because of the short Angevin mantle he wore. In 1150 he was made duke of Normandy. The following year, on his father's death, he inherited Geoffrey's Angevin territories. By his marriage in 1152 to Eleanor of Aquitaine, divorced wife of King Louis VII of France, Henry added Guienne, Aquitaine, and lands in s. France to his possessions. Through his mother, who had been designated her father's heiress but was deprived of the succession by Stephen of Blois, Henry claimed the English kingship. In 1153 he defeated the armies of Stephen in England and compelled the king to choose him as his successor; on the death of Stephen in the following year, Henry became king. During the first few years of his reign Henry devoted himself to quelling the disorder that had developed during Stephen's reign and to enlarging his English possessions. He regained some N. counties previously ceded to King Malcolm IV of Scotland and conquered Wales.

From 1157 until 1180 Henry II was involved in conflict with King Louis VII of France over French provinces to which Henry laid claim. Meanwhile, he carried on a quarrel with Thomas à Becket (q.v.), Archbishop of Canterbury, concerning ecclesiastical courts. The dispute began in 1163 over the question of trying "criminous clerks", or ecclesiastics accused of crime. By the Constitutions of Clarendon (see CLARENDON, CONSTITUTIONS OF), the supreme authority was fixed in the royal, not the ecclesiastical, courts. Thomas à Becket refused to approve the Constitutions and was accordingly so persecuted that he fled to France in 1164. Fearing papal interdiction on his dominions, Henry effected a reconciliation with the archbishop, who returned to England in 1170. Before the question of the "criminous clerks" could be settled, Becket was murdered by four knights loyal to Henry but not acting on his orders. Nevertheless, Henry was held responsible and probably undertook the conquest of Ireland at that time to temporarily escape censure. As a result of the murder, Henry had to accede on the question of ecclesiastical authority and in 1174 had to perform penance at the archbishop's shrine.

From 1173 until his death the king was troubled by a succession of rebellions headed by his sons and furthered by King Philip II of France and by Queen Eleanor, who was hostile to her husband because of his faithlessness. Despite the internecine strife, caused partly by the Becket affair and partly by the king's close-handed distribution of lands and titles to his sons, Henry did not lose the loyalty of his people. His death was hastened by his discovery that his favorite son and erstwhile ally, John, was secretly aiding Henry's son and heir apparent, Richard, and his allies against Henry. Henry made a number of valuable administrative reforms, especially in the judicial branch of the government. See ENGLAND: *History*.

HENRY III (1207–72), King of England from 1216 until 1272, member of the house of Anjou, or Plantagenet, and son of King John and of Isabella of Angoulême. He succeeded to the throne at the age of nine, on the death of his father. During part of his minority the kingdom was ruled by the regent William Marshal, Earl of Pembroke; Peter des Roches, Bishop of Winchester, was Henry's guardian. After Marshal's death in 1219 the justiciar, Hubert de Burgh, was the chief power in the government. During the regency the French, who occupied much of E. England, were expelled and rebellious barons were subdued.

Henry was declared of age in 1227. In 1232 he dismissed Hubert de Burgh from his court and commenced ruling without the aid of ministers. Allied with the papacy, Henry supported the exaction of money from the English clergy by the Church and shared the returns with the Pope. He displeased the barons by filling government and church offices with foreign favorites and by squandering money on Continental wars, especially in France. The barons refused to supply subsidies without placing conditions on their grants; consequently, Henry borrowed from the clergy, the towns, and the Jewish merchants. The publication, sometime after 1255, of Henry's scheme to place his son Edmund Crouchback on the throne of Sicily finally aroused the barons to action. Led by Simon de Montfort, Earl of Leicester, they forced Henry to agree to the Provisions of Oxford, whereby the king temporarily transferred his power to an oligarchy of nobles. However, Henry soon found an opportunity to repudiate his oath, with papal approval. After a brief period of war, the matter was referred to the arbitration of King Louis IX of France, who annulled the Provisions. Simon de Montfort accordingly led the barons into war in 1264 and defeated Henry at Lewes, took him prisoner, and compelled him to submit to a virtual dictatorship by the Earl of Leicester. In the following year Simon summoned a Parliament, the first in which the boroughs were represented. In that same year the king's son and heir, Edward, reorganized the royal party and, reopening the war, defeated and killed Simon de Montfort at Evesham. The barons agreed to a compromise with Edward and his party in 1267. From then on Edward was actually king, and when his father died, he succeeded him as Edward I.

Despite internal warfare, art and learning flourished during Henry's kingship; Roger Bacon and Robert Grosseteste (qq.v.) were teachers at Oxford in that period, and the eastern portion of Westminster Abbey was rebuilt under Henry's ægis. See ENGLAND: *History*.

HENRY IV, surnamed BOLINGBROKE, called by many of his contemporaries HENRY OF LANCASTER (1367–1413), King of England from 1399 until 1413, member of the house of Lancaster, son of John of Gaunt and of Blanche, daughter of Henry, Duke of Lancaster. About 1380 he married Mary Bohun, one of the heiresses of the Earl of Hereford. From 1387 until 1390 he was a leader of the party opposing his cousin King Richard II. Henry subsequently took part in several wars in Lithuania and made a pilgrimage to Jerusalem. After his return to England he joined the king's party and was made Earl of Hereford in 1397. Because of a quarrel with the Duke of Norfolk, Henry was exiled for six years by King Richard, who nevertheless promised that Henry would not be deprived of his inheritance. However, when Henry's father died in the next year, Richard confiscated the estates willed to Henry. The exile thereupon raised an army, invaded England, and captured his cousin, who subsequently abdicated from the throne. On being chosen king by Parliament in 1399, Henry became the first constitutional monarch of England and the founder of the Lancastrian dynasty of kings. In that same year a Welsh revolt began under the leadership of Owen Glendower (q.v.), but was soon suppressed by the king. In 1400 Henry put down a revolt of discontented nobles, most of whom he had executed. The Scots, who instigated a war against the English crown, were defeated at Homildon Hill in 1402. In the following year the Percy family, under the leadership of Sir Henry Percy, rebelled against Henry because they were dissatisfied with the rewards for service he had bestowed upon them; they were overcome in the battle of Shrewsbury, during which Sir Henry's son and namesake, called Hotspur, was killed. Wars and rebellions persisted after that date but diminished in number. During his reign Henry IV persecuted the Lollards (q.v.). In the last years of his reign he was an invalid.

HENRY V (1387–1422), King of England from 1413 until 1422, member of the house of Lancaster and son of Henry IV. When his father acceded to the throne in 1399, he received several titles, among them Duke of Lancaster and Prince of Wales. Henry led the English forces in the defeat of Owen Glendower (q.v.) and the Percies at Shrewsbury in 1403. Until 1408 he was active in combating the Welsh revolt. In 1410–11, during the period of his father's illness, Henry headed the royal council, governing almost as a regent. A political quarrel with Henry IV in 1411 resulted in the removal of the prince from his position in the council. On succeeding his father in 1413 Henry V restored the son of Sir Henry Percy (Hotspur) to his lands and titles and honorably reburied at Westminster Abbey the remains of Richard II, who was dethroned by Henry IV and, on dying in 1400, was interred without a state funeral at King's Langley. The new king continued his father's policy of persecuting the Lollards (q.v.), executing their leader, Sir John Oldcastle, in 1417.

In 1415 Henry warred against France, winning in that same year the battle of Agincourt (q.v.). Two years later he invaded and conquered Normandy, and in 1419 he captured Rouen. He concluded a peace treaty at Troyes in 1420 with the French king, Charles VI, obtaining the king's eldest daughter, Catherine of France, in marriage and securing the regency of France and the promise of succession to the French throne on the death of the king. With King Sigismund of Hungary, he ended the Western Schism (see SCHISM, WESTERN) by securing the election of Pope Martin V. When he visited England in 1421, leaving his brother the Duke of Clarence as governor of Normandy, the French rose in opposition against English rule and defeated the Duke at Beaugé. Henry returned to France for a third campaign, during which he became ill and died at Bois de Vincennes. He was, at the time of his death, the most influential ruler in western Europe.

Shakespeare's interpretation of Henry in the play *Henry IV* is generally considered in-

King Henry IV of England

King Henry V of England leading his army at Harfleur in 1415, in the war against France

correct in several respects. The frivolity ascribed to the prince by the playwright in *Henry IV* is negated by the fact of Henry's early activity in politics as well as in war. A transformation in the character of the prince on his accession to the throne, such as that portrayed by Shakespeare in *Henry V*, did not actually occur. However, Henry did turn against his erstwhile friend Sir John Oldcastle (q.v.), the probable model for the character of Falstaff.

HENRY VI (1421–71), King of England (1422–61; 1470–71), and of France (1422–35), a member of the house of Lancaster, son of Henry V and Catherine of France. While still an infant he succeeded his father to the throne of England and his grandfather, Charles VI, to that of France, being placed under the protectorship of his uncles John, Duke of Bedford, and Humphrey, Duke of Gloucester. The kingship of Henry in France was contested by his uncle Charles VII. Henry was crowned king of England in 1429 and king of France in 1431. After 1429, when Joan of Arc aroused the French people by her heroism, the power of England weakened in France. This decline was accelerated in 1435, when the Duke of Bedford, regent for Henry in France, died and the Duke of Burgundy deserted the English cause, allying himself with Charles VII. Under the guidance of Cardinal Beaufort, Henry began to take part in government affairs, supporting the cardinal's peace policy in order to save at least Guienne and Normandy. His marriage with Margaret of Anjou in 1445 was

unpopular in England as the bride brought no dowry and one of the conditions of the marriage was the surrender of some English territory in France. By 1453 all that remained in English hands in France was Calais.

Economic unrest and usurpation of property by great nobles led in 1450 to a rebellion in England by the men of Kent under the leadership of Jack Cade (q.v.). They demanded that Richard, Duke of York, next in line of succession to the throne, replace Henry VI. The rebellion was put down, but from that time on Richard continued to be the favorite of the people. In 1454 Henry went insane. Until he recovered his sanity a year later, Richard of York acted as protector of the kingdom. The Wars of the Roses (see ROSES, WARS OF THE) between the houses of Lancaster and York began in 1455. After intermittent warfare Henry was captured by the Yorkists at Northampton and was compelled to acknowledge Richard of York as his successor. Enraged because her son was thereby deprived of the crown, Queen Margaret renewed the war, her forces causing Richard's death at Wakefield and triumphing over the Yorkists at St. Albans in 1461. Richard's son Edward subsequently became leader of the Yorkists, proclaimed himself King Edward IV, and won the battle of Towton, ending the reign of Henry.

Henry and Margaret escaped to Scotland, where they remained until 1464. In that year he returned to take part in an unsuccessful rebellion against Edward. Henry was taken prisoner in 1465 and detained in the Tower of London. Margaret subsequently secured the aid of Richard Neville, Earl of Warwick, who, in 1470, drove Edward from the kingdom. Although then imbecilic, Henry became king and ruled until he was recaptured, dethroned, and returned to the Tower by Edward in 1471. Henry died soon afterward, supposedly murdered by order of Edward IV. Zealously interested in promoting education, Henry founded Eton in 1440 and King's College, Cambridge, in 1441.

HENRY VII, often called HENRY TUDOR, and known until his accession as HENRY, EARL OF RICHMOND (1457–1509), King of England from 1485 until 1509, first king of the house of Tudor, son of Edmund Tudor, Earl of Richmond, and of Margaret Beaufort, direct descendant of John of Gaunt. After the Yorkist Edward IV seized the English throne from Henry VI in 1471, Henry Tudor, a Lancastrian, took refuge in Brittany. He became head of the house of Lancaster on the death of Henry VI in 1471, remaining the chief rival for the English throne after the accession of Richard III. Taking advantage of the indignation aroused against Richard III whose nephews, the sons of Edward IV, were murdered in the Tower of London in 1483, presumably by order of Richard, Henry crossed over to England, where he gathered an army of supporters. In 1485, at Bosworth, he met and defeated Richard III, who was killed during the battle. Henry Tudor was subsequently crowned Henry VII in London. In the following year he married the Yorkist heiress, Elizabeth, eldest daughter of Edward IV, uniting the houses of York and Lancaster and ending the Wars of the Roses (see ROSES, WARS OF THE).

After his accession Henry had to contend with several uprisings, notably those led by the impostors Lambert Simnel (q.v.), who claimed to be the Earl of Warwick, and Perkin Warbeck, who pretended he was the Duke of York. In 1494 Henry sent Sir Edward Poynings to Ireland to re-establish English control in that country. Henry managed to maintain friendly relations with Austria and Spain on the one hand and their enemy, France, on the other, throughout most of his years of kingship. In 1501 he married his eldest son, Arthur, to Catherine of Aragon, daughter of Ferdinand and Isabella. Seven years after Arthur's death in 1502, Henry negotiated a marriage for Catherine with his second son, later Henry VIII.

During his reign Henry encouraged commerce and exploration, winning the support of the middle classes. He imposed heavy taxes in order to suppress intrigues and rebellions. Later in his reign, however, avarice led him to indulge in extortionist practices, and he acquired great wealth. An autocratic king, he summoned only seven parliaments during his reign. The establishment in 1487 of the Star Chamber (q.v.) was one of several means by which Henry strengthened the royal power.

HENRY VIII (1491–1547), King of England from 1509 until 1547, of the house of Tudor, the son of Henry VII and Elizabeth of York. A papal dispensation was secured in 1503 to allow the betrothal of Henry to his brother Arthur's widow, Catherine of Aragon. Six years later Henry succeeded his father to the throne and subsequently married Catherine. The attractiveness of person, fondness for sport and the hunt, military prowess, and hearty personality of "Bluff King Hal" endeared him to his subjects in the beginning of his reign. A student of the Renaissance, he entertained at his court the disciples and teachers of the new learning. Withal Henry was devoutly religious, and in 1521 he was given the title Fidei Defensor ("Defender of the Faith") by Pope Leo X for writing *Assertio Septem Sacramentorum,* a treatise against Martin Luther.

In 1511 Henry joined his father-in-law, King Ferdinand of Spain, and the papacy, Austria, and Venice in the Holy League against France, the traditional enemy of England. Henry personally led the English forces in 1513 through a victorious campaign in N. France. Meanwhile, King James IV of Scotland invaded England but was defeated and killed by the English at Flodden Field (q.v.). Finding himself deserted by his allies in 1514, Henry married his sister Mary to King Louis XII of France, with whom he formed an alliance. He subsequently appointed the archbishop of York, Thomas Wolsey (q.v.), lord chancellor and commissioned him to direct foreign policy. With the accession in 1519 of Charles I of Spain to the throne of the Holy Roman Empire, hostilities between King Francis I of France and Charles became inevitable (see CHARLES V). Despite the efforts of Wolsey to win for England the role of arbiter, and despite the magnificently staged interview of Henry and Francis on the Field of the Cloth of Gold (q.v.), Henry chose to side with his wife's nephew, Charles, in the war which opened in 1521. The English participated in the campaigns of 1522 and 1523. However, riots broke out in England in protest against Henry's attempt in 1525 to raise a large loan for military purposes, and England's full prosecution in the war was halted. Henry consequently made peace with France in that same year.

In 1527 Henry made manifest his desire to divorce his wife, on the grounds that the papal dispensation making the marriage possible was invalid. The chief reason for the divorce was Catherine's failure to produce a male heir. Her only surviving child was a girl, Mary, whose chance of succession in England, where no woman had ever mounted the throne, was doubtful. Furthermore, Henry had fallen in love with Anne Boleyn, a young and beautiful lady-in-waiting of the queen. Knowing that Pope Clement VII, who was then a prisoner of Charles V, could not invalidate Henry's marriage without displeasing his captor, Henry appointed Wolsey and Lorenzo Campeggio, a papal legate, to try the case in an English legatine court. The case was eventually summoned to Rome by the Pope. When in that same year the treaty of Cambrai acknowledged Charles the victor over Francis I in Italy, and the prospect of securing a papal annulment seemed hopeless, Henry dismissed Wolsey, making Sir Thomas More (q.v.) lord chancellor and appointing Thomas Cromwell (q.v.) his chief adviser, both men favoring ecclesiastical reform within the Church.

Henry then proceeded to dissolve one by one the ties that bound the English church to the papacy. With the aid of parliamentary legislation Henry first secured control of the clergy, compelling that group in 1532 to acknowledge him as head of the English church and to submit any new canons to his approval. In the following year Henry secretly married Anne Boleyn, who was crowned queen after Thomas Cranmer (q.v.), Henry's obedient archbishop of Canterbury, declared the marriage with Catherine of Aragon void and that with Anne valid. An act of succession affirmed the archbishop's declaration and established Anne's progeny as heirs to the throne. In 1534 Pope Clement VII refused to sanction the divorce of Henry, whom he excommunicated. However, by an act of supremacy in that year, Henry repudiated the jurisdiction of the Pope, making himself the supreme ecclesiastical authority in England. The English people were required to affirm under oath the contents of the acts of 1533 and 1534. Sir Thomas More and St. John Fisher were executed for refusing to accept the religious supremacy of the English monarch, al-

Henry VIII (by Hans Holbein the Younger)

though they were willing to accept the succession of Anne's and Henry's children. In 1536 Henry dissolved the lesser monastic communities and by 1539 abolished the remaining monasteries, despite the occurrence of the Pilgrimage of Grace, an uprising in protest against that action. Monastic property was sold or given to the nobles in exchange for their support.

Although he altered the character of the English church, Henry did not wish to introduce Protestant doctrine into England. Those who refused to accept Catholic teachings as well as those who rejected Henry's authority over the Church were executed. Henry promulgated in 1536 the Ten Articles, containing a creed which generally adhered to the old order. In 1539 he published the Six Articles, a body of statements reaffirming the Catholic view of certain disputed points of doctrine. The licensing of an English translation of the Bible, the issuance of Cranmer's litany, and the translation into English of certain parts of the traditional service were the only other important changes made in the orthodox religion during Henry's lifetime.

Meanwhile, Henry had acquired several more wives. Charging Anne Boleyn with incest and adultery, he had the mother of the future Queen Elizabeth executed in 1536. A few days after Anne's death, Henry married Jane Seymour, who died in 1537 after bearing Henry's only son, Edward. A marriage was arranged in 1540 with Anne of Cleves in order to form a tie between England and the Protestant princes of Germany. Because she was ugly, Henry divorced her after several months, marrying Catherine Howard in that same year. Catherine Howard, however, was executed in 1542 for having been unchaste prior to marriage and having committed adultery. In the following year Henry married his sixth wife, Catherine Parr, who survived him.

Between 1542 and 1546 Henry was involved in war with Scotland and France. His troops defeated the Scots at Solway Moss in 1542 and later took Edinburgh. They captured Boulogne from the French in 1544, and when peace was made in 1546 Henry received an indemnity from France.

At the close of his reign Henry was gross, egotistical, and despotic. Much of the wealth he received from secularization of monastic property was spent on revelry. However, he retained the loyalty, if not the love, of his subjects. Under Henry the country prospered materially and the masses of the people received equitable treatment in legal matters. Because he encouraged naval growth, Henry is known as the father of the English navy. See ENGLAND: *History*.

HENRY I (1008–60), King of France from 1031 until 1060, member of the Capet (q.v.) family, son of Robert II and grandson of Hugh Capet. From the beginning of his reign until 1039 he was occupied in putting down rebellions. Between 1035 and 1047 he assisted William the Bastard (later William the Conqueror) in establishing his authority over rebellious Norman nobles. Henry later grew jealous of William's power and went to war against him in 1054. He was defeated by William in 1058.

HENRY II (1519–59), King of France from 1547 until 1559, member of the house of Valois, second son of Francis I, born at Saint-Germain-en-Laye. Between 1526 and 1530 he and his brother, the dauphin Francis, were held as hostages in Spain (see FRANCIS I). He married Catherine de Médicis in 1533 and three years later, on the death of the dauphin, became heir to the throne. When his father died in 1547, Henry succeeded to the kingship. He was largely influenced during his reign by his mistress, Diane de Poitiers, and by Duc Anne de Montmorency, constable of France. An ardent Catholic, he persecuted the Protestants and showed favor toward the Guise (q.v.) champions of the Catholic cause, François de Lorraine and his brother Charles Cardinal de Lorraine. In 1550 Henry went to war with England and recovered Boulogne, which had been taken by the English during the reign of Henry VIII. Two years later he seized the bishoprics of Metz, Toul, and Verdun from the Holy Roman emperor Charles V. Engaging in a second war with the English in 1557–58, Henry deprived them of Calais and Guines, their last possessions in France. While King Philip II of Spain was busy consolidating the dominions in Spain, Italy, and the Low Countries given him by his father, the emperor Charles V, Henry took the opportunity to attack Italy and the Netherlands in the period 1556 to 1559. The French troops were defeated in Italy and in the Low Countries, and the wars with Philip II were terminated in 1559 by the treaty of Cateau-Cambrésis (q.v.). Henry died as a result of a wound received in a tournament.

HENRY III (1551–89), King of France from 1574 until 1589, third son of Henry II and Catherine de Médicis, born at Fontainebleau. At an early age he was given the title Duc d'Anjou. He took part in the victories over the Huguenots at Jarnac and at Moncontour in 1569. In 1572 he aided his mother in planning the Massacre of St. Bartholomew (see ST. BARTHOLOMEW, MASSACRE OF). He was elected king of Poland in 1573 but after one year of kingship returned to France to become the French ruler on the death of his brother Charles IX. The wars between the Catholics and Protestants continued throughout his reign. When the king's brother, the Duc d'Alençon, joined the Huguenots, Henry was compelled in 1576 to conclude the peace of Beaulieu, according more privileges to the Huguenots. That peace was confirmed by the edict of Bergerac in the following year.

Displeased with the number of privileges granted the Huguenots in the peace of Beaulieu, the Catholic party, under the leadership of Henri I de Lorraine, Duc de Guise (q.v.), formed the Holy League (q.v.), and in 1579–80 renewed war with the Huguenots. The war ended in a renewal of the terms of the edict of Bergerac. The League was revived in 1584, when the Duc d'Anjou died, leaving the Huguenot Henry of Navarre heir to the throne. In the following year the king excluded Henry of Navarre from the succession and repealed all the privileges granted to the Huguenots, causing Henry of Navarre to begin the War of the Three Henrys against the League. After the termination of the war in 1587 Henry III found his power being rivaled by that of the Duc de Guise. In 1588, on the Day of Barricades, when the citizenry of Paris revolted against the king under the leadership of the Duc de Guise, Henry III was allowed by the Catholic leader to flee the city and thereby to escape being dethroned in favor of the Guise leader. However, the king subsequently had the Duc de Guise and his brother the Cardinal de Lorraine put to death. This action aroused the hatred of Catholic France, and Henry III placed himself under the protection of Henry of Navarre, whom he declared to be his successor. The two Henrys then became joint leaders of a Huguenot army. While marching toward Paris on August 1, 1589, Henry III was wounded by a fanatical monk, Jacques Clément, and died the following day.

HENRY IV, often called HENRY OF NAVARRE (Fr. HENRI DE NAVARRE) and sometimes known as HENRY THE GREAT (1553–1610), King of Navarre, as Henry III, from 1572 until 1589, and King of France, as Henry IV, from 1589 until 1610, the first of the Bourbon line. He was born in Pau, Béarn, the son of Anthony of Bourbon and Jeanne d'Albret. After the death of his father in 1562, Henry was placed under the control of his mother, a zealous Calvinist, who employed tutors sympathetic to her religious views to instruct her son. As a member of the Huguenot army, Henry participated in the religious wars between 1568 and 1570. After the death of the Huguenot chief, Louis I de Bourbon, Prince de Condé, at Jarnac in 1569, Henry was declared titular leader of the Huguenots, with Admiral Gaspard de Coligny actually in command. In 1572 Jeanne d'Albret died and Henry became king of Navarre. Over the protests of both Protestants and Catholics, Henry married Margaret of Valois, sister of King Charles IX of France, in that same year. The Massacre of St. Bartholomew (see ST. BARTHOLOMEW, MASSACRE OF) took place within a week after the marriage, and Henry was forced to espouse Catholicism in order to save his life. For four years following that event he was retained at the French court, as a virtual prisoner. When he finally escaped in 1576, he joined the Protestants in Gascony, where he repudiated his enforced conversion and resumed command of the Huguenot army.

On the death of the Duc d'Alençon in 1584 Henry became heir presumptive to the French throne. Because the Holy League (q.v.) was renewed in protest against Henry of Navarre becoming the royal heir, King Henry III proclaimed Henry of Navarre ineligible to succeed to the throne, causing the outbreak of the War of the Three Henrys, so called because it involved the Holy League chief, Henry of Guise, King Henry III, and Henry of Navarre. The war ended in 1587 with the Protestant victory at Coutras. In the next year, after the murder of Henry of Guise and his brother the Cardinal de Lorraine by the king's guards, an understanding was arranged between Henry III and Henry of Navarre, who subsequently proceeded, as joint leaders of the Huguenot army, to lay siege to Paris.

Henry III was assassinated in 1589, and Henry of Navarre succeeded to the throne as Henry IV. However, his kingship was contested by the Catholics, against whom he was obliged to wage war in order to secure his royal title. Henry IV was victorious over the Holy League at Arques in 1589 and at Ivry in 1590, but Spain intervened on the side of the League and defeated his plans until he professed himself a Catholic in 1593. The declaration of conversion caused the important cities of the kingdom to surrender in succession, with Paris capitulating in 1594. "Paris," the light-hearted but astute monarch is reputed to have said, "is well worth a Mass". The war with the League, however, continued until 1596. Peace was concluded with Spain at Vervins two years later. On April 13, 1598, Henry IV signed the Edict of Nantes (q.v.), which secured the Protestants liberty of conscience and guaranteed the administration of impartial justice.

In 1600 Henry married Marie de Médicis as his second wife. The rest of his reign was devoted to recovery from the damage of civil war. Henry, a popular ruler, encouraged industry, made territorial gains, and accomplished the centralization of administration. Under his aegis, the Duc de Sulley (q.v.) reorganized the financial system. At the time of his death Henry, in alliance with the Protestant Union of Germany, was preparing to make war on the ancient enemies of France, the Hapsburg rulers of Austria. He was assassinated by a religious fanatic, François Ravaillac.

HENRY I, called HENRY THE FOWLER (876?–936), Duke of Saxony from 912 until 936, son of Duke Otto of Saxony and the first of the Saxon line of German kings, ruling Germany from 919 until 936. Henry succeeded his father as duke of Saxony, lord of all of Thuringia, and lord of part of Franconia. Following the death of Emperor Conrad I in 918, Henry was chosen king of Germany by the Franconian and Saxon nobles, ultimately securing the approval of the rest of the German nobles. In 924 Henry secured a nine-year truce from warfare with the Magyars. During that period he transformed many of the small towns of Germany into fortified cities, containing trained troops of mounted warriors. His military preparations were successfully tested on the defeat of the Wends in 929. When the Magyars invaded Thuringia in 933, Henry defeated them so decisively that they never again invaded the northern duchies and for a long time made no inroads in the rest of Germany. He defeated the Danes in the following year, compelling them to pay him tribute. In order to retain the loyalty of the German nobles, he confirmed many of their privileges and acted as mediator in many of their disputes. Although he never received the Imperial crown, Henry the Fowler is generally recognized as one of the Holy Roman emperors.

HENRY II, called THE SAINT (973–1024), King of Germany and Holy Roman Emperor from 1002 until 1024, last of the Saxon emperors, son of Henry II, Duke of Bavaria. On the death of the childless Otto III, King of the Germans, Henry was elected to succeed him. From 1003 until 1018 he carried on intermittent warfare with King Boleslav I of Poland over the latter's seizure of certain German territories, regaining all but one of the territories taken by Boleslav. In 1004 Henry invaded Italy to fight against the Lombard king, Ardoin, who was in revolt. After he returned to Germany he engaged in war with his brothers-in-law over the seizure by one of the archbishopric of Treves. He had to contend also with rebellions, notably that led by Rudolph of Burgundy, who at length agreed to the union of Burgundy with Germany after his death.

Henry invaded Italy a second time in 1014 and deposed Ardoin, having himself crowned king of the Lombards. He then proceeded to Rome, where he recognized Pope Benedict VIII as the official pope in opposition to Gregory, the antipope, and was crowned Holy Roman emperor by Benedict. In 1021 Henry undertook a third expedition to Italy to help Pope Benedict against the Greeks in s. Italy. During his reign Henry was active in church reform and established a number of monasteries and schools. He was canonized by Pope Eugenius II in 1146.

HENRY III, called THE BLACK (1017–56), Holy Roman Emperor from 1039 until 1056, son of Conrad II. In 1026 he was designated to succeed his father as German king, and two years later was crowned joint ruler of Germany, becoming sole ruler on the death

of his father in 1039. When in 1041 the Bohemians invaded the lands of Henry's vassals, the Poles, Henry brought them to submission, compelling the Bohemian king to recognize his suzerainty. Between 1043 and 1045 Henry campaigned successfully to restore the deposed Hungarian king to his throne and for a short time afterward controlled Hungary. In 1046 he was requested to arbitrate the conflict caused by three rival claimants to the papacy. Setting aside the three antipopes, he appointed a German bishop, who, as Pope Clement II, crowned Henry as Holy Roman emperor. Throughout the rest of his reign Henry appointed the succeeding popes. Returning to Germany, he had to contend with domestic rebellions, notably those led by Godfrey, Duke of Upper Lorraine, who sought to possess all of Lorraine. Henry supported the attempts of the Church to check clerical abuses, and strengthened the power of the papacy to a point that proved disadvantageous for his son, Henry IV (q.v.).

HENRY IV (1050–1106), King of Germany and Holy Roman Emperor from 1056 until 1106, son of Henry III. During his minority his mother, Agnes of Poitou, ruled in his name. After Henry came of age in 1065 he crushed a rebellion in Saxony. About that time began the struggle between the pope and the emperor for temporal power in the Empire (see HOLY ROMAN EMPIRE). Despite the papal decree that lay investiture would be punished by excommunication, Henry appointed prelates in various parts of Italy in 1075. On being reprimanded by Pope Gregory VII, Henry convoked a German council at Worms in 1076 to depose the pope. This act resulted in the excommunication of Henry and the release of his subjects from allegiance to him. Thereupon, the nobles formed a coalition, threatening not to recognize Henry unless he could secure absolution by February of 1077. By dressing as a penitent and standing barefoot in the snow for three days outside the castle of Canossa, where Pope Gregory VII was staying, Henry was able to obtain readmission to the communion of the Church.

The German nobles, however, elected Rudolph of Swabia to replace Henry, causing civil war. In 1080 the pope recognized the kingship of Rudolph and re-excommunicated Henry. After the death of Rudolph in that same year, Henry continued the war in Italy, capturing Rome in 1082. Two years later he declared Pope Gregory VII deposed and had the German bishop Guibert elected antipope under the title of Clement III. After being successively crowned Holy Roman emperor by Guibert and being driven from Rome by Robert Guiscard (q.v.), Henry returned to Germany and there participated in a long series of civil wars, in which his sons eventually turned against him. In 1104, following the renewal of Henry's excommunication by Pope Paschal II, Henry's son and namesake, who had been elected German king in 1098, refused to recognize the authority of his father as emperor. During the conflict which subsequently followed, Henry IV was taken prisoner by his son in 1105. Escaping in the next year, Henry IV solicited aid from various sources, including England, Denmark, and France. He died at Liège while gathering an army.

HENRY V (1081–1125), King of Germany and Holy Roman Emperor (1106–25), the son of Emperor Henry IV, and the last of the Franconian dynasty. When his brother Conrad was deposed from the German kinship in 1198, Henry was named to replace him, swearing not to engage in Imperial affairs while his father was still alive. However, he revolted against his father in 1104, and on the death of the latter in 1106, was made sole ruler.

In 1110 he agreed to respect the decree of Pope Paschal II against lay investiture, providing the pope would crown him and that the Church would surrender all its secular property and its feudal rights within the Empire. Because the latter demand raised such a furor among the clergy when it was announced to them on the day of coronation, Paschal refused to crown Henry, who thereupon departed from Rome, taking the pope with him. In order to gain his freedom, the pope allowed Henry the power of investiture, but in 1112 he retracted his concessions and excommunicated Henry. Taking advantage of Henry's excommunication, many of the German princes rebelled between 1112 and 1116. Although northern Germany was in revolt in 1116, Henry invaded Italy to seize the territories left to the papacy by Matilda of Tuscany. After driving Pope Paschal from Rome, he had himself recrowned in 1117 by the archbishop of Braga, whom he set up as the antipope, Gregory VIII, after the death of Paschal in 1118. He was accordingly excommunicated by the official pope, Gelasius II.

On returning to Germany Henry concluded peace with his former domestic enemies. By the Concordat of Worms in 1122 he established a compromise with the papacy, abandoning his papal nominee, Gregory VIII, and

Henry VI of Germany (from old manuscript)

being reinstated in the communion of the Church. In the last years of his reign the emperor was involved in conflicts with Lothair of Saxony; and, allied with King Henry I of England, whose daughter Matilda he married in 1114, he carried out an expedition against King Louis VI of France.

HENRY VI (1165–97), King of Germany and Holy Roman Emperor from 1190 until 1197, and King of Sicily from 1194 until 1197, the son of the Hohenstaufen emperor Frederick I. He was entitled king of the Romans in 1167, and on his marriage to Constance of Sicily in 1186, he was entitled king of Italy. Three years later, when his father departed on the Third Crusade, Henry became regent for him. At that time he became involved in war with Henry the Lion (q.v.), with whom he made peace in 1190. In the following year, after the death of Frederick I, Henry was crowned Holy Roman emperor at Rome. Claiming the crown of Sicily through his wife, Henry then advanced against Tancred, who had been made king of Sicily on the death of King William II. Henry failed to take Naples and was forced to return to Germany, where he found the Guelphs and the nobles of the s. Rhineland, including Henry the Lion, in revolt. In 1192 the em-

Henry VII of Luxemburg (on the horse in the foreground) at the siege of Florence, 1313 (miniature from an old manuscript)

peror captured and held for ransom Richard Cœur de Lion (Richard I of England), brother-in-law of Henry the Lion. On releasing Richard in 1194, the emperor was able to bring Henry the Lion to terms and thus restore peace in Germany. Using the ransom collected from Richard, Henry gathered a large army and invaded Italy, where he found Tancred dead. With little difficulty he conquered Sicily and was crowned king. In 1195 he launched a Crusade to the Holy Land and campaigned in Italy and Germany for recruits. Henry tried unsuccessfully in 1196 to make the imperial crown hereditary in the Hohenstaufen family. However, he did succeed in obtaining the coronation of his son Frederick II as king of the Romans. While in Italy in 1196–97 seeking support for his Crusade he put down a revolt in s. Italy and sent the main body of his army to the Holy Land, but before he could set out on the Crusade, he died.

HENRY VII, known also as HENRY OF LUXEMBURG (1275?–1313), Count of Luxemburg (as Henry IV), and King of Germany and Holy Roman Emperor from 1308 until 1313, first of the line of Luxemburg. On the death of Albert I in 1308, Henry was elected German king, being crowned at Aix-la-Chapelle in 1309. In the following year he deposed the ruler of the kingdom of Bohemia and placed on the throne his son John, whom he married to Elizabeth, daughter of Wenceslaus II, king of Bohemia (1278–1305). Henry next embarked on the grand scheme of reviving the union of Germany and Italy which had existed under the Hohenstaufen emperors. Many Italians, notably Dante, welcomed his plan as a means of terminating the strife between the Guelphs and Ghibellines (q.v.) in Italy. Holding himself above both factions,

Henry secured the homage of both the Guelph and Ghibelline leaders and was crowned king of the Lombards in 1311 and Holy Roman emperor in 1312. However, the activities of the Guelphs soon forced the emperor into the Ghibelline camp. Allied with Frederick II of Sicily in 1312–13, Henry prepared an attack on Robert of Naples, leader of the Guelphs. However, he died before the attack was begun.

HENRY, or (Port.) HENRIQUE (1512–80), King of Portugal from 1578, fifth son of Emanuel I (q.v.). Henry was educated for the priesthood and at the age of twenty-seven was consecrated bishop of Évora and appointed Grand Inquisitor of Portugal. Under his direction the Inquisition became a powerful force in Portugal, and Henry was made a cardinal in 1545. From 1562 to 1578 he acted as regent for his nephew Dom Sebastian, who was three years old when he became king. Henry succeeded to the throne when Sebastian was killed during a battle with the Moors. The cardinal was an ineffective ruler during his short reign, and Portugal became a Spanish possession following his death. See PORTUGAL: *History*.

HENRY, called HENRY THE NAVIGATOR, or (Port.) HENRIQUE O NAVEGADOR (1394–1460), Prince of Portugal, third son of King John I, born at Oporto, noted as the patron of navigators and explorers. He participated with distinction in the conquest of Ceuta, Morocco, in 1415. Subsequently he made his residence at Sagres, near Cape St. Vincent, and there established an observatory and a school for navigators. Henry not only developed greatly the science of navigation but he also made improvements in the art of shipbuilding. He made no voyages himself, but, under his direction, many important expeditions were undertaken along the West African coast, as far south as 15° north of the equator. The pupils and captains of Henry reached the Madeira Islands in 1420, doubled Cape Bojador in 1434, sailed to Cape Blanco in 1441, rounded Cape Verde, in Senegambia, in 1445, and reached the mouth of the Gambia River about 1446. The impulse Henry gave to navigation continued for more than fifty years after his death and resulted in the circumnavigation of Africa and the opening of a new trade to the East. See COMMERCE; DIAS, BARTHOLMEU; GAMA, VASCO DA.

HENRY, JOSEPH (1797–1878), American physicist, born in Albany, N.Y., and educated at Albany Academy. He was appointed professor of mathematics and natural philosophy at Albany Academy in 1826 and professor of natural philosophy at Princeton University in 1832. The foremost American physicist of his day, he did his most valuable work in electromagnetism. Henry discovered the principle of electromagnetic induction a few years before Michael Faraday (q.v.) announced his discovery of electromagnetically induced currents, but Faraday published his findings first and is credited with the discovery. However, the discovery of the phenomenon of self-induced induction, which Henry announced in 1832, is accredited to him, and the unit of inductance is named the *henry* in his honor.

Henry experimented with and improved the electromagnet which had been invented in 1823 by William Sturgeon in England. By 1829 he developed electromagnets of great lifting power and efficiency and essentially of the form used later in dynamos and motors. He also developed electromagnets capable of magnetizing iron at a distance from the source of current, the forerunners of the electromagnetic telegraph. He actually constructed in 1831 the first practical electromagnetic telegraph, with which he operated a bell in his office. He also devised and constructed the first electric motor, an oscillating machine with automatic commutator, the forerunner of modern electric motors. In 1842 he recognized the oscillatory nature of an electric discharge. In addition to his wide range of research in inductance and other electrical phenomena, his interests extended to a variety of subjects, including meteorology, sun spots, and the velocity of projectiles.

In 1846 Henry was elected secretary and director of the newly formed Smithsonian Institution, serving in those positions until his death. Under his direction activity in many fields of science was stimulated. He organized meteorological studies at the Smithsonian Institution, and was the first to use the telegraph to transmit weather reports, to indicate daily atmospheric conditions on a map, and to make weather forecasts from meteorological data. The successful meteorological work of the Smithsonian Institution led to the creation of the U.S. weather bureau. Henry took a leading part in the organization of the National Academy of Sciences. He was also active in founding the American Association for the Advancement of Science and the Philosophical Society of Washington. See DYNAMOELECTRIC MACHINERY; ELECTRICITY; INDUCTION; TELEGRAPH.

HENRY, O., pseudonym of William Sydney Porter (q.v.).

HENRY, PATRICK (1736–99), American Revolutionary orator and patriot, born in Hanover County, Va. He was largely self-educated. From 1751 until 1760 he was successively a storekeeper and a farmer. Failing at both occupations, he undertook the study of law in 1760, and, after a period said to have extended over no more than six weeks, he was admitted to the Virginia bar.

By 1763 he had become a prominent lawyer in Virginia. In 1765 he became a member of the Virginia House of Burgesses, where he introduced resolutions against the Stamp Act, concluding his proposal speech with: "Cæsar had his Brutus; Charles the First his Cromwell; and George the Third—may profit by their example." In answer to the cries of treason from the conservative members who considered his resolutions presumptuous, Henry retorted, "If this be treason, make the most of it." His resolutions were carried by a small majority and printed in the colonial newspapers as the "Virginia Resolves". Re-elected to the House of Burgesses in 1769, Henry joined with the radical faction which was ready to precipitate an open rupture with Great Britain. When the House of Burgesses was dissolved in 1774, he became a member of the Revolutionary provincial convention of Virginia. Before the provincial convention in 1775 he urged the adoption of resolutions establishing a state of defense in the colonies

Prince Henry of Portugal (from an old print)

N.Y.U. Hall of Fame
Portrait bust of Patrick Henry

with a speech famous for these words: "I know not what course others may take, but as for me, give me liberty or give me death!"

Henry was subsequently made chairman of a committee to prepare a defense plan for Virginia. Between 1774 and 1776 he was a delegate to the first Continental Congress. From 1776 until 1779 and again from 1784 until 1786 he served as governor of the Commonwealth of Virginia, the constitution of which he assisted in writing. During the first gubernatorial term he sent George Rogers Clark (q.v.) on his expedition to the Northwest. As a delegate to the Virginia convention for the ratification of the U.S. Constitution in 1788, Henry opposed that instrument on the ground that it threatened the rights of States and individuals. Largely through his efforts, the provisions known as the Bill of Rights were adopted as the first ten amendments to the Constitution. He was offered many governmental posts, including appointments as U.S. senator in 1794, and U.S. secretary of state and chief justice of the U.S. Supreme Court in 1795. However, he declined those offices, continuing his law practice. In 1799 Henry was elected to the Virginia legislature but died before taking his seat.

HENRY'S LAW, a law concerning the nature of solubility of gases in liquids, formulated by the English chemist William Henry (1774–1836). It states that when the temperature is kept constant the weight of a gas that dissolves in a liquid is proportional to the pressure exerted by the gas on the liquid. For example, at a pressure of one atmosphere and a temperature of 20° C., 0.0434 grams of oxygen dissolve in a liter of water; at a pressure of ten atmospheres and a temperature of 20° C., 0.434 grams (or ten times 0.0434) of oxygen dissolve in a liter of water. If a gas, such as hydrogen chloride or ammonia, is extremely soluble in water, Henry's law does not apply. Compare RAOULT'S LAW.

HENRY THE LION, or (Ger.) HEINRICH DER LÖWE (1129–95), Duke of Saxony from 1139 until 1180, and of Bavaria from 1156 until 1180, son of Henry the Proud, born in Ravensburg. At the age of ten he succeeded his father in the duchy of Saxony, which his mother and grandmother administered for him until 1146. In 1147 Henry demanded of the Diet of Frankfort the restoration of the Duchy of Bavaria, which had been taken from his father. On being refused, Henry engaged in unsuccessful warfare against Emperor Conrad. However, Conrad's successor, Frederick I, became a close friend of Henry and restored the duchy to him in 1156. Henry subsequently aided Frederick in wars in Poland and Italy between 1157 and 1159. Possessing territories extending from the North Sea and the Baltic to the shores of the Adriatic, some German and others Italian, Henry was a formidable figure in the Empire. Accordingly, a league of nobles, archbishops, and bishops was formed against him in 1166, but in two years of warfare against the league Henry was triumphant. About that time he separated from his first wife and in 1168 married Matilda, daughter of King Henry II of England. In 1172–73 he made a pilgrimage to Jerusalem. By refusing to aid Emperor Frederick I in an Italian expedition, Henry instigated a quarrel (1175–76) between himself and the emperor. As a result, Henry was placed under the ban of the Empire and deprived of most of his possessions in 1180 and forced into exile in 1182 and 1189, spending most of his time in England. Returning to Germany shortly after the second exile, Henry took part in a rebellion of German nobles against Emperor Henry VI, but made peace with the emperor at Fulda in 1190. Henry was a capable ruler; one of his greatest accomplishments was the colonization of northern Germany.

HEPARIN, an anticoagulant substance obtained from the livers of dogs and cattle, and present also in large amounts in the muscles and lungs of man. The drug was first prepared by the American physiologist William Henry Howell in 1918, and has since been used to prevent clot formation during transfusions and operations on blood vessels, and in cases of thrombosis and frostbite. Researches upon victims of the atomic bomb in Hiroshima indicate that radiation causes an overproduction of heparin which lowers the blood-clotting ability of the body and leads to hemorrhages.

Heparin differs in its action from dicumarol (q.v.), another anticoagulant widely used today; it stops clotting quickly but its effect soon ceases, whereas dicumarol does not begin to act until several hours have passed and maintains its action for several days.

HEPATICA (Gr. *hepatikos*, "liver"), genus of perennial herbs, commonly called liver-leaf, belonging to the family Ranunculaceae. Hepaticas have thick, heart-shaped, evergreen leaves, each with three lobes, somewhat reminiscent of the three lobes of the liver. They grow in open woodlands and bloom in early spring. Hepaticas can be transplanted to gardens from the wild state or propagated by seeds or division of roots. The two North American species are distinguished from each other by the shape of the leaves: *H. triloba* has rounded lobes and *H. acutiloba* has pointed lobes. Both species bear delicate purple, blue, pink, or white flowers. A European species, *H. angulosa,* frequently cultivated in U.S. gardens, has toothed leaves and pale-blue flowers. Hepaticas are attacked by the late spore stages of a rust fungus, *Tranzschelia punctata;* earlier spore stages of this rust attack stone fruit such as almond, cherry, plum, peach, and apricot, and hepatica is often for this reason eradicated from the neighborhood of orchards.

HEPATICAE, scientific name of a primary subdivision of the bryophytes, comprising simple, mosslike plants commonly called liverworts. Liverworts grow in shaded, moist places all over the world; a few liverworts are floating plants, but most of them live in deep forests. The typical liverwort plant is a leaflike, flat growth called a *thallus.* It obtains minerals and moisture from the soil by means of rootlike hairs called *rhizoids.* Reproduction is accomplished by the union of gametes produced by sex organs called *antheridia* and *archegonia* and by spores which are produced in structures called *sporangia* (q.v.).

Botanists divide the liverworts into three distinct orders: (1) Marchantiales, or thallose liverworts; (2) Jungermanniales, or leafy liverworts; and (3) Anthocerotales, or hornworts. The Marchantiales consist of plants having simple, thick, disklike bodies. Several genera produce small, cuplike structures, called *cupules,* on the upper surface of the thallus. Cupules contain small globular structures called *gemmae,* which germinate to produce new thalli. Most Jungermanniales have leafy thalli, resembling those of mosses (q.v.). Anthocerotales, comprising three genera, have simple thalli which produce long, hornlike sporangia. Antheridia and archegonia of hornworts bear a closer resemblance to those of ferns than to those of other liverworts, and so many botanists consider hornworts to be the ancestors of ferns. See BRYOPHYTA.

HEPATITIS. See LIVER; JAUNDICE.

HEPBURN, AUDREY (1929–), British actress, born in Brussels, Belgium, and educated at the Conservatory of Music in Arnhem, the Netherlands. She lived in the Netherlands from 1939 until 1948, when she removed to England. She made her stage debut as a chorus girl in the London production of the American musical *High Button Shoes* and subsequently played small parts in British films and revues. Though virtually unknown, she was the personal choice of the French novelist Colette for the starring role in *Gigi* (1951), an American play adapted from Colette's story of the same name. She won instant critical acclaim for her portrayal of Gigi. For her performance as Princess Anne in *Roman Holiday* (1953), her first American film, she received the Motion Picture Academy Award for best actress of the year. In 1954 she starred in the Broadway production of *Ondine,* a play by the French author Jean Giraudoux, and in the American film *Sabrina.*

HEPBURN, KATHARINE (1909–), American actress, born in Hartford, Conn., and educated at Bryn Mawr College. She made her debut in *The Czarina* in 1928, in Great Neck, N.Y. She scored a notable success in the role of Antiope in *The Warrior's Husband* (1932), at the Morosco Theater, New York City, and shortly afterward accepted a contract to act in motion pictures. In succeeding years she alternated between stage and screen appearances. Among the theatrical productions in which she subsequently appeared are *The Lake* (1933); *Jane Eyre* (1936); *The Philadelphia Story* (1939), in which she gave one of her finest performances in the part of Tracy Lord; and *Without Love* (1942). She was also starred in the film version of *The*

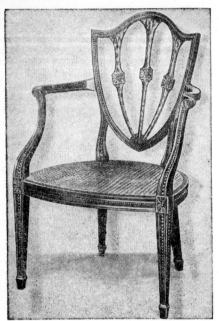

Metropolitan Museum of Art

A Hepplewhite chair

Philadelphia Story (1939), in which she won the award of the N.Y. Film Critics for the best performance by an actress in 1940. Among other motion pictures in which she was starred are *A Bill of Divorcement* (1933); *Morning Glory* (1933), for which she received the Motion Picture Academy Award; *Mary of Scotland* (1936); *Stage Door* (1937); *Holiday* (1938); *Keeper of the Flame* (1943); *Dragon Seed* (1944); *State of the Union* (1948); and *African Queen* (1952).

HEPHÆSTUS, in Greek mythology, the god of fire and metalwork. He is represented by the Greek epic poet Homer as lame, walking with the aid of a stick, and panting as he goes. Hephæstus was the son of Zeus, father of the gods, and of Hera, queen of heaven. According to Homer, Hera was so disgusted with her child's deformity that she cast him down from Mount Olympus. He fell into the sea, where he was cared for by the sea divinities Thetis and Eurynome. Another version, also given by Homer, represents Hephæstus as having been hurled from heaven by Zeus for siding with Hera against him. Hephæstus subsequently returned to Olympus, where he married Charis (Grace). In later legend, however, he is united with Aphrodite, apparently for the contrast between the awkward, grimy

smith and the goddess of beauty. In classic art, Hephæstus is usually depicted with a beard, and wearing a round, tight-fitting cap and a brief, sleeveless garment. See also VULCAN.

HEPPLEWHITE, GEORGE (d. 1786), English cabinetmaker. He learned the art of furniture making in Lancaster; subsequently he established a shop for furniture making in the parish of St. Giles, Cripplegate, London. Hepplewhite is regarded as one of the best of English designers and makers of furniture. The furniture of his design is characterized by a classic simplicity and delicacy. In particular, Hepplewhite chairs are distinguished for their comparatively small size; the shield or heartshape of their backs; their slender legs, often tapering to a spade foot; and their painted or inlaid ornamentation. Many of his best designs are contained in the posthumously published volume *Cabinet-maker and Upholsterer's Guide* (1788). See CHAIR: *Modern Chairs*; FURNITURE: *18th-century England*; INTERIOR DECORATION.

HEPTATEUCH (Gr. *hepta,* "seven"; *teuchos,* "book"), a term applied to the first seven books of the Old Testament, particularly to an abridgement and translation of these books, together with the Book of Job, into Anglo-Saxon, made by Ælfria, an English ecclesiastical writer, in the late 10th and early 11th centuries. The word is formed on the analogy of Pentateuch (q.v.), the first five books of the Old Testament.

HERA, in Greek mythology, the sister and wife of Zeus, and queen of the Olympian gods. She was the goddess of marriage and childbirth. In Homer's *Iliad,* she aids the Greeks in the Trojan War, venting her wrath upon the Trojans because Paris of Troy awarded the fatal apple of discord to Aphrodite, the goddess of love and beauty. Hera is the mother of Hephæstus, the god of fire, of Ares, the god of war, of Hecate, a moon, earth, and underworld goddess, and of Hebe, the goddess of youth and cupbearer to the gods. She is represented by Homer as jealous and illtempered. As the goddess of lawful marriage she persecutes the illegitimate offspring of Zeus, notably Heracles and Dionysus. She conspires against Zeus, who retaliates by hanging her up in heaven with golden fetters on her hands and a pair of anvils on her feet. The union of Zeus and Hera, celebrated widely throughout ancient Greece in the Sacred Marriage (Gr. *hieros gamos*), is the prototype of human wedlock. Identified with the successive phases of woman's life, Hera was variously worshiped as *Parthenos* (the virgin), *Teleia* (the goddess of the connubial state), *Eileithyia* (the goddess of parturition), and *Chera* (the widowed). The cult of Hera was universal throughout the Greek world, but was especially prominent at Argos, Mycenæ, and Sparta.

HERACLES or **HERAKLES.** See HERCULES.

HERACLITUS (about 540–475 B.C.), Greek philosopher, born in Ephesus in Asia Minor. Because of the loneliness of his life, and the obscurity and misanthropy of his philosophy, he was called the "dark philosopher" or "weeping philosopher", as distinguished from Democritus (q.v.), the "laughing philosopher".

Heraclitus was in a sense the founder of Greek metaphysics, though his ideas stem from those of the Ionian school (q.v.). He postulated fire as the primal substance or principle which through condensation and rarefaction creates the phenomena of the sensible world, and added to the "being" of his predecessors the concept of "becoming" or flux, which he took to be a basic reality underlying all things, even the most apparently stable. In ethics he introduced a new "social" emphasis, holding virtue to consist in a subordination of the individual to the laws of a universal, reasonable harmony. Though his thought was strongly tinged with elements of popular theology, he attacked the notions and ceremonies of the popular religion of his day.

Only one work, *On Nature,* is definitely attributable to Heraclitus; numerous fragments of this work were preserved by later writers, and collected editions of all of his surviving fragments may be found in several modern editions, including *Heraclitii Ephesii Reliquiae* (1877, ed. by I. Bywater) and *Die Fragmenter der Vorsokratiker* (4th ed., 1922, ed. by Hermann Diels). See also GREEK PHILOSOPHY: *Ionian School.*

HERACLIUS (about 575–641), a Byzantine emperor, born in Cappadocia. In 610 he headed a revolt against the tyrant Phocas, slew him, and ascended his throne. At this time the Empire was in great straits. The Avars threatened it on the N.W., and the Persians invaded its frontiers from the Euxine to Egypt. In 620 he concluded a treaty with the Avars, and set about disciplining an army. Two years later Heraclius took the field against his eastern enemy, and utterly routed the generals of Persia.

The fame of Heraclius was then at its height, but the rise of the Mohammedan power in Arabia brought a new enemy against the old Empire, where religious dissensions created factions whose strife weakened the state. In his efforts to mediate between the orthodox party and the Monophysites, Heraclius sought to impose the Monothelite doctrine on the Empire, arousing thereby great disturbances in the capital (see MONOTHELITISM). Before the close of his life Syria, Palestine, Mesopotamia, and Egypt were in the hands of the caliphs. See BYZANTINE EMPIRE.

HERALDRY, a term used to designate all of the numerous duties and functions of heralds; in this article, however, the term is restricted to the narrower field of armorial bearings.

Symbolic and ornamental figures similar to those used in heraldry have been used as tribal or national emblems and standards since ancient times. The ancient Thracians used the sow; the Romans, the eagle; the Goths, the bear; the French, first the lion and later the fleur-de-lis. The practice of carrying personal armorial devices on shields and banners began during feudal times, when it was necessary for a knight to be recognized at a distance; see FEUDALISM. Such insignia were depicted on shields borne in the Third Crusade in the 12th century; in the following century the practice was introduced of embroidering the family insignia on the surcoat worn over the coat of mail, giving rise to the expression *coat of arms.* In England armorial insignia were assumed by knights as they pleased until early in the 15th century, when King Henry V restrained the practice. In 1483 King Edward IV established the Heralds' College, to which he delegated the supervision of armorial bearings. In addition to individuals, organizations entitled to coats of arms are families, kingdoms, lordships, towns, episcopal sees, abbeys, and corporations.

The entire display of a person's arms is called an *achievement of arms.* It includes the escutcheon, the helmet, the crest, the motto, the mantling, the supporters, and the crown or coronet (see below). Of these parts the escutcheon is most important.

The term "escutcheon" is derived from the French *écusson,* which signified a shield with arms portrayed upon it, as distinguished from a plain shield. It is usually in the shape of a conventionalized shield, except in the arms of churchmen, where it is generally oval, and in the arms of ladies, where it is lozenge-shaped. To facilitate description, heralds divided the shield from above downward into chief, fess, and base, and from right to left (i.e., the right and left of the wearer of the shield, rather than of the observer), into dexter, middle or pale, and sinister. The shield bears various *charges* (see below), or figures, represented in different *tinctures*.

The term "tincture" includes the representation of metals, colors, and furs. Two metals are in common use: *or,* gold; and *argent,* silver. They are represented in painting by yellow and white, respectively; in uncolored drawings or engravings, gold is represented by white stippled with fine black dots and silver by plain white. The principal colors are *gules* or red, *azure* or blue, *sable* or black, *vert* or green, and *purpure* or purple. A charge emblazoned in the natural color of the object represented is said to be *proper.* The furs are *ermine* and *vair.* Colors and furs are also represented in uncolored drawings by conventional hatchings and figures; see illustration.

Tinctures

CHARGES. Every figure depicted on an escutcheon is called a charge. Charges are classified by heralds as *honorable ordinaries,* plain geometrical divisions of the *field;* as *subordinaries;* and as *common charges.*

Honorable Ordinaries. These simple geometrical figures, instead of being taken from extraneous objects, represent the wooden or metal strengthening braces of ancient shields. In some of the oldest escutcheons, an honorable ordinary constitutes the only charge. Ordinaries may be delineated by straight lines or by *partition lines* of irregular forms, called *engrailed, invected, wavy* or *undy, nebuly, indented, dancetty, raguly, dovetailed, embattled* or *crénelé,* and *potented;* see illustration.

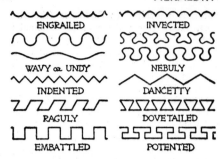

Partition lines

Nine honorable ordinaries are, in general, recognized by heralds.

(1) The *chief* constitutes the upper part, about one third, of the shield, separated by a partition line from the field. It has a diminutive, the *fillet,* a band about one fourth the width of the chief, running horizontally across the shield between chief and fess.

(2) The *fess* is a horizontal band occupying the middle third of the shield. Like the other ordinaries, its partition lines may be straight or irregular.

(3) The *pale* is a central stripe running from the top to the bottom of the shield and occupying one third of the width of the shield. The pale has two diminutives: the *pallet,* one half the width of the pale; and the *endorse,* one half the width of the pallet.

(4) The *bend* is a band running diagonally across the shield from dexter chief to sinister base. Its diminutives are the *bendlet* or *garter,* one half its width; the *cost* or *cotise,* one half of the bendlet; and the *riband,* one half of the cotise. The *bend sinister* is a diagonal band from sinister chief to dexter base. Its diminutives are the *scarp,* one half its width, and the *baton,* one half the width of the scarp and stopping short of the edge of the shield at both ends.

(5) The *bar* is a horizontal band running across the shield. It differs from the fess in being narrower, and in never being placed in the middle of the shield. The bar is seldom used singly; in pairs, they are called *bars gemelles.* The diminutives of the bar are the *closet,* about one half its width, and the *barrulet,* about one fourth.

(6) The *chevron* is composed of two stripes forming an inverted V. Its diminutives are the *chevronel* of one half, and the *couple close* of one fourth its width.

(7) The *cross* is a combination of pale and fess. It is varied in many different ways: al-

most four hundred distinct variations are recognized by heralds. Most of these lesser crosses, however, are common charges, rather than ordinaries. Among the commonest varieties are the *cross fleury,* with each of the four ends terminating in a fleur-de-lis; the *cross patonce,* with each end bearing three points; the *cross potent,* with each end crossed to form the letter T; and the *cross crosslet,* with each arm crossed to form a small cross. These and other crosses are said to be *fitchy* when the bottom arm terminates in a sharp point. See also CROSS.

(8) The *saltire,* or St. Andrew's cross, is a diagonal cross formed by a combination of a bend dexter and a bend sinister.

(9) The *pile* is a wedge with point downward. In a single uncharged pile the base of the wedge is about one third the width of the shield; when charged, the pile may be as much as double that width.

Field. The field of an escutcheon may be of two or more tinctures, divided by one or more partition lines. When the division is in the direction of one of the ordinaries, the shield is said to be *parted,* or *party, per* that ordinary; for example, a shield parted vertically in two halves is *party per pale.* Party per cross, however, is more commonly called *quarterly;* if one of the divisions is, in turn, quartered, the original division is called a *grand quarter.* A shield parted per cross and per saltire is called a *gyronny of eight,* and each segment is called a *gyron.* When the shield is completely divided into a number of equal parts by lines in the direction of a pale, bend, bar, or chevron, it is said to be *paly, bendy, barry,* or *chevronny,* and the number of divisions is specified, as, for example, a paly of six *or* and *sable.* A field divided by vertical and horizontal lines is called *checky,* and one divided by intersecting diagonal lines is called *lozengy* or *fusilly* (see *lozenge,* below). A field strewed with an indefinite number of small charges so as to produce a pattern is said to be *semé* of that charge; when strewed with bezants, billets, cross crosslets, or drops, however, it is called *bezanty, billetty, crusily,* or *gouttée.* Specific terms are applied to drops of different tinctures: silver, *gouttée d'eau* (sprinkled with water); red, *de sang* (blood); blue, *de larmes* (tears); and black, *de poix* (pitch). *Fretty* describes a field covered with an open network of diagonal interlaced ribbons.

Subordinaries. No sharp line of demarcation exists between honorable ordinaries and subordinaries, or between the latter and common charges.

The *bordure,* or border, is often considered as an honorable ordinary. It consists of a band encircling the shield, and often bears small charges. Its diminutive, the *orle,* is narrower and does not touch the edges of the shield. The diminutive of the orle is the *tressure,* which is usually borne double, and often embellished with fleurs-de-lis.

The *quarter* consists of the dexter chief quarter of the shield. Occupying less than a full fourth of the shield, the figure is called a *canton,* and if quarter or canton is parted per bend, each triangle is called a *gyron.*

Flanches consist of the dexter and sinister flanks of the shield, cut off by curved lines. The diminutives are *flasques* and *voiders.*

The *lozenge* is a figure with four equal sides and its vertical apexes acute. When a lozenge is *voided,* that is, represented only in outline with the tincture of the field showing in the center, it is called a *mascle;* when it is pierced with a round opening it is called a *rustre.* A charge similar to the lozenge, but much narrower in relation to its height, is known as a *fusil.*

A small shield charged upon the escutcheon is called *inescutcheon;* it may be charged in turn, or plain.

A *billet* is a small rectangular charge with height about twice its width.

Among the charges considered by some to be subordinaries and by others to be common charges are the *pall* and *roundle.* The pall is a Y-shaped charge, representing the archepiscopal insignium conferred by the pope upon metropolitans; see ARCHBISHOP. Roundles are small circular charges, which are distinguished by different names according to their tinctures: when they are of gold, they are called *bezants;* of silver, *plates;* of red, *torteaux;* of blue, *hurts;* of purple, *golps;* of green, *pommes;* and of black, *pellets* or *ogresses.* A voided roundle is an *annulet.*

Common Charges. Common charges are more or less conventional representations of familiar objects which, in some way, portray the history or character of the individual or family. One of the most important of such charges is the *lion,* a symbol of royalty, used by sovereigns and granted by them to favored retainers as a mark of honor. The earliest known armorial representation of the lion is on the seal (about 1164) of Philip I, Duke of Flanders. Later it was adopted by the rulers of England, Scotland, Norway, Denmark, Wales, and other European states. The earliest position of the heraldic lion was *rampant,* that is, represented as erect, facing right (dexter), and with only one foot on the ground. *Salient* is similar to rampant, except that both hind feet are on the ground. Represented as walking to the right, a beast of prey is *passant*, and a beast of the chase, as a stag, is *trippant*. A crouching beast is *couchant* if the head is raised, and *dormant* if the head is resting on the forepaws. No specification is made when the head is shown in profile looking forward, but when looking toward the observer it is called *gardant*, and looking backward, *regardant*. Two lions rampant placed face to face are called *combatant*, and back to back, *addossé*. Lions are often *crowned* or *gorged* (collared) with a crown or coronet. Animals used as heraldic charges include the bear, bull, boar, goat, dog, fox, horse, and hedgehog, and occasionally the elephant, camel, mole, ape, cat, and mouse.

The heads and limbs of animals are often borne as heraldic charges, and may be either *couped*, i.e., cut off in a straight line, or *erased*, with a jagged cut. A *leopard's face* shows none of the neck and fronts the observer. A *stag's head* borne full faced, with none of the neck portrayed, is said to be *caboshed*. *Bears' heads* are usually represented muzzled.

The *eagle*, by far the commonest of heraldic birds, is generally represented *displayed*, or with wings spread. The *allerion* and *martlet*, originally the eagle and swallow respectively, became in time unreal birds, the former without claws or beak, and the latter without legs or beak. Many other birds are used as charges, notably the falcon, the pelican, the swan, the cock, and the raven. The *pelican*, when represented in her nest feeding her young with her blood, is said to be *in her piety*. A *peacock* borne *affrontée* (full faced) with his tail spread is *in his pride*. In general, birds are shown *close, rising,* or *volant* (flying).

Fishes and reptiles also occur as charges; the former are said to be *naiant*, if depicted in a horizontal position, and *haurient*, if vertical. The *dolphin*, regarded in heraldry as the king of fish, is usually represented *embowed*, or curved. The *escallop shell*, or *clam*, was the symbol of a pilgrim in the times of the Crusades, and is shown on many escutcheons. Serpents occur in various attitudes, and in the arms of the Visconti family are depicted *vorant* (devouring) a child. Among the imaginary animals frequently used as charges are dragons, griffins, wyverns, unicorns, harpies, and mermaids.

Armorial charges also include the human body and its parts, as, for example, in the Dalzell family arms, *argent, a naked man proper,* and in the escutcheon of the Isle of Man, *three legs conjoined*.

Trees, plants, leaves, and flowers are all common heraldic charges. *Trefoil, quatrefoil,* and *cinquefoil* are conventional representations of flowers of three, four, and five petals respectively. Trees are often *eradicated* (uprooted) and sometimes depicted *on a mount*. A *garb* is a sheaf of grain: unmodified the term designates a sheaf of wheat ("corn" in British usage); other grains are specified as a *garb of oats*. Leaves, as those of the laurel, are often borne in threes. A *trefoil* with three leaflets and a stalk is said to be *slipped*. The *rose* became prominent in English heraldry from having been the badge of the rival houses of York and Lancaster, but the most famous floral device is the fleur-de-lis, adopted as a badge by King Louis VII of France in 1150.

Many charges represent articles connected with the occupation or position of the individual, as swords, bows and arrows, helmets, battle-axes, and lance heads for knights, and miters and crosiers for bishops and abbots. The *sun* surrounded by rays is *in his splendor,* and is usually depicted as having a human face. The moon is represented by a *crescent* with cusps pointing upward; if the cusps point toward dexter, it is called an *increscent,* if toward sinister, a *decrescent*. The five-pointed star is seldom used, as it is indistinguishable from the *mullet,* or spur rowel, except that the latter is sometimes pierced. The conventional star is the *estoile,* which is shown with six wavy rays.

EXTERNAL ORNAMENTS. In addition to the escutcheon, the achievement of arms may include the *helmet,* the *crest,* the *motto,* the *mantling,* the *supporters,* and the *crown* or *coronet*.

The *helmet,* the natural accompaniment of the shield in representing a warrior, was added to arms before the beginning of the 14th century. After the end of the 16th century, its form and position were modified in British heraldry to indicate the rank of the bearer; thus, helmets of knights and princes are portrayed full faced, and those of peers and gentlemen, in profile.

The *crest* is the most ancient of armorial bearings. It was worn by the warrior chiefs of Greek and Roman antiquity, and served not only as a mark of rank but also as a conspicuous emblem in battle, around which soldiers might rally. In heraldry the crest is represented attached to the top of the helmet, and always in profile (even when the helmet is full faced); its base is surrounded by a *wreath,* a circlet

Honorable ordinaries and subordinaries of heraldic escutcheons

of twisted ribbons tinctured of the principal metal and color of the shield.

The *motto*, originally the war cry of the bearer, is now a phrase or sentence containing an allusion to the family, the arms, or the crest. It is placed in a *scroll* either above the crest or below the shield.

The *mantling* is an embellishment of scrollwork flowing down from the helmet on both sides of the shield. It originally represented a scarf, military mantle, or robe of state.

The *supporters* are figures placed on each side of the shield. They were, originally, mere decoration, but later came to indicate the head of a family of distinction.

The *crown, coronet,* and *miter* are adjuncts of the arms of persons entitled to wear them. Any collar or badge of an order to which the bearer may have a right is also properly portrayed in his achievement. The collar is shown surrounding the shield; badges are suspended from it.

BLAZONRY. In tournaments of the Middle Ages, whenever an unknown knight arrived, it was the duty of the herald to *blasen* (blow) a trumpet for attention, and then describe to the assemblage the bearings on the knight's escutcheon. From this practice the term "blazonry" came to designate the accurate and specific description of a coat of arms.

In describing an *achievement of arms,* the name of the person, domain, or institution bearing the arms is given first. The blazoning of the escutcheon is then given, describing first the field with specification of its tinctures and the shape and direction of its partition lines. The description of the charges follows, starting with the principal charge, which is assumed to be in the center of the shield unless otherwise specified. In general, ordinaries are given first, except for chief, canton, and bordure, which are described last. For example: France, ancient, azure, semé of fleurs-de-lis, or; Erskine, argent, a pale, sable; Gainsborough, or fretty gules, a canton, ermine.

When two identical charges are mentioned, they are placed *in pale,* that is, in a vertical line, unless otherwise specified; three are placed *in pile,* two above and one below. An ordinary may *debruise* (overlie and partly hide) a charge of the field; in such case the charge is mentioned first. By heraldic convention, repetition is avoided: when a tincture recurs in a description, *of the first, of the second* (tincture mentioned), or *of the field* is substituted; to avoid repetition of a number, the phrase *as many* is used. For example: Anglesey, sable, on a cross engrailed between four eagles displayed, argent, five lions passant gardant, of the field; Leith, or, a crosscrosslet fitchy, sable, between three crescents in chief, and as many lozenges in base, gules.

Differencing. From the earliest days of heraldry, only the head of a family had the right to inherit unchanged the entire paternal arms. In the early times junior branches of the family *differenced* their arms by changing certain tinctures, or by substituting charges, as three mullets for three billets. In modern times younger sons wear the paternal arms with a *difference,* or *mark of cadency;* see CADENCY. The difference of the eldest son is the *label,* a narrow bar with pendants, usually three, borne in chief. It covers any other charges, as it is considered a temporary mark, sewed over the shield, rather than charged upon it. The differences of the second and younger sons are, respectively, crescent, mullet, martlet, annulet, fleur-de-lis, rose, cross moline (a cross with the ends of the arms split and curled back), and octofoil.

Marshaling of Arms. The proper arrangement of such arms as are to be combined in one escutcheon is called *marshaling of arms.* In early heraldry it was the practice to display no more than one coat of arms on an escutcheon. However, if the wife was an heiress (i.e., without brothers and therefore entitled to inherit the paternal arms), the arms of husband and wife were sometimes displayed side by side on separate escutcheons. This practice was followed by *dimidiation,* in which both shields were parted per pale and the dexter half of one was joined to the sinister half of the other. A notable result of dimidiation is the double-headed eagle borne by the Austro-Hungarian, German, and Russian empires: this charge was produced by the dimidiation of an imperial eagle facing dexter with a similar eagle facing sinister. Dimidiation was followed, in turn, by *impaling,* in which both coats were shown entire in the halves of a shield parted per pale.

The blazoning of different coats on a shield divided both horizontally and vertically, called *quartering,* began about the middle of the 14th century. The divisions of the shield are called quarters and are numbered horizontally from dexter chief to sinister base. Sovereigns quarter their shields to show dominion, sometimes showing more than twenty coats in a single escutcheon. The commonest reason for quartering, however, is to indicate descent from heiresses who have married into the family. In the case of a single quartering, the paternal arms are shown in the first and fourth quarters; the maternal arms in the second and third. The third and fourth quarters may, after generations, be occupied by the arms of a second and third heiress. When the coat of the heiress is already quartered, it is placed entire in the appropriate quarter which is then called a *grand quarter.* Although the arms of certain European families may show as many as thirty coats marshaled into a single escutcheon, the practice in British heraldry is to select only the most important.

HERAT, capital of the province of the same name, Afghanistan. The city of Herat is located on the banks of the Hari Rud, about 60 miles w. of the Iranian border and the same distance s. of the U.S.S.R. border. It is thought to have been founded by Alexander the Great in the 3rd century B.C. In the 7th century A.D. it was captured by the Mohammedans. In 1381 the Mongol conqueror Tamerlane (q.v.) made it his capital. Under his reign it became a center of Persian art and learning. The Afghans captured Herat in 1749. Principal architectural features of the city are the old city walls and gates, the Janima Musjid or Great Mosque, and the tomb of the Islamic saint, Abdullah Ansari. The city is a trading center for the grain, fruit, vegetables, and sheep of the surrounding agricultural area. In recent years deposits of chrome ore have been discovered in the province. Area of province, 2403 sq.m.; pop. (1948 est.) 1,142,343. Pop. of city (1948 est.) 75,632.

HÉRAULT, maritime department of s. France, bordering on the Golfe du Lion. It is crossed in the N. by the Cévennes Mts., which rise to a maximum height of 4250 ft. above sea level and then slope S.E. to the Mediterranean plains. The principal rivers are the Hérault, the Orb, and the Livron. Hérault is served by several railroads and canals. It has the greatest acreage of vineyards of any department in France. Mulberries are grown for the raising of silkworms, and olives and chestnuts also are produced. Quarries supply marble, limestone, and gypsum, and marshes provide abundant salt. Tanning, the distilling of wine, the weaving of cotton and woolen cloth, the spinning of silk, fishing, and the manufacture of casks, soap, and fertilizers are among the chief industries of the department. Montpellier, the capital, and Béziers (qq.v.), Sète (pop. in 1946, 29,914), and Agde (6687) are the principal towns. Area, 2402 sq.m.; pop. (1953 est.) 484,000.

HERB, botanical term applied to any seed plant which does not develop secondary wood in its aboveground parts. The original classification of plants into herbs, shrubs, and trees goes back to the time of the Greek naturalist Theophrastus (q.v.). The term is applied by pharmacists to any plant or plant part which has medicinal properties. Plant parts which are boiled for use as food or seasoning are called culinary herbs or potherbs.

HERBARIUM, a collection of dried plants, usually classified according to region of origin. The purpose of an herbarium is to preserve plants which may not be kept in the fresh state, to serve as a reference collection against which other specimens may be checked. Plant specimens are pressed and dried between sheets of coarse, semiabsorbent cardboard. The dried plants are mounted on sheets of smooth, heavy paper by means of adhesive strips. Loose bits of plant material, such as fruits and seeds, are placed in an envelope attached to the herbarium sheet. Each sheet is carefully labeled with the name of the plant, date and place of collection, name of collector, and other pertinent data such as the habitat in which the plant grew.

HERBART, JOHANN FRIEDRICH (1776–1841), German philosopher and educator, born in Oldenburg, and educated at the University at Jena. After leaving Jena he tutored for several years in Switzerland, where he came under the influence of Johann Heinrich Pestalozzi (q.v.). In 1805 he was appointed professor of philosophy at the university at Göttingen. Herbart went to Königsberg in 1809 to hold a similar post. In 1833 he returned to Göttingen, where he remained until his death.

Herbart's system of philosophy stems from the analysis of experience. The system includes logic, metaphysics, and esthetics as co-ordinate elements. He rejected all concepts of separate mental faculties, substituting the concept that all mental phenomena result from interaction of elementary ideas. In applying his philosophy to education, Herbart believed that educational methods and systems should be based on psychology and ethics: psychology to furnish necessary knowledge of the mind, and ethics to be used as a basis for determining the social ends of education. Herbart's principal works are *Allegemeine Pädagogik* (1806), *Hauptpunkte der Metaphysik* (1806), *Lehrbuch zur Psychologie* (1816), *Psychologie als Wissenschaft* (1824–25), and *Allegemeine Metaphysik* (1828–29). See EDUCATION.

HERBERT, the name of a prominent family of English noblemen. Its members include the earls of Pembroke, the marquises of Powis, the earls of Carnarvon, and the barons Herbert of Cherbury. Among the more important members of the family are the following.

1. WILLIAM HERBERT (1580–1630), 3rd EARL OF PEMBROKE. He was a favorite courtier of King James I, and was chamberlain of the royal household from 1615 to 1625, and lord steward from 1626 until his death. He was active in the great exploration and trading companies of his day, including the East India Company and the Virginia Company. He was chancellor of Oxford University from 1617; Pembroke College was named in his honor. He was patron of Ben Johnson and Philip Massinger, and is sometimes identified with the "Mr. W.H." to whom Shakespeare's *Sonnets* were inscribed. The edition of Shakespeare's plays known as the First Folio (1623) was dedicated to him and his brother Philip (1584–1650), who became 4th Earl of Pembroke.

2. WILLIAM HERBERT (1617–96), 1st MARQUIS OF POWIS, grandson of a cousin of the 3rd Earl of Pembroke. He was created Earl of Powis in 1674. As the recognized head of the Roman Catholic aristocracy in England, he was suspected of complicity in the Popish Plot, and was imprisoned in the Tower of London from 1678 to 1684. Restored to royal favor after the accession of King James II in 1685, he was made privy councillor in 1686, and Marquis of Powis in 1687. In the following year he accompanied James II into exile and was named Duke of Powis by the dethroned king.

3. EDWARD HERBERT (1583–1648), 1st BARON HERBERT OF CHERBURY, soldier, diplomat, and philosopher, educated at Oxford University. He was English ambassador to France from 1619 to 1624, and was created Baron Herbert of Cherbury in 1629. Although he accompanied King Charles I on the Scottish expedition in 1639–40, he was later granted a pension by Parliament. His most important philosophical work, *De Veritate* (1624), was the first purely metaphysical treatise to be written by an Englishman, and it brought him the name of the "Father of Deism". In it he advanced an antiempirical theory of knowledge, and held the common principles of all religions to be apprehended by instinct, and to include the existence of God, duty of worship and repentance, and future reward and punishment; these principles, he maintained, were vitiated by superstition and dogma. He also wrote fresh and graceful poems, an *Autobiography* (1624), and *Life of Henry VIII* (1649).

4. GEORGE HERBERT (1593–1633), brother of Edward, poet, educated at Trinity College, Cambridge University. He entered holy orders, and in 1630 he received the rectory of Bemerton, Wiltshire. Almost all of his extant poetry is included in *The Temple, or Sacred Poems* (1633), a collection of 160 poems of a religious character. He also wrote a book of principles for the guidance of rural clergymen, *The Country Parson* (published posthumously, 1652).

5. HENRY WILLIAM HERBERT (1807–58), author, son of William Herbert (1778–1847), 1st Earl of Carnarvon, and grandson of Henry Herbert (1734–94), 10th Earl of Pembroke. He was born in London, England, and educated at Caius College, Cambridge University. He emigrated to the United States in 1831, and for eight years taught Greek and Latin in a private school in New York City. In 1833 he established the *American Monthly Magazine*, which he edited until 1836. In 1834, under the pen name Frank Forester, he began writing books on sports and sketches of outdoor life. His more serious literary work included a series of historical novels and translations from the classics and from contemporary French novelists. His works include *Two Brothers: A Tale of the Fronde* (1835), *Cromwell* (1837), *Field-Sports of the United States and the British Provinces* (1848), *The Deerstalkers* (1849), *The Cavaliers of England* (1852), and *The Puritans of New England* (1853).

6. HENRY HOWARD MOLYNEUX HERBERT (1831–90), 4th EARL OF CARNARVON, Conservative statesman, educated at Christ Church, Oxford University. As colonial secretary from 1866 to 1867 and 1874 to 1878, he introduced bills for the federation of the North American Provinces and of South Africa, and for the abolition of slavery on the Gold Coast. He was lord lieutenant of Ireland in 1885–86, and favored limited self-government. He wrote *The Druses of the Lebanon* (1860), and verse translations of Homer's *Odyssey* and Æschylus' *Agamemnon*.

7. GEORGE EDWARD STANHOPE MOLYNEUX HERBERT (1866–1923), 5th EARL OF CARNARVON, Egyptologist, educated at Trinity College, Cambridge University. In 1906 he began a life-long association with Howard Carter (q.v.) in Egyptian archeological excavation. Before their work was interrupted by World War I, they discovered near Thebes the tombs of several princes and kings of the XIIth and XVIIIth Dynasties. Resuming work in another part of the Valley of the Kings after the war, they made further discoveries, and in 1922 uncovered the tomb of Tutankhamen (q.v.), almost untouched by the grave robbers of earlier ages. He wrote *Five Years' Exploration at Thebes* (1912).

HERBERT, VICTOR (1859–1924), Irish-American violoncellist, conductor, and composer, born in Dublin. He studied at the Stuttgart Conservatory in Germany, and was a private cello pupil of Bernhard Cossmann. He toured France, Italy, and Germany as a soloist, and in 1883 he became first cellist in the Stuttgart Court Orchestra, remaining at Stuttgart for three years, during which time he also studied composition. In 1886 he went to New York City, and obtained the position of first cellist in the orchestra of the Metropolitan Opera House, where his wife, Therese Herbert-Förster, had been engaged to sing German opera. His most important composition of this period was his second cello concerto, in E minor, which he played with the New York Philharmonic Orchestra in March, 1894. In 1898 he became conductor of the Pittsburgh Symphony Orchestra, but retired from that position in 1904 to devote himself to composition.

He wrote more than forty highly popular operettas, of which some of the best known are *The Fortune-Teller* (1898, revived 1930), *Babes in Toyland* (1903, revived 1930; motion picture 1934), *The Red Mill* (1906, revived 1945–47), and *Naughty Marietta* (1910, revived 1931; motion picture 1937). He also wrote two grand operas, *Natoma* (produced in Philadelphia, 1911) and *Madeleine* (produced in New York City at the Metropolitan Opera House, 1914), and many orchestral works, which did not, however, attain the popularity of his operettas. In addition to his composing and conducting activities, Herbert helped to organize the American Society of Composers, Authors and Publishers (ASCAP).

HERCULANEUM, a city of ancient Italy, situated at the N.W. base of Mt. Vesuvius, about 5 miles E. of Naples. The name of the city was derived from the local worship of Hercules. Few facts have been discovered concerning the earliest history of Herculaneum, but historians consider it to have been founded by Phenicians and later occupied by Oscans and pre-Hellenic Greeks. According to archeological evidence, the Samnites, a pre-Roman Italian tribe, conquered the city together with the territory now included in the present-day Italian region of Campania. In the 4th century B.C., Herculaneum came under Roman domination. The city was severely damaged in 63 A.D. by a violent earthquake, and in 79 A.D. it was buried, with the neighboring cities of Pompeii and Stabiæ, by lava during an eruption of Mt. Vesuvius.

Herculaneum now lies at a depth of from 40 to 100 ft. below the surface of the ground,

Musical Courier

Victor Herbert

which consists of volcanic rock deposits composed of sand and ashes consolidated by water. Above the site are the modern villages of Portici and Resina, part of the suburbs of Naples. The remains of the buried city were first discovered in 1706, when, during the digging of a well, fragments of the ancient mosaics were found. Systematic excavations of the ruins began in 1738, and have proceeded intermittently since that time. Many archeological and art treasures have been uncovered by successive excavators, and in 1911 King Victor Emanuel III and the Italian government contributed large grants to furthering scientific excavation. The government subsidized another series of excavations in 1927. Most of the outstanding works of art and a celebrated library of papyri were, however, discovered in the 18th century. Among the art relics excavated at Herculaneum, which far exceed those found at Pompeii in historical interest and value, are the statues of Æschines, Agrippina, the Sleeping Faun, the Six Actresses, Mercury, a group called the Satyr, and busts reputed to be those of Plato, Scipio Africanus, the emperor Augustus, Seneca, and Demosthenes. These treasures, together with many others and other objects, such as vases and domestic im-

Farnese Hercules, famous statue in Naples

plements, are displayed in the National Museum at Naples. See ARCHEOLOGY.

HERCULES, a constellation in the northern hemisphere, lying between Lyra and Boötes. The most interesting object in this constellation is a globular star cluster called Messier 13. Hercules also contains a variable, a Herculis, which oscillates between magnitudes 3.1 and 3.9; a binary, ζ Herculis, with yellow and blue components of the third and sixth magnitudes respectively and a period of about thirty-five years; and a star, 95 Hercules, notable for its changes in color. The last-named was first observed by Sir William Herschel in 1780. Its two components, both of magnitude 5.5, were at that time bluish white and white; about 1855 they changed to orange and green respectively, and color changes in them continued until both became pale yellow, their color at the present time. The direction of the sun's course through space is toward a point in Hercules.

HERCULES, in Gr. HERACLES or HERAKLES (*Hera,* the goddess; *kleos,* "glory"), in classical mythology, the Latin name of a Greek hero, noted for his strength, and the subject of innumerable legends. Hercules was the son of Zeus and Alcmene, wife of Amphytrion (q.v.). Zeus, father of the gods, intended Hercules to be king of Argos, but Hera, the jealous consort of Zeus, gained the throne for Eurystheus by a trick. Through the machinations of Hera Hercules became a servant of Eurystheus. To secure his freedom, he was forced to perform certain enormously difficult tasks which the king set for him. These tasks, called the "labors of Hercules", were variously described and set at different numbers by Greek writers until Pisander, a poet of the 7th century B.C., established the number definitively as twelve in an epic poem on the adventures of Hercules.

The twelve labors of Hercules are (1) the destruction of the invulnerable Nemean lion; (2) the destruction of the Lernæan Hydra; (3) the capture of the Erymanthian boar; (4) the capture of the hind of Cerynea; (5) the destruction of the man-eating Stymphalian birds; (6) the procurement of the belt of Hippolyta, queen of the Amazons; (7) the cleansing of the Augean stables; (8) the capture of the Cretan bull; (9) the capture of the man-eating mares of Diomedes; (10) the capture of the red cattle of Geryon; (11) the procurement of the golden apples of the Hesperides; and (12) the capture of Cerberus, watchdog of the gates of Hades. This group of twelve exploits became an integral part of Greek religious mythology.

According to classical mythology, Hercules undertook other adventures on his own account. He killed a sea monster which ravaged Troy and, when the city refused to give him a promised reward, destroyed Troy. In another legend, he rescued Alcestis from Hades. He was also one of the Argonauts. The manner of his death is the subject of a well-known myth. The centaur Nessus tried to violate Deianira, wife of Hercules, and the hero shot him with a poisoned arrow. The dying centaur thereupon told Deianira to dip a garment into his blood, which he said was a powerful love charm, but was, instead, a strong poison. Later, his wife sent the garment to Hercules, who was seized with such agonies on putting it on that he threw himself on a funeral pyre on Mt. Œta and expired. After death, he joined the gods, with Hebe as his wife. According to Homer, his phantom, armed with bow and arrow and a golden baldric wrought with wild boars and lions, became a source of terror to the dead in Hades.

The Greek cult of Hercules regarded him sometimes as mortal and sometimes as divine. An exceedingly ancient cult of Hercules in Italy, however, regarded him uniquely as a god of traders and merchants. He was also regarded by the Romans as a god of victory. According to Roman legend, Hercules visited Italy on his way from the raid on the cattle of Geryon, and there killed a monster, Cacus, who had terrorized the people. The hero then instituted worship of himself as a substitute for a noisome religion involving human sacrifice.

In art, Hercules is usually represented as an enormously strong man with muscular limbs and curly hair; in most statues he wears the skin of the Nemean lion and carries a huge club. The most famous statue, called the Farnese Hercules, was found in the ruins of the baths of Caracalla at Rome in 1599, and is now in the National Museum of Naples. This statue, the work of the 1st-century B.C. sculptor Glycon of Athens, is thought to be a copy of another work by Lysippus.

HERCULES BEETLE. See RHINOCEROS BEETLE.

HERCULES'-CLUB, common name of several plants which bear branches or fruits having a real or fancied resemblance to clubs. The name is most often applied to members of the genus *Zanthoxylum,* also called prickly ash. The genus comprises several shrubs and small trees having prickly leafstalks. Male and female flowers are borne on separate plants. The fruit is a pod. Northern prickly ash, *Z. americanum,* also called toothache tree, is an aromatic shrub bearing clusters of small, yellow-green flowers. It is native to N.E. United States. Southern prickly ash, *Z. clava-herculis,* is a small, prickly tree which grows in S.E. United States. It bears small, white flowers in cymes. The angelica tree, *Aralia spinosa,* and the bottle gourd, *Lagenaria vulgaris,* are also called Hercules'-club; see ARALIA; BOTTLE GOURD.

HERCULES, PILLARS OF. See PILLARS OF HERCULES.

HERDER, JOHANN GOTTFRIED VON (1744–1803), German philosopher and man of letters, born in Mohrungen, East Prussia, and educated at the University of Königsberg (now Kalingrad). His first important work, *Fragmente über die Neuere Deutsche Literatur* (1767), published while he was serving as an assistant pastor at Riga, was notable for its advocacy of the emancipation of German literature from all foreign influences. Herder later became the leader of a new literary movement known as the *"Sturm und Drang"* movement (see GERMAN LITERATURE: *The Classical and Romantic Period*), which sought to free German writing particularly from the influence of French classicism. His teachings

were a source of inspiration to many young German writers, most notably Johann Wolfgang von Goethe (q.v.). In 1776 Goethe obtained for him an appointment as general superintendent and court preacher at Weimar, where Herder spent the rest of his life. His writings extend over a wide range of subjects and include *Über den Ursprung der Sprache* (1772), a study of the nature and origins of language; *Stimmen der Völker in Liedern* (1778–79), a collection of popular poetry and folk songs; *Vom Geist der Hebräischen Poesie* (1778–79), a critical appraisal of Hebrew poetry; and *Ideen zur Philosophie der Geschichte der Menschheit* (4 vols., 1784–91), his chief contribution to philosophic theory.

HEREDIA, JOSÉ MARIA DE (1842–1905), French poet, born of Spanish parents, near Santiago de Cuba. In 1859 he went to Paris, where he studied at the École des Chartes. He became a disciple of the poet Leconte de Lisle and was thenceforth associated as a leader of the Parnassians (q.v.), a school of poets who believed in the repression of emotions and concentration on form in their works. Hérédia was one of the greatest masters of the French sonnet. His collection of fifty sonnets, *Les Trophées* (1893), is remarkable in modern literature for its rich, melodic language and restrained classical form. Hérédia took much of his subject matter from scenes of his youth in Havana and from episodes in the Spanish conquests of the New World. He translated the *History of the Conquest of New Spain* (1877–87) by Bernal Diaz del Castillo, and wrote the prose romance *La Nonne Alferez* (1894). He became a member of the Institute of France in 1894, and librarian of the Bibliothèque de l'Arsenal, Paris, in 1901.

HEREDITY, transmission of physical and mental traits from parents to offspring. Traits which are determined by heredity may be modified by environmental influences during the lifetime of an organism, but these modifications are not passed on to succeeding generations. The scientific study of heredity is sometimes called "genetics", a name coined by the English biologist William Bateson (1861–1926). Animals and plants which reproduce sexually almost always produce offspring which are similar to the parents and to one another in major characteristics, such as number of legs or kind of fruit, but somewhat dissimilar in specific characteristics, such as color of hair or size of flowers.

Physical Basis of Heredity. All higher organisms are aggregations of small cells which are visible under a high-powered microscope. Every living cell is the result of the division of a pre-existing cell. All the cells of a human being, for example, result from the repeated division of a single cell, called the *zygote,* which was formed at conception; see FERTILIZATION. The zygote is identical in structure with the cells produced by its successive divisions. Each cell consists of a layer of living material called the *cytoplasm,* surrounding a centrally located body called the *nucleus.* Each nucleus contains a fixed number of minute threadlike objects called *chromosomes* (q.v.). Chromosomes vary in size and shape, but two chromosomes of each kind are present in every normal nucleus. For example, every normal cell in the human body contains twenty-four pairs of chromosomes, whereas every normal fruit fly cell contains four pairs. Each chromosome contains many small, discrete particles called *genes,* which are visible under an electron microscope. Each gene (q.v.) is located at a particular place on a particular chromosome, and has the potentiality of expressing an hereditary trait in two or more ways.

The process of growth and development by which a single-celled zygote becomes a many-celled adult (see EMBRYOLOGY) is accomplished by a type of cell splitting called *mitosis;* in mitotic division each chromosome divides into two equal parts. The two parts travel to opposite ends of the cell, and when division is complete each of the resulting cells has the same number of chromosomes and the same genes as the original cell; see CELL DIVISION.

Higher organisms such as man, which reproduce sexually, are formed from the union of sex cells called *gametes.* Gametes are produced by cells located in organs called *gonads.* In man, for example, the female gonads, called the *ovaries,* produce gametes called *ova* or *eggs,* and the male gonads, or *testes,* produce gametes called *spermatozoa* or *sperms.* Gametes are produced by a special type of division of gonad cells, called *meiosis,* which differs from mitotic division in one significant respect: in meiosis one chromosome from each pair of chromosomes is transmitted to each of the resulting gametes, and so gametes contain exactly one-half the number of chromosomes found in the other cells of the body. When two gametes unite in fertilization, the resulting cell, called a zygote, contains the same number of chromosomes as do the body cells of the parent. For example, ordinary body cells of man contain 48 chromosomes,

gametes contain 24 chromosomes, and zygotes contain 48 chromosomes.

The union of gametes brings together two sets of genes, one from each parent. When a gamete from a red-flowered sweet pea, carrying a gene *R,* for red, unites with another gamete carrying *R,* the offspring is *RR* (red). When a gamete from a white-flowered sweet pea, carrying a gene *W,* for white, unites with another gamete carrying *W,* the offspring is *WW* (white). When a gamete from a red-flowered sweet pea unites with a gamete from a white-flowered sweet pea, the offspring will contain both genes *RW,* producing a pink-flowered plant. The pink-flowered plant cannot produce gametes carrying genes for pink, however, because pink is the result of the interaction of genes *R* and *W.* Gene factors, such as *R* and *W,* which are located at the same position on paired chromosomes, are called *alleles.* When an organism has a pair of similar alleles for a given trait, such as a sweet pea having the constitution *RR* or *WW,* it is said to be *homozygous* for that trait; when it has dissimilar alleles, such as *RW,* it is said to be *heterozygous* for that trait.

Dominance. In the above example, the effect of *R* and *W* were equal in determining the flower color of sweet peas. Most pairs of alleles are unequal in effect, so that one of the alleles is expressed whenever it is present, regardless of the presence of the other allele. The allele which is always expressed is called the *dominant* allele, and the allele which is expressed only when the dominant is absent is called the *recessive* allele. For convenience, alleles are usually designated by a single letter; the dominant allele is represented by a capital letter and the recessive allele by a small letter. Thus red is *R* and white is *r.* For example, when purebreeding red-flowered garden pea, *RR,* is crossed with purebreeding white-flowered garden pea *rr,* the offspring are all red-flowered, *Rr.* The parental red-flowered plants look exactly like the red-flowered offspring, but do not have the same genetic constitution. The expressed characteristic of the plant (such as red flowers) is called the *phenotype* and the actual genetic constitution (such as *RR* or *Rr*) is called the *genotype.* When heterozygous plants, *Rr,* are crossed with one another, the offspring are produced in an approximate ratio of three red plants to one white plant. Half the gametes produced by the heterozygous plant are *R* and the other half are *r.* When these gametes are dispersed at random, they unite ac-

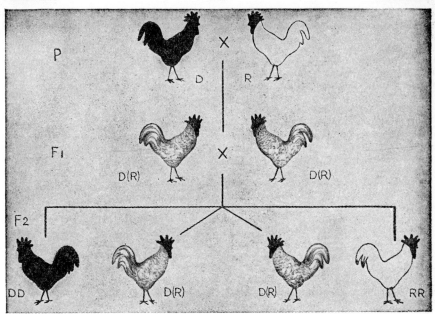

An example of Mendelian heredity in Andalusian fowls, in which incomplete dominance is shown. P, parents; D, black; R, white; F₁, hybrid generation; D(R), "blue" hybrids; F₂, second filial generation; DD, pure dominant black; RR, pure dominant white.

cording to the laws of chance. The action of the gametes may be expressed mathematically as $(\frac{1}{2}R + \frac{1}{2}r)^2$, which yields offspring in the ratio $\frac{1}{4}RR + \frac{1}{2}Rr + \frac{1}{4}rr$. The RR and Rr plants, which together comprise three quarters of the offspring, produce red flowers, and the rr plants, which comprise one quarter of the offspring, produce white flowers.

Many characteristics of organisms are dependent on the influence of more than one gene, but as long as the genes involved are on different chromosomes, the independent behavior of each gene is exactly the same as in the case of flower color in garden peas. Thus, when two hypothetical genes, A and B, are present as heterozygotes, a plant $AaBb$ will produce the following gametes: $\frac{1}{4} AB$, $\frac{1}{4} Ab$, $\frac{1}{4} aB$, $\frac{1}{4} ab$. This proportion of gametes, uniting at random, would give the following offspring: $\frac{1}{16} AABB$, 2/16 $AABb$, $\frac{1}{16} AAbb$, 2/16 $AaBB$, 4/16 $AaBb$, 2/16 $Aabb$, $\frac{1}{16} aaBB$, 2/16 $aaBb$, $\frac{1}{16} aabb$. The phenotypes resulting from these genotypes are: $\frac{9}{16}$ expressing characters A and B, $\frac{3}{16}$ expressing A but not B, $\frac{3}{16}$ expressing B but not A, and $\frac{1}{16}$ expressing neither A nor B. This proportion of phenotypes, called the 9:3:3:1 ratio, is common among crosses involving two genes located on different chromosomes in the same organism.

Linkage. When two genes occur on the same chromosome they are said to be *linked,* and are expected to behave as a unit as long as the chromosome retains its integrity. Thus, when genes C and D occur on the same chromosome, a pair of chromosomes in a heterozygous organism can be designated (CD) (cd). Gametes formed by the organism would contain either (CD) or (cd). In a cross between (CD) (cd) and (cd) (cd), with each chromosome behaving as a unit, the expected offspring are: $\frac{1}{2}$ (CD) (cd) and $\frac{1}{2}$ (cd) (cd); no $Cdcd$ or $cDcd$ are formed. Instances of this kind are occasionally found when the two genes are very close to one another on the chromosome. When the genes are farther apart, linkage is not complete. Thus, if there is complete linkage, the results of such a cross would be 50% (CD) (cd) (showing both characters) and 50% (cd) (cd) (showing neither character). If the genes are unlinked (on different chromosomes), the same cross would produce 25% (CD) (cd) (both characters), 50% (Cd) (cd) or (cD) (cd) (one character), and 25% (cd) (cd) (neither character). If linkage is partial, intermediate results would be obtained, such as 45% (CD) (cd), 10% (Cd) (cd) or (cD) (cd), and 45% (cd) (cd). Geneticists have found that most genes on a single chromosome are only partially linked, and that the weakness of the linkage is proportional to the distance between the genes. The breaking of such a linkage, called *crossing over*, is due to exchange of material between two chromosomes of a pair. This process of chromosome exchange can be seen under a microscope during meiosis. Crossing over almost invariably occurs during meiosis (with a few exceptions, such as production of fruit fly spermatozoa); but if two genes are close together, a break is unlikely between them, and linkage may be nearly complete. By statistical analysis of the percentage of crossing over in such crosses the distance between genes may be measured, and the location of genes on chromosomes may be determined in this manner.

Gene Action. The action of genes is seldom a simple relationship in which a single gene controls a single trait. Many genes are known to affect more than one trait. For example, a gene which produces white eyes in the common laboratory insect *Drosophila* (q.v.), also produces effects on fertility, color of testes, and shape of sperm sacs. Many characteristics, such as flower color in sweet pea, require the simultaneous action of two genes for expression. Varieties which are purple-flowered require the action of gene *P*, to produce purple pigment, but no pigment is produced if gene *C* is not also present. A sweet pea having *C* and *P* will therefore produce purple flowers, but sweet peas having *C* without *P*, *P* without *C*, or neither *C* nor *P* will produce white flowers.

Many genes which affect a single trait when separate will interact to produce an entirely different trait when they are together. The comb shape of domestic poultry, for example, is determined by the presence or absence of two genes. When gene *R* only is present, a fowl has a low, regular "rose" comb; when gene *P* only is present, a fowl has a higher, three-ridged "pea" comb; when both *R* and *P* are present, a fowl has a "walnut" comb, which resembles a walnut meat; and when neither *R* nor *P* is present, a fowl has a single, erect blade, called a "single" comb.

Several genes, called inhibiting genes, are known to prevent the expression of other genes. White Leghorn poultry, for example, are homozygous for a gene *C*, for color, but are also homozygous for an inhibiting gene, *I*, which prevents the expression of color;

the White Leghorn genotype is *CCII*. White Wyandotte poultry, on the other hand, do not carry an inhibitor, but lack a gene for color; the White Wyandotte genotype is *ccii*. Hybrids between White Wyandottes and White Leghorns, having the genotype *CcIi*, are white; the offspring of these heterozygotes, however, are 13/16 white and $\frac{3}{16}$ colored. Only the *CCii* and *Ccii* offspring (which possess *C* but lack *I*) are colored.

Lethal Genes. Genes which cause the death of the organisms which carry them are known as lethals. Approximately one quarter of offspring resulting from crosses between yellow house mice die in an embryonic stage. The three quarters which survive are produced in a ratio of two yellow to one dark. The result is explained by the supposition that yellows are heterozygous for yellow fur color, having the genotype *Yy*. In a mating between two yellows, the offspring expected are $\frac{1}{4}YY$: $\frac{1}{2}Yy$: $\frac{1}{4}yy$. *Y* is therefore a dominant gene which is lethal when homozygous; yellow mice which survive are *Yy*, and dark mice are *yy*.

Quantitative Inheritance. Hereditary traits which are expressed as variations in quantity or extent, such as weight, size, or degree of pigmentation, are usually dependent on several genes. In many of these instances, the number of allele-pairs which contain at least one dominant gene determines the extent of expression of the trait. The height of a plant, for example, may be determined by a series of four genes, *A*, *B*, *C*, and *D*, and may average ten inches in height when the genotype is *aabbccdd*. Each allele pair which contains a dominant will increase the average height by four inches, and so a plant which is *AABBccdd* would be eighteen inches tall, and a plant *AABBCCDD* would be twenty-six inches tall. Dominance is often incomplete in such instances, so that *AaBbCcDd* may be shorter than *AABBCCDD*. Inheritance of quantitative characteristics which depend on several genes is called *multiple-factor inheritance*. Many kinds of hybrid plants succeed in attaining unprecedented weights and sizes in the first hybrid generation, but return to their old characteristics during subsequent generations. The theory of multiple-factor inheritance explains this phenomenon of "hybrid vigor" by supposing that the increase in the first hybrid generation is due to a combination of completely dominant alleles which did not exist in either of the parent strains. For example, if the hypothetical plant mentioned above had the genotype *AABBccdd*, it would average eighteen inches in height. Another strain, *aabbCCDD,* would also average eighteen inches in height. Either strain, regardless of the number of generations inbred, would maintain the same average height. When a cross is made between *AABBccdd* and *aabbCCDD,* the hybrid is *AaBbCcDd,* which would average twenty-six inches in height. In the following generation, however, the possible gametes vary genetically from *ABCD* to *abcd* and all genotypes from *AABBCCDD* to *aabbccdd* would result. The amount of variation in height would therefore range from ten to twenty-six inches, but very few would appreciably exceed eighteen inches in height. When multiple-factor traits are bred to a state of complete homozygosity, as in *AABBCCDD,* they will continue to breed true at the high level, if self-fertilized or inbred. Homozygosity cannot be obtained for most traits, however, because several members of a multiple-factor complex will usually be linked genes, which are difficult to breed to homozygosity.

Chromosome Action in Heredity. Considerable genetic variation is controlled by the behavior of chromosomes as discrete units, rather than merely as carriers of genes. Sex, for example, is determined by the action of a single pair of chromosomes. (Gene-controlled abnormalities of the endocrine system may alter the basic heredity, especially the expression of secondary sexual characteristics, but cannot completely reverse sex.) Body cells in man contain 48 chromosomes. In the human female, these chromosomes consist of 24 pairs, but in the male there are 46 paired chromosomes (23 pairs), and two chromosomes which are dissimilar in size. The 23 pairs of chromosomes which are alike in both male and female are called *autosomes.* The remaining pair of chromosomes, in both sexes, are called the *sex chromosomes* or *heterochromosomes.* The sex chromosomes in the female are identical in appearance, and are called *X chromosomes;* one of the sex chromosomes in the male is an X chromosome, but the other is shorter, and is called the *Y chromosome.* When gametes are formed, each egg produced by the female, who is *XX,* contains an *X* chromosome, but the sperms produced by the male, who is *XY,* can contain either an *X* or *Y* chromosome. Male offspring result from the union of an egg (bearing an X chromosome) with a sperm which bears a Y chromosome. Female offspring result from the union of eggs with sperms which bear X chromosomes

Modifications of this mechanism occur in plants and lower animals. Moths, for example, have XX males and XY females. Poultry have XX males, and females, designated X-, which lack the Y chromosome altogether.

Sex-Linkage. The human Y chromosome is approximately one third as long as the human X chromosome. As a result, two thirds of the genes on the X are not present on the Y; the Y chromosome is, in effect, an X chromosome lacking two thirds of its length. Hereditary characteristics which are carried by genes located on the portion of the X which has no corresponding portion on the Y are *sex-linked.* The disease called *hemophilia* (q.v.) in humans is carried by a sex-linked recessive gene, *h.* A female with *HH* or *Hh* is normal; a female with *hh* has hemophilia, but this genotype is usually lethal. When a male carries *h* on his X chromosome, there is no allele present on the Y to offset it, and so hemophilia is expressed. Such a hemophiliac male has the genotype *h-,* as far as gene *h* is concerned; a normal male has the genotype *H-.* When a normal male marries a female who is heterozygous for expression of gene *h,* the offspring of the marriage are *HH* and *Hh* (girls), *H-* (normal boys), and *h-* (hemophiliac boys). The characteristic is not expressed in *Hh* girls because of the presence of the dominant normal gene, *H. Hh* women are called carriers, because they transmit hemophilia to half their sons. Queen Victoria of England, who was an ancestor of many hemophiliac members of European royalty, had the genotype *Hh.* Several other abnormal conditions, such as red-green color blindness, hereditary myopia, night blindness, and ichthyosis, have been identified as sex-linked traits in man.

Chromosome Alterations. Chromosomes occasionally alter in form. A section of a chromosome may become detached from the main body and later reunite with it. When the portion has turned in the opposite direction before uniting, it is called an *inversion;* when it reunites with the main body at a different position than it previously occupied, it is called a *translocation.* Occasionally a portion will reunite with the other chromosome of the pair. The chromosome to which it originally belonged is said to have a *deficiency,* and the chromosome to which it is later attached, and which has the portion in question represented twice, is said to have a *duplication.* These chromosomal rearrangements often have a visible hereditary effect. A characteristic in *Drosophila,* called Bar because bar-shaped eyes are produced instead of normal oval eyes, was originally considered a gene effect by geneticists, but later researchers discovered that the characteristic was caused by a duplication on the chromosome which carries the characteristic. Another characteristic in *Drosophila,* called Notch-wing, is caused by a deficiency on the X chromosome. When a female having one normal and one deficient X chromosome is crossed with a male having normal X and Y chromosomes, those of the male offspring which inherit the deficient X chromosome from the female parent die.

Mutation. The transmission of existing hereditary traits follows definite patterns when undisturbed, but the evolutional history of every organism indicates that new traits arise periodically. Biologists have assigned the term *mutation* to changes in genetic structures of organisms which produce new characteristics. Geneticists originally restricted the term mutation to gene changes, but it is now apparent that changes which take place in chromosomes are of equal importance.

Gene mutations are changes, probably chemical, which alter the expression of characteristics by genes. Mutations are said to be spontaneous, because agents which cause gene mutations are largely unidentified. In 1927 the American geneticist H. J. Muller produced gene mutations in *Drosophila* by use of X-rays, and similar results have since been obtained by application of radioactivity rays, ultraviolet-light rays, and heat rays. The amount of radiation produced in nature, however, is insufficient to account for the amount of mutation which occurs. Most genes have been found, by statistical surveys of large populations, to be quite stable; rates of mutation are very low. The rate of mutation from *H* to *h* in human hemophilia, for example, is about one mutation per 100,000 genes. The average rate of mutation in several *Drosophila* genes is one per 1,000,000, ten times as great as that of the hemophilia gene. Mutation is never the loss of a gene, but always a change in expression. A gene which has mutated can mutate back to its original form. A single gene may mutate in several ways; the resultant alleles created by these mutations are called *multiple alleles.* For example, a gene which produces red eyes in *Drosophila* can mutate to produce white eyes, eosin eyes, or any of at least ten other color variations. The action of genes is not wholly independent and the mutability of a gene may be influenced by the presence or absence of other genes.

The majority of gene mutations are harmful to the organisms which carry them. They are, however, usually recessive and so are not expressed as visible characteristics unless two recessive genes are brought together in a mating to produce homozygous recessive offspring. This result is most likely to occur in *inbreeding,* the mating of closely related organisms which may have inherited the same recessive gene from a common ancestor. Mutations rarely occur simultaneously in more than one gene of an organism; this fact indicates that even when genes are caused to mutate by the effects of change in environmental conditions, the change does not affect all genes equally. Two members of a gene pair usually mutate independently; if a mutation of *R* to *r* occurs in a cell of genetic constitution *RR,* the resulting cell is usually *Rr.* It is apparent from these facts that gene mutation can never produce new species within a short period of time; a large complex of gene mutations (and, probably, other factors) which have survival value is necessary to produce a distinctly new organism.

Spontaneous changes in chromosomes, called chromosome mutations, include (1) changes which take place within chromosomes, such as deficiencies, duplications, inversions, and translocations, and (2) changes in the number of chromosomes. The normal number of chromosomes in nongametic cells of higher plants and animals is called the *diploid* or *2n* number. Gametes, having half this number of chromosomes, are said to be *haploid* or *1n.* When a 2n, gamete-producing cell in plants fails to divide in the usual manner to produce 1n gametes, it may produce 2n gametes. When 2n gametes unite, a 4n (*tetraploid*) zygote is produced, but when a 2n gamete unites with a normal (1n) gamete, a 3n (*triploid*) zygote is produced. Continued doubling of chromosomes eventually results in plants which are 5n (*pentaploid*), 6n (*hexaploid*), 7n (*heptaploid*), 8n (*octoploid*), and so on. All organisms having chromosome numbers higher than 2n are called *polyploid,* and the process which produces them is called *polyploidy.* Polyploidy is the only process known under which new species arise in a single generation. It is largely confined to hermaphroditic organisms, such as most flowering plants and a few invertebrate animals. The principles of polyploidy are useful in the artificial evolution of new species by plant breeders; natural evolution of new species of

Australian Information Service

An albino native of the Trobriand Archipelago, near New Guinea. Homozygous recessive albinism is common among these people, and others in this group may carry such genes.

flowering plants has apparently been largely due to polyploidy. Existing species of wheat, for example, have 14, 28, or 42 chromosomes; the 14-chromosome species are diploid, the 28-chromosome species are tetraploid, and the 42-chromosome species are hexaploid. Similarly, the violet genus includes species which have 12, 18, 24, 30, 36, 42, 48, 54, or 96 chromosomes. Plant polyploids are characteristically larger, thicker, and more sturdy than their diploid ancestors.

Human Heredity. The inheritance of physical characteristics in man is one of the most important but least developed aspects of genetics. Investigators of human heredity have no opportunity to direct the sequence of matings from generation to generation, and so information on human pedigrees is obtained from relatively unsatisfactory observation of small family groups. Furthermore, the length of a human generation is between twenty and forty years, contrasted with two weeks, the approximate length of a *Drosophila* generation. Most human characteristics are trans-

mitted by multiple-factor inheritance; identification of separate genes is almost impossible without performing breeding experiments. Despite these barriers to scientific investigation, the modes of transmission of several known traits have been determined.

The inheritance of blood groups has been investigated extensively. A,B,O blood groups are determined by a set of three alleles, only two of which are present in any one human being. There are four major blood groups in the A,B,O series: O, A, B, and AB. The genotypes which correspond to these blood groups are:

Blood Group	Genotypes
O	*oo*
A	*AA* or *Ao*
B	*BB* or *Bo*
AB	*AB*

Gene *o* is recessive to *A* and *B,* but genes *A* and *B* are equally dominant and so the genotype *AB* expresses both genes equally. Knowledge of inheritance of blood groups has

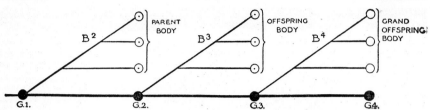

The principle of germinal continuity. G_1, G_2, G_3, and G_4 represent successive generations of germ cells, each giving rise to new germ cells plus body cells, represented by B_2, B_3, and B_4. Environmental influence on the body does not affect germ cells.

become useful as a means of exonerating men who are falsely accused of fathering illegitimate children. The following table indicates the method of exclusion:

If the baby is	and the mother is	the father cannot be
O	O, A, B	AB
AB	A	A, O
AB	B	B, O
AB	AB	O
A	B	B, O
A	O	B, O
B	A	A, O
B	O	A, O

A few other normal human characteristics, such as left-handedness and red hair, are controlled by recessive genes, but most genetically identified traits are abnormalities. Red-green color blindness and myopia are controlled by sex-linked recessive genes similar to the gene which causes hemophilia. Migraine, certain types of hereditary deafness, albinism, and certain types of feeble-mindedness and anemia are caused by recessive genes. Some types of hereditary baldness, formerly thought to be sex-linked because the characteristic is expressed only in males, have been found to be controlled by recessive genes; the requisite genes to produce baldness may be carried by women, but are never expressed by them.

Eugenics. The science of the control of human breeding for the purpose of improving the biological characteristics of human populations uses the principles of genetics in formulating its theories. The effectiveness of methods proposed by eugenists is small because it is not possible to eliminate deleterious hereditary traits from human pedigrees by means short of controlled mass breeding. The practical value of eugenics is restricted to prevention, in individual cases, of obviously bad traits. In the type of feeble-mindedness which can be carried by a recessive gene, for exam-

ple, the trait is expressed by homozygous recessive individuals, and so several countries forbid parenthood to feeble-minded persons. Feeble-mindedness can never be entirely eliminated by this method because two mentally normal people, each carrying a single recessive gene for feeble-mindedness, can produce feeble-minded offspring. The reduction in the proportion of homozygous recessives carrying a deleterious trait in a large population depends on the percentage carrying that trait; a trait which is expressed by a large percentage of a population can be greatly reduced, but one that is expressed by a small percentage cannot be reduced significantly. For example, in a population containing 25 percent feeble-minded people, denial of parenthood to feeble-minded people for ten generations would reduce feeble-mindedness to 0.7 percent of the total population, provided that there is no mutation from normal to feeble-minded. Undesirable recessive traits, however, usually express themselves in a small percentage of a population, such as 0.1 percent (one in 1000). Elimination of homozygous recessives, in this case, would reduce the incidence of the trait to 0.06 percent after ten generations. Thus, when the original percentage of homozygous recessives is 25, there is a 97 percent reduction in ten generations, but when the original percentage is 0.1, the reduction is only 41 percent.

Cytological Inheritance. Not all hereditary characteristics are determined by genes or even by chromosomes. Asexual methods of reproduction (q.v.), such as spore production in lower plants and propagation by cuttings in higher plants, merely transmit stable genetic patterns from organism to organism. Certain snails, such as *Limnaea peregra*, show a peculiar type of delayed inheritance. *Limnaea* shells may coil to right or left, depending on their genotype, but expression of the genotype occurs not in the snail but in its offspring. The variegated (white-spotted) leaves of several plants, such as *Pelargonium,* are determined by hereditary factors which are not carried by the chromosome, but in the cytoplasm of leaf cells. The inheritance of leaf color depends on reproduction of small cytoplasmic *plastids.* When a plastid in a young leaf cell mutates from "green" to "colorless", all the plastids which are formed from successive divisions of the original plastid may remain colorless. Large areas of leaves occupied by such colorless plastids are white.

History. Early theories of heredity were based on pure speculation. The ancient Greek philosopher Aristotle and the *preformationists* of the 17th century, for example, thought that the gamete produced by one of the parents contained a miniature offspring, similar to the parent in all respects except size. The theory of preformation collapsed when the cellular nature of organisms and of gametes was established by observation; see CELL. Scientists realized that gametes do not contain small replicas of the characteristics they transmit, but merely act as agents for the transmission of substances which determine these characteristics. Speculation on the mechanism of hereditary transmission continued, during the 18th and 19th centuries, mostly without the support of experimental evidence. Jean Baptiste Lamarck proposed that changes caused in an organism by environmental influences are passed on to the offspring; see LAMARCKISM. Charles Darwin felt that heredity is at least partially determined by environmental influences. Although he did not insist that environment was the sole determining factor, he suggested, in his theory of *pangenesis,* that each cell of the body continually emits minute particles, called gemmules, which travel throughout the body and finally reach the gonads, where they enter the gametes. According to this theory, all parts of the body contribute influences which are transmitted to succeeding generations. Pangenesis is essentially similar to Lamarckism, and both theories are easily discredited; humans who have lost a leg, for example, do not produce offspring who lack a leg. The last of the major speculative theories of heredity was proposed by the German zoologist, August Weismann, in 1892. He believed that changes in the germ plasm (q.v.) which are caused by external influences are transmitted from one generation to the next, but that changes imposed on the body by external influences rarely affect the germ plasm. Weismann assumed that the primary constituents in a germ plasm were minute particles, similar to the present-day conception of genes, which he called "biophores".

Modern study of genetics began in 1900, when several plant breeders independently discovered a technical paper written by an Austrian monk, Gregor Mendel (q.v.). The paper, published in 1866, described a series of experiments with garden peas which Mendel had completed in 1865. Mendel discovered that hereditary characteristics behave as if they were determined by particles which are present in pairs in ordinary body cells, but present singly in gametes. He stated that such pairs *segregate* in the meiotic divisions which produce gametes, and rejoin at random in fertilization; see MENDEL'S LAW. Mendel's results were substantiated through repetition of his experiments by many biologists. During the early years of the 20th century, geneticists found that Mendel's law can be applied to hereditary transmission in practically all plants and animals. Following these discoveries, Thomas Hunt Morgan and coworkers, working with the fruit fly, *Drosophila melanogaster,* discovered that sex-linked traits are carried on X chromosomes, that genes are arranged in linear order on all chromosomes, and that genes on a single chromosome behave as a single unit. By performance of literally millions of linkage experiments involving billions of flies, geneticists have prepared accurate "maps" of the location of about 1000 genes on the four chromosomes of this insect. *Drosophila* has become the most popular subject for hereditary experimentation because it has a short breeding cycle, has only four chromosome pairs, is easy to breed, and has exceptionally large salivary-gland chromosomes.

During the period when Mendel's results were being substantiated, a Dutch botanist, Hugo DeVries, proposed that spontaneous changes in genotype observed in evening primroses were due to changes in gene expression which he named mutations. Later geneticists found that variations in evening primrose were actually due to chromosomal behavior, but the principles of DeVries' theory stimulated experimentation to determine the cause of other mutations. Morgan and his coworkers were responsible for discovering a large number of naturally occurring mutations in *Drosophila,* and knowledge of the nature of mutation has been broadened further by the work of H. J. Muller on artificially induced mutations in the same insect.

Recent Developments. The most dramatic occurrence in recent genetics was the photographing of probable genes by use of an electron microscope in 1949. Prior to this time, evidence for the existence of genes was based entirely on observation of the results of gene action. Although little is yet known about the physical and chemical structure of the gene, this discovery makes possible the investigation of methods of isolating genes for intensive study.

Great strides were made in the development of hybrid plants during the 1940's. Many hybrid plants which have desirable characteristics are sterile, due to the inability of gamete-producing organs to bring forth functional gametes. This inability results from the dissimilarity between the chromosomes contributed by the two strains used to produce the hybrid. When chromosomes are doubled to form a tetraploid, however, one set of chromosomes from each parental strain is available for each gamete, and so functional gametes are formed. Geneticists have found that tetraploidy can be induced by application of several chemical compounds, such as colchicine (q.v.), podophyllin (see MAY APPLE), β-indoleacetic acid, and acenaphthene. Agriculturists and horticulturists soon adapted use of these compounds to the development of many fertile hybrid plants.

In the field of pure genetical research, a large body of basic information has been accumulated through use of sac fungi, such as *Neurospora* and *Penicillium* (q.v.), as experimental plants. These sac fungi grow rapidly and have a high mutation rate. The mutants, most of which have abnormal metabolism, can be easily isolated in culture media similar to those used for bacteria. Each mutant gene controls the production of a single enzyme necessary to normal metabolism. Lacking this enzyme, the mutant is unable to synthesize a particular substance necessary to its life, and so requires the presence of this substance in its food supply; the normal organism thrives without the same substance. By 1948, several scientists were "making mutants to order" by inducing mutations in culture media lacking specific nutrients in the presence of an agent such as penicillin which kills only growing organisms. The desired mutants, unable to grow in such a medium, nonetheless survive other organisms, and can then be isolated and be transferred to a medium in which they can thrive.

An American geneticist, Tracy Sonneborn, discovered that many hereditary traits in *Paramecium* (q.v.) are carried in the cytoplasm, rather than in chromosomes. Corresponding work with other unicellular plants and animals indicates that cytoplasmic inheritance is probably widespread in lower organisms.

A group of plant breeders in Russia, led by Trofim Lysenko, president of the Soviet Academy of Agricultural Sciences, began a political-scientific movement to reject Mendelian theory as a basis for practical breeding. The movement became a subject of international discussion in 1948 when Lysenko's theories became the basis of genetical education in Russia. Lysenko adopted a viewpoint similar to that expressed by Darwin in his theory of pangenesis, claiming that he was able to produce new plant varieties by subjecting them to changes in environment. According to his pronouncements, environmental effects on seeds or even entire plants are transmitted to succeeding generations. His conclusions, however, proved unfounded when his experiments were repeated. Observers from other countries who were permitted to view several of his experiments saw evidence of careless technique, and saw no adequate basis for his conclusions. Lysenko's technical papers are characterized by frequent interruptions for vituperative attacks on non-Soviet geneticists, political attacks on Soviet Mendelian geneticists, and purely political digressions. His theories were denounced, in 1948, by many celebrated geneticists, including H. J. Muller in America and Eric Ashby in Great Britain.

See BREEDING; PLANT BREEDING. Also see biographies of most of the biologists mentioned in this article.

HEREFORD, city, municipal borough, and county seat of Herefordshire, England, situated on the Wye R., 144 m. by rail w.n.w. of London. The town was founded in the 7th century by the West Saxons, and since 676 it has been an episcopal see. Hereford was incorporated in 1597. Between the 13th and 16th centuries it was an important center for the wool trade. The great cathedral at Hereford was begun in the 11th century and was improved and enlarged in later centuries. With the choirs of the Gloucester and Worcester cathedrals, the Hereford cathedral choir participates in an annual music festival, held successively in each of the three cities. Just outside the city is the White Cross, erected in 1347 to commemorate the termination of the Black Plague. Hereford was the birthplace of Nell Gwyn and of David Garrick (qq.v.). Pop. (1951 prelim.) 32,490.

HEREFORDSHIRE, or HEREFORD, county of s.w. England, drained by the Wye, the Frome, and the Teme rivers. The Malvern Hills, rising to a height of 1194 ft. above sea level, and the Black Mountains, which are more than 2000 ft. above sea level in places, are the principal ranges of the county. More than four fifths of the area is cultivated, much of the land being devoted to pasture, orchards, and fields of hops. Herefordshire is noted for its cattle, horses, and sheep. The breed of cattle known as Hereford cattle originated there. Industries other than agriculture include the quarrying of limestone, iron founding, and the manufacture of agricultural implements and paper. During the 7th century, after the invasion of the West Saxons, Herefordshire was settled by a tribe called the Hecanas. It probably became a county during the reign of King Athelstan. Among the important towns of the county are Hereford (q.v.), the county seat, and Leominster (pop., about 6000). Area, 842 sq.m., pop. (1951) 127,092.

HERESY, a religious doctrine opposed to the authorized dogma of a particular church, especially a doctrine held by a person professing faith in the teachings of that church. The term originally designated a doctrine chosen by private judgment (Gr. *Hairesis*, "choosing for oneself"), and is used in this sense in the Acts of the Apostles, but in the Epistles and all later Christian writings it is used in the opprobrious sense of a heterodox belief held in opposition to the teaching of the Church.

With the establishment of Christianity in the Roman Empire, heresy came to be considered as a crime against the state, punishable by the civil law. The same concept was held, generally, in countries with an established church (see ESTABLISHMENT, ECCLESIASTICAL) until it lost its force with the general adoption of the Protestant principle of private interpretation of the Scriptures and denial of the authority of the ecclesiastical body in all matters of belief.

In the Roman Catholic Church, the term heretic is applied only to members of that church who profess heterodox doctrines and not to their descendants or remote followers.

See separate articles on important heresies and heresiarchs, such as ARIUS; ALBIGENSES; GNOSTICISM; ICONOCLASM; MONARCHIANISM; MONOPHYSITES; MONOTHELETISM; WALDENSES.

HERGESHEIMER, JOSEPH (1880–1954), American novelist, born in Philadelphia, and educated at a Quaker school. After studying art and living for some years in Italy, he be-

came a professional writer about 1907. His first novel, *The Lay Anthony* (1914), an idealized romance, was a success. His best-known novels, mostly popular romances, include *The Three Black Pennys* (1917), *Java Head* (1919), *Linda Condon* (1919), *Cytherea* (1922), *The Bright Shawl* (1922), *Tampico* (1926), *The Party Dress* (1929), *The Limestone Tree* (1931), *Tropical Winter* (1933), and *The Foolscap Rose* (1934). He also wrote short stories, travel sketches, and the autobiographical work *From An Old House* (1925).

HERKIMER, NICHOLAS (1728–77), American Revolutionary soldier, born in German Flats (now Herkimer), N.Y. He was a leader in the American struggle against the British crown prior to the Revolution, and he was appointed brigadier general of the militia of Tryon County, N.Y., in 1775. In August, 1777, he led his troops to the relief of Fort Stanwix, then besieged by a British force, but was ambushed at Oriskany, N.Y. He received a mortal wound during the ensuing battle. The village of Herkimer was named in his honor.

HERMAPHRODITISM, in biology, the presence in one individual, plant or animal, of both male and female gonads or organs of sex-cell production. The term is derived from the legend of Hermaphroditus (q.v.).

Hermaphroditism occurs in the great majority of flowering plants: "monoclinous" plants have hermaphrodite or perfect flowers (q.v.), each of which has both male and female elements (stamens and carpels), and "monoecious" plants have flowers containing only male elements and others containing only female elements, both occurring on the same plant. Only a few flowering plants are "dioecious" (not hermaphroditic). Most hermaphroditic plants have some device such as dichogamy (q.v.) which insures cross-pollination; however a few, such as the violet and the evening primrose, are habitually self-pollinated.

Hermaphroditism habitually occurs in many invertebrate animals, in hagfishes and tunicates, and in sea bass of the genus *Serranus*. It occurs occasionally in other fishes, in frogs, toads, and certain newts among the amphibians, and rarely in higher forms of animal life. Hermaphrodite animals are rarely self-fertilizing; in most cases the spermatozoa and ova mature at different times (successive hermaphroditism) or the male and female external organs are located so that self-fertilization is impossible. Among the invertebrates, sponges, coelenterates, some mollusks, and earthworms

4th-century B.C. Greek sculpture of Hermes

are regularly hermaphroditic. Flatworms have a complete set of male and female gonads in each segment and regularly fertilize themselves.

The females of many species of both plants and animals regularly or occasionally reproduce independently of males; this phenomenon, called parthenogenesis, is, however, entirely different in nature from hermaphroditism.

True functional hermaphroditism is rare or absent in higher animals. Animals, called "hermaphrodites", are occasionally seen which appear to be intermediate in form between males and females; but such animals are usually sterile, and, when fertile, probably never produce both fertile eggs and fertile sperm. Such organisms are often called "intersexes" or "sex-intergrades"; intersexes in the fruit fly have been shown to arise from inheritance of an abnormal ratio of "maleness" (autosomes) to "femaleness" (X chromosomes); see HEREDITY. Cases of intersexual individuals, called "false hermaphrodites", have been observed in human medical practice; they may be produced by inherited factors, but often show functional disturbance of the endocrine glands, especially of the pituitary or adrenal glands. Because of the complete homology between male and female sex organs, it may be difficult to tell whether a human "hermaphrodite" is a female with overdeveloped clitoris

or a male with underdeveloped penis, cleft scrotum, and nondescendant testes; see TERATOLOGY.

HERMAPHRODITUS, in Greek mythology, the son of Hermes, the messenger of the gods, and of Aphrodite, the goddess of love. In his fifteenth year, Hermaphroditus traveled from his home on Mount Ida to Caria in s.w. Asia Minor. There he rejected the love of the nymph Salmacis, in whose fountain he bathed. Salmacis then embraced the youth, praying to the gods that she might be forever united with him. The result was a being half male and half female. This is the form, set down by Polyclitus, a Greek sculptor of the 5th century B.C., in which Hermaphroditus is represented in classic art. The dual divinity was a favorite subject for statuary in the late Greek and Greco-Roman periods.

HERMES, in Greek mythology and religion, a god, son of Zeus and Maia, identified by the Romans with Mercury. His cult probably originated in Arcadia, where legend says he was born in a cave of Cyllene (Mt. Ziria). There he was worshiped particularly as the god of fertility.

Throughout ancient literature, art, and religious cult, Hermes is represented as a god of versatile gifts and many attributes. He is most frequently characterized as the messenger and herald of the gods on Olympus, though he was also considered the protector of sheep and cattle, in which capacity he often appears carrying a ram. As a pastoral god Hermes is closely connected with Pan and the nymphs. Many titles and epithets in Homer's *Iliad,* such as "bestower of good things", refer to his attributes as the god of fertility. In the *Odyssey* Hermes is represented as the conductor of the dead to Hades, and the Athenians held a festival in honor of Hermes and the souls of the dead. Hermes was also considered the god of dreams, to whom the Greeks offered a libation before going to sleep, and was often represented in literature as the god of science and invention. Homer and Hesiod mention him as the god of eloquence. Many writers dwell on Hermes' trickery, theft, and cunning, representing him also as the god of sudden good luck and of treasures casually come upon.

Like Apollo (q.v.), Hermes was a patron of music, and the inventor of the cithara. Together with Apollo and Heracles, Hermes presided over athletic contests, and his statues were common sights in the stadia and gymnasia of Athens.

In ancient art and sculpture Hermes is generally represented as a strong, bearded youth wearing a long chiton and a winged cap. In his role as herald he bears the herald's staff; in his pastoral capacity he carries a sheep over his shoulder. After the 5th century B.C. Hermes was represented as a vigorous young athlete, beardless and nude. The most famous statue of Hermes is that by Praxiteles (q.v.) in the museum at Olympia, Greece, in which the god is represented in the nude, carrying the infant Dionysus (q.v.).

HERMIONE, the name of several beautiful women in myth and fiction. **1.** The only daughter of Menelaus, prince of Sparta, and of his beautiful wife, Helen of Troy. Hermione was married against her will to the hero Neoptolemus (Pyrrhus), son of Achilles, in fulfillment of a promise made by her father. According to a later tradition, Hermione was carried off by Neoptolemus, who was killed by Orestes, to whom she had already been promised. **2.** The unjustly accused and much-injured wife of Leontes, the jealous King of Sicily, in *A Winter's Tale* by William Shakespeare. **3.** In Jean Baptiste Racine's drama *Andromaque,* the betrothed of Pyrrhus and rival of Andromache (q.v.).

HERMIT CRAB or **ROBBER CRAB,** common name for any of the marine decapod crabs in the family Paguridae and for several terrestrial crabs in the family Coenobitidae. They are found on, or just off, the coasts of Europe and the Americas. Hermit crabs are armorless animals, the largest of which attain a length of about six inches. They insert their abdomens into the empty shells of snails and carry the shells about with them for protection. The abdomens of the crabs are soft and asymmetrical, flexed and twisted to fit into the whorls of the borrowed shells. Their abdominal appendages are especially modified for keeping the shell firmly supported on the body.

Hermit crabs are often forced to seek new shells because they have outgrown their old ones; they change their housing whenever chancing upon another shell into which they can fit. The hermit crab inserts its claws into the opening of the new shell, and then raises it, emptying it of pebbles and stones which may injure the crab's naked skin. Several hermit crabs will often fight for the possession of a new shell. Annelid worms often share a shell with the hermit crab. Sea anemones commonly live on the upper surface of the shell, subsisting on the remains of the crab's food and by means of their stings protecting the crab from other animals, such as the small crustaceans of the genus *Sacculina* (order Cir-

ripedia) which attack the gonads of crabs. Unlike most other animals, the hermit crab is capable of regenerating its gonads if they are destroyed. Most hermit crabs are marine. The few terrestrial forms are tropical and belong to the same family as the coconut crab (q.v.). The common American species of hermit crab is *Pagburus pollicaris;* the common English species is *Eupagurus bernhardus.*

HERMITE, CHARLES (1822–1901), French mathematician, born in Dieuze, Meurthe, and educated at the Lycée Louis-le-Grand and the École Polytechnique. From 1848 to 1876 he was connected with the École Polytechnique in various capacities, and during this period, from 1862 to 1873, was *maître de conférences* at the École Normale Supérieure. From 1869 until 1897 he held the chair of higher algebra at the University of Paris.

Hermite's major work was on the theory of functions; his first important writing in this field secured for him an election to the Academy of Sciences. He also worked on the theory of algebraic forms and on the theory of numbers. Two of his important achievements were his solution of equations of the fifth degree by using elliptic functions, which definitively settled the question of the solubility of quintic equations (compare ABEL, NIELS), and his proof, in 1874, that *e* (q.v.) is not an algebraic number. The latter paved the way for Ferdinand Lindemann's proof in 1882 that π (see PI) is not an algebraic number. Hermite's works include *Sur l'Équation du 5ème Degré* (1866), *Sur la Fonction Exponentielle* (1874), and *Sur Quelque Applications de la Théorie des Fonctions Elliptiques* (1877–82).

HERMIT THRUSH, SOLITARY THRUSH, or RUFOUS-TAILED THRUSH, common name for a small North American thrush, *Hylocichla guttata,* usually found in places not inhabited by man, such as evergreen forests and the sides of mountains. The hermit thrush lives in Canada and N. United States during the summer but travels as far south as Guatemala in the wintertime. It is about seven inches long, brownish green above and white below, with the breast and throat speckled with black. The hermit thrush characteristically raises and lowers its chestnut-red tail when alarmed. During migratory flights the bird utters a deep note; at its nest it sings a beautiful, complex song for which it is famous. The nest is usually placed in a hole in the ground which the bird has lined with evergreen needles or moss; it is built of grass, twigs, and bark, cemented together with mud. Three or four bluish eggs are laid in one clutch.

American Museum of Natural History

The hermit thrush

HERMON, MOUNT (Ar. *Jebel esh-Sheikh,* "old man mountain", or *Jebel eth-Thelj,* "snow mountain"), mountain of the Anti-Lebanon range, s. Syria. The highest of its three summits reaches a height of 9232 ft. above sea level. The mountain is noted for its majestic beauty and has been the inspiration for much imagery in Hebrew poetry. Remains of ancient temples, one probably dedicated to Baal and several bearing Greek inscriptions, are found on its slopes. Mount Hermon is believed to have been the site of Christ's transfiguration.

HERMONTHIS. See KARNAK.

HERNANDEZ. See FERNANDEZ.

HERNDON, WILLIAM HENRY (1818–91), American lawyer, born in Greensburg, Ky., and educated at Illinois College. In 1844 he was admitted to the bar, and in the same year began his law partnership with Abraham Lincoln, which was formally maintained until Lincoln's death. Herndon was an active worker in the antislavery cause and influenced Lincoln's ideas on slavery. He was elected mayor of Springfield, Ill., in 1855. After Lincoln's death he gathered reminiscences of the President's boyhood and youth from many sources and wrote the biography *Herndon's Lincoln: The True Story of a Great Life* (with Jesse W. Weik, 3 vols., 1889). Herndon's papers and letters relating to Lincoln were edited by the lawyer and scholar Emanuel Hertz (1870–1940), and were published under the title *The Hidden Lincoln* (1938).

HERNE, town of North Rhine-Westphalia, West Germany, in the Ruhr (q.v.) valley, 15 m. by rail N.N.W. of Dortmund. It is a center of the Ruhr coal industry, and also contains factories producing ammonia and boilers. Following World War II Herne was included in the British zone of occupation. Pop. (1950) 111,591.

HERNIA, the protrusion from the body cavity of one or more of its tissues or organs. Hernias may be produced accidentally, as the result of the rupture or destruction of the tissues of the body wall, but such condition is rare. The great majority of hernias result from congenital weaknesses of the sustaining tissues or incomplete closure of passages which should have closed during fetal life, but which have persisted.

Most *congenital hernias* are abdominal, and are produced by exertion or muscular strain sufficient to cause the opening of the weak or incompletely closed passage, and the subsequent escape of a loop of intestine. These hernias, often called "ruptures", are classified according to location, such as inguinal, femoral, or umbilical hernias. Abdominal hernias, particularly inguinal hernias, are much commoner among men than among women.

If a hernia takes place through a sac or weak spot which has not been present at birth it is said to be an *acquired hernia;* for example, after abdominal surgery the abdominal wall is sometimes left in a weakened condition along the line of the incision and a ventral, or incisional, hernia is likely to result.

From the standpoint of treatment, hernias are classified according to their condition. *Reducible hernias* can be returned to the body cavity by gentle manipulation and kept in place with a truss (q.v.), whereas *irreducible hernias* cannot be replaced and can be relieved only by surgery. A *strangulated hernia* is one in which the blood supply to the contents of the herniated sac has become interrupted and inflammation, or, in long-continued cases, gangrene, has set in. When a hernia becomes strangulated, swift surgical treatment is imperative.

In children, an important site of hernia is through the incompletely closed fontanels of the skull (q.v.). The membranes enclosing the brain may protrude through the fontanel and, in severe cases, some of the brain substance may be contained in the hernial sac. Such a condition is known as *meningocele,* and is very serious. Meningoceles may also form along the spinal column. Various other organs of the body may also herniate, producing such conditions as *cystocele,* hernia of the bladder, and *gastrocele,* hernia of the stomach.

HERO. See GREEK RELIGIOUS MYTHOLOGY; ROMAN RELIGIOUS MYTHOLOGY; SCANDINAVIAN MYTHOLOGY.

HERO, in Greek legend, a priestess of Aphrodite, the goddess of love, at Sestos. Hero loved and was beloved by Leander (q.v.), whose home was at Abydos, across the Hellespont (Dardanelles). The priestess was bound to celibacy, and therefore could not wed Leander. Every night the young man swam to Hellespont to visit his beloved, guided by a lamp that burned on her tower. One stormy night a high wind extinguished the beacon, and Leander was drowned in the strait. His body was washed ashore beneath Hero's tower, and in her grief, the priestess cast herself into the sea and perished.

HEROD AGRIPPA I (about 10 B.C.–44 A.D.), King of Judæa from 41 to 44 A.D., the son of Aristobulus II (see MACCABEES) and Berenice, the daughter of Salome. His early years were spent at the court of Emperor Tiberius Claudius Nero Cæsar in Rome. There, because of his spendthrift habits, he incurred heavy debts which at length necessitated his retirement to Palestine. In the closing years of Tiberius' reign Herod Agrippa returned to Rome and was appointed companion to the emperor's grandson, Gaius Cæsar (afterward the Emperor Caligula). Upon Caligula's accession to the throne in 37 A.D., Herod Agrippa received from him the tetrarchies of Philip the Tetrarch and Lysanias, with the title of king, the Roman Senate adding the honorary rank of prætor. In 40 A.D. he obtained the fortified tetrarchy of Herod Antipas (see HEROD ANTIPAS); and in the following year the new Roman emperor, Tiberius Claudius Drusus Nero Germanicus, gave Herod Agrippa the additional territory of Judæa and Samaria. He was thus finally in possession of the whole region over which his grandfather, Herod the Great, had ruled. To preserve peace, Herod Agrippa adopted a pro-Jewish policy. His extreme personal piety and official furtherance of Jewish interests endeared him to the people but earned him the strong disfavor of both the Roman civil population and the Roman troops in his domains.

HEROD AGRIPPA II (27–100? A.D.), King of Judæa from 50 to about 100 A.D., the son

of Herod Agrippa I. He received his early education at the court of Emperor Tiberius Claudius Drusus Nero Germanicus in Rome. Because of Agrippa's extreme youth at the time of his father's death, Claudius was persuaded not to give him the succession. The whole of Palestine thus passed under direct Roman rule. In 50 A.D., however, two years after the death of his uncle Herod, king of the small district of Chalcis in w. Syria, Agrippa received the kingdom which had thereby been vacated. He surrendered it in 53 A.D., receiving in return the former tetrarchy of Philip the Tetrarch, son of Herod the Great, together with the tetrarchy of Lysanias and the domains of the Roman governor of Syria, Publius Quintilius Varus. In 56 A.D. the Roman emperor Nero Claudius Cæsar Drusus Germanicus augmented these territories with the cities of Tiberius and Julias in Galilee and Tarichæa in Perea, and surrounding lands and villages. In common with the other Herods, Agrippa launched numerous architectural projects, improving his capital, Cæsarea Philippi, which he renamed Neronias, and adorning the city of Berytus (Beirut) in Phenicia. Unlike his father, he gave no special consideration to the interests of the Jews, manifesting, in fact, a general indifference to the religious issues of his time. During his reign, however, the Temple at Jerusalem was completed. Agrippa endeavored to combine Hellenism (q.v.) and Judaism. He strove to dissuade the Jews from carrying out their war with Rome, and continued loyal to Rome even after the Galilean cities had deserted him. He was rewarded for his allegiance at the conclusion of the war by a northward extension of his territory, and in 75 A.D. he was honored with the rank of prætor. It was before Herod Agrippa II and his sister Berenice that the apostle Paul was brought in Cæsarea, on the eve of his deportation to Rome, as related in the New Testament (Acts 26).

HEROD ANTIPAS (fl. 1st cent. A.D.), son of Herod the Great and the Samaritan Malthace, and younger brother of Herod Archelaus. He was tetrarch of Galilee and Perea from 4 B.C. to 40 A.D. Though comparatively little is known of his rule, he appears to have governed ably. Antipas possessed his father's cunning, but lacked the latter's diplomacy and talent for war. Antipas divorced his first wife, daughter of Aretas, King of the Nabatæans, and married Herodias, wife of his half brother Herod Philip (not Philip the Tetrarch), thus precipitating a war with Aretas in which An-

Ancient Greek bust of Herodotus

tipas was routed. He was censured for his marriage by John the Baptist (q.v.), whose execution Antipas was enticed into ordering through the machinations of Herodias. Later, at the urging of his ambitious wife, Antipas went to Rome and demanded of Emperor Caligula that he be favored, as had Herod Agrippa I, with the title of king. Instead, he was deposed and banished by Caligula to Lugdunum (Lyons) in Gaul. Antipas is the Herod most frequently mentioned in the New Testament. It was to him that Jesus was sent by Pontius Pilate, the procurator of Judæa (Luke 23:7-15).

HERODAS or **HERONDAS** (fl. 3rd cent. B.C.), Greek poet, probably a native of the island of Cos. He was the author of short, humorous, dramatic sketches of everyday life called *mimes,* written in the old Ionic dialect and in choliambic verse (see VERSIFICATION). These mimes represented a new Greek literary form, and contain, in less than a hundred lines each, a definite character portrayal and a diverting incident.

HERODIAN (fl. 3rd cent. A.D.), a Greek historian. He held office under the Roman government, and wrote with a practical knowledge of the events and circumstances which he describes. His history, in eight books, covers the years 180 to 238, from the death of Emperor Marcus Aurelius to the accession

of Gordianus III. The work was first made known to the Western world in the translation of the 15th-century Italian Humanist Angelus Politianus.

HERODIANS, in Jewish history, a political party which, during the first century of the Christian era, supported the policy of the Herodian rulers of Judæa, to fuse Judaism with Hellenism. Together with the Pharisees (q.v.), the Herodians opposed the belief in Jesus as the Messiah, fearing that the Christian doctrines emphasizing the spiritual equality of all men before God would cause the breakdown of the existing social and political structure.

HERODOTUS (fl. 5th cent. B.C.), Greek historian, born in Halicarnassus, originally a Doric colony in s.w. Asia Minor, but at that time under the domination of Persia. Herodotus was thus by birth a Persian subject. His uncle, Panyasis, an epic poet, was put to death about 457 B.C. for conspiring against the Persian tyranny. Herodotus thereupon went into exile, and is said to have made his temporary home on the Greek island of Samos, then under Athenian control. Between 464 and 447 (although the dates cannot be established with any exactitude) the historian is believed to have traveled extensively in Greece and Asia Minor. He visited Ægina, Thasos, Crete, Delos, Rhodes, Paros, Samothrace, Cerigo, and Cyprus in the Greek Archipelago; journeyed from Sardis to Susa, capital of the Persian Empire; explored the western shores of the Black Sea to the mouth of the Dnieper R., traversed Thrace and Scythia; and made a lengthy sojourn in Egypt. The starting points, direction, and extent of his travels are not precisely known, but these peregrinations provided him with valuable first-hand knowledge of practically all the regions described in his famous work, entitled *History.* About 447 Herodotus went to Athens, then the center and focus of culture in the Greek world. There he gave readings from his unfinished historical works, winning the admiration of the most illustrious men of Greece and the personal friendship of the poet Sophocles (see GREEK LITERATURE). In the year 444 Herodotus joined the colony which the Athenian statesman, Pericles, was founding at Thurii (Thurium) in Magna Græcia, s. Italy. About his subsequent life almost nothing is known. It was presumably devoted to the completion and publication of his *History.* According to tradition, his death occurred at Thurii, probably around 424.

Herodotus was called by the Roman orator and statesman, Marcus Tullius Cicero, the father of history (q.v.). He was the first historian to grasp firmly a great international theme, making use of legendary, local, antiquarian, geographic, and ethnologic lore, derived in part from predecessors, but widely supplemented with knowledge gained in his own travels. Both ancient and modern critics have paid tribute to the grandeur of design and nobility of style which characterize the work of Herodotus (see GREEK LANGUAGE).

HEROD THE GREAT (73?–4 B.C.), King of Judæa from 37 to 4 B.C. He was the second son of Antipater and Cypros, an Arabian woman. Upon the assassination of Antipater in 43 B.C., a period of intrigue and warfare ensued. Antigonus, son of Aristobulus II, and last scion of the Hasmonæan dynasty (see MACCABEES), supported by the Parthians (see PARTHIA), contested the Roman-backed Herodian rule in Judæa. The Parthians invaded Palestine, Antigonus ascended the throne, and Herod escaped to Rome. There, in 39 B.C., at the instance of the Roman soldier and statesman Marcus Antonius, he was proclaimed king of Judæa by the Roman senate. Not until 37 B.C., however, did Herod succeed in putting down the forces opposed to him. With Roman aid he broke the Hasmonæan power and accomplished the execution of Antigonus. He then sought to consolidate his position with the Jews by wedding Mariamne, a princess of the Hasmonæan line.

The first years of Herod's reign were troubled because of the hostility of the Sadducees and Pharisees (qq.v.) and the enmity of the surviving members of the Hasmonæan house, who secured a friend in Cleopatra, Queen of Egypt. Herod ultimately prevailed against his adversaries, however, partly through murder and confiscation of property, partly through political strategy, but mainly through the defeat of Cleopatra and Marcus Antonius (first the lover and then the ally of the Egyptian queen) at the hands of the Roman statesman Gaius Octavius, afterward the Emperor Augustus. Following the victory of Octavius at Actium in 31 B.C., Herod was confirmed as ruler of Judæa, the Maccabee Hyrcanus II, former high priest and political opponent of Herod, was put to death, and the last of the Hasmonæans were suppressed. Jealousy rather than political expediency caused Herod to order the execution of his wife, Mariamne, whom he passionately loved.

The years from 25 to 13 B.C. were for the most part prosperous. During this period the king devoted himself to a great number of architectural projects, including the construction at Jerusalem, Jericho, and Cæsarea of theaters, amphitheaters, and hippodromes for the Grecian games inaugurated in honor of Augustus. To protect the frontier of Judæa against Arab incursions, he built or rehabilitated a chain of fortresses which were later to prove of great value to the Jews in their insurrection against Rome. He began the rebuilding of the Temple in Jerusalem with close regard for the religious scruples of the people. The final years of Herod's reign were embittered by the ceaseless and complicated political intrigues within his palace. On his last visit to Rome he obtained the consent of Augustus to dispose of his kingdom as he saw fit. A few hours before Herod died he made a will, in which he gave Judæa, including Samaria and Idumæa, to his son Archelaus, with the title of king; Galilee and Perea to Antipas, brother of Archelaus, with the title of tetrarch; and Gaulanitis, Auranitis, Trachonitis, Batanea, and Panias to Philip (known as Philip the Tetrarch). This will was confirmed by Emperor Augustus, and despite disorders on the part of the people, who desired to be rid of Herodian rule, was put into effect.

HEROIN, a trade-mark name applied to a narcotic, diacetylmorphine, derived from morphine. It is a white, crystalline powder with a bitter taste, soluble in water and alcohol. Heroin is more toxic and habit forming than morphine, and has greater analgesic and euphoric properties per gram than any other narcotic. For these reasons it has become the main drug of addiction in many parts of the world. In recent years the medicinal use of heroin has been largely discontinued as part of the international drive for narcotics control. The manufacture and use of heroin was outlawed in the United States in 1924. Similar legislation was passed by many other countries; by 1954 only a few nations, including the United Kingdom, Canada, France, Belgium, and Japan, had failed to ban the manufacture and consumption of heroin.

Heroin poisoning was generally fatal until the discovery in 1954 that a recently developed drug, known as nalorphine, is effective as an antidote. Nalorphine, a derivative of morphine, was previously recognized as an antidote to various other narcotics. See DRUG ADDICTIONS; MORPHINE; NARCOTICS.

HERON, common name for any tall, gaunt wading bird in the family Ardeidae of the Stork order, found in swamps and marshes

The great blue heron

and on mudbanks in all warm parts of the world. Included among the herons are several groups of birds more commonly known as bitterns, boatbills, and egrets (qq.v.); see also NIGHT HERON.

Herons have elongated necks and legs, and somewhat resemble cranes (q.v.), but are smaller. They fly with their necks bent in an S shape and with their heads supported between their shoulders. Their bills average eight inches in length and are sharp-edged and pointed. Herons have four long, clawed toes on each foot, three of which are directed forward, and the fourth backward. The claw on the middle of the forward toes has a rough, comblike inner margin which is used in preening the heron's soft plumage. Herons often have a headdress of feathers, some of which during the breeding season grow into long, hanging plumes. The birds mate and nest yearly in the same place, in a large group known as a *heronry*. Most species construct their loose, flat, platform-style nests high in the branches of a swamp tree. Notable exceptions are the bitterns which place their nests among reeds on the ground. Two to six pale-blue eggs are laid in a clutch. The young are covered with white or yellow powder down at birth and bear little resemblance to the adults. They have the habit of regurgitating at any strange animal which approaches them. Herons subsist on fish, small amphibi-

ans, small snakes, and mice. Most species do not stalk their prey but wait in shallow water or on land, spearing it with their long bills as it comes past them.

Eleven genera of herons are found in North America. One of the best known is the great blue heron, *Ardea herodias,* which is widely distributed in North America and winters as far south as N. South America. This bird is about 4 feet long, and has a wing span of about 6 feet. Above it is bluish gray; below, white streaked with black. Its crown is white, with a black crest; the sides of its head are black and its face is slate blue. Its legs and feet are black. During the mating season two feathers of this bird's crest become long and threadlike. Another well-known American species is the green heron or shitepoke, *Butorides virescens,* with a similar range. The bird is 17 inches long, and is shiny green above and reddish brown below. The great white heron, *A. occidentalis,* is a large, completely white heron, about 4½ feet long, found in Florida, Mexico, and the West Indies. Common among the mangrove trees of the Louisiana bayous is the Louisiana heron, *Hydranassa tricolor,* which is slightly over 2 feet in length. It is bluish gray above with a white rump, and is white below. Its crest is light brown in color and several plumes extend back as far as the tail. This bird often flies north as far as New England at the end of the mating season. The little blue heron, *Florida caerulea,* is common in S.E. United States. It is about 2 feet long, and is slate blue above and reddish brown below.

The common European heron, *Ardea cinerea,* is about 3 feet long and is similar in coloring to the great blue heron. It was formerly hunted with peregrine falcons (q.v.). Several species of herons in the genus *Tigrisoma* are common in Central and South America. They are known as tiger herons, or tiger bitterns, because their plumage is tinted and striped like that of a tiger.

HERON'S-BILL. See ERODIUM.

HEROPHILUS (fl. 300 B.C.), Greek anatomist and surgeon, born at Chalcedon (Kadiköi) in Bithynia, and educated under Praxagoras, one of the followers of Hippocrates. He practiced in Alexandria, and was one of the founders of a school of anatomy there. Herophilus was one of the first to perform post-mortem examinations, and is also said to have practiced vivisection upon condemned criminals. He distinguished between the sensory and motor functions of nerves and nerve trunks, and accurately described the eye, brain, liver, and pancreas, and the salivary and genital organs. His works included commentaries on Hippocrates and treatises on obstetrics and on the causes of sudden death. See GREEK LITERATURE: *The Hellenistic Period*.

HÉROULT, PAUL LOUIS TOUSSAINT (1863–1914), French metallurgist and inventor, born in Normandy and educated at the École des Mines in Paris. Héroult invented, independently of Charles M. Hall (q.v.), an electrolytic process for refining aluminum, patenting his process in 1887. He also invented an electric-arc furnace used in the manufacture of alloy steels; see ELECTRIC FURNACE.

HERPES (Gr. *herpein*, "to creep"), name applied to any of a number of skin diseases characterized by a creeping or spreading area of blister formation. The name is especially applied to cold sores, or fever blisters, known as *herpes simplex,* and to shingles, known as *herpes zoster.*

Fever blisters are eruptions of very small blisters which commonly appear during the course of or after illnesses such as the common cold, pneumonia, malaria, meningitis, and typhoid fever. They usually appear on the nose, lips, face, ears, or genitals, and are caused by a virus which is carried about by most persons, but which probably causes the eruption only when the physical resistance of an individual is lowered. Fever blisters appear with no preliminary pain other than a slight tingling, and persist for about four days, at the end of which time they clear without leaving scars. Treatment for recurrent cold sores includes the administration of vitamin-B complex, antibiotics, vaccinations, and drying agents, such as calamine lotion.

Shingles are blisters about the size of a pinhead grouped in areas measuring from ¼ in. to 1 in. in diameter. They are usually found on one side of the thorax (upper trunk), along the course of an inflamed sensory nerve, but may be found along the path of inflamed sensory nerves anywhere in the body. Shingles result after impulses from the damaged nerves to the skin cause the skin cells to produce a toxic substance similar to histamine (q.v.). Nerve damage leading to shingles may be brought on by mechanical injury, by chemical poisoning, or by viruses or bacterial toxins. Pain is usually felt before the eruption of shingles and may persist for many months; the blisters heal in about 2 weeks, but often leave scars. Treatment consists of the use of palliative medication. Although there is no known cure for shingles, cortisone

was reported in 1954 to bring fast relief from pain and to prevent complications.

HERPETON. See WATER SNAKE.

HERRERA, FERNANDO DE, called EL DIVINO (about 1534–97), Spanish poet, born in Seville. He was known especially for his odes and sonnets, written partly in imitation of the poetry of Garcilaso de la Vega. Herrera's odes on the naval battle of Lepanto (1571) and on Don John of Austria, the victorious commander in that battle, are regarded as masterpieces. In 1580 was published his annotated edition of De la Vega's poems.

HERRERA Y TORDESILLAS, ANTONIO DE (1559–1625), Spanish historian, born in Cuéllar. Philip II of Spain appointed him first historiographer of the Indies and chronicler of Castile. The historian's principal work is *Historia General de los Hechos de los Castellanos en las Islas y Tierra Firme del Mar Océano* (1601), considered an accurate account of the Spanish in America from 1492 to 1554. He is also known for *Descripción de las Indias Occidentales* (1601), concerning the West Indies.

HERRICK, MYRON T(IMOTHY) (1854–1929), American political leader and diplomat, born in Huntington, O., and educated at Oberlin College and Ohio Wesleyan University. From 1878 to 1886 he practiced law in Cleveland, O., and in the latter year turned to railroad, industrial, and banking activities. During this period Herrick began to interest himself in politics. From 1903 to 1905 he was governor of Ohio, and in 1912 he was appointed ambassador to France by President William H. Taft. He continued to hold this post under the Democratic administration of President Woodrow Wilson, and at the outbreak of World War I assumed charge of the embassies of Germany, Austria, and other nations of the Central Powers. Until relieved in December, 1914, Herrick maintained headquarters in Paris, even at a time during the Marne offensive when the French government moved to Bordeaux. After his return to America he devoted much of his time to war relief activities. In 1921 he was again appointed ambassador to France by President Warren G. Harding, and remained in office until his death. In 1927 he received Charles Lindbergh (q.v.) in Paris at the end of the latter's famous transatlantic flight.

HERRICK, ROBERT (1591–1674), English lyric poet, born in London, and educated at Westminster School and Cambridge University. In 1629 he became vicar of Dean Prior in Devonshire, but in 1647, during the Civil

War, was deprived of the living because of his royalist sympathies. Following the restoration of King Charles II, Herrick was reinstated at Dean Prior, where he resided from 1662 until his death.

Herrick occasionally contributed small poems to such contemporary anthologies as *Lachrymæ Musarum* (1649) and *Wit's Recreations* (1650). His chief work is the volume *Hesperides, or the Works both Human and Divine of Robert Herrick* (1648). Within the same book, but under a separate title page bearing the date 1647, was printed a group of religious poems by him. The entire collection contains over 1200 short poems, ranging in form from epistles, eclogues, and epigrams to folk songs and love poems. Herrick's themes are pastoral, dealing mostly with English country life and village customs. Many of his love poems, as "Gather ye Rosebuds" and "Corinna's Going a-Maying", have become famous, and are considered unique among this form for style, melody, and feeling.

HERRING, common name for any marine, teleost fish in the large family Clupeidae, the most economically important group of fish to North America and w. Europe. The family contains over two hundred species, all valued as food, including the menhaden, the pilchard (the young of which are the common sardines), and the shad (qq.v.). They are abundant throughout the North Atlantic Ocean, in the North and Baltic seas, and in the North Pacific Ocean. Most of the clupeids are about one foot long when mature; the largest species, the shad, reaches thirty inches in length. They are characterized by a single short dorsal fin in the middle of the upper margin of the body, and by an anal fin similarly located below. The head is scaleless, and the slender body is covered with thin cycloid scales in which rings of organic material, rich in guanine, are laid down each season. By counting these rings, scientists can determine the age of clupeids, which live as long as twenty years. They swim near the surface of the water in huge schools, containing millions of individuals, and feed on plankton (minute, floating invertebrates). During the breeding season the schools approach the coasts to spawn in shallow water. Each female lays about thirty thousand eggs on the rough, gravelly sea floor. The eggs are covered with a sticky substance which causes them to adhere to the bottom. The young remain near the coast until they are one year old, when they go out to the deep sea, the temperature of which influences their sexual maturation. North Sea herring mature at three

to four years of age, Baltic Sea herring at five to eight, and herring found farther north in the Bering Sea mature even later. Herring of southerly seas die at an earlier age than those inhabiting more northerly regions; consequently those found in the north grow to a larger size.

The fishing, processing, and marketing of different species of the Herring family is a major industry in the U.S., England, Scotland, Norway, Denmark, Holland, Germany, France, and Portugal (see FISHERIES). Besides fresh and salted herring, the products of this industry on the market include "red herring", which has been smoked until it is hardened; "kippered herring", which is slightly salted and partially smoked; "bloaters", which are large herring, heavily salted and partially smoked; and canned sardines.

The term "herring", when unqualified, usually refers to the common or sea herring, *Clupea harengus*. This fish, abundant in the Atlantic Ocean and found on the coast of the U.S. north of South Carolina, grows to a length of one foot and is bluish green above, silvery below. Its young, and the young of the European sprat, *C. sprattus*, are often called "whitebait", and are considered table delicacies. The Pacific herring, *C. pallasii*, found from Alaska to Mexico, is a similar fish. The fall herring, *Pomolobus mediocris*, so called because it spawns in the fall, is found south of Cape Cod. The blueback, *P. aestivalis*, also known as the summer or glut herring, is unusual because it ascends into fresh water to spawn. Another common herring is the branch or spring herring, or alewife (q.v.).

The name herring is also applied to several fresh-water fish, such as the lake herring, or cisco (q.v.), of the Great Lakes, and the rainbow herring, a smelt (q.v.). The chimera (q.v.) is sometimes called "king of the herrings".

HERRING GULL, or SILVERY GULL, common name for a large gull (q.v.), *Larus argentatus*, abundant on both sides of the North Atlantic Ocean, on inland waters in North America, and in the North Pacific Ocean from Japan to the Bering Straits. The adult herring gull, which is about two feet long, is silvery gray above and white below. Its bill is yellow; its wings are tipped with black and streaked with white; and its legs and feet are orange. Young herring gulls are dark brown, streaked with gray. Herring gulls commonly follow ships out of harbor to pick up garbage. They normally subsist on fish, but also eat shellfish, turnips, potatoes, and grain. At high tide they float on the surface of the water, and when the tide ebbs they congregate on the shores. The cry of the herring gull is loud, high-pitched, and hoarse. Herring gulls breed in the spring in large communities off the coasts of N.E. United States, and travel south in late summer and early fall, wintering in Cuba.

HERRINGS, BATTLE OF THE. See FASTOLF, SIR JOHN.

HERRIOT, ÉDOUARD (1872–   ), French statesman and man of letters, born in Troyes, and educated in Paris at the Lycée Louis le Grand and the École Normale Supérieure. He entered politics in 1904 as a member of the municipal council of Lyon and in the same year was elected mayor of Lyon, an office he held continuously from 1905, except for the period from 1942 to 1945 when he was a prisoner of the German conquerors of France. Herriot was one of the most eminent and active political leaders of his time. He was the leader of the Radical Socialist Party of France. From 1919 he was a member of the chamber of deputies; he was premier of France in 1924–25 and again in 1932; and president of the chamber of deputies from 1936 to 1940. In the last-mentioned office he refused to collaborate with the Nazis after their conquest of France or with the French Vichy government under Marshal Pétain, and openly protested against Pétain's dictatorship and collaboration with the Germans. Herriot was arrested by the Germans in 1942 and kept interned in France and Germany until 1945, when he was liberated by Soviet troops. He was an important witness in 1945 in the trials of Pétain and other French collaborationists. Herriot was a deputy to the constituent assembly which wrote the constitution for the Fourth French Republic. The same year he was elected a deputy to the first national assembly to meet under the new constitution. In 1947 he was elected leader or speaker of the national assembly and held that office until 1954. Herriot became a member of the Institute of France in 1946. As a man of letters he is known chiefly for his book on the Jewish-Alexandrian philosophy, *Philon the Jew* (1897), and the biography *The Life of Beethoven* (1929). Other works are *Outline of the History of French Literature* (1905), *United States of Europe* (1930), *Message to the Free Countries* (1942), and *In Those Days* (autobiographical, 1952).

HERSCHEL, a family of English astronomers, including the following.

1. SIR WILLIAM HERSCHEL, originally FRIED-

French Embassy, Information Division
Édouard Herriot

RICH WILHELM HERSCHEL (1738–1822), born in Hanover, Germany. His early education was limited, but he studied music and became a skilled performer on several instruments. At the age of nineteen he went to England, where he worked as a teacher of music, band conductor, and finally, after 1766, as organist at the Octagon Chapel in Bath. While at Bath he became interested in astronomy, and devoted all his spare time to the study of astronomy and mathematics. Unable to procure adequate instruments, he constructed and constantly improved his own telescopes. In 1774, with the aid of his sister, Caroline, he began a comprehensive and systematic survey of the heavens. In 1781 he discovered a new planet, which he named Georgium Sidus in honor of George III, and which was later named Herschel, but which is now universally called Uranus. A year later he was appointed private astronomer to the king. He erected a telescope at Slough with a 48-inch mirror and a focal length of 40 feet. Using this instrument, he discovered two satellites of Uranus and the sixth and seventh satellites of Saturn. He studied the rotation period of many planets and the motion of double stars, and also catalogued over 800 double stars. He also studied nebulae, contributing new information on their constitution and increasing the number of observed nebulae from about 100 to 2500. Herschel was elected a Fellow of the Royal Society in 1781, was knighted in 1816, and in 1821 became the first president of the Royal Astronomical Society. He is considered the virtual founder of sidereal astronomy.

2. CAROLINE LUCRETIA HERSCHEL (1750–1848), born in Hanover, sister of William Herschel. She received only the rudiments of an education in her youth, because her mother believed it sufficient that a girl be trained in household duties. However, in 1772 she joined her brother, William, and from then on was of great assistance to him in his research in astronomy. She independently discovered seven comets, and several of the nebulae and stars included in her brother's catalogues. In 1828 she was granted the gold-medal award by the Royal Astronomical Society and was soon afterward chosen an honorary member of the Royal Society.

3. JOHN FREDERICK WILLIAM HERSCHEL (1792–1871), born in Slough, son of William Herschel, and educated at St. John's College, Cambridge. After working in mathematics and spending a short time studying law, he applied himself to astronomy. He re-examined the double stars and nebulae observed by his father and added many more to the latter's catalogues. In order to complete the survey of the heavens undertaken by his father he led an expedition to the Cape of Good Hope in 1834 to study the stars of the southern hemisphere, and published the results in 1847. He became president of the Royal Astronomical Society in 1848. He was also interested in chemistry and photography and discovered the solvent action of sodium hyposulfite on silver salts, the basis of the fixing process in photography. He was also the first to apply the terms positive and negative to photographic images.

HERSEY, JOHN (RICHARD) (1914–), American author and journalist, born in Tientsin, China, and educated at Yale and Cambridge universities. He joined the staff of the weekly news magazine *Time* in 1937, and during World War II he served as a *Time* correspondent in both the Pacific and European theaters of operations. Subsequently he was a senior editor of *Life* and editor of the magazine '47 and '48. Hersey is the author of *Men on Bataan* (1942) and *Into the Valley* (1943); vivid accounts of the war in the Pacific; *A Bell for Adano* (1944; Pulitzer Prize, 1945), a novel about the Allied occupation of Italy; *Hiroshima* (1946), a graphic report on the atomic bombing of that Japanese city; *The Wall* (1950), a novel about the fate of the

Jewish community of Warsaw under the Nazis during World War II; and *The Marmot Drive* (1953), a symbolic novel set in a modern New England town.

HERSHEY, LEWIS BLAINE (1893–), American army officer, born in Steuben County, Ind., and educated at Tri-State College, Ind. In 1910 he took a position as a country school teacher in Steuben, Ind., and was a high school principal in Flint, Ind., from 1914 to 1916. He served in the Indiana National Guard from 1911 to 1916, and in 1916 was commissioned first lieutenant in the U.S. army. By 1940 he had advanced through the grades to lieutenant colonel. Between 1923 and 1927 Hershey was assistant professor of military science and tactics at Ohio State University and between 1936 and 1940 he was a member of the War Department general staff. In 1936 he was appointed secretary and executive officer of the Selective Service Commission, and in 1940 he was promoted to brigadier general in recognition of his work in drawing up plans for the Selective Service System. He was appointed director of the Selective Service System in 1941 and promoted to major general in 1942. In 1947 he became director of the Office of Selective Service Records, and in 1948, of the new Selective Service System.

HERTER, ALBERT (1871–1950), American mural and figure painter, born in New York City. He studied with Carroll Beckwith at the Art Students' League, New York City, and in Paris with Jean Paul Laurens. He became an associate of the National Academy after receiving many awards for his work, which was noted for its decorative inventiveness. A large mural in the Gare de l'Est, Paris, commemorating World War I, was donated by Herter to France in memory of his son. Among his later works were a set of mural panels for the Supreme Court room of the Wisconsin Capitol and an allegorical decoration in the St. Francis Hotel, San Francisco. He also designed and produced tapestries at his Herter Looms. His painting "Two Boys" is at the Metropolitan Museum of Art, New York City.

HERTFORDSHIRE or **HERTFORD,** or HERTS, county of S.E. England. It is traversed in the N.W. by an extension of the Chiltern Hills. The river Lea, which is the principal stream of Hertfordshire, flows generally E. across the county and, turning S. southeast of Ware, forms part of the county's E. boundary. Other important rivers are the Colne and

Stort rivers, tributaries of the Thames. The county originated as a military district which was created around a fortress established at the town of Hertford by the Anglo-Saxon king Edward the Elder during the 10th century. It is first mentioned as a county in the Saxon Chronicle of 1011. Agriculture is the chief industry of Hertfordshire. Silk and paper are the principal manufactures; brewing, tanning, brickmaking, straw-plaiting, the processing of lime, and the quarrying of marl also are carried on in Hertfordshire. In addition to the county seat, Hertford (pop., 1951 prelim., 13,890), Hemel Hempsted (25,523), Cheshunt (23,016), and St. Albans (44,106) are the most important towns. Area, 632 sq.m.; pop. (1951 prelim.) 609,735.

HERTOGENBOSCH, 'S (Fr. *Bois-le-Duc*), capital of North Brabant Province, the Netherlands, located at the confluence of the Dommel and the Aa rivers, about 30 miles s.s.e. of Utrecht. The city contains several medieval buildings and was, for a time, the residence of the Dutch scholar Desiderius Erasmus. Pop. (1953 est.) 61,143.

HERTWIG, Oskar (1849–1922), German embryologist, born in Friedberg, and educated at the universities of Jena, Zurich, and Bonn. In 1878 he became a professor at Jena, and in 1888 professor of anatomy in Berlin, where he founded and was the director of the Anatomical Institute (1888–1921). Hertwig was the first to show that fertilization comes about by the uniting of two equivalent nuclei: that of the egg and that of the sperm. He laid the foundations of the germ-layer theory, showing the growth of the various body tissues from differentiated layers of cells in the embryo. He made investigations into the malformations of vertebrate embryos, and demonstrated the similarities in the development of the male and female gametes in the hairworm, *Ascaris*. Hertwig's works include: *Beiträge zur Kenntnis der Bildung, Befruchtung und Theilung des Tierischen Eies* (1876), *Studien zur Blättertheorie* (with R. Hertwig, 1879–83), and *Allgemeine Biologie* (1912).

HERTZ, Gustav (1887–), German physicist, nephew of Heinrich R. Hertz. He was educated at the universities of Göttingen, Munich, and Berlin. In 1928 he was appointed director of the Physical Institute, Berlin Technische Hochschule, and in 1935 he became director of the research laboratory of the Siemens Works in Berlin, manufacturers of electrical equipment. He collaborated with James Franck (q.v.) in research on the effects of the impact of electrons on atoms, and for this work Hertz and Franck were awarded the Nobel Prize for physics in 1925. In 1947 Hertz was engaged by the government of the U.S.S.R. to continue his work in atomic research.

HERTZ, Heinrich Rudolph (1857–94), German physicist, born in Hamburg, and educated at the University of Berlin. He was an assistant to Hermann Helmholtz (q.v.) in the physics laboratory of the Berlin Institute from 1880 to 1883, and in the following two years lectured on theoretical physics at the University of Kiel. Between 1885 and 1889 he was a professor of physics at Karlsruhe Polytechnic, and after 1889 was professor of physics at the University of Bonn. Hertz studied the work of James Maxwell (q.v.) on electromagnetic wave theory, and in 1887, using the spark of an induction coil, succeeded in producing and detecting electromagnetic waves, later called hertzian waves. He studied the properties of electromagnetic waves and showed experimentally that they possessed many of the properties of light, i.e., measurable velocity and wave length, reflection, refraction, and polarization. Hertz' demonstration of the existence of electromagnetic waves was originally of purely theoretical interest as confirmation of Maxwell's theory of the electromagnetic nature of electricity and light, but his discoveries later led to the development of radio. See Waves, Electromagnetic.

HERTZOG, James Barry Munnik (1866–1942), South African soldier and statesman, born in Wellington, Cape of Good Hope Province, and educated at Victoria College and Amsterdam University. From the time of his first public office, a judgeship in the Orange Free State to which he was appointed in 1895, Hertzog was a leader of the Old Boer element of South Africa. He served throughout the Boer War, from 1899 to 1902, and at its close voted against a negotiated peace with the British. He endeavored to keep anti-British feeling alive after hostilities were ended, and, as attorney general and director of education in the Orange River Colony (now the Orange Free State) from 1907 to 1910, attempted unsuccessfully to impose an official bilingualism of Dutch and English upon the schools under his charge. Using frank racist appeals, and uncompromisingly rejecting government proposals for the development of South Africa within the framework of the British Empire, Hertzog succeeded in increasing the strength of his party, which he

Theodor Herzl

called the Nationalist party, to sixty-three seats in parliament in 1924. A coalition with the Labor party gave him a majority in that year, and he came to power as prime minister, holding the post until 1939. At the outbreak of World War II Hertzog opposed a declaration of war against Germany. He was voted down in parliament, however, and resigned his ministry in favor of Jan Smuts (q.v.). For the remainder of his life he was a leader of the movement within the Union for a negotiated separate peace with Germany.

HERVIEU, PAUL ERNEST (1857–1915), French novelist and playwright, born in Neuilly-sur-Seine, and educated at the Lycée Condorcet, Paris. He was admitted to the bar in 1877 and in 1881 was secretary to the French Legation in Mexico. He wrote some of his early works under the pen name of Éliacin. His novels, in which he was sharply critical of the life of the French upper classes, include *L'Inconnu* (1886), *Flirt* (1890), *Peints par Eux-Mêmes* (1893), *L'Armature* (1895), and *Amitié* (1900). His dramas deal with social problems, such as those arising from divorce and from the conflicts between parents and children. Among his plays are *Les Tenailles* (1895); *L'Énigme* (1901); *Le Dédale* (1903), subsequently performed in New York City as *The Labyrinth; Connais-Toi* (1909); *Bagatelle* (1912); and *Le Destin est Maître*

(1914). In 1900 he was elected a member of the Institute of France.

HERZEGOVINA. See BOSNIA.

HERZL, THEODOR (1860–1904), Austrian writer and journalist, famous as the founder of modern political Zionism, born in Budapest, Hungary, and educated in Vienna. Herzl became well known as a writer of plays, essays, and short stories, and in 1891 was appointed Paris correspondent for the Vienna *Neue Freie Presse*. In 1894 he reported the trial of Alfred Dreyfus (q.v.) for his newspaper. The violent anti-Semitism resulting from the Dreyfus affair deeply affected Herzl, who was a Jew. Until that time, he had believed that gradual assimilation of the Jews with the Christian peoples of Europe was the most practicable solution for the problem of anti-Semitism (q.v.). The trial convinced him that the problem could be solved only if the Jews became a separate national group, with sovereignty over their own territory. He returned to Vienna in 1895 and a year later became literary editor of the *Neue Freie Presse*. Most of his time, from then on, was devoted to Zionism. He wrote *Der Judenstaat* ("The Jewish State") in 1896, and the territory he finally selected for the future Jewish state was Palestine, because of its associations with Jewish history.

In 1897 Herzl organized and presided over the first Zionist congress, at Basel, Switzerland, and for the rest of his life headed the Zionist organization. In his official capacity, he procured audiences with Pope Leo XIII, Emperor William II of Germany, Sultan Abdul-Hamid II of Turkey, and other leaders to ask for support in the acquisition of Palestine as a Jewish homeland. His death was occasioned by his strenuous labors in behalf of Zionism, and he is regarded as the first and one of the greatest influences in the movement which led to the creation of the state of Israel (q.v.) in 1948. Herzl's other works on Zionism include *Alt Neuland* ("Old Newland") written in 1902. See ZIONISM.

HESIOD (8th cent. B.C.), the founder of Greek didactic poetry, and, after Homer (q.v.), the earliest Greek poet whose work has survived. He was born in Ascra, near Mt. Helicon in Bœotia, whence his father had migrated from the Æolian town of Cyme in Asia Minor. Following his father's death, Hesiod left Ascra in consequence of a dispute with his brother Perses over the division of the family estate, and settled in Naupactus. There, as in his youth, he tended sheep and led a farmer's life.

Except for what Hesiod reveals of himself in his poetry, little is definitely known of his life. Modern scholars place him in the Homeric age of Greek literature (q.v.). His first poem, *Works and Days,* is the earliest example of its type, and is composed of 828 verses in Homeric hexameter. The work embodies Hesiod's experiences as a Bœotian farmer, interspersed with many episodes of allegory and fable. Its main theme, developed principally in a didactic style, is that of honest labor and husbandry. Hesiod's work also charts a religious calendar of months, citing days that are propitious and unpropitious for certain farming tasks. The *Works and Days* was the prototype of a long series of poems of the so-called "practical" type by other writers, including the *Georgics* of Vergil (q.v.).

Hesiod's *Theogony* ("Origin of the Gods"), a poem of 1022 verses inspired by sacred traditions, is an attempt to systematize the large and amorphous body of Greek myths, and to incorporate into the Greek pantheon the newer divinities unknown to the Homeric poems. The poem recounts the creation of the world out of chaos, and the birth and genealogy of the gods. The closing portion of the poem contains a list of the daughters of Zeus, father of the gods, who bore sons to mortals; it forms the introduction to a lost poem, the *Catalogue of Women.* This poem, a few fragments of which survive, treats of the mortal women who had become the mothers of heroes and gives an account of the heroes' exploits.

Of other works by Hesiod only titles and fragments remain, and even these, some scholars believe, may have been written by Hesiod's many imitators, who as a group were called the Hesiodic school. In this group are the didactic poem *Maxims of Cheiron;* the genealogical poem *Ægimius;* and the mythical poems *Marriage of Ceyx* and *Descent of Theseus to Hades.* Though generally regarded as inferior to Homer in power of language, imaginative grasp, and grandeur of conception, Hesiod nevertheless occupies an honored place in Greek literature for his moral precepts and his sententious, colloquial style.

HESPERIDES, in Greek mythology, the name of the sisters who, in an island garden far in the west, aided by the ever-vigilant dragon Ladon, protected the tree of the golden apples which Gæa, or Earth, produced as a wedding gift for Hera, queen of heaven, on the occasion of her marriage to Zeus, father of the gods. According to the earliest version of the myth, the Hesperides were the daughters of Erebus, or Darkness, and Nyx, or Night. The number and names of the maidens varied. Apollonius of Rhodes, a Greek epic poet of the early 2nd century B.C., gives three, called Ægle (Radiance), Erytheïs (Redness), and Hespera (Evening); but Apollodorus, an Athenian grammarian of the 2nd century A.D., lists four, including Ægle, Erytheia (a variant of Erytheïs), Hestis (goddess of the hearth), and Arethusa (a wood nymph transformed into a fountain).

HESPERIS. See DAME'S VIOLET.

HESS, DAME MYRA (1890–), English pianist, born in London. She began her training at the Guildhall School of Music under Julian Pascal and Orland Morgan, and in 1902 won a scholarship to the Royal Academy of Music, where she studied under Tobias Mattlay for five years. She won immediate success at her debut in 1907, given in Queen's Hall, at which she played the Beethoven *Concerto in G,* with the orchestra under the direction of Thomas Beecham. She subsequently made concert tours throughout Europe and (after 1922) the United States. With Tobias Mattlay she established in London the Myra Hess scholarship for young pianists. Myra Hess had an unusually large repertoire, and was particularly noted for her playing of the sonatas of Scarlatti, the "48" of Bach, and the concertos of Mozart.

HESS, RUDOLF (1894–), German fascist leader, born in Alexandria, Egypt. He went to Germany at the age of fourteen, and upon the outbreak of World War I enlisted in the German army. His first meeting with Adolf Hitler occurred shortly thereafter, when both were serving in the same regiment. In

British Information Services

Myra Hess at the piano

1921 he joined the National Socialist Party (see NATIONAL SOCIALISM) which had just been formed by Hitler and his associates. He participated in the attempt of the Party to overthrow the Bavarian government by force in 1923, and was incarcerated with Hitler in the prison at Landsberg am Lech. While serving his sentence, he took down, at Hitler's dictation, a large part of the work which later became famous as *Mein Kampf.*

Hess ably abetted Hitler in the struggle which culminated in the rise of the National Socialists to power in January, 1933, and in April of that year was appointed Hitler's deputy in charge of the Party organization. In the following year he was elevated to the rank of minister of the Reich and appointed a member of the Cabinet Council. Hitler named him third deputy of the Reich in 1939, placing him immediately below Hermann Göring (q.v.) in the line of succession to absolute power in Germany.

Two years later, when World War II was reaching its height, Hess made a solo airplane flight to Scotland; upon his immediate arrest as a prisoner of war he announced that he had been commissioned by Hitler to persuade the British government to cease hostilities with Germany and join the Germans in an assault on the Soviet Union. At the war crimes trial held at Nuremberg in 1945–46, he was convicted as a major war criminal, and was sentenced to life imprisonment in Spandau Prison, Berlin.

HESS, VICTOR FRANZ (1883–   ), Austrian physicist, born in Waldstein, Austria, and educated at the universities of Graz and Vienna. After lecturing and teaching in various universities in Austria from 1907 to 1921, he came to the U.S. and became director of research for the U.S. Radium Corporation in New York City, and consultant to the U.S. Bureau of Mines. He returned to Austria and became professor of physics at the universities of Graz and Innsbruck from 1925 to 1931 and 1931 to 1937 respectively. In 1938 Hess became professor of physics at Fordham University in New York City. He was one of the earliest workers in the field of cosmic rays. As early as 1911 he made measurements of cosmic-ray activity at altitudes as great as 30,000 feet. He was awarded half the Nobel Prize for physics in 1936. He is the author of *Conductivity of the Atmosphere* (1928) and *Biological Activity of Cosmic Rays* (with J. Eugster, 1940).

HESS, WALTER RUDOLF (1881–   ), Swiss physiologist, born in Frauenfeld, and edu-

cated at the universities of Lausanne, Bern, Berlin, Kiel, and Zurich. He served as professor of physiology and as director of the Physiological Institute at the University of Zurich from 1917 until his retirement in 1951. Hess is best known for his studies on the functioning of the nervous system. In 1949 he shared the Nobel Prize in physiology and medicine with the Portuguese neurologist Antonio Caetano Moniz.

HESSE, a region of s.w. Germany, comprising the former state of Hesse (q.v.) and the former Prussian province of Hesse-Nassau; also the name of a former ruling family of landgraves. Derived from *Hessi,* the designation applied to a Frankish tribe of antiquity, the name began to figure in German history during the 12th century, when the region formed a part of the landgraviate of Thuringia. Hesse was established as a separate landgraviate in 1247 by Duchess Sophia, niece of the Thuringian ruler Henry Raspe. Her son, called Henry the Child, became in 1263 the first male landgrave of Hesse. During the 16th century the rulers and people of the landgraviate played an important part in the Protestant Reformation. The Landgrave Philip the Magnanimous founded, in 1527, Marburg University, a Protestant institution. Following Philip's death, in 1567, the landgraviate was partitioned among his four sons. Two of these branches of the family subsequently became extinct, and their holdings were absorbed by the surviving lines, the houses of Hesse-Darmstadt and Hesse-Cassel (qq.v.).

HESSE (Ger. *Hessen*), successively a state of the German Republic, of the Third Reich, and, after May 23, 1949, of the Federal Republic of Germany (West Germany), situated in the s.w. section of the country. As formerly constituted, Hesse consisted of the province of Oberhessen, separated from the remainder of the state by territory belonging to the Prussian province of Hesse-Nassau (q.v.), and of the provinces of Starkenburg and Reinhessen, separated from each other by the Rhine R. Oberhessen is partly occupied, in the E., by the Vogelsberg, an uplift of volcanic origin. The principal summit of this uplift, which is adjoined on the w. by the fertile valley of the Wetter R., is the Taufstein (2533 ft.). Spurs of the Taunus Mountains bound the Wetter valley on the w. Reinhessen consists largely of fertile uplands, noted for their vineyards. Starkenburg is traversed by various spurs of the Odenwald. In addition to wine grapes, the principal agricultural products of Hesse include rye, wheat, oats, barley, potatoes, fruit, tobacco, and flax. The region has a variety of mineral deposits, notably manganese, iron, salt, and lignite. Darmstadt (q.v.) was the capital of the former state of Hesse, which had an area of 2969 sq.m. and a population (1939) of 1,469,921.

From 1567 to 1806 the territory of Hesse comprised the landgraviate of Hesse-Darmstadt (q.v.). The landgraviate was reconstituted as a grand duchy in 1806 and, retaining this status, became part of the German Empire in 1871. After the collapse of the German Empire, at the close of World War I, the grand duchy was transformed into a state of the Weimar Republic. Hesse was allocated to the American occupation zone following the defeat of the Third Reich in World War II. Subsequently, most of the former Prussian province of Hesse-Nassau was merged with the former state. On December 1, 1946, the merged territories were established as the new state of Hesse, with Wiesbaden (q.v.) as the capital. Area, 7931 sq.m.; pop. (1950) 4,323,801.

HESSE, HERMANN (1877–), German novelist and poet, born in Calw, Swabia. He attended several schools but abandoned each in turn in order to educate himself through reading and to be free to write. In 1911 he made a trip to India to make a study of Indian mysticism. Hesse's early novels, among which are *Peter Camenzind* (1904), *Unterm Rad* (1905), *Nachbarn* (1908), and *Knulp* (1915), are characterized by musical prose, sensitive scenic description, and an atmosphere of nostalgic melancholy. Among his later novels are *Demian* (1919), a psychoanalytical novel; *Siddhartha* (1923), the story of a search for spiritual happiness; *Ded Steppenwolf* (1927), a novel violently criticizing the spiritually barren modern world; *Narziss und Goldmund* (1930), a tale contrasting spiritual and mundane life; and *Glasperlenspiel* (1943). His two volumes of poetry, *Gedichte* (1922) and *Trost der Nacht* (1929), belong to the Romantic school of German poetry. Hesse was awarded the Nobel Prize for literature in 1946.

HESSE-CASSEL, successively a landgraviate and electorate of Germany, and the name of the ruling family. The landgraviate was established in 1567 by William IV, son of Philip the Magnanimous. Constituted an electorate in 1803, Hesse-Cassel retained this status, except for a brief period during the Napoleonic Wars, until 1866, when it was absorbed by Prussia. The landgraves included Maurice, William V, William VI, William VII, Charles I, Frederick I, who was also king of Sweden (1720–51), and Frederick II, the ruler who furnished Hessian troops to the British during the American Revolution. Among the electors were William II and Frederick William, who was deposed by the Prussians. Under Prussian rule, Hesse-Cassel became part of the province of Hesse-Nassau.

HESSE-DARMSTADT, successively a landgraviate and grand duchy of Germany, and the name of the ruling family. The grand duchy, generally identical with the former German state of Hesse, was absorbed into the German empire in 1871. A branch of the house of Hesse, the Hesse-Darmstadt line was founded by George I in 1567. His successors as landgrave included Louis V, George II, Louis VI, Ernest Louis, Louis VIII, Louis IX, and Louis X. Among the rulers of the grand duchy, which was established in 1806, were Louis I (the Landgrave Louis X), Louis II, and Louis Ernest, who abdicated in 1918.

HESSE-NASSAU, formerly a Prussian province, situated in w. central Germany, and comprising, since December 1, 1946, a part of the state of Hessen in the American occupation zone of Germany. On the incorporation of Hesse-Nassau into the new state of Hessen, the rural districts of Oberwesterwald, Unterlahnkreis, Unterwesterwald, and St. Goarshausen became part of the state of Rhineland-Palatinate in the French occupation zone of Germany. The province of Hesse-Nassau was formed in 1867–68 from various territories, including Hesse-Cassel, the duchy of Nassau, and the free city of Frankfurt am Main, which were won by Prussia in the Seven Weeks' War. A hilly region, with an area of 6502 sq.m., this section of Germany is thickly forested and contains a variety of mineral deposits, notably manganese, coal, iron, and copper.

HESSIAN FLY, a small, mosquitolike, nematocerous fly, *Mayetiola destructor,* of the family Cecidomyiidae. In the larval state it is more destructive to wheat in the U.S. than any other insect pest, and also damages rye and barley crops. Annual loss due to the ravages of the Hessian fly amounts to about $50,000,-000. The fly first appeared in the U.S. in Long Island toward the end of the 18th century. It takes its common name from the belief held by Americans at that time that it was imported in the bedding straw sent to the Hessian mercenary troops from their native land. At present the Hessian fly is widely distributed in the wheat-growing regions of the U.S., and is also found in Canada, Europe, N. Africa, w. Asia, and New Zealand.

Two, or occasionally three, generations of Hessian flies appear yearly. The adult first appears in March in the Southern States, in May in Michigan. It is about 1/10 in. long, dark brown to black, with long, beaded antennae and sparsely veined wings. The female lays its cylindrical, pink eggs, about 1/50 in. in length, on the leaves of wheat plants. The adult flies live from several days to a fortnight, their life being longest in warm, humid weather. The eggs hatch in about three weeks, and the pink larvae, which turn white in three or four days, move down the plant to the roots or to the space between the leaf base and the stem. They then bore into the stem and suck the sap, weakening the plant until the upper portions break off. The larvae, which grow to about ¼ in., pupate toward the end of June or beginning of July; the larval skin hardens, turns brown, and encloses the developing insect in a shell similar in appearance to the outer coat of a flaxseed, whence the common term "flaxseed stage" for the pupal period. The new adults emerge in late August or early September, mate, and lay their eggs. The larva of this generation usually pupates in late October and remains in the "flaxseed stage" till the following spring, but occasionally, during a mild winter, it continues to develop and produces a third generation.

HESSONITE. See GARNET.

HESTIA, in Greek mythology, the goddess of the hearth. She was the eldest daughter of the Titan Cronus, and of Rhea, daughter of Uranus (heaven). Hestia was wooed by Poseidon, god of the sea, and by Apollo, the divinity of music, poetry, and oracular wisdom. To escape their suit she vowed eternal virginity, upon which Zeus, father of the gods, selected her to preside at all sacrificial altar fires. Though Hestia did not figure prominently in legend, her cult was widely diffused throughout Greece. Every community had its common hearth where the sacred fire burned.

HESTON AND ISLEWORTH, municipal borough of Middlesex County, England. The two towns, which form a residential suburb of London and are about 10 m. by rail distant from that city, were united in 1927 and created a municipal borough in 1932. Both are market-gardening centers. Isleworth contains breweries and soap works. Pop. (1951 prelim.) 106,636.

HESYCHASTS (Gr. *hesychastes,* "quietist"), a mystic sect of monks which arose in the Eastern Church, especially at Mount Athos, Greece, during the 14th century. The members of the sect held that a hidden divine light lay in the soul. This light they declared to be the energy of God Himself. They sat on the earth in a certain fixed position and contemplated their navels, in the belief that after a time the divine light would be manifested. Belief in the divine light was decreed an article of faith by the Council of 1351; this decision was reaffirmed in 1368, and ever since this belief has been a part of the doctrine of the Greek Orthodox Church.

HETEROCERA. See MOTH.

HETEROGAMY. See GAMETE.

HETEROPTERA. See BUG.

HETEROSPORY. See SPORE.

HEUCHERA, genus of North American perennial herbs belonging to the family Saxifragaceae, named after Johann Heinrich von Heucher, an 18th-century German botanist. Members of the genus are commonly called alumroot because of the astringent properties of their roots. Alumroots have heart-shaped leaves, clusters of small flowers in feathery panicles, and one-celled capsular fruits. The common alumroot, *H. americana,* grows in rocky woodlands of E. United States. It has small, greenish flowers, a five-parted calyx, five petals, five orange-tipped stamens, and a single pistil. Coral-bells, *H. sanguinea,* is the common alumroot of w. United States, and is cultivated in gardens all over the U.S. The bell-shaped flowers have coral-pink sepals in the wild type; cultivated varieties have white, coral, or crimson flowers.

HEVEA, genus of tropical trees belonging to the family Euphorbiaceae, the source of most natural rubber. All the trees of the genus are native to South America, and many are extensively cultivated in tropical regions of South America, S.E. Asia, the East Indies, and central Africa, as a source of rubber. The most widely cultivated species is *H. brasiliensis.* The trees have trifoliate leaves and bear petalless flowers in loose panicles. The fruit is a brown capsule which explodes when ripe, ejecting seeds to distances sometimes exceeding 50 feet. Rubber latex is carried in tubes which entirely encircle the tree beneath and throughout the inner bark layers. See RUBBER.

HEVELIUS, HEWEL, or HÖWELCKE, JOHANNES (1611–87), Polish astronomer, born in Danzig. He studied law at the University of Leiden, and, after traveling about Europe, settled in Danzig in 1634. There he became a brewer and town councilor. His chief interest was astronomy, and in 1641 he began to construct a well-equipped observatory in his house. His studies of the moon's surface and his discovery of the moon's libration in longitude, recorded in *Selenographia* (1647), are said to have laid the foundation for the study of lunar topography. He also observed sunspots, catalogued many stars, discovered four comets, studied the phases of Saturn, and was one of the first to observe the transit of Mercury. Among his writings are *Prodromus Cometicus* (1665), *Cometographia* (1668), *Annus Climactericus* (1685), and *Prodrumus Astronomiæ*, a catalogue of 1564 stars, published posthumously in 1690.

HEVESY, GEORG VON (1885–   ), Hungarian physicist, born in Budapest, and educated at the University of Budapest, the Technical High School in Berlin, and the University of Freiburg. In 1918 he was appointed professor, and in 1920 associate, in the Institute of Theoretical Physics at the University of Copenhagen. While he held this position he was a professor at the University of Freiburg from 1926 to 1930, Baker lecturer at Cornell University from 1930 to 1934, and an associate at the Institute of Theoretical Physics in Copenhagen under Niels Bohr from 1934 to 1944. He was appointed associate professor at the Institute of Research in Organic Chemistry, Stockholm, in 1944. Von Hevesy worked on the separation of isotopes (q.v.) and their use as tracers in chemical and biological research. He made the first application of radioactive tracer methods to biological research in 1923. In 1922 he discovered, with the Dutch physicist Dirk Coster, the element hafnium (q.v.). He was awarded the 1943 Nobel Prize in chemistry for his work in radioactivity. He is the author of *Manual of Radioactivity* (2nd ed. 1932), *Selten Erden und Atombau* (1927), *Chemical Analysis with X-Rays and Its Application* (1931), and *Radioactive Indicators* (1948).

HEWES, JOSEPH (1730–79), American Revolutionary leader, born in Kingston, N.J., and educated at Princeton College. In 1763 he moved to Edenton, N.C., and in the same year was elected to the North Carolina legislature. In 1774 he was elected to the Continental Congress, and with the exception of a brief period when he declined to serve, held office until his death. He was one of the signers of the Declaration of Independence.

HEWITT, ABRAM STEVENS (1822–1903), American industrialist and political leader, born in Haverstraw, N.Y., and educated at Columbia College. After teaching mathematics at Columbia in 1843, he studied law, and was admitted to the bar in 1844. Defective eyesight prevented him from practicing law, and

with a college classmate he organized a firm manufacturing iron girders and beams. Hewitt brought from England a process for making gun-barrel iron which he made available to the U.S. without profit during the Civil War. In 1871 he first became prominent in public affairs as a leader in the reform group in Tammany Hall (q.v.) during its reorganization. From that year until his death he was a leader in the movement for national and municipal reform. From 1875 to 1879, and again from 1881 to 1886, he was a member of the House of Representatives. In 1886 Hewitt was elected mayor of New York City, defeating Henry George and Theodore Roosevelt (qq.v.). His subsequent break with Tammany Hall cost him a renomination to this office, and his independent campaign for re-election in 1888 met with defeat. Hewitt was also active as a philanthropist; he made liberal donations to, and acted as secretary and trustee of, the Cooper Union for the Advancement of Science and Art (q.v.), which was founded by his father-in-law, Peter Cooper (q.v.).

HEXAPODA. See INSECT.

HEXATEUCH, a term used to describe the first six books of the Bible: Genesis, Exodus, Leviticus, Numbers, Deuteronomy, and Joshua. These books are considered as a literary whole because they describe the history of the Jews from Creation through the reconquest of Palestine. The terms Pentateuch, describing the first five, and Octateuch, describing the first eight books of the Bible, were used in antiquity; Hexateuch is a term coined by modern students of the Scriptures. See BIBLE.

HEYDRICH, REINHARD (1904–42), German fascist official, known as "The Hangman", born in Halle. He entered the German navy in his early youth, and served in the intelligence division until 1931, when he joined the National Socialist Party (see NATIONAL SOCIALISM). Three years later the chief of the Gestapo, Heinrich Himmler (q.v.), appointed Heydrich to the post of deputy chief. Heydrich later became notorious for the ruthless brutality with which he stamped out all opposition to the Nazi regime. He became Reich protector of Bohemia and Moravia in September, 1941, and inaugurated a program of merciless extermination of all dissenting elements. His sanguinary career was ended by assassination in June of the following year; shortly afterward, in reprisal for his death, the Nazis demolished the Czechoslovakian village of Lidice (q.v.) and executed its entire male population.

HEYMANS, Corneille (1892–   ), Belgian physiologist, born in Ghent, Belgium, and educated at the universities of Ghent and Vienna, and at Western Reserve Medical School. Heymans began his career as a physician and lecturer in the early 1920's. In 1930 he was appointed professor of pharmacodynamics at the University of Ghent, and during World War II, from 1940 to 1944, served as head of the medical department of the Belgian Relief Commission. For his studies in the physiology and pharmacology of respiration and circulation, together with his detection of the importance of the sinus aorta mechanism in respiration (q.v.), Heymans was awarded the Nobel Prize in physiology and medicine in 1938. He is the author of *Le Sinus Carotidien* (1933).

HEYSE, Paul von (1830–1914), German novelist, poet, and dramatist, born in Berlin, and educated at the University of Berlin. During a great part of his career he was under the patronage of the Bavarian kings Maximilian II and Ludwig II. Heyse was noted for the realism and structural perfection of his writings. He was particularly known for his novelettes, of which he wrote about 120, many of them in verse. The most famous of his prose novelettes is *L'Arrabiata* (1855); others are *Das Mädchen von Treppi* (1858) and *Der Weinhüter von Meran* (1864). His novels include *Kinder der Welt* (1872). He wrote numerous poems, narrative and lyric, and about sixty plays. He also did translations from English, Spanish, and particularly Italian, literature. Heyse was an opponent of the naturalistic and impressionistic movements in German literature of the last quarter of the 19th century; the counterattacks upon him of members of these schools caused him to lose considerable literary prestige in Germany. In 1910, however, Heyse was awarded the Nobel Prize for literature, the first German writer to obtain this honor.

HEYWARD, DuBose (1885–1940), American writer, born in Charleston, S.C. His native city was the background for several of his colorful novels of the life of Negroes in Southern city slums. In his first novel *Porgy* (1925), he made effective use of the Gullah Negro dialect of South Carolina. He later wrote the novels *Angel* (1926), *Mamba's Daughters* (1929), *Peter Ashley* (1932), *Lost Morning* (1936), and *Star Spangled Virgin* (1939). In collaboration with his wife, Dorothy Heyward, he wrote a dramatization of his novel *Porgy*, which was produced under that name in New York City in 1927 and

won the Pulitzer Prize. This play was the basis for the libretto of the opera *Porgy and Bess* (1935) by the American composer George Gershwin. Also in collaboration with his wife, Heyward dramatized *Mamba's Daughters;* the play bore the same title as the novel and was produced in New York City in 1939. Heyward was also the author of a volume of verse, *Skylines and Horizons* (1924).

HEYWARD, Thomas, Jr. (1746–1809), American political leader, born in St. Luke's Parish, S.C., and educated in his native town and in London, England, where he finished his law studies. From 1775 to 1778 he represented North Carolina in the Continental Congress, and was one of the signers of the Declaration of Independence. He served as circuit court judge in North Carolina from 1779 to 1789. He was a member of the State convention for framing a constitution in 1790, and in the following year retired from public life.

HEYWOOD, John (1497?–1580?), English dramatist and epigrammatist, born probably in North Mimms, Hertfordshire. He was a friend of the statesman Sir Thomas More, through whom he was introduced to the court of King Edward VI and Queen Mary, where he became a favorite: in 1528 he was granted an annual £10 royal pension. Shortly after the accession (1558) of Queen Elizabeth, Heywood left England for Malines, Belgium, where he spent the rest of his life.

Heywood wrote several short dramatic pieces, known as interludes, to be performed at court, including *The Four P's* (printed 1569), *The Play of the Wether* (1533), *The Play of Love* (1533), and *The Dialogue of Wit and Folly*. These interludes are regarded as the precursors of English comedy. Heywood was also the author of the well-known *Epigrammes* (1562), a collection of over 600 epigrams and proverbs. He may also have been the author of the two interludes *The Pardoner and the Frere* and *Johan Johan* (both printed anonymously, 1533). His other works include a number of ballads, among them *Willow Garland,* and a long allegorical poem entitled *The Spider and the Flie* (1556), which represented Roman Catholics as the flies and Protestants as the spiders, with Queen Mary depicted as the maid destroying the spiders.

HEYWOOD, Thomas (1574?–1641), English dramatist and miscellaneous writer, born in Lincolnshire, and educated at Cambridge University. In 1598 he was a member of the lord admiral's company of actors in London, and in 1619 was an actor in the queen's company. By his own testimony he wrote more than 220 plays for the English stage. He exhibited a remarkable talent for quick dramatic construction and for fanciful situations, and was most successful in the writing of domestic dramas. His chief plays include the comedies *The Royal King and the Loyal Subject* (1637), and *The Wise Woman of Hogsdon* (1638); the tragedies *A Woman Killed with Kindness* (1603), *The English Traveller* (1633) and *The Rape of Lucrece* (1608); and the chronicle histories *Edward IV* (2 parts; 1600, 1605) and *The Troubles of Queen Elizabeth* (1605). Heywood was also the author of a series of pageants (1637); several poems, including *Great Britain's Troy* (1609) and *The Hierarchy of the Blessed Angels* (1635); compilations and translations; and *An Apology for Actors* (1612).

HEZEKIAH (Heb. *Hizqīyāh*, "God has strengthened"), **EZECHIAS** or **EZEKIAS** (740?–692? B.C.), King of Judah (720?–692? B.C.), the son and successor of Ahaz (q.v.). During the early part of his reign, Hezekiah waged war successfully on the Philistines (2 Kings 18:8). The most important event of his reign was the invasion of Judah by Sennacherib (q.v.), King of Assyria, about 700 B.C. Hezekiah, allied with the Philistines and the Chaldæans, defied the power of Assyria shortly after Sennacherib became king. The Assyrian ruler completely routed the coalition, re-established the authority of Assyria, and forced Hezekiah to pay a heavy tribute (2 Kings 18:13, 20:12-19). In a second expedition against Judah, about 690 B.C., the Assyrians were routed, before they could attack, by a disaster, described in the Old Testament as a visitation of an angel which destroyed 185,000 men, and by the Greek historian Herodotus as a plague of field mice. Hezekiah is noted as a great religious reformer. He was probably influenced by the Prophet Isaiah, who lived during his reign.

HIALEAH, a city of Dade Co., Fla., situated on the edge of the Everglades, about 8 m. by rail N.W. of Miami. It is one of the important communities in the Miami winter-resort area, and is noted for its horse-racing track, Hialeah Park. Pop. (1950) 19,676.

HIAWATHA, a legendary chieftain of the Iroquois (q.v.) Indians, said to have lived in the 15th century. He is credited with having brought about the union of the Five Nations of the Iroquois for their mutual protection against the aggressive and stronger Algonquin Indians. According to legend, Hiawatha employed miraculous powers to protect his people from the evil forces of nature; he also instructed the Iroquois in the arts of medicine, agriculture, and navigation. The Indian hero was the inspiration for Henry Wadsworth Longfellow's famous poem *Hiawatha* (1855).

HIBBING, a village of St. Louis Co., Minn., situated 75 miles N.W. of Duluth. It is served by two railroads, and maintains a municipal airport. Hibbing lies in the heart of the Arrowhead resort country, noted for its lakes and forests, and is surrounded by the Mesabi Iron Range. The Hibbing district produces approximately 25% of all the iron ore produced in the U.S. Mining operations in the village and surrounding area are chiefly by the open-pit method. Within the village is the largest open-pit mine in the world, 3 m. long, ½ to 1 m. wide, and about 435 ft. in depth. Lumbering, dairying, and poultry raising are additional industries in the region, and the village contains woodworking shops. Iron ore in commercial quantities was first discovered in the vicinity of the present village in 1891. Hibbing was laid out in 1893 and incorporated in the same year. The Duluth, Mesaba and Northern Railroad reached the village in 1894, and the first shipment of iron ore was made in 1895. Pop. (1950) 16,276.

HIBERNATION, the relatively dormant condition resembling sleep in which many animals pass the winter months. The extent of dormancy varies greatly in different hibernating species. For example, the dormouse goes into a profound state of torpor which may last as long as twenty-five weeks, and from which it can be awakened only with difficulty. Its body temperature may drop to 40° F. (4° C.), its metabolic rate drops to about 10% of its normal rate, and its respiration and heartbeat are greatly slowed. However, another hibernator, the hedgehog, often forages for food during comparatively warm nights in midwinter, and females of some species of bears give birth while hibernating. During the winter months hibernating animals live principally on fats stored within their bodies, emerging in spring with only 60% to 70% of the autumn weight.

Among the environmental factors which necessitate hibernation, lack of food is probably more important than cold, especially among the warm-blooded animals. Hibernators are known in almost every group of animals except the birds. Mammals hibernate in recesses offering protection from weather and other animals. Reptiles and certain fish bury themselves in soft, moist earth below the depth of frost penetration. Many insects pass the winter in the pupal stage.

Estivation is a comatose condition similar to hibernation in which many tropical animals pass the hot, dry season during which food or moisture is not available.

HIBERNIA, IVERNA, JUVERNA, or IERNE, names by which Ireland was designated by the classical writers of Greece and Rome. The Greek philosopher Aristotle mentioned two islands in the Atlantic Ocean beyond the Pillars of Hercules which were called "Albion, and Ierne, beyond the Celtæ". The Roman geographer Pomponius Mela stated that the herbage of Hibernia was so luxuriant that the cattle feeding upon it sometimes burst. The most important of all classical writers on Hibernia, however, was Claudius Ptolemæus, an Alexandrian geographer of the 2nd century A.D., who gave a more or less accurate description of the country, including the names of the principal rivers, promontories, seaports, and inland towns.

HIBERNIANS IN AMERICA, ANCIENT ORDER OF, a Roman Catholic fraternal and benevolent society for Americans of Irish birth or descent, founded in 1836 at New York City, and reorganized under the above name in 1851.

The Order was established primarily to support the movement for Irish national independence, and for many years was a principal source of financial support of the Land League of Ireland, one of the constituent organizations in that movement. It sought also to promote the study of the Gaelic language and Gaelic literature in the United States, and endowed chairs in the Gaelic language and in Irish history at the Catholic University of America, Washington, D.C. The Order attained its largest membership during the first decade of the 20th century, when about 150,000 men and 70,000 women were enrolled. During this period, the annual disbursements of the Order for charitable and educational purposes were in excess of $2,600-000, and its annual expenditures for sickness and death benefits exceeded $1,100,000. After the establishment of the Irish Free State in 1922, however, the patriotic aims of the Order were largely fulfilled, and thereafter membership declined rapidly. In a recent year, about 42,000 members were enrolled.

HIBISCUS, genus of plants, commonly called rose mallows, belonging to the Mallow family. The genus is native to warm, temperate regions of the Northern Hemisphere. The hibiscus flower is characterized by a five-pointed calyx which is surrounded by a set of colored bracts growing just beneath it, giving the appearance of a double calyx. The large, showy flowers have five petals, a column of fused stamens with kidney-shaped anthers, and several pistils. The fruit is a many-seeded, five-celled pod.

Shrubs of *Hibiscus* are extensively cultivated throughout civilized countries of the temperate Northern Hemisphere. Rose of Sharon or shrubby althea, *H. syriacus,* is a tall Asiatic shrub with smooth leaves. Cultivated varieties have flowers in colors ranging from white to yellow, rose, red, and purple. The Chinese hibiscus, *H. rosa-sinensis,* a shrub or tree which grows as tall as 30 feet, is the official flower of Hawaii. It produces huge, showy flowers. Chinese hibiscus is cultivated in the U.S.; in northern parts the shrub dies back to the ground each autumn. The musk mallow, *H. abelmoschus,* is an annual herb growing as tall as 6 feet. It bears large yellow flowers with crimson centers, and is widely cultivated in Florida and the West Indies.

Several species of *Hibiscus* grow in the wild state in North America. The swamp rose mallow, *H. moscheutos,* is a tall perennial herb with ovate leaves and rose-colored flowers. It grows along lake shores, river banks, and swamp edges in E. United States. Rose of Sharon frequently escapes from cultivation, forming thickets along roadsides and in wet waste places.

Okra (q.v.) is the fruit of a plant of the closely related genus *Abelmoschus;* it is sometimes considered a species of *Hibiscus.*

HICCUP or **HICCOUGH,** paroxysmal involuntary contraction of the diaphragm (q.v.). The characteristic sound associated with hiccups is caused by contractions of the vocal cords which arrest the flow of air into the pharynx. Mild cases of hiccups last for a few minutes, but severe cases may last for days or, rarely, months. Mild hiccups are commonly induced by slight stomach upsets; severe cases are associated with various postoperative abdominal conditions, organic or functional diseases of the brain and spinal cord, and various mental and toxic disorders. The contraction of the diaphragm which causes hiccups is caused by stimulation of the phrenic nerve by the brain or irritation of the phrenic nerve by any organ which lies along the course of the nerve. Mild cases usually disappear without treatment, but hiccups which last several days are often treated by applying pressure to the phrenic nerve. Stimulation of the autonomic nervous system by inhaling air rich in carbon dioxide sometimes stops an attack of hiccups. Most of the commonly accepted "cures" for hiccups are useless, with the exception of breathing into a paper bag and rebreathing the exhaled air; this treatment causes increased inspiration of carbon dioxide. In excessively prolonged cases, the phrenic nerve is stimulated electrically, or temporarily blocked by anesthesia; if this treatment fails, the nerve is usually severed.

HICKORY, common name for trees of the genus *Carya,* belonging to the Walnut family. The genus comprises about eighteen species native to North America and China. It includes some of the most valuable timber and nut-producing species in the United States. Hickory trees have tough, hard wood and bear large, pinnately compound leaves. Flowers are borne in separate inflorescences on the same tree; male flowers are borne in small catkins and female flowers are borne in clusters of two to five.

The most valuable nut-producing hickory is *C. illinoensis,* the pecan (q.v.). The shagbark, *C. ovata,* produces most of the nuts marketed as "hickory" nuts. It is a tall tree, 65 to 90 feet in height, which grows in E. United States. Shagbark nuts are white, globular, and thin-shelled. Big shellbark or king nut, *C. laciniosa,* which grows 65 to 100 feet tall, is native to N.E. United States. Shellbark nuts are white or yellowish and have thick shells. Mockernut, *C. alba,* which grows 65 to 100 feet tall, is native to E. United States. It bears light-brown nuts which have very thick shells. The pignut (q.v.), *C. glabra,* produces nuts which are palatable when young but bitter when mature. The bitternut or swamp hickory, *C. cordiformis,* is a tall tree, 50 to 95 feet in height, producing white, thin-shelled, bitter nuts. It is native to rich, wet woods throughout temperate North America.

HICKORY SHAD, GIZZARD SHAD, or **MUD SHAD,** common name for any fish in the genus *Dorosoma* of the family Clupeidae. The hickory shad, which is found in both fresh and salt water in eastern and central North America, is characterized by a stomach resembling that of seed-eating birds (see GIZZARD) internally, and looking like a large hickory nut externally. The best-known species is *D. cepedianum,* which is 15 in. long when fully grown.

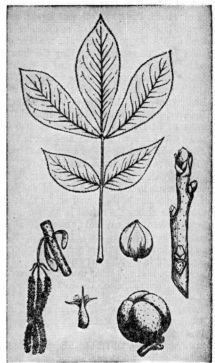

Nature Magazine

Parts of the hickory tree (Carya ovata)

The name hickory shad is also sometimes applied to the fall herring (q.v.).

HICKS, ELIAS (1748–1830), American Quaker minister, born in Hempstead, Long Island, N.Y. He became a well-known preacher by the time he was twenty-seven. His vigorous preaching during his tours of the United States and Canada (after 1775), his attacks against slavery, and his inclination toward Unitarianism in religious doctrine gained him a wide following. In 1827, when the Society of Friends split into conservative and liberal sects, the latter, comprising Hicks' followers, became known as the Hicksites. Hicks was the author of *Observations on Slavery* (1811). His *The Letters of Elias Hicks* was posthumously published in 1834. See FRIENDS, SOCIETY OF.

HICKS, WILLIAM, known as HICKS PASHA (1830–83), British soldier in the Egyptian army, commander in chief of Egyptian forces during the insurrection of the Mahdists (see MAHDI) in 1883. Hicks served in the British army in India from 1849 to 1880, when he retired from the service with the honorary rank of colonel. In 1882 he entered the service of Tewfik Pasha, Khedive of Egypt, and a year later was appointed commander in chief of the Egyptian army in the Sudan. Hicks was charged with quelling the insurrection led by Mohammed Ahmed, a Moslem fanatic who claimed to be the Messiah. The British commander won what seemed a decisive victory near Khartoum in April, 1883. However, in November, when he crossed the desert of El Obeid with a force of 10,000, Hicks was betrayed into an ambuscade and killed, and almost his entire army massacred.

HICKSITES. See HICKS, ELIAS.

HIDALGO, a state of central Mexico. It is mountainous in the N. and E., and consists of rolling plains in the s. and w. Its mineral regions are among the richest in Mexico, producing silver, copper, gold, mercury, zinc, lead, antimony, manganese, iron, coal, and marble. Among the important agricultural crops raised in Hidalgo are cereal grains, coffee, cotton, maguey, sugar cane, and tobacco. The chief towns include the capital Pachuca (q.v.), Mineral del Monce (pop. in 1940, 13,536), Tulancingo (12,552), and Tula (3386). Area of the state, 7056 sq.m.; pop. (1950) 850,394.

HIDALGO Y COSTILLA, MIGUEL (1753–1811), Mexican priest and revolutionist, born in Corralejos, and educated at Valladolid. In 1779 he was ordained a priest and was given charge of the parish of Dolores, in Guanajuato. During the next thirty years he was known as a pious churchman who worked to improve the economic condition of his poor parishioners, mostly Indians. In 1809 Hidalgo joined one of the patriotic societies which were nominally established to promote Mexican loyalty to the Spanish crown during Napoleon I's invasion of Spain. The society was, however, secretly dedicated to freeing Mexico from the oppression of the Spanish colonial government. On Sept. 16, 1810, Hidalgo led hundreds of his parishioners in a successful attack on the prison of Dolores. Carrying a banner depicting Our Lady of Guadalupe, patron saint of Mexico, the priest proclaimed a crusade and was joined by thousands of Mexican natives. He captured the towns of Guanajuato and Guadalajara and with an army of 80,000 marched on Mexico City. The rebels won the first battle for the city, but Hidalgo's excommunication and the dissension in the rebel army disrupted the insurgent forces, which were forced to retreat. The priest took his last stand near Guadalajara in Jan., 1811, where his army was com-

pletely routed by a small force of Spanish soldiers. Hidalgo fled north, but he was captured and shot. After the establishment of the Mexican republic, in 1824, the priest was regarded almost as a saint. The town of Guadalupe Hidalgo was named for him, and the town of Dolores became Dolores Hidalgo. The day on which he proclaimed his revolt (Sept. 16) is celebrated as the Mexican Independence Day. See MEXICO: *History*.

HIDDENITE. See SPODUMENE.

HIERATIC WRITING. See HIEROGLYPHICS.

HIERO or **HIERON,** the name of two rulers of Syracuse. **1.** HIERO I (d. 466 B.C.), Tyrant from 478 to 466 B.C., successor to his brother Gelon (q.v.). Hiero, known for his military craft, had, before his accession to power, distinguished himself at the battle of Himera (q.v.) in 480 B.C. The victory of his fleet over the Etruscans at Cumæ, on the Italian coast, in 474 B.C., preserved the independence of the Greek colonists in Italy. Hiero made Syracuse the greatest city in Sicily. He relocated entire cities and about 475 B.C. founded the city of Ætna. In 472 B.C. the Syracusan army defeated Thrasydæus, Tyrant of Æragas (modern Agrigento), and Hiero became supreme ruler of the island. The tyrant was known as a cruel ruler, but he was noted for his patronage of poets and philosophers, including such great writers as Pindar and Æschylus.

2. HIERO II (about 308–215 B.C.), King from 270 to 215 B.C., the illegitimate son of Hierocles, a Syracusan noble. He fought under Pyrrhus (q.v.), King of Epirus, against the Roman invaders of Sicily (278–75 B.C.), and after the departure of Pyrrhus in 275 B.C. was chosen commander of the Syracusan army. Hiero's military successes against the Italian mercenary troops, the Mamertines, resulted, in 270 B.C., in his election as king by the grateful citizens of Syracuse. In 264 B.C. Hiero allied himself with the Carthaginians in besieging the Mamertines at Messana (Messina), but the Romans, supporting the Mamertines, defeated the Syracusan army. A year later Hiero concluded a treaty with Rome, and he remained a Roman ally thereafter. During the first and second Punic Wars between Rome and Carthage, Hiero assisted his allies with money and troops and was awarded great honors by the Romans. The Syracusan king was known as a wise and just ruler. He employed his relative, Archimedes (q.v.), to construct powerful war engines which, in 214 B.C., almost frustrated the Roman siege of Syracuse (q.v.).

HIEROGLYPHICS, characters in a system of writing which consist of representations of objects rather than purely conventional signs. The term is also applied to the system of writing using such characters, and especially to the writing of the ancient Egyptians and of the early Indians of Mexico (see MAYAS). The writings of other North American Indians were pictorial, but did not amount to a hieroglyphic system; the writings of ancient Babylonia (see CUNEIFORM) and China (see CHINESE LANGUAGE AND LITERATURE) were originally picture writings, but at an early date they were simplified and conventionalized to the extent of losing their hieroglyphic character.

The hieroglyphic writing of ancient Egypt was already well developed at the time of Menes (about 3400 B.C.), the first historical king of Egypt. It consisted of *pictograms,* signs representing objects or associated ideas, and *phonoglyphs,* signs representing the sounds of the words for the object depicted. In the Egyptian language, as in other North African and Near East tongues, the essential meaning of a word was represented by its root, the consonant framework stripped of prefixes, suffixes, and vowels. Thus the hieroglyph for ear, representing the root *sdm,* was used not only for "hear" and "hearing", but also for "to paint the eyes", with the root *śdm.* In order to specify the meaning intended, which was not always clear from the context, the symbols for each word included one or more *determinatives;* thus the hieroglyph for man acted as a determinative to indicate that the hieroglyph associated with it represented a man's name; a book (a roll of papyrus) was the determinative signifying that an abstract meaning was intended, and a book with an ear represented "hearing". Other common determinatives included those for motion, force, buildings, inhabited places, and foreign countries.

Two forms of hieroglyphic writing were in common use, the *epigraphic,* or *monumental,* hieroglyphics, which were carved or painted on stone or wood with precise detail, and the *hieratic,* or cursive, form, written on papyrus with a blunt reed pen. Monumental hieroglyphics were carved in vertical columns read from top to bottom, or in horizontal lines, from right to left. Occasionally, only on balanced tablets flanking a central figure, one tablet contained hieroglyphics carved from right to left, and the other from left to right. The hieratic form, conventionally inscribed from right to left, was in use as early

Hieroglyphics on an ancient Egyptian tablet

as the first dynasty, and had become common by 2500 B.C. Although it was intended as a precise transcription of hieroglyphics sign by sign, it was gradually modified until in time little resemblance remained. About the 6th century B.C. another form of script, the *demotic,* came into common use, and the hieratic, previously used for all purposes, was restricted to the transcription of religious writings. Demotic was a more cursive and conventionalized development from the hieratic script, and, like the other forms of hieroglyphics, was written from right to left. It remained in use until the 5th century A.D. After that time knowledge of hieroglyphic writing was lost, and was not rediscovered until the decipherment of the Rosetta Stone (q.v.) in the 19th century; see EGYPTIAN ARCHEOLOGY; EGYPTIAN LANGUAGE AND LITERATURE.

HIERONYMITES, the name of any of several associations of hermits in Spain and Italy deriving their name from St. Jerome (q.v.), whom they regarded as their patron and example. All of these groups lived according to an Augustinian discipline with supplementary rules taken from the writings of St. Jerome.

The most important group was organized from the Tertiaries or third order of Franciscans (q.v.), and established themselves about the beginning of the 14th century in the mountains near Toledo, Spain. In 1374 they obtained the approval of Pope Gregory XI to form communities and build monasteries, and by 1415 had constructed twenty-five cloisters containing some of the most famous monasteries on the Iberian peninsula, including a royal monastery in the Escorial (q.v.) built by Philip II, and one near Lisbon which became the burial place of the Portuguese royal family. A female branch of the order was founded by Maria Gracias (died 1426). At its height this group exercised great influence at both the Spanish and Portuguese courts, but it began to fall into decay after the 15th century, and was eventually suppressed by the Vatican.

HIERONYMUS, Saint Eusebius. See Jerome, Saint.

HIGGINSON, Thomas Wentworth (1823–1911), American clergyman, author, and soldier, born in Cambridge, Mass., and educated at Harvard College and the Harvard Divinity School. From 1847 to 1850 he was a Unitarian pastor in Newburyport, Mass., but in the latter year, moved by intense abolitionist conviction, he resigned his pastorate to run unsuccessfully for Congress. After holding another pastorate in Worcester, Mass., from 1852 to 1858, he abandoned the ministry to take up antislavery agitation, especially in Kansas. At the outbreak of the Civil War, Higginson enlisted as a captain in a regiment of Massachusetts volunteers; from 1862 to 1864, when he was discharged because of a wound received in 1863, he served as colonel in command of the first regiment of freed slaves to fight for the Union. At the close of the war he turned to literature, distinguishing himself as a prolific man of letters and an advocate of the political rights of women. Among his numerous works are *Army Life in a Black Regiment* (1870), *Women and Men* (1887), *Henry Wadsworth Longfellow* (1902), and *John Greenleaf Whittier* (1902).

HIGH COMMISSION, COURT OF, in the former judicial system of England, an ecclesiastical tribunal established to punish heresy, schism, and other offenses against the peace and dignity of the church; see Ecclesiastical Courts. It was created in 1559 in the reign of Queen Elizabeth; in the following years it became an instrument of oppression of opponents of the Established Church, particularly of the Puritans. The Court of High Commission was abolished by Parliament in 1641, was re-established by King James II in 1686, and was finally abolished three years later following the outbreak of the Glorious Revolution (q.v.).

HIGHHOLE. See Flicker.

HIGHLANDERS, various regiments of the British army, originally recruited in the Highlands (q.v.) of Scotland, with dress uniforms which include the traditional Scots tam-o-shanters and kilts. Among the most famous of the Highland regiments are the Royal Highlanders, founded in 1729, commonly called the Black Watch (q.v.) because of the dark tartan they wear, and the Gordan Highlanders, founded in 1796 by the Duke of Gordon.

HIGHLAND FLING, a folk dance of Scotland, danced particularly by natives of the Scottish Highlands. Three or four persons take part in the dance, which is performed to the same music as that used for the Scottish dance known as the strathspey. The expression "fling" comes from the characteristic step of the Highland fling. The participant places one hand on his hip and holds the other elevated above his head, the hand curving downward. He hops alternately on each leg, beginning with the one opposite the elevated hand; as he hops he touches the ground with the toe of the free leg, then brings the free foot up and flings it first around the front of the opposite knee and then around the back. When he hops on the other leg, he alternates the position of his hands, placing upon the hip the one that was elevated, and elevating the other hand.

HIGHLAND PARK, a city of Wayne Co., Mich., completely surrounded by Detroit. It is a manufacturing center, and a residential suburb of Detroit. The principal industries are the manufacture of automobiles, boats, tools, and candy. Highland Park was incorporated in 1918. Pop. (1950) 46,393.

HIGHLANDS, the designation for the mountainous portion of Scotland extending N. and W. of the Grampians (q.v.). The region has no political or civil boundary, and is separated by only a vague line of demarcation from the division called the Lowlands. The people of the Highlands maintained a substantial independence from those of the Lowlands for many centuries, based on ethnological, linguistic, and cultural differences. From the Stone Age until the 11th century A.D. the Highlands were penetrated by continuous Scandinavian invasions which left a permanent effect upon the racial composition of

British Information Services

Dancing the traditional Highland fling in a contest at Ballater, Aberdeenshire, Scotland

the people of the region. The persistence of the Gaelic language among the Highlanders served to isolate them further from other Scotsmen. They have long been popular subjects for poets and writers of fiction, being most memorably treated in the poems and novels of Sir Walter Scott (q.v.). The city of Inverness (q.v.) is customarily considered to be the capital of the Highlands.

HIGH POINT, a city of Guilford Co., N.C., situated in the Piedmont region, 19 miles S.E. of Winston-Salem and 99 miles N.W. of Raleigh. It is served by three railroads, and by major air lines at the Greensboro-High Point airport. High Point is called the "Furniture and Hosiery Capital of the South". The city contains about ninety furniture factories, manufacturing all varieties of wooden household furniture, and over thirty hosiery mills. Among other industrial products are overalls, shirts, men's clothing, mattresses, box springs, pillows, veneers, plywoods, art glass, glass furniture and novelties, mirrors, paints, enamels, varnishes, building materials, toys, paper boxes, dyes, chemicals, embossed labels and seals, yarns, textiles, and weaving and knitting equipment. The city is the site of the semiannual Southern Furniture Exposition. High Point College (Methodist), in the city, was established in 1924. Notable buildings include the Southern Furniture Exposition

Building, in which a permanent furniture exhibit is maintained, and the Springfield Quaker Meeting House, containing a historical collection.

High Point was settled in 1853 and received its name as a result of being the highest point on the original survey for the old North Carolina Railroad between Goldsboro and Charlotte. It was incorporated in 1859, and the first furniture factory was established there in 1888, marking the beginning of the city's industrial growth. Pop. (1950) 39,973.

HIGH PRIEST, in a religious hierarchy, the head of a priesthood. The term is particularly used to connote the head of the Jewish priesthood in ancient Israel. Until about the 6th century B.C., the Jews had no central religious authority. After the second Temple was built, in 516 B.C., the chief priest of Jerusalem came to be considered the head of the theocracy and the official representative of the nation, then under Persian domination. During this period, the Pentateuch, the Law of Moses, was revised to make the office of high priest a hereditary dignity of the family of Moses, through the patriarch's brother Aaron. The office is recorded as having descended to Aaron's third son, Eleazar, and thenceforward in the line of Eleazar (Ex. 28). The priesthood was kept in the family of Aaron until the subjugation of Israel by the Greeks and, later, by the Romans, when foreign rulers began to confer the office as they pleased.

The regulations for the office are set down in Lev. 8, 9, and 21. The high priest was permitted to marry only a virgin of his own tribe, and he was forbidden any impure contact that might defile him. His functions consisted principally of the administration of the Temple and the Jewish religion. Only he could enter, once a year on the Day of Atonement, the Holy of Holies, where the sacred Ark was kept, and there consult the Urim and Thummim (q.v.). He wore a costume of great splendor, except when he entered the Holy of Holies, at which time he wore a simple white robe. He proclaimed divine revelations, he alone being permitted to consult God directly. Though he had no official judicial power, appeal to him could be made in any matter, and no important decision affecting national policy could be taken without his consent.

The Roman religion also required a high priest, who was called the Pontifex Maximus. In Mormonism, all the priests of the Melchizedek priesthood are called high priests (see MORMONS).

HIGH RELIEF. See RELIEF.

HIGH SCHOOL. See EDUCATION, NATIONAL SYSTEMS OF: *United States;* EDUCATION, SECONDARY.

HIGH SEAS, in international law, the open sea, including the whole extent of the sea not the exclusive property of any particular country. The rule of international law is that every country bordering on the sea has exclusive sovereignty over that sea for a distance of 3 m. from its shores; and that all the sea beyond, up to a distance of 3 m. from the shores of other countries, is open or common to all countries. The Supreme Court of the United States has held the term "high seas" to apply to the waters of the Great Lakes beyond a distance of 3 m. from the shores of the United States and Canada.

Within the territorial limits of 3 m. the courts of the nations contiguous to the sea have jurisdiction; beyond the three-mile limit international law prevails. A number of treaties with other countries, negotiated by the United States during the Prohibition (q.v.) era of the 1920's, gave the United States the right to board vessels, suspected of transporting intoxicating liquors illegally, outside the three-mile limit as far as 12 m. from the shores of the United States.

HIGH TREASON. See TREASON.

HILARION, SAINT (about 290–371), Palestinian monk and hermit, born in Tabatha, near Gaza, and educated in Alexandria, where he became a convert to Christianity. He visited St. Anthony in the Egyptian desert, and on his return to Palestine in 307, Hilarion became the first monk and hermit in that country. He lived as an anchorite in the desert marshes near Gaza for many years and attracted many disciples by his piety and the miraculous cures attributed to him. In order once more to achieve solitude Hilarion went to Egypt in 356, but his retreat was discovered by his followers. Again he set out in search of solitude, traveling first to Sicily, then to Epidaurus in Dalmatia, and finally to Cyprus, where he died. His feast is celebrated in the Roman Catholic Church on October 21.

HILARY, SAINT (d. about 367), Christian prelate and Doctor of the Church, born in Poitiers. Of pagan parentage, Hilary was a convert to Christianity. About 353 he was unanimously elected bishop of Poitiers, and immediately began a rigorous suppression of the heresy of Arianism (see ARIUS) in his diocese. In 356 Hilary's Arian opponents secured his banishment to Phrygia, but even in exile he retained control of his diocese. In 359 he attended the synod of Seleucia, where he delivered a scholarly and vigorous defense of orthodoxy. He returned to Poitiers in 361, and continued until his death to attack the theories of the Arian heretics. Among his writings on this controversy are the epistles *De Synodis* or *De Fide Orientalium* (358) and *De Trinitate,* both written during his exile, and the *Contra Arianos vel Auxentium Mediolanensem Liber.* His feast is celebrated Jan. 14.

HILDA or **HILD,** SAINT (614–80), English abbess, born in Northumbria. Converted to Christianity by St. Paulinus, she became the abbess of Hartlepool in 649 or 650, and in 657 she founded the monastery and convent of Whitby, over which she ruled until her death. During her rule the abbey of Whitby was a gathering place for important ecclesiastics and scholars; the poet Caedmon was a resident of the monastery, which was the site of an important synod in 664.

HILDEBRAND, name of Pope Gregory VII (see GREGORY).

HILDEBRAND, ADOLF VON (1847–1921), German sculptor, born in Marburg. He studied art in Nuremberg, Munich, and Berlin, and from 1874 to 1892 had a studio in Florence. His work is characterized by realism and also the repose and balance of classic form. Among his works are the statue "Young Man" (National Gallery, Berlin); monumental works, including an equestrian statue of Bismarck (Bremen), the Wittelsbach Fountain (Munich), a fountain at Strasbourg with the statue "Father Rhine", a monument to Brahms (Meiningen); and portrait busts, including those of Clara Schumann and Arnold Böcklin. Hildebrand was the author of *Das Problem der Form* (1893), an analysis of the optical laws governing the representation of form, which has widely influenced art theorists and critics.

HILDEGARD, SAINT (about 1098–1179), German abbess, born in Böckelhelm, and educated at the Benedictine convent of Disibodenberg. She became abbess of Disibodenberg in 1136, and later founded the convent of Rupertsberg, near Bingen. St. Hildegard is renowned for her mystical experiences, which were recorded between 1141 and 1150 by her friend the monk Godefridus and were first published in 1513 under the title *Scivias*.

HILDESHEIM, town in Lower Saxony, West Germany, on the Innerste R., at the base of the Harz Mts. and 18 m. by rail S.E. of Hanover. In 822 it became the seat of a bishopric and in the early 11th century the town was walled by one of its bishops, St. Bernward. After becoming a free city of the Holy Roman Empire in the 13th century, Hildesheim was accorded municipal rights (1249) and in that same period entered the Hanseatic League (q.v.). In succeeding years the bishops of the town enlarged its territory by warfare. The bishopric of Hildesheim was secularized in 1801 and twelve years later incorporated within the kingdom of Hanover. The Roman Catholic cathedral and the church of St. Michael date from the 11th century and the church of St. Godehard from the 12th. Among the important municipal buildings are the *Rathaus,* or town hall, and the *Knochenhaueramthaus,* which formerly served as the butchers' guildhall. Many of the houses, with high gables and overhanging upper stories, were built in the Middle Ages. Present-day Hildesheim is chiefly industrial, manufacturing agricultural tools, bricks, paper, stoves, machines, cigars, textiles, and beer, and processing foodstuffs, sugar, and leather. The town is an episcopal see. Following World War II it was included in the British Zone of Occupation. Pop., about 72,000.

HILDRETH, RICHARD (1807–65), American journalist and historian, born in Deerfield.

Mass., and educated at Harvard College. After reading in law at Newburyport, he established himself as a lawyer in Boston, but he gave up his practice in 1832 to edit the *Boston Atlas.* Hildreth vigorously supported and influenced the movement for the separation of Texas from Mexico, which gave rise to the Mexican War (1846–48), and became a prominent abolitionist. He left the *Boston Atlas* in 1840 to devote himself to writing and for a time (1840–43) lived in British Guiana, where he edited two newspapers. From about 1857 to 1860 he was a member of the staff of the New York *Tribune.* After the inauguration of Abraham Lincoln in 1861, Hildreth was appointed U.S. consul at Trieste, Italy. His greatest work is *History of the United States* (6 vols., 1849–56), an account of American history from 1492 to 1821. Other works include *The Slave* (1834), a famous anti-slavery novel; *Despotism in America* (1840), a study of slavery; and *A Theory of Politics* (1853).

HILL, AMBROSE POWELL (1825–65), American soldier, born in Culpeper Co., Va., and educated at the U.S. Military Academy at West Point. He served in the Mexican and Seminole wars, and from 1855 to 1860 with the U.S. Coast Survey. In 1861, just prior to the outbreak of the Civil War, Hill resigned from the army to become a colonel in the Confederate service. He fought with distinction in many major campaigns and in 1863 he was made a lieutenant general, commanding a corps of Lee's army; in that year his troops led the attack which began the Battle of Gettysburg. Hill was killed in action during the fighting around Petersburg.

HILL, ARCHIBALD (1886–   ), English physiologist, born in Bristol, and educated at Trinity College, Cambridge University. From 1920 to 1923 he was professor of physiology at the University of Manchester, and from 1923 to 1925 he held the same position at University College, London. From 1926 to 1951 he served as research professor of the Royal Society and as secretary of the Royal Society from 1935 to 1945. Hill contributed valuable research in physiology and biophysics; for his work on the production of lactic acid associated with the expenditure of energy in muscular activity, he shared the 1922 Nobel Prize in physiology and medicine with Otto Meyerhof (q.v.).

HILL, DAVID JAYNE (1850–1932), American educator and diplomat, born in Plainfield, N.J., and educated at the University of Lewisburg (now Bucknell University). He taught classics and rhetoric at this university, and was afterward president of the university from 1879 to 1888. From 1888 to 1896 he was president of the University of Rochester, and from 1898 to 1903 he was assistant secretary of state. During part of his stay in Washington he was professor of European diplomacy in the School of Comparative Jurisprudence and Diplomacy there. Subsequently Hill served as U.S. minister to Switzerland from 1903 to 1905, to the Netherlands from 1905 to 1908, and to Germany from 1908 to 1911. His writings include *World Organization as Affected by the Nature of the Modern State* (1911), *A History of Diplomacy in the International Development of Europe* (3 vols., 1905–14), and *The Problem of a World Court* (1927).

HILL, JAMES JEROME (1838–1916), American railway executive and financier, born near Guelph, Ontario. He left his home as a youth for a business career in Minnesota, and in 1870 organized a group of river steamboat lines which were the first to open up communication between St. Paul and Winnipeg. Eight years later he helped to form the syndicate which ultimately built the Canadian Pacific Railway. In subsequent operations Hill secured control of the St. Paul, Minneapolis, and Manitoba Railroad, rising in the years between 1879 and 1890 from the post of general manager to that of president. In the latter year his line became a part of the Great Northern System of railroads and steamship lines, and from 1888 to 1893 Hill figured as the principal promoter of the Great Northern's growth. He was president of the system from 1889 to 1907, and chairman of its board of directors from 1907 to 1912. His far-flung operations, which eventually included not only railroads and shipping lines but stock-exchange manipulations, mining, and banking, caused him to become known as the "Empire Builder".

HILLARY, SIR EDMOND P. (1919–), New Zealand apiarist and mountain climber, born in Auckland, and educated at Auckland Grammar School. During World War II he served in the New Zealand air force. An experienced skier and mountaineer, he participated in expeditions to the Himalaya in 1951 and 1952. He joined the British Mt. Everest Expedition of 1953 as one of the chief climbers. Together with the Nepalese Sherpa mountain climber Tensing Norkay, he reached the summit on May 29, 1953. Hillary was later knighted by Queen Elizabeth II of Great Britain for his achievement.

HILLEL (fl. 30 B.C.–9 A.D.), Jewish rabbi and teacher, the first scholar to systematize the interpretation and explanation of Scriptural law. According to the Talmud, Hillel was born in Babylonia and, when he was about forty years of age, migrated to Palestine in order to study Scriptural law at the Jerusalem schools. In time, he became a leading authority on the law and, about 30 B.C., was elected president of the Sanhedrin, the supreme council of the Jews. The school of Scriptural interpretation founded by Hillel supported a liberal view of the law, in opposition to the rigid views held by the school of Shammai (q.v.), another great scholar of the day. The conflict between the two schools endured for about a century after Hillel's death and was finally decided in favor of Hillel by Gamaliel (q.v.) of Jabneh. Hillel is reputed to have exercised a great influence on Jesus, many of whose sayings are very similar to the teachings of the great rabbi.

HILLMAN, SIDNEY (1887–1946), American labor leader, born in Zagare, Lithuania. He came to the United States at the age of twenty, and became a labor-union organizer in the men's clothing industry. He was elected president of the Amalgamated Clothing Workers of America in 1915, and led the strikes which resulted in the establishment of the 48-hour week in New York City in 1916 and the 44-hour week in 1919. Subsequently, he attained nationwide prominence as a leader of the American Federation of Labor (q.v.). In 1935 he was one of the leaders of the group of unions which disaffiliated from the AFL to form the Congress of Industrial Organizations (q.v.). He later became a vice-president of the CIO, and in 1939 was elected chairman of the executive council of the Textile Workers' Union of America. In 1941 President Roosevelt appointed him codirector, with William S. Knudsen, of the Office of Production Management. A year later, when that agency was superseded by the War Production Board, Hillman became director of the Labor Division of the latter agency.

HILLQUIT, MORRIS (1869–1933), American lawyer and socialist leader, born in Riga, Latvia. He came to the United States in 1886, and was educated at the New York University Law School. He joined the Socialist Party in 1888, and in 1897 was the leader of a group of right-wing members who opposed the radical leadership of the party, and who broke away to form the Social Democratic Party (the present Socialist Party). Hillquit became chairman of the national executive committee, and represented the party at seven successive congresses of the Socialist International. He was a leading pacifist during World War I, and was Socialist candidate for the mayoralty of New York City in 1917 and 1932. His writings include *History of Socialism in the United States* (1903), *Socialism in Theory and Practice* (1909), *Socialism Summed Up* (1912), and *From Marx to Lenin* (1921).

HILO, seaport and county seat of Hawaii Co., situated on the N.E. coast of Hawaii Island, Territory of Hawaii. Its harbor, a crescent-shaped bay, is one of the best in the Territory. The tropical forests surrounding the city and the volcanoes of Mauna Loa and Mauna Kea rising up behind Hilo add to the beauty of the city, which is an important tourist center. The canning of pineapples is the principal industry; canned pineapple, sugar, and coffee are exported. Pop. (1950) 27,198.

HILTON, JAMES (1900–1954), English author, born in Leigh, Lancashire, and educated at Cambridge University. He wrote a number of very popular novels, including *And Now Goodbye* (1931), *Lost Horizon* (1933; motion-picture version, 1937), *Goodbye, Mr. Chips* (1934; motion picture, 1939), *Random Harvest* (1941; motion picture, 1942), *The Story of Dr. Wassell* (1944), *So Well Remembered* (1946), *Morning Journey* (1951), and *Time and Time Again* (1953).

HILVERSUM, city of North Holland Province, the Netherlands, located on the Zuider Zee, 18 m. by rail S.E. of Amsterdam. It is a residential suburb and a summer resort. Several radio-broadcasting stations are situated in the city. Among the important manufactured products of Hilversum are carpets and woolens. Pop. (1953 est.) 91,967.

HIMALAYA, usually, although less correctly, called THE HIMALAYAS (Skt. *hima,* "snow"; *alaya,* "abode"), a mountain system containing the highest peaks in the world, and consisting of several parallel and converging ranges in south central Asia. The mass of the Himalaya proper extends S.E. and E. from the Indus River to the Brahmaputra River, a distance of about 1500 m. On the north it descends to the elevated plateau of Tibet; on the south to the lowland drained by the Ganges and the Indus rivers; its average width is about 100 to 150 m. The mean elevation of the range is from 16,000 to 18,000 feet above sea level, but many peaks are known which are more than 25,000 feet above sea level. Among them are Nanda Devi in Ku-

maun, Annapurna, Dhaulagiri, and Everest in Nepal, Godwin-Austen in Kashmir, and Kinchinjunga on the borders of Sikkim and Nepal; see individual articles on these mountains.

The Himalayan mountain system is divided into three parallel zones extending the entire length of the system from west to east. They are the *Great Himalayas* in the north, which include the main ranges and highest peaks, and rise above the snow line to an average elevation of about 20,000 ft.; the *Lesser Himalayas* to the south, which comprise the intricate middle ranges of the chain, at an average elevation of about 12,000 to 15,000 ft.; and the *Outer Himalayas,* which lie between the Lesser Himalayas and the plains at an average height of 3000 to 4000 ft. At the south base of the Outer Himalayas three distinct regions separate the true mountains from the plains of Hindustan. They are the *Dhuns,* a belt of detritus; *Saul Wood,* a wooded belt stretching along a great part of the range; and the *Terai,* a swampy lowland belt north of the Ganges river.

Occasional snowfalls occur in the mountains at elevations as low as 2500 ft. above sea level, and snow falls every winter at elevations over 6000 ft. The snow line in the Great Himalayas lies at about 16,200 ft. on the southern face of the range, and at about 17,400 ft. on the northern (the difference in these altitudes being due to the dry atmosphere of Tibet). The high main range of the Himalaya forms a vast screen, which intercepts and condenses nearly all the moisture carried by the southwest monsoons which blow from the Indian Ocean from May to October; this moisture is deposited on the southern face of the mountains. At Cherra Punji (q.v.), for example, which is about 4200 ft. above sea level, the mean annual rainfall is about 430 in., and over 900 in. were registered in 1861. The rainfall varies, however, at different stations and altitudes, with a low point of about 30 in. per year in the region where the Indus issues from the mountains. In Tibet, on the other hand, an arid zone exists beyond the northern barrier of the range in which the average rainfall is for the most part well below 10 in. per year.

The altitude of the Himalaya also affects temperature. The climate of the southern side varies from subtropical at the base and in valleys, through temperate at a height of about 7000 ft. (the height of most of the Himalayan hill stations), to frigid at about 12,000 to 15,000 ft.; above the snow line, frost and intense cold are found the year round. In Tibet, conditions quite different from those of the

Canadian Pacific Railway

Ice-capped peaks in the Himalaya mountains

southern side prevail: even at 15,000 ft. frost is permanent only from November to May, while at 12,000 ft. the temperature rises in the summer months to a mean of about 60° F. The daily range of Tibetan temperature is very wide; differences of 50° or even 60° are not uncommon, and the temperatures of the dry surface soil vary even more widely.

Glaciers are found in every part of the Himalayan system above the snow line. Though for the most part they appear to be in retreat, some glaciers in the Kinchinjunga group reach down to about 13,000 ft. and some in Kumaun to about 12,000 ft., while a few isolated glaciers in Kashmir reach as low as 8000 ft. A number of the glaciers are as long as fifteen miles, and a few have been mapped which are thirty miles and longer. The passes through the Himalaya, which often lie along or across these glaciers, are the highest in the world; their average height is about 10,000 ft. The highest known, the Ibi-Gamin pass into Garhwal, is 20,457 ft. above sea level, and the highest pass used for traffic is the Parang pass in Spiti (18,000 ft.). All the passes over 16,000 ft. are closed by snow from November to May. Small glacial lakes are abundant along the passes and at the heads of the gorges; the chief

lakes of the system, however, lie at comparatively low altitudes; they are Naini Tal in Kumaun and the Lake of Kashmir, which are 6520 and 6125 ft. above sea level respectively.

The geologic structure of the Himalaya consists chiefly of gneiss, mixed with mica schist in the north and bands of granite and syenite in the south. While the upheaval of the system probably commenced in early geologic time, the principal uplift occurred in the middle or late Tertiary period, in the same epoch in which the Alpine system of Europe was raised. The chains developed from north to south in a series of stages, during each of which mountains were pushed forward along great east-west fault lines over the beds at their southern bases, and the sub-Himalayan ridges to the south of the main chains are due to the repeated crumpling and folding of these beds. Even today the system has not reached a state of equilibrium; the frequency of earthquakes along the main fault lines, especially in the central range, indicates that the development of the Himalaya is still in process.

The Brahmaputra and Indus river systems have their chief sources in the seasonal melting of the Himalayan snows, and are in flood at the hottest season of the year when the moisture they supply is most needed. Thus the warm, damp climate characteristic of the Indian peninsula is in part at least due to the great mountain system to the north. Upon the mountains themselves trees and cultivated grains ordinarily attain their highest limits at about 11,800 ft. and shrubs at about 15,200 ft., though a few flowering plants are found at elevations as high as 19,500 ft. Tea is cultivated along the entire southern face of the system, the best grades being produced at 2000 to 3000 ft.

The fauna of the system, like the flora, overlaps with that of the Indian peninsula along the outer ranges, but for the most part the animals of the main ranges, particularly on the Tibetan side, are northern in affinity. Both bird and insect life abounds throughout the year even above the snow line, and tigers and apes are found up to 11,000, and leopards up to 13,000 ft. On the higher passes and peaks, however, only animals especially adapted to the rigors of intense cold and strong winds can endure; they include the yak, the pika, and several breeds of hairy dogs which have been domesticated and used to drive herds over passes as high as 18,000 ft. Hibernation in burrows beneath the snow and surface soil is common at heights with extreme seasonal variations in temperature.

The great height of the Himalaya, and the apparent impossibility of reaching its summits, stimulated the ancient Hindus to attribute supernatural properties to its peaks, which were associated with the history of some of their deities. In the Puranas (q.v.) the Himalaya was personified and the fabulous mountain Meru was placed to the north of it. As the abode of Siva (q.v.), the Himalaya was designated as the goal of pilgrims journeying to win that god's favors.

HIMATION. See COSTUME: *Grecian.*

HIMEJI, city of Hyogo, w. Honshu Island, Japan, located w. of Kobe. Among its chief manufactures are leather and cotton goods. Pop. (1950) 212,100.

HIMERA, an ancient city on the N. coast of Sicily, not far from Panormus (modern Palermo). It was founded in 648 B.C. by colonists from Messana (Messina) and exiles from Syracuse. In 481–480 B.C. the tyrant Terillus was expelled from Himera by the invading Theron of Agrigentum, who thereupon became tyrant. Terillus then invoked the aid of the Carthaginians, who dispatched a large army under Hamilcar. The forces of Carthage were defeated, however, by a force of Syracusan Greeks under the command of Gelon. Thrasydæus, son and successor of Theron, brought a large body of Dorian Greek emigrants to Himera in 476 B.C. A few years later, Thrasydæus was deposed by Hiero I, king of Syracuse and brother of Gelon. The city appears to have been prosperous during the remainder of the 5th century. In 408 B.C. Himera was demolished by the Carthaginian general Hannibal, who in the following year built a new city, Thermæ Himerææ (Baths of Himera), about eight miles west of the former site; the name, now Termini Imerese, was derived from the famous hot springs in the city in which the mythical hero Hercules was said to have bathed. Thermæ Himerææ remained in the possession of Carthage until it was taken by the Romans during the First Punic War.

HIMMLER, HEINRICH (1900–45), German fascist official, known chiefly as the head of the Gestapo (q.v.). He joined the National Socialist, or Nazi, Party in 1925, and from 1926 to 1930 was its director of propaganda. In 1930 he was elected a member of the Reichstag and became chief of the *Schutzstaffel,* an elite military force of the party. As head of the Gestapo from 1936 to 1945, he carried out a ruthless program for the extermination of Jews and the suppression of all opposition to the Nazi regime. The German dictator Adolf Hitler appointed him deputy head of the government in 1939, and in 1944 Himmler became director of home-front operations and chief of the German armed forces operating within the borders of Germany. In April, 1945, he attempted, through the medium of the Swedish government, to negotiate the surrender of the German armed forces to Great Britain and the United States. Shortly thereafter he was captured by the British army. He was scheduled to stand trial with the other German leaders as a major war criminal, but committed suicide before the trial.

HIMYARITES, an ancient Arabian tribe which inhabited a kingdom in extreme s.w. Arabia, and became rulers of s. Arabia about 115 B.C. The Himyarites were of great antiquity; their inscriptions on stone are dated as far back as 700 B.C. In the 4th century A.D., the Himyaritic dynasty was overthrown by an Abyssinian invasion. Some of the Himyarites accepted Judaism and founded a new kingdom in Saba, or Sheba, in s. Arabia. The Jewish kingdom was conquered by the Abyssinians in 525 A.D., and the Himyarites were assimilated into northern Arabian tribes. See ARABIA: *History*; SABÆANS.

Paul Hindemith

HINCKLEY, urban district of Leicestershire, England, located 14 m. by rail s.w. of Leicester. It is a center for the hosiery industry, and also contains shoe-manufacturing establishments. Mineral springs and coal mines are in the vicinity. Pop. (1951 prelim.) 39,088.

HINDEMITH, PAUL (1895–   ), German violist and composer, born in Hanau. He studied with Arnold Mendelsohn and Bernhard Sekles at Hoch's Conservatorium in Frankfort. At the age of thirteen, while at the conservatory, he gained practical experience by playing in dance bands and at theaters and cinemas. From 1915 to 1923 he was concertmaster and then conductor of the Frankfort Opera. In 1921, with Licco Amar, he organized the famous Amar Quartet, in which Hindemith played the viola. He composed many chamber-music works during this time, and began to acquire an international reputation as a composer. In 1927 he became a teacher at the Berlin Hochschule, a post he held for ten years. In 1934, under the Nazi regime, his work came under government ban in Germany because of its uncompromising modern style. He came to the U.S. in 1939 and three years later became head of the Music Department of Yale University.

Hindemith is considered one of the leading figures in modern music. He has been designated an atonalist (see ATONALITY), and some of his compositions show tendencies in that direction; however, in the main his work stays in the sphere of tonality, especially that written after 1935, when his *Violin Sonata in E* was published. He wrote many compositions for the theater, symphony orchestras, chamber groups, choruses, and voice; one of his best-known works is the symphony *Mathis der Maler*. He was the author of several theoretical works, including *The Craft of Musical Composition* (1941), *Traditional Harmony* (1943), and *Composer's World* (1952).

HINDENBURG, PAUL (LUDWIG HANS ANTON VON BENECKENDORFF UND) VON (1847–1934), German military and political leader, born in Posen. He was educated at the cadet school in Wahlstatt, Silesia, and the cadet academy in Berlin. He entered the Prussian army in 1866 and took part in the Seven Weeks' War (1866) between Prussia and Austria, and the Franco-Prussian War (1870–71). From 1871 to 1911 he advanced in rank from captain to general of infantry in the German imperial army. In 1911 he retired, but was recalled in 1914, on the outbreak of World War I. General Hindenburg commanded the German forces in East Prussia and led them to victory over the Russian armies at Tannenberg (1914). He was rewarded with promotion to the rank of field marshal and the Order of Merit. In 1916 he became German chief of staff and thereafter, with General Erich Ludendorff, first quartermaster general, was responsible for the direction of all German forces for the remainder of the war. In March, 1917, Hindenburg established the German armies in western Europe in a system of trenches across northern France known as the "Hindenburg Line", which the Allied armies did not break until October, 1918.

Hindenburg again retired in 1919. In 1920 he published his autobiography, *Out of my Life,* in which he stated that the German army's defeat in World War I had been due primarily to the revolution (1918) behind the lines, which had overthrown the Empire and established the German Republic. This theory was later used by Adolf Hitler (q.v.) to encourage the German people in World War II. In 1925 Hindenburg was elected the second president of the German Republic. Although a convinced monarchist, Hindenburg did not seek a restoration of the Hohenzollern dynasty, which the revolution of 1918 had overthrown, but sought German political unity under the Republic. However, he was strictly conservative in economic matters, and defended the interests of the East Prussian large property owners, a group known as the 'Junkers". In 1932 he defeated Adolf Hitler for the presidency, but Hitler's National Socialist (Nazi) Party was so powerful that in January, 1933, Hindenburg appointed Hitler chancellor of Germany. Hitler shortly afterward gained control of the Reichstag, which voted him dictatorial powers, whereupon Hindenburg's office lost its meaning. He died the following year.

HINDI, an Indo-European language which, with its component dialects, is spoken in the central States of the Indian Union by over 60,000,000 people. The language is divided into two main branches, *Eastern Hindi* and *Western Hindi,* both derived from variant forms of Prakrit. Eastern Hindi possesses an extensive and important literature, which reached its peak in a simple, vigorous poetry produced about the beginning of the 17th century; since that time, it has been the language most used in northern India for epic poetry. Its most important literary dialect is called Awadhi. Western Hindi comprises four main dialects: Kanauji, Braj Bhasha, Bundeli, and a vernacular Hindustani spoken around Delhi. The first two, like Awadhi, are important literary tongues of northern India; as a broad rule, the literatures they contain, along with most of the classical literature of India, is of a religious character. The Hindustani language (q.v.) developed from an obscure dialect of Western Hindi.

HINDI, artificial subdialect of the Hindustani language, adopted in 1949 as the official language of the Union of India. See HINDUSTANI LANGUAGE.

HINDUISM, the generic designation for the vast complex of theological, metaphysical, philosophical, ethical, cultural, and social institutions comprising the predominant religious system of India (see INDIA: *History).* The fundamental features of Hinduism are reverence for the sacred scriptures known as the Vedas (q.v.); the scrupulous observance of various regulations concerning diet, marriage, and burial; and the conscientious performance of specified rites, sacraments, and divine invocations. The caste system (see CASTE), for centuries a characteristic institution of Hinduism, is being progressively liberalized in consequence of the reforms instigated by Mohandas Karamchand Gandhi (q.v.). Hinduism is often used synonymously with Brahmanism (q.v.), although the latter term is more correctly restricted to the orthodox faith of the Brahmans (q.v.), which is closer to traditional Vedic belief than are the newer and more popular forms of worship constituting Hinduism.

The Sanskrit word *dharma* (law, duty, morality, piety) precisely indicates the scope and spirit of Hinduism. Originally a reform movement, like Buddhism and Jainism, and like these two great heterodox religions, a protest against the excessively formalistic and sectarian tendencies of Brahmanism, Hinduism began as a monotheistic faith based on the gospel of love. The chief written sources of Hinduism are the great epics the *Ramayana* and *Mahabharata* (qq.v.), and particularly the sections of the latter work known as the *Bhagavad-Gita* and *Harivansha* (qq.v.); the *Puranas* (see PURANA) and other sectarian treatises such as the *Bhakti* of the commentators Sāndilya and Nārada; and speculative and exegetical dissertations by the founders of various Hindu sects.

The first or epic period of Hinduism, starting about the 3rd century B.C., was marked by the development of two main creeds, popular and philosophical. The popular creed was mythological in its orientation, and its supreme aim was to select the most powerful god of the Vedic pantheon around whom the other divinities could be grouped. Two gods in particular vied for this central position, Vishnu and Siva (qq.v.). In the *Ramayana* the ascendancy of Vishnu is an accomplished

Paul von Hindenburg

Brit. Info.; Ewing Galloway

HINDUISM

Above: Hindu tending the fire at a burning ghat, section of ghat used by Hindus for cremation of the dead. Left: Modern Hindu temple at Sarnath, India, four miles from city of Benares, visited by thousands of Hindu pilgrims each year.

fact; in the *Mahabharata,* however, the rival claims of Siva are clearly recognized. Brahma (q.v.), though occasionally regarded as superior to both the other gods, gradually lost his mythological identity and became a philosophical abstraction, the symbol of the supreme principle of the universe.

The philosophical creed of Hinduism in the epic period promulgated the idea that the union (or, more properly, reunion) of the individual soul (*atman*) with the supreme soul (*Brahman,* neuter form of Brahma) may be facilitated by peculiar modes of breathing, particular postures, protracted fasting, and other physical disciplines. These ritualistic practices comprise the system of Yoga (q.v.).

The concept of the reunion of the individual soul with the supreme soul, a doctrine basic to the majority of Indian speculative philosophies, is founded on the assumption that the individual soul must become absolved of all guilt before it can again be merged with the perfect being whence it emanated. However, as the individual soul is unable to achieve this purification in the short space of one human life, it must pass through as many successive incarnations as are required to eliminate all the evils which keep it from absorption into the supreme soul. This doctrine of transmigration (q.v.) is the logical consequence of a religious system which holds the human soul to be consubstantial with God. The cycle of births and deaths, called *samsara,* is frequently symbolized in Hindu art and literature by a rotating wheel. When the purified soul has atoned for all the deeds (*karma*) which inexorably set the pattern of its future incarnations, *samsara* is annihilated and Nirvana (q.v.) attained.

The second stage in the development of Hinduism, extending roughly from the 6th to the 16th century, is known as the Puranic period. The name is derived from the *Puranas,* a class of sacred scriptures in verse which, with the *Tantras,* a series of philosophical tracts in the form of dialogues between the god Siva and his wife Durga, succeeded epic Hinduism and supplanted Buddhism. The philosophical creed of Puranic Hinduism was enriched by the Advaita Vedanta (see VEDANTA), a system of idealistic monism (see MONISM) which was elaborated by the 9th-century Hindu scholar, Sankara Acharya, from his Upanishadic commentaries (see UPANISHADS). According to Sankara, the phenomenal world is an illusion (*maya*) rooted in beginningless ignorance (*avidya*). The only true reality, Sankara maintains, is Brahman, or absolute being, with which the purified soul is identical. The Advaita Vedanta thus opposes an unconditioned, incogitable Brahman to the qualified, anthropomorphic Brahma of the Upanishads, who, as a personal deity, is held to be a concession to the unenlightened masses. For the enlightened soul, the ritualism of popular worship has no importance. Sankara's doctrine found support in many quarters, but as it tended to subvert established religious authority, it also had numerous adversaries.

With respect to the popular creed, on the other hand, the Puranic period of Hinduism was one of general decline. Its pantheon was nominally the same as that of the epic period; but whereas the epic period was characterized on the whole by harmonious relations among the major deities, the Puranic period exhibited them in a state of discord indicating the destruction of the original concepts personified by the epic gods. The legends of the epic period relating to these gods became, in the Puranic period, amplified and distorted according to the sectarian tendencies of the masses; and the divine character of the gods as disclosed in the *Ramayana* and *Mahabharata* was increasingly alloyed with mundane involvements. Popular worship, whether preserving a semblance of decorum, as with the devotees of Vishnu, or surrendering itself to unbridled license, as with the zealous adherents of Siva and Durga, became empty ceremonialism having little or no connection with the Vedic scriptures by which it purported to be inspired. It is this popular creed of the Puranic period which constitutes the Hinduism of the great mass of worshipers of present-day India. See also the articles on BUDDHISM; INDIAN LITERATURE; INDIAN MYTHOLOGY; INDIAN RELIGION.

HINDU KUSH, a range of mountains extending about 500 m. westward from the Himalaya, and sometimes reckoned as a part of that range. It stretches from the upper Indus R. in the east to the Bamian pass in the west, between latitudes 34° and 36° N. and longitudes 68° and 74° 30′ E., lying for most of its length within the borders of Afghanistan. For the first 100 m. west of the plateau region of the Pamirs (q.v.), it is a flat-topped watershed, with lakes and no prominent peaks, and with passes ranging in altitude from 12,-500 to 17,500 ft. above sea level. Farther westward it becomes higher, and its plateau summit breaks up into peaks, many of them over 20,000 ft. high. The highest peak in the range, Tirich Mir, in Chitral State, Northwest Frontier Province, Pakistan, lies in this portion; it is over 25,200 ft. above sea level. This part of the Hindu Kush is intersected by many passes.

The Hindu Kush consists mainly of granites and schists, and was probably uplifted in Tertiary time. Its general structure indicates conditions of uplift and subsequent denudation similar to those which prevailed in the western Himalaya. The range is of later origin than the Himalaya, however, and is in part marked by overthrusts of Cretaceous limestones upon Cenozoic shales and clays. Many important waterways and river systems have their sources within the Hindu Kush; among them are the Oxus R., which has its source in the northern ridges, and parts of the tributary system of the Indus R., which flow down the southern slopes.

The conquests of Alexander the Great (q.v.) extended to the Hindu Kush, and the range was called the Caucasus by geographers and historians of that period. A certain confusion seems to have existed at the time between the Hindu Kush and the Colchian Caucasus; both chains were considered a part of a larger Alpine barrier which crossed Asia from west to east. Except for modern times, during which its first 200 m. have formed a part of the southern border of Afghanistan, the range has never been of great political importance.

HINDU MUSIC. See INDIA, MUSIC OF.

HINDUSTANI LANGUAGE, a name given by Europeans to a dialect originally derived from western Hindi (q.v.), and now the common language, or *lingua franca,* of India. It is in no sense a hybrid "pidgin" speech, but a distinct language enriched by borrowings; it is still considered a living dialect of western Hindi, though its adoption as an official language during the Mogul empire introduced a period of intensive borrowing, mostly from Arabic and Persian, and the use of an adapted Arabic script.

The most important subdialect of Hindustani is called *Urdu;* it is the standard form of the speech used by Mohammedans. Urdu contains more Persian words and grammatical constructions than any other of the subdialects. It has tended to remain more restricted than the standard speech, for it is not acceptable to patriotic Hindus and, because of its large Persian element, can be written conveniently only in a Persian script. An artificial subdialect developed in modern times especially for use by Hindus is called Hindi (not to be confused with the Hindi language); in formulating it, its inventors deliberately avoided a Persianized vocabulary, but introduced so many borrowings from Sanskrit (probably in an attempt to "purify" the language) that Hindi, like Urdu, is intelligible only to persons especially educated in it; moreover, Hindi must be transcribed in Dēvanāgarī. Thus, while educated Mohammedans may read and speak a Persianized Hindustani called Urdu, and educated Hindus a Sanskritized Hindustani called Hindi, standard Hindustani remains a *lingua franca* understood by both and by many Europeans, and basic to widespread communication throughout India. It may be transcribed today in both Perso-Arabic and Dēvanāgarī scripts. Hindi in the Dēvanāgarī script was adopted in 1949 as the official language of the Union of India.

Hindustani is an analytic language, like all other modern Indian languages, and like Persian and English. Words are generally conjugated and declined by postpositions, affixes, and periphrases. There are two genders, two numbers, two voices, and nine tenses in common use.

Hindustani, unlike most other languages spoken by a great variety of peoples and subject to many external influences, has successfully adopted foreign words and forms as casual additions to speech without basic change in form or content. Some of the older Persian and Arabic borrowings have been given terminations characteristic of the parent Hindi language, but modern borrowings from Europeans have been restricted in the main to nouns, particularly substantive nouns, which are spelled phonetically or according to corrupt native pronunciations, and declined as though they were indigenous nouns. The earliest Western language in contact with Hindustani was Portuguese; French and Dutch elements subsequently appeared, but the effect of all three was relatively slight. English, on the other hand, is of the greatest importance in modern Hindustani. Some words borrowed from English have already appeared in the literature of the language, and despite recent political changes (see INDIA), bilingualism is increasing among educated Indians, and the bulk of modern technical vocabularies is being borrowed from the English language.

HINNY. See MULE.

HIPPARCHUS. See HIPPIAS.

HIPPARCHUS (190–120 B.C.), Greek astronomer, born in Nicæa in Bithynia. Only fragments of his writings are still in existence, but the records of his researches are preserved in the *Syntaxis* of Ptolemy. In addition to his many contributions to astronomy (q.v.), he laid the foundations of trigonometry.

HIPPIAS (d. about 490 B.C.), Tyrant of Athens (527–510 B.C.), son and successor of Pisistratus (q.v.). Upon the death of his father, Hippias became ruler of Athens with his brother, Hipparchus. Hipparchus was assassinated in 514 B.C., during an attempt to overthrow the tyranny (see HARMODIUS AND ARISTOGITON), and Hippias avenged the murder by ruling thenceforward as a despot, imposing oppressive taxes, selling public offices, and putting to death whomever he suspected of intriguing against him. After making several unsuccessful attempts against him, the Alcmæonidae, a powerful Athenian family, received aid from Sparta and overthrew Hippias in 510 B.C. The tyrant and all his relatives were exiled from Attica. Hippias went to the court of Darius I of Persia and helped persuade the Persian ruler to attack Greece (see GREECE: *History of Ancient Greece*). He accompanied the Persian expedition to Greece in 490 B.C. and persuaded the Persians to land at Marathon.

HIPPOCRATES (460?–377? B.C.), Greek physician, born on the island of Cos. Hippocrates was the most celebrated physician of antiquity; he was and is still called "the father of medicine". He was the son of a

Hippocrates refuses to be bribed by the Persians, who try to lure him away from Greece.

certain Heraclides, and descent from Hercules was claimed for him on his mother's side; this confusion in his ancestry is typical of the accretions of legend which are attached to his name. Little is known of his personal history. After spending some time in traveling through different parts of Greece, and practicing in Thrace, Thessaly, Athens, Delos, and elsewhere, he seems to have settled and practiced at Cos, and finally died at Larissa in Thessaly. Hippocrates was an influential author and teacher; he established the high reputation of the medical school at Cos, and his work and name were touchstones of objectivity and ethical standards in the disputes between sects and doctrines which were characteristic of Hellenistic science. See HIPPOCRATIC OATH; DISEASE; GREEK LITERATURE.

HIPPOCRATIC OATH, an oath appearing in the Hippocratic collection, which in classical times was taken by young men entering the study of medicine. A similar oath was used in the Middle Ages, and many contemporary medical schools impose the Hippocratic oath as an admonition and an affirmation to which their graduating classes assent. At one time the oath was ascribed to Hippocrates (q.v.), but modern research has shown that the version we possess was composed at a later period than his; some authori-

ties date it as late as the 3rd century A.D. The oath is as follows:

"I swear by Apollo, the physician, by Æsculapius, by Hygieia, Panacea, and all the gods and goddesses, that according to my ability and judgment I will keep this oath and stipulation. I will look upon him who shall have taught me this art even as one of my parents. I will share my substance with him, and I will supply his necessities, if he be in need. I will regard his offspring even as my own brethren, and I will teach them this art, if they would learn it, without fee or covenant. I will impart this art by precept, by lecture, and by every mode of teaching, not only to my own sons but to the sons of him who has taught me, and to disciples bound by covenant and oath, according to the law of medicine. The regimen I adopt shall be for the benefit of my patients according to my ability and judgment, and not for their hurt or for any wrong. I will give no deadly drug to any, though it be asked of me, nor will I counsel such, and especially I will not aid a woman to procure abortion. With purity and holiness will I pass my life and practice my art. I will not cut a person who is suffering with stone, but will leave this to be done by those who are practitioners of such work. Whatsoever house I enter, there will I go for the benefit of the

Ringling Bros. & Barnum & Bailey Circus

The common brown or gray hippopotamus with its great jaws opened, waiting to be fed

sick, refraining from all wrongdoing or corruption, and especially from any act of seduction, of male or female, of bond or free. Whatsoever things I see or hear concerning the life of men, in my attendance on the sick or even apart therefrom, which ought not to be noised abroad, I will keep silent thereon, counting such things to be as sacred secrets. While I continue to keep this oath inviolate, may it be granted to me to enjoy life and the practice of my art, respected always by all men; but should I break through and violate this oath, may the reverse be my lot."

HIPPOLYTA, in Greek mythology, queen of the Amazons (q.v.), and the daughter of Ares, god of war. She was slain by the hero Hercules when he took from her, as the sixth of his twelve labors, the girdle given to her by her father. According to another legend, Hippolyta, at the head of her army of Amazons, invaded the ancient state of Attica, and being defeated, retired to the town of Megara, where she died of grief. A third legend

represents her as becoming the betrothed of the Attic hero Theseus. This version is the one used as a partial basis for the plot of *A Midsummer Night's Dream* by William Shakespeare.

HIPPOLYTUS, in Greek mythology, the son of Theseus, slayer of the Minotaur, and Antiope, or (in other versions) her sister Hippolyte, queen of the Amazons. Hippolytus was a mighty hunter and devoted servant of Artemis, goddess of the chase. His father Theseus had married Phædra, daughter of the Cretan king Minos. Phædra became enamored of her stepson, Hippolytus, and when he spurned her advances, she committed suicide, leaving a tablet in which she accused him of having attempted to ravish her. Theseus thereupon invoked his father, Poseidon god of the sea, to bring about the destruction of Hippolytus. Accordingly, as the young man was driving his chariot along the seashore at Trœzen, Poseidon caused a monster to rise from the sea and terrify the horses Hippolytus was thrown from the chariot, became ensnared in the reins, and was dragged to his death by the plunging steeds. In an alternate version of the story, Hippolyte did not commit suicide before the death of her stepson, but took her life in contrition after he had been killed. A tradition among the ancient inhabitants of Epidaurus represented Artemis as having persuaded Asclepius, god of medicine and healing, to restore Hippolytus to life. Euripides, a Greek dramatist of the 5th century B.C., wrote two plays on the theme, one of which is lost. Other playwrights to treat the legend were the Roman Seneca and the Frenchman Jean Baptist Racine.

HIPPONAX (fl. 6th cent. B.C.), Greek poet born in Ephesus. In 540 B.C. he was exiled from his native city by the tyrant Athenagoras, and he moved to Clazomenæ (near Smyrna), where he remained for the rest of his life. Hipponax was the reputed inventor of parody (q.v.), and also of a halting iambic the *scazon* or *choliambus* (see VERSIFICATION). He was well known for his biting scurrilous verses. According to the Roman historian Pliny, two artists, Bupalus and Athenis, made a statue of Hipponax ridiculing his ugliness, whereupon the poet retaliated with such vituperative verses that they hanged themselves in despair.

HIPPOPOTAMUS, or RIVER HORSE, common name of either of two species of artiodactylous mammals comprising the family Hippopotamidae, found only in Africa. The hippopotamuses are heavy-bodied, short-legged, short-tailed animals, resembling pigs (to which they are closely related) more than horses. They have large heads, with small eyes, small ears, and nostrils surrounded by sparse, bristly hairs and equipped with special flaps which close down when the animal goes under water. The eyes and the ears are located on the top of the head. The mouth is huge and contains long, pointed incisor and canine teeth; the canine teeth of the lower jaw are tusklike, about 30 in. in total length and almost 8 lbs. in weight in adults of the common hippopotamus, and are valued as ivory. The bare skin reaches a thickness of 2 in. and is used in the making of leather whips, known as "sjamboks". The feet are four-toed. The meat of the hippopotamus is edible and tastes like beef.

The common brown or gray hippopotamus, *Hippopotamus amphibius,* once widely distributed throughout Africa and now found chiefly in Ethiopia, is one of the largest four-footed animals. It reaches a length of 14 ft. and weight of over 4 tons; because of its short legs it stands no higher than 5 ft. tall at the shoulder. Its stomach is over 10 ft. long. This animal is semiaquatic, spending most of the day with only its eyes, ears, and nostrils above the surface of a river, and capable of remaining under water for as long as five minutes. During the day it feeds on aquatic vegetation, and often swims over 25 miles in search of food. At night it emerges to feed on land plants; it is fond of sugar cane and corn, and sometimes enters plantations, where it does more damage by trampling the plants than it does by feeding. It has occasionally been seen in mountain rivers at heights of over 5000 ft. above sea level, and at temperatures near freezing. Common hippopotamuses travel in large herds numbering as many as forty individuals. The cow bears one young at a time, and fights ferociously if the calf is attacked. Old bulls, like old elephants, sometimes go berserk and attack other hippopotamuses or men. The species is widely hunted; natives kill it by harpooning, or in pitfalls, or by fencing it in and starving it to death.

The pigmy hippopotamus, *Choeropsis liberiensis,* is about half the size of the common hippopotamus. It is found only in w. Africa, especially in Liberia. Above it is black, with a greenish sheen; below it is yellowish green. It is less aquatic in habit than the common hippopotamus, and is found in cool forests and in marshlands. Pigmy hippopotamuses almost always travel in pairs, rarely forming a herd.

Remains of many fossil hippopotamuses have been found in European and Indian deposits of the Pliocene and Pleistocene epochs; fossils found in England seem to be of the same species as the present-day common hippopotamus.

HIROHITO (1901–), Emperor of Japan (1926–). He was educated at the Imperial Education Institute in Tokyo. Hirohito visited Europe in 1921, becoming the first Japanese prince to leave his native land. He governed Japan as regent from 1921, when his father, Emperor Yoshihito, retired from office because of ill health, to 1926, when Yoshihito died and Hirohito succeeded to the throne (see JAPAN, *History*). He designated his reign as the period of *Showa* ("light and peace"). Hirohito married in 1924; the heir to the throne, Prince Akihito, was born in 1933.

Hirohito's reign in Japan was marked by the growing ascendancy of a militaristic party of statesmen and leaders of the army and navy. This militaristic clique was largely responsible for the policy of expansion by conquest which led to the establishment by Japan of the puppet state of Manchukuo in 1934 (see CHINA: *History: The Republic*); the Sino-Japanese War (1937–45); and Japan's attack upon the United States (1941) and participation in World War II on the side of Germany and Italy. On August 15 (Tokyo time), 1945, following the second atom-bomb attack upon Japan, Hirohito issued a proclamation to the Japanese people informing

Wide World Photo

Emperor Hirohito and the Empress Nagako

them of the surrender of all Japanese forces to the United Nations, and on September 2 he ordered all Japanese troops to lay down their arms.

In 1945 the state Shinto religion, according to which the emperor is of divine origin, was brought to an end through order of Gen. Douglas MacArthur, Supreme Commander of the Allied Powers, and on January 1, 1946, Hirohito publicly disclaimed such divine origin. By the new constitution which went into effect on May 3, 1947, the emperor's powers, theretofore those of an absolute monarch, were limited to those of a constitutional monarch. Although he still remained at the head of the Japanese government, Hirohito was among those Japanese military and political leaders who were implicated in the charge of planning and waging aggressive war; in its verdict concerning the defendants, the International Military Tribunal ruled (November 12, 1948) that Hirohito had opposed the Japanese warlords in some of their aggressive designs and that his consent to their major militaristic plans had been obtained largely by deceit on the part of his premier, Hideki Tojo.

HIROLA. See HARTEBEEST.

HIROSHIGE, ANDO (1797–1858), Japanese landscape artist and designer of wood-block prints. He was the last important figure of the Ukiyoye school. Before 1820 he worked principally on prints and figures. Thereafter, he began printing large landscapes in color, particularly a series of views of Tokyo, in which he created a variety of atmospheric effects, such as moonlight, snow, mist, and rain. This work made him popular in his own country and was also an important influence on the work of the French Impressionist school and on the American painter James A. McNeill Whistler. A large number of his prints are in the Metropolitan Museum, New York City, and in many other collections.

HIROSHIMA, a city and a prefecture of the same name in western Honshu, Japan, located about 160 miles s.s.w. of Kobe. The city of Hiroshima, one of the principal ports of the Inland Sea, maintains a large trade in lacquer and bronze ware. It is an important center of religious worship, much of which is carried on in the temples and torii of a nearby islet dedicated to the goddess Benten. A few miles south of the city, on the same bay, lie a large naval arsenal and base, and within the city itself a great many military industrial plants were concentrated during World War II; it was chosen by the U.S. as the

site for the first military use of the atomic bomb, on August 6, 1945 (see ATOMIC ENERGY: *Nuclear Explosions*). Area of prefecture, 3257 sq.m.; pop. (1947) 2,011,498. Pop. of city (1940) 343,968; (1945) 137,197.

HIRSCH, EMIL GUSTAV (1851–1923), American rabbi, born in the Grand Duchy of Luxemburg. He came to the United States as a young man, and was educated at the University of Pennsylvania and later at the universities of Berlin and Leipzig. He was appointed rabbi of the Sinai Congregation, Chicago, in 1880, and became widely known as a leader of the Jewish Reform movement (see JUDAISM). He was the first American rabbi to discard the observance of Saturday as the Jewish Sabbath, and to hold services in the synagogue on Sunday. Among the publications which he edited at various times are the *Reformer,* published in New York City, and the *Reform Advocate,* published in Chicago. From 1892 until his death, he was professor of rabbinical literature and philosophy at the University of Chicago.

HIRSCH, BARON MORITZ, known also by the French form of his name, MAURICE DE HIRSCH (1831–96), German businessman and philanthropist, born in Munich, and educated at Brussels. In 1855 he entered the employ of the international banking firm of Bischoffsheim and Goldschmidt of Brussels, London, and Paris, and accumulated a large fortune through investments in railways, copper mines, and other enterprises. His interest was later aroused by the oppression of his Jewish coreligionists in several European countries, especially Russia, and he became a contributor to philanthropic organizations established to help them. Hirsch was one of the principal supporters of the Alliance Israélite Universalle, and founded the Jewish Colonization Society. To the latter organization, which had as its goal the resettlement of Russian Jews in agricultural colonies outside of Russia, he made two successive contributions totaling over £9,000,000. In 1891 he established, with an endowment of almost $2,500,000, a trust fund in New York City for the benefit of Jews entering the United States. The organization set up to administer this endowment, known as the Baron de Hirsch Fund, has carried on a variety of activities, assisting Jewish immigrants to obtain American citizenship, finding them homes and employment, and maintaining trade schools for Jewish youths.

HIRTIUS AULUS (90?–43 B.C.), Roman statesman and historian, the writer of a continuation of Julius Cæsar's *Commentaries on the Gallic War.* Hirtius was a close friend of Cæsar and served under the Roman general as a legate during the campaigns in Gaul. During the war between Cæsar and Pompey (49–48 B.C.), Hirtius protected Cæsar's interests in Rome. A year after the assassination of Cæsar in 44 B.C., Hirtius was elected a consul. He supported the Senate and Octavian (later the Emperor Augustus) against Mark Antony for the control of Rome. The consul was killed during the battle of Mutina, in which Antony was decisively defeated. In addition to writing the eighth book of the *Commentaries,* Hirtius is thought by historians to have written some parts and commissioned the writing of other parts of the last two books, which concern Cæsar's African, Alexandrian, and Spanish campaigns.

HIRUDINEA. See LEECHES.

HISPANIOLA, an island of the West Indies, lying E. of Cuba and W. of Puerto Rico. It was named La Española (Little Spain) by Christopher Columbus, who discovered it on December 6, 1492. Politically, Hispaniola is divided into the separate governments of Haiti (q.v.), occupying the western third of the island, and the Dominican Republic (q.v.).

The aboriginal inhabitants of Hispaniola were Indians, engaged principally in farming and fishing. They gradually became extinct as a result of the widespread persecution and exploitation to which they were subjected by the early Spanish colonists. Thereafter, Negro slaves were imported to take the place of the Indian laborers. In time the Spanish migrated from Hispaniola to South America, and for about a hundred years the island was virtually deserted. In 1697, by the peace of Ryswick (q.v.), which concluded the war between Louis XIV of France and the Grand Alliance, a portion of Hispaniola which had been occupied by French adventurers, as Saint Dominique, was formally ceded to France. The French fostered the production of coffee, sugar, and cotton, and developed a flourishing trade. Intermarriage between the French colonists and the Negroes produced a class known as *mulattoes,* who, being free, became owners of property, and in 1789 were granted political rights by the French national assembly in Paris. The French landlords and planters of Hispaniola, called *colons,* objected vigorously to the political recognition of the mulattoes, and a bitter struggle was precipitated between the two groups. The colons appealed to the British for assistance, where-

upon the latter, together with the Spanish, occupied a portion of the island.

Pierre Dominique Toussaint L'Ouverture (see TOUSSAINT L'OUVERTURE), a Negro who had gained his freedom in the emancipation of the Hispaniolian slaves decreed by the new French republican government in 1793, espoused the cause of France, and succeeded in driving the British and Spanish invaders from the island. In recognition of his services he was elevated to the office of governor of Hispaniola. After a victorious war against the mulattoes, who had opposed his authority, Toussaint proclaimed himself master of the island. Napoleon I, who had come to power in France meanwhile, dispatched General Charles Victor Emmanuel Leclerc to replace Toussaint as governor. Although he put up a determined resistance, Toussaint was finally captured and deported to France, where he died in prison.

In 1802 Leclerc succumbed to yellow fever. His successor was defeated by the Negro general Jean Jacques Dessalines (q.v.), who, in 1804, expelled the French, proclaimed the independence of the island, the name of which was changed to Haiti, and assumed the title of emperor. Two years later, in consequence of his tyrannous rule, Dessalines was assassinated by Henri Christophe (q.v.), a Negro and former lieutenant under Toussaint L'Ouverture. Christophe then assumed control of the northern part of Haiti, taking the title of king in 1811; the southern part of the island was established as a republic by the mulatto Alexander Sabès Pétion. Following the death of Christophe in 1820, the mulatto Jean Pierre Boyer (q.v.), the successor of Pétion, brought the entire island under his control. Boyer ruled until overthrown by revolution in 1843. A year later the eastern part of the island declared its independence, forming the Republic of Santo Domingo, now the Dominican Republic. The island, as a geographic unit, assumed its former name, Hispaniola. Area of the island, about 29,530 sq.m.

HISTAMINE, or HISTAMINE PHOSPHATE, a synthetic amine (beta-imidazolyl-ethylamine, ergamine, or ergotidine) found in minute quantities in ergot (q.v.) and putrified meat products. Although histamine is produced synthetically for medicinal purposes, it is a normal constituent of almost all animal body cells. It is probably produced by bacterial action in the intestinal tract; the body is able to destroy it by enzymatic action and to neutralize its toxic effects, probably by a secretion of adrenalin. In response to certain stimuli the cells release histamine, which immediately effects a dilation of the blood vessels. This dilation is accompanied by a lowering of blood pressure and an increased permeability of the vessel walls, so that fluids escape into the surrounding tissues. This reaction may result in a general depletion of vascular fluids, causing a condition known as histamine poisoning or histamine shock. Allergic reactions show many similarities to histamine poisoning, and the two may be basically allied. The two conditions are treated similarly. Among the new antihistamine drugs used in allergy therapy are benadryl, pyrobenzamine, ephedrine, and chlor-trimeton.

The reaction time to subcutaneous injections of histamine is used as a test for circulatory deficiency characteristic of diseases such as diabetes. Histamine also causes contraction of involuntary muscles, especially of the genital tract and gastrointestinal canal, with an accompanying secretion by associated glands. Because histamine stimulates the flow of gastric juices, it is used diagnostically in patients with gastric disturbances. The ability of the body to localize infections may be due to the secretion of histamine and the subsequent increased local blood supply and increased permeability of the blood vessels. Histamine is sometimes used in the treatment of chronic rheumatism, arthritis, myositis (muscle inflammation), certain types of dermatitis, and in particular of various types of allergies. The last-named use is based on the hypothesis that such treatment will bring about a gradual desensitization of the body to the toxic effects of histamine, but many biologists doubt the ultimate value of such therapy. See ALLERGY.

HISTIÆUS (d. 494 B.C.), Tyrant of the city of Miletus (q.v.) during the reign of Darius I of Persia. In 513 B.C. Histiæus was charged with guarding a bridge of boats on which the Persian army, invading Scythia, crossed the Danube R. Other tyrants and the Athenian general Miltiades tried to persuade Histiæus to destroy the bridge, but he refused. When Darius returned, he rewarded the Milesian with the rule of the island of Lesbos (now Mytilene) and a district in Thrace. Later, the tyrant's increased power made the Persians uneasy. Histiæus was invited to the court of Darius at Susa, and detained there for thirteen years. In 500 B.C. the tyrant intrigued to free himself. He instigated a revolt against Persia in Ionia and persuaded the Persians that he alone could quell the revolt. Once free, His-

tiæus openly made war on Persia as a pirate, establishing headquarters at Byzantium. After several years he was captured by the Persian general Harpagus and crucified at Sardis.

HISTOLOGY, the microscopic study of animal and plant tissues, comprising groups of cells differentiated for co-operative performance of a particular biological function. Histology, the study of the structure and processes of interrelated cells, thus differs from cytology (q.v.), the study of individual cells. Histology is closely connected with embryology, anatomy and physiology, and pathology, inasmuch as it affords techniques which enable the biologist to study respectively the development of tissues into organs, the functioning of the tissues within an organ, and the changes in tissues during disease. Biopsy (q.v.) and histological studies after autopsy give the scientist valuable information about disease processes and about tissue changes which have led to death.

Histology originated in the 17th century in the work of Marcello Malpighi and of Anton van Leeuwenhoek (qq.v.). The science progressed slowly until the 19th century, when the compound microscope began to assume its present form, and when the *microtome,* an instrument for slicing thin portions of tissue, was invented by Johannes Evangelista Purkinje (q.v.). In 1907 the American biologist Ross Granville Harrison discovered that living tissues could be cultured, i.e., grown outside of the parent organ. This discovery introduced a new era in histology and has led to many important discoveries; see, for example, LINDBERGH, CHARLES A.

Five principal groups of tissues are found in the animal body: epithelium, which is found in all the lining and secreting areas of the body; connective tissues, which include bone, cartilage, and other supporting structures; muscle tissue; nerve tissue; and the fluid tissues, blood and lymph. Tissues are also classified on the basis of their embryological origin; see EMBRYOLOGY. See separate articles on most of the tissues mentioned. For plant tissues, see MORPHOLOGY OF PLANTS.

HISTORY (Gr. *historia,* "information, inquiry, history"), a systematic narrative or account of past events, particularly of those affecting nations, institutions, arts, and sciences. Because history links these events with a philosophical examination of their causes, such as social and economic conditions, racial affinities, and physical environment, it is differentiated from annals or chronicles, which merely record events. In general, history is loosely divided into three main chronological periods: *ancient,* from the beginning of records to about 500 A.D.; *medieval,* until about 1500; and *modern.*

History is primarily inductive; it proceeds from a body of concrete facts, which critical study connects according to the sequences of time and causation. Historical facts come from various sources: remains, such as artifacts (i.e., primitive tools and art objects), buildings, or religious monuments; documents, such as business or official papers, or letters; literatures; traditions, either written or handed down by word of mouth; law codes; and contemporary writings of any description, particularly annals, chronicles, and biographies. The historian arranges these facts in logical order and interprets them critically, in accordance with the results of his arrangement. However, the human element involved in critical interpretation is so large a factor that history can never be an exact science, and few historians reach the same conclusions. Another factor in the divergence of historical writing is the increasing scope of human knowledge through the ages, each new science or study contributing to a knowledge of man as a social being and of man in his relation with the physical world.

The first known historian, the so-called "Father of History", was the Greek Herodotus (q.v.), who lived in the 5th century B.C. Herodotus, however, was primarily a narrator, recording some events with great accuracy, but mingling so many fabulous happenings with his narratives that he is alternately known as the "Father of Lies". Thucydides (q.v.), the next great Greek historian, was the first to apply philosophical reasoning to an historical narrative, and he is known as one of the foremost historians of all times. A third notable Greek historian was Xenophon (q.v.), a Greek general who recorded what he had himself observed. Among the leading Roman historians were Julius Cæsar, Livy, and Tacitus (qq.v.); of the three, Tacitus is considered the greatest because, like Thucydides, he sought an underlying causal meaning in the political and social events he recorded.

No great historical writing was done from the fall of the Western Roman Empire, in the 5th century A.D., to the Renaissance, and medieval events were recorded in an indiscriminate manner in annals, chronicles, or in such famous documents as the English Domesday Book (q.v.). With the revival of scholarship during the Renaissance began a new school of political and historical thinkers who learned their historical method from rediscovered classical models. Two Italians, Niccoló Machiavelli and Francesco Guicciardini (qq.v.), became particularly notable, and the writing of history again developed into the interpretation of political, social, and constitutional trends.

In the 18th century the English historian Edward Gibbon (q.v.) wrote one of the masterpieces of historical scholarship, *The Decline and Fall of the Roman Empire.* François Voltaire, David Hume, Charles de Montesquieu, and William Robertson (qq.v.) are considered brilliant historians of the same century. In the 19th century, concurrently with the development of natural sciences, history began to develop into a systematic science. Barthold Niebuhr and Leopold von Ranke (qq.v.) became outstanding as pioneer scientific historians in Germany, and the German philosopher Georg Hegel (q.v.) developed a celebrated theory of history based on his philosophical concept of the Absolute Idea. Karl Marx (q.v.), the German political philosopher and founder of modern socialism, expounded an economic, materialistic view of history. Victor Duruy and Bon Louis Henri Martin (qq.v.), French scholars, distinguished themselves with their clear, scientific historical writing. In Great Britain, Thomas Macaulay, James Froude, and Thomas Carlyle (qq.v.) were landmarks of 19th-century historical thought. In the United States such historians as Francis Parkman and Henry Adams (qq.v.) became noted for their simple, incisive style and objective treatment (see AMERICAN LITERATURE).

During the 20th century history has become bound to an increasing degree with economics and sociology. Notable contemporary historians in the United States are such writers as Harry Elmer Barnes, Charles Austin Beard, James Breasted, Sr., Henry Steele Commager, Carlton J. H. Hayes, John Bassett Moore, David Saville Muzzey, Allan Nevins, and James Harvey Robinson (qq.v.). One increasingly important school of historians led by the English scholar Arnold Toynbee (q.v.) has attempted to discover the patterns of history in the study of cultures instead of national groups, and cultural history is tending to take the place of the rational history of the 19th century.

HITLER, ADOLF (1889–1945), German political and military leader, born in Branau, Upper Austria, and naturalized a German citizen in 1932. His father was an Austrian,

whose name is believed to have been originally Schicklgruber, and his mother was a Bavarian.

In his youth Hitler was a failure as an
artist, an architectural draftsman, and a businessman. In World War I he served in a
Bavarian regiment, receiving two German
decorations for bravery and a promotion to
gefreiter (Br., lance corporal; U.S., private
first class). After the war he entered politics,
founding with six others the National Socialist German Workers' party (see NATIONAL
SOCIALISM) or "Nazi" party, which had as
its purposes the cure of the domestic economic
and political ills of Germany, and the improvement of its inferior international position after its defeat in World War I (see
GERMANY: *History*) by imposition on the
country of a form of fascism (see FASCISM:
General Features). With the aid of the German general Erich Ludendorff and other
sympathizers, Hitler, in November, 1923, attempted to seize control of the Bavarian
government in Munich. The revolt failed and
Hitler was sentenced to five years' imprisonment for treason and was confined in the
fortress of Landsberg, Bavaria. He was pa-
roled after serving nine months. During his
imprisonment, he dictated to his secretary
Rudolf Hess (q.v.) the work *Mein Kampf*,
in which he set forth his intention of not only
making Germany strong internally, but also
of making it the ruler of all Europe and
eventually of the entire world; he also explained in detail exactly how and by what
steps he intended to bring about the fulfillment of these aims. The book had wide circulation in Germany and was of aid in bringing about the subsequent growth of the Nazi
party.

From 1928 to 1932, principally under Hitler's leadership and with the backing of important German industrialists, Nazi representation in the Reichstag greatly increased;
and although Hitler was defeated for the office of president of the German Republic in
1932 by Field Marshal Paul von Hindenburg
(q.v.), in the following year Hindenburg appointed him chancellor. In 1934, on the death
of Hindenburg, Hitler abolished the presidency, combining its functions with those of
the chancellorship, and assumed the title of
"Der Führer", or "supreme leader", of the
German people. Under his dictatorship the
domestic policy of the Third Reich, which
had taken the place of the Republic in 1933,
included a violent anti-Semitic program, economic reorganization, and rearmament. In

foreign affairs under Hitler's leadership Germany rapidly increased its power and territory of Europe, following out with remarkable fidelity the plans laid down in *Mein
Kampf*. After reoccupying the Rhineland zone
between France and Germany (March, 1936),
annexing Austria (March, 1938), and then
Czechoslovakia (March, 1939), Germany invaded Poland (Sept. 1, 1939). The invasion
brought on World War II (q.v.); see also
EUROPE: *History, Modern*. By the middle
of 1941 Germany had conquered Poland, Denmark, Norway, the Netherlands, Luxemburg,
Belgium, France, Greece, and Yugoslavia.

In June, 1941, Germany invaded Russia,
and in December of that year Hitler personally took command of the German military
forces. His conduct of the campaign against
Russia was disastrous for Germany. In 1943
Russia was able to begin a counteroffensive
which eventually, in conjunction with the
Allied invasion of the German-held Continent
(1944), brought about the total defeat of
Germany (1945). Hitler escaped an attempt
to assassinate him in 1944 by a military group
within the Nazi party, but toward the end of
the war is believed to have suffered a nervous
breakdown. He remained in Berlin when the
Russians entered the city toward the end of
April, 1945, and on April 30 committed suicide, together with his former mistress Eva
Braun, whom he had married the previous
day. No positive identification of his remains
has ever been made, but no reason has appeared to doubt these facts of his death.

HITTITE LANGUAGE, a dead Indo-European language of N.E. Asia Minor, surviving
in cuneiform and hieroglyphic inscriptions on
tablets and monuments excavated at sites
within the ancient empire of the Hittites
(q.v.). The first important finds in the language were made by expeditions led by the
German Assyriologist Hugo Winckler (q.v.)
from 1906 to 1907 (when royal archives containing nearly ten thousand clay tablets were
discovered) and from 1911 to 1912. In 1915
the Czech archeologist Bedrich Hrozný
(q.v.) announced that he had deciphered the
language and found it to be Indo-European,
and two years later he produced a Hittite
grammar which in effect proved his conten-
tion of Indo-European affinity. Hrozný's arguments, however, were not those of a professional Indo-Europeanist, and his first
statement of them was extreme and somewhat inexpert; his position and even the accuracy of some of his readings were attacked
by the great majority of students. By about

Right: A Hittite relief carving of the sky god Teshub, discovered at Babylon. Above: Carving of a female warrior at Boghaz Keui, once the capital of the Hittites.

1925, a Hittite vocabulary and an essentially Indo-European grammar for the language had been worked out to the satisfaction of most philologists, proving the validity of Hrozný's decipherment and theory. Intensive investigations of both the vocabulary and the grammar of the Hittite language are still being carried on.

Linguistic scientists are not yet certain of the precise position of Hittite in Indo-European philology. Its records, which date back to 1400 B.C., are among the oldest known of an Indo-European language, and Hittite constructions, displaying striking parallels to and divergences from those of the western Indo-European languages, have suggested to some scholars that Hittite may have broken away from the parent language, Proto-Indo-European, before any other known Indo-European tongue. If this is true, Hittite must have passed through a longer period of independent development than such languages as Sanskrit, Greek, and Latin. Moreover, only a small part of the identified vocabulary of Hittite appears to be Indo-European; the majority of the words stem from some unidentified source, presumably an indigenous language or group of languages of Asia Minor.

HITTITES (Heb. *Hittīm*), an ancient people of uncertain origin, who, between 2000 B.C. and 1200 B.C., conquered and ruled an empire in Asia Minor which rivaled the contemporary Egyptian and Babylonian empires in power and influence. The term itself is of Biblical origin and is used in the Old Testament to describe not the Hittite conquerors, but the natives of Khatti, a city or country in E. Asia Minor. Heth, in Hebrew the singular of *Hittīm,* is mentioned (Gen. 10:15) as the son of Canaan, indicating that the Khatti or Biblical Hittites belonged to the peoples who inhabited Syria during the Hebrew invasion, and that they were regarded as akin to the Phenicians and Amorites.

Most of the historical data concerning the empire-building Hittites has come from Egyptian, Babylonian, and Assyrian sources. Hittite monuments and inscriptions were excavated during the 19th century, though they were not deciphered until 1915. From these sources, archeologists and historians have succeeded in outlining a general history of the Hittites during their ascendancy. Some of the mystery which surrounds them has resulted from the confusion, in ancient inscriptions of other civilizations, between them and the original inhabitants of Khatti. Egyptian monuments, for example, depict the Hittites with large, aquiline noses and sloping foreheads, a physical type which is thought characteristic of the Khatti Hittites rather than their invaders.

Research indicates that the invading Hittites may have come from regions north of the Black and Caspian seas. This hypothesis is borne out by the fact that the Hittite language (q.v.) belongs to the group of Indo-European languages. Other languages represented in Hittite archives are Khattish and Khurrish, both non-Indo-European, and Lûish, akin to Hittite. The juxtaposition of these languages, together with the data in Hittite and other inscriptions, indicates that the invaders entered and conquered Cappadocia about 2000 B.C. During the next two centuries, the Hittites established themselves in Asia Minor with their capital at Pteria (modern Boghazkeui). About 1800 B.C. the Hittite king Tlabarnash extended his empire to the Mediterranean Sea. Successive kings continued the Hittite march eastward, and by 1758 B.C. all of Babylonia was a Hittite province. The Hittite invasion caused the migration of Syrian peoples, known as the Hyksos, who conquered Egypt during the 18th century B.C. (see EGYPT: *History*). By the 14th century B.C. the Hittite Empire was the greatest power in the Near East. Inevitably the Hittites clashed with the power of Egypt. About 1290 B.C., near the city of Kadesh, the Hittite king Hattusil led an army against the Egyptians under Ramses II. After the battle, the two rulers concluded an alliance and Ramses married Hattusil's daughter in 1277 B.C. Amicable relations between the two great empires continued until about 1195 B.C., when the Hittites joined the confederacy of peoples that attacked Egypt, according to an Egyptian inscription which declares that the prince of the Hittites was captured in battle. Internal dissension and Assyrian attacks in the 13th and 12th centuries B.C. resulted in the end of Hittite domination in Asia Minor. Strong, independent Hittite kingdoms existed for several centuries after the fall of the empire, but Carchemish, the last of them, was conquered by the Assyrian ruler Sargon II in 717 B.C.

The Hittite culture, which has been the subject of many archeological studies during the 20th century, was strongly influenced by contemporary civilizations, notably that of Babylon, from which the Hittites borrowed their cuneiform (q.v.) script. Hittite religion and art are mixtures of elements taken from other cultures. Though Hittite adaptations of these elements resulted in a uniformly high level of culture by the 13th century B.C., the empire did not produce a great civilization of its own.

HIVES. See URTICARIA.

HOANG-HO. See HWANG-HO.

HOARHOUND. See HOREHOUND.

HOATZIN or **HOACTZIN,** a South American bird, *Opisthocomos cristatus,* which constitutes a suborder Opisthocomi of the order Galliformes. The adult bird is about 14 in. long and is generally dark olive with white markings above and chestnut markings below. It somewhat resembles a small pheasant, but has a long, erectile crest of loose feathers on its crown. Its wings and legs are short, its feet are large, and its tail is long and wide, broadly bordered with yellow. The bird feeds on the fruit and leaves of several trees found along the banks of the Amazon River. Unlike other birds, the hoatzin grinds its food in its muscular crop rather than its gizzard. The adult gives off a musky, offensive odor which has led to native common names which, translated, signify "stinkbird" and "stinking pheasant". The hoatzin is arboreal; although it occasionally flies in slow and clumsy fashion, it prefers climbing among the branches of trees. As the wing feathers develop, the claws degenerate; the adults utilize their clawless wings in climbing much as the young use their claws.

HOBAN, JAMES (1762?–1831), American architect, born in County Kilkenny, Ireland, and educated at the University of Dublin. He settled in Charleston, S.C., before the American Revolution, and in 1792 moved to Washington, D.C. He is best known as the architect who, between 1792 and 1799, designed and directed the building of the mansion for the President, later known as the White House. He rebuilt the White House after it was burned by the British in 1814. He was also one of the architects who worked on the design and execution of the Capitol building.

HOBART, capital of Tasmania, located on the S.E. coast, in Buckingham County, on Storm Bay at the mouth of the Derwent R. The city is the seat of the Anglican bishopric of Tasmania and of the Roman Catholic archbishopric of Hobart. The University of Tasmania, established in 1890, is located in Hobart. The harbor is the largest one of the island. The principal exports are wool, ores, lumber, grain, hops, and fruit. Imports are coal, tin, sugar, tea, and manufactured products. In Hobart are foundries, tanneries, flour mills, sawmills, and factories producing woolen goods. The city was founded in 1804 and named for Lord Robert Hobart, then British secretary for war and the colonies. In 1853 Hobart was made a municipality, and in 1857 it became a city. Pop. (1953 est.) 93,480.

HOBART, GARRET AUGUSTUS (1844–99), American lawyer and statesman, 24th Vice-President of the United States, born in Long Branch, N.J., and educated at Rutgers College. He was admitted to the bar in 1869, and practiced law in Paterson, N.J. Over a period of twenty years, starting in 1871, he was city counsel of Paterson, a member of the New Jersey State Assembly, and vice-president of the State Senate. He was elected vice-president of the United States in 1896 when William McKinley was elected President, and as an intimate friend and counselor of President Mc-Kinley exercised strong influence on the conduct of public affairs. He died before the expiration of his term of office.

HOBART COLLEGE. See SENECA, COLLEGES OF THE.

HOBBEMA, MEINDERT (1638–1709), Dutch painter, born in Amsterdam, where he lived during his entire career. Hobbema and Jakob van Ruisdael (q.v.) are considered the two greatest masters of Dutch landscape painting. The two artists were friendly and the work of Hobbema was influenced by that of Ruisdael. Hobbema painted scenes of the village countryside, in which cottages, huts, and ruined castles are surrounded by trees and foliage. Pools and particularly water mills were also among his favorite motives, and clear skies full of great white clouds form the background of many of his pictures.

At the age of thirty Hobbema married the cook of Lambert Reynst, the burgomaster of Amsterdam. Through the influence of the burgomaster he received a municipal appointment as wine gauger, gauging foreign wine-casks in the Amsterdam measure, and thereafter he abandoned his artistic career.

One of his finest paintings, "The Avenue Middelharnis", is hung, with many other examples of his work, at the National Gallery, London; his excellent "Landscape with a Ruined Castle" is in the Frick Museum, New York City. His work is also to be found in the Rijksmuseum at Amsterdam, the Antwerp Museum, the Louvre at Paris, and the Chicago Art Institute.

HOBBES, THOMAS (1588–1679), English philosopher, born in Malmesbury, and educated at Magdalen Hall, Oxford University.

Thomas Hobbes

He was born prematurely, reputedly because of the fright of his mother at reports of the approach of the Spanish Armada; to this circumstance Hobbes attributed the excessive timidity which plagued him all his life. In 1608 he became the tutor of William Cavendish, later Earl of Devonshire; in the following years he made several tours through France and Italy with his pupil and, later, with the latter's son. During his travels he met and talked with several of the advanced thinkers of the time, including Galileo Galilei, René Descartes, and Pierre Gassendi. In 1637, on one of his periodic returns to England, Hobbes became interested in the constitutional struggle between the king and Parliament. He immediately set to work on "a little treatise in English" in defense of the royal prerogative. This work was privately circulated in 1640 under the title *The Elements of Law, Natural and Politique* (published 1650). Hobbes became fearful that Parliament might have him arrested because of his book, and he fled to Paris, where he remained in voluntary exile for eleven years.

In 1642 he finished his *De Cive,* a statement of his theory of government; the work was circulated privately, but was not printed until 1647. From 1646 to 1648 he was mathematics tutor to the Prince of Wales, later Charles II. Hobbes' best-known work, *Leviathan, Or the Matter, Form and Power of a Commonwealth* (1651), was a forceful and detailed exposition of his doctrine of sovereignty. The work was received by the followers of the exiled Charles as a justification of the Commonwealth, and excited the suspicions of the French authorities by its attack on the papacy. Again fearful of arrest, Hobbes fled back to England.

In 1660, when the Commonwealth ended and Hobbes' former pupil acceded to the throne, Hobbes again came into favor. However, in 1666, Commons passed a bill requiring investigation and report of "such books as tend to atheism, blasphemy and profaneness . . . and in particular the book . . . of Hobbes called the *Leviathan*". The measure caused Hobbes to burn many of his papers, and to withhold from publication three of his works: *Behemoth: The History of the Causes of Civil Wars of England; Dialogues . . . of the Common Laws of England;* and a metrical *Historia Ecclesiastica*. At the age of eighty-four, Hobbes amused himself by writing an autobiography in Latin verse, and within the next three years he translated into English verse the *Iliad* and the *Odyssey* of Homer.

Hobbes' philosophy represents a reaction against the liberty of conscience of the Reformation which, he contended, brought anarchy. It effected the breach of English philosophy with scholasticism and laid the foundations of modern scientific sociology by its attempt to apply to man, as both maker and matter of society, the principles of physical science which govern the rest of the material world. Hobbes developed his politics and ethics from a naturalistic basis; he held that all men fear each other, and for this reason must submit to the supremacy of the state in both secular and religious matters. See ETHICS.

HOBBLEBUSH. See VIBURNUM.

HOBBY, OVETA CULP (1905–), American soldier, born in Killeen, Texas, and educated at Mary Hardin Baylor College and Texas Law School. At the age of twenty she was elected to the Texas House of Representatives, in which she served for six years. In 1931 she became research editor of the *Houston Post,* a newspaper with which she was associated for many years, serving successively as book editor, assistant general editor, and executive vice-president. In the same year she married William P. Hobby, a former governor of Texas. She was a member of the Texas Legislature again from 1939 to 1941, and then worked with the War Department Bureau of Public Relations. In 1942 she was appointed director of the U.S. Women's Auxiliary Army Corps, and in 1943 she was commissioned colonel and given charge of the newly organized U.S. Women's Army Corps, in which she

served until 1945. President Dwight D. Eisenhower appointed her head of the Federal Security Agency in January, 1953. In April, 1953, when the agency was transformed into the Department of Health, Education, and Welfare, she became a cabinet member.

HOBOKEN, a city of Hudson Co., N.J., situated on the Hudson R., adjoining Jersey City on the s. and opposite the lower part of New York City, with which it is connected by several ferries and tunnels. It is served by seven railroads and by ocean-going steamers. Harbor facilities of Hoboken include extensive dry docks, and the piers of major steamship companies; among the industrial establishments in the city are large shipyards and marine shops. Other important industries in Hoboken are printing, food processing, and the manufacture of paper boxes and containers, chemicals, varnishes, furniture, lead pencils, and iron castings. The city is the site of Stevens Institute of Technology, opened in 1870 and endowed by Edwin Stevens, son of John Stevens, the founder of Hoboken.

The region of the present city was known to the Indians as Hobocan Hackingh, "the land of the tobacco pipe", from the pipes made there from local stone. The first white settlers were the Dutch, who came there after 1635, when the land was purchased by the Dutch West India Company. In 1643 the Dutch were driven out by the Indians, from whom the land was repurchased in 1658 by Peter Stuyvesant, administrator of New Netherlands. It was acquired by Samuel Bayard, a New York merchant, in 1711, and in 1784, after the confiscation of the property by the State of New Jersey because of the Tory sympathies of Bayard's descendants, it was purchased by John Stevens, who laid out a town on the site in 1804. During the early part of the 19th century Hoboken was a noted resort and contained the villas of many prominent New Yorkers. It was incorporated as a town in 1849 and as a city in 1855. Pop. (1950) 50,676.

HOBSON, JOHN ATKINSON (1858–1940), English economist, born in Derby, and educated at Oxford University. He lectured from 1887 to 1897 on English literature and economics for the University Extension Delegacy, and for the London Society for the Extension of University Teaching. He became widely recognized as one of the foremost socialist theoreticians in England. Two of his works, *The Evolution of Modern Capitalism* (1894) and *Imperialism* (1902), were regarded by the Bolshevik leader Nikolai Lenin as contributions to the theory of Marxism. But in views expressed in other works, notably *Economics and Ethics* (1929), he took issue with a number of Marxist economic theories. He rejected the revolutionary solution of contemporary social problems advanced by the Marxists and advocated a solution of the business cycle of prosperity and depression through the purchase by the state of monopolistic enterprises. Among other writings by Hobson in addition to those identified above are *Problems of Poverty* (1891), *Problems of a New World* (1921), *God and Mammon* (1931), and *Confessions of an Economic Heretic* (1938).

HOBSON, RICHMOND PEARSON (1870–1937), American naval officer, born in Greensboro, Ala. After graduation from the U.S. Naval Academy and postgraduate study abroad, Hobson organized a course for officers in the field of naval construction. He served with distinction in the Spanish-American War and became a popular hero after he tried to trap a Spanish fleet in the harbor of Santiago, Cuba, by sinking a collier at its entrance. Returning to the U.S., Hobson was the subject of a series of wild demonstrations in a number of cities during which he was kissed by thousands of hysterical women. Hobson left the Navy in 1904, and served as a member of Congress from Alabama from 1907 to 1915. He introduced the first proposed amendment to the Constitution which would have banned the sale of alcoholic beverages. In his latter years Hobson was an outspoken advocate of American naval supremacy and of the prohibition of spirituous liquors.

HOCHE, (LOUIS) LAZARE (1768–97), French general, born in Montreuil near Versailles. He enlisted in the *Gardes Françaises* at the age of sixteen and served with distinction until this corps was disbanded at the commencement of the French Revolution in 1789. After serving in various regular army regiments, Hoche was commissioned in 1792. In the following year he was made a general and put in charge of the French forces fighting against the Prussians in Lorraine. Later in the same year he was placed in command of the Army of the Rhine and administered a crushing defeat to the Prussians. In 1794 he was accused of treason and imprisoned in Paris; a few months later, after the fall and execution of Robespierre, Hoche was reinstated and led an army against the Royalists in La Vendée. Within two years he had entirely stamped out Royalist opposition in the western part of France. In 1796 Hoche was reappointed to the command of the Army of the Rhine and waged a successful campaign against the Austrians. He returned to Paris for a few months as minister of war, and then returned to his military command on the Rhine, where he died of tuberculosis.

HO CHI MINH (1892?–   ), Indochinese revolutionist, born in Annam. He became a communist in Paris during World War I. In the 1920's he studied revolutionary tactics in Moscow and organized Annamese nationalist refugees in s. China. He founded the Indochinese Communist Party at Hong Kong in 1930. Soon after the Japanese occupation of Indochina in World War II, the party, under Ho's leadership, established the Viet Minh, a united front organization consisting of communists and anti-Japanese and anti-French nationalists; as its head Ho led the resistance movement in Viet Nam. Ho became president of the newly proclaimed Republic of Viet Nam (q.v.) in 1946. He led the Viet Minh forces in the ensuing war (1946–54) against the French. See INDOCHINA, ASSOCIATED STATES OF: *History.*

HOCKEY, a game in which two opposing groups of players attempt to drive a ball, puck, or other small object through the goal of the opponent by means of sticks. Various forms of hockey were well known among the ancient Greeks and Persians. Similar games were played in Europe during the Middle Ages. The game was called *hoquet* in France and was adopted by the English, who altered the name to "hockey". Early forms of hockey were played on open fields, a form of the game now called *field hockey. Ice hockey* probably arose in Europe during the 18th century, but its present form originated in Canada during the 19th century.

Modern field hockey, as a formalized game, began about 1875 in England. Since then the game has become popular in the British Isles, Western Europe, and the British dominions. In the United States, however, field hockey is played almost exclusively by women. The game is played on a field 90 to 100 yards long and 50 to 60 yards wide. Each team is composed of eleven players; usually five of these are forwards, two are fullbacks, three are halfbacks, and one is goalkeeper, but the formation may be changed by the captain. The game is divided into two periods of thirty minutes each. The teams change goals at the end of the first half. A goal is located at the center of each goal line; each goal consists of two upright posts, 7 feet high, joined at the tips by a horizontal crossbar 4 yards wide. A net is attached to the crossbar, the uprights, and the ground behind the goal. The object

Toronto Maple Leaf goalkeeper stops puck in an ice-hockey game with the New York Rangers.

ball is a small, white, leather-covered sphere, weighing between 5½ and 5¾ ounces, with a circumference of about 9 inches. Each player carries a stick, not exceeding 28 oz. in weight, curved at one end. A point is scored whenever a team knocks the ball, by means of sticks, between the uprights and below the crossbar of the goal being defended by the opposing team. Officials at a field hockey game include two umpires, two linesmen, and two scorekeepers. Rules of field hockey do not provide for overtime play when the score is tied.

Ice hockey, one of the fastest of all games, is played entirely on skates. The game is played on an oval rink slightly over 200 feet long and about 85 feet wide. The rink is surrounded by a board wall about 4 feet high. The two goal nets, each of which is attached to a frame 4 feet high and 6 feet wide, are slightly over 10 feet from the ends of the rink. The playing area is divided into three zones, each of which is 60 feet long. The zone nearest a team's goal is called its defense zone, the central zone is called the neutral zone, and the farthest zone, nearest the opponent's goal, is called the attacking zone.

Each team consists of six players, including a center, two forwards, two defense men, and a goalkeeper. Each player carries a wooden stick having a shaft no more than 53 inches long and a blade no more than 14¾ inches long. A puck is used in ice hockey instead of a ball. It consists of a small disk of hard rubber, 3 inches in diameter and 1 inch thick. A point is scored when the puck is driven into the opponent's goal net.

Play is begun with a "face-off" in which the referee drops the puck between the opposing centers. The puck is driven or passed across the ice by means of hockey sticks. The puck may not be touched with the hands during play by any player except a goalkeeper. It may not be driven by a player from one zone to the next, but must be passed to a teammate in the next zone; if this rule is violated, the puck is said to be "offside", and play is interrupted. Play is resumed with a face-off at the place where the offside occurred. The game is divided into three twenty-minute periods, with a change of goals at the end of each period. If the game is tied at the end of the third period, an additional ten-minute period is played; if the tie is not broken at the end of this period, the game ends in a tie. Penalties are given for excessive roughness or other infractions of the rules by banishing the offending player from the ice for a fixed number of minutes. The penalized player's team may not use a substitute during the player's penalty period. The chief official of an ice hockey game is the referee, whose decisions are final.

HODEIDA, city and one of the principal seaports of Yemen, Arabia, located on the Red Sea, about 100 miles N. of Mocha. Hodeida is the chief landing place for African pilgrims on their way to the Islamic holy city of Mecca, located about 500 miles N.W. of the city. Coffee and hides are the principal exports. Pop. (1948 est.) 26,000.

HODGES, COURTNEY HICKS (1887–   ), American army officer, born in Perry, Ga., and educated at the U.S. Military Academy at West Point. He enlisted in the regular army in 1906 and rose through the ranks to brigadier general in 1940, major general in 1941, and lieutenant general in 1943. He participated in various campaigns in France during World War I as battalion and regimental commander, and served with the army of occupation in Germany in 1918. During World War II he was commanding general of the tenth Army Corps from 1942 to 1943, and later commanded the Third Army and the First Army through many European campaigns.

HODGKIN'S DISEASE, a general disease characterized by malignant neoplastic growth of cells in the lymph nodes, which may involve the lymphatic tissue of any organ of the body. Enlargement of the cervical glands is often the first sign of the condition. In many cases, however, the condition is entirely confined to the internal lymph glands. The spleen is frequently enlarged. The cause of Hodgkin's disease is still as obscure as it was when Thomas Hodgkin (1798–1866), an English physician, described the disease in 1832. The condition is usually restricted to persons between the ages of fifteen and thirty-five, but has been observed in patients as old as sixty. Complete recovery is extremely rare. Untreated cases usually die within three years, but the lives of patients treated with X-rays and nitrogen mustards have been prolonged for ten years or longer. See CANCER.

HODLER, FERDINAND (1863–1928), Swiss figure and allegorical painter, born in Gurzelon. In 1881 he studied with Barthélemy Menn in Geneva, where he learned to paint in the classical manner. A visit to Spain in 1877 acquainted him with the art of the Spanish masters, and in the same year he achieved his first success when he exhibited his painting "Wrestlers" in Paris. In 1900 he received a gold medal at the Paris Universal Exposition.

For the next few years Hodler devoted himself to the painting of Swiss village scenes and episodes. Subsequently he gave new liveliness and interest to historical painting, celebrating the heroism of the Swiss soldiers of the Middle Ages in such works as the large fresco "The Retreat from Marignano", in the National Museum, Zurich. The work of his late years became more decorative in character as he turned to the painting of large, allegorical figure compositions. He is generally regarded as the greatest modern Swiss painter. Important examples of his late style are "Day" and "Night" in the Berne Museum; many other paintings by him are in the Kunsthaus, Zurich.

HOE, the name of a family prominently connected with the manufacture and improvement of the printing press in America. Its most important members are the following. **1.** ROBERT HOE (1784–1833), born in Leicestershire, England. He emigrated to the U.S. in 1803, worked for a time as a master carpenter, and subsequently was an associate in a business which shifted from carpentry to the manufacture of a hand printing press. In 1823 he became sole proprietor of the business. A skillful mechanic, Hoe constructed and introduced the original Hoe press, and was apparently the earliest American machinist to use steam as a motive power in his plant. **2.** RICHARD MARCH HOE (1812–86), son of Robert Hoe, born in New York City. He entered his father's factory at the age of fifteen, and eventually succeeded him as head of the firm. In 1847, in an attempt to secure greater speed in printing, he introduced presses using revolving cylinders, which replaced the old flat-bed models, and as subsequently improved were called the Hoe rotary or "lightning" presses. Shortly thereafter he developed the web press, which superseded the former invention, printing on both sides of a sheet, and containing apparatus for cutting and folding sheets. The web press became the basis of the modern newspaper press. **3.** ROBERT HOE (1839–1909), nephew of Richard March Hoe, born in New York City, and educated in Europe. He became head of the family firm in 1886, and carried on the improvements in printing presses and processes which had been initiated by his grandfather and uncle. Under his direction were developed the rotary art press, a multicolor press for printing colored illustrations, and a number of improvements in the efficiency and speed of newspaper presses. He was also a collector of art objects and of rare books and manuscripts; during his career as a connoisseur he participated in the founding of the Metropolitan Museum of Art in New York City and amassed a personal collection valued at several million dollars. His interest in book making as a fine art led to his participation in organizing the Grolier Club in 1884 and his election as its first president.

For a description of some of the printing presses produced by the Hoe firm, Robert Hoe & Co., see PRINTING.

HOF, a town of Bavaria, West Germany, on the Saale R., 30 miles N.E. of Bayreuth. It is an important center of the cotton- and wool-spinning industry, and also contains flour mills, sugar refineries, sawmills, ironworks, chemical works, breweries, and machine shops. In the vicinity of the town are large iron mines and marble quarries. After World War II Hof was assigned to the United States Zone of Occupation. Pop. (1950) 60,867.

HOFER, ANDREAS (1767–1810), Tirolese patriot, born in St. Leonhard in the valley of Passeier, in the Austrian Alps. He fought in the Austrian army in the wars against the French (1796–1805), and rose to captain of militia. When by the Peace of Pressburg in 1805 Tirol was transferred to Bavaria, Hofer became the leader of resistance to Bavarian rule. He raised a force of Tirolese and in 1809 drove the Bavarian army out of Tirol. In spite of assurances to the contrary, given to Hofer by the Austrian emperor Francis, Tirol was surrendered to the French by the armistice of Znaim, and a force of 40,000 French and Bavarian troops attempted to occupy the territory. Hofer defeated the new invasion and for two months ruled Tirol under the emperor of Austria. The treaty of Schönbrunn, however, again ceded Tirol to Bavaria, and French troops occupied the country. Hofer revolted once more, but was defeated, and took refuge in the mountains. Two months later he was betrayed to the French, who took him to Mantua. There he was court-martialed and shot.

HOFER, KARL (1878–), German painter, born in Karlsruhe. He studied with Hans Thoma, and from 1907 to 1913 he lived in Paris, where he was influenced by the works of Paul Cézanne and Pablo Picasso. After 1919 Hofer developed a highly individual style of painting, severe and thoughtful, and careful in structure. He also used broad masses of color in the manner of the Expressionists. Among his most famous paintings are "Night Club", "Melon", and "The Yellow Flag". His works are in the Berlin and Dresden galleries, Germany, in the Rome National Museum of Modern Art, Italy, and in the Zurich Art Museum, Switzerland.

HOFFMAN, MALVINA (1887–), American sculptor, born in New York City. She studied with Auguste Rodin (q.v.), and by 1911 had achieved international fame with her "Pavlowa Gavotte", "Bacchanale Russe",

and "La Peri", sculpture groups depicting rhythm and movement in the dance and inspired by the Russian ballerina Anna Pavlova, her close friend. In 1920 she carved the large monument "Sacrifice", in memory of the Harvard University men who died in World War I. Later the Field Museum of Chicago commissioned her to portray the races of man in sculpture. She was helped in this important undertaking by the prominent British anthropologist Sir Arthur Keith, and by 1932 she had completed the work after traveling widely throughout the world.

Her sculpture is marked by intensity of feeling combined with perfect control over mass and detail. She created busts, memorials, animal sculpture, and fountain pieces. Her "Pavlowa Gavotte" is in the Detroit Institute of Fine Arts, Mich.; 100 bronzes comprising "Races of Man" are in the Field Museum, Chicago; and a bust of Ignace Jan Paderewski is in the American Academy at Rome. She is also represented by work in the Brooklyn Museum, New York City, in the Carnegie Institute, Pittsburgh, and in the Luxembourg, Paris.

HOFFMAN, PAUL GRAY (1891–), American businessman and government official, born in Chicago, Ill. He studied at the University of Chicago in 1908–09, and in 1911 joined the sales staff of the Studebaker Corporation. By 1935 he had risen to the position of president of the firm. At various times he also served as chairman of the Automotive Safety Foundation, director of the Federal Reserve Bank of Chicago, director of the New York Life Insurance Company, vice-president of the Automobile Manufacturers Association, and member of President Truman's Advisory Committee on Foreign Aid. In 1948 President Harry S. Truman appointed him head of the Economic Cooperation Administration, the agency of the U.S. government responsible for the supervision of the European Recovery Program (q.v.). He served as president of the Ford Foundation from 1951 to 1953. His writings include *Peace Can Be Won* (1951).

HOFFMANITES. See FRIENDS OF THE TEMPLE.

HOFFMANN, AUGUST HEINRICH, known as HOFFMANN VON FALLERSLEBEN (1798– 1874), German poet, philologist, and literary historian, born in Fallersleben, and educated at the universities of Göttingen and Bonn. He was professor of German at the University of Breslau from 1830 to 1842, when he was dismissed because of the liberal political views he expressed in his *Unpolitische Lieder* (1841–42). He lived and worked in a number of German cities before taking up permanent residence at Korvei, where from 1860 he was librarian of the Duke of Ratibor. His philological and historical works include *Fundgruben für Geschichte Deutscher Sprache und Literatur* (2 vols., 1830–37) and *Geschichte des Deutschen Kirchenliedes bis auf Luther* (1832). He is best known for his lyric poetry on subjects taken from everyday life. Among his poetic writings are *Kinderlieder* (1843–47), *Liebeslieder* (1851), and *Vaterlandslieder* (1871). He wrote the words and adapted the music for the song which became (1922) the German national hymn, *Deutschland, Deutschland, Über Alles* (1841). He was also the author of the autobiography *Mein Leben* (6 vols., 1868–70).

HOFFMANN, ERNST THEODOR WILHELM (1776–1822), German author, illustrator, and composer, born in Königsberg. For his musical compositions he used the name of Ernst Theodor Amadeus Hoffmann, in honor of Wolfgang Amadeus Mozart. As a young man, Hoffmann practiced law in Posen until forced to abandon his profession because of some satiric caricatures he drew of important citizens. Subsequently he lived in a number of German and Polish cities, earning his livelihood by painting, music criticism, and composition. In 1816 he became councilor of the court of appeals at Berlin. He is best known, however, as a writer. Beginning with 1814 he wrote a number of fictional works which were among the most characteristic and influential produced by the Romantic movement in German literature (see GERMAN LITERATURE: *The Classical and Romantic Period*). Hoffmann's fiction dealt with the grotesque, startling, marvelous, and morbid in life, and is noted for its lyrical prose, its flights of imagination, and its satiric quality. In his first book, *Phantasiestücke in Callots Manier* (4 vols., 1814–15), a collection of music criticism and short stories, illustrated by himself, appeared some of his best-known short stories, including *Don Juan, Ritter Gluck,* and *Das Märchen vom Goldenen Topf.* His other works include the novels *Die Elixiere des Teufels* (1816) and *Lebensansichten des Katers Murr* (1820–22, unfinished); and the collections of stories *Nachtstücke* (2 vols., 1817) and *Die Serapionsbrüder* (4 vols., 1819–21). Hoffmann was also the composer of the opera *Undine* (1816), to a libretto by Baron Friedrich Heinrich Karl de La Motte-Fouqué. He is best known as the author of the fantastic tales on which the French composer Jacques Offenbach based his opera *Les Contes d'Hoffmann* (1881, *"Tales of Hoffmann"*).

HOFMANN, AUGUST WILHELM VON (1818–92), German chemist, born in Giessen, and educated at the University of Göttingen. He was an assistant to the famous chemist Justus von Liebig at Giessen until 1845, when he became a docent in chemistry at the University of Bonn. In the same year Hofmann was appointed director of the newly established Royal College of Chemistry in London, and he held that position until 1864. The following year he accepted a professorship in chemistry at the University of Berlin. He founded the German Chemical Society in 1868.

Hofmann was one of the great organic chemists of his time. He worked with coal-tar products, from which he isolated benzene and aniline, and which he used in the synthesis of artificial dyes. He studied and clarified the chemistry of amines, and he discovered an important reaction (for converting amides to amines containing one fewer carbon atoms) which is now called the Hofmann reaction. He also discovered many organic chemicals, including allyl alcohol and formaldehyde. Hofmann was also a great teacher, and his *Introduction to Modern Chemistry* (1865) brought about important reforms in the methods of teaching chemistry. He was knighted in 1888. Among his writings are *A Handbook of Organic Analysis* (1853), *The Life Work of Liebig in Experimental and Philosophic Chemistry* (1876), and *Zur Erinnerung an Vorangegangene Freunde* (1889).

HOFMANN, JOSEF CASIMIR (1876–   ), Polish-American concert pianist and composer, born in Cracow. His first teacher was his father, who was a professor at the Warsaw Conservatoire and conductor of the Warsaw opera. Later he studied theory and composition, and at the age of sixteen became a pupil of Anton Rubinstein. He made his first public appearance as a pianist at the age of six and began a long career of concert tours throughout Europe and America; his American debut was made at the Metropolitan Opera House in 1887. He was noted for his interpretative ability in all schools of music.

Hofmann became an American citizen in 1926 and in the same year became director and teacher at the Curtis Institute of Music in Philadelphia, with which he was associated until 1938. Under the pseudonym of Michel Dvorsky he composed a symphony and many works for the piano.

HOFMANNSTHAL, HUGO VON (1874–1929), Austrian poet and playwright, born in Vienna, and educated at the University of Vienna. His early lyric and dramatic poetry, distinguished for melodious and colorful language and for its complex spiritual moods, established the Romantic school of poetry and drama in Austria, in German literature as a whole he was the earliest of the Neoromantic or late Romantic writers. Among his works are the dramas in verse *Gestern* (1892), *Der Tod des Tizian* (1901), *Elektra* (1903), *Das Gerettete Venedig, nach Thomas Otway* (1904), and *Jedermann* (1912), produced by Max Reinhardt (q.v.); and the book of lyric verse *Ausgewählte Gedichte* (1903). He is also noted as the librettist of six operas by the modern German composer Richard Strauss: *Elektra* (produced 1909), *Der Rosenkavalier* (1911), *Ariadne auf Naxos* (1912), *Die Frau Ohne Schatten* (1919), *Die Aegyptische Helena* (1928), and *Arabella* (1933).

HOFMEYR, JAN HENDRIK (1845–1909), South African statesman, born in Cape Town, and educated at the South African College. As editor of the *Volksvriend* and later of the *Zuid Afrikaan* and *Zuid Afrikaansche Tidjschrift* he was the most influential journalist in Cape Colony. From 1879 to 1895 he was a member of the Cape parliament and, because of his control of the Afrikander Bund, a political group formed in 1882, he was the leader of the Dutch party in Cape Colony. Hofmeyr worked for a fusion of the British and Dutch elements and a federation of the various colonies in South Africa. He supported bilingualism and it is largely due to his influence that there are two official languages in South Africa, English and Afrikaans (q.v.), a Dutch dialect.

Starting in 1890, Hofmeyr collaborated with Cecil Rhodes, who became premier of Cape Colony with the support of the Afrikander Bund. In 1895 Hofmeyr resigned his seat in parliament and his presidency of the Bund because the members of the Bund had become increasingly dissatisfied with Rhodes' policies. However, after the Jameson Raid, Hofmeyr severed his alliance with Rhodes in 1896 and became president of the Bund. After the outbreak of the Boer War, he neither repudiated nor supported the outspoken anti-British attitude of the Bund, and he soon withdrew to Europe. Toward the end of the war he returned to South Africa, and took an active part in negotiations to establish the Union of South Africa (q.v.).

HOG, a mature specimen of the domestic swine, a member of the family Suidae (q.v.), which is extensively raised in most parts of the world as a food animal. Young swine are usually called pigs, but in common usage the three terms, swine, hog, and pig, are often used interchangeably. Hogs are cloven-hoofed animals with heavy, round bodies and short legs. Their skins are thick and partially covered with coarse bristles. The head of the hog has a comparatively long, flexible snout containing the nostrils and the mouth, which has 44 teeth.

Young hogs are frequently called *shoats*. The adult male hog is usually called a *boar* and the female adult hog a *sow*. The exact genesis of the domestic hog is not known, but zoologists believe that the animal is a cross between the wild boar of Europe, *Sus scrofa,* and the Asiatic wild boar, *Sus cristatus.* The economic value of the hog is considerable. Its fresh flesh, known as pork, is a staple meat, and is also smoked or otherwise cured and eaten as ham and bacon. Lard, the fat of the hog, is one of the most important edible fats. Hog intestines are used as sausage casings, and other portions of the animal including the head and feet are regarded as delicacies. The hog's hide, when tanned, becomes the handsome and durable leather known as pigskin, used extensively in the manufacture of luggage and gloves. The stiff bristles from the hide are made into paint brushes.

Wild boars were first domesticated by the Chinese in approximately 2900 B.C. In Europe they were probably domesticated independently at a somewhat later date. Archeologists believe that these animals were first domesticated as scavengers and only later came to be regarded as food animals. Hogs are omnivorous and can live on vegetable and animal garbage. Another reason for the popularity of the hog as a farm animal is that it reproduces more rapidly and matures earlier than any of the other common meat-producing animals.

Breeds. A large number of breeds of hogs have been developed in various parts of the world to meet local conditions of climate and pasturage. In the U.S. eight separate breeds are widely raised: the *Berkshire,* an English breed with a black body and white face and markings, which matures early but is not very prolific; the *Chester White,* a pink-skinned, white-bristled breed developed in Chester Co., Pa., which grazes well, is very prolific, and matures early; the *Duroc Jersey,* another

The Rural New Yorker

VARIOUS BREEDS OF DOMESTIC HOG. *Top, left: Chester White. Top, right: Berkshire. Bottom, left: Spotted Poland China. Bottom, right: Duroc Jersey.*

breed of U.S. origin, red in color, hardy, and maturing to substantial weights; the *Hampshire,* a breed from England with a black body belted with a white band about the body and front legs, remarkable for its ability to thrive on pasture; the *Poland China,* developed in Warren Co. and Butler Co., Ohio, a black breed with white feet, which in mature boars may reach weights of 1000 lbs.; the *Spotted Poland China,* similar to the Poland China but having numerous white spots on the body; the *Tamworth,* a red breed of English origin with a maximum of lean meat in its long deep body; and the *Yorkshire,* an English breed of white hogs which, like the Tamworths, are particularly suited to bacon production.

Feeding Hogs. In modern farming practice, hogs are not fed on garbage but are given a carefully balanced ration containing proteins, carbohydrates or fats, and minerals. Approximately 400 lbs. of balanced feed are needed to add 100 lbs. to the weight of a hog. In the U.S., corn is the most important component of hog feeds, but rye, barley, vegetable oils and oil cakes, alfalfa, milk products such as skim milk and dried milk, tankage, and fish meal are also employed as components of hog rations. A typical feed mixture for hogs being fattened for slaughter might include 85 lbs. of ground corn, 5 lbs. of tankage or fish meal, 5 lbs. of linseed meal, and 5 lbs. of alfalfa hay. Hogs are also fed on forage crops such as alfalfa, clovers, rape, soybeans, and bluegrass.

Diseases of Hogs. Like other domestic animals, hogs are subject to a number of diseases, some of which are also dangerous to human beings who may eat meat from infected animals. The most serious disease to which hogs are prone is hog cholera, a highly contagious and fatal disease caused by a filtrable virus. Prior to the year 1905 as much as 13 percent of the hogs in the U.S. succumbed to hog cholera in a single year. In 1905, however, the Bureau of Animal Industry of the U.S. Dept. of Agriculture developed an effective serum for this disease. Another serious disease of hogs is swine erysipelas, an illness, characterized by skin outbreaks, fever, and swollen joints, to which human beings are also subject. The bacillus causing this disease is known and a serum has been developed which gives immunity for a few weeks. Hogs are also subject to several kinds of enteritis, particularly a form of dysentery commonly called the scours, which affects young pigs. The cause of this disease is not known but it is apparently partly due to faulty nutrition of the young animals. The disease caused by the organism *Brucella abortis,* which also affects cattle and man, is less common in hogs than in cows but is important because the disease can be readily transmitted to men and women who are tending or slaughtering the infected animals; see UNDULANT FEVER. The U.S. Public Health Service estimates that approximately half the cases of human undulant fever in this country are traceable to hogs. Hogs fed on uncooked garbage are prone to infestation by a number of internal parasites, of which the most dangerous are the nematode worms called Trichinae which form cysts in the muscles. Trichinae can be passed on from hogs and other animal hosts to men eating the flesh of the infected animal. Presence of Trichinae in the human body can cause the disease called trichinosis. Trichinosis may be avoided by thoroughly cooking pork and other hog-flesh foods to kill the parasites. Vesicular exanthema, a highly contagious disease which affects only swine, is also spread through feeding uncooked garbage. The symptoms closely resemble the more dangerous foot-and-mouth disease (q.v.).

HOGAN, BEN (1912–   ), American professional golf player, born in Fort Worth, Texas. He was the leading money winner among American golfers in 1940, 1941, 1942, and 1946; was a member of the U.S. Ryder Cup team in 1941 and its captain in 1947; won the Professional Golfers' Association championship in 1946 and 1948, the U.S. open championship in 1948, 1950, 1951, and 1953, and the British open championship in 1953.

HOG APE, a name for the mandrill. See BABOON.

HOG APPLE. See MAY APPLE.

HOGARTH, WILLIAM (1697–1764), English painter and engraver, born in London. Upon finishing his apprenticeship to a silversmith in 1718 he turned to engraving, first becoming known in 1726 by his plates for Samuel Butler's novel *Hudibras.* About 1728 Hogarth began painting, producing small group scenes such as "The Wanstead Assembly" and "The Politician". In 1734 he established his reputation as a painter of English manners and customs by two series of paintings, "A Harlot's Progress" and "The Rake's Progress". He also made popular sets of engravings from these paintings, and soon became acclaimed as a brilliant satirist of moral follies.

In 1736 he painted, on the staircase of St. Bartholomew's Hospital, "The Good Samaritan" and "The Pool of Bethesda", two of his most ambitious works. He engraved plates for Jarvis' translation of *Don Quixote.* In 1745 his most famous series appeared, "The Marriage à la Mode", in a set of six paintings and an equal number of engravings. Hogarth's remarkably exuberant satire, his pungent details of everyday life, and his mastery of complex scenes find their highest expression in this work. To this period also belong many of Hogarth's portraits.

In 1753 he wrote *The Analysis of Beauty,* in which he tried to establish a fixed standard for principles of esthetics. Four years later he was appointed sergeant painter to King George II. From 1762 until his death Hogarth was engaged in political feuds with the newspaper editor John Wilkes and the poet Charles Churchill. His last engraving, "The Bathos", intended as a farewell work, was published in 1764. On his monument is an epitaph written by his friend, the actor David Garrick. Though Hogarth painted some exceptional portraits, such as "The Shrimp Girl" and "Self-portrait with a Dog" (National Gallery), his greatest achievement is as a caustic commentator on the customs and moralities of his time. Most of his important paintings are in the London galleries and museums, including the famous "Garrick as Richard III" and "Sigismonda".

HOGG, JAMES, known as THE ETTRICK SHEPHERD (1770–1835), Scottish poet, born in Ettrick, Selkirkshire. He had no education; as a boy he herded sheep and worked on his father's farm, and from 1790 to 1799 he himself was a shepherd at Yarrow, where his employer encouraged his gift for composing songs. His first poem, *Donald M'Donald,* was published anonymously in 1800. In the following year he visited Edinburgh, and arranged for the publication of a collection of his songs, which appeared as *Scottish Pastorals* (1801). In 1802 he met Sir Walter Scott, who was visiting Ettrick in search of material for his own work; Hogg was sufficiently encouraged by Scott to write a volume of poems and ballads, *The Mountain Bard* (1807).

Hogg settled in Edinburgh in 1810, and took up writing for a living; in that year appeared his *Forest Minstrel.* On the appear-

Metropolitan Museum of Art

"The Cockpit," engraving by William Hogarth

ance of the volume of poems *The Queen's Wake* (1813), his reputation as a poet was firmly established. He was a close friend of the literary men of the day, including Scott, Lord Byron, Robert Southey, William Wordsworth, and John Wilson. Through the writings of Wilson, who so characterized him in his *Noctes Ambrosianæ,* Hogg became known as the Ettrick Shepherd.

Hogg is regarded as one of the great pastoral poets and songwriters of Scotland. His other poetical works include *Pilgrims of the Sun* (1815), *The Poetic Mirror* (1816), *Queen Hynde* (1826), *The Shepherd's Calendar* (1829), and *Lay Sermons* (1834). He was also the author of the prose works *The Three Perils of Man* (1822) and *Domestic Manners and Private Life of Sir Walter Scott* (1834), and of a number of tales.

HOG-NOSED SNAKE or **HOGNOSE,** common name of any of four species of short, thick-bodied, harmless, North American colubrine snakes in the genus *Heterodon.* The hog-nosed snake is characterized by a flattened snout with a strong, triangular plate slanting diagonally upward from the tip of the snout to the crown. The maximum length is about 3½ ft. The general color pattern is

highly variable in design but dull in hue. The hog-nosed snakes have extensible anterior ribs which they keep close at their sides when at rest, but which they inflate, giving them a cobralike appearance when excited. A loud hissing and weaving of the head to and fro increase their sinister appearance, causing them to be feared by people who do not know that they are harmless. If this behavior does not frighten away the disturber, the snake rolls onto its back and feigns death. The popular names applied to the hog-nosed snake because of its frightening appearance include "puffing adder", "spreading adder", "flat-headed adder", "hissing adder", "blowing viper", and "sand viper". The hog-nosed snake inhabits dry, sandy regions and burrows into the ground with its specially adapted snout. It feeds chiefly on toads and frogs. The female lays its cylindrical eggs, about 1 in. long, in the sand, and the young hatch in three or four days.

The commonest species of hog-nosed snake is *H. contortrix,* found from s. New England to Florida and westward to the Missouri and Mississippi rivers. *H. simus* is found in the Southern States westward to the Mississippi River. *H. nasicus* inhabits the region between

Montana and N. Mexico, and *H. browni* is found only in S. Florida.

HOGNUT, common name of plants which have nutlike underground tubers (see EARTH-NUT), and of a species of hickory tree which is also called pignut (q.v.).

HOG PLUM, SPANISH PLUM, or BRAZILIAN PLUM, common name of trees and shrubs of the genus *Spondias,* belonging to the Cashew family. Hog plums are native to the tropical Western Hemisphere and the South Pacific islands. The common hog plums, *S. lutea,* and *S. purpurea,* bear plumlike yellow fruits which are common food for hogs in the West Indies. Another hog plum, *S. dulcis,* also called the Tahiti apple, is native to the South Pacific islands.

HOHENZOLLERN, royal family of Germany, originating as a family of counts in Swabia in the 11th or 12th century and named for their ancestral castle, Zollern (later Hohenzollern), located near Hechingen, Swabia. The first to bear the name was probably Wezel of Zolorin, or Zollern. In 1227 one of the Hohenzollern counts, Conrad III, was awarded the burgraviate of Nuremberg by his friend the Holy Roman emperor and thus two branches of the family, the Swabian and the Franconian, were established, the Swabian being the elder branch. Through marriage and purchase of lands Conrad's domains were augmented by his Franconian heirs, who supported the Hohenstaufen and Hapsburg rulers of the Empire between the 12th and 15th centuries. One of the Franconian Hohenzollerns, Burgrave Frederick (VI) of Nuremberg, became elector and margrave of Brandenburg (q.v.) as Frederick I in 1417. He was succeeded by eleven electors, the last, Frederick III, securing the kingship in Prussia (q.v.) as Frederick I in 1701. In the century and a half after Frederick's death in 1713, Frederick William I, Frederick II the Great, Frederick William II, III, and IV, and William I held the Prussian throne. William I became ruler of the German empire in 1871 and his successors, Frederick III and William II, were also German emperors, the latter abdicating in 1918.

The Swabian branch of the Hohenzollerns, which ruled the petty principalities of Hohenzollern-Hechingen and Hohenzollern-Sigmaringen, was relatively unimportant in German history. In 1849 Charles Anthony, prince of Hohenzollern-Sigmaringen line of the Swabian branch, ceded his principality to the Prussian king. His son Leopold was considered as candidate for the Spanish throne in 1870. His second son, Charles, became Carol I, King of Romania, in 1866; Charles' descendants retained the throne until the abdication of King Michael in 1947. The Hohenzollern-Hechingen line of the Swabian branch became extinct in 1869. See GERMANY: *History.*

HOKKAIDO, formerly YEZO or EZO, one of the principal islands of the Japanese archipelago, situated due S. of Sakhalin, from which it is separated by Soya Strait, and due N. of Honshu, from which it is separated by Tsugaru Strait. The southernmost of the Kurile Islands lie off the N.E. coast of Hokkaido. The island has a coastline of about 1530 m., and is characterized topographically by a complexity of mountain systems and extensive lowlands. Among the outstanding plains regions, totaling more than 3,370,000 acres, are those bordering the Ishikari and Tokachi rivers, the largest streams of the island. Of the various mountain ranges of Hokkaido, the Kurile Range is especially noteworthy. This range, a volcanic uplift, contains a number of extinct, quiescent, and active volcanoes. The active peaks are Komagatake (3822 ft. above sea level), Tarumai (2969 ft.), Esan (2067 ft.), and Noborbetsu (1148 ft.). Tokachi (8200 ft.), in the N. central region, is the highest summit on Hokkaido. Due to the influence of the prevailing N.E. winds and cold ocean currents, climatic conditions on the island are unusually severe, particularly during the fall and winter seasons. Heavy falls of snow occur during this period. The Ainu (q.v.), a primitive, indigenous race of Japan, inhabit parts of the island. Sapporo (q.v.) is the administrative center of Hokkaido, and Hakodate (q.v.) is the largest city and chief seaport. Area of Hokkaido, including that of some sixty-eight small adjacent islands, about 34,275 sq.m.; pop. of Hokkaido (1947) 3,852,821.

HOKUSAI (1760–1849), Japanese painter, draughtsman, and designer of wood-block prints, born in Yedo. He is considered the outstanding figure of the Ukiyoyè school. Hokusai entered the studio of Shunsho in 1775 and there learned the new, popular technique of woodcut printing. From 1796 to 1802 he illustrated a large number of books with colored plates and made thousands of colored single-sheet prints. His vast amount of work pictured the stories, traditions, legends, and habits of the simple people. In these prints he displayed a quickness of invention, a free linear style, and great dexterity. His most typical wood-block prints, large screens

Metropolitan Museum of Art

"View of Mount Fuji from Todo Bay," by the Japanese painter Hokusai

and landscape paintings, were done from 1830 to 1840. The free curved lines in his work gradually became a series of spirals imparting the utmost freedom and grace to his work, as in "Raiden, the Spirit of Thunder", considered one of his finest works. In his late works Hokusai used large, broken strokes for his lines and a dry method of color, creating a more somber type of painting such as his large "Group of Workmen Building a Boat". Among his best-known works are the fifteen volumes of "Mangwa" sketches and the series of block prints known as "The Hundred Views of Mount Fuji". Besides its influence on the Japanese art of the time, his work was an important factor in Western art of the late 19th century.

HOLBEIN, HANS, THE YOUNGER (1497 ?–1543), German portrait painter, born in Augsburg. He was taught painting by his father Hans Holbein the Elder. In 1521–22 he painted frescoes in the City Hall at Basle, and the following year he painted a portrait of the Dutch scholar Erasmus which the latter sent to the English statesman Sir Thomas More in 1525. A year later, carrying letters of introduction to More from Erasmus, Holbein visited England, where he lived for some time as a guest of More, painting many fine portraits of More and his friends. In 1528 Holbein returned to Basle and paint-

ed the notable portrait of his wife and two children (now in the Basle Museum). However, the bitter religious controversies of the time put an end to the patronage of art in Basle, and in 1531 Holbein again visited England. There he painted portraits of the merchants of the Steelyard (the London establishment of the Hanseatic League) and received a commission to execute two large decorative paintings. Unfortunately all his fresco and decorative works have been either lost or destroyed.

His portrait of Thomas Cromwell, Earl of Essex, brought him recognition at the court, and by 1536 he was fully established as one of the painters to King Henry VIII. During this period he painted a portrait of Henry's wife Jane Seymour, and of many important court figures. In 1538 Holbein was sent to Belgium by the king to paint the portrait of Queen Christina of Denmark and in 1539 to Flanders to paint Anne of Cleves; the latter portrait (now in the Louvre) is said to have decided the king in his choice of a wife.

Holbein's greatest fame rests on his remarkable series of 89 portraits of well-known court figures, drawn in red chalk and India ink, which are housed in the royal collection at Windsor Castle. For clear, incisive draughtsmanship and sensitive character portrayals these drawings remain unsurpassed and have

"Jean de Dinteville," painting by Hans Holbein the Younger

established Holbein as one of the supreme masters in the field of portraiture. His early death is generally attributed to the plague of London in 1543.

HOLBERG, Ludvig (1684–1754), Danish writer, considered the founder of Danish literature, born in Bergen, Norway, and educated at the universities of Copenhagen and Oxford. He became professor of metaphysics at the University of Copenhagen in 1718; professor of public eloquence in 1720; and rector of the university in 1735. In 1747 he was created baron of Holberg.

Holberg's use of his native language in writing drama, poetry, and historical works established Danish as a literary language. At a time when plays on the Danish stage were given only in German or French, Holberg wrote more than a dozen plays which were successfully performed in his native tongue. These plays include the well-known comedy *Henrik and Pernille* (1724). Holberg's poem *Pedar Paars* (1719), a satire on contemporary manners, is considered a classic of Danish literature. Other satiric works are the poems *Metamorphosis* (1726) and *Nicolai Klimii Iter Subterraneum* (1741). After 1727, Holberg wrote a series of scholarly philosophical and historical works. These include *Description of Denmark and Norway* (1729), *Description of Bergen* (1737), and *Moral Reflection* (1744). His last work was his *Letters* (5 vols., 1748–54).

HOLCROFT, Thomas (1745–1809), English writer and dramatist, born in London

and self-educated. He worked as a shoemaker and stableboy at Newmarket, and subsequently as a tutor in the house of the philanthropist Granville Sharp. After working as a prompter at a theater in Dublin he acted in comedy parts with groups of traveling actors; later he began writing plays. He wrote more than thirty in all, including *The Crisis* (1778), which was presented at Drury Lane, and *Duplicity* (1781); his most successful play was *The Road to Ruin* (1792), one of the first melodramas to be produced in England. He also wrote a number of novels, including *Alwyn* (1780), and translated many works from other languages, among them Goethe's *Hermann und Dorothea* (1801) and Johann Kaspar Lavater's *Physiognomische Fragmente* (1793). In 1794, because of activities in behalf of the French Revolution, he was charged with treason, but was subsequently acquitted without trial.

HÖLDERLIN, (Johann Christian) Friedrich (1770–1843), German poet, born in Lauffen on the Neckar. He studied theology at Tübingen, but did not become a clergyman. The poet Friedrich von Schiller published some of Hölderlin's early verse in periodicals which he edited, and also obtained for him a position as tutor. In 1804 Hölderlin was appointed librarian to the landgrave of Hesse-Homburg. Hölderlin became insane in 1807 and never recovered. His poetry is characterized by the intense subjectivity of the German "Sturm and Drang" period (see German Literature: *The Classical and Romantic Period*), but at the same time is influenced by the spirit of restraint and balance of the arts of Greek antiquity. Hölderlin used no rhyme but wrote in a form known later as "free verse" (q.v.). His work is a link between the German classical and romantic schools. He is known principally for his lyrics, among which are *An die Hoffnung* and *Der Blinde Sänger*. His principal larger works are *Hyperion*, a romantic story in the form of letters (2 vols., 1797 and 1799), and *Der Tod des Empedokles*, an unfinished tragedy.

HOLDOVER. See Landlord and Tenant.

HOLGUÍN, city of Oriente Province, Cuba, located about 25 miles s.s.w. of the Atlantic Ocean port of Gíbara and 65 miles N.W. of Santiago de Cuba. Holguín was settled in 1720, and became a city in 1751. It is the trading center for the tobacco, corn, cattle, and cabinet wood of the surrounding area. Pop. (1943) 171,997.

HOLIDAY, a day set apart as a religious anniversary, or for the commemoration of some extraordinary event or distinguished person, or for some reason of public policy; see FEASTS AND FESTIVALS; BANK HOLIDAYS. Holidays are characterized by a partial or total cessation of work and of normal business activities, and are generally accompanied by public and private ceremonies.

Originally, in ancient times, holidays were predominantly religious in character and were called holy days, whence "holiday" is derived. Subsequently holidays commemorating historical occasions or distinguished persons outnumbered religious holy days. Today the outstanding holiday of the Christian, Mohammedan, and Hebrew peoples is one of religious observance, taking place on Sunday (q.v.), Friday, and Saturday, respectively.

In the United States, Sunday is not only a religious holiday, but is the only common-law holiday. Other legal holidays are designated by legislative enactment or by executive proclamation. Congress and the President designate the legal holidays for the District of Columbia and the Federal Territories, but are without power to declare national holidays. However, Independence Day and other holidays are observed on a national scale as a result of action by the States. In the case of Thanksgiving Day the President proclaims the calendar date and requests national observance, and the States thereupon usually enact the necessary legislation. Federal statutes frequently specify certain days as holidays for purposes related to the legislation.

The following are the principal legal holidays, in addition to Sunday, observed in the United States, its Territories, and its possessions.

Jan 1. *New Year's Day*. Observed in all States, the District of Columbia, and Territories.

Jan. 20. *Inauguration Day*. Observed in the District of Columbia only.

Feb. 12. *Lincoln's Birthday*. Observed in Arizona, Arkansas, California, Colorado, Connecticut, Delaware, Illinois, Indiana, Iowa, Kansas, Kentucky, Maryland, Michigan, Minnesota, Missouri, Montana, Nebraska, Nevada, New Jersey, New Mexico, New York, North Dakota, Ohio, Oregon, Pennsylvania, South Dakota, Tennessee, Texas, Utah, Vermont, Washington, West Virginia, Wisconsin, Wyoming, Alaska, Hawaii, and the Virgin Islands.

Feb. 22. *Washington's Birthday*. Observed in all States except Idaho, and in the District of Columbia and Territories.

March or April. *Good Friday*. Friday immediately preceding Easter. Observed in Ar-

kansas, California, Connecticut, Delaware, Florida, Illinois, Indiana, Louisiana, Maryland, Minnesota, New Jersey, North Dakota, Pennsylvania, Tennessee, and Territories.

May 30. *Memorial* or *Decoration Day*. Observed in all States, the District of Columbia, and Territories, with the following exceptions: Alabama, Georgia, Mississippi, and South Carolina.

July 4. *Independence Day*. Observed in all States, the District of Columbia, and Territories.

Sept. *Labor Day*. First Monday of the month. Observed in all States, the District of Columbia, and Territories.

Oct. 12. *Columbus Day*. Observed in Alabama, Arizona, Arkansas, California, Colorado, Connecticut, Delaware, Florida, Georgia, Illinois, Indiana, Kansas, Kentucky, Louisiana, Maryland, Massachusetts, Michigan, Minnesota, Missouri, Montana, Nebraska, Nevada, New Hampshire, New Jersey, New Mexico, New York, North Dakota, Ohio, Oklahoma, Oregon, Pennsylvania, Rhode Island, Texas, Utah, Vermont, Virginia, Washington, West Virginia, Wisconsin, Wyoming, and Puerto Rico.

Nov. 2-8. *Election Day*. First Tuesday after the first Monday in the month in most States; see ELECTIONS. Observed in all States, except Alabama, Connecticut, Georgia, Kansas, Kentucky, Maine, Massachusetts, Mississippi, Missouri, Nebraska, New Mexico, Utah, Vermont, and the District of Columbia.

Nov. 11. *Armistice Day*. Observed in all States, the District of Columbia, and Territories. It is also observed as *Victory Day* in Tennessee.

Nov. *Thanksgiving Day*. Fourth or last Thursday of the month. Observed in all States, the District of Columbia, and Territories.

Dec. 25. *Christmas Day*. Observed in all States, the District of Columbia, and Territories.

In many States the anniversary of the admission of the State to the Union is celebrated as a legal holiday, and is usually called Admission Day. A number of States commemorate other important events in their history; in Vermont the Battle of Bennington, fought in the Revolutionary War, is commemorated annually on August 16; in Louisiana the Battle of New Orleans of the War of 1812 is commemorated on January 8. Throughout the United States, the birthdays of great men, other than those noted above, are also celebrated on legal holidays set apart for that purpose. The following days are usually observed but are not legal holidays.

American Indian Day. Observed on the fourth Friday in September.

Armed Forces Day. Observed on the third Saturday in May.

Child Health Day. Observed on May 1.

Constitution Day. Observed on Sept. 17.

Father's Day. Observed on the third Sunday in June.

Flag Day. Observed on June 14.

Halloween. Observed on Oct. 31.

I Am An American Day. Observed on the third Sunday in May.

Mother's Day. Observed on the second Sunday in May.

National Aviation Day. Observed on Aug. 19.

National Freedom Day. Observed on Feb. 1.

National Maritime Day. Observed on May 22.

Pan-American Day. Observed on April 14.

St. Patrick's Day. Observed on March 17.

St. Valentine's Day. Observed on Feb. 14.

HOLINSHED or **HOLLINGSHEAD,** RAPHAEL (d. about 1580), English chronicler, born probably in Cheshire. He came to London about 1560 and was employed by Reginald Wolfe, a printer, as his assistant in the compilation of a universal history. After the death of Wolfe in 1573, Holinshed continued the work, publishing it in an abridged form as the *Chronicles of England, Scotland, and Ireland* (1578). He had been assisted in the task by William Harrison, among others. A revised edition of the *Chronicles* was published in 1587, after Holinshed's death. It contained some passages disagreeable to Queen Elizabeth, who ordered them excised. An edition in six volumes was published in London in 1808 with the excised passages restored. The fame of the *Chronicles* rests upon their use as a source of historical material by Shakespeare and other Elizabethan dramatists.

HOLLAND, a city of Ottawa Co., Mich., situated on lake Macatawa, 6 m. from Lake Michigan and 25 m. by rail s.w. of Grand Rapids. It has steamer connections with Great Lakes ports. Holland lies in an agricultural area producing fruit, sugar beets, poultry, and dairy products, and is an important manufacturing center. The principal industries in the city are the manufacture of furniture, shoes, patent medicines, cosmetics, boats, furnaces, oil burners, stokers, concrete vaults, and metal products. Numerous vacation resorts are situated in the vicinity of the city, and the tulip gardens in the parks and residential sections of Holland attract many visitors to its annual tulip festival. The city is the site of Hope College (q.v.) and Western Theological Seminary of the Dutch Reformed Church. The Netherlands Museum in the city contains Dutch historical relics. Holland was settled in 1847 by a group of dissident religious refugees from the Netherlands under the leadership of the Rev. A. C. Van Raalte. It was chartered as a city in 1867. Pop. (1950) 15,858.

HOLLAND. See NETHERLANDS, THE.

HOLLAND, BARONS. See Fox, family.

HOLLAND, CLIFFORD MILBURN (1883–1924), American civil engineer, born in Somerset, Mass., and educated at Harvard University. Between 1906 and 1908 he was assistant engineer in the building of the Battery-Joralemon Street tunnel in New York City, and afterward was in charge of construction of a section of the Fourth Avenue Subway in Brooklyn. From 1914 to 1919, as tunnel engineer of the Public Service Commission of New York, he was in charge of construction of the double subway tunnels under the East River. In 1919 he was appointed chief engineer of the New York State and New Jersey Interstate Bridge and Tunnel Commission, and directed construction of the vehicular tunnel under the Hudson River, connecting lower Manhattan and New Jersey. A short time after his death this tunnel was named the Holland Tunnel in his honor. See TUNNEL.

HOLLAND, JOHN PHILIP (1840–1914), Irish-American inventor, born in County Clare, Ireland, and educated at the Christian Brothers' School in Limerick. From 1858 to 1872 he taught in Ireland, and in the following year emigrated to the U.S., and taught school for five years in Paterson, N.J. Holland was ardently devoted to the cause of Irish independence; in the hope of destroying the sea power of England he directed his attention to the submarine as an offensive naval weapon. His first design, offered to the U.S. Navy in 1875, was rejected as impracticable; but he continued his experiments with the aid of a subsidy from the Fenians (q.v.), and in 1881 launched his first successful submarine, the *Fenian Ram,* on the Hudson River. A defective power system rendered this craft useless for extended naval operations. In 1893 Holland received his first contract from the U.S. Navy for the development of a usable submarine; working in conjunction with naval officers, he eventually completed the *Holland,* a submarine with internal-combustion engines for surface power and an electric motor for undersea power, which was launched in Elizabeth, N.J., in 1898. The *Holland* and several other submarines constructed by him were subsequently purchased by the U.S. government. See Submarine.

HOLLAND, THE PARTS OF, administrative county of s.e. Lincolnshire (q.v.), England. The county seat is Boston (pop. 1951 prelim., 24,453). Area, 419 sq.m.; pop. (1951) 101,545.

HOLLINGWORTH, Harry Levi (1880–), American psychologist, born in De Witt, Nebr., and educated at the Nebraska Wesleyan University, the University of Nebraska, and Columbia University. He taught psychology at Columbia University after 1907, and became a full professor in 1921. Hollingworth was both an educational psychologist and a leader in the application of scientific psychology to industry. His works include *Advertising, Its Principles and Practice* (1915), *Vocational Psychology* (1916), *Applied Psychology* (1917), *Psychology, Its Facts and Principles* (1928), *Educational Psychology* (1932), *The Psychology of the Audience* (1935), and *Psychology and Ethics* (1949).

HOLLY, common name of the plant family Aquifoliaceae, and of its typical genus, *Ilex.* The Holly family consists of dioecious or hermaphroditic trees and shrubs with small, four to eight-parted, white or greenish flowers. The fruits are berrylike drupes. The genus *Ilex* contains plants commonly called holly. English holly, *I. aquifolium,* is a small, hermaphroditic, Eurasian tree with thick, glossy, dark-green, spiny leaves and bright-red fruits. In medicine, the bark is used as a febrifuge and the berry is used as an emetic and purgative. The common American holly, *I. opaca,* is similar to English holly, but has duller, less spiny leaves. It is native to e. United States, where it has been harvested so extensively that several States enforce protective laws. Both species of holly are extensively cultivated for ornamental purposes; the leaves and fruits are used in wreaths or sprigs for Christmas decoration. Several other members of the

Nature Magazine

The hollyhock

genus which are native to the U.S. are called inkberry or winterberry (qq.v.). Leaves of a South American species, *I. paraguayensis,* have stimulant properties similar to tea leaves and are used to make an aromatic beverage called maté (q.v.).

HOLLYHOCK, common name of a biennial or perennial herb, *Althaea rosea,* belonging to the Mallow family. It is native to China and is cultivated in gardens of Europe and the United States. Hollyhocks are tall and erect, usually growing 5 to 9 feet in height. The single stems and the undersides of the heart-shaped, wrinkled leaves are hairy; the large, axillary flowers are borne on short stalks in the summer. Each flower has five sepals which are united at the base, five showy petals, and many stamens and pistils. The fruit is a kidney-shaped schizocarp.

Hollyhocks are grown from seed or root-cuttings. Most common varieties of hollyhock have single blossoms, but newer garden varieties are double-flowered. Color of flowers varies; white, yellow, salmon, rose, red, violet, and purple are common, and a few varieties are almost black.

Young hollyhock plants are susceptible to attacks of slugs and several fungus diseases. Hollyhock rust, *Puccinia malvacearum,* causes yellowing of foliage, and sometimes entirely destroys the soft parts of the leaves. The rust

Fruit and leaves of English holly

can be controlled by clearing the garden of all old hollyhock stalks and destroying all common mallow (q.v.), which is an alternate host of the rust. Hollyhock anthracnose, a leaf spot disease caused by the imperfect fungus *Colletotrichum althaeae,* is also controlled by cutting or burning old stalks.

HOLLYWOOD, the N.W. part of Los Angeles (q.v.), Calif., bordered on the N. by the Hollywood Hills, on the S. by Melrose Avenue, on the E. by Vermont Avenue, and on the W. by Fairfax Avenue. Its name derives from the holly which grows in the adjacent hills. Originally an independent village, Hollywood was incorporated in 1903. In 1910, however, it surrendered its charter and became a part of Los Angeles. In 1911 the first motion-picture studio was established in the Hollywood area, and the community soon became noted as the center of the motion-picture industry of the U.S. In Hollywood studios, which number about twenty, is produced a substantial percentage of all the motion pictures made in America. The community is also a major radio-broadcasting and television center. It is the site of many fine residences, parks, and theaters. Griffith Park, one of the largest natural parks located within a city, contains the Griffith Observatory and Planetarium; De Longpre Park contains a shrine to the one-time motion-picture idol Rudolph Valentino. Hollywood Bowl, occupying a natural amphitheater in the Hollywood Hills, is the site of an annual summer music festival and of numerous cultural events. Many theaters in the area contain interesting relics and mementos of past motion pictures. Sunset Boulevard, the main thoroughfare, and Vine Street contain many well-known restaurants, motion-picture offices, and radio-broadcasting studios.

HOLM, HANYA (1898?–   ), German-American dancer, educated at the Dalcroze Institute in Hellerau and the Mary Wigman Institute in Dresden. She became co-director and head of the faculty at the Mary Wigman Institute, and collaborated with Mary Wigman in the production of several large-scale dance works, the most important of which was *Totenmal,* presented in Munich in 1930. In the following year Holm came to America to establish a branch of the Wigman school, and in 1932 set up a studio of her own in New York City. She also conducted classes at Columbia and New York universities, at the Bennington College School of the Dance, at Adelphi and Mills colleges, and at the Colorado College of Education.

Most of her theater work in America was subsidized by dance foundations and institutions, particularly the Bennington Festival at Bennington, Vt., and the Fine Arts Center at Colorado Springs, Col. She developed a highly experimental and personal choreographic style with roots in the austere theory of Mary Wigman; her dance group performed works characterized by original and novel musical accompaniments, and by abstract and occasionally surrealist decors. The first important work of her American period was *Trend* (1937); among her subsequent compositions were *Orestes and the Furies* (1943) and *What Dreams May Come* (1944). In 1952 she secured a copyright on her choreography for the musical play *Kiss Me, Kate,* the first dance script to be so registered by the Library of Congress. See DANCE: *Interpretive Dancing.*

HOLMES, OLIVER WENDELL (1809–94), American man of letters, born in Cambridge, Mass., and educated at Phillips Andover Academy and at Harvard College. In 1836, after more than two years of study and travel in Europe, he received a medical degree from the Harvard Medical School, and began the practice of medicine in Boston. From 1838 until 1840 he was professor of anatomy at Dartmouth College, and from 1847 to 1882 professor of anatomy and physiology at the Harvard Medical School. His essay *The Contagiousness of Puerperal Fever* (1842) was a landmark in the history of medicine, and contributed to the introduction of aseptic techniques in obstetrics and later in surgery (compare SEMMELWEIS, IGNAZ PHILIPP).

Holmes lived in Boston for most of his life, and his name was intimately associated with that city. His fame as a writer of light, witty verse and as a raconteur was purely local until 1857. In that year the poet James Russell Lowell established the *Atlantic Monthly,* for which Holmes began writing a series of papers, twelve in all, entitled *Autocrat of the Breakfast Table.* These essays, which were published in book form in 1858, achieved immediate popularity for their witty, lively expression of ideas, as well as for their characteristic New England flavor. Holmes achieved recognition, both in the U.S. and in England, as a brilliant writer, and thenceforth dominated Bostonian literary and social circles. He belonged to a group of distinguished men of letters including Ralph Waldo Emerson, Lowell, John Greenleaf Whittier, and Louis Agassiz. The essays were followed in the next year by *The Professor at the Breakfast Table* (published in book form, 1860), and later, by *The Poet at the Breakfast Table* (1872). Because of the

Wyeth, Inc.

Above: Oliver Wendell Holmes reading his famous essay "The Contagiousness of Puerperal Fever" before the Boston Society for Medical Improvement in 1843 (from a painting by Dean Cornwell).

Right: Bust of Holmes by Edmond T. Quinn.

success and fame of the first series, the most original and popular, Holmes is still often called "the Autocrat".

In his first novel, *Elsie Venner* (1861), a picture of New England character, Holmes attacked the stern Calvinistic dogmas of earlier days. His other novels include *The Guardian Angel* (1867) and *The Moral Antipathy* (1885). Holmes is also the author of the volumes of poetry *Songs in Many Keys* (1862), *Songs of Many Seasons* (1875), *The Iron Gate and Other Poems* (1880), and *Before the Curfew and Other Poems* (1887); of the essays *Soundings* (1864), *Pages from an Old Volume of Life* (1883), and *Our Hundred Days in Europe* (1887); and of the biographies *John Lothrop Motley* (1879) and *Ralph Waldo Emerson* (1885). He wrote many well-known poems, including "Old Ironsides", "The Chambered Nautilus", "Dorothy Q", "The Deacon's Masterpiece", "The Last Leaf", and the hymn "Lord of all being! throned afar".

HOLMES, OLIVER WENDELL (1841–1935), American jurist, son of Oliver Wendell Holmes (q.v.), born in Boston, Mass., and educated at Harvard College. He served three years in the Civil War, fighting with the Union Army at Ball's Bluff, Antietam, and Fredericksburg, and attaining the rank of lieutenant colonel. In 1867 he was admitted to the bar, and began the practice of law in Boston. He edited *The American Law Review* from 1870 until 1873. In 1880 he was a lecturer on common law at the Lowell Institute in Boston. He became professor of law at the Harvard Law School in 1882, but resigned in the same year to accept an appointment as associate justice

Brown Brothers

Oliver Wendell Holmes, American jurist

of the Massachusetts Supreme Court; he served until 1899, when he became chief justice. In 1902 he was appointed associate justice of the U.S. Supreme Court, and he held the position until his retirement in 1932.

As a member of the Supreme Court Holmes was distinguished for his great legal learning, sound judgment, humor, and power of expression; he was known as a liberal interpreter of the Constitution. His Lowell lectures, collected as *The Common Law* (1881), became internationally known. His *Collected Legal Papers* were published in 1920, and *The Dissenting Opinions of Mr. Justice Holmes* in 1929.

HOLMES, SHERLOCK. See DETECTIVE STORY; DOYLE, SIR ARTHUR CONAN.

HOLMES, WILLIAM HENRY (1846–1933), American anthropologist and archeologist, born in Harrison Co., O., and educated at the McNeely Normal College. After teaching for some years, he was on the staff of the U.S. Geological Survey from 1872 to 1899. For the ensuing nine years he served the Bureau of American Ethnology as an archeologist. From 1894 to 1902 he was a curator and later the head curator of the department of anthropology at the Field Museum of Natural History in Chicago. In 1902 he rejoined the Bureau of American Ethnology as its chief. From 1910 to 1920 Holmes was both head curator of an-

thropology at the U.S. National Museum and curator at the National Gallery of Art, and from 1920 until his death was the director of the National Gallery of Art. His works include *Pottery of the Ancient Pueblos* (1886) and *Handbook of Aboriginal American Antiquities* (1918).

HOLMIUM, an element, member of the rare-earth group of elements, symbol Ho, atomic number 67, atomic weight 164.9, valence 3. It was discovered by the Swedish chemist Per Teodor Cleve (1840–1905) in 1879. Holmium is one of the least abundant of the rare-earth metals, ranking 43rd in order of abundance of the elements in the earth's crust. It occurs in gadolinite and other minerals containing rare earths. Holmium oxide, Ho_2O_3, a grayish-white powder, and a few salts, such as the sulfate, have been prepared. See RARE EARTHS.

HOLOGRAPH. See WILL.

HOLOTHURIOIDEA, the class of the phylum Echinodermata which contains the sea cucumbers, or sea slugs, cucumber-shaped or sausage-shaped animals comprising over 500 species. Holothurians are found in salt water in all parts of the world, and range in size from several inches to $3\frac{1}{2}$ feet in length; some of the larger species are considered delicacies in the Orient, and are used in the preparation of soups (see TREPANG).

Holothurians differ from other echinoderms in being bilaterally rather than radially symmetrical. Their bodies are rubbery, without bony skeletons, and contain a few scattered ossicles (calcareous supporting elements). Like other echinoderms the holothurians have projecting *tube feet* on all portions of their bodies, especially concentrated about their mouths. The tube feet of echinoderms contain parts of the circulatory system and are used in locomotion; in holothurians the tube feet about the mouth are modified into tentacles which contain receptors for the sense of smell, and which are used to push food into the mouth. Most holothurians breathe by means of internal *respiratory trees,* ramifying organs which lead from the cloaca into the body cavity. Contractions of the cloaca force water into the respiratory trees; these empty the water into the body cavity, where it mixes with the body fluids and imparts its oxygen to them. Some species have *Cuvierian organs,* cloacal enlargements of the respiratory trees which, when the animal is in danger, are extruded from the body and form sticky masses of threads in which any threatening animal may be entangled. Holothurians feed on minute invertebrates which they find in the sand of the ocean bottom.

The commonest holothurians belong to the orders Dendrochirota and Aspidochirota. Dendrochirota is widely distributed in shallow waters, and is characterized by branching tentacles. A well-known species in this order is *Thyone briareus,* a brown sea cucumber, about 5 in. long and 1½ in. thick, found off the Atlantic coast. Other species in this order include several in the genus *Cucumaria* (q.v.), the most important being *C. frondosa,* about 2 in. long, which is common off America and Europe. Aspidochirota is found in shallow tropical waters and is characterized by tentacles only slightly branched at the tip, forming a shieldlike end plate. *Holothuria* is the typical genus of this order.

Pelagothurida is the most unusual order, containing the only holothurians adapted to a free-swimming adult life. Elasipoda is a deep-sea order. Molpadida and Synaptida (or Apoda) are burrowing orders; holothurians in Synaptida are slender, wormlike animals. which have no tube feet.

HOLST, GUSTAV THEODORE (1874–1934), English composer, born in Cheltenham. In 1893 he entered the Royal College of Music, at which he studied piano, organ, and theory. Two years later he won a scholarship for composition, and studied with Sir Charles Villiers Stanford. In 1903 Holst became music master at a school in Dulwich, and subsequently held many teaching directorships, including posts at Morley College, the Royal College of Music, and Reading College. He conducted many of his own works at concerts, and made appearances in the U.S. at the University of Michigan, Ann Arbor, and throughout Europe. His numerous compositions include symphonies, operas, orchestral suites, and church music. He is best known for his orchestral suite *The Planets.*

HOLY ALLIANCE, a league formed after the fall of Napoleon, at the instance of Alexander I of Russia, by the sovereigns of Russia, Austria, and Prussia, to regulate the relations of the states of Christendom by the principles of Christian charity. The document was drawn up by Alexander, and was signed at Paris in Sept., 1815, by Francis I of Austria, Frederick William III of Prussia, and by Alexander. In addition to the original signatories, Naples, Sardinia, France, and Spain acceded to the provisions of the alliance, and it received the commendation, though not the signature, of the prince regent (later George IV) of Great Britain. Prince Klemens Wenzel Metternich, Austrian minister of foreign affairs, used the Alliance as an instrument to further his reactionary policies. In the name of the Holy Alliance, Austria, in 1821, crushed the popular revolutions in Naples, Piedmont, and France, and in 1823 restored absolutism in Spain. Meaningless in itself, the Holy Alliance soon ceased to have any importance.

HOLY COMMUNION. See LORD'S SUPPER.

HOLY CROSS, COLLEGE OF THE, a Roman Catholic institution of higher learning for men, founded in 1843 and situated in Worcester, Mass. The college is conducted by the Fathers of the Society of Jesus. Its curriculum places special emphasis on classical studies and includes courses in the liberal arts and sciences leading to bachelor's and master's degrees. In a recent year, the faculty was composed of 104 men, and the student enrollment was over 1700.

HOLY CROSS, CONGREGATION OF THE, a Roman Catholic order of priests and lay brothers, formed in France in 1836 by the union of the Brothers of St. Joseph (Josephites) and the Fathers of the Holy Cross (Salvatorists). In addition to their religious life, the members devote themselves to teaching and missionary work. The congregation was introduced into the United States in 1841 by the French missionary Edward Frederick Sorin (1814–93), who established near South Bend, Ind., a foundation which became the University of Notre Dame. The congregation also maintains colleges in Washington, D.C., Oregon, Wisconsin, Ohio, Louisiana, and Texas, and numerous secondary schools.

HOLY CROSS NATIONAL MONUMENT, a national monument established in 1929 in the Rocky Mountains in Colorado, about 75 miles s.w. of Denver. It contains the Mountain of the Holy Cross (13,978 ft. above sea level), a peak of the Sawatch Range. The monument area of 1392 acres contains also the two snow-filled ravines, crossing each other at right angles and forming the cross from which the mountain derives its name. The snowy cross is visible from a distance of 30 to 40 miles.

HOLY GHOST or **HOLY SPIRIT,** in theology, the third Person of the Divine Trinity, "proceeding from the Father and the Son". In orthodox belief the Holy Spirit is God, but distinct from the Father and the Son in the same manner as the Son is distinct from the Father. The work of the Holy Spirit is the sanctification and regeneration of the souls of all mankind. See TRINITY, DOCTRINE OF THE.

HOLY GRAIL. See GRAIL, THE HOLY.

HOLY GRASS, common name of fragrant perennial grasses belonging to the genus *Hierochloë*. Vanilla grass, *H. odorata,* was formerly strewn in front of church doors of northern Europe on saints' days. It is a short grass growing from creeping rootstocks and bearing spikelets in pyramidal panicles. It grows in meadows throughout the temperate regions of North America and Eurasia. Vanilla grass was formerly used for basketmaking and mat weaving by the Seneca Indians. *H. alpina* is a similar shorter grass which grows in alpine areas of Europe and N.E. United States.

HOLY LAND. See PALESTINE.

HOLY OFFICE, CONGREGATION OF THE, the division of the *Curia Romana* of the Roman Catholic Church (q.v.) having jurisdiction over matters of doctrine and dogma. The Holy Office deals with questions of heresy and suspected heresy; it decides matters connected with marriage and divorce, and compiles the Index of prohibited books (q.v.).

HOLYOKE, a city of Hampden Co., Mass., situated on the Connecticut R., 8 miles N. of Springfield. It is served by two railroads, and an airport in the vicinity affords airline service. The city is one of the leading paper-manufacturing centers of the world. It is especially noted for the manufacture of fine writing paper, in addition to card, tissue, and glazed paper. Other important industries are the manufacture of paper machinery, cutlery, tools, boilers, heaters, thread, and cotton, silk, satin, woolen, and rayon goods. The Holyoke Museum of Natural History and Art contains notable collections of paintings, musical instruments, wildlife, and Indian articles. The city lies at the foot of Mt. Tom (1214 ft.), which provides excellent facilities for skiing; nearby is Mt. Tom State Reservation, covering 1800 acres, with facilities for fishing, swimming, and picnicking, in addition to winter sports. The site of the present city was first settled about the end of the 17th century, and was at first a part of Springfield and then of West Springfield. Its importance as a manufacturing center dates from the construction in 1849 of the Holyoke Dam across the river, which has a drop of 60 ft. at Holyoke. The building of the dam, a stone structure with a length of 1017 ft., was a major accomplishment at the time, and the water power thus furnished provided the basis of Holyoke's industries. The town was separated from West Springfield and incorporated in 1850; in 1873 it was chartered as a city. Pop. (1950) 54,661.

HOLY ORTHODOX CATHOLIC AND APOSTOLIC CHURCH, the official name of the Eastern, Greek, or Orthodox Church. See ORTHODOX CHURCH.

HOLY ROMAN EMPIRE, in general usage, the designation applied to an amorphous political entity of w. Europe, originated by Pope Leo III in 800 A.D., and in nominal existence more or less continuously until 1806. For purposes of historical accuracy, it should be noted that, in its initial stages, the organization was styled "Empire of the West" and "Roman Empire"; and that the epithet "Holy" did not appear in the official title until 1155.

The establishment of the Holy Roman Empire represented, as the original styling implies, an attempt to resuscitate the Western Roman Empire, which had collapsed in 476 (see ROME). Throughout the turbulent period, known in history as the Dark Ages, that followed the removal of Romulus Augustulus from the Western throne by Odoacer, the traditional concept of a temporal realm coextensive with the spiritual dominions of the Church had been kept alive by the bishops of Rome, later referred to as the popes (see PAPACY). The Byzantine Empire (q.v.), the eastern division of Imperial Rome, retained, during part of the period, nominal sovereignty over the territories formerly under the control of the Western Empire, and many of the Germanic tribes which had seized these territories gave formal recognition to the overlordship of the Byzantine rulers. Partly because of this circumstance and for other reasons, including dependence on Byzantine protection against the Lombards (q.v.), the bishops of Rome also recognized the sovereignty of the Eastern Empire for an extended period after the enforced abdication of Romulus Augustulus.

With the coalescence of groupings of the Germanic tribes into independent Christian kingdoms during the 6th and 7th centuries, the political authority of the Byzantine emperors became practically nonexistent in the w. The spiritual influence of the western division of the Church expanded simultaneously, in particular during the pontificate (590–604) of Gregory I (q.v.). As the political prestige of the Byzantine Empire declined, the papacy grew increasingly resentful of interference by secular and ecclesiastical authorities at Constantinople in the affairs and practices of the western Church. The consequent feud between the two divisions of the Church attained critical proportions during the reign (717–41) of Emperor Leo III, who sought to abolish the use of images in Christian ceremonies. Roman resistance to Leo's decrees culminated (730–32) in a complete rupture with Constantinople. After severance of its ties with the Byzantine Empire, the papacy nourished dreams of a revivified Western Empire. Evidence exists, indeed, that certain of the popes weighed the possibility of launching such an enterprise and assuming the leadership of the projected state. In the absence of the prerequisite organizational apparatus and confronted with a hostile Lombardy, the Church hierarchy, abandoning the idea of a joint spiritual and temporal realm, finally decided to confer imperial status on the then dominant w. European power, the kingdom of the Franks (q.v.). Several of the Frankish rulers had already, in various ways, demonstrated their fidelity to the Church (see CHARLES MARTEL), and Charlemagne (q.v.), who ascended the Frankish throne in 768, had displayed ample qualifications for the exalted office, notably by the conquest (772) of Lombardy and by the expansion of his dominions to imperial proportions.

On December 25, 800, Pope Leo III crowned Charlemagne Emperor of the West, establishing both a precedent and a political structure that were destined to figure decisively in the affairs of central Europe. The precedent, inauguration of the papal prerogative in the selection and coronation of the emperors of the West, endured for nearly 700 years. In its primary stage, the resurrected Western Empire endured, as an effective political entity, less than 25 years after the death (814) of Charlemagne. The reign of his son and successor Louis I was marked by intensive feudal and fratricidal strife, climaxed, in 843, by the partition of the Empire. (For an account of the growth, vicissitudes, and final dissolution of the Frankish realm, see FRANCE: History).

Despite the dissension within the newly created Western Empire, the popes maintained the Imperial organization, except for an interlude extending from 877 to 881, for more than a century after the death of Louis I, conferring the title mainly on rulers of the Carolingian (q.v.) dynasty. The emperors exercised little authority beyond the confines of their personal dominions, however. After the reign (915–24) of the Lombard ruler Berengar I, who was crowned emperor by Pope John X, the Imperial throne remained vacant for nearly four decades. The East Frankish Kingdom, or Germany, capably

St. Peter bestowing the stole on Pope Leo III, founder of the Holy Roman Empire, and the standard on Charlemagne, crowned Holy Roman emperor by Leo (from early mosaic)

led by Henry I (q.v.) and Otto I, emerged as the strongest power in Europe during this period. Besides being a capable and ambitious sovereign, Otto I was an ardent friend of the Church, as revealed by his appointment of clerics to high office, by his missionary activities E. of the Elbe R., and, finally, by his military campaigns, at the behest of Pope John XII, against Berengar II of Lombardy. In 962, in recognition of Otto's services, John XI awarded him the Imperial crown and title.

Thus resurrected, the Empire of the West, at first an unstable political union of Germany and Italy and later a loose union of Germanic states, remained in almost continuous existence for more than 800 years. During the Italo-German phase, the Empire played a significant role in central European politics and ecclesiastical affairs. A central feature of the history of this period was the mortal struggle between the popes and the emperors for control of the Church. All of the emperors were German kings, and because Imperial duties and ambitions inevitably required their full attention, national interests were neglected. As one result, Germany, which might have been transformed into a strong centralized state, degenerated into a multiplicity of minor states. In 1155 Frederick I Barbarossa, one of the greatest of the emperors, added "Holy" to the Imperial designation, ostensibly to increase the sanctity of the crown. (For accounts of these and related events, see GERMANY: *History;* ITALY: *History;* GUELPHS AND GHIBELLINES; WELF; see also the biographical sketches of most of the Holy Roman emperors, whose names are tabulated at the end of this article.

The Holy Roman Empire had little real importance in European political and religious developments after the Great Interregnum, the event that signalized papal victory in the protracted struggle with the Empire. Beginning (1273) with Rudolph I, the first of the Hapsburg (q.v.) dynasty, various German kings laid claim to the Imperial title and, in several instances, these claims were recognized by the popes. The office was little more than honorary, however, and inasmuch as the Empire comprised a loose confederation of sovereign states and principalities, Imperial authority was strictly nominal. Louis IV (q.v.), who assumed the title in 1314, successfully challenged the power of the papacy and, for a brief period, restored the prestige of the Empire. During the reign of Charles V (q.v.), the Empire encompassed territories as extensive as those of Charlemagne. But dynastic rather than ecclesiastical principles composed the chief cohesive element in the Imperial structure of Charles V. The medieval concept of a temporal state coextensive and in harmony with the spiritual dominions of the Church survived solely as a theory. As the Protestant Reformation gained headway, even the theory lost practical meaning. In its final phase, the Holy Roman Empire performed certain useful purposes, including the maintenance of a measure of unity among the component states (see DIET; ELECTORS, GERMAN IMPERIAL). The later emperors, all rulers of Austria (q.v.) and concerned mainly with aggrandizement of their personal dominions, were mere figureheads. Futile armed intervention against the French Revolution (q.v.) constituted the last important venture of the Empire in European politics. In the words of the French writer Voltaire, the contemporary Holy Roman Empire was "neither Holy, nor Roman, nor an Empire". Because of

well-founded fears that Napoleon I (q.v.) intended to annex the Imperial title, Francis II, the last of the emperors, formally dissolved the Empire on August 6, 1806.

HOLY ROMAN EMPERORS

Name	Dynasty	Reign
Charlemagne	Carolingian	800–14
Louis I	"	814–40
Lothair I	"	840–55
Louis II	"	855–75
Charles II	"	875–77
Charles III	"	881–87
Arnulf, King of Germany (crowned emperor 896)	"	887–99
Louis III, King of Germany*	"	899–911
Conrad of Franconia, King of Germany*	"	911–18
Henry I, King of Germany*	Saxon	919–36
Otto I (crowned 962)	"	936–73
Otto II	"	973–83
Otto III	"	983–1002
Henry II (crowned 1014)	"	1002–24
Conrad II (crowned 1027)	Franconian	1024–39
Henry III (crowned 1046)	"	1039–56
Henry IV (crowned 1084)	"	1056–1106
Henry V (crowned 1111)	"	1106–25
Lothair II (crowned 1133)	"	1125–37
Conrad III*	Hohenstaufen	1138–52
Frederick I (crowned 1155)	"	1152–90
Henry VI (crowned 1191)	"	1190–97
Philip of Swabia*	"	1198–1208
Otto IV** (crowned 1209)	Guelph	1198–1215
Frederick II (crowned 1220)	Hohenstaufen	1215–50
Conrad IV*	"	1250–54
(The Great Interregnum, 1254–73)		
Rudolf I*	Hapsburg	1273–91
Adolf I*	Nassau	1292–98
Albert I*	Austria	1298–1308
Henry VII	Luxemburg	1308–13
Louis IV**	Wittelsbach	1314–47
Frederick of Austria**	Austria	1314–26
Charles IV (crowned 1355)	Luxemburg	1347–78
Wenceslaus	Bohemia	1378–1400
Rupert of the Palatinate*	Wittelsbach	1400–10
Sigismund (crowned 1433)	Luxemburg	1411–37

Holyrood Palace in Edinburgh, Scotland

Albert II*	Hapsburg	1438–39
Frederick III	"	1440–93
(crowned 1452)		
Maximilian I***	"	1493–1519
Charles V	"	1519–56
(crowned 1520)		
Ferdinand I	"	1556–64
Maximilian II	"	1564–76
Rudolf II	"	1576–1612
Matthias	"	1612–19
Ferdinand II	"	1619–37
Ferdinand III	"	1637–57
Leopold I	"	1658–1705
Joseph I	"	1705–11
Charles VI	"	1711–40
Charles VII	Wittelsbach	1742–45
Francis I	Hapsburg-Lorraine	1745–65
Joseph II	" "	1765–90
Leopold II	" "	1790–92
Francis II	" "	1792–1806

  * *Not crowned as emperor.*
  ** *Rival king of Germany.*
 *** *Last Holy Roman emperor crowned by
   the pope.*

HOLYROOD PALACE, the former residence of the Scottish kings, located in Edinburgh, Scotland. It occupies the site of the
Augustinian Abbey of the Holy Rood erected
by the Scottish king David I in 1128. On the
site of the abbey, according to legend, David
I was miraculously saved from the attack of
a hunted stag by the interposition of the lost
holy cross or rood, which fell from the stag's
antlers into the king's hands, and at the sight
of which the animal turned and fled. The sole

remains of the abbey are the ruins of the
church, which anciently was a safe refuge for
criminals and remained so for debtors until
the abolition of imprisonment for debt in 1880.
The palace was built by James IV of Scotland (1473–1513), destroyed by fire in 1650,
and rebuilt by King Charles II of England
between 1671 and 1679.

HOLY SEE, or ROMAN SEE, in the Roman
Catholic Church, the diocese of Rome which,
as the official see of the pope, is the center of
government for the Church. It is also called
the *Apostolic See* or *See of Peter*, from its
foundation by St. Peter about 42 A.D. Each of
St. Peter's successors (including the popes of
Avignon) has borne the title "Bishop of
Rome". In a wider sense the term "Holy See"
signifies the papal power, either in the person
of the pope or as delegated to the various
offices of the Roman Curia; see ROMAN CATH-
OLIC CHURCH: *Curia Romana.*

HOLY SEPULCHER, the tomb where Jesus
Christ was buried after His crucifixion. The
traditional site of both Calvary and the tomb
was covered by a basilica erected by the Emperor Constantine in 326. The basilica was
destroyed by the Persians in 614; it has since
been replaced by the church of the Holy
Sepulcher on the same site, about a hundred
yards northwest of the Gate of Ephraim in
the "second wall" of Jerusalem.

HOLY SEPULCHER, KNIGHTS OF THE,
an order of knighthood instituted in 1496,
probably by Pope Alexander VI, for the purpose of protecting the Holy Sepulcher (q.v.)
in Jerusalem. According to tradition the or-

der was founded by the French Crusader God-frey of Bouillon (q.v.). The knights of the order were held to strict rules of honor, faith, and purity, and received unusual privileges, including exemption from taxes. The pope at first had the sole right to nominate candidates, but he later shared the right with the Franciscan Order and then with the Roman Catholic patriarch in Jerusalem. Since 1905 the members of the Knights of the Holy Sepulcher have been chosen by the Roman Catholic patriarch in Jerusalem, who is also guardian of the Holy Sepulcher; the pope retains the right to nominate candidates. The badge of the order is worn suspended by a black ribbon, and consists of a red Jerusalem cross, surmounted by a crown; between the arms of the cross are four smaller Latin crosses.

HOLY SPIRIT. See HOLY GHOST.

HOLY WATER, water blessed by a bishop or priest, and prescribed for use in the ritual of nearly every blessing in the liturgies of the Catholic churches. As water is the natural agent for cleansing, the use of holy water is representative of internal purification. Under the Jewish Mosaic Law sprinkling the hands and face with water before entering the sanctuary was prescribed for all persons who were ritually unclean, and the practice was adopted in the Christian Church as early as the 2nd century.

HOLY WEEK, in Christian liturgy, the week immediately preceding Easter, beginning with Palm Sunday and including Maundy Thursday and Good Friday. The ceremonies of Holy Week commemorate the passion and death of Jesus Christ. The week was originally called "Passion Week", but that designation is now given to the week preceding Palm Sunday, starting with Passion Sunday.

HOMAGE. See FEUDALISM.

HOME ECONOMICS. See DOMESTIC ECONOMY.

HOMEL. See GOMEL.

HOMEOPATHY, or HOMOEOPATHY, a system of medical practice based on the principle that diseases can be cured by drugs which produce in a healthy person the same pathological effects that are symptomatic of the disease. This doctrine of similarity, *similia similibus curantur,* was first formulated by Samuel Hahnemann (q.v.) in 1796. Homeopaths also believe that small doses of a drug are more efficacious in curing a disease than large doses. For example, opium, which induces an extreme tendency to sleep, accompanied by profuse perspiration and delirium, cures a fever accompanied by the same symptoms. According to the theory, a very small dosage of opium is more efficacious than a large one.

Homeopathy was introduced into the United States by a physician, Hans B. Gram, in 1825. The American Institute of Homeopathy, the national society of homeopathic physicians, was founded in 1844. Schools of medicine teaching the homeopathic system are recognized in Europe and the United States today, but the dichotomy between homeopathy and allopathy has been greatly reduced.

HOMER (between 1200 and 850 B.C.), traditional epic poet of ancient Greece. Seven ancient cities claimed him, but his birthplace and the age in which he lived are unknown. According to legend, "Homer", assuming for the sake of convenience that he was one person (see HOMERIC QUESTION), was a divinely inspired poet, blind, old, and poor, who made his living as an itinerant singer. Another tradition states that he competed in song with Hesiod (q.v.).

Whatever his identity, it is clear from his two epic masterpieces, the *Iliad* and the *Odyssey* (qq.v.), that Homer was not describing contemporary events, but was drawing upon traditional material handed down from the Greek prehistoric period. Judging also from the skillful artistic construction of the two epics, he probably had access to an existing body of oral poetry. The perfected use of the hexameter is a further indication that this metrical form was the recognized medium for epic poetry, dating from an earlier period of Greek literature (q.v.).

The first evidence of a written text of the *Iliad* and the *Odyssey* dates from the late 6th century B.C., in Athens. In that city, every four years, both poems were recited at the Panathenæa (q.v.) by professional rhapsodists, presumably from a written text, which may well have been prepared from other oral or written versions then in existence. The texts of the *Iliad* and *Odyssey* as they exist today date from the version prepared about 150 B.C. by the Alexandrian critic Aristarchus of Samothrace (q.v.), which may or may not be identical with that used earlier in Athens.

The Homeric narrative of the siege and destruction of the city of Troy as presented in the *Iliad* is related to a real siege which took place about 1200 B.C. Soon after these events a large body of heroic songs or lays came into existence, forming the historical nucleus of the *Iliad* and *Odyssey.* However, it is impossible to determine which part of the Homeric poems is history and which is fiction and folklore, so well are these elements blended in the artistic whole. Both epics are in the style of ancient oral poetry. The emphasis is placed on the major theme, flow of narrative, and especially on dramatic action; details are generic rather than particular. The language is rich, simple, and dignified, but the Homeric dialect is not any definite spoken speech of a particular place or time. It is rather a traditional dialect, mainly Ionic, though with a sprinkling of Æolic forms, as well as an element of very old Greek; see GREEK LANGUAGE. In the main, too, the dialect of Homer is one molded by the needs of the dactylic hexameter.

Homer's characters, such as Achilles, Hector, Nestor, Odysseus, Helen, Andromache, and Penelope (qq.v.), are vivid personalities, and have remained as universal figures throughout the centuries. The Homeric portrayals of the gods, such as Zeus, Apollo, Hera, Poseidon, and Athena (qq.v.), became the ideal types for all subsequent representations of those deities in poetry, painting, and sculpture. To the ancient Greeks Homer was the Bible and Shakespeare in one; many cultivated Greeks knew the *Iliad* by heart. Even at the height of the Attic drama (see DRAMA: *Greek Drama*) the *Iliad* and *Odyssey* were not overshadowed but were recited to great audiences. In modern times the works of Homer have influenced almost every school of Western poetry and literature.

The so-called Homeric Poems, a large body of epic poetry dealing with the sack of Troy and other aspects of the Trojan War, are the work not of Homer but of various other poets who drew on a traditional body of legend. Only fragments of these later epics exist.

HOMER, WINSLOW (1836–1910), American figure and marine painter, water colorist, and illustrator, born in Boston. Beginning as a lithographer's apprentice in 1855, he became a well-known illustrator for *Harper's Weekly* and other periodicals, to which he contributed from 1858 to 1876. For *Harper's* he was a Civil War correspondent (1862–64); his experiences during the war supplied him with themes for early pictures. His first oil paintings date from 1862, an important example being "Croquet" (1866), a work of bold realism and striking color. He painted some Negro genre pieces and other scenes of Southern life in Virginia between 1876 and 1880, visited England in 1881–82, and finally, in 1884,

Hellenistic bust of Homer

settled at Pront's Neck, Maine, where he began his series of large marines.

Homer's main themes were the forest and sea, the woodsmen and fishermen, all painted with fidelity and power. After subsequent trips to Florida and Bermuda, he painted a series of water colors in which he captured the intensely bright atmosphere with simple, vivid washes of color. Among his famous sea pieces are "Eight Bells" and "West Wind", both at the Addison Gallery, Andover, Mass. Large groups of his water colors are at the Chicago Art Institute and at the Metropolitan Museum of Art, New York City. "Tornado-Bahamas", a dramatic water color at the Metropolitan Museum, is his most popularly known work.

HOMERIC QUESTION, the controversy surrounding the identity of the traditional Greek epic poet Homer (q.v.). The critical study of Homeric texts began as early as the 6th century B.C., and almost all ancient critics provided commentaries (*scholia*) to the texts of the *Iliad* and *Odyssey* (qq.v.). In the modern period, however, the Homeric question relates specifically to the large body of scholarly literature and discussion occasioned by the theories of the German scholar Friedrich August Wolf (q.v.). In his *Prolegomena ad Homerum* (1795), Wolf expounded the theory that the *Iliad* and *Odyssey* are the work not of one but of several poets, arguing that the

"Eight Bells," painting by Winslow Homer

two poems were put together out of pre-existing materials by subsequent editors. Wolf's theory gave rise to a new and minute examination of the Homeric texts by many scholars everywhere, who elaborated other theories on the question.

HOME RULE. See IRELAND; IRELAND, REPUBLIC OF; UNITED KINGDOM.

HOMESTEAD, a borough of Allegheny Co., Pa., situated on the Monongahela R., 6 miles S.E. of the center of Pittsburgh. It is served by six railroads and by river barges, and is connected with Pittsburgh by a bridge. Homestead and several adjoining boroughs comprise the "Homestead District", an important industrial unit. The production of steel is the major industry in the area; iron, mill machinery, coal-mining machinery, engines, castings, car wheels and axles, valves, precision tools, cement blocks, brick and tile, cigars, and paper boxes also are produced. In the district is one of the largest steel plants in the world, covering 290 acres and containing 100 miles of railroad track.

A town was laid out on the site of the present borough of Homestead in 1870, and in 1879 a glass factory was established there. In 1881 the Homestead Steel Works was built, which in 1883 was acquired by Carnegie,

Phipps and Co., of which Andrew Carnegie (q.v.) was the principal owner. A dispute between the company and its employees in 1892 resulted in one of the most violent strikes in U.S. labor history. The strike was carried on by the National Amalgamated Association of Iron and Steel Workers and lasted more than four months. On July 6, during the course of the strike, a riot occurred in which several men were killed and wounded, and on July 12 the State militia was called out by the governor and the borough was put under martial law. The strike ended in a victory for the company and the plant was reopened in November (see STRIKES). Pop. (1950) 10,046.

HOMESTEAD LAWS, in U.S. history, the collective name for a series of Federal enactments, the purpose of which was to enable citizens without capital to acquire homesteads. The first homestead law was enacted by Congress in 1862; it provided that any citizen, either the head of a family or twenty-one years of age, could acquire a tract of public land, not exceeding 160 acres. As a condition for acquiring title to the land, the homesteader was obliged to settle on and cultivate the homestead for a period of at least fourteen months. The law expressly declared that no land so acquired could be levied against by creditors for the satisfaction of debts contracted prior to the issuance of the land grant. Other Federal homestead laws, subsequently enacted, were essentially modifications of the act of 1862. The Federal homestead laws are important in U.S. history chiefly because they provided an incentive, in the form of easily obtainable land, for the settlement of the West.

HOMESTEAD NATIONAL MONUMENT, a national monument in S.E. Nebraska, established in 1939 as a memorial to the hardships endured by the early settlers of the West. It is situated 3 miles N.W. of Beatrice. The monument covers an area of 163 acres and contains the first homestead settled under the Homestead Law of 1862, which opened up millions of acres of public land to Civil War soldiers and others. Daniel Freeman, a Federal soldier, filed the first claim under the law, and settled on a site within the present monument area.

HOMICIDE, in criminal law, the killing of a human being by the act, procurement, or negligence (q.v.) of another. As appears from this definition, homicide is a generic term, comprehending not only the crimes of *murder* and *manslaughter,* but also the taking of a human life under circumstances justifying the act or in a sense excusing its commission. Killing under such circumstances, not amounting to murder or manslaughter, is described as *justifiable* or *excusable homicide.* The penalties for homicide vary from State to State and range from death sentences to terms of imprisonment. See MANSLAUGHTER; MURDER.

HOMILETICS, the science of composing and delivering sermons. The term is derived from the homily (q.v.), an informal explanation of the Scriptures in the early Christian Church.

HOMILY, an informal sermon on a portion of the Scriptures, designed to explain the literal meaning and derive the spiritual or moral significance of the text. The practice of reading the Scripture in the synagogue and explaining its lessons in popular form prevailed among the Jews before the Christian Era, and was adopted by the Christian Churches from the earliest times. Ancient collections of homilies are numerous, and much of the literature of the Middle Ages is homiletic. The *Homilies of the Church of England* are collections of sermons, published in 1547, which are frequently consulted in controversies concerning the doctrines of the Anglican Church.

HOMINIDAE (Lat. *homo,* "man"), the family of primates containing man. The only extant species is *Homo sapiens;* the family also includes several extinct species of which fossil remains have been discovered. Among these extinct species of man are several in the genus *Homo,* and others in the genera *Pithecanthropus* (Java man), *Sinanthropus* (Peking man), and *Eoanthropus* (Piltdown man); see MAN, ANCIENT. The characters which distinguish the Hominidae from the other primates include possession of an enlarged, nonopposable great toe on the foot, and possession of a prominent ridge on the lower jaw (the chin). Man has a larger brain than any of the other primates, and, except for the gibbon, is the only one of them with an erect posture.

HOMOEOPATHY. See HOMEOPATHY.

HOMOGENIZATION. See MILK.

HOMOOUSIAN, in Christian theology, the doctrine that in the divine Trinity the Son is of the same substance or essence as the Father, or, as expressed in the Nicene Creed (q.v.), is "consubstantial with the Father". In the 4th-century controversies over the nature of the Trinity, the homoousian doctrine was upheld by St. Athanasius (q.v.; see also ATHANASIAN CREED) against Arius (q.v.), who held the *heteroousian* doctrine that the Father and the Son differ in essence. During the same controversies a compromise doctrine, called *homoiousian,* was held by the Semi-Arians, who believed the Father and the Son to be similar in essence, but not of the same essence. The homoousian doctrine was upheld at the Council of Nicæa in 325, and was reaffirmed at the Council of Constantinople in 381 and has since remained the orthodox belief.

HOMOPTERA. See BUG.

HOMOSPORY. See SPORE.

HOMRAI. See HORNBILL.

HOMS (anc. *Emesa*), town of Syria, located 90 miles N. of Damascus and about 35 miles S. of Hama. It was noted in ancient times for its temple to the sun god, of which the Roman emperor Heliogabalus, a native of Homs, was at one time a priest. The town was made a Roman colony under Emperor Caracalla in the early part of the 3rd century. Rebelling Syrian forces under Queen Zenobia were defeated there by the Roman army of Emperor Aurelian in 272. In 636 the town was captured by the Arabs. The chief industry of the present-day town is the manufacture of silk. Pop. (1952 est.) 261,904.

HONAN, inland province of China, located in the s.w. portion of the great plain of China. It is watered by the Hwang Ho, or Yellow River. The province is fertile and is one of the most densely populated regions in China. People and crops in E. Honan are constantly menaced by the danger of flood from the Hwang Ho and the Hwai, a river in the s. part of the province. The chief agricultural products of Honan are grains, hemp, and cotton. Iron and coal mining and the manufacture of silk and cotton goods are among the most important industries. Much of Honan, including the capital, Kaifeng (q.v.), was occupied by the Japanese during the Sino-Japanese War of 1937. During the armed conflict between the Communists and Nationalists in China following World War II Honan was taken and occupied by the Communist forces. Area, 59,444 sq.m.; pop. (1952 est.) 77,000.

HONDO. See Honshu.

HONDURAS, a republic of N. Central America, bounded on the w. by Guatemala, on the N. by the Caribbean Sea, on the E. by Nicaragua, and on the s. by Nicaragua, El Salvador, and the Pacific Ocean. The capital and chief city of Honduras is Tegucigalpa (q.v.). Other important cities are San Pedro Sula, Choluteca, Juticalpa, and Santa Rosa. The principal port is Amapala (q.v.), on the Pacific coast. Atlantic coast ports include Ceiba, Puerto Cortés. Tela, and Trujillo (q.v.). Area, about 44,411 sq.m.; pop. (1952 est.) 1,513,000, of whom about 86 percent are mestizo (of mixed Spanish and Indian blood), 10 percent Indian, 2 percent Negro, and 2 percent White.

Except for two coastal strips, one extending 400 m. along the Caribbean Sea, the other 40 m. along the Pacific Ocean, Honduras is a plateau, consisting of broad, fertile plains broken by deep valleys, and rising to mountains that reach an elevation of 10,000 ft. in the volcanic ranges on the Nicaraguan frontier. The watershed between the rivers on the Atlantic and the Pacific sides is far to the s., and most of the drainage is to the Atlantic Ocean. Navigable Atlantic rivers include the Ulua and the Segovia. The former river drains approximately a third of the country. The Cordillera traverses Honduras irregularly in a N.W. and S.E. direction. The climate is healthful and generally temperate in the uplands of the interior. In the low-lying coastal regions, however, the temperature is

higher and the humidity oppressive. The dry season prevails from November to May, the remainder of the year being rainy.

Bananas (constituting about 35% of the value of Honduran exports in 1952–53) and coffee (about 25%) are the country's major crops. Banana production is virtually a monopoly of the United Fruit and the Standard Fruit and Steamship companies, both of which are American-owned. Other agricultural products are corn, coconuts, rice, tobacco, oranges, lemons, henequen, and sarsaparilla. The extensive forests of Honduras yield great quantities of valuable timber. Hardwoods, such as mahogany, walnut, rosewood, and guayacan, grow along the s. coast, in N.E. Honduras, and in the valleys of the interior. Among the softwoods, pine, white pine, and cedar are found in abundance in the interior. Fertile pasture lands provide the basis for increasingly productive dairy-farming and cattle-raising industries. Silver, gold, and lead are mined. Other mineral resources, largely unworked, are iron, zinc, coal, copper, lead, and antimony. Manufacturing industries are small-scale, and produce candles, soap, matches, cigarettes, yarns, and cotton goods for domestic use.

The balance of trade in Honduras is somewhat unfavorable, imports exceeding exports. Exports, valued at about $54,338,000 in 1952–53, include bananas, coconuts, coffee, livestock, gold, silver, mahogany, and pine. Imports, valued at about $57,468,000, include raw materials, manufactured articles, foodstuffs, and beverages. The United States furnishes Honduras with about 71% of imports and receives about 75% of Honduran exports.

The population of Honduras is composed predominantly of mestizos. The ruling class, however, is of almost pure Spanish descent. The majority of the Negro inhabitants are British subjects, formerly brought in for work on the low-lying banana plantations; the practice has now been discontinued. With the exception of certain isolated Indian tribes dwelling in the remote interior, the majority of the population speak Spanish.

Education is free and compulsory for children between the ages of seven and fifteen. Institutions furnishing instruction include 2214 primary schools, 32 secondary and normal schools, and 7 colleges. The National University at Tegucigalpa maintains schools of engineering, pharmacy, medicine, economics, and law. The Honduran government is taking steps to combat the country's high rate of illiteracy, estimated at 63% in 1953. The

Pan American World Airways

The cathedral of San Miguel on the Plaza Morazan in Tegucigalpa, Honduras

prevailing religion is Roman Catholicism, but complete freedom of worship for all faiths is guaranteed under the constitution.

The railroads of Honduras, mostly owned by the fruit companies, are employed principally in the transportation of bananas and run for a length of 816 m. along the N. coast. The mountainous character of the country has made aviation an important means of communication. There are 15 local airports, 1 large international airport, and many small landing fields. The total length of roads was 1124 m. in 1952. The country is linked with the highway systems of Nicaragua, Guatemala, and El Salvador by the Pan American Highway. Lake Yojoa and a number of rivers are navigable by small vessels.

Honduras is governed under the constitution of 1936. Legislative power is vested in the unicameral congress of deputies, composed of forty-nine members elected for six

years by popular vote. While congress is not in session, a permanent commission of five members transacts routine and emergency business. The president, holding executive power, is popularly elected for six years; the term may be extended by vote of congress.

History. The coast of Honduras was discovered by Christopher Columbus in 1502. The first settlement was made in 1524 by Cristóbal de Olid, a lieutenant of the Spanish explorer Hernando Cortes. Olid had been dispatched from Mexico to take possession of the country in the name of his commander. He founded the town of Triunfo de la Cruz, but was induced by reports of rich gold and silver mines to establish an independent government. On receiving intelligence of Olid's defection, Cortes set out in person to bring his lieutenant to terms. After a difficult march of six months over the mountains and rivers of Mexico and Central America, he reached

Ewing Galloway

Above: Mestizo family outside their palm-leaf hut in Honduras.
Left: Spraying an insecticide on banana plants in northern Honduras.

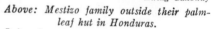

the colony in the spring of 1525. There Cortes reasserted his own authority, founded the town of Natividad de Nuestra Señora, on Caballos Bay, and returned to Mexico in 1526. A royal governor was appointed to administer the province. The gold and silver mines of Honduras proved valuable, but the colony developed slowly under Spanish rule. In 1539 the province was made a part of the Captaincy General of Guatemala. The laws enacted for the protection of the natives were systematically disregarded.

In 1821 Honduras revolted from Spain and was annexed to the Mexican Empire. Two years later, the country joined the federation of Central American States, a union which lasted until 1839. Between 1849 and 1851, Honduras formed an alliance with El Salvador and Nicaragua, ending in 1863 in war among the contracting parties. Because of the strategic geographical position of Honduras with respect to the other countries of Central America and its consequent ability to affect the balance of power, the ruler of each neighboring Central American state has consistently sought to install his own puppet as president of Honduras. In 1874 Marco Aurelio Soto, the Guatemalan candidate, was elected president of Honduras, and was returned to office for two successive terms. Between 1883 and 1903 the country was torn by revolutions and civil disorders. In the latter year, General Manuel Bonilla was elected to the presidency on a platform of domestic pacification and progress. The program was not realized, however, and Honduras, allied with El Salvador, was soon involved in a war against Guatemala, resulting in the overthrow of the Bonilla regime. In 1911 Bonilla led a revolt against President Miguel R. Dávila, whereupon the United States intervened to secure an adjustment of the difficulties. A peace conference was arranged, and following Bonilla's death in 1913, Dr. Francisco Bertrand became president.

In World War I Honduras, following the example of the United States, declared war upon Germany, but did not actively engage in the conflict. The republic subsequently signed the Treaty of Versailles, and became a member of the League of Nations. General Rafael López Gutierrez became president in 1919 as the result of a Liberal revolution. At the expiration of his term three years later, he attempted to perpetuate himself in office, thereby precipitating civil war. The United States again intervened to mediate the dispute, at the same time declaring that it would withhold diplomatic recognition from a revolutionary regime. Following the elections of 1924, Dr. Miguel Paz Barahona, a Conservative, was installed as president. Serious revolutions occurred in 1931 and 1932, but were effectively put down. In 1936 President Tiburcio Carías Andino, with a view to continuing himself in office beyond the expiration of his term, exerted pressure on congress to ratify a new constitution, one of the major provisions of which was the extension of the presidential tenure from four to six years. The vice-president and members of congress were similarly affected. In the same year Honduras withdrew from the League of Nations. Mounting political unrest in 1937, sparked by severe economic depression, culminated in a serious revolt against the dictatorial regime of President Carías Andino. The insurrection was quelled by drastic measures, and its leader, General Justo Umana, fled to Guatemala. Despite continued tension, Carías Andino maintained a firm hold upon his office. In August, 1937, a boundary dispute between Nicaragua and Honduras was inflamed by the issue of a Nicaraguan postage stamp depicting a map of Nicaragua in which the territory at issue was marked "in dispute". The threat of war was averted by the mediation of the United States, Costa Rica, and Venezuela.

Pursuing its policy of co-operation with the United States, the Honduran government enforced stricter curbs upon pro-Axis activities throughout 1941. In June, the German and Italian consulates in Honduras were closed, and six months later the Honduran congress unanimously ratified a declaration of war on Japan, Germany, and Italy. Curtailment of demand for Honduran exports because of the World War II emergency severely affected the country's economy. Financial and technical assistance furnished by the United States helped in some measure to moderate the economic crisis. Through the office of the Coordinator of Inter-American Affairs at Washington, D.C., projects were initiated for the expansion of fruit, vegetable, and livestock production in Honduras. In November, 1943, the Honduran government announced the frustration of a plot to assassinate President Carías Andino. The year 1944 was notable for the introduction of twelve new crops into Honduran agriculture, the most important of which was abaca, a plant furnishing fiber from which rope and hawsers are made. In addition, thousands of acres were planted with Hevea rubber trees under the sponsorship of the United Fruit Company.

Honduras signed the Charter of the United Nations on June 26, 1945, becoming one of the fifty-one original member states of the U.N. In 1947 Honduras became a signatory of the Treaty of Rio de Janeiro (see RIO JANEIRO, TREATY OF). President Carías Andino announced early in 1948 that he intended to retire from public life, and general elections were scheduled for October. Juan Manuel Gálvez, the minister of war, won the nomination of the government-backed Nationalist Party. The Liberal Party entered the campaign but, accusing the government of violating electoral guarantees, withdrew its candidate shortly before the election. Gálvez received a large majority of the votes cast; he was inaugurated on Jan. 1, 1949. In his inaugural address he outlined a broad program of improvements in various fields, including agriculture, communications, education, and social welfare. In October the congress approved legislation imposing taxes on individual incomes. The government granted (No-

Arthur Honegger

vember) several agricultural-development concessions to a subsidiary of the United Fruit Co. Widespread criticism of this move and certain policies of the administration led (1950) to official reprisals against dissidents, particularly members of the Liberal Party. In 1951 Honduras signed the charter of the Organization of Central American States and in conjunction with Costa Rica, Panama, Guatemala, and El Salvador founded an institute to combat malnutrition in Central America. The congress approved (May, 1952) a $10 million appropriation for construction of a network of national highways.

Disagreements within the Nationalist Party during 1953 culminated in the emergence of two factions, one headed by President Gálvez, the other by Carías Andino. The Liberal Party, assiduously championing civil rights and agrarian reforms, broadened its following during the year. Relations with Guatemala worsened in 1953, mainly as a result of Guatemalan charges that Honduras had extended aid to Guatemalan refugees plotting against the leftist Arbenz Guzman regime.

Honduras and the United States concluded a military-aid pact on May 20, 1954, and a few days later the U.S. government, alarmed over the arrival of large cargoes of military equipment in Guatemala from Red Poland, air-lifted various types of small arms and ammunition to Honduras. On June 18 detachments of anticommunist Guatemalan exiles, operating from bases in Honduras, launched a successful rebellion against the Arbenz Guzman government.

The Liberal Party and each faction of the Nationalist Party nominated candidates for the presidency in 1954. None of the candidates obtained an absolute majority in the voting, which took place on Oct. 10. Consequently, under constitutional processes, selection of the country's next president became the responsibility of the congress. The latter was scheduled to meet later in the year.

HONDURAS, BRITISH. See BRITISH HONDURAS.

HONEGGER, ARTHUR (1892–), French composer, born in Le Havre. He studied at the Zurich Conservatory from 1909 to 1911. In 1912 he entered the Paris Conservatoire, where he studied harmony, counterpoint, and fugue under André Gédalge and Charles Marie Widor, and orchestration under Vincent d'Indy. In 1920 he became a member of the group known as Les Six (see SIX, LES). Beginning as a composer of the Impressionist school, Honegger gradually evolved a personal style characterized by austerity, dramatic power, and ability to describe realistically in music various aspects of contemporary life. The last-named quality is exemplified in his two orchestral compositions *Pacific 231* (1923, a musical description of a steam engine) and *Rugby* (1928). His other works include the oratorio *Le Roi David* (1925), the opera *Judith* (1925), and a number of symphonies and ballets. He is regarded as one of the most important composers of the French school of the first half of the 20th century.

HONEY, a sweet, thick, liquid substance manufactured by bees to feed their larvae and to subsist on during the winter. Nectar of flowers is ingested by worker bees, and converted to honey in special sacs in their esophagi. It is stored and aged in combs in their hives. Bee honey is an important constituent of the diet of many animals, such as bears and ratels, and is put to many uses by man. Other insects, especially bugs, manufacture honey from flowers, from the honeydew of plants, or from the sweet secretions elaborated by other insects; this honey is of little economic importance.

Bee honey is composed chiefly of fructose, glucose, and water, in varying proportions; it also contains several enzymes and essential oils. The color and flavor depend on the age of the honey and on the source of the nectar. Light-colored honeys are usually of higher quality than darker honeys; white honey is derived from the Californian white sage, *Salvia apiana.* Other high-grade honeys are made by bees from orange blossoms, clover, and alfalfa. A well-known, poorer-grade honey is a dark variety elaborated from buckwheat.

Honey has a fuel value of about 1520 calories per pound, and a specific gravity of 1.45 to 1.49 at ordinary room temperature (68° F. or 20° C.). It readily picks up moisture from the air, and is consequently used as a moistening agent for tobacco. Glucose crystallizes out of honey on standing at room temperature, leaving an uncrystallized layer of dissolved fructose. Honey to be marketed is usually heated by special processes to about 150° F. (65.6° C.) to dissolve the crystals and is then poured into containers hermetically sealed to retard crystallization.

The fructose layer in crystallized honey ferments readily at temperatures of 60° F. (15.6° C.) or over (see FERMENTATION). Fermented honey is used in the production of honey wine or mead (q.v.).

Honey is marketed in the original comb as "comb honey", or centrifuged out of the comb and sold as "extracted honey". "Chunk honey" consists of pieces of comb honey suspended in extracted liquid honey. See BEE.

HONEY BADGER. See RATEL.

HONEYCOMB CORAL. See HALYSITES.

HONEYCOMB MOTH, BEE MOTH, or **WAX MOTH,** common name of a moth, *Galleria mellonella,* in the family Pyralididae, so called because its larvae live in the combs of bees. The distribution of the honeycomb moth is almost world wide. The adult moth is about ¾ in. long and has a wing span of about 1¾ in. Its forewings are purplish and its hind wings tan. The female honeycomb moth enters a beehive at night, while the bees are asleep, and lays its eggs. The larvae feed at night on the wax of the hive and on the wastes of the bees, and spend the daytime concealed in tunnels made of silk.

HONEYDEW MELON. See MUSKMELON.

HONEY EATER or **HONEYSUCKER,** common name for any oscine bird in the family Meliphagidae, found in Australia, New Zealand, the Malay Archipelago, and the islands of the central Pacific Ocean. The birds have long, forked tongues with which they scoop nectar and small insects from the inside of flowers. Their bills are long, down-curved, and sharp. They build loose, cup-shaped nests on bushes and in trees; the females lay from two

to five eggs in one nesting, light buff spotted with dark brown.

The best-known honey eaters are the friarbird, wattlebird, and the parson bird, *Prosthemadera novaeseelandiae,* of New Zealand. The last-named is so called because of a white, collarlike fringe of feathers on each side of its throat. The bird is satin black with white shoulders, and is about 15 in. long. It often imitates the calls of other birds. Other well-known honey eaters include the bellbirds, *Anthornis melanura,* of New Zealand, and *Manorina melanophrys,* of Australia; and the soldierbird, *Myzomela sanguineolenta,* of Australia.

HONEY GUIDE, INDICATOR, or **MOROC,** common name for any small, dull-colored bird in the family Indicatoridae of the Woodpecker order, found in Africa, Asia, and the East Indies. The bird is about 10 in. long and has a short bill. The female deposits her eggs in the nests of other birds. A common species is *Indicator major.* The honey guide has a fondness for honey, and men are often able to locate beehives by following it.

HONEY LOCUST, common name of North American leguminous trees of the genus *Gleditsia,* belonging to the Senna family. The common honey locust, *G. triacanthos,* grows as tall as 140 feet, and has branches covered with strong, forked spines. Its leaves are pinnately compound, with rounded leaflets. The flower comprises a short, three- to five-lobed calyx, three to five greenish petals, three to ten stamens, and one pistil. The fruit is an elongated, brown or black, leathery pod containing several flat, black seeds and a sweet pulp. Honey locust is native to deep woods of northeastern and central U.S. It is planted extensively in parks; small specimens are often heavily pruned to form hedges.

The water locust, *G. aquatica,* is a smaller tree, 25 to 35 feet tall, which grows in swamps and river basins of southern U.S. Its leaves and flowers are similar to those of common honey locust, but it has slender thorns which are usually unforked, shorter leaflets.

Several other leguminous trees and shrubs are sometimes called honey locust, including mesquite (q.v.), black locust, and clammy locust; see LOCUST.

HONEYSUCKLE, common name of plants of the genus *Lonicera,* and of the family Caprifoliaceae to which they belong. The genus contains more than one hundred species, all native to temperate regions of the Northern Hemisphere. Honeysuckles are twining or erect shrubs having smooth, opposite leaves. The flowers of many species are showy and fragrant, and consist of a five-toothed calyx, a funnel-shaped, five-lobed, tubular corolla, five stamens inserted on the corolla lobes, and a single pistil. The fruit is a many-seeded berry.

The common honeysuckle, in England also called woodbine and eglantine, is *L. periclymenum,* a native of Europe cultivated in the United States. It is a popular climber, with white, yellow, and cream-colored flowers which have a heavy fragrance. The American honeysuckle, *L. dioica,* is a smooth twiner which bears purple or yellow-green flowers. The perfoliate honeysuckle, *L. caprifolium,* has remarkable upper leaves; pairs of opposite leaves unite to form a single leaf through which the stem passes. This twiner is a native of s. Europe, extensively cultivated in eastern U.S. as an early-flowering variety. The trumpet honeysuckle, *L. sempervirens,* is a native of s.e. United States having large, fragrant, scarlet flowers. The Japanese honeysuckle, *L. japonica,* is a creeping vine used popularly as ground cover on slopes. It has spread alarmingly, ruining large areas of woodland; herbicides are effective in controlling it; see WEEDS. Several other Asiatic species are erect shrubs. *L. tartarica,* the Tartarian honeysuckle, bears pink or white flowers which give rise to dark-red berries. The fragrant honeysuckle, *L. fragrantissima,* is a strong Asiatic shrub which grows as high as eight feet. It bears leathery leaves and cream-colored flowers. Cultivated honeysuckles are usually grown from seeds, cuttings, or layers.

Several unrelated plants with fragrant flowers are also commonly called honeysuckle, such as *Diervilla,* the bush honeysuckle, and *Azalea* (q.v.), the swamp honeysuckle.

HONG KONG, a British crown colony comprising the island of Hong Kong and the small Stonecutter's Island (combined area, 32 sq.m.), and also Kowloon peninsula (3 sq.m.) and the New Territories (359 sq.m.) on the mainland of China. Hong Kong Island, located at the mouth of the Canton, or Pearl R., some 90 miles s.e. of Canton, extends about 11 m. from e. to w. and has a width of from 2 to 5 m. It is separated from the mainland by the narrow Lyemun Pass. The New Territories, composed for the most part of agricultural areas, and including the waters of Deep Bay and Mirs Bay and a number of islands, were leased to Great Britain by the Chinese government in 1898 for a period of 99 years. In addition, considerable areas have been reclaimed at Wanchai, Kowloon Bay, and North Point. The capital and chief city of Hong Kong colony is Victoria (q.v.), which extends some 5 m. along the n. shore of the island of Hong Kong. The only other city of importance is Kowloon (q.v.).

The total area of the colony is about 391 sq.m.; pop. (1952 est.) 2,250,000 (including about a million Chinese refugees), composed predominantly of Chinese, and containing British, Indian, Portuguese, and American inhabitants.

The principal importance of Hong Kong derives from its excellent natural harbor, covering an area of 17 sq.m., and constituting the only satisfactory seaport between Shanghai and Indochina. The size and strategic location of the harbor have made it a gateway between West and East, and a clearing point for commerce throughout s. China and the w. Pacific. With the exception of import duties levied on hydrocarbon oils, toiletries, tobacco, alcoholic beverages, and non-British automotive vehicles, the port facilities of Hong Kong are free.

The greatest portion of the industry of Hong Kong is the importing of goods for re-export. The chief items of commerce are textiles, piece goods, drugs and chemicals, Chinese medicines, minerals and ores, metals, paper and paper products, tanning and dyeing materials, oils and fats, and foodstuffs. Among the products of China transshipped from Hong Kong to markets in the United States, Europe, and other parts of the world are tea, peanut oil, wood oil, hides, firecrackers, feathers, tin (processed in Hong Kong), and wolfram ore. Export articles manufactured in Hong Kong itself include shirts, undershirts, socks, rubber-bottomed canvas shoes, and flashlight batteries. Other industries are the building and repairing of ships, and the manufacture of cement, paint, and matches. Virtually every maritime country in the world maintains regular passenger and shipping services to and from Hong Kong. The bulk of the trade is normally with the United Kingdom.

Roughly 20% of the total land area of the colony is under cultivation, for the most part in the New Territories. Rice, sugar cane, and vegetable crops are rotated. Production is severely limited by primitive agricultural implements and procedures. Fishing, both coastal and deep-sea, is carried on by a large segment of Hong Kong's population dwelling on junks or sampans in Victoria harbor and adjacent bays.

Although within the tropics, Hong Kong has a subtropical climate because of the s.w. mon-

Pan American World Airways

Rickshaws on a business street in the British crown colony of Hong Kong

soon, a moist, warm, equatorial wind which prevails from May to August. The mean annual temperature is 72° F., with a range from 59° F. in February to 82° F. in July. The rainy season is in the summer, the heaviest precipitation occurring between the months of May and September. Typhoons are not uncommon, and frequently visit the island with great destruction.

Education in Hong Kong is not compulsory, but all schools are required to be registered with the Department of Education. There are four types of schools: government schools, staffed and operated by the department of education; grant schools, maintained by missionary organizations through government grants; government-subsidized schools, with classes conducted in the Cantonese dialect; and private schools. Other institutions of learning include two teachers colleges and a training college. The University of Hong Kong, established in 1912, has faculties of arts, medicine, and engineering; enrollment in 1953 totaled 982.

Hong Kong Colony had 432 miles of roads in 1953, of which approximately 180 miles

are on Hong Kong Island, about 140 miles in the New Territories, and about 112 miles in Kowloon. Hong Kong Island is also served by busses, electric streetcars, and cable cars.

The colony of Hong Kong is administered by a governor with the aid of a twelve-member executive council and a legislative council of seventeen.

Before the British occupation, Hong Kong was the site of a small fishing community, and served as a haven for pirates and opium smugglers. British vessels first utilized the island's harbor as a naval base at the time of the Opium War (q.v.) between Great Britain and China. By the Treaty of Nanking (1842), which brought the Opium War to an end, Hong Kong was ceded to the British. Eighteen years later, after the second Opium War, Great Britain acquired Kowloon and Stonecutter's Island, and in 1898 obtained the New Territories under a long-term lease.

Hong Kong became a refuge for political exiles from the mainland of China following the establishment of the Chinese Republic in 1911.

A period of intense Chinese nationalism ensued, marked by antagonism toward all foreign countries, and from 1925 to 1927 a Chinese boycott denied British shipping access to the ports of s. China. With the seizure of Manchuria by Japan in 1932, however, and the outbreak of the Sino-Japanese War in 1937, China turned to Great Britain and other European countries for its military supplies, and the diplomatic relations between the British in Hong Kong and the Chinese became progressively more friendly. Throughout 1937 hundreds of thousands of Chinese, displaced by Japanese invasion of their country, sought refuge in Hong Kong. Meanwhile, Great Britain instituted an extensive program to strengthen and expand the defenses of the colony against possible Japanese attack.

The outbreak of World War II in September, 1939, further dislocated the economic life of Hong Kong, already seriously affected by the Sino-Japanese conflict. The threat of Japanese aggression against Hong Kong was intensified in the following year when 10,000 Japanese troops occupied most of the coastal zone on the mainland of China, severing communication of the colony with the Chinese interior. In the following weeks some 4000 Americans and Europeans (for the most part women and children) were evacuated from Hong Kong by way of Manila, Philippine Islands, and military reinforcements arrived to strengthen the garrison. The defense program was accelerated, and great tunnels were bored in the island's cliffs to shelter the civilian population from air raids.

Early in 1941 emergency foodstocks were accumulated, great quantities of ammunition were stored, and all approaches to Hong Kong Island were mined. On December 8, one day after Japan's surprise attack on Pearl Harbor, Hawaii, nine Japanese aircraft bombed Kowloon. After several days of intensive fighting, Japanese ground forces dislodged British troops from Kowloon and the New Territories on the mainland, forcing them to retire to Hong Kong Island. On December 25, following a brief siege, the British were obliged to surrender. The Japanese, upon their occupation of Hong Kong, proceeded to convert it into a military bastion and supply station for their projected campaigns in East Asia. Their operations were largely hampered, however, by the action of United States submarines and China-based U.S. bombing planes. Reliable eyewitnesses escaping from Hong Kong carried to the outside world reports of atrocities perpetrated by the Japanese upon captured British officers and European and Chinese ci-

vilians. The British reoccupied Hong Kong following the unconditional surrender of Japan on Aug. 14, 1945.

During the immediate postwar period Hong Kong swiftly regained its status as a major Far Eastern entrepôt. Numerous economic dislocations resulted, however, from the Nationalist-Communist civil war in China. Hundreds of thousands of Chinese took refuge in the colony before and after the Red victory (1949). Foreign trade decreased steadily between December, 1950, when the U.S. imposed a ban on trade with Red China, and July, 1952. Thereafter shipments of nonstrategic goods to Communist China mounted in volume.

HONOLULU, CITY AND COUNTY OF, capital, city, and county of the Territory of Hawaii, coextensive with Oahu Island and certain other islands of the Hawaiian chain, and situated about 2090 miles s.w. of San Francisco, Calif. The city proper occupies a magnificent site on the s. coast of Oahu and extends inland to the Koolau Mountains, a range with an extreme elevation of about 3100 feet above sea level. An extinct volcanic crater, known as the Punchbowl, is situated within the environs of the city, and Diamond Head, a headland 761 feet above sea level, dominates the E. approach to the harbor. Honolulu harbor, almost completely enclosed by a natural breakwater of coral reefs, has extensive facilities and equipment for the receipt and discharge of waterborne freight. At the crossroads of transpacific shipping routes, the port is reached regularly by passenger lines and cargo carriers operating from all parts of the world. The port is also the terminus of an interisland steamship line, a regular point of call of several transpacific air-transport services, and the center of transpacific cable and wireless services. Among the principal exports shipped from Honolulu are sugar, canned pineapple fruit and juice, molasses, coffee, and canned fish. Imports include automobiles, petroleum, machinery, chemicals, textile products, paper and wood products, rice, flour, and other foodstuffs. The leading manufacturing industries in the city are canning, sugar refining, and the making of food-processing machinery. A number of minor industrial establishments are engaged in the production of various items for the domestic market.

Because of its equable climate (mean annual temperature, about 75° F.) and low annual precipitation, Honolulu is a favorite resort city, visited by thousands of tourists and vacationists yearly. The climate is especially favorable for persons suffering from pul-

Merchant Street in the city of Honolulu, Oahu Island, Territory of Hawaii

monary disorders. Among the points of interest of the city are the Territorial Capitol, formerly the residence of the Hawaiian royal family, and the surrounding civic center; the Bernice Pauahi Bishop Museum, noted for its collections of zoological, ethnographical, and historical materials related to the Hawaiian Islands; the public parks and gardens, containing a profusion of exotic tropical flora; the University of Hawaii, the chief institution of higher learning in the Territory; and Waikiki, an internationally famous bathing and pleasure resort. Pearl Harbor (q.v.), a huge naval base and the object of the surprise Japanese attack (December 7, 1941) which brought the United States into World War II, is situated 7 miles w. of the city proper. About 20 m. to the w. is Schofield Barracks, the principal United States Army post in the Territory. Area of Oahu Island, 604 sq.m.; pop. of city (1951 est.) 315,345.

HONSHU or **HONDO,** the largest island (sometimes referred to as the mainland) of Japan, bounded on the N. by Tsugaru Strait, which separates it from Hokkaido Island, on the E. by the Pacific Ocean, on the S. by the Inland Sea and the Strait of Shimonoseki, which separates it from Shikoku and Kyushu islands, and on the w. by the Sea of Japan. The coastline of the island has a total length

of about 5900 m. and is deeply indented, with many excellent harbors. Like all of the islands of Japan, Honshu is extremely mountainous. In the central mountain mass, often called the Japanese Alps, occur the loftiest peaks of Japan. Mount Fuji (q.v.) or Fujiyama, the highest summit of the country, has an elevation of 12,395 ft. above sea level. Asamayama, the largest volcano of Japan, is situated on the island, about 85 miles N.W. of Tokyo. A number of other peaks, some of which are extinct or quiescent volcanoes, exceed 8000 feet. The Tone, Shinano, and Kiso rivers, among the largest of Japan, are situated on Honshu, and the island also contains numerous lakes, which are noted as summer-resort areas.

Extending over approximately eight degrees of latitude, Honshu has wide regional variations of climate. Severe winters, with considerable snow, are common w. of the central uplift and in N. portion of the island. South of Tokyo, where the minimum temperature frequently falls to 22° F., climatic conditions are generally milder, except at extreme altitudes. Under the influence of the s.w. monsoon, the summers are usually moist and hot, with extreme temperatures as high as 95° F. Annual precipitation, heaviest between June and September, often exceeds 60 inches in the E. central region. Considerably more than half of the population of Japan resides on Honshu. Besides Tokyo, the leading cities of the island include Osaka, Nagoya, Kyoto, Yokohama, Kobe, and Hiroshima (qq.v.). Area, including that of nearly 200 small adjacent islands, 87,293 sq.m.; pop. (1947) 58,769,968. See JAPAN.

HONTHORST, GERARD VAN (1590–1656), Dutch painter, born in Utrecht. He studied painting in Rome, where he was influenced by the work of Caravaggio. His paintings, particularly of night scenes, won great popularity. On his return to Utrecht in 1623 he was elected dean of the painters' guild of St. Luke, and opened an art school which attracted many students. In 1628 he was invited to England by Charles I, and subsequently painted allegorical pictures for the walls of Whitehall Palace. For the King of Denmark he painted a series of works illustrating Danish history. In his late years he devoted himself entirely to portrait painting. He is represented by paintings in the Amsterdam Museum, the Berlin and Dresden galleries, the Uffizi Gallery in Florence, and the Louvre in Paris.

HOOCH, PIETER DE (1629–after 1677), Dutch genre painter, born in Rotterdam. From 1654 he was a member of the Guild of St. Luke at Delft, where he painted his finest works, illustrating simple middle-class life and domestic scenes. He was noted for his painting of distinctive interiors, in which the typical effect is strong sunlight falling into a room and illuminating a standing figure, often a maidservant, or a family group seated at a table. De Hooch, in his work, captured the simple, expressive gestures of people occupied with their daily chores, and enhanced his quiet interiors with sharp patterns of golden light. In the painting of genre interiors he ranks second only to his great Dutch contemporary, Jan Vermeer (q.v.). De Hooch worked in Amsterdam during his later years; although he utilized similar subject matter in his paintings, the examples of this period are generally considered less noteworthy than his superb Delft productions. He is represented by work in the principal museums of the world, including the Louvre, Paris; the Amsterdam Museum, Holland; the National Gallery, Washington, D.C.; and the Metropolitan Museum of Art, New York City.

HOOD, JOHN BELL (1831–79), American army officer, born in Owingsville, Ky. He was graduated from the U.S. Military Academy at West Point in 1853, and held a commission in the U.S. Army until the outbreak of the Civil War, when he joined the Confederate Army. He was promoted to the rank of brigadier general in 1862, and for his able command of the "Texas Brigade", particularly at the Battle of Gaines' Mill, the second Battle of Bull Run, and the Battle of Antietam, was commissioned major general. He fought at Gettysburg and Chickamauga, and in 1864 served as lieutenant general under General Joseph E. Johnston. Just before the siege of Atlanta, Hood replaced Johnston in command of the Army of Tennessee in the defense of Atlanta against the army of Union General William T. Sherman. Hood was defeated and forced to retreat from Atlanta, and after his loss of the battles of Franklin and Nashville, Tenn., he asked to be relieved of his command. After the war he was a commission merchant in New Orleans. He wrote a book entitled *Personal Experiences in the United States and Confederate Armies,* published posthumously in 1880.

HOOD, THOMAS (1799–1845), English poet and humorist, born in London. After working in a mercantile office, in 1818 he was apprenticed to an uncle who was an engraver; his experience in the latter position enabled him subsequently to illustrate several of his own works. He served as subeditor of the *London Magazine* from 1821 until 1823, during which period he joined the literary group including Charles Lamb, Thomas De Quincey, David Hartley Coleridge, and William Hazlitt. Hood's first work, *Odes and Addresses to Great People* (1825), shows the influence of the poet John Keats (q.v.), as does his volume of poetry *The Plea of the Midsummer Fairies . . . and Other Poems* (1827).

Hood had great talent both as a serious poet and as a humorous writer. He won his reputation as a humorist through the series of the *Comic Annual,* a publication which he undertook in 1830 and edited until 1842; in these writings Hood deftly caricatured both current events and contemporary figures. In another annual, the *Gem,* which Hood had undertaken to edit in 1829, appeared *The Dream of Eugene Aram, the Murderer* (1831), a poem which attracted attention to Hood's serious poetical talents. Also in the serious vein are the well-known *Song of the Shirt* (1843, in *Punch*), *Bridge of Sighs* (1846), and *Song of the Labourer,* poems which revealed Hood's sympathy with the sufferings of the industrial workers of his time, among whom his name was honored.

Hood lived on the Continent from 1835

until 1840, because of ill health. During that period he continued writing and editing the *Annuals*. On his return to England he edited first the *New Monthly Magazine,* and then, in 1844, started *Hood's Magazine.* His other works include the novel *Tylney Hall* (3 vols., 1834); the collection of short stories *National Tales* (2 vols., 1837); *Hood's Own, or Laughter from Year to Year* (1838); the volume of humorous sketches *Up the Rhine* (1840); and the comic poem *Miss Kilmansegg* and collected miscellaneous pieces *Whimsicalities* (1844).

HOODED CROW, Dun Crow, Gray Crow, or Hoodie, common name of a crow, *Corvus cornix,* abundant in England and N. Europe, so called because its black head, wings, and fore parts look like a hood against the gray remainder of its body. The bird is about 19 in. long. Like the carrion crow, *C. carone,* with which it frequently interbreeds, the hooded crow feeds on dead flesh, and also eats small birds and their eggs. The female hooded crow lays about five green eggs, mottled with brown.

The name hooded crow is sometimes applied to the Indian house crow, *C. splendens,* a slightly smaller bird with similar coloring. The house crow is occasionally domesticated and is useful as a scavenger.

HOODED WARBLER, a wood warbler, *Wilsonia citrina,* of eastern U.S., so called because the male has black markings extending from the crown and neck to the throat and breast in the shape of a hood. The male is greenish brown above, reddish yellow on the abdomen. The forehead and sides of its head are yellow. The female bird differs from the male in not having the black hood; yellow or gray replaces it. The hooded warbler is 5½ to 6 in. long and has a powerful, beautiful song. It feeds on insects, often catching them in mid-air. It nests near the ground in low bushes.

HOOD, MOUNT, peak in the Cascade Range, located in Clackamas and Hood River counties, Ore., about 50 miles S.E. of Portland. It rises to a height of 11,245 ft. above sea level, and is the highest point in Oregon. Mt. Hood is a recreation center, attracting skiers in the winter and mountain climbers in the summer.

HOOF-AND-MOUTH DISEASE, another name for foot-and-mouth disease (q.v.).

HOOGHLY, or Hugli, a river of West Bengal, India, the most westerly of the channels by which the Ganges R. (q.v.) reaches the Bay of Bengal, and its principal channel of navigation. It is formed near Santipur, about 40 m. above Calcutta, by the confluence of the Nadia rivers, three western deltaic distributaries of the Ganges, comprising the Bhagirathi, Jalangi, and Churni rivers. The Hooghly is navigable by ocean vessels from its mouth to Calcutta, a distance of about 80 m. Navigability is maintained, however, by constant engineering operations, especially at the mouth of the river, where shoals and a seven-foot bore which arises during the monsoon season afford hazards to shipping.

HOOGHLY, or Hugli, a town and district of West Bengal State, Union of India. The town, which forms a single municipality with the town of Chinsura, is situated on the Hooghly R., 24 m. by rail N. of Calcutta. Hooghly-Chinsura is the site of Hooghly College. Among the buildings in the municipality are a monastery, and several structures dating from the period of the Dutch occupation of Chinsura, which was formerly the principal Dutch settlement in Bengal. The town of Hooghly was founded by the Portuguese in the 16th century, and Chinsura was settled by the Dutch in 1656. The Hooghly district is watered by the Damodar and Rupnarayan rivers, in addition to the Hooghly R. Extensive marshes cover the low-lying areas between the high lands along the rivers. The chief crops of the district are rice and jute, and the principal industrial establishments, situated mainly along the banks of the Hooghly, are jute factories. Area, 1206 sq.m.; Pop. (1951) 1,554,320. Pop. of Hooghly-Chinsura, about 49,000.

HOOKE, Robert (1635–1703), English physicist, born on the Isle of Wight, and educated at Oxford University. He served as assistant to the physicist Robert Boyle (q.v.) and assisted him in the construction of the air pump. In 1662 Hooke was appointed curator of experiments to the Royal Society and served in this position until his death. He was elected a Fellow of the Royal Society in 1663, and was appointed professor of geometry at Oxford University in 1665. After the Great Fire of 1666 he was appointed surveyor of London, and designed many buildings, including Montague House and Bethlehem Hospital.

Hooke anticipated some of the most important discoveries and inventions of his time, but failed to carry many of them through to completion. He formulated the theory of planetary motion as a problem in mechanics, and grasped, but failed to develop mathematically, the fundamental theory upon which Sir Isaac Newton formulated the law of gravitation. He also anticipated the wave theory of light and observed the phenomena of interference and diffraction. Among his more positive contributions are the correct formulation of the theory of elasticity, the kinetic hypothesis of gases, and the nature of combustion. He invented and improved many instruments, especially astronomical instruments. He was the first to use the balance spring for the regulation of watches and devised improvements in pendulum clocks. Among his writings are *Micrographics* (1666) and *Lectiones Cutlerianæ* (1678).

HOOKER, JOSEPH (1814–79), American army officer, born in Hadley, Mass., and educated at the U.S. Military Academy at West Point. During the Mexican War he was brevetted lieutenant colonel for gallantry. At the outbreak of the Civil War he was appointed brigadier general of volunteers, and in 1862 he became brigadier general in the U.S. Army. His skillful leadership and personal bravery won for him the sobriquet of "Fighting Joe".

In January, 1863, Hooker was assigned by President Abraham Lincoln to the command of the Army of the Potomac. He rehabilitated and organized this Army, but his command on the battlefield failed to show those qualities which had distinguished him as a corps and division commander. At the Battle of Chancellorsville (q.v.) the defeat of the Union troops was in large measure due to Hooker's vacillation and inability to cope with the surprise actions of the Confederate leadership. In deference to Lincoln's lack of confidence in him and the pressure of public opinion in the North, Hooker resigned his command of the Army of the Potomac. He was given command of the Eleventh and Twelfth Corps, later combined to form the Twentieth Corps. Hooker fought with distinction of the Battle of Chattanooga and at the so-called "Battle of the Clouds" on Lookout Mountain, and was brevetted major general in the regular army. He was given charge of the Northern Department, then of the Department of the East, and finally of the Department of the Lakes. A paralytic attack caused him to retire from active service in 1868, with the full rank of major general in the regular army.

HOOKER, SIR JOSEPH DALTON (1817–1911), British botanist, son of Sir William Jackson Hooker, born in Halesworth, Suffolk, and educated at Glasgow University. After graduation in 1839 he joined, as assistant surgeon, an Antarctic expedition led by Sir James Ross (q.v.). He returned to Great Britain in 1843 and during the ensuing seventeen years published descriptions of the floras of Antarctica, New Zealand, and Tasmania. Hooker was appointed botanist to the Geological Survey of Great Britain in 1846 and surveyed unexplored regions in the Himalayas from 1847 to 1851. He was appointed assistant director of the Royal Botanic Gardens at Kew in 1855, and succeeded his father as director, serving in that post from 1865 to 1885. Hooker was influential in inducing Charles Darwin to publish the *Origin of Species*. He was president of the Royal Society (London) from 1873 to 1878. In 1907 he was awarded the Order of Merit by Edward VII. His principal writings include *Outlines of the Distribution of Arctic Plants* (1862), *Genera Plantarum* (with George Bentham, 1862–83), *Student's Flora of the British Isles* (1870), and *Flora of British India* (1907).

HOOKER, RICHARD (1554?–1600), English theologian, born in Heavitree, Devon, and educated at Corpus Christi College, Oxford University. He took holy orders in 1582, and was made master of the Temple, London, in 1585. In 1591, Hooker was transferred to the rectory of Boscombe, Wiltshire, where he wrote the first four books of his *Laws of Ecclesiastical Polity,* published in 1594. He moved to the rectory of Bishopsbourne, Kent, in 1595. The fifth book of his *Polity* was published in 1597, and the final three books were published after his death. Early editions of the latter three were extensively altered by editing, and the first definitive edition of all eight books was published by Isaak Walton (q.v.) in 1666. The modern standard edition, done by John Keble (q.v.), was published in 1836. The immediate purpose of Hooker's *Polity* was to defend the Anglican form of church organization against Presbyterian attack. The lasting value of the work stems from its recognition that natural law is unchangeable and eternal, but that positive law, including law affecting forms of government, can be altered when change is necessary and expedient.

HOOKER, THOMAS (1586?–1647), American Congregationalist clergyman, born in Leicestershire, England, and educated at Emmanuel College, Cambridge University. He was pastor of several churches from 1620 until 1630, when he was called to appear before the Court of High Commission for nonconformist views. He fled to Holland, where he preached for three years, and then sailed for New England, settling in New Towne (later Cambridge), Mass. He was chosen pastor of the first church in New Towne, and served from 1633 to 1636, when he migrated with his congregation to Connecticut and settled in Hartford. He was the leader of the new settlement in Hartford and of the surrounding Connecticut towns, and had a leading part in framing the "Fundamental Orders", which served as the constitution for Connecticut. Hooker was also influential in the organization of United Colonies of New England, the first attempt at federal government in America. A few of Hooker's many writings are *The Soule's Preparation for Christ* (1632); *A Survey of the Summe of Church Discipline,* a defense of the New England churches which greatly influenced the development of Congregationalism in America, pu'lished in 1648; and *An Application of Redemption,* published in 1657.

HOOKWORM, any of several related parasitic worms of the class Nematoda, particularly those of the genera *Ankylostoma, Necator,* and *Uncinaria.* These worms take their name from the hooklike appendages which surround their mouths. As intestinal parasites they are responsible for diseases of men and animals; see HOOKWORM DISEASE.

HOOKWORM DISEASE, a disease caused by parasitic invasion of the intestine by hookworms of the species *Necator americanus, Ankylostoma duodenale,* and, occasionally, *A. braziliense* or *A. ceylonicum.* Hookworm disease, which is marked by pronounced anemia, was formerly prevalent in the southern portion of the U.S. and is still endemic in many tropical and subtropical countries. The disease is occasionally found among miners in temperate regions. The eggs of hookworms are deposited on the earth in the feces of people suffering from the disease. The eggs develop into larvae which subsist on fecal matter and which have a life of several weeks to several months. These larvae are able to penetrate the skin of any person who touches them; infection is most commonly caused by walking bare-footed in contaminated areas or by handling human feces used as fertilizer. Entering the body, the larvae travel through the blood stream to the lungs, and from there, by way of the bronchial tubes and trachea, to the digestive tract. The larvae then attach themselves to the walls of the intestine and develop in about a month into adult worms.

The symptoms of hookworm disease are caused primarily by the blood which the worms drain from the intestinal walls. The anemia may at times be severe. The disease usually causes apathy and malnutrition and,

in children results in underdevelopment.

In many tropical countries, notably in Asia and Latin America, hookworm disease is a public health problem of the first importance, since in some cases as much as 95 percent of the population may be affected. In 1948 medical authorities estimated that in all parts of the world, 457,000,000 people were afflicted with hookworms. The disease can be prevented by sanitary measures including the disposal or disinfection of fecal matter, the avoidance of contaminated areas, and the wearing of shoes. The disease is successfully treated with anthelmintics (drugs which expel the worms from the intestine) plus dosages of iron salts. Compare SCHISTOSOMIASIS.

HOONOOMAUN. See LANGUR.

HOOP ASH. See CELTIDACEAE.

HOOPER, WILLIAM (1742–90), American Revolutionary leader, born in Boston, and educated at Harvard College. He practiced law in North Carolina, and was elected to the State legislature in 1773. A year later he was elected to the Continental Congress and held office until 1777, when he resigned. Hooper was one of the signers of the Declaration of Independence. In 1786 he was one of the federal judges appointed to settle the territorial dispute between Massachusetts and New York.

HOOPOE, common name of any Old World coraciiform bird in the family Upupidae; both the common name and the family name are imitative of the bird's cry. The hoopoes, which are found in Europe, Asia, and N. Africa, are about 1 ft. long. Their feathers are in many shades of color, varying according to the species. Their characteristic features are a very long, down-curving bill and a large, central, feathery crest, running from the forehead to the back of the crown. The crest can be folded or spread out at will. Hoopoes nest in holes in trees and the crannies of walls and

American Museum of Natural History
Hoopoe (Upupa marginata)

are noted for the filthiness of their nests, which both parents and offspring fill with excrement. They feed on worms and insects. Several species are eaten in Europe. The best-known species of hoopoe is *Upupa epops*, which is black above and white below. Its head and crest are cinnamon tan, the crest being tipped with black and white. The wings are black, banded with white.

Several African coraciiform birds, constituting the family Phoeniculidae, are known as wood hoopoes. They resemble true hoopoes but have no crest. *Phoeniculus senegalensis*, a common species, is about 18 in. long.

HOOP SKIRT. See CRINOLINE.

HOOP SNAKE. See MUD SNAKE.

HOOVER, HERBERT CLARK (1874–   ), thirty-first President of the United States, born in West Branch, Iowa, and educated at Stanford University. In 1897 he went to Australia as a mining engineer for an English syndicate, and in 1899 the Chinese government appointed him director general of mines. His government work was terminated by the Boxer uprising, and he returned to private practice, engaging in mining operations in many parts of the world. He became associated with numerous successful mining companies and was managing director of several of them.

At the outbreak of World War I Hoover was living in Europe; he was appointed to organize and direct the American Relief Committee which aided the repatriation of more than 200,000 American tourists left in Europe as a result of the breakdown of transportation caused by the war. Soon afterward he was made head of Belgian Relief, and was entrusted with the expenditure of nearly a billion and a half dollars to purchase and supply food and clothing to the people of that wartorn nation. Upon the entry of the United States into the war, President Woodrow Wilson recalled Hoover and appointed him Federal Food Administrator. After the war he was made director general of the American Relief Administration, providing food and necessities to the peoples of Europe impoverished by the war.

In 1921 Hoover was appointed secretary of commerce by President Warren G. Harding, and served through the administration of President Calvin Coolidge; he resigned in 1928 when he was nominated by the Republican Party as candidate for the Presidency. The campaign was bitter, not so much because of Republican action, but because of internal dissension in the Democratic Party

over the nomination of Alfred E. Smith. Hoover won by a popular vote of twenty-one to fifteen millions, and by an electoral vote of 444 to 87. At his inauguration on March 4, 1929, he took an affirmation of office rather than the customary oath, which the precepts of his Quaker religion forbade.

The first few months of Hoover's administration were marked by the reopening of international negotiations for limitation of naval armaments, the appointment of a National Law Enforcement Commission to study

Wide World Photo

President Herbert Hoover

the effects of national prohibition, and the establishment of a Federal Farm Board. His administration was principally marked by the stock market crash of 1929, and the ensuing economic depression. Among his efforts to combat the depression were the establishment of the Reconstruction Finance Corporation and a moratorium on the repayment of the war debts. The continuance of the depression was chiefly responsible for Hoover's defeat by Franklin D. Roosevelt (q.v.) in his campaign for re-election in 1932.

After his defeat Hoover retired to private life for the duration of the Roosevelt administration. He emerged from retirement in

1946 at the request of President Harry S. Truman to undertake a study of world food supplies to enable the U.S. government to administer effectively relief for thirty-eight war-damaged countries. In 1946–47 he headed a U.S. government commission to study the entire structure of the Federal government and to submit recommendations for its reorganization in the interests of economy and efficiency. After work of more than a year the Hoover Commission submitted a series of reports over the period of November, 1948, to March, 1949, containing a comprehensive plan for government reorganization. Among the recommendations of the report were consolidation of many departments and agencies, establishment of more cabinet posts to relieve the President of unnecessary detail work and supervision of minor agencies, and a plan to increase the attractiveness of government careers to capable men. In 1954 he became chairman of the Robert A. Taft Memorial Foundation.

Hoover's writings include *The Challenge to Liberty* (1934), *Addresses upon the American Road, 1945–48* (1949), and *Memoirs* (Vols. 1–3, 1951–52).

HOOVER, JOHN EDGAR (1895–   ), American criminologist and government official, notable as the director of the Federal Bureau of Investigation. He was born in Washington, D.C., and studied law at George Washington University. In 1917 he was admitted to the bar, and in the same year he joined the staff of the U.S. Department of Justice. Two years later he was appointed a special assistant to the U.S. attorney general, and in 1921 he was named assistant director of the Investigation Section of the Department of Justice. In 1924, when the Section became the Federal Bureau of Investigation, Hoover was made director of the Bureau. He subsequently instituted many of the techniques and procedures which made the Bureau famous for its efficient apprehension of criminals. During the 1930's he supervised the investigations which led to the capture of many of the most dangerous criminals in the nation, including the bank robber John Dillinger. In World War II the counterespionage and antisabotage operations conducted under his direction by the FBI were successful in preventing interference by Nazi and Japanese agents with the war effort of the United States. After the war, he directed the Bureau in an exhaustive series of investigations designed to curb subversive activities both within the Federal government and in private industries and institutions. His writings include *Persons in Hiding* (1938) and articles in magazines, police journals, law reviews, and encyclopedias.

HOP, common name of twining perennial herbs of the genus *Humulus,* belonging to the Hemp family. Hop plants have rough stems and heart-shaped, three to seven-lobed leaves. Male and female flowers are produced on separate plants. Male flowers are borne in loose panicles, each flower comprising five sepals and five stamens. Female flowers, comprising scalelike sepals and solitary pistils, are borne in catkins. The hop fruit is an achene. The female fruiting catkin, which is the hop of commerce, is covered with a fine yellow powder called *lupulin* or *hop flour*. Lupulin, which gives the hop its bitter flavor and aroma, is used as a sedative in medicine. The common hop, *H. lupulus,* is native to Eurasia and is naturalized in N. and W. United States, S. Australia, and S. Brazil. The American hop, *H. americanus,* is native to temperate North America. Several unrelated plants are commonly called hop, including bryony (q.v.) and black medick (see MEDICK). The "hop plant" is sweet marjoram (see MARJORAM).

Cultivation. Catkins of common and American hop are extensively cultivated as a source of "hops" used in brewing. Cultivation of common hop is carried on throughout suitably warm areas of Europe, North America, Australia, and New Zealand. In normal times, Germany, England, and the United States are leading hop-producers. Cultivation of American hop is common only in the Pacific States. Average annual production of all hop in the United States is about 50,000,000 pounds.

Hop must be grown in areas having an abundant rainfall during the growth period and abundant sunlight during the fruiting period. Hop is usually grown from cuttings, which are planted in rows about two yards apart in late winter or early spring. Only female plants produce catkins usable in commerce, but a few male plants are included in each hop field because fertilized catkins grow larger and more rapidly than unfertilized catkins. Hop plants are trained to strings suspended above the rows. Catkins become crisp and aromatic in late summer or early fall and are then ready for harvesting. On most modern hop plantations, catkins are picked by portable hop-picking machines which cut off the entire aboveground portion of the plant. As the vine moves into the machine, the catkins and leaves are stripped from the stems by revolving drums covered with wire strippers. The leaves are separated from the catkins by mesh belts which carry the catkins to outlets which open into sacks. The catkins are then carried to kilns or air-drying chambers powered by large fans, where they are dried by hot-air currents. Aromatic oils of hop are lost at high temperatures, and so kilns and air-drying chambers are kept at less than 110° F. When drying is completed, the hop catkins are ready for market; see BEER; BREWING.

HOPE, ANTHONY. See HAWKINS, SIR ANTHONY HOPE.

HOPE, BOB, professional name of LESLIE TOWNES HOPE (1903–), American comedian, born in Eltham, England, and educated in the public schools of Cleveland, Ohio. He began his career in vaudeville; in 1927 he made his Broadway debut in *The Sidewalks of New York* (1927), a revue. Subsequently he was featured in such productions as *Ballyhoo* (1932), *Roberta* (1934), *The Ziegfeld Follies* (1935), and *Red, Hot, and Blue* (1936). Hope appeared in numerous motion pictures after 1937, including *The Big Broadcast of 1938, Road to Singapore* (1940), *My Favorite Blonde* (1942), *Paleface* (1947), *Road to Bali* (1952), and *Casanova's Big Night* (1954). Meanwhile, he became the star of his own radio show (1938), and after 1950 he appeared regularly on television. Hope received numerous awards for entertaining the armed forces and for many charity benefit performances. He is the author of *They've Got Me Covered* (1941), *I Never Left Home* (1944), *So This Is Peace* (1946), and *Bob Hope's Own Story: Have Tux, Will Travel* (1954).

HOPE COLLEGE, coeducational institution of higher learning situated in Holland, Mich. Maintained by the Reformed Church in America, it was opened as a school in 1851 and received its charter as a college in 1866. It offers courses leading to the baccalaureate degree in the liberal arts. In 1953–54 the total enrollment was 815, including 736 full-time students, and the faculty numbered 62. In the same period the endowment was $1,079,-303 and the library contained 47,000 volumes.

HOPEH (formerly CHIHLI), a province of China, bordering the Gulf of Pohai on the E. and Shansi Province on the w. The terrain consists largely of a level plain, the only hilly areas being confined to the extreme w. and N. Fertile and well watered, the Hopeh lowlands are intensively cultivated. Wheat, corn, and millet comprise the principal field crops, and many varieties of fruits and vege-

tables are grown. The province contains rich deposits of coal and iron ore. Paoting (formerly Tsingyuan, q.v.) is the capital. Hopeh was occupied by the military forces of Japan in 1937, shortly after the outbreak of the Sino-Japanese War, and remained under Japanese control until the end of World War II. The armies of the Chinese Republic were expelled from the province by Communist forces early in 1949, during the civil war between the Chinese Nationalists and Communists. Area, 54,812 sq.m.; pop. (1952 est.) 29,790,000.

HOPI, or MOQUI, a tribe of pueblo Indians (q.v.) of the Shoshonean stock, dwelling in six villages in north-central Arizona. A seventh village is occupied by members of the unrelated Tewa tribe who were driven from their homes by the Spaniards in the 17th century; the seven villages taken together, lying on three high mesas, have been objects of intensive study by explorers and ethnologists as examples of typical advanced pueblo culture.

The Hopi tribe is the only branch of the Shoshonean stock which has adjusted successfully to pueblo life. In traditions, social organization, and customs they are almost identical with the other pueblo Indians, and in modern times they have maintained their aboriginal pueblo culture, which is now far better preserved than that along the Rio Grande. The Hopis are industrious farmers, and harvest and store large crops of corn, beans, pumpkins, and in recent times some fruits, such as peaches. They also weave baskets and blankets, and are skillful potters and carvers. Hopi houses are built of stone roughly cut and laid, and are finished in plaster by the women. Their ceilings are supported by beams and cross poles, and consist of a compressed mixture of brush and clay. The floors are sometimes flagged and the interior walls are generally whitewashed with gypsum and sometimes ornamented in simple geometric bands. In primitive Hopi houses the doorways, which were the only sources of light, were sometimes built in T-shapes; windows covered with selenite were introduced under Spanish influence, and the modern houses generally have glass windows and hinged doors.

Each of the Hopi pueblos has three chiefs, restricted to communal, ceremonial, and military leadership respectively, and holding their positions for life. The tribe is grouped in exogamous clans technically known as "incest groups"; within each clan exists a kinship relationship so strong that intermarriage be-

Amer. Mus. Nat. Hist.

Museum group showing the village life of the Hopi Indian.

tween members of a clan is forbidden. The clans themselves are usually coupled in pairs, and these links are sometimes strong enough to justify larger exogamous groupings. Marriage is monogamous, and the lines of descent by which clans are defined are reckoned through the mother.

Like that of all other pueblo Indians, the religion of the Hopis is pagan, and consists in worship of the forces of nature and in techniques for propitiating and influencing the upernatural powers which represent them. Ancestor worship plays an important role in their ceremonies, and in their historic period Christian influences have been felt, particularly in the dating of ceremonies and the observance of saints' days. Private rites are held in ceremonial chambers called *kivas* (which differ from the *kivas* of other pueblo tribes in being rectangular rather than circular in shape and entirely rather than partially subterranean), whereas public services and dances are commonly performed in the open air. The most important of these ceremonies are the *katcina* or *kachina* mysteries (the *katcina* is the spirit of an ancestor, usually the eponym of a clan, represented in ceremonies by a masked and painted dancer, or by a small, carved, wooden doll which is painted and decorated with feathers), midsummer and midwinter rituals of sun and fire worship, and the celebrated snake dances. In these dances, which are attended by thousands of visitors every summer, live rattlesnakes

are used as representatives of the Sky God, and the dances themselves are designed to bring down rain for the Hopi crops. They are among the most spectacular of all American Indian ceremonies; the snakes, which are not deprived of their fangs or poison glands, are handled fearlessly, usually with no serious consequences, and at certain points are carried in the dancers' mouths. See also ZUÑI.

HOPKINS, ESEK (1718–1802), American naval officer, born in Scituate, R.I. He was a brigadier general in the Revolutionary War until December, 1775, when he was commissioned the first commander in chief of the Continental navy. He commanded the first squadron sent out by the colonies, and succeeded in capturing the forts at New Providence in the Bahamas and destroying important British military stores, ordnance, and ammunition. In June, 1776, however, he was censured by the Continental Congress for inactivity and failure to harass enemy ships. Continued difficulties in manning and equipping the few ships in the American navy prevented him from getting ships ready for sea, and in December, 1776, the American fleet was blockaded in Narragansett Bay. He was suspended from command in March, 1777, after criticizing the Congress and failing to answer a citation to appear before it, and was dismissed from service in January, 1778. He was afterward prominent in Rhode Island political affairs.

HOPKINS, Sir Frederick Gowland (1861–1947), English biochemist, born in Eastbourne, and educated at the University of London. From 1905 to 1910 he was a tutor at Emmanuel College, Cambridge University, and after 1910 he occupied the post of prelector in physiological chemistry created specially for him at Trinity College, Cambridge. His research covered many phases of biochemistry. A method for the quantitative determination of uric acid, which he developed, was applied to a variety of physiological and pathological problems. His research on the production of lactic acid in muscular contractions was extremely important in the study of the chemistry of muscular action. He succeeded in isolating the amino acid tryptophane from proteins, and in 1921 he isolated the peptide glutathione from living tissue and showed its importance in the oxidation process in living cells. Hopkins was the first to demonstrate the existence of essential amino acids, and also of certain "accessory food factors" necessary in a balanced diet which were later known as vitamins. He was awarded academic honors in many countries. He was made a fellow of the Royal Society in 1905, and president of that society in 1931. In 1925 he was knighted and in 1929 he shared with Christian Eijkman the Nobel Prize for physiology and medicine.

HOPKINS, Gerard Manley (1844–89), English Jesuit and poet, educated at Oxford University. He became a member of the Roman Catholic Church in 1866 and was ordained a priest in 1877. Hopkins was appointed professor of Greek at Dublin University in 1884. He was the author of a number of short poems which are highly individual in style and which extended the technique of English poetry by a number of innovations in rhythm. None of his poems was published during his lifetime, but after his death the English poet laureate Robert Bridges had several of them published in an anthology of English 19th-century poetry. A nearly complete edition of the poems of Hopkins was published in 1918, and a complete edition in 1930. Among his most characteristic poems are *Pied Beauty, Felix Randal, Dun Scotus' Oxford, The Windhover, The Wreck of the Deutschland,* and *Vision of the Mermaids.*

HOPKINS, Harry Lloyd (1890–1946), American government official, born in Sioux City, Iowa, and educated at Grinnell College. Until 1931 he was engaged in social welfare work. Among posts occupied by him in this field were that of director in New York City for the Association for Improving the Condition of the Poor, executive secretary of the New York City Board of Child Welfare, divisional director of the Red Cross in New Orleans, and director of the New York Tuberculosis and Health Association.

During the economic depression of the 1930's, Governor Franklin D. Roosevelt of New York State appointed Hopkins director of the State Temporary Relief Administration in 1931, and chairman in the following year. After Roosevelt was inaugurated President in 1933 he appointed Hopkins head of the Federal Emergency Relief Administration; two years later Hopkins was made head of the Works Progress Administration. From 1938 to 1940 he was secretary of commerce.

During World War II Hopkins served as Lend-Lease Administrator and as a member of the War Production Board and the Pacific War Council. He was also an influential Presidential assistant, and accompanied Roosevelt on the latter's trips to Teheran in Iran and Yalta in the Crimea, in 1944 and 1945 respectively, to consult with Premier Josef Stalin of the Soviet Union and Prime Minister Winston Churchill of Great Britain. Roosevelt also sent Hopkins as a personal envoy on a number of important diplomatic missions. On one such mission he laid the groundwork for the conference of the heads of state of the victorious powers, held subsequent to Roosevelt's death and after Germany's defeat, at Potsdam, Germany.

HOPKINS, Johns (1795–1873), American financier and philanthropist, born in Anne Arundel Co., Md. He lived on a farm until he was seventeen, when he went to Baltimore and worked in his uncle's grocery store. He started his own grocery business, and in 1822 founded the house of Hopkins & Brothers. After 1847, having amassed a large fortune, he became an influential figure in railroad and banking affairs. He left his fortune for the founding of two institutions which perpetuate his name, Johns Hopkins University and Johns Hopkins Hospital, both in Baltimore.

HOPKINS, Samuel (1721–1803), American clergyman and founder of Hopkinsian theology, born in Waterbury, Connecticut, and educated at Yale College. He studied theology with the elder Jonathan Edwards (q.v.), and qualified for preaching in Congregationalist churches in 1742. He served as pastor in Housatonic (now Great Barrington), Mass., from 1743 to 1769, when opposition to his theological opinions resulted in his removal. He spent the remainder of his life as pastor in

Newport, R.I. He was an active opponent of slavery, despite having been a slaveholder in his early manhood.

Hopkins is best known for his system of theology, expounded in his *System of Doctrines Contained in Divine Revelation, Explained and Defended* (1793). He attempted to reconcile the occurrence of sin with the Calvinist dogma of predestination, which assumes that all activity is predetermined by God. He believed that a single sin, although reprehensible in itself, may serve a Divine purpose in promoting greater ultimate good. Thus, the murder of a tyrant is a sin, as such, but since it is predestined by God, it must be assumed that He intended an ultimate benefit. The actions of God, in Hopkins' theology, are not necessarily understandable by humans, nor is sin which is committed as part of God's plan excusable. Hopkins believed that virtue consisted in carrying out the plan of God, and that humans should therefore be willing to suffer damnation in His service. Hopkins' other writings include several pamphlets and addresses, and *Life and Character of Jonathan Edwards* (1799).

HOPKINS, STEPHEN (1707–85), American Colonial statesman, born in Providence, R.I. His public life began with his election to the Rhode Island Assembly in 1733. From 1751 to 1754 and at various times thereafter he was chief justice of the superior court of Rhode Island. He served nine one-year terms as governor of the colony between 1755 and 1768. During this period, he joined the struggle against British policy in America. His pamphlet *The Rights of the Colonies Examined* (1765), which attacked the Stamp Act, achieved wide circulation, even being reprinted in London. He was a member of all the Continental Congresses from 1774 to 1780, and was a signer of the Declaration of Independence. Hopkins was a founder of the *Providence Gazette,* for which he wrote (beginning in 1765) a *History of the Planting and Growth of Providence.*

HOPKINSIANISM. See HOPKINS, SAMUEL.

HOPKINSON, FRANCIS (1737–91), American composer, author, and politician, born in Philadelphia, and educated at the College of Philadelphia (now the University of Pennsylvania). It is not known who were his music teachers, but he is believed to have studied with James Bremner. He was the composer of *My Days Have Been So Wondrous Free,* the first piece of secular music produced in America, and of the *Temple of Minerva,* considered the first American opera. an "oratori-

Billiard Association of America
William Hoppe at the billiard table

cal entertainment" first performed in 1781.

A lawyer by profession, Hopkinson was active politically. He signed the Declaration of Independence (1776), was a member of the Convention that framed the Constitution of the United States, and designed the first official American flag (see FLAG OF THE UNITED STATES). He held various posts in the newly established American government, and from 1779 to 1789 was a judge of admiralty for Pennsylvania. Hopkinson wrote a number of brilliant political satires attacking the British, such as the *Letter Written by a Foreigner on the Character of the English Nation* (1777), *The Battle of the Kegs* (verse, 1778), and *Date Obolum Bellisario* (1778). His later writings include several satires on post-Revolutionary life in the United States; among these are *Modern Learning Exemplified* (1784) and *A plan for the Improvement of the Art of Paper War* (1786).

HOPPE, WILLIAM F. (1887–   ), American billiardist, born in Cornwall-on-the-Hudson, N.Y. Hoppe was regarded by many of his contemporaries as the greatest billiard player of all time. He won his first world championship, in 18.1 balkline play, in 1906, and held the 18.1 and 18.2 balkline championships intermittently for the following eighteen years. He was undisputed world champion of 14.1 balkline (1914), cushion caroms (1933), and 71.2 balkline (1938). Hoppe held the world championship in three-cushion billiards in 1936, 1940 to 1944, and 1947 to 1952. He retired from tournament play in 1952. In both league and tournament play, he set the world record for high average score with an average of 1.36 points per inning in 1945. See BIL-LIARDS.

HOPPER, DEWOLF, in full WILLIAM DE-WOLF (1858–1935), American actor, born in New York City. In 1879 he made his debut in *Our Boys,* and soon achieved celebrity as a comedian. He was for some years associated with the famous comedy team of Weber and Fields, and he later starred at the head of his own company in such roles as Mr. Pickwick. From 1912, when he appeared as Reginald Bunthorne in *Patience,* Hopper was famous as an interpreter of the comic roles in the operas of Gilbert and Sullivan, and from 1921 to 1925 his company engaged in a Gilbert and Sullivan revival. Hopper's recitation of *Casey at the Bat* was one of the most cele-brated monologues of his time in the Amer-ican theater. He wrote *Once a Clown, Al-ways a Clown* (with W. W. Stout, 1927).

HOPPER, EDWARD (1882–), American painter and etcher, born in Nyack, New York. He studied in New York with William Chase, Kenneth Hayes Miller, and Robert Henri. Hopper is well known for his paintings of quiet suburban scenes such as "Sunday Morning", in the Whitney Museum, New York City. By the use of sunlight Hopper gave a homely warmth to commonplace sub-jects. He won many prizes and is represented by paintings in the Metropolitan Museum, New York City, the Chicago Art Institute, the Phillips Gallery, Washington, D.C., and many other museums. He was included in the exhibit "19 Living Americans" at the Mu-seum of Modern Art in 1929.

HOPPNER, JOHN (1758–1810), English por-trait painter, born in Whitechapel. He was as-sisted in his art studies by King George III and began exhibiting at the Royal Academy in 1780. He was appointed portrait painter to the Prince of Wales in 1789 and elected full academician in 1795. His only rival as the outstanding portrait painter of his day was Sir Thomas Lawrence (q.v.), who also worked for the court. Hoppner was greatly influenced in his style by the paintings of Sir Joshua Reynolds (q.v.). To Reynold's dignified real-ism Hoppner added boldness of execution, gracefulness, and brilliance of tone and color. He was unable to develop his fine gift for landscape art, which is revealed in many chalk sketches, because the prevailing fashion of the day forced him to earn his income ex-clusively in the field of portrait painting. Some of his principal portraits are those of

the Prince of Wales, the Duke and Duchess of York, the Duke of Wellington, and Wil-liam Pitt. His works are in the National Gal-lery, Hampton Court, and St. James's Palace, London, in the Metropolitan Museum of Art, New York City, and in many other English and American museums.

HOP TREE, common name of *Ptelea tri-foliata,* a tall shrub belonging to the Rue family, native to temperate regions of North America. Leaves of the hop tree are composed of three oval leaflets which are covered with down when immature. The small greenish-white flowers, which are borne in terminal cymes, have three to five sepals, three to five petals, three to five stamens, and two pistils which are fused at the base. The fruit is an elongate, winged samara containing two seeds. Both flower and fruit contain small glands which produce a bitter, acrid, essential oil. The bitter fruits were formerly used as a substitute for hop catkins; see HOP.

HORACE, in full QUINTUS HORATIUS FLAC-CUS (65–8 B.C.), Roman lyric poet and satirist, son of a freedman, born in Venusia, Lucania, and educated in Rome and subsequently in Athens, where he studied the Greek philoso-phers and poets. When Julius Cæsar was as-sassinated in 44 B.C. Horace left Athens to join the republican army raised by Marcus Junius Brutus (q.v.) in Macedonia. There he was made a military tribune in command of a sixth part of a Roman legion, and fought at the Battle of Philippi (42 B.C.). Before the final defeat of Brutus' army by Mark An-tony (see ANTONIUS, MARCUS) and Octavius (see AUGUSTUS), Horace returned to Italy. He became employed as a clerk, and began to write poetry.

His friendship with the great poet Vergil, then poet laureate, brought Horace into the com-pany of the statesman Gaius Cilnius Mæcenas (q.v.), who befriended him, became his pa-tron, and introduced him to the Emperor Augustus. The latter frequently commissioned Horace for literary assignments, and Horace soon became an important figure in the lit-erary and social life of Rome. In about 33 B.C. Mæcenas gave him a farm and villa among the Sabine Hills, to which he often re-tired for reflection and writing. Many of his poems reflect his fondness for nature and ex-tol the pleasures of country life.

Horace ranks as one of the great Roman poets. He began as an imitator of Greek models, at a time when all branches of Latin poetry were based on Greek models; he sub-sequently exhibited such a gift for irony, wit, and rhythmical expression, that after Vergil's death (19 B.C.) he was undisputed poet laureate of Rome. His works fell into four categories: satires, epodes, odes, and epistles. In his *Satires* (35 B.C.) he perfected the use of the Greek hexameter (q.v.) in Latin satirical verse; he satirized various types of people, but with tolerance and urbanity, showing no anger or impatience. The *Epodes* (30 B.C.) are lyrical in form, and lampoon various contemporary personages. Horace's chief poetical works are the *Odes* (23 and 15 B.C.). Lyrical in form, they are in Greek meters, some adapted from and many directly in imitation of the poets Anacreon, Simonides, Alcæus, and Sappho. In the *Odes* Horace treats of the themes of mutability, friendship, and country pleasures, and of Roman history. Famous for their rhythm, irony, and cultivated urbanity, the *Odes* were greatly admired and often imitated by the English poets of the 18th and 19th centuries; see ENGLISH LITERATURE. The ode *Carmen Sæculare,* written in 17 B.C. at the request of the Emperor Augustus, was sung or chanted aloud by a chorus at the secular games in Rome.

Horace's last extended work is the *Epistles,* written about 20 B.C., late in his literary career. Like the *Satires* they are in hexameter, and show Horace in the role not so much of poet as of literary and social critic. He is the philosopher of the golden mean, seeking Epicurean (see EPICURUS) pleasures, but always advocating moderation, even in the pursuit of virtue. The subjects of the *Epistles* are similar to those of the *Satires,* and reveal the social moods and events of contemporary Roman life. The best known of this group of works is the *Epistle to the Pisos* (19 B.C.?), better known as *Ars Poetica,* a letter extolling the Greek masters, explaining how difficult and serious is the poetic art, and giving technical advice to would-be poets. The terse and felicitous language used by Horace has given rise to many well-known expressions, for example, *carpe diem* ("enjoy today") and *dulce et decorum est pro patria mori* ("it is sweet and fitting to die for one's country").

HORDALAND, county of s.w. Norway, located on the North Sea. Included within it is the region of Hardanger Fiord (q.v.). The county seat is Bergen (q.v.). Area, 6021 sq.m.; pop. (1950) 198,047.

HOREB. See SINAI.

HOREHOUND, or HOARHOUND, common name of *Marrubium vulgare,* a plant belonging to the Mint family, and of confections and extracts made from its dried leaves and flowers. Horehound is native to Eurasia and is naturalized in waste places of N.E. United States. It is an herbaceous perennial growing about one foot tall, bearing grayish-white, pubescent (hoary) leaves. The small white flowers, borne in whorled clusters, have a ten-veined, tubular calyx, an asymmetrical corolla, four stamens, and a pistil. The fruit is a nutlet. The leaf surfaces are dotted with small glands which contain an aromatic essential oil. The leaves also contain lignin, tannin, resins, and a bitter constituent called *marrubiin.* Horehound is used in medicine as a syrup tonic and as an anthelmintic.

Several other mints are commonly called horehound. The black or fetid horehound, *Ballota nigra,* is similar in appearance to *M. vulgare,* but has purple flowers and a foul odor. It is a native of Europe which is naturalized in N.E. United States. The bugleweeds, belonging to the genus *Lycopus,* are sometimes called water horehounds; see BUGLE.

HORIZON, in popular usage, the circular line formed by the apparent meeting, at a great distance from the viewer, of the sky and the surface of the earth. This circle is best visible at sea, where the line dividing the visible surface of the ocean from the sky is called the *sea horizon.*

Astronomers and navigators call the horizon described above the *apparent, local,* or *visible horizon.* For their purposes, and particularly for the precise location of heavenly bodies, this popular definition is inexact, and an arbitrary circle called the *celestial, rational,* or *true horizon* is substituted, the position of which may be determined by the use of a plumb line. The celestial horizon is the circle of the celestial sphere exactly halfway between the zenith and the nadir (which are respectively the points of the sphere cut by the plumb line extended indefinitely upward and downward). In reference to the celestial horizon, see ALTITUDE.

HORMONES, substances secreted directly into the blood by various organs of the animal body, which control in great measure the development and activities of the body. They are also called endocrines, or "internal secretions", to distinguish them from the glandular products which are delivered to a free surface or a duct as, for example, the products of the sweat glands or the kidneys. The term hormones was originally applied only to those internal secretions which have a stimulating effect; it has been extended, however, to include *chalones,* which have inhibitory effects. Hormones are necessary for normal development, metabolism, and reproduction, and even for the maintenance of health and of life itself. They influence bodily function, and interact to maintain among themselves a state of dynamic equilibrium. Hormones are catalytic in action (see CATALYST; ENZYME), producing their effects in minute concentrations. Their distribution through the blood stream results in a response which, though slower than that of a nervous reaction, is often maintained over a longer period of time.

The principal organs involved in the production of hormones are the pituitary body, or hypophysis; the thyroid gland; the parathyroids; the adrenal, or suprarenal, bodies; the pancreas; the gonads, or male and female reproductive glands; the placenta; and, under certain conditions, the mucous membrane of the small intestines.

The pituitary gland is made up of three parts: an anterior and a posterior lobe, and the *pars intermedia*. The anterior lobe is considered the master gland of the endocrine system. It controls the growth of the skeleton, regulates the rate of secretion of the thyroid, and affects the action of the gonads, the adrenals, the parathyroids, and the pancreas. It also secretes prolactin except when inhibited by the progesterone secreted by the placenta (see below); prolactin stimulates the formation of milk in well-developed lacteal glands. The *pars intermedia* of the pituitary secretes a hormone having a chromatophore-dispersing action. The posterior lobe produces hormones which increase blood pressure (*pressor* factor), prevent excessive secretion of urine (*antidiuretic* factor), and stimulate contraction in uterine muscle (*oxytocic* factor). Several of the pituitary hormones are opposed in effect to other hormones, as, for example, the diabetogenic factor which inhibits the effect of insulin. See PITUITARY BODY.

The hormone of the thyroid gland (q.v.; see also THYROXINE) stimulates general metabolism; it also increases the sensitivity of various organs, especially the central nervous system, and has a pronounced effect on the rate of metamorphosis (i.e., the change from infantile to adult form). The secretion of the thyroid hormone is controlled primarily by the anterior lobe of the pituitary, but is also affected by the hormones of the ovaries and, in turn, affects the development and function of the ovaries.

The hormone of the parathyroid glands (q.v.) controls the concentration of calcium and phosphate in the blood.

Insulin (q.v.) is the hormone of the pancreas. It acts with other enzymes to promote combustion of sugar in the tissues, and affects the metabolism of proteins and fats. See SUGAR, METABOLISM OF.

The adrenal glands are anatomically divided into two parts, an outer cortex and an inner medulla. Extracts of the cortex contain hormones, which control the concentrations of salts and water in the body fluids and are essential for the maintenance of life in an individual; see CORTISONE. The cortical hormones are also necessary for the formation of sugar from proteins and its storage in the liver, and for maintenance of resistance to physical, emotional, and toxic stresses. The cortex also elaborates hormones which affect secondary sexual characteristics. The medulla, which is functionally and embryologically independent of the cortex, produces adrenalin (q.v.), which has an action similar to that of stimulation of the sympathetic nervous system (see AUTONOMIC NERVOUS SYSTEM).

The gonads, under the influence of the anterior lobe of the pituitary, produce hormones controlling sexual development and the various processes of reproduction. The hormones of the testes control the development of the secondary sexual characteristics of the male; see TESTOSTERONE; ANDROSTERONE. The hormones of the ovaries are produced primarily in the ovarian follicles. Estrogenic hormones, produced by the *granulosa* cells, include *estradiol,* the most important, and *estrone, estriol, equilène,* and *equilenin,* which are related chemically to estradiol and are similar in action but much less potent. Estrogenic hormones interact with those of the anterior lobe of the pituitary to control the cycle of ovulation. During this cycle the corpus luteum is produced, which in turn secretes *progesterone* (q.v.), and thus controls the cycle of menstruation (q.v.). Progesterone is also formed in large amounts by the placenta during gestation; it causes development of the mammary glands and, at the same time, inhibits the secretion of prolactin by the pituitary. The placenta also secretes a hormone similar to one produced by the pituitary and called A.P.L. (anterior-pituitary-like), which inhibits ovulation. This hormone is present in the blood in substantial quantities, and is excreted readily by the kidneys; it is the basis of such tests for pregnancy as the Aschheim-Zondek test (q.v.).

A special group of hormones is secreted by the mucous membrane of the small intestines at a certain stage of digestion. They act to coordinate digestive activities, controlling the motility of the pylorus, duodenum, gall bladder, and bile duct. They also stimulate formation of the digestive juices of the small intestines and of the external secretion of the pancreas.

Deficiency or excess of any one of the hormones upsets the chemical equilibrium which is essential to health, normal growth, and, in extreme cases, to life. The method of treating diseases arising from endocrine disturbances is called *organotherapy;* it involves the use of preparations of animal organs and synthetic products, and has achieved marked, and at times spectacular, success. See separate articles on such diseases as ADDISON'S DISEASE; CRETINISM; DIABETES; GIGANTISM; GOITER; MYXEDEMA.

Hormones have also been discovered to play an important part in the physiology of plants. Plant hormones often possess a chemical structure related to that of animal hormones of similar function; for example, the estrogenic hormones of animals strongly stimulate the flower and seed production of certain plants. A plant hormone, isolated (1953) in the blossoming stage of development, has been found to prevent plant distortion by inhibiting tumorlike growths. The possible effect of this hormone on the control of animal tumors is being investigated in cancer research. See PHYSIOLOGY.

HORN, usually called FRENCH HORN, a brass wind instrument with a funnel-shaped mouthpiece and spirally coiled tubing about 12 feet in length with a widely flaring bell. Its tonal quality is soft and resonant, the mellowest of that of all brass instruments.

The name stems from the *natural horn,* an instrument having a single note and twelve harmonics (q.v.); called the *cor de chasse,* it was used in 16th-century France by royal hunting parties. The developments making possible the modern orchestra horn were the work of two Germans: Anton Hampel, who in Dresden in 1770 discovered that additional tones could be played by stopping the bell of the horn with the hand (thus the name *hand horn*); and Wilhelm Blümel, who in Saxony in 1813 worked with the first model of the modern *valve horn,* eliminating the cumbersome crooks and added tubing which had been necessary previously to allow playing in all keys. The tone of the modern valve horn, much softer than that of the early orchestra horn, is the result not only of the reversal of the bell by Hampel to permit hand

N.Y. Philharmonic-Symphony Society
Playing the French horn

stopping, but also of the valve action, which creates a less brilliant, more muffled tone. Thus horn parts written by Johann Sebastian Bach or George Frederick Handel now sound quite different from what was intended in the original scoring. Stopping or muting of the horn has been used in modern music by such composers as Maurice Ravel and Claude Debussy, but to obtain change of quality rather than pitch.

The first orchestral use of the pre-Hampel instrument was in Dresden (1711), and contemporary French musical literature refers to the horn as the *cor allemand* (German horn). Jacques Halévy's opera *La Juive* (1835) was the first score for the modern French valve horn. The customary pair of horns used before the time of Ludwig van Beethoven has been increased to orchestral sections of from six to eight men. Horns are most often employed in the key of F with a range of about three octaves, and because of their resonant quality have since 1945 come into fairly common use in dance orchestras.

HORN, ACOUSTIC. See SPEAKER.

HORNADAY, WILLIAM TEMPLE (1854–1937), American zoologist, born in Plainfield, Ind., and educated at Iowa State Agricultural College. From 1882 to 1890 he was chief taxi-

The homrai, a hornbill of the East Indies

dermist of the U.S. National Museum and from 1889 to 1890 he served also as superintendent of the National Zoological Park in Washington, D.C. In 1896 he was appointed director of the New York Zoological Park in the Bronx, N.Y., a position he held until 1926, when he retired. Hornaday was influential in establishing game preserves and promoting legislation for the conservation of wildlife. His writings include *The Extermination of the American Bison* (1887), *Taxidermy and Zoological Collecting* (1891), *Our Vanishing Wild Life* (1913), *The American Natural History* (1914), and *Wild Life Conservation in Theory and Practice* (1914).

HORNBEAM, common name of trees and shrubs of the genera *Carpinus* and *Ostrya*, belonging to the family Betulaceae. Plants of both genera are sometimes called ironwoods. The American hornbeam *C. caroliniana*, also called blue beech or water beech, is a tree or tall shrub having very hard wood, smooth, gray bark, and leaves resembling those of the beech. It bears male and female flowers on separate catkins. The fruits are one-seeded nuts. American hornbeam is native to forests of N.E. United States. The common hornbeam, *C. betulus*, is a similar plant native to temperate regions of Eurasia. The American hop hornbeam, or leverwood, *O. virginiana*, bears hoplike male catkins on branches produced the preceding year. The solitary female flowers are borne at the ends of new shoots. Hop hornbeam has birchlike leaves and brown bark, but is similar in other respects to *Carpinus*. The hornbeams are little used for timber, but shrubby hornbeams are often cultivated as hedge plants.

HORNBILL, common name of any large coraciiform bird in the family Bucerotidae, characterized by a long, shell-like, horny bill surmounted by a hollow horny projection or

"casque". Hornbills are found in Africa, s. Asia, and the East Indies. The Hornbill family is divided into two subfamilies: Bucorvinae, containing the terrestrial ground hornbills (q.v.); and Bucerotinae, containing arboreal species. Hornbills are 2 to 5 ft. long, and are usually black and white in color. They feed on fruit and small animals. The hornbills are noted for their peculiar nesting habits; the female nests in a hollow tree, the opening of which the male plasters over with clay mixed with salivary secretions, leaving only a small opening. While the single, large white egg is being hatched, the male hornbill feeds the female through the opening. The food is first ground in his gizzard, and then regurgitated and given to the female.

The rhinoceros hornbill, *Buceros rhinoceros*, of the East Indies, is well known for its casque, which is turned upward at the anterior end, and looks somewhat like the horn of a rhinoceros. The bird is about 5 ft. long. Other common species are the homrai, *Dichoceros bicornis*, of the East Indies, and the helmet hornbill, *B. vigil*, which is the only species with a solid casque.

HORNBLENDE. See AUGITE.

HORNBLOWER, or HORNWORM, the larva of a hawk-moth (q.v.).

HORN, CAPE. See CAPE HORN.

HORNED FROG, common name for any large South American frog in the genus *Ceratophrys*, characterized by a stiff, hornlike, upright extension of the eyelid. About a dozen species are known, all strikingly colored. The best-known species is *C. cornuta*, found in Brazil, which has larger horns than any other species. It averages 7 in. in length, and is tinted with mottled shades of brown and green.

HORNED PHEASANT. See TRAGOPAN.

HORNED SNAKE. See MUD SNAKE.

HORNED TOAD, more properly but less commonly called **HORNED LIZARD,** common name for any of the short-legged, short-tailed,

Horned toad (Phrynosoma solare)

Above: Hornet (Vespa crabro). Right: A hornets' nest hanging from beams of a roof.

North American lizards in the genus *Phrynosoma* of the Iguana family, characterized by large spines on the crown and temples, and stiff, erectile, smaller spines along the back. The body is wide and flattened. The horned lizards inhabit the dry, hot desert regions of w. United States and Mexico. They are very active in the daytime and burrow into the sand at night to avoid the desert cold; specimens in captivity become torpid and will not eat when kept at temperatures below 75° F. Horned lizards hibernate in burrows in the sand in wintertime, and mate in spring or early summer. Females of northerly species hatch their eggs within their bodies; females of southerly species lay about two dozen eggs in holes in the sand, where they are hatched by the heat of the sun. Horned lizards feed on insects and are especially fond of ants. When excited they squirt thin streams of blood, sometimes to a distance of 5 ft., from the corners of their eyes, without injury to themselves.

The common horned lizard, *Phrynosoma cornuta,* is widely distributed throughout w. United States. It reaches a maximum length of 6 in. and a width of 2½ in. The general body color varies among different specimens, but most lizards in this species have a longitudinal yellow stripe running over their heads and backs, and four pairs of large tan patches, of which one pair is on the shoulders, and the other three are along the sides. The regal horned toad, *P. regale,* has flat spines regularly placed on its head in the shape of a royal crown. It is one of the largest of the horned lizards, reaching a length of 7 in. Both the common and regal horned lizards are egg layers. The pygmy horned lizard, *P. douglassii,* which is about 2 in. long, is found farther north than any of the other horned lizards; its spines are reduced to small tubercles and it gives birth to living young.

HORNED VIPER. See CERASTES.

HORNET, name generally applied to any social wasp in the family Vespidae, characterized by a powerful sting, and by a large nest constructed of paper which the insects manufacture from partially digested fibers of growing plants. Technically the name hornet is restricted to *Vespa crabro,* a native of Europe, which first appeared in eastern U.S. about 1850. This hornet attains a length of over an inch, and is reddish brown streaked with clay yellow. Its nest, which is made of brown paper, is built in the hollows of trees, in crevices in rocks, or in artificial sheltered places, such as between the beams and roof of a barn. It feeds on insects and their larvae, and on ripe fruit.

Several wasps in the genus *Vespula* are commonly called hornets. The bald-faced or white-faced wasp, *V. maculata,* widely distributed throughout the U.S., is about 1¼ in. long, and is black, with white markings on most of its segments and on its face. Its nest, made of gray paper, is large, often over a foot long, and is usually suspended from a limb of a tree. "Yellow jackets" are so called because their bodies are marked with large areas of yellow. Unlike the bald-faced wasp the yellow jackets construct their nests close to or under the ground. A single yellow jacket nest usually contains about 15,000 individuals (see INSECT: *Social Insects*). In several species, such as *V. austriaca* and *V. adulterina,* no workers are produced and the female lays its eggs in the nests of other wasps, where the young are fed by "foster" workers.

HORNEY, KAREN, *nee* DANIELSEN (1885–1952), German-American psychiatrist, born in Hamburg, and educated at the University of Freiburg. She was an instructor at the Institute for Psychoanalysis in Berlin from 1920 to 1932, when she emigrated to the United States. After serving as associate director of the Chicago Institute for Psychoanalysis for two years, she taught at the New York Psychoanalytic Institute from 1934 to 1941. Starting in 1935 she also lectured at the New School for Social Research in New York City. She was appointed dean of the American Institute for Psychoanalysis in 1941 and a professor at New York Medical College in 1942.

Horney founded a neo-Freudian school of psychoanalysis based on the belief that neuroses are the result of emotional conflicts arising from disturbances in personal relationships. She believed that such disturbances are conditioned by the culture in which a neurotic lives rather than by the instinctual drives postulated by Freud. Among her writings are *The Neurotic Personality of Our Time* (1936), *New Ways in Psychoanalysis* (1939), *Self-Analysis* (1942), *Our Inner Conflicts* (1945), and *Neurosis and Human Growth* (1950). See PSYCHOANALYSIS.

HORN FLY, or TEXAS FLY, common name of a small dipterous fly, *Lyperosia irritans*, in the Housefly family. The horn fly is common in Europe; it first appeared in the U.S. about 1887 in Pennsylvania, and was thought at that time to have come from Texas. Horn flies are now found as far west as Idaho. Adult horn flies are often seen lighting on the heads of cattle at the bases of the horns, where they cluster and suck blood. The horn fly is about ¼ in. long and is slate gray with yellowish markings. The female horn fly lays its eggs in cow dung on which the larvae feed.

HORNPIPE. 1. A folk dance popular in England from the 16th to the 19th century. It was danced in a triple meter (3/2 or 3/4), but during the 18th century the meter was changed to common time (4/4); in this latter rhythm the hornpipe was popular as a solo dance among British sailors. The hornpipe was used in musical works by such composers as George Frederick Handel and Henry Purcell. **2.** A primitive reed instrument, originally called "stock-horn" and "pibgorn", in use during the early 18th century in Scotland and Wales. The instrument was made of wood or bone, with a cylindrical tube having eight finger

holes, and extended into a bell made of animal horn.

HORNSBY, ROGERS (1896–   ), American professional baseball player, born in Winters, Tex. He began playing professional baseball at the age of eighteen, and in 1915 became second baseman for the St. Louis team of the National League. Subsequently he played with the New York, Boston, and Chicago teams of the National League and the St. Louis team of the American League. He was manager of all the above-mentioned teams, except the New York team, and of the Cincinnati Reds. As manager of the St. Louis National League club, he guided it to the world's championship in 1926. Hornsby is considered one of the greatest right-hand batters baseball has ever known. In his nineteen years in the National League he led the league in batting seven times; three times he had a batting average of over .400, a feat achieved by only two other players in the history of baseball. In his National League career he played in 2192 games, for a batting average of .359. He was elected to the Baseball Hall of Fame in 1942. Hornsby wrote *My Kind of Baseball* (1953).

HORNSEY, a municipal and parliamentary borough of Middlesex County, England, forming a residential suburb of London, located 6 miles N. of St. Paul's Cathedral. Pop. (1951) 98,134.

HORN SILVER. See CERARGYRITE.

HORNTAIL, or WOOD WASP, common name for any hymenopterous insect in the family Siricidae, closely related to the sawflies. The horntail differs from the sawfly chiefly in having a strong, drilling ovipositor (egg-laying organ) rather than a sawing ovipositor. The insect derives its name from the shape of the ovipositor, which it uses to excavate cavities in diseased trees. The larvae hatch and pupate within these cavities, and emerge as late as two years later, leaving a hole about ¼ in. in diameter in the timber. Thus emerging, they often damage stored timber in lumberyards and even injure furniture which had been newly constructed of green wood. The adults are much larger than sawflies; a common species, the pigeon horntail, *Tremex columba,* averages 2¼ in. in length, and has a wing span of about 2¼ in. Compare SAWFLY.

HORNWORT FAMILY. 1. Common name applied to a family of flowering plants, the Ceratophyllaceae. It comprises a single genus, Ceratophyllum, of submerged aquatic herbs which are native to ponds and streams of Europe and are naturalized in similar habitats in N.E. United States. The common hornwort,

C. demersum, has stalkless leaves divided into three slender, hornlike forks. Male and female reproductive organs are borne on separate flowers of each plant. Male flowers consist of ten to twenty stamens protected by a whorl of bracts. Female flowers consist of a simple pistil having a single, one-celled ovary, protected by bracts. The fruit is one-seeded achene, containing a partly developed embryo having several small, undeveloped leaves. **2.** Common name of a family of horned liverworts, the Anthocerotaceae, which have a hornlike sporophyte plant arising from the female reproductive organ of the gametophyte plant; see HEPATICAE.

HOROLOGY, the science of measuring time by such devices as the clepsydra, clock, dial, watch (qq.v.), chronometer, and hourglass.

HOROSCOPE, in astrology, in strict usage, that part of the ecliptic which is ascendant (rising in the east) at any given moment. In practice, astrologers have directed their attention only to those moments at which events occur whose outcome is to be predicted (such as the birth of a child); and the term has generally been extended to denote a figure of the heavens, based on the twelve "houses" of the heavens and showing the relative positions of the planets and the signs of the zodiac (q.v.), by means of which astrological predictions may be made. Astrologers cast horoscopes both to predict the future in general and to answer specific horary questions. A nativity (i.e., a horoscope drawn up on the basis of the exact moment of birth) is supposed to be of special importance in predictions concerning a specific individual. See ASTROLOGY.

HOROWITZ, VLADIMIR (1904–   ), Russian-American concert pianist, born in Kiev. He received his musical education at the Kiev Conservatory, where he studied under Felix Blumenfeld. At the age of twenty he began a series of concert tours of Europe, and soon became known as a virtuoso of the highest rank. In 1928 he made his U.S. debut with the N.Y. Philharmonic Orchestra, and later made several tours of the U.S. as well as Europe. He married Wanda, daughter of the conductor Arturo Toscanini, in 1933. Horowitz is considered one of the foremost virtuosos of all time and is particularly known for his interpretation of romantic and modern music.

HORSE, the common name of vertebrates of the family Equidae in the order Perissodactyla, especially the species *Equus caballus,* the domestic horse. No true horses have ever been found in a natural state; so-called "wild horses" living in various parts of the world are probably all the descendants of domesticated horses that have reverted to an untamed state. On the other hand, several wild species of the same genus are known, including the ass, the zebra (qq.v.), the onager, Przhevalski's horse, the quagga (which recently became extinct), and the tarpan. The ancestry of the domestic horse is uncertain, and zoologists do not know whether the present species represents a single evolutionary development or the result of the interbreeding of several species in prehistoric times when horses were first domesticated.

Mature male horses are called stallions and mature female horses mares. Newly born horses are known as foals, young horses are called colts, and young mares are sometimes known as fillies. Most male horses which are not to be used for breeding purposes are castrated or gelded and are then called geldings. Small horses are often called ponies, but properly speaking this term is limited to a few specific diminutive breeds.

Anatomy. The most marked anatomical characteristic of the modern horse is the possession of only a single digit or toe on each of its four feet. This toe, which corresponds to the middle digit of the human hand, is much enlarged and is protected by a horny hoof that surrounds the front and sides of the toe. Vestigial splints corresponding to the second and fourth digits are situated on either side of the foot above the hoof. Fossils of early prehistoric ancestors of the modern horse indicate that the animals had four toes on their forefeet and three toes, with vestigial remains of two more, on their hind feet.

The skull of the horse is long, and the facial bones are twice the length of the cranium. The mandible, or lower jaw, is long and has a broad, flat plate at its lower hind end. The spine is composed of seven cervical, eighteen dorsal, six lumbar, five sacral, and fifteen caudal vertebrae. Horses have forty-four teeth: three incisors, one canine, four premolars, and three molars on each side of each jaw. The incisors, which are used for cropping grass and other herbage, grow in the form of a semicircle. A pronounced gap or diastema exists between the canine teeth and the premolars in which the metal bit used for controlling the horse is placed when the animal is ridden or driven. All the teeth have long crowns and comparatively short roots.

Prehistoric Horses. The evolution of the horse can be traced back by means of fossil remains to *Eohippus,* a horse about the size

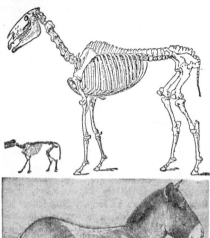

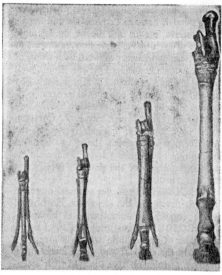

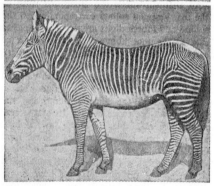

ANIMALS RELATED TO THE HORSE

Top, left: Scale drawing of the skeletons of an Eohippus (left) and a modern horse. Above: Possible steps in the evolution of hind foot of the horse. Left to right, Eohippus; Mesohippus; Miohippus; Pliohippus. Left, middle: The kiang (Equus kiang), a wild ass native to the Tibetan highlands. Left, bottom: Grevy's zebra, an inhabitant of the mountains of northeast Africa.

means of land bridges between Asia and America which existed at various times during the Tertiary period. Horses were prevalent on this continent until Pleistocene times, but the family then died out, possibly as the result of some form of epizootic disease.

Cave dwellings in Europe indicate that horses were plentiful on that continent during the early Stone Age. Dismembered skeletons of horses have been found in and near such dwellings in sufficient number to show that horses were frequently killed and eaten. In Neolithic times, when Europe was largely forested, the number of horses evidently declined. Remains of the Bronze Age include bits and other pieces of harness and clearly demonstrate that horses had become domestic animals in this period.

History. The first horses were introduced into Babylonia in about 2000 B.C. and into Egypt approximately 300 years later. The animals were brought into Egypt by the Hyksos, a tribe of conquerors which originated in

of a small dog, which lived in Eocene times. In Miocene times it was succeeded by *Miohippus* and *Anchitherium*, which in their turn gave place to the Pliocene *Pliohippus,* the direct evolutionary ancestor of the modern horse. Each of these developmental stages showed an increase in general size and a shrinkage in the size of the supplementary toes present in *Eohippus.* See EVOLUTION.

The original home of the prehistoric horses was apparently in Asia, but members of the tribe crossed into the American continent by northeastern Syria. These Egyptian and Babylonian horses were the forerunners of the swift horses of the Near East and northern Africa, broadly termed the Arab breed. Experts believe that another strain of horses was also domesticated in Europe. These were heavily built and slower but more powerful than the Arab breed, and are regarded as the early ancestors of the various modern breeds of draft horses employed for plowing and other heavy work. Some authorities also believe that a third ancestral strain found in the British Isles was the prototype of the various breeds of modern ponies.

During the early part of the Christian era and down to about the 17th century in most parts of Europe, the native horses were used for military mounts, for hauling heavy loads, and as pack animals. The heavy structure and strength of these horses adapted them to such work. During the same period the Arabic world had developed their smaller, fast-galloping breeds, which were introduced into Spain after the Mohammedan conquest of that country in the 8th century. The horses bred in Spain became famed for their speed and endurance, and individual animals were imported into England and other parts of Europe as early as the 12th century. The first systematic attempts to produce an improved breed of horses, however, did not take place until the end of the 17th century, when Arab stallions were imported to England and France for the specific purpose of breeding them with mares of the local stock.

The first horses to be introduced into America were of the Arab type and were brought by the Spanish conquistadors in the 16th century. Both Hernando Cortes, the Spanish conqueror of Mexico, and Hernando de Soto, who discovered the Mississippi River, are believed to have abandoned some of their horses during their expeditions, and these may have been the source of herds of wild horses found in various parts of western North America. Horses left by the Spaniards also ran wild on the pampas of South America around the Plata River. The English settlers, especially the early Virginia colonists, also imported a large number of horses, but at first used them chiefly as food. In 1646 less than 300 horses existed in all the English colonies of North America. Later, however, more horses were shipped to the colonies and horses were bred locally.

Types of Horses. In the last 300 years horse breeders have made continuous attempts to improve the various breeds of horses and to develop strains that are particularly suited for various kinds of work and sport. The result has been an increasing number of types of horses, many of them highly specialized. They include saddle and harness horses especially adapted for racing at the gallop and at a pace trot; hunters bred for endurance as well as speed; carriage horses; draft horses for pulling heavy loads; polo ponies and cow ponies, small fast horses which can be trained to the complicated maneuvers of roping and the game of polo; and a number of types of saddle horses which are capable of being trained to special gaits.

Gaits. Horses are capable of a variety of gaits. In order of speed the normal gaits are: walk, single-foot, canter, pace, trot, and gallop. The *walk* is a gait in which the feet are lifted and advanced in the following order: left fore, right hind, right fore, left hind. In an ordinary walk two of the horse's feet are on the ground at all times, and three feet for part of the time. When a horse is walking very slowly all four of his feet may be on the ground at the same time. A horse going at the *single-foot* lifts and places his feet right hind, right fore, left hind, left fore, and at no time has more than two feet on the ground at once. The *canter, pace, trot,* and *gallop* can best be understood by reference to the table below. The table represents the successive stages of these gaits and shows which feet are on the ground during these stages. In the table Lf equals left fore, Rf equals right fore, Lh equals left hind, Rh equals right hind, and O equals no feet on the ground.

Canter. Rh, Rh Rf, Rh Rf Lh, Rf Lh, Rf Lh Lf, Lh Lf, Lf, O, Rh.

Pace. Rh, Rh Rf, O, Lh, Lh Lf, O, Rh.

Trot. Rf, Rf Lh, Lh, O, Lf, Lf Rh, Rh, O, Rf.

Gallop. Lh, Rh Lh, Rh, Rh Lf, Lf, Lf Rf, Rf, O, Lh.

Both the single-foot and the pace are sometimes referred to as a *rack* or *amble,* and the gallop, which for most horses is the fastest gait, is also sometimes called a *run.*

Breeds. The breed called the Arab is often divided into three sub-breeds according to the regions from which the horses come. *Turks* come from European Turkey and Asia Minor, *Arabs* from the regions between Damascus and the Euphrates River, and *Barbs* from the Barbary states of North Africa. Arabs in general are comparatively small horses, standing between 58 and 60 in. at the shoulder (14½ to 15 hands in the terms commonly used by horsemen). They have re-

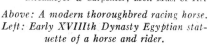

Strohmeyer & Carpenter; Met. Mus. of Art

Above: A modern thoroughbred racing horse.
Left: Early XVIIIth Dynasty Egyptian stat-
uette of a horse and rider.

markable powers of endurance and are swift
gallopers, but not so fast as the Thoroughbred or the American Standardbred, which
have been bred for racing.

The English hunter and the American saddle horse are sometimes referred to as breeds
but are properly types of horses. Thorough-

breds are sometimes used as hunters and saddle horses, as are crosses between Thoroughbreds and harness horses. The important
qualities of a hunter are endurance, fair speed,
and the ability to walk, canter, trot, and gallop. Saddle horses are usually higher in the
shoulder than draft horses and are commonly
trained to use five gaits.

The breeds of draft horses are more distinct
than those of saddle horses. They include the
Belgian, the Shire, the Clydesdale, and the
Percheron. The Belgian is one of the largest
of horses, reaching a shoulder height of 68
or more inches and weights of as much as
2500 lbs. The English Shire is about the same
size and is distinguished by having legs covered with long hair. Both of these breeds
represent refinements of the original native
horses of their countries of origin. Clydesdales
are smaller than either of the above breeds.

This breed was founded in Scotland by crossing native horses with Belgian and Shire horses. The Percheron is also a smaller horse, standing about 66 in. at the shoulder. It is a native of the former district of La Perche in northwestern France and was produced by crossing Arabian horses with the old Flemish breed of which the Belgian is the modern representative.

Several breeds of small horses commonly called ponies are native to Great Britain; among them are the Shetland, the Dales, the Welsh, the Dartmoor, and the New Forest. The smallest of the ponies is the Shetland, which is only about 42 in. in height at the shoulder.

Horses as Food. The flesh of horses closely resembles beef and is often regarded as being more delicate than beef in flavor. Horsemeat is eaten by human beings in most countries of the world where horses exist, but in some areas, such as the U.S. and England, a prejudice exists against this meat, and some religious groups such as the Jews forbid its use. In many parts of Asia a nourishing drink called kumiss is prepared by fermenting and sometimes distilling mare's milk.

See also HORSEMANSHIP; HORSE RACING.

HORSE BOT, common name for the larva or bot of any of three species of flies, known as horse botflies, in the family Gastrophilidae. Horse bots are internal parasites of horses and mules, and often cause the death of these animals by covering the absorptive surfaces of the alimentary tract.

The common horse botfly, *Gastrophilus equi* (sometimes known as *G. intestinalis*), is found throughout the U.S., and is especially abundant in late July and early August. It is about ¾ in. long, and is black and yellow in color, with brown wings. The female lays its eggs on hairs on the legs, or sometimes the flanks or shoulders, of horses. The eggs hatch in about seven days if rubbed and licked by a horse; they require both friction and moisture for hatching. The horse carries the newly hatched larvae into its mouth, where they burrow in the tongue for three to four weeks, at the end of which time they drop to the stomach and attach themselves to the stomach wall by means of small hooklets until mature. When ready to pupate, the pink and yellow larvae release their hold and pass out in the animal's feces.

The nose fly, *G. haemorrhoidalis,* is the most annoying of horse botflies; it is abundant in the north-central U.S. It is about ¼ in. long, and has a black, yellow, and orange body. The female lays its eggs, which require only moisture to hatch, on the upper lips of equine animals. The larvae appear in about two days and burrow through the lips of horse until they reach the internal membrane, in which they remain for more than six weeks. They then drop to the stomach and upper intestine in which they live until several days before they are ready to pupate; at pupating time they drop to the rectum of the horse and reattach themselves to the anus, causing the horse much pain.

The third species of horse botfly is the chin fly.

In order to prevent infestation of horses with horse bots the animals should be sponged with hot water to remove unhatched eggs, and should be fed capsules containing carbon disulfide, which poisons horse bots, causing them to pass out of the alimentary tract before being ready to pupate. Compare SHEEP BOT; OX BOT.

HORSE CHESTNUT, common name of trees of the genus *Aesculus,* belonging to the Soapberry family. The genus is native to temperate regions of Eurasia and North America. Horse chestnuts have large, opposite, compound leaves, each composed of five to seven palmate leaflets. The flower has a five-lobed, tubular calyx, four or five spreading, unequal petals, six to eight stamens, and a three-celled pistil. The fruit, which is a leathery capsule covered with soft spines, contains one to three large seeds which resemble chestnuts.

The common horse chestnut, *A. hippocastanum,* is a native of s.e. Asia which was introduced to w. Europe at the end of the 16th century, and to North America during the colonial period. It is a valuable ornamental tree, extensively planted in parks, parkways, and lawns because of its rich foliage and erect racemes of reddish-white flowers. The tree grows as high as 100 feet and extends its branches widely. The wood is too soft to be of great value as lumber. The bark is bitter and astringent, containing the glycoside *aesculin,* $C_{15}H_{16}O_9 \cdot 2H_2O$, which has been used in tanning and dyeing. The seeds are unpleasantly bitter, and contain large quantities of saponin (q.v.) and starch. Other members of the genus native to North America are usually called buckeye (q.v.).

HORSEFLY, GADFLY, or BREEZE FLY, common name for any of over 2000 species of brachycerous flies constituting the family Tabanidae, which is world-wide in distribution. Many of the horseflies are large insects with broad heads, flattened bodies, and large, brilliantly colored, compound eyes. The females have a long proboscis adapted for biting. They live on the blood of animals. Male horseflies, which do not bite, subsist on the nectar of flowers. Female horseflies place their eggs on plants in wet regions in summertime. The larvae, which are characterized by protruding knobs circling each segment, drop to the moist ground or into water after hatching and feed on insects. They hibernate during winter and pupate in spring after attaining a length of about 2 in. Adults emerge in June.

Many of the larger horseflies in North America belong to the genus *Tabanus,* and are often called "greenheads" because of their large, bright-green eyes. *T. lineola,* a common species, is about ¾ in. long; *T. atratus* is about 1¾ in. long.

The small horseflies in the genus *Chrysops* are commonly called "deer flies", "strawberry flies", or "ear flies". The most important species is *C. discalis,* which is the principal vector in the transmission of tularemia, or deer-fly fever, from rodent to rodent. The insect is grayish yellow, brown, and black, and is about ⅓ to ½ in. long.

HORSE GENTIAN. See FEVERWORT.

HORSEHAIR WORM. See HAIRWORM.

HORSE LATITUDES, name applied to either of two belts of calms in the neighborhood of 30°N. and 30°S. latitude, near the trade-wind belts. They are characterized by high pressure, low humidity, light variable winds, and calms, and are sometimes called the tropical belts of calms.

HORSE MACKEREL. See TUNNY.

HORSEMANSHIP, the art of riding and driving horses and of training horses to bridle and bit, saddle, and driving harness. The art of horseback riding or equitation is of very remote origin, but the various components of harness which permit the modern horseman to exert delicate and precise control of the animal which he is riding or driving are comparatively recent in origin. The earliest riders used no form of saddle or stirrups but rode bareback or on a cloth or blanket. The horses were guided by means of halters and later by reins and bits. Saddles were introduced in the 4th century A.D. and stirrups about 300 years later. Prior to the use of stirrups, riders vaulted into the saddle or used mounting blocks from which they climbed upon their steeds. Modern methods of riding originated in Italy in the 16th century, and the so-called

haute école methods of training and riding were further developed in the imperial riding school in Vienna and the French military riding school.

Fundamentals of Riding. The expert horseman maintains his position on the horse by means of his balance in the saddle and by gripping the horse's body between the knees and thighs. The stirrups are used only for convenience in mounting and dismounting and as a rest for the feet. The stirrups are so adjusted that the toes are slightly higher than the heels. The reins are held in the left hand and the horse is directed to left or right by a slight pressure of the reins on the side of the neck. At a walk the rider sits almost erect in the saddle, urging the horse forward by a light pressure of the knees; a similar seat is used for the canter. When the horse is trotting, the rider leans slightly forward and "posts", that is, rises slightly by springing the knees in time with the horse's gait. In some schools of riding, and particularly in the western U.S., the rider does not post to the trot but maintains his seat firmly. At a gallop, the rider leans forward slightly more than at the trot or canter and shortens the reins to maintain better control.

Riders invariably mount their horses from the left or *on* side. Grasping the reins with the left hand and placing that hand on the horse's neck, the rider puts his left foot in the stirrup and his right hand on the rear portion of the saddle, and then swings himself into place.

Horse Training. The training or breaking of a young horse to saddle or to harness consists largely in gradually accustoming the animal to the various unfamiliar pieces of harness and saddlery and then to carrying or pulling a weight. First a simple halter is placed on the colt's head, and he is permitted to run free until he is no longer frightened. The reins, first a single one and then a double, are attached to the halter and the horse is controlled as he runs or walks in a circle. Finally the bit is placed in the horse's mouth and the full head harness is installed. When the animal has become accustomed to this harness, he is given his first lesson in obedience to the reins. The final stage of preliminary training is to acquaint the horse with the feel of a saddle and then the weight of a rider. The forcible breaking of older horses, in which a horse is saddled, bridled, and ridden without previous training, is sometimes practiced, but this method is generally regarded as primitive and unsatisfactory.

Wide World Photos

HORSEMANSHIP. *Top: A prize pair of harness ponies at the National Horse Show in Madison Square Garden, N.Y.C. Bottom: An army officer making a skilled jump, in England.*

Advanced training of horses may include training in changing gait at the rider's command and in such advanced maneuvers as turning rapidly and jumping. In training for jumping, the horse is first taught to jump small barriers while running free and is then led to leap successively higher obstacles. The horse is finally ridden over small fences or walls, assisted in his jumping by the rider, who urges the horse to the jump and helps it to keep its balance in the air by shifting the position of his body.

Horsemanship in Racing. The modern jockey who rides in races employs an entirely different seat from that used for ordinary riding. The jockey rides with extremely short stirrups and crouches far forward over the horse's neck. This seat enables the horse to extend its neck to the fullest extent and gives the freest play to both the fore and hind legs. The crouching jockey also offers less wind resistance than a rider sitting upright.

Fancy Horsemanship. The *haute école* school of riding, mentioned above, includes the mastery of a large number of maneuvers such as *caracoles* (half turns or zigzag turns) which demand skill and training on the part of both rider and horse. The general purpose of this training is to make the rider complete master of his mount and to make the horse completely obedient to the wishes of the rider. Other forms of fancy horsemanship include acrobatics such as leaping on and off the back of a moving horse, standing on its back, or riding two or more horses at once while standing on their backs. Such feats have little relationship to practical horsemanship.

The forcible breaking of horses, in which animals are ridden without preliminary training, has been largely abandoned as unsatisfactory, but survives in the "bronco busting" exhibitions in rodeos. In these exhibitions the so-called "wild horses" are usually beasts that have been trained to buck.

HORSENS, a town of Aarhus County, s.e. Jutland, Denmark. The town is located 32 m. by rail s.w. of the town of Aarhus, at the head of Horsens Fiord. Horsens contains a good harbor. Textiles, soap, organs, engines, and electrical apparatus are manufactured in the town, and tobacco and dairy products are processed. Horsens contains several religious edifices dating from the 13th century. Pop. (1950) 35,898.

HORSEPOWER, a unit of power defined as the ability to perform work at the rate of 33,000 foot-pounds per minute, or 550 foot-pounds per second. It is the unit used in stat-

ing the power of an engine or other prime mover. An engine working at the rate of 99,000 foot-pounds per minute delivers 3 H.P. The value of 33,000 foot-pounds per minute was adopted by James Watt (q.v.), who found in practical tests that a strong horse could pull a load of coal at the rate of 22,000 foot-pounds per minute; he arbitrarily raised this figure by a factor of one-half. In the metric system the horsepower is defined as 4500 kilogram-meters per minute, which is equivalent to 32,549 foot-pounds per minute or 0.986 of an ordinary horsepower. In Europe, this metric unit is sometimes called *force de cheval* or *cheval-vapeur*. The electrical equivalent of a horsepower is 746 watts.

Indicated horsepower is the theoretical efficiency of an engine, i.e., the mathematically calculated power developed in the cylinder or cylinders of an engine. *Brake horsepower* represents the effective power available for doing work, i.e., the indicated horsepower less the amount of power absorbed in driving the engine itself; it is measured directly by means of a dynamometer (q.v.). Engine ratings are given in terms of brake horsepower. Most automobile engines in the U.S. are rated between 60 and 150 H.P. Airplane engines have higher power; the B-50, for example, has four engines, each with a rating of about 3000 H.P. A large ocean liner, such as the *Queen Mary,* runs at 150,000 H.P. Small electric motors used in households for running sewing machines, electric mixers, small lathes, and other equipment usually deliver a fraction of a horsepower. So-called horsepower ratings, calculated on the basis of arbitrary formulas depending on cylinder volume or piston area, are sometimes used for purposes of assessing taxes or limiting classes in competition. For example, British automobile engines are rated on such a system, and have an actual brake horsepower about four to six times the rated horsepower.

HORSE RACING. From remote antiquity speed contests between horses both ridden and driven have taken place in all countries in which horses have been domesticated. The earliest mention of horse racing in a European source is in the *Iliad* of Homer, which indicates that the sport was known to the Greeks approximately ten centuries before the Christian era. References to such contests in Oriental countries occur in even earlier works. Undoubtedly the horses competing in early races were chariot horses and military mounts. Since the 18th century A.D., how-

Wide World Photo

Horses jumping a hurdle in the Liverpool Foxhunters' Steeplechase at Aintree, England

ever, racing has been almost entirely confined to strains of horses which have been bred especially for speed. The most important of these breeds is the Thoroughbred, a type of horse first produced in England by crossing small, speedy Arabian horses with larger animals of local origin. The pedigrees of Thoroughbred horses are studied with great care. All Thoroughbreds have as common ancestors one or more of three stallions of Eastern origin imported into England about the beginning of the 18th century. These fathers of the modern race horse were named after their owners and the countries from which they came and are known as the Byerly Turk, the Darley Arabian, and the Godolphin Barb (from Barbary on the north coast of Africa). The Godolphin Barb, originally a gift from the Emperor of Morocco to Louis XIV

of France, was discovered drawing a cart in the streets of Paris by an Englishman who bought the horse for about $15.

The rules of the English Jockey Club require that no horse may be listed in the General Stud Book of the club unless its ancestry can be traced to one or another of these three horses. As a result a number of Thoroughbreds bred in the U.S. (among them the famous Man o' War) are not eligible for such listing, and are not regarded as Thoroughbreds in England.

Types of Racing. Modern horse racing is one of the most highly organized and commercialized of sports. In general four major types of racing are recognized: *flat racing, steeplechasing, hurdle racing,* and *harness racing.* Flat races are contested by saddle horses on a level track or course. Steeplechases are

Trotter and sulky driver in a harness race in the United States

ridden over courses having a number of obstacles such as fences, walls, and ditches over which the horses must leap. Hurdle races are also jumping races, resembling steeplechases but using only fences as obstacles. Harness races are contested by horses drawing light, two-wheeled carts called sulkies; in this type of race the horses are not permitted to gallop, but must maintain one of two gaits, a trot or a pace.

In addition to the major types of horse racing, several other forms of contest are sometimes held. Among such contests are the wild-horse races occasionally featured in rodeos, and quarter-horse races, short sprint races for the specially trained horses used as work horses on cattle ranches.

Flat Racing. Of all the forms of horse racing, flat racing has the greatest popular appeal, particularly in the U.S. In a recent postwar year 34 tracks for flat racing in 16 States were members of the Thoroughbred Racing Associations. These tracks conducted a total of over 3000 days of racing and nearly 24,000 individual races. The number of horses entered in the races was over 17,000. The total attendance at the tracks was nearly 27 million persons.

Flat races were formerly contested at varying distances up to four miles or more, but are now run almost entirely at distances between six furlongs (¾ mile) and twelve furlongs (1½ miles). Race tracks are usually of dirt and are oval in shape; all but the shortest races are run around one or more turns.

Steeplechasing and Hurdle Racing. These forms of racing are more popular in England than in the U.S., but some U.S. tracks run such races occasionally and other classic races are held over cross-country courses. The usual steeplechase course is between two and four miles in length.

Harness Racing. This is a particularly American form of horse racing which increased markedly in popularity during the 1930's and 1940's. In a recent postwar year approximately 20 major and 800 minor tracks held harness-race meetings, with about 15,000 horses competing. The total attendance at the tracks was in the neighborhood of 16,500-000 people.

Formerly the winner of a harness race was determined by racing three or more one-mile heats, but in recent years a single heat of one mile is usual. The tracks used for harness racing are in general similar to those on which flat races are run, and in some instances both flat- and harness-race meetings are run on the same track.

Records. The fastest official times for horses running on the flat include: ¼ mi., 20⅘ sec.,

Big Racket, 1945; ½ mi., 45⅖ sec., Tie Score, 1945; 1 mi., 1 min. 33⅗ sec., Citation, 1950; 1¼ mi., 1 min. 58⅕ sec., Noor, 1950; 1½ mi., 2 min. 23 sec., The Bastard, 1929; and 2 mi., 3 min. 15 sec., Polazel, 1924.

The fastest mile ever trotted by a harness horse was 1 min. 55¼ sec. This record was set by Greyhound in 1938. The one-mile record for pacers is 1 min. 55 sec. and was made by Billy Direct, also in 1938.

No generally established records are kept of the speed of steeplechasers or hurdle racers, because the courses over which such races are run vary in difficulty.

See also GAMBLING.

HORSE-RADISH, common name of a tall perennial herb, *Radicula armoracia,* belonging to the Mustard family. The herb is native to E. Europe and is cultivated all over Europe and the U.S. It has very large, lance-shaped leaves. Each of the small, white flowers comprises four sepals, four petals, six stamens, and a two-celled pistil. The fruit is a globe-shaped pod. The pungent roots of horse-radish are ground for use as a condiment. If used immediately, ground horse-radish root need not be preserved, but bottled horse-radish is usually preserved in vinegar. Horse-radish is used as a base for other condiments and sauces, in combination with ground beets, mustard, catsup, or thick, bland sauces.

HORSE-RADISH TREE, common name of a tropical East Indian tree, *Moringa oleifera,* belonging to the family Moringaceae. It is cultivated in the West Indies and other tropical countries. The horse-radish tree has fragrant white flowers and edible fruits. The edible root has a pungent flavor similar to that of horse-radish and is used for the same purpose. The seeds are a source of *oil of ben,* a fixed oil which is used in perfumery. Australian trees of the genus *Codonocarpus,* belonging to the Pokeweed family, produce pungent foliage and are also called horse-radish trees.

HORSESHOE CRAB or **HORSEFOOT.** See KING CRAB.

HORSESHOE FALLS. See NIAGARA FALLS.

HORSESHOE PITCHING. See QUOITS AND HORSESHOE PITCHING.

HORSETAIL. See EQUISETUM.

HORTENSIUS, QUINTUS (114–50 B.C.), Roman lawyer and orator. Soon after his admittance to the bar at the age of nineteen, he won a reputation by successfully defending Nicomedes III, king of the Roman dependency of Bithynia, against the charge of corrupt administration. Hortensius was one of the leaders of the aristocratic party, and rose to be quæstor in 81, ædile in 75, prætor in 72, and consul in 69. Until the year 70 he was considered unequaled as an orator. In that year he was opposed by Marcus Tullius Cicero (q.v.), in the case of the Sicilian governor, Gaius Verres; Hortensius attempted to defend Verres against charges of cruelty and dishonesty in office, but Verres was convicted on the basis of Cicero's first speech. Later, however, Cicero joined the same party as Hortensius, and the two lawyers often worked together in court.

HORTHY, MIKLÓS (Eng. NICHOLAS), VON NAGYBÁNYA (1868–   ), Hungarian admiral and statesman, born in Kenderes in E. Hungary, and educated at the Naval Academy of Fiume. During World War I he rose to become admiral of the Austro-Hungarian navy. After the war he returned to Hungary and organized a counterrevolution against the Bolshevist government of Béla Kun. Horthy was made commander in chief of the Hungarian armed forces in 1919, and in 1920 the National Assembly elected him regent. As regent, Horthy defeated attempts of the ex-king Charles to regain the throne, and the Hungarian government declared the right of the Hapsburg dynasty to the throne to be forfeit. From that time Horthy ruled the country as regent for a legally nonexistent king. Through Horthy's efforts, Hungary joined the Axis Powers (q.v.) in 1940; in 1944, when the tide of World War II turned against them and Horthy attempted to make a separate peace between Hungary and the United Nations, Hungary was occupied by German troops, and Horthy was deposed as regent. He disappeared, reportedly as a prisoner of the Germans, until the following year, when he was captured in Bavaria by the U.S. Army. He was held in protective custody until the end of 1945, and was then released. He did not return to Hungary, but continued to interest himself in Hungarian politics; for example, in 1949 he made a public statement in behalf of Josef Mindzsenty, a Roman Catholic cardinal who had been accused of treason by the communist government of Hungary and sentenced to life imprisonment. See HUNGARY: *History.*

HORTICULTURE, the practice of cultivation of plants in gardens and orchards. Although horticulturists use information and methods developed by botanical scientists (see BOTANY), horticulture is a practical art. Horticulture may be loosely divided into three fields: (1) *olericulture,* the growing of vegetables; (2) *pomology,* the growing of fruit; and (3) *floriculture,* the growing of flowers. The principles of floriculture are used in conjunction with those of landscape gardening in the maintenance of ornamental gardens. Workers in all horticultural activities use new varieties of plants developed by plant breeders; see PLANT BREEDING.

Vegetable-growing. Vegetables are produced by truck farms, for commercial distribution; in market gardens, for consumption in nearby areas; and in home gardens, for family consumption. Truck farms were unknown in the U.S. prior to the Civil War, but with the ensuing development of efficient methods of transportation and refrigeration, truck farming became a major industry. Cities too large to be supplied by ordinary farms and gardens of surrounding areas are markets for truck-farm produce. Vegetables commonly grown on truck farms are those which can be produced at a relatively low cost per acre, such as cabbage, broccoli, Brussels sprouts, cauliflower, asparagus, eggplant, beets, peas, tomatoes, peppers, and various melons and squashes. Crops are usually grown in large, relatively level fields where rows can be widely spaced to permit cultivation with power machinery. Many truck farmers employ semi-portable irrigation units, constructed of lightweight metal spray tubing attached to portable power pumps. Practically all vegetable crops require the addition of fertilizer (q.v.) to supply mineral elements which are lacking in the soil. Most of the principal truck-gardening regions of the U.S. are situated in milder climates than the markets they supply. Southernmost areas produce vegetables ready for shipment at the beginning of the year. The harvesting time for vegetables occurs about one week later for each successive hundred miles northward.

Market gardens are small farms, located near large urban centers, which produce high-grade fresh vegetables, such as lettuce, celery, endive, spinach, Swiss chard, bunch beets and carrots, radishes, onions, and tomatoes. Production costs and acreage values are high in market-garden areas, and so cultivation is restricted to crops which bring a high financial return. Reduced transportation costs due to the proximity of the market do not reduce costs sufficiently to allow market gardens to compete with truck farms. Market gardens must, therefore, produce vegetables which cannot be grown on truck farms, are not in

season on truck farms, are too perishable for transportation over long distances, or are superior in quality to those produced on truck farms. Because production costs require a large crop return, space is conserved in market gardens by planting rows close together. Most of the weeding must be done with hand tools, and cultivation is carried on with wheel hoes or small garden tractors. Garden plots are carefully fertilized and irrigated to insure highest quality and quantity of produce.

Home gardens are common in the U.S. and become especially prevalent in times of emergency. During World War II, for example, the number of home vegetable gardens, called "victory gardens", exceeded 18,000,000 in the United States. Almost every American farm has a home garden in which vegetables other than those grown in the fields are raised, including both vegetables to be used fresh and vegetables to be canned or otherwise preserved for winter use. Home gardens are also popular in thinly settled urban and suburban areas. Two harvests are usually produced in a single growing season from well-regulated home gardens. Early varieties of vegetables, such as onions, spinach, Swiss chard, radishes, beets, peas, and sweet corn, reach a mature stage in time to make way for late varieties of peas, string beans, cabbage, celery, turnips, cucumbers, pumpkins, and squash. Tomatoes, peppers, asparagus, parsley, carrots, parsnips, cauliflower, kale, kohlrabi, and eggplant are other popular home-garden plants. Some gardeners reserve a corner of their plot for culinary herbs, such as chives, basil, marjoram, sage, and thyme. Small home gardens can readily be fertilized, cultivated, and irrigated intensively enough to produce any vegetables which can grow in the climate in which the gardens are located.

Fruitgrowing. Fruit (q.v.), according to strict botanical definition, includes many edible plant parts, such as tomatoes, peppers, and eggplants, which are commonly regarded as vegetables. The term fruitgrowing applies to production of edible fruits, other than nuts, which are sweet or have other qualities which make them suitable for use, raw or cooked, as desserts. Most large fruits and many small fruits raised commercially are borne on trees and bushes in orchards (q.v.). A few small fruits grow in specialized situations; grape (q.v.), for example, grows in vineyards, cranberry (q.v.) grows in bogs, and strawberry (q.v.) grows in beds. Many fruit trees and bushes, such as apple, cherry, orange, blackberry, and blueberry, have a graceful appearance or beautiful foliage or flowers, and are used in gardens for both decorative and fruit-producing properties. All native nut-bearing trees are used to some extent for their shade-giving and decorative properties in addition to their food value.

Flower Growing. Commercial production of flowers is an important industry in the U.S., yielding an annual crop worth about $500,000,000. Most of this output is sold by florists as cut flowers or potted house plants. Home flower gardens are a common feature of land areas adjoining dwellings all over the U.S. Cultivated flowers are most often grown in large central beds or narrow bordering beds. Except in very large gardens in which the grower has enough space to devote large areas to plantings of one species, a mixture of several species occupies a single bed. A carefully planned bed contains species which bloom at different periods of the growing season. The general color effect of floral beds is influenced by the season of the year. The proportion of white-flowered species, for example, is greatest during the earliest part of the growing season, but decreases beginning in early summer. Red-flowered species predominate in late summer, decline in early fall, and again predominate in late fall. Annual plants, such as cosmos, nasturtium, petunia, and zinnia, are replaced by reseeding yearly. Biennials and many perennials, such as aster, columbine, hollyhock, phlox, Oriental poppy, and primrose, grow for more than one season without further planting. Other perennials, such as dahlia and gladiolus, are less hardy, and in temperate climates the roots and bulbs from which they are grown are usually removed from the soil at the end of the growing season and stored over winter.

Practical Problems. All phases of horticulture share most of the same problems. Insect pests must be controlled by use of insecticides (q.v.); plant diseases must be controlled by use of fungicides (q.v.) and by eradication of other plants which support disease fungi; and noxious weeds (q.v.) must be eliminated by use of herbicides and by manual removal. Propagation material may consist of seeds, cuttings, bulbs, or entire plants. Trees are seldom grown from seeds or cuttings; young trees are ordinarily obtained from a nursery (q.v.), and transplanted.

Soil is prepared for planting by applying sufficient fertilizer to make up any mineral deficiencies in the soil, by adding sufficient humus-bearing material to make up organic deficiencies, and by treating the soil to make it either more or less acid. For soilless horticulture, see HYDROPONICS. Specific methods of cultivation are slightly different for every plant; see separate articles on individual plants. Finally, the continued propagation of plants depends on employment of various methods of reproduction, including reproduction by seeds and reproduction by bulbs, cuttings, grafting, or layering (qq.v.). See LANDSCAPE GARDENING; SOILS AND SOIL MANAGEMENT.

HORUS, Egyptian divinity represented in art as having the head of a hawk. He was the god of day, and was diversely considered as elder brother and as the child of Osiris. See EGYPTIAN RELIGION.

HOSEA or **OSEE** (fl. 8th cent. B.C.), the first of the minor Hebrew prophets. Hosea prophesied during and after the reign of Jeroboam II (q.v.), ruler of Israel, the northern kingdom of ancient Palestine. The Old Testament mentions him nowhere except in the book which bears his name. According to the Book of Hosea, the prophet was a citizen of Israel, and son of Beeri. The Book is divided into two main parts. In the first division, including Chapters 1-3, the prophet compares apostate Israel with an adulterous wife: Israel is always unfaithful to God, but God continually forgives. Biblical scholars consider the allegory to be an actual statement of Hosea's married life. The remainder of the book is given to denunciation of the moral degradation of Hosea's time and a prophecy of salvation for those who are truly Godfearing and righteous.

HOSIERY. See STOCKING.

HOSPITAL, an institution providing medical, surgical, or psychiatric care for patients ill enough to be confined to bed or to need constant observation and attention. Hospitals thus differ from dispensaries or clinics which patients merely visit for treatment. In many cases, however, outpatient clinics and dispensaries are directly affiliated with and share the quarters of hospitals.

History. Some authorities state that as long ago as 4000 B.C. temples of the god Saturn were used as houses of refuge for the sick and infirm and as training schools for doctors. Later the temples of Æsculapius, the Greek god of medicine, served the same purpose. Historical records also show that hospitals existed in India under Buddhist auspices as early as the 3rd century B.C. A general growth of hospitals came in the first centuries of the Christian era. In the 4th century A.D. hospitals were founded in Cæsarea and in Rome. The

The Hôtel Dieu, a 7th-century hospital in Paris (from a 16th-century wood engraving)

subsequent rise of the monastic orders also resulted in the creation of hospitals, which, together with hospices and schools, functioned as an integral part of the monasteries which built them. Elsewhere other hospitals were founded under the direction of the church, such as the Hôtel Dieu in Paris, built under the direction of St. Landry, the bishop of Paris, in 600 A.D. During the period of the crusades, religious orders were created which had as their chief duty the care of the sick, and these orders built a number of hospitals, particularly in the Mediterranean area. The most famous of these orders was the Knights Hospitalers of St. John of Jerusalem; see HOSPITALERS. Throughout the Middle Ages, the Renaissance, and even later, the administration of hospitals was almost entirely in the hands of the church.

Beginning in the 18th century, municipal hospitals operated by the civil authorities began to make their appearance, particularly in England. In the U.S., various small private hospitals were operated by churches and by individual physicians, but not until 1751 was the first public hospital, the Pennsylvania Hospital in Philadelphia, opened through the efforts of Benjamin Franklin and the Philadelphia doctor Thomas Bond. The first public hospital in New York City, the New York Hospital, was planned in 1769 but was not opened until 1791.

From the middle of the 19th century onward, the number of hospitals, particularly in the U.S., greatly increased, principally because of the discovery of anesthesia and aseptic surgical techniques. During the first half of the 20th century the demand for hospital service expanded further with the spread of prosperity and with the introduction of various forms of hospitalization insurance (q.v.; see also BLUE CROSS PLANS).

Types of Hospitals. Early hospitals often grouped all patients in a single ward, regardless of the diseases from which they suffered, but today certain types of patients are usually segregated in separate institutions to facilitate the particular treatments they require and to lessen the danger of infection of one patient by another. Tuberculosis patients are almost always treated in sanatoriums devoted entirely to the cure of that disease, as are patients suffering from leprosy. Hospitals for communicable diseases have facilities for segregating individual patients; and orthopedic hospitals are equipped with the various kinds of apparatus required in the treatment of bone and muscle disorders. A large number of hospitals, mostly government-financed, are given over entirely to the treatment of mental disease. Other special hospitals are devoted exclusively to ear and eye diseases, cancer, and the diseases of children. In addition most U.S. communities of more than a few thousand inhabitants have general hospitals which are equipped to give general medical, surgical, and maternity care. Such hospitals range from small village hospitals with ten to twenty beds to large city medical centers which have thousands of beds and combine five or more separate hospitals in one institution.

Modern hospitals can also be divided according to their sponsorship. The majority of U.S. hospitals are nonprofit institutions operated by community or religious groups. The Federal, State, and city governments operate another group of hospitals (see VETERANS' ADMINISTRATION), and a small proportion of the country's hospitals are operated as profit-making institutions by individuals or corporations.

The Modern Hospital. In the 20th century the custodial care of chronic and incurable invalids has been undertaken largely by nursing homes; hospitals concentrate their services in caring for the acutely sick and injured, and those requiring surgery. A modern general hospital, even of moderate size, is a complex institution. In addition to its purely medical functions, the hospital must also provide shelter, heat, food, and other services to its patients and its staff. A substantial area of a hospital building is given over to boiler rooms, laundries, kitchens, cafeterias, linenrooms, staff quarters, and storerooms. The medical services require space for laboratories, X-ray and other diagnostic equipment, a pharmacy, operating rooms, delivery rooms for obstetric cases, accommodations for various

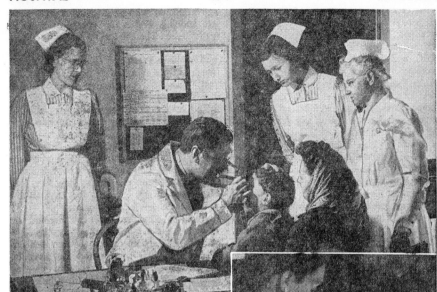

Columbia-Presbyterian Med. Cen.

IN A MODERN HOSPITAL

Above: A physician examining a child's eyes at a clinic. Right: A laboratory worker engaged in a research project. Below: Surgeon and assistants performing an operation.

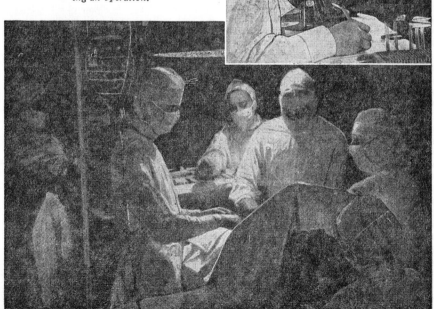

types of treatment such as physical and occupational therapy, a pathology room, and a morgue. Patients' accommodations include wards, semiprivate (generally two to six beds) and private rooms, isolation rooms, ordinary nurseries, nurseries for premature babies, lounges and waiting rooms, sun rooms, diet kitchens, nurses' stations, and flower rooms. The hospital administration must have offices for accounting and record keeping. Many sizable hospitals include schools of nursing which require dormitory, classroom, and laboratory accommodations for the students. Quarters for resident members of the staff such as nurses and resident physicians must also be provided.

In a typical hospital the various facilities are grouped for maximum efficiency. The lowest floor of the hospital usually houses the kitchen, laundry, boiler room, and other housekeeping offices, and often a small emergency operating room for accident cases. Administrative offices and X-ray and other diagnosis rooms are on the next floor, as are the offices and consulting rooms of the outpatient clinic. The floors above are devoted to patients' rooms and the special facilities of the various medical services. Medical patients, surgical patients, maternity patients, and child patients are commonly separated, either in different wings or on different floors of the hospital building. Operating suites are sometimes located on the same floor as the surgical patients and sometimes placed separately at the top of the building to obtain a maximum amount of daylight.

Hospital Administration. Although hospitals operate under a variety of administrative arrangements, the organization given below is typical of many nonprofit community hospitals.

The governing body of the hospital is a board of trustees or governors composed of prominent citizens of the community. This board has general control of the hospital finances and operation. The administrative details are delegated to a superintendent (usually not a physician) who administers all phases of the hospital's operation except medical matters. All aspects of the medical operation of the hospital are in the charge of the chief of the medical staff, a doctor appointed by the board of governors. The chief of staff, in consultation with the governors, selects the hospital's medical board, the group of doctors who have qualified for the privilege of treating patients at the hospital. The only full-time physicians on the staff are usually "interns"

and "residents" who are undergoing postgraduate training, and a few specialists such as pathologists. The chief of staff is also responsible for the selection and training of interns and residents. Frequently each specialized staff (such as the surgical, obstetrical, or neurological) authorized to practice at the hospital has its own chief. The nursing staff is administered by a superintendent of nurses who assigns nurses to various duties and who may also be responsible for the direction of the hospital's school of nursing. In larger hospitals, the work of running the hospital is further divided among other subordinate administrators, professional staff members, and technicians. Many hospitals also have an affiliated social-service department.

Hospital administration has become so complex that a number of universities give special postgraduate courses to train men for the field. Similar courses are also given in some universities and colleges to prepare graduate nurses for administrative duties.

Statistics. In the period from 1909 to the entry of the U.S. into World War II the number of hospitals in this country increased from 4359 to 6358 and the total patient capacity ("beds", in hospital parlance) increased even more, from 421,065 to 1,324,381. A large proportion of this increase was in hospitals for mental diseases and for mental defectives; approximately one third of the hospital beds in the U.S. are in institutions of this type. In a recent postwar year 6280 hospitals of all types, having a total of 1,468,714 beds and 84,145 bassinets for newborn babies, admitted a total of 15,153,452 patients. The average number of patients in hospitals at one time during this same year was 1,239,454 or about 79 percent of the total hospital accommodations available. In that year New York had the largest number of hospitals of any State in the Union: 155 government-operated institutions and 367 others with a total of 203,214 beds. States with the next largest number of hospitals were California, Texas, Pennsylvania, and Illinois. See HOSPITALIZATION; MEDICINE; PUBLIC HEALTH.

HOSPITALERS. See SAINT JOHN OF JERUSALEM, KNIGHTS OF.

HOSPITALET, city of the province of Barcelona, Catalonia, Spain, located several miles s.w. of Barcelona. Pop. (1946 est.) 59,740.

HOSPITALIZATION INSURANCE, the contract between a subscriber and an insuring agency which guarantees limited payment of hospitalization expenses incurred by the subscriber alone, or by the subscriber and his dependents. The two most important types of hospitalization insurance in the United States are *hospital service plans,* provided by various hospital service associations, and *group hospital expense insurance,* underwritten by insurance companies. In a recent year there were about 90 nonprofit hospital service associations approved by the Hospital Service Plan Commission of the American Hospital Association; they insured more than 33,000,000 persons, including subscribers and their dependents. In the same year, group hospital expense insurance plans covered over 7,000,000 persons. Both types of hospitalization insurance are offered to individual subscribers at premium rates higher than those for group insurance. Smaller group plans are offered to members of fraternal orders, labor unions, and employees associations; some of the plans are operated by the latter organizations and others are arrangements by the associations with insurance companies.

Hospital service associations usually furnish specified services with fixed maximum limits of cost. Insurance company contracts usually provide benefits specified in dollars. Neither type of coverage is intended to replace benefits payable to the insured under Workmen's Compensation acts (see WORKMEN'S COMPENSATION), and so both types cover only nonoccupational injuries and sickness. Many hospital service associations and most insurance companies have arrangements for coverage of supplementary surgical and obstetrical expenses on payment of extra premiums.

Hospital Service Plans. Specific services and fee schedules differ in various hospital service plans. Blue Cross Plans (q.v.) are typical of hospital service plans. The following description does not apply to any specific plan, but to Blue Cross Plans in general.

Cooperative arrangements are made, by a Blue Cross Plan, with the majority of hospitals in a community; the hospitals which are members of the plan are committed to provide specified services to subscribers. No member hospital is expected to relax its usual admission policies. Services provided consist of room and board in semiprivate accommodations, general nursing care, ordinary drugs and dressings, anesthesia (when administered by a hospital employee), use of operating room, and X-ray and laboratory examinations. Services are provided up to full value (such as seven dollars a day) for a maximum of 21 to 30 days in any contract year; services for additional periods, such as 90 days, are provided up to a fixed percentage of full value. Subscribers who are hospitalized in nonmember hospitals, or who occupy private sickrooms, are required to pay the difference between insurance rates and actual cost.

Benefits for maternity and elective operation cases are available after a specified waiting period, which is usually ten months. No benefits are available for certain excluded hospital admissions, such as those for purely diagnostic purposes, pulmonary tuberculosis, venereal diseases, communicable diseases which require isolation or quarantine, or functional nervous and mental disorders.

Enrollment of employees as group subscribers is limited to establishments in which a fixed minimum number of employees, such as five, wish to enroll. Monthly premium rates depend on the extent of coverage desired. At least three types of contract are usually available to subscribers: (1) individual contracts, without maternity benefits; (2) man and wife contracts, without maternity benefits; and (3) family contracts, which cover husband, wife (including maternity benefits for the wife), and all unmarried children between the ages of 90 days and 18 years. Applications for hospitalization insurance are accepted up to age sixty-five. Subsequent coverage is provided up to any age, if subscription is continuous.

Insurance Company Plans. The most common form of group hospital expense insurance is a master policy, issued to an employer, which covers eligible employees who wish to subscribe. Such groups of employees must usually total twenty-five or more, and must constitute at least three quarters of all eligible employees. The policy may provide benefits for the employee alone, or for the employee and his dependents. The basic benefit is a payment of a fixed amount for each day the subscriber is hospitalized up to the maximum number of days specified in the policy. In addition to the basic benefit, there is usually provision for reimbursement of related expenses, such as cost of drugs, dressings, anesthetics, and laboratory examinations, up to a total of five or ten times the value of a single day's benefit. Premium rates for group coverage depend on the maximum number of days of care permitted, the extent of allowances for related services, the percentage of women in the group, and the type of industry in which the group is employed. Rates for coverage of dependents are based primarily on the composition of the subscriber's family, and whether or not maternity benefits are desired. Maternity benefits are limited, and often are conditioned upon a waiting period. Age limits are not set for this type of insurance, but continued coverage depends on continuance of employment.

HOST (Lat. *hostia,* "sacrifice"), in ecclesiastical usage, a thin wafer of bread used in the celebration of the Lord's Supper (q.v.). In the Roman Catholic Church the host is a circular wafer of unleavened bread, stamped with a symbolic device such as the Lamb, the cross, or the monogram IHS (standing for "Jesus" in Greek); in the Orthodox Church, leavened bread is used. This difference in practice was one of the grounds of separation of the Eastern and Western Churches; see SCHISM, GREAT. See also ELEVATION OF THE HOST.

HOTCHKISS, BENJAMIN BERKELEY (1826–85), American inventor and ordnance maker, born in Watertown, Conn. After working in several arms factories, including that of Samuel Colt, he set up his own factory in New York City. Hotchkiss opened an arms factory in Paris in 1870 and there produced a large number of rapid-firing naval guns of his own design. These guns, which were made for one-, three-, and six-pound projectiles, were first made for the U.S. Navy and later became part of the standard armament of most of the world's navies. These so-called Hotchkiss guns were later supplanted by other guns of larger caliber.

HOTH, in Norse mythology, a sightless god, the twin brother of Balder, god of peace and light, whom he dearly loved. Everything in creation had taken a solemn oath not to harm Balder, except the mistletoe. One day Loki, god of mischief, placed in the hand of Hoth a shaft of mistletoe, and directing the aim of the blind god, caused the death of Balder.

HOTHOUSE. See GREENHOUSE.

HOT SPRINGS, or properly, CITY OF HOT SPRINGS NATIONAL PARK. See HOT SPRINGS NATIONAL PARK.

HOT SPRINGS NATIONAL PARK, the name of a city and of a national park in Arkansas. The city, county seat of Garland Co., is situated on the Ouachita R., in a valley at the E. base of the Ouachita Mountains, 58 miles s.w. of Little Rock. It is served by two railroads, and maintains a municipal airport. The mountains which encircle the city rise to a height of 1200 ft. above sea level, and insure a mild climate throughout the year. The city almost completely surrounds the national park for which it is named, and is a famous health and pleasure resort, and the site of the executive headquarters of the Ouachita National Forest. Lakes Catherine and Hamilton, created by the construction of a dam across the Ouachita R., are on the outskirts of the city. The lakes have a combined shoreline of 340 m., along which are numerous vacation cottages. Among the places of interest in the city are an ostrich farm and an alligator farm, and the Oaklawn Park race track.

The park, established by Congress as Hot Springs Reservation in 1832 and made a national park in 1921, covers 1016 acres and contains forty-seven curative springs. The thermal springs issue from a small area at the s.w. base of Hot Springs Mountain at an average flow of 1,000,000 gallons a day and with an average temperature of more than 140° F. They are practically identical in chemical composition, containing over twenty mineral constituents. The sixteen bathhouses, eight in the city and eight in the park, receive equal quantities of water from a central system, and are operated under Federal government regulations. The Army and Navy General Hospital at Hot Springs, established in 1882 and one of the largest general hospitals in the U.S., as well as the first to be built, is also supplied with water from the springs. The Federal government maintains a museum in the park, with geological displays. Facilities for many forms of recreation, including fishing, swimming, hunting, golf, tennis, horseback riding, and boating, are provided within the park area and in the adjoining region.

The Spanish explorer Hernando de Soto is said to have visited the springs in 1541, and to have found that their medicinal qualities were long known to the Indians. In 1803 the Hot Springs area became a part of the U.S. as a result of the Louisiana Purchase, and in 1807 the first permanent settlement was established on the site. The Hot Springs Reservation was created in 1832 to preserve the waters free from monopoly and commercial exploitation. Although the U.S. government thereby undertook the administration of the spa, the City of Hot Springs National Park operates under its own municipal and State laws. The reservation and town were physically and administratively separated in 1877. The City of Hot Springs National Park was chartered in 1879. It is visited annually by about 325,000 persons. Pop. (1950) 29,307.

HOTSPUR, a surname of Sir Henry Percy (1364–1403). See PERCY, family.

HOTTENTOT BREAD. See ELEPHANT'S-FOOT.

HOTTENTOTS, members of the South African race which was in possession of what is now the greater part of the Cape of Good Hope Province when it was first visited and colonized by Europeans. At the present time they are scattered throughout the western half of South Africa.

The Hottentots are related to both the Bushmen and the Bantus (qq.v.), and may have sprung from an ancient cross between the two peoples. They exhibit, however, a consistent set of physical characteristics, which has been thoroughly investigated and described by physical anthropologists. The skin, like that of the Bushmen, is yellowish, brown, or brownish gray, but never black; the hair is long and woolly; the cheek bones are prominent; the eyes are dark or black and wide apart; the nose is broad and flat and the nostrils thick; the mouth is large, with heavy, upturned lips and considerable prognathism; the chin is pointed, and the jaw receding. The head is dolichocephalic, and somewhat greater than that of the Bushmen in cranial capacity. The women are characterized by enormously overdeveloped buttocks, a condition known as steatopygy. In stature the Hottentots average a little over five feet; they are accordingly short, but not dwarfish.

Modern Hottentot culture has been greatly affected by contact with Europeans and incursions and conquest by neighboring warlike tribes, particularly the Bantus. The occupation of the lowlands by Dutch and English settlers has driven most of them into mountains and waste places, and as a people they are slowly dying out; see, however, BASTAARDS; GRIQUAS. They are divided into a number of tribes under separate chiefs, each occupying its own territory and leading a nomadic pastoral life. Trade is carried on by barter in cattle, which are for the most part raised for milk, their chief food. Most of the meat they eat is procured by hunting, and they gather a variety of wild roots and fruits.

Within a tribe the Hottentots are organized in exogamous tribes, and practice cross-cousin marriage. Lines of descent are reckoned through the father. Their religion is a combination of animism and the personification of the natural forces which produce rain. The Hottentots believe in the existence of the soul after death and in a ruler of all things who in one form came out of the east. Their graves, therefore, are oriented. During every visit to a cemetery they add to a pile of memorial stones, a practice which has enabled students to trace with some accuracy the course of their nomadic wanderings and large-scale migrations. Though the Hottentots have no priestly class and no temples or places of united worship, they have medicine men, witch doctors, and sorcerers who are called in to heal the sick by magic. An extensive folklore exists, having many resemblances with that of the neighboring Bantus.

The Hottentot language embraces three principal dialects: the Nama, which is the most important, the Kora, and the Cape dialect, now extinct. The language is usually considered to be substantially independent of all other languages and families. Certain of its features, particularly the existence of grammatical gender, apparently show the effect of Hamitic languages (q.v.), and largely conjectural attempts have been made to prove cultural and physical admixture with or descent from the Hamites (q.v.). The most distinctive feature of the language, however, is a phonetic element shared with the Bushmen. It consists of clicks occurring at the beginnings of over seventy-five percent of the words, made by pressing the tongue against the teeth, the palate, or the sides of the upper jaw, or by doubling the tongue backward, and in all cases followed by an explosive noise. These clicks render the language almost impossible for Europeans to imitate accurately; indeed, the name Hottentot stems from the efforts of the Dutch to imitate these sounds. The language as a whole is agglutinative and rich in relational suffixes which closely resemble true inflections. As in the Indochinese and some African languages, differences in meaning are often expressed by changes in pitch.

HOT-WATER HEATING. See HEATING, VENTILATION, AND AIR CONDITIONING.

HOUDINI, HARRY (1874–1926), American magician, born in Appleton, Wis. His real name was Erich Weiss, but he took the name of Houdini after the French magician Houdin. He began his career in 1882 as a trapeze performer, and later became world famous for his performances of feats of magic. He showed astounding ability in extricating himself from handcuffs, ropes, locked trunks, and bonds of any sort. At one time he had himself roped and then locked in a packing case, which was bound with steel tape and dropped into the harbor off the Battery in New York City. He appeared on the surface of the water in 59 seconds.

Houdini attributed all of his feats of magic to natural, physical effects and explained how many of his tricks were performed. He exposed the tricks of fraudulent spiritualistic mediums, often producing "spiritualistic" phenomena himself which he explained in non-mystical, physical terms. Before he died Houdini arranged a definitive test of spiritualism. He devised a ten-word code which he would communicate to his wife, if possible, within ten years after his death. After he died various mediums maintained that they were able to establish contact with him, but none was able to transmit to his wife the prearranged code. He left his library of magic, one of the most valuable in the world, to the Library of Congress. Among his writings are *Miracle Mongers and Their Methods, A Magician Among the Spirits, The Unmasking of Robert Houdin,* and *Handcuff Secrets.*

HOUDON, JEAN ANTOINE (1741–1828), French portrait sculptor, born in Versailles. He won the Prix de Rome in 1761 and studied in Italy until 1769. After his return to Paris, in 1771 he exhibited his bust of Denis Diderot, the first of a long series of sculpture portraits of eminent men of his time. In 1778 he made busts of Voltaire and of Benjamin Franklin and the death mask of Jean Jacques Rousseau. By this time Houdon was renowned as the greatest portrait sculptor of his day. He was invited to America, where in 1785 he made from life the famous statue of George Washington, residing at the latter's Mount Vernon estate for several weeks. He also made likenesses of Thomas Jefferson, when the latter was American envoy to Paris in 1789, and of Napoleon. Clarity, sensitive modeling, and penetrating characterization are the outstanding qualities of Houdon's sculpture. His works, and copies made from them, are to be found in museums, libraries, and public buildings in the U.S. and Europe.

HOUND, the name of one of the two classes of sporting dog (q.v.) or dogs used for hunting purposes. Most sporting dogs of the hound type follow their quarry by scent; a few breeds follow it by sight. See AFGHAN HOUND; BASSET HOUND; BEAGLE; BLOODHOUND; BORZOI; DACHSHUND; DEERHOUND, SCOTTISH; FOXHOUND; GREYHOUND; NORWEGIAN ELKHOUND; OTTERHOUND; SALUKI; WHIPPET; and WOLFHOUND, IRISH.

HOUNDFISH, name applied to several dog-fishes (q.v.), also known as "hounds" and "houndsharks", and to the garfish (q.v.).

HOUND'S-TONGUE, or DOG'S TONGUE, common names applied to herbs of the genus *Cynoglossum,* belonging to the Borage family. The common hound's-tongue, *C. officinale,* has tongue-shaped upper leaves. It bears reddish-purple flowers having a five-parted calyx, five-lobed corolla, five stamens, and a solitary pistil. The fruits are large nutlets. Common hound's-tongue is native to Europe and naturalized in pastures and waste grounds of N.E. United States. The yellow clintonia, *Clintonia borealis,* is also called hound's-tongue; see CLINTONIA. Wild vanilla, *Trilisa odoratissima,* a vanilla-scented herb, is sometimes called dog's-tongue; see VANILLA.

HOUR, a measure of time equal to the twenty-fourth part of an astronomical day (q.v.). As there are two kinds of days, the solar and the sidereal, there are two corresponding kinds of hours. A sidereal hour (employed only by astronomers) is shorter than a solar by 9.856 seconds. The solar hour now in use, which remains stable throughout the year, is a relatively modern innovation. Until the 18th century an hour was usually taken as the twelfth part of the period between sunrise and sunset or between sunset and sunrise, and varied with the seasons. Hours are divided into sixty equal minutes (q.v.).

HOUR ANGLE, the angle at the celestial pole between a given hour circle (q.v.) and the celestial meridian, measured westward from the meridian. Hour angles are used in the location of celestial bodies.

HOUR CIRCLE, any great circle of the celestial sphere which passes through the celestial poles. The celestial meridian, for example, is that hour circle which passes through the zenith of the observer. For the location of celestial bodies, a system of hour circles can be constructed which is independent of the rotation of the earth and the position on the earth of an observer; such a system is usually preferred by astronomers to one based upon the horizon (q.v.). Twelve hour circles, dividing the celestial equator into twenty-four equal spaces of fifteen degrees, or one hour, each, are often drawn through the poles of a globe or model of the heavens.

The term "hour circle" is also applied to a circle graduated in hours, minutes, and seconds, which is attached to the polar axis of a telescope employing equatorial mounting (q.v.). It is used to measure the right ascension of stars.

HOURI (Ar. *hūrīyah*), one of the beautiful maidens who, according to the Mohammedan faith, dwell in Paradise and reward true believers with their companionship after death. The houris are said to repose on gorgeous couches in pavilions of pearl. They are not fashioned of clay, like ordinary women, but of musk, saffron, incense, and amber. The houris are perennially young and free from physical defect, and have the power to conceive and bear children at will. Although later Mohammedan theologians were offended by this unabashedly sensual depiction of Paradise, and endeavored to place an allegorical interpretation upon the houris, it is abundantly clear from the authoritative pronouncements of Mohammed himself that to the prophet and his immediate followers the maidens of Paradise had substantial reality.

HOURS, BOOK OF, name given to liturgical or devotional books containing prayers, psalms, and excerpts from Scripture to be read or recited at the canonical hours. Such books were popular during the Middle Ages, and are still used in certain Eastern churches; in the Roman Catholic Church, however, such devotions have been gathered into the Breviary (q.v.). During the 14th to the 16th centuries, books of hours were often richly illuminated; they were important in the history of art because the miniatures, landscapes, and formal illumination they contained constituted the first step in the development of painting in France; see FRENCH ART AND ARCHITECTURE. Among the most important such books still surviving is the *Très Riches Heures* of Jean de France, Duc de Berry, which was illuminated by the 15th-century Belgian painters, the Limburg brothers; this book of hours is now in the Condé Museum in Chantilly.

HOURS OF LABOR or **HOURS OF WORK,** in labor economics, the length of the working day and the working week. The determination of standard hours of work constitutes one of the principal problems in the fields of labor-management relations and social legislation in virtually all countries. Before the development of factories and the factory system (q.v.) of production in Europe in the 19th century, most industrial work was of the nature of handicrafts and was conducted by artisans in small shops; see GUILD. The number of daily and weekly hours of work of the artisans was regulated by the guilds in the interests of the guildmasters and, except on the part of reformers, was regarded as a matter for the exclusive determination of the guilds. Serfs, peasants, farmers, and agricultural laborers worked from "sun to sun", I.E., from dawn to dusk.

The number of hours of labor became an important social consideration only after the Industrial Revolution (q.v.) and the development of a large social group dependent for its existence on working for wages. In 1800, both in England and the United States, a 14-hour working day in industry was commonplace for women and children as well as men, and even longer hours prevailed in some establishments, particularly in textile mills. In England a number of Parliamentary enactments, called Factory Acts and sponsored by humanitarians and reformers, shortened the hours of labor performed by children and women. In 1802 the first legislation of this kind ever to be enacted anywhere limited the hours of children to 12 a day; in 1819 the hours of children between the ages of nine and sixteen were limited to 72 a week; in 1825 children were given a half holiday on Saturday; and in 1831 the hours of work for all employees under eighteen years of age were reduced to 69 a week. During the 1840's the Chartists (see CHARTISM) led the English workers in a series of militant struggles for a 10-hour day. Thereafter in England the pressure of workers organized in trade unions was the principal factor in effecting a reduction of the workday and the work week.

Agitation by workers for shorter working hours developed in the United States in the 1820's. In 1827 the Mechanics Union of Trade Associations of Philadelphia went on strike for a 10-hour day. A series of strikes for the same objective, which took place in the 1830's when the workday averaged between 12 and 14 hours, culminated in 1840 in an executive order by President Martin Van Buren instituting a 10-hour day for Federal employees. The first State laws establishing shorter hours were enacted to eliminate abuses in the employment of children; see CHILD LABOR. These laws were followed by others intended to limit the hours of women. Most of this legislation was subsequently invalidated by the courts as being in violation of freedom of contract. At the time of the Civil War the average number of hours worked in a week was 72 in agriculture and 64 in industry and commerce. During the industrialization of the country following the Civil War, pressure by workers for a shorter working day increased. By 1890 the 10-hour day and the 60-hour week were common in industry; the average number of hours in a work week in agriculture was about 70. The constant agitation for shorter hours bore fruit at the end of the 19th century in a reversal of the attitude of the courts toward legislation limiting the work week and workday. The courts declared that the health of workers was a matter affecting the public welfare, and that laws intended to preserve it were a legitimate exercise of the police powers of the government. This attitude made possible the subsequent enactment of important acts establishing normal standards of and legal limits for the workday and work week. Further progress in the achievement of shorter hours lay in the struggle for the 8-hour day.

The Eight-Hour Day. The movement for a working day of 8 hours originated among the Australian workers in 1856, and was taken up in 1866 by the International Workingmen's Association (q.v.) led by Karl Marx. The National Labor Union in the United States in 1866 and the Trades Union Congress in England in 1869 publicly advocated an 8-hour day. In the United States a Congressional enactment in 1866 provided for an 8-hour day for all Federal government employees. From the 1880's first the Knights of Labor (q.v.) and then the American Federation of Labor pressed demands for legislation for an 8-hour day. Congress, in 1916, under the threat of a general railroad strike, passed the Adamson Act providing an 8-hour day for railroad trainmen; this was the first Federal enactment establishing the 8-hour day.

In the United States as in Great Britain, however, the 8-hour day was realized not primarily by legislative enactment but through collective bargaining by labor unions and employers. By the end of World War I the 8-hour day and a work week of 48 hours prevailed in most industries in the United States and Great Britain. Conspicuous exceptions were the maritime industry and agriculture.

In 1919 the first proposals for a world-wide 8-hour day were adopted by the International Labor Conference sponsored by the League of Nations, meeting in Washington, D.C. These proposals called for a limitation of the hours of work in industrial undertakings to 8 per day and 48 per week; the recommendations, however, were not confirmed by the countries represented at the conference. In 1935 the Conference recommended the universal adoption of an 8-hour day and a 40-hour week.

During the economic depression of the 1930's agitation for a 5-day work week was widespread, particularly in the United States, where labor leaders demanded that unemployment be relieved by the spread of available work to more employees. In 1933 the Federal National Recovery Administration (q.v.), in its codes regulating the administration of industries, reduced the hours of work in many industries to 40 per week; the working day was established at 8 hours. Some labor unions during this period obtained a 35-hour week through collective bargaining; the American Federation of Labor declared that 30 hours per week should be the maximum. After the invalidation of the NRA by the U.S. Supreme Court, the Federal government in 1936 and 1938 established a 40-hour week for workers employed in enterprises engaged on government contracts, and for workers employed by firms in interstate commerce; see WALSH-HEALEY ACT; FAIR LABOR STANDARDS ACT.

HOUSATONIC RIVER, river rising in the Berkshire Hills, N.W. Massachusetts, and flowing generally s. through that State and Connecticut until, after a total course of about 150 m., it empties into Long Island Sound between Devon and Stratford, Conn. It is noted for its scenic beauty and as a source of water power.

HOUSE, a man-made structure used as a dwelling place. Permanent dwellings are usually called houses, but semipermanent or portable habitations, including those used by primitive tribes, are usually described by specific names such as wigwams, lodges, or tents. Permanent dwellings of flimsy construction are referred to as huts; small, simple dwellings are often called cottages; and more pretentious habitations, manors or mansions. A distinction is frequently made between houses in which individuals or families live for extended periods of time and hotels or inns which provide transient lodgings. From the legal point of view a single apartment in a multiple-unit dwelling is sometimes regarded as a house and in certain cases single rooms or the premises in which a business is conducted are also defined as houses. In common speech, however, a house is a single detached dwelling unit, and the separate dwelling units found under a single roof in multiple tenements or apartment houses are called apartments or flats.

History. Archeological research indicates that primitive man built several different kinds of dwellings to suit the climate and the other conditions under which he lived. In many temperate countries natural caves were used for shelter and were frequently improved by the addition of rude stone walls roofed with sticks or hides and set up outside the mouths of the caves. Huts of many descriptions were also made from timber frames covered with skins, bark, or a thatch of straw or reeds. The huts were sometimes constructed on piling over shallow water at the edges of lakes. In the earliest primitive times huts

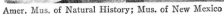
Amer. Mus. of Natural History; Mus. of New Mexico

PRIMITIVE HOUSES. *Above: A food-storage house of the Maori, aborigines of New Zealand. Right: A Philippine native tree house. Below: Houses in a Pueblo Indian village in New Mexico.*

consisted of but a single room, but later several huts were grouped under a common roof with narrow spaces between them, and, later still, interior partitions were employed to separate the hut into rooms. The availability of different building materials affected the construction of primitive houses. In forested lands huts were built in the familiar log-cabin pattern with walls made of notched logs. In warm countries where clay was available, walls were made of sun-dried brick. Certain Eskimos used snow as a material for building their winter houses or igloos. Other primitive forms of house include the skin tents with light wooden frameworks, used by the Indians of the U.S. and the nomadic tribes of Asia, and sod houses which were excavations roofed with sod set on wooden beams. See PUEBLO.

With the rise of civilization in Western Asia, Egypt, and the lands around the Ægean Sea, simple primitive houses gave way to more complicated forms. The houses of Mesopotamia in the period between 2000 and 1000 B.C. were made of sun-dried and baked brick reinforced with reeds and timbers. One common form of house of this period was a tall hut with a high, dome-shaped roof. Another consisted of a series of rooms surrounding one or more open interior courts. Egyptian houses of the early dynasties of the empire (between 3000 and 2000 B.C.) were built either with a central court, or, more commonly, in the form of a compact block of rooms. In some instances, houses were built in the shape of an L surrounding two sides of a rectangular yard or court which was enclosed with walls on the other two sides. The materials were similar to those used in Mesopotamia. In Crete and other Ægean countries, from about 2000 B.C., the court type of house dominated the architecture, but houses of the block type were also occasionally built.

Throughout the classical age of Greek and Roman civilization almost all houses were of the court type. The open court itself was surrounded by a covered colonnaded passageway called the peristyle, and the various rooms opened off from the peristyle. At the beginning of the Christian era houses were often two or more stories in height, particularly in crowded cities. The materials used for building were stone and brick masonry, timber, and tile.

The Roman influence in house architecture continued in Europe down to the Middle Ages, particularly in towns. The great houses or castles of feudal lords, usually built in the country, were, however, heavily fortified (see FORTIFICATION AND SIEGECRAFT). The houses of serfs and peasants were commonly simple structures of one or two rooms with masonry walls and thatched or sodded roofs. As the age of feudalism ended, more elaborate farmhouses were built, usually in the form of a rectangular farmyard enclosed by sheds, barns, storerooms, and the house itself, which was usually a building of two stories. French farmhouses of this period were commonly built of stone, but those of Scandinavia and Germany were made of wood or of half-timber construction in which timber supports were combined with masonry and the timbers themselves were exposed. Town houses were usually built several stories high because of crowding and the increased value of land. Such houses frequently had front and back rooms on each floor, connected by galleries around an open court or light well. A typical house of the period had a shop or store at the front of the first floor and a kitchen at the rear, a living room on the second floor over the shop and sleeping rooms at the rear, and attic and storage space on the third floor. The house was equipped with glazed windows, one or more chimneys, and, usually, a well in the courtyard.

The chief change in architecture at the time of the Renaissance was in the large houses of nobles and other wealthy men. The dark, thick-walled, small-windowed castles of feudal times gave way to houses which had extensive windows and balconies to provide light and air, and which were embellished and enriched with various types of architectural ornamentation. At the same time, architects became more adept in planning the interiors of their houses for the convenience and comfort of the occupants. Living, sleeping, eating, and cooking rooms were planned with relation to one another. The manor houses of England, beginning in about the 16th century, displayed floor plans and arrangements of rooms that are essentially modern. On the continent of Europe in the 17th century and later, comfort was often sacrificed to architectural elegance and impressiveness. A typical French town house of the 17th century was built with a monumental gateway leading into an open courtyard, back of which was situated the house proper. Behind the house was a large enclosed garden. Many examples of such private houses or hôtels particuliers still exist in the cities of France.

House architecture in colonial America in general reflected the architecture of England, but with differences dictated by the conditions of life in the New World. In Virginia, the houses of well-to-do colonists resembled typical English country houses. Farther north, however, as in New England, houses were built that were more suitable for the severe winters encountered. Typically, these houses were compact in plan, with low ceilings and small rooms to conserve heat. Smaller houses with two or four rooms in each story were built around a single chimney which frequently provided flues for fireplaces in each room. Larger houses had one or more chimneys at each end of the building. The façades of these New England houses were commonly symmetrical with the entrance door at the center and evenly spaced windows at either side. Earlier New England houses were almost universally of wood frame construction, but in the 18th century many brick houses were built, particularly in towns.

Modern Houses. Since the Industrial Revolution, and particularly in the last century, two strong tendencies have been observed in the architectural design of houses. One tendency is to decrease the amount of living space occupied by the individual family, partly because of the expense of domestic servants; the other is to divide the living space into smaller, low-ceilinged rooms. These tendencies are a natural outcome of the growth of cities and have resulted in two characteristic forms of modern domestic architecture: the large urban apartment house, containing small dwelling units for a large number of families; and the small, closely spaced houses of the suburbs, detached or "attached" in rows (forming a single structure), each on its own small plot of ground.

In the second quarter of the 20th century both social planners and architects gave much attention to the problems of housing, particularly in urban and industrialized areas. Both private builders and government agencies recognized the need for coordinated planning that would provide economical houses and other dwelling units which had adequate light, air, and recreational facilities. Many notable urban and suburban housing developments have been built, both by private investors and with government funds, in which the design has been fitted to the needs of the entire community. Notable among such developments are the "greenbelt" towns outside of Washington, D.C., Cincinnati, Ohio, and Milwaukee, Wis., built by the Resettlement Administration of the U.S. Department of Agriculture. These towns are complete communities, with integral utility, recreational, and other facilities, in which all the land is community-owned and the size of the town is deliberately limited. These towns take their name from a broad surrounding belt of agri-

Floor plan (right) and exterior (below) of a modern house designed by Marcel Breuer, famous European architect, built and displayed in the garden of the Museum of Modern Art, N.Y.C.

Museum of Modern Art

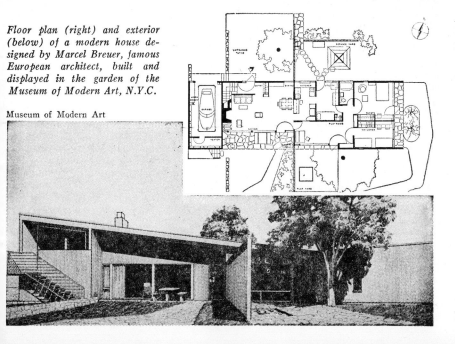

cultural land which insures protection against the encroachment of outside building. A privately built planned community of the same general type is the town of Radburn, N.J., near New York City. Within cities and towns a large number of coordinated apartment-house groups have been built, both as income-producing properties and as low-cost, government-financed housing. One of the largest of such developments was built by a life-insurance company in New York City in the late 1940's.

Modern House Design. In the late 19th and early 20th centuries, particularly in the U.S., architects tended to design the interiors and exteriors of houses as separate units. The interior was equipped with modern kitchen and plumbing facilities, central heating, gas, and electrical devices and was then enclosed in an exterior shell modeled after a Spanish ranch house, a Normandy farmhouse, a Swiss chalet, or a half-timbered English town house of Tudor times. Modern architects, however, following the lead of such pioneers as the German Walter Gropius, the Swiss Le Corbusier, the Finn Eliel Saarinen, and the American Frank Lloyd Wright, have endeavored to combine the interiors and exteriors of their houses to produce a useful and beautiful structure.

The interiors of modern houses are designed for ease of housekeeping and cleaning, for convenience of movement, and for the special requirements of their inhabitants. The exteriors are designed to harmonize with the sites on which they are placed, to take advantage of views, sunlight, and prevailing breezes, and to provide privacy for the inhabitants in crowded communities. Modern house architects have also taken full advantage of the many modern structural materials, such as plywood, glass brick, stainless steel, aluminum, and lightweight concrete, and modern insulating materials. Improved heating, ventilating, and air-conditioning systems are built into the houses, as are rubbish- and garbage-disposal devices and automatic laundries. A wide variety of materials is used in building, but emphasis is usually placed on those materials which are native or traditional to the locality, such as native stones and woods.

Forms of House Structure. By far the most common form of construction for single-family houses in the U.S. is the wooden-frame structure. Such frames can be finished off with a single layer of brick (brick veneer), with shingles, or with clapboard. Stone or brick masonry construction is sometimes used for larger houses. Houses with masonry walls of hollow cement blocks were built extensively after World War II. Interior finish is usually plaster on lath, either painted or papered, although plywood, gypsum boards, or fiber boards are sometimes used. Wood paneling, which was formerly employed extensively as an interior finish, is now found only in large, expensive houses. Floors are commonly made of hardwood boards, but ceramic tile, asphalt tile, rubber tile, and linoleum are also employed for floor finishes, especially in kitchens and bathrooms. In larger dwellings such as apartment houses, steel-frame construction is the rule for all modern buildings. Such buildings are faced with masonry and have interior partitions of hollow tile. The interior finish is commonly the same as that of small houses.

Prefabricated Houses. Beginning in the 1930's architects and engineers made a number of experiments in the design and construction of "prefabricated houses"—standardized houses in which entire wall sections or other units of the completed house are constructed at a central factory and then assembled into a completed building at the house site. This application of the principles of mass production to house construction is economically very desirable because it avoids the high labor costs and material wastes inherent in the building of houses by conventional contract methods. Prefabrication also permits the use of efficient and inexpensive structural methods such as stressed metal wall panels which would be difficult and uneconomical for individual houses.

During World War II the armed services made extensive use of prefabricated housing units including such types as the Quonset hut, a semicylindrical building made of sheets of corrugated metal. In general widespread use of prefabricated houses is hampered by local building codes in which specifications are stated in terms of conventional frame or masonry construction and which do not allow the use of stronger and lighter materials.

HOUSE, EDWARD MANDELL (1858–1938), American diplomat, born in Houston, Texas, and educated at Cornell University. He took an active part in State political councils in Texas, but did not seek public office. He was called "Colonel House" because he was a colonel on the staff of Governor Culberson of Texas. House entered national politics by taking an active part in securing the Presidential nomination for Woodrow Wilson in 1912, and although he did not hold a cabinet post he became one of the President's chief advisers. In 1914, shortly before the outbreak of World War I, and again in 1915 and 1916, he represented President Wilson in diplomatic missions to Europe. When the United States entered the war in 1917 he was special U.S. representative at the interallied conference for coordination of war activities. In 1918–19 House was a member of the American Peace Commission at Paris and helped draft the Treaty of Versailles. He was a member of the commission that framed the covenant of the League of Nations and was a member of the Commission of Mandates in 1919. He retired from public life shortly thereafter. Among his writings are *Philip Dru* (1912) and *What Really Happened in Paris* (with Charles Seymour, 1921). The *Intimate Papers of Colonel House,* a selection of his papers, was edited by Charles Seymour and published in 1926–28.

HOUSEBREAKING, in criminal law in the United States, the forcible breaking into a house (q.v.) with felonious intent. Housebreaking by night is called burglary (q.v.). The penalties for housebreaking are determined in the criminal codes of the States and vary for short terms for first offenders to life imprisonment for habitual criminals.

HOUSEBURNING. See ARSON.

HOUSE CENTIPEDE, common name for any long-legged, long-antennaed centipede in the genus *Scutigera* of the family Scutigeridae. House centipedes are found in the moist portions of houses, especially closets and cellars, in most parts of the world, and are valuable as destroyers of roaches, flies, and other insects. Although their bite is mildly venomous, they almost never bite human beings. The best-known species is *S. forceps,* which is about 1½ in. long. See CENTIPEDE.

HOUSE CROW. See HOODED CROW.

HOUSE FINCH, or LINNET, a small bird, *Carpodacus mexicanus,* of the Finch family, one of the commonest and most familiar of all birds throughout western U.S., from the Great Plains to the Pacific coast. The bird is about 5½ in. long. The female is light brown above and white below; the male has a similar color pattern, but has a bright-red head, breast, and rump. Both male and female sing; the song of the male is beautiful, far superior to that of the female. The house finch nests in trees, and in holes and crannies about houses; whence arises its common name. It subsists on the seeds of weeds.

HOUSEFLY, TYPHOID FLY, or **DISEASE FLY,** a hairy, dipterous fly, *Musca domestica,* commoner about human habitations throughout the world than any other fly. It often is a carrier of such diseases as typhoid fever, cholera, dysentery, and anthrax. The adult reaches a length of slightly over ¼ in. The body of the male is dark gray above, and tan and lighter gray below. The female is dark gray above, and lighter gray marked with red and black below. The eyes, which are closer together in the male than in the female, are brownish red. Houseflies do not bite; they subsist chiefly on the liquid portions of decaying organic matter. The adult fly transmits disease by contaminating food with disease organisms which it has either picked up on its hairy legs, or ingested and then regurgitated. The female lays an average of 150 white eggs, about 1/25 in. long, in horse manure or other decaying substance. The eggs hatch in about twelve hours into white, legless larvae called maggots, which grow to ½ in. in length. The maggot pupates in five days, and the new adult emerges in another five days if the weather is warm, or in a month or more if weather conditions are unfavorable. The housefly may hibernate at any stage of its life cycle. On the average twelve generations of houseflies are produced in one year.

The name housefly is also applied to several other species of flies found about houses. The biting housefly or stable fly, *Stomoxys calcitrans,* is in the same family (Muscidae) as the common housefly and resembles it closely. Unlike the common housefly it has biting mouthparts and subsists on the blood of horses and cattle. It is most frequently found about stables and often enters human habitations, especially in rainy weather, whence another common name, "Storm fly". The lesser housefly, *Fannia canicularis,* in the family Anthomyiidae, resembles the common housefly but is somewhat smaller. It is most abundant in late spring and early summer. Contrary to popular opinion, this fly never grows to the size of the common housefly. Compare FLESH FLY. See also D.D.T.; ENTOMOLOGY, MEDICAL; INSECTICIDES.

HOUSEHOLD GODS, among the ancient Romans, the divinities supposed to watch over the domicile and the family. See LARES AND PENATES.

HOUSELEEK, common name of *Sempervivum tectorum,* a perennial climbing plant belonging to the Orpine family. Houseleek, also known as hen-and-chickens, is native to

Europe and is naturalized in waste places of E. United States. Its leaves are produced in thick, basal rosettes, from which flower-bearing stalks arise. The flowers are pink, rose, or purple, and usually consist of six sepals, six petals, twelve stamens, and six pistils. Houseleeks produce fertile seed, but the ordinary method of reproduction is by prostrate lateral branches called offsets, which root at some distance from the parent plant and produce new rosettes which lead an independent existence. In cultivation, houseleek is frequently planted in rock gardens.

HOUSEMAID'S KNEE. See JOINTS.

HOUSE OF COMMONS. See PARLIAMENT.

HOUSE OF LORDS. See PARLIAMENT.

HOUSE OF REPRESENTATIVES. See CONGRESS OF THE UNITED STATES.

HOUSE SNAKE. See MILK SNAKE.

HOUSE SPARROW. See ENGLISH SPARROW.

HOUSING, the provision of permanent shelter for human habitations, especially in large numbers. The term also includes the social, economic, and political problems involved in meeting adequately the need for dwellings of the large, low-income groups of the population. The history of housing is inseparably connected with the social and economic development of mankind.

At the dawn of civilization, when nomadic tribes settled down in permanent habitations, they gathered their dwellings in small groups for social, economic, or military reasons, forming the agricultural village. As trade developed, merchants and artisans gathered in larger villages, and the industrial city came into being. The buildings of the ancient cities were mostly one-story, one-family houses, which contained the workshop, as well as the habitation of the family. Even in ancient Mesopotamia cities were laid out on a large scale, with well-constructed streets and with piping for water supply and for sewage. Later, as city planning (q.v.) advanced, separate sections were assigned to the different trades and industries. Ancient cities were of necessity surrounded by defensive walls, and the impossibility of moving the walls imposed a physical limitation on the size of the city. As commerce and industry continued to draw more inhabitants into the city, houses were built with as many stories as construction techniques would permit, and were crowded with inhabitants from cellar to roof.

With the fall of the Roman Empire, the barbarian invasions, and the plagues of the Middle Ages, city populations markedly decreased, and a more agricultural economy, typified by the feudal manor house surrounded by retainers' cottages, prevailed. The Industrial Revolution, however, caused a renewal of the urban shift in population, and cities of crowded multifamily houses again became the rule.

The rise in land prices attendant upon urban development led in the modern city to a development of apartment houses and tenements. Low-income families are forced to live in restricted quarters, and the requirements of hygiene and morality are often neglected. A large proportion of their income is expended for rent, particularly by the poorest families; for example, in the period preceding World War I, the average European worker paid about fifteen percent of the family income for rent, while the average middle-class family paid only eight percent.

The problem of providing adequate housing for the great bulk of the population arises from the condition that in times of prosperity, although demands for housing increase, construction of new housing declines from competition with the more profitable industrial construction, and wages lag behind building costs to such an extent that rents cannot be increased sufficiently to make new construction profitable.

Governmental activity in the field of housing began in several European countries with a form of rent control during the inflationary period following World War I. Fixing rents was successful in reducing the proportion of income expended for housing, and assisted greatly in restoring the stability of the national currencies, but, by reducing the gross income from rented property to a point below even bare maintenance costs, it drove private capital out of the field and resulted in an acute housing shortage. Housing for the great bulk of the population came to be regarded as a public utility, and various methods of public administration of housing programs and of public aid to private enterprise were tried, but, generally, with indifferent success.

United States. Much of the housing of Colonial times was inadequate and unsanitary, and the urban trend of population, caused by the 19th-century development of the factory system (see FACTORY AND FACTORY SYSTEM), was reinforced by immigration from Europe. Agitation for governmental regulations to improve conditions, however, was not widespread until the middle of the 19th century (see BUILDING ACTS), and not generally effective until the early years of the 20th century, when Tenement House Laws were enacted by various States and cities.

Aside from such regulations, government agencies left housing to private enterprise until World War I, when a shortage of housing for war workers caused the Federal government, through the Housing Division of the Shipping Board and the U.S. Housing Corporation, to build 15,764 family units which, after the war, were sold to private individuals. With the wartime and postwar decline in housing construction, however, the shortage of housing amounted by 1921 to a million and a quarter dwellings. The shortage caused congested living conditions, and in several areas (in the States of Maine, Massachusetts, and Wisconsin, and in Washington, D.C., and New York City), rent-control measures were enacted. California formed a State corporation to build low-cost houses for returning veterans and finance them at favorable terms; New York instituted a program of tax exemption to aid limited-dividend housing corporations.

Aid to housing became a policy of the Federal government with the passage in 1932 of the Emergency Relief and Construction Act. The program was extended in 1933 under the National Industrial Recovery Act, which set up the Federal Emergency Administration of Public Works (later Public Works Administration), and authorized its administrator to construct, finance, or aid any slum-clearance project. Among similar agencies established about that time were the Home Owners Loan Corporation, to relieve the distress of home owners unable to refinance their mortgages, and the Federal Housing Administration, to stimulate building with private capital by insuring mortgage loans.

The Housing Act of 1937 established the United States Housing Authority to finance the projects of State and municipal housing authorities by loans, up to ninety percent of the cost of the project, to be amortized over sixty years. When this aid was not sufficient to make the housing available to low-income families, the USHA was authorized by the Act to make further annual grants, requiring corresponding contributions from the local authority. To insure that the housing would be available to low-income groups, regulations were established requiring the exclusion of families with income greater than five times the cost of rent and utilities (six times, when the family contained three or more dependent minors). By 1939, when the USHA was placed under the jurisdiction of the Federal Works Agency, it had made grants providing housing for 102,000 families in 129 communities.

Under the rearmament program for World War II, The Federal Works Agency engaged in the provision of housing for workers in national-defense industries. Much of this housing was provided by new construction; in several cases entire new communities were built. The buildings were mostly of permanent construction, but, especially when no postwar use was in prospect, semipermanent and temporary structures were erected. In the postwar housing shortage, however, many of the temporary structures were continued in use, and temporary military constructions, such as barracks, were converted into living quarters for returning veterans and their families. Activity in new construction of housing expanded, and in 1946 more than 670,000 new family units were started.

In 1947 the Federal housing agencies were consolidated into the Housing and Home Finance Agency, which consisted of the Federal Housing Administration, the Public Housing Agency (qq.v.), and the Home Loan Bank Board. Under the impetus of government aid administered by these agencies, and with the gradual return to normal supply of building materials and supplies, housing construction accelerated. Construction of 849,000 nonfarm family units was started in 1947, and in 1950 1,396,000 units were built, an all-time peak; the previous record, 937,000 units, was established in 1925. In 1953 the total was 1,103,800 units.

In the period of 1947 to 1949, the Housing and Home Finance Agency, through its subsidiary bodies, also engaged in the disposal to private individuals and corporations of more than 440,000 family units of wartime emergency construction still remaining in government hands. Among these government-held properties were 2200 family units in the so-called "greenbelt" communities: Greenbelt, Md., near Washington, D.C.; Greendale, near Milwaukee, Wisc.; and Greenhills, near Cincinnati, Ohio. These communities were started during the depression by the Resettlement Administration of the Federal government and were intended to serve as models of planned suburban communities, or satellite towns, for moderate-income workers in the nearby cities. They were laid out, on a plan similar to that of Radburn, N.J., with particular attention given to the arrangement of residential areas in respect to stores, schools, and churches, with separation of pedestrian

Brown Brothers

A. E. Housman (from a pencil sketch)

and vehicular traffic, and with the provision of adequate park and playground areas.

Another important factor in postwar housing development was the increase in carefully planned private housing developments built not for speculation but as long-term investments by financial institutions and insurance companies.

HOUSING AND HOME FINANCE AGENCY, an independent agency of the U.S. government, created in July, 1947. It superseded the National Housing Agency, which had been created early in 1942 in accordance with the First War Powers Act of 1941. The Housing and Home Finance Agency is entrusted with the administration of all housing functions of the Federal government; its duties include the co-ordination of housing policies and programs with the general economic and fiscal policies of the government. It is composed of the following units: the National Housing Council, the Home Loan Bank Board, the Federal Housing Administration (qq.v.), and the Public Housing Administration. At the head of the Housing and Home Finance Agency is an administrator, who has responsibility for the supervision of the constituent agencies and also for the operation and disposition of temporary housing erected by the government during World War II.

HOUSMAN, ALFRED EDWARD (1859–1936), English classical scholar and poet, elder broth-

er of Laurence Housman (q.v.). Alfred Housman was educated at Oxford University. From 1892 to 1911 he was professor of Latin at University College, London, and from 1911 to 1936 at Cambridge University. Housman was considered one of the foremost English classical scholars of his time. He wrote extensively for periodicals devoted to classical studies, and edited editions of the Latin poets Juvenal, Lucan, and Manilius. Housman was the author of several volumes of poetry remarkable for their simplicity of diction, lyric beauty, and pessimistic thought. The first, *A Shropshire Lad* (1896), was slow to find popularity, but by the time of publication of the second volume, *Last Poems* (1922), the individual character of Housman's work had become appreciated and the volume was an instant success; today Housman occupies a permanent place in English literature. Two volumes of his verse appeared posthumously, *More Poems* (1936) and *Collected Poems of A. E. Housman* (1940).

HOUSMAN, LAURENCE (1865–   ), English author and artist, born in London, and educated at South Kensington. He was the younger brother of Alfred Edward Housman (q.v.). Laurence Housman was a book illustrator, poet, novelist, and playwright. Among the books he illustrated are *Jump to Glory Jane* (1892) by George Meredith, and *Goblin Market* (1893) by Christina Rossetti. His works include the volumes of verse *Spikenard* (1898) and *Mendicant Rhymes* (1906), and the novels *An Englishwoman's Love Letters* (1900) and *Sabrina Warham* (1904). He is perhaps best known for his plays, which include *Prunella* (in collaboration with Harley Granville-Baker, 1906), *Victoria Regina* (1934), and *Jacob* (1942). Housman was also the author of a memoir of his brother, *A. E. H.* (1937); *Samuel the Kingmaker* (1944); *Back Words and Fore Words* (1945); *The Family Honour* (1950); and *Old Testament Plays* (1951).

HOUSSAY, BERNARDO ALBERTO (1887–   ), Argentine physiologist, born in Buenos Aires, and educated at the National University of Buenos Aires. He was on the faculty of that university from 1907 to 1946, when, having fallen out of favor with the government, he was retired, ostensibly because he was eligible for an old-age pension. From 1944 he was director of the Institute of Biology and Experimental Medicine. Houssay is known for his research on snake and spider bites; however, the work for which he was awarded half of the 1947 Nobel Prize in medicine was done on diabetes. Houssay showed the significance of the hormone produced by the frontal lobe of the pituitary gland in causing this disease. See SUGAR, METABOLISM OF.

HOUSSAYE, the name of two French men of letters, father and son. **1.** ARSÈNE, originally ARSÈNE HOUSSET (1815–96), born in Bruyères. From 1849 to 1856 he was administrator of the Comédie Française, the national theater of France. He was the author of many novels; of biographies of Voltaire, Mademoiselle de la Vallière, and others; of *Histoire du Quarante et Unième Fauteuil de l'Académie Française* (1855); and of *Confessions* (1885–91), an autobiography. **2.** HENRI (1848–1911), historian, born in Paris. He is noted for his works on the Napoleonic period, which include *1814, Histoire de la Campagne de France et la Chute de l'Empire* (1888); *1815* (three parts, 1893, 1899, and 1905); and *Iéna et la Campagne de 1806* (1912). Henry Houssaye became a member of the Institute of France in 1895.

HOUSTON, inland seaport, port of entry, and county seat of Harris Co., Tex., situated at the head of the Houston Ship Channel, 57 miles w. of Galveston Bay and the Gulf of Mexico. It is served by seven railroads, by major air lines, and by coastal and ocean steamship lines. The tidal channel which extends along the San Jacinto R. and Buffalo Bayou, connecting the port of Houston with the Gulf, has been continuously widened and deepened since 1919. It provides a turning basin in Houston's harbor with a minimum depth of 34 ft. In addition, the city is a terminal of the Intracoastal Canal, giving it access to the Mississippi R. and other important inland waterways.

Houston is the largest city of Texas, and one of the leading seaports and industrial centers of the U.S. It ranks first among the ports of Texas in tonnage and diversity of exports, and is a leading petroleum-refining center, and a concentration point and processing center for cotton. Rice, sulfur, livestock, and lumber are other basic commodities of the city's trade, shipping, and industry. In addition to petroleum refineries and tank farms, cotton compresses, storage warehouses, and cottonseed-oil mills, the city contains flour mills, grain elevators, meat-packing plants, food-processing plants, rice mills, breweries, pulp and paper mills, railroad shops, shipyards, foundries, machine shops, printing and publishing plants, and plants producing oil-field equipment, synthetic

rubber, paint, chemicals, cement, iron, steel, iron and steel products, metal containers, clothing, fertilizers, and furniture.

Educational and medical institutions in Houston include Rice Institute (q.v.), one of the largest privately endowed universities in the U.S.; the University of Houston, established in 1934; the Houston College for Negroes (1926); Baylor Medical College, the school of dentistry of the University of Texas; and the Texas Medical Center, which includes a large U.S. Naval Hospital. Among cultural institutions are a museum of fine arts and a museum of natural history. The municipal park area covers approximately 3000 acres, and includes a well-stocked zoological garden. The San Jacinto Monument and Museum, a historic State park at the San Jacinto Battlefield, is situated 23 miles E. of Houston. The monument, which is 570 ft. in height, commemorates the decisive victory won by the Texans over Mexican forces on April 21, 1836.

Houston was founded shortly after the Bat-

In the business section of Houston, Texas

Sam Houston (from an old print)

tle of San Jacinto, and was named in honor of Gen. Sam Houston, hero of that battle. In 1837 it became the first capital of the Republic of Texas, remaining the capital until 1839. It was incorporated as a city in 1840, and was again the capital from 1842 to 1845, when the seat of government was returned to Austin. In 1928 Houston, one of the most thriving cities of the United States, was the site of the National Democratic Convention. Population of the city (1940) 384,514; (1950) 596,163.

HOUSTON, DAVID FRANKLIN (1866–1940), American educator and public official, born in Monroe, N.C., and educated at South Carolina College and Harvard University. From 1894 to 1902 he was professor of political science at the University of Texas, of which, from 1905 to 1908, he served as president. Between 1902 and 1905 he was president of the Agricultural and Mechanical College of Texas. Houston was chancellor of Washington University from 1908 to 1916. In 1913 he was appointed secretary of agriculture in President Woodrow Wilson's cabinet, and he held this post until 1920, when he was appointed secretary of the treasury. He resigned from the latter post in 1921 after the election of Warren Harding to the presidency in 1920. He was the author of *A Critical Study of Nullification in South Carolina* (1896) and *Eight Years with Wilson's Cabinet.*

HOUSTON, SAM(UEL) (1793–1863), American soldier and political leader, born in Rockbridge County, Va. After his father's death in 1806 his family moved to Tennessee, and when he was about fifteen years of age young Houston ran away from home to avoid working as a clerk in a trader's store. He then lived with the Cherokee Indians of E. Tennessee for about three years. During the War of 1812 he enlisted in the U.S. Army as a private, served under Andrew Jackson in fighting the Creek Indians, and was promoted to lieutenant.

He entered a law office in Nashville after the war and was admitted to the bar. From 1823 to 1827 Houston represented Tennessee in Congress, and in 1827 was elected governor of the State. In 1829, three months after he was married, he and his wife separated; he then resigned his governorship, without explanation, and returned to live with the Cherokees, who formally adopted him as a member of their nation. He later represented the Cherokees in Washington to expose the frauds practiced upon them by government agents.

In 1832 he was commissioned by President Jackson to negotiate treaties with the Indian tribes in Texas for the protection of American traders. He decided to settle in Texas, and became a popular leader and an outstanding figure in its early history. In November, 1835, he was chosen commander in chief of the Texan army in the Texan Revolution against Mexico; his victory at San Jacinto and capture of Antonio Lopez de Santa Anna (q.v.) won the Texans their independence. Houston was elected president of Texas in 1836 and served until 1838, when his term expired; he was elected again in 1841 and served for three years. With the admission of Texas as a State of the Union in 1845, Houston was elected one of its first U.S. senators, serving from 1846 to 1859. In 1859 he was elected governor of Texas. He opposed secession of the State from the Union, and in March, 1861, after the outbreak of the Civil War, when he refused to swear allegiance to the Confederacy, he was declared deposed. The city of Houston, Texas, was named in his honor during his first term as president of Texas.

HOVENWEEP NATIONAL MONUMENT, a national monument in s.w. Colorado and s.e. Utah, established in 1923. It comprises 299 acres, about equally divided between the two States. In the Colorado portion are the Keely Canyon group, containing five large prehistoric masonry buildings on the canyon rim and several small cliff dwellings in the canyon walls; and the Hackberry Canyon group, with high-walled towers honeycombed by many chambers. In Utah are the Cajon Canyon group and the Ruin Canyon group. Among the prehistoric relics in the latter is a building, known as Hovenweep Castle, with walls 20 ft. high and 66 ft. long, several towers, and large rooms.

HOWARD, name of a distinguished family of English noblemen. The head of the family is the duke of Norfolk, premier duke and hereditary earl marshal of England; other lines include the earls of Northampton, Nottingham, Arundel, and Carlisle. The family traces its ancestry to Sir William Howard, or Haward (d. 1308), a justice of common pleas in 1297. His descendant Sir Robert Howard married the daughter of Thomas Mowbray, Duke of Norfolk; their descendants were given the dukedom. Among the important members of the family are the following.

1. JOHN (1430?–85), 1st Duke of Norfolk (of the Howard line), also known as Jack of Norfolk. He was knighted in 1461, and was created baron by King Henry VI in 1470. He fought in France for Edward IV in 1475, but on Edward's death he supported Richard III, who made him Duke of Norfolk and earl marshal of England in 1483. He died with Richard in the battle at Bosworth, and his titles were attainted by the victorious Henry VII. **2.** THOMAS (1443–1524), 2nd Duke of Norfolk, Earl of Surrey, son of the 1st duke. He supported King Edward IV, and was created Earl of Surrey in 1483. At the battle at Bosworth, he was wounded and taken prisoner; his titles were attainted, and he was imprisoned until 1489. On his release his earldom was restored, and he was placed in command of the defense of the Scottish border. In 1513 he led the forces which defeated the Scots at Flodden Field, and in the following year the attainder of his father was reversed, and he became Duke of Norfolk. **3.** THOMAS (1473–1554), 3rd Duke of Norfolk, Earl of Surrey, eldest son of the 2nd duke. He commanded the English vanguard at Flodden Field, and was made earl when his father regained the family dukedom. On the death of his father in 1524 he succeeded to the dukedom, and became the most powerful peer in England. Norfolk led the party opposed to the policies of Cardinal Wolsey, and favored the divorce of King Henry VIII from Catherine of Aragon and the king's marriage to Anne Boleyn,

Norfolk's niece. He became president of the king's council in 1529, and as lord steward he presided at the trial and execution of Anne Boleyn. In 1536 he repressed the rebellion of the Pilgrimage of Grace, and in 1540 he arrested Thomas Cromwell (q.v.). He led the English forces on expeditions into Scotland in 1542 and into France in 1544. With the execution of his niece Catherine Howard (q.v.), he lost his influence at court, and, when his son Henry Howard (q.v.) was arrested for treason, he was charged with complicity, and was condemned and attainted with his son. His son was executed, but the subsequent death of the king prevented the execution of Norfolk. He was held in prison throughout the reign of Edward VI, but on the accession of Queen Mary in 1553 he was released and his lands and titles were restored. **4.** THOMAS (1536–72), 4th Duke of Norfolk, son of Henry Howard. He succeeded to the dukedom on the death of his grandfather, the 3rd duke. In 1568 he became president of the commission appointed by Queen Elizabeth to investigate the affairs of Mary, Queen of Scots. The following year he was arrested and imprisoned, by order of Elizabeth, for plotting to marry Mary, who was at that time in his custody. After his release in 1570 he began negotiations with Philip II of Spain in regard to Philip's proposed invasion of England. His plot was discovered in 1571 and he was arrested; he was beheaded the following year.

5. HENRY (1540–1614), 1st Earl of Northampton, younger brother of the 4th Duke of Norfolk. He was suspected of complicity in his brother's plot to marry Mary, Queen of Scots, and was arrested several times. His attack on judicial astrology, *A Defensative against the Poyson of Supposed Prophecies* (1583), was declared to contain treason and heresy, and led to his imprisonment for a time. After the accession of James I, however, he received many honors; he was created earl in 1604, and was made lord privy seal in the same year. He was commissioner at the trials of Sir Walter Raleigh, of Guy Fawkes, and of Henry Garnett. **6.** CHARLES (1536–1624), 1st Earl of Nottingham, 2nd Baron Howard of Effingham, nephew of the 3rd Duke of Norfolk. He succeeded to the barony on the death of his father, William Howard (1510?–73), and was made knight of the Garter in 1574. In 1585 he became lord high admiral, and commanded the English fleet in the defeat of the Armada (q.v.) in 1588. With Robert Devereux (q.v.),

2nd Earl of Essex, he commanded the English naval expedition which in 1596 sank the Spanish fleet and sacked the city of Cadiz. In 1601 he took a leading part in suppressing the rebellion of Essex. He served on many royal commissions, including those for the trial of Mary, Queen of Scots, in 1586, for the trial of Essex in 1601, for the union of England and Scotland in 1604, and for the trial of the conspirators of the Gunpowder Plot (q.v.) in 1606. **7.** PHILIP (1557–95), 13th Earl of Arundel (1st in Howard line), eldest son of the 4th Duke of Norfolk. Prevented by the attainder of his father in 1572 from inheriting the dukedom, he became Earl of Arundel on the death of his maternal grandfather in 1580. He was suspected of plotting against the government of Queen Elizabeth and was ordered by the queen to remain under house arrest. He attempted to leave England in 1584, and was arrested and sentenced to life imprisonment. He was released after a time, but was rearrested on a charge of high treason and condemned to death. He died in prison. **8.** THOMAS (1585?–1646), 2nd Earl of Arundel, Earl of Surrey and Norfolk, son of Philip. At the accession of King James I, he was given the earldoms of his father and the baronies of his grandfather, 4th Duke of Norfolk. In 1641 he left England and settled in Padua. For contributing large sums of money to the cause of Charles I, he was made Earl of Norfolk in 1644. He is known chiefly as a collector of works of art; his collection, including the famous Arundel Marbles, was the first large-scale collection gathered in Great Britain. His grandson Thomas (fl. 1660) became 5th Duke of Norfolk in 1660 by reversal of the attainder of 1572; Thomas' brother Henry (1628–84), 6th Duke of Norfolk, presented the Arundel Marbles to Oxford University in 1667.

9. CHARLES (1629–85), 1st Earl of Carlisle. He was the great-grandson of Lord William Howard (1563–1640), third son of the 4th Duke of Norfolk. Charles distinguished himself in 1651, fighting for the Commonwealth in the battle of Worcester; he became a member of the council of state in 1653, and a member of Cromwell's House of Lords in 1657. In 1659 he favored the restoration of the monarchy, and in 1661 King Charles II created him Baron Dacre of Gilsland, Viscount Howard of Morpeth, and Earl of Carlisle. He served as ambassador to Russia, Sweden, and Denmark in 1663-64, and as governor of Jamaica from 1677 to 1681. **10.** FREDERICK (1748–1825), 5th Earl of Carlisle.

In 1778 he headed the commission sent by Lord North to attempt a reconciliation with the North American Colonies. He was viceroy of Ireland from 1780 to 1782, and later was active in the opposition to the ministry of William Pitt the younger. He was the author of several poems, and the tragedies *The Father's Revenge* (1783) and *The Stepmother* (1800). **11.** GEORGE WILLIAM FREDERICK (1802–64), 7th Earl of Carlisle, born in London, and educated at Christ Church, Oxford University. He was undersecretary for Ireland from 1835 to 1841, and succeeded to the earldom in 1848. He was viceroy of Ireland from 1855 to 1858, and again from 1859 to 1864. Interested in the problem of juvenile delinquency, he established a model reformatory on his estate. He wrote a lecture, *The Life and Writings of Pope* (1851); a tragedy, *The Last of the Greeks* (1828); and a book of travels, *Diary in Turkish and Greek Waters* (1854).

HOWARD, BRONSON CROCKER (1842–1908), American playwright, born in Detroit, Mich. He worked on the staff of various New York newspapers until 1870, when his play *Saratoga,* produced by Augustin Daly, met with considerable success. This production, the first native American drama to achieve serious recognition from theatrical producers, paved the way for the development of the American theater in the latter part of the 19th century. Among Howard's other plays are *The Banker's Daughter* (1878); *Young Mrs. Winthrop* (1882); *One of our Girls* (1885); *The Henrietta* (1887), a satire on the American business world; *Shenandoah* (1889), a drama of the Civil War; and *Aristocracy* (1892), a satire on American Anglomania. *Shenandoah* was produced by Charles Frohman, and was instrumental in establishing Frohman's career as a producer.

HOWARD, CATHERINE (1520?–42), Queen of England as the fifth wife of Henry VIII. She was a granddaughter of Thomas Howard, 2nd Duke of Norfolk, and, because her father was poor, was brought up chiefly in the home of her grandmother, the Duchess of Norfolk. There she entertained several lovers, among them her music teacher, her cousin Thomas Culpepper, and a retainer of the Duchess. Catherine's meetings with the king were arranged by Stephen Gardiner, Bishop of Winchester, and, after the divorce of Anne of Cleves on July 9, 1540, Henry and Catherine were married on July 28. In November, 1541, Catherine was accused of immoral conduct; she admitted prenuptial indiscretions, but denied marital infidelity. Two of her lovers were executed, but the queen was cleared. Later, evidence of her misconduct after marriage was produced; a bill of attainder passed Parliament, and Catherine was beheaded.

HOWARD, HENRY (about 1517–47), English soldier and poet, by courtesy Earl of Surrey after 1524 when his father, Lord Thomas Howard (see HOWARD, family), became 3rd Duke of Norfolk. Howard received a classical education at the English and French courts, and in 1532 he married Lady Frances de Vere, daughter of the 15th Earl of Oxford. He served in the war with Scotland in 1542, and in 1543 fought in Flanders with the English army on the side of the Holy Roman emperor Charles V, who was seeking to acquire the Netherlands for the empire. The following year he was field marshal under his father's command, and was wounded at the siege of Montreuil, in the Pas de Calais; in 1545 and 1546 he was commander of the garrison of Boulogne. Howard and his father were arrested for treason on charges brought by their enemies at the English court, and in 1547 they were condemned and Howard was executed.

His love poems, like those of Sir Thomas Wyatt (q.v.), with whom Howard shares the honor of having introduced the sonnet form into English literature, show the influence of Italian models. His translation of the second and third books of the *Æneid* was written in blank verse of five iambic feet, the first use of this form in English. Forty of his poems were printed in 1557 in *Songs and Sonettes written by the ryght honorable Lorde Henry Howard late Earle of Surrey, and other,* and in the same year his translations from Vergil appeared as *Certain Bokes of Virgiles Aeneis turned into English meter.*

HOWARD, OLIVER OTIS (1830–1909), American army officer and administrator, born in Leeds, Me., and educated at Bowdoin College and the U.S. Military Academy at West Point. He was assistant professor of mathematics at West Point from 1857 to 1861. At the outbreak of the Civil War he became colonel of the Third Maine Volunteers and commanded a brigade in the first Battle of Bull Run. As brigadier general of volunteers he participated in the Peninsular campaign, and received a wound which necessitated the amputation of his right arm. He was later promoted to the rank of major general of volunteers, and in 1863, as commander of the Eleventh Army Corps, took a conspicuous part in the battles of Chancellorsville and Gettysburg. He then served in the Chattanooga campaign. In 1864 he commanded the right wing of General William T. Sherman's March to the Sea, and at the end of the year was appointed brigadier general in the regular army and brevet major general.

After the war, from 1865 to 1874, he was commissioner of the Freedman's Bureau (q.v.). He was active in the founding of Howard University (q.v.) and served as president of that institution from 1869 to 1874. He was subsequently superintendent of the U.S. Military Academy at West Point in 1881 and 1882. In 1886 he was appointed major general in the regular army and in 1894 he retired from the service. In 1895 he founded the Lincoln Memorial University at Cumberland Gap, Tenn.

HOWARD, ROY WILSON (1883–   ), American newspaperman, born in Gano, Ohio, and educated at the Manual Training High School in Indianapolis. In 1902 he joined the staff of the Indianapolis *News* as a reporter, and, after working for various papers in Indianapolis, St. Louis, and Cincinnati, became the New York correspondent of the Scripps-McRae League in 1906. Later in the same year he became the New York City manager of the Publishers' Press Association. In 1907, when that organization was absorbed by the United Press Association, he remained its New York manager. Five years later he was appointed general manager of the United Press Association, and in 1921 became chairman of its board and business director of the Newspaper Enterprise Association, and of all the Scripps-McRae (now Scripps-Howard) chain of newspapers. He was editor and president of the New York *World-Telegram* from 1931, and president of the Scripps-Howard newspapers from 1936 to 1952.

HOWARD, SIDNEY COE (1891–1939), American playwright, born in Oakland, Calif., and educated at the University of California and Harvard University. During World War I he served as an officer in the American aviation service. In 1919 he joined the staff of *Life,* a magazine of humor, and his first play, *Swords,* was produced in 1921. He became a feature writer on the staff of the *New Republic* and of *Hearst's International-Cosmopolitan* magazine in 1923. His play *They Knew What They Wanted* (1925, revived 1949) won the Pulitzer Prize for 1925. Among his other theatrical works are *The Silver Cord* (1926), *Yellowjack* (1928), *Half-Gods* (1929),

N.Y.U. Hall of Fame

Portrait bust of Elias Howe

The Late Christopher Bean (1933), *Dodsworth* (from the novel by Sinclair Lewis, 1934), and *Paths of Glory* (with Humphrey Cobb, 1935). Howard also adapted for the American stage several plays from the French, Spanish, and Hungarian, and wrote the screen adaptations of such popular novels as *Arrowsmith, Dodsworth,* and *Gone with the Wind.* The Playwrights Company, of which he was a member, established the Sidney Howard Memorial Award in his honor in 1940; the award is presented annually to a new playwright who has written a play of merit produced during the current season.

HOWARD UNIVERSITY, a coeducational institution of higher education for Negroes, founded in Washington, D.C., in 1867, and named for its first president, Oliver Otis Howard (q.v.). The functions of the university, formerly controlled by the Department of the Interior, were transferred to the Federal Security Agency in 1940. The institution offers courses leading to bachelors' and masters' degrees in the liberal arts; civil, electrical, and mechanical engineering; law; pharmacy; and theology. It is supported by a combination of private funds and Congressional appropriations. In 1953–54 there were 4317 students enrolled, all attending classes full time, and the faculty numbered 357. In the same period the endowment was $1,721,433 and there were over 291,000 volumes in the library.

HOWE, ELIAS (1819–67), American inventor, born in Spencer, Mass. When he was seventeen, Howe apprenticed himself to a manufacturer of textile machinery in Lowell, Mass., and learned the trade of machinist. In 1837, while he was employed in a watchmaking shop, he conceived the idea for a sewing machine and spent all his spare time in the next five years in its development. He obtained a patent for the machine in 1846 and, after building only four of them in the U.S., went to England, where he sold his patent rights to a corset manufacturer for $1250. In 1849 Howe returned to the U.S., and found that his patents had been infringed and that a number of sewing machines had been built and were in use. He instituted lawsuits and finally, after expensive and lengthy proceedings, won his suits and derived considerable wealth from his invention.

HOWE, JOSEPH (1804–73), Canadian editor and statesman, born in Halifax, Nova Scotia. Howe learned the printing business in the office of his father's paper, the *Weekly Chronicle,* and in 1828 he became owner and editor of the *Nova Scotian* (after 1843 amalgamated with the *Morning Chronicle*). In his trenchant editorials in this paper, Howe advocated many liberal reforms and sponsored the development of Nova Scotian communications. He became a member of the Nova Scotian provincial assembly in 1836, and spent the next twelve years working for the reformation of the Nova Scotian government, advocating responsible government for his fellow citizens. This reform was granted by the British Empire in 1848, and Howe served as provincial secretary from 1848 to 1854, when he was appointed chief commissioner of railways. From 1860 to 1863 Howe was prime minister of Nova Scotia; he spent the following six years opposing the confederation of Nova Scotia with Canada but, when his cause was finally defeated, in 1869, accepted the post of president of the council in the Canadian government. Later in the same year he became Canadian secretary of state, and in 1873, a few weeks before his death, he was appointed lieutenant governor of the province of Nova Scotia.

HOWE, JULIA WARD (1819–1910), American poet and reformer, born in New York City. From an early age she contributed poetry to magazines and periodicals. In 1843 she married the philanthropist Samuel Gridley Howe and from that time on she was associated with him in his humanitarian work and in editing the Boston *Commonwealth,* an antislavery paper to which she contributed poems, editorials, and essays. During the Civil War, in February, 1862, the *Atlantic Monthly* published her best-known poem, *The Battle Hymn of the Republic,* which immediately achieved great popularity among the Union troops, who sang it to the tune of *John Brown's Body.* From 1868 on she was associated with the movement for women's emancipation, and she was a founder and for many years a president of both the New England Women's Club and the Association for the Advancement of Women. In 1872 she was a delegate to the World's Prison Reform Congress in London, and in the same year founded the World Peace Association. She lectured widely in support of these causes, occasionally preaching in Unitarian churches. Among her works are the collection of poems *From Sunset Ridge: Poems Old and New* (1898) and the biographical works *A Memoir of Dr. Samuel Gridley Howe* (1876), *Life of Margaret Fuller* (1883), *Reminiscences* (1899), and sketches of *Representative Women of New England* (1905).

HOWE, RICHARD, EARL HOWE (1726–99), English admiral, born in London. He entered the navy in 1740 and served in the Seven Years' War. In 1770 he became a rear admiral, and in 1775 vice-admiral. The following year Howe was appointed commander of the American coast, and there, with an inferior force, he resisted a powerful attack by French ships under the command of Comte Jean Baptiste d'Estaing. He became First Lord of the Admiralty in 1783 and received an earldom in 1788. Upon the outbreak of war with France in 1793, he took command of the English fleet and gained a spectacular victory in the battle of the "Glorious First of June".

HOWE, SIR WILLIAM, 5th VISCOUNT HOWE (1729–1814), British army officer, born in London. Howe entered the army in 1746 and gained distinction as one of the most brilliant junior officers in the service. In 1775 he was second in command under General Thomas Gage (1721–87) and commanded British troops in the Battle of Bunker Hill (q.v.); later in that year he succeeded Gage as commander in chief of all British forces in America. In 1776 he defeated the Americans on Long Island, took the City of New York, and won the battles of White Plains and Brandywine. During the winter of 1777–78, when Washington had set up quarters at Valley Forge, Howe stayed in Philadelphia with his troops. He was severely criticized for this inactivity, and in the spring of 1778 he re-

signed and returned to England claiming that he had not received sufficient support from the home government. Four years later he was commissioned lieutenant general of ordnance and in 1793 was made a full general. He was a member of Parliament for Nottingham (1758–80), holding his seat even while in America.

HOWELLS, WILLIAM DEAN (1837–1920), American man of letters, born in Martin's Ferry, Ohio. After learning the printing trade from his father, he worked successively, beginning in 1851, as a compositor and a writer on several small Ohio newspapers; from 1856 to 1861 he wrote for the *Ohio State Journal* at Columbus. Following the Presidential nominations in 1860, he wrote a campaign biography of Abraham Lincoln, and was later appointed U.S. consul at Venice, Italy. Returning to the U.S. in 1865, he became assistant editor of the literary magazine, *Atlantic Monthly,* in 1866, and was its editor in chief from 1871 through 1881. After resigning from his editorship, he devoted the rest of his life to writing, and achieved a pre-eminent position in American literature through his realistic fiction and his many works of literary criticism.

Howell's work in the field of fiction comprised more than thirty novels, the first of which were comedies of manners and studies of contrasting character types. In this category belong *The Lady of the Aroostook* (1879), *A Fearful Responsibility* (1881), and *Dr. Breen's Practice* (1881). After 1881, when he began serializing his stories in the *Century*

William Dean Howells

Magazine, Howells wrote novels containing realistic descriptions of American life. The chief works of this period were *A Woman's Reason* (1883), a study of Boston Back Bay society; and *The Rise of Silas Lapham* (1885), a study of a typical self-made businessman. With the novel *Annie Hilburn* (1889), dealing with class contrasts in a New England town, Howells became increasingly interested in the problems of industrialism and labor. He subsequently wrote several other novels treating social and economic problems, including *A Traveler from Altruria* (1894) and *Through the Eye of the Needle* (1907). His last novel, *The Leatherwood God* (1916), dealt with the Ohio of his youth. Howells' critical works include *Criticism and Fiction* (1891), in which he summed up his literary credo and defended realism; *My Literary Passions* (1895); and *Literature and Life* (1902). He also contributed many short stories to magazines; and his stay in Italy resulted in several works, including *Venetian Life* (1866), *Italian Journeys* (1867), and *Modern Italian Poets* (1887).

HOWITZER. See ARTILLERY; ORDNANCE.

HOWLING MONKEY, HOWLER, STENTOR, or ALOUATTE, common name of any of several species of South and Central American monkeys comprising the genus *Alouatta* of the family Cebidae. These monkeys have a powerful characteristic roar which can be heard at least two miles away. Their hyoid bone (the bone supporting the tongue) is enlarged and hollow, and opens into a greatly dilated voice box; the capacious hyoid and voice box provide two huge resonating chambers for the production of sound. Externally the animal is large and heavy, reaching a length of three feet, excluding the long, prehensile tail, and a body weight of over twenty pounds. Its black face is bearded with long black hair in the adult, but beardless in the young monkey. The lower jaw is very wide, and the neck is swollen. The body and tail are covered with thick fur except for the underside of the tip of the tail, which is bare and rough in order to obtain firm support when the animal swings from limb to limb. Howling monkeys live in trees in groups led by one powerful male. They feed on leaves and fruit.

The best-known species of howling monkey is the red howler, *Alouatta macconnelli,* which is metallic red in general color, and has a black face and black feet and hands. The ursine howler, *A. ursina,* is a common Brazilian species. Other howlers include the guariba, or guereba, *A. caraya,* and the araba, *A. straminea.*

HOWRAH, city and district of West Bengal State, Union of India. The city is located on the Hooghly River, which separates it from Calcutta (q.v.), of which it is an industrial suburb. Jute, cottonseed oil, and machinery are produced in the city. The district of Howrah is both agricultural and industrial. It is served by three railroads and by a canal connecting the Hooghly R. with the city of Midnapore. Area of district, 561 sq.m.; pop. (1951) 1,611,373. Pop. of city (1951) 433,630.

HOXIE, VINNIE REAM (1847–1914), American sculptor, born in Madison, Wisconsin. She studied in Paris with Léon Joseph Florentin Bonnat and in Rome. She won a $30,000 government competition for a statue of President Lincoln; the first woman sculptor to receive such a commission, she executed a life-size figure which is in the rotunda of the Capitol at Washington, D.C. Congress later commissioned her to make the heroic statue of Farragut in Farragut Square, Washington. Among her other works were many portrait busts and medallions of prominent Americans, and a number of classical statues. In 1911 she executed the statue of Sequoyah to represent the State of Oklahoma in the statuary hall in the Capitol at Washington.

HOY, second-largest of the Orkney Islands (q.v.), Scotland, situated 2 miles s.w. of Pomona Island. It is 13 m. long and 6 to 8 m. wide. Along the Atlantic coast red sandstone cliffs rise as high as 1000 ft. above sea level. A portion of sandstone detached from this line of rocky coast, and called the Old Man of Hoy, rises 450 ft. above sea level, and is a famous landmark for seafarers. The loftiest peak on the island is Ward Hill (1564 ft.), situated inland. Also in the interior of the island is a sandstone block, the Dwarfie Stone, out of which rooms, apparently once inhabited, were carved. Long Hope, near the s. end of the island, is a fine natural harbor. Area, 62 sq.m.; pop. (1931) 955.

HOYLE, EDMOND (1672–1769), English writer on card and other games. Few details of his life are known. He lived in London for a while, partially supporting himself by giving lessons in the game of whist (q.v.). He drew up for his pupils a *Short Treatise on the Game of Whist,* published in 1742, which systematized the rules of the game in the form followed until 1864. Hoyle also organized the rules of various other games, including backgammon, piquet, and chess. He wrote a book on games which passed through many editions, and which continued to be revised long after his death. Books of game rules are still published today bearing the name of Hoyle.

HRABANUS MAURUS. See RABANUS MAURUS.

HRADEC KRÁLOVÉ (Ger. *Königgrätz*), administrative center of a region of the same name, Czechoslovakia, situated on the Elbe R., about 65 miles N.E. of Prague. The city contains a medical school, which is a branch of Prague University. Hradec Králové is an industrial center containing sawmills, tanneries, and establishments manufacturing machinery, pianos, candles, soap, and confectionery. The city also is the trading center of a rich agricultural region. Area of region, 1986 sq.m.; pop. (1947) 552,780. Pop. of city (1947) 51,480.

HRDLIČKA, ALEŠ (1869–1943), American anthropologist, born in Humpeletz (now Humenné), Bohemia, and educated in medicine in New York City. From 1894 to 1898 he investigated institutionalized insane and mentally defective individuals for the State of New York, and from 1899 to 1903 was in charge of physical anthropology for an expedition sent by the American Museum of Natural History in New York City to southwestern U.S. and Mexico. In 1903 he became assistant curator in charge of the division of physical anthropology at the U.S. Museum in Washington, D.C., and from 1910 until 1942, when he retired, was curator. For the remainder of his life he held the post of associate in anthropology at the Smithsonian Institution.

Hrdlička was one of the foremost anthropometrists in American anthropology; in 1918 he founded, and thereafter edited, the *American Journal of Physical Anthropology,* and he was the founder, in 1929, and first president of the American Association of Physical Anthropologists. He completed an important anthropological survey of Alaska, and was an exponent, largely on anthropometric grounds, of several controversial theories about the evolution and diffusion of ancient man. Among them are the theories that the majority of American Indians were of Asiatic origin, that the Neanderthal man did not represent a species distinct from modern man, and that the beginnings of civilization occurred in Europe rather than in Asia or Asia Minor. Among Hrdlička's important writings were *Physical Anthropology*

(American) (1919), *Anthropometry* (1920), and *Old Americans* (1925).

HROZNÝ, BEDŘICH or FRIEDRICH (1879–1952), Czech archeologist and Orientalist, born in Leszno, Poland, and educated at the universities of Prague, Vienna, Berlin, and London. His earliest field trip was made in 1904 in northern Palestine; in the following year he began to teach at the University of Vienna, and in 1919 was appointed professor of cuneiform research and ancient oriental history at Charles University in Prague. Hrozný's name is most closely associated with his famous solution of the problem of deciphering the Hittite language (q.v.) and his proof that it is an Indo-European tongue. He wrote his first translations and analyses of the language in 1915, basing them upon archeological finds in the cuneiform script made by Hugo Winckler (q.v.) and the German Oriental Society. Though Hrozný's claims were long attacked, his success in deciphering new texts and the support he received from eminent authorities eventually won acceptance of his conclusions. Among his works are *Die Sprache der Hethiter* (1916), *Über die Völker und Sprachen des Alten Chatti-Landes* (1920), and *Hethiter und Inder* (1928).

HSINKING. See CHANGCHUN.

HSÜAN T'UNG, name assumed by PU-YI or PU-I (1906–   ), tenth and last Chinese emperor of the Ch'ing or Manchu dynasty, on his accession to the throne. He was the nephew of the previous emperor, Kuang Hsü, and in 1908 was chosen to succeed to the throne by the Empress Dowager Tzu Hsi; his father, Prince Ch'un, was appointed regent. Though a policy of reform was adopted by the imperial government, the revolution of 1911–12 forced his abdication and established the Republic. From 1912 Hsuan T'ung lived in Peking (now Peiping), studying the Chinese classics and Occidental subjects. At the suggestion of his English tutor he adopted the first name Henry, adding it to his personal name of Pu-yi, and in 1922, immediately after his marriage to Elizabeth Yuang, a member of the Manchu nobility, with full imperial ritual, he abandoned all the ancient Chinese customs. After 1924, when the title of emperor was officially abolished and he was driven from Peking, he was known as Henry Pu-yi. He subsequently lived in the Japanese Concession at Tientsin. In 1931 he was moved to Dairen by the Japanese. In 1932 the Japanese made him chief executive of the puppet state of Manchukuo, of which he was crowned emperor in 1934.

At the end of World War II, in 1945, the Russian army captured him, and in the following year he was released to the authorities of the International War Crimes Tribunal in Tokyo. He testified that the Japanese had forced him into the position of puppet emperor by threats against his life, charging that they had poisoned his wife and forced him to marry a Japanese girl, but admitted that he had signed a contract relinquishing his Manchu dynastic rights in Manchuria to the Japanese in return for the throne of Manchukuo. He was subsequently returned to Russian custody.

HUALAPAI. See WALAPAI.

HUAMBISA, a tribe of South American Indians, of the Jivaroan linguistic stock, dwelling on the borders of Peru and Ecuador, around the junction of the Santiago and upper Marañón rivers at the upper limits of navigation of the Amazon River. They joined the Jivaro (q.v.) tribes in their revolt against Spanish rule in 1599, and took part in the sack of Sevilla del Oro, during which 7000 Spanish women were carried off by the Indians. Evidence of intermarriage with these women still remains in the fair skins and beards of the Huambisa, Jivaro, and several other tribes of the region. The Huambisa continued their incursions into the territories of their white neighbors until well into the 19th century; in 1843 they massacred the entire population of Santa Teresa, a town between the Santiago and Maroni rivers. At the present time they maintain a hostile and nearly complete isolation from both their Indian and white neighbors.

HUASTEC, an isolated tribe of Mayan linguistic stock, living along the Atlantic coast in the state of Vera Cruz in N. Mexico, south of Tampico and the Panuco river. Their language, still spoken by about 20,000 Indians, appears to be an archaic form of other Mayan languages, and some ethnologists believe that the Huastecs were left behind in the great southward migration of the Mayan peoples toward Yucatan and Guatemala. The indigenous Huastecan culture has been shown to be inferior to that of the Mayan peoples as a whole; their conquest by the Aztecs in the middle of the 15th century, with the consequent assimilation of those Toltec-Aztecan culture patterns adaptable to a lowland life, has made their pre-Columbian history exceptionally difficult to trace. In historic times the Huastecs submitted to the Spanish conquerors at an early period in the colonization of Mexico, and were one of the first Indian tribes to become converted to the Christian religion.

HUBBARD, ELBERT GREEN (1856–1915), American writer, editor, and printer, born in Bloomington, Ill. As a youth he worked in print shops and as a free-lance newspaperman in Chicago, and he later worked for a soap factory in Buffalo, N.Y., eventually becoming a partner in the firm. After selling his interest in the soap business Hubbard traveled for some time and finally settled in East Aurora, N.Y. There, in 1895, he founded the Roycroft Shop which produced *de luxe* editions of the classics. Hubbard founded, edited, and wrote, from 1895 until his death, the monthly magazine *The Philistine*; he also wrote, from this time on, a series of monthly biographical sketches known as the *Little Journeys,* which eventually filled fourteen volumes. Among his best-known works are *A Message to Garcia* (1899), an inspirational pamphlet describing the exploit of the American lieutenant Andrew Rowan in delivering a message to the Cuban general Calixto García-Iñiguez; *Time and Chance* (1899); and *The Man of Sorrows* (1904). Hubbard died in the sinking of the S.S. *Lusitania* (q.v.) by a German submarine.

HUBBELL, CARL OWEN (1903–), American baseball player, born in Carthage, Mo. In 1928 Hubbell joined the New York Giants, and remained with them for his entire playing career, which ended in 1943. His great success was due largely to his almost perfect control of the so-called screwball (a pitch which rolls off the inside of the middle finger with a reverse spin). Hubbell was a left-handed pitcher, although he batted right-handed. He pitched a total of 535 games, of which he won 253 and lost 154, a percentage of .621. He was elected to the Baseball Hall of Fame (q.v.) in 1947. Immediately after his retirement, Hubbell was appointed supervisor of the Giant farm system for developing new players in minor-league baseball teams.

HUBERT, SAINT (d. about 727), bishop of Maastricht and Liége. According to the legends told of his life, he was an official of the Austrasian court, and was passionately addicted to hunting. One Good Friday, when he was hunting in spite of the solemnity of the day, a miraculous stag, bearing a luminous crucifix between its antlers, is said to have appeared before him, causing him to be converted from his worldly ways and to spend the rest of his life in holy orders. It is a known fact that he was appointed to the see of Maastricht and Liége in 708. The many conversions with which he is credited earned him the title "Apostle of the Ardennes", and he was said to have cured hydrophobia by means of a miraculous stole he received from heaven. About a hundred years after his death his remains were removed from Liége to a Benedictine abbey on the site of the miraculous apparition of the stag, and the abbey and neighboring village are now known as Saint-Hubert. The incident of the apparition is the subject of a well-known painting by Pieter Brueghel the Elder. Saint Hubert is the patron of hunters, and his feast is celebrated on November 3.

HUBERT DE BURGH. See BURGH, HUBERT DE.

HUC, ÉVARISTE RÉGIS (1813–60), French Roman Catholic missionary, explorer, and writer, born in Toulouse. He entered holy orders and joined the Congregation of the Mission of Saint Vincent de Paul, or Lazarist Fathers. In 1839, shortly after his ordination, he went to China with the Lazarist Fathers' missionary expedition, and spent the following five years in China and Mongolia. In 1844, with a Tibetan convert and Father Joseph Gabet, another Lazarist, Huc set out to explore Tibet. After two years of arduous travel, the three men, disguised as lamas, reached Lhasa, where the Tibetan authorities permitted them to open a chapel, but the Chinese ambassador exerted his influence and had them sent back to Canton. Huc's health had been impaired by the rigors of his travels, and he returned to France in 1852. His account of his voyage, *Souvenirs d'un Voyage dans la Tartarie, le Thibet, et la Chine pendant les Années 1844–46* (2 vols., 1850), was violently attacked as inaccurate, but later explorations confirmed his observations. He also was the author of *L'Empire Chinois* (2 vols., 1854) and *Le Christianisme en Chine, en Tartarie, et au Thibet* (4 vols., 1857–58).

HUCKLEBERRY, common name applied to shrubs of the genus *Gaylussacia,* belonging to the Heath family, named after the French chemist, Joseph Louis Gay-Lussac. The shrubs are native to temperate North America. The pale purple or pale red flowers, borne in racemes, have a five-parted calyx, five-cleft tubular or bell-shaped corolla, ten stamens, and a solitary pistil. The blue to black fruit contains ten bony, seedlike nutlets. Lower surfaces of huckleberry leaves are sprinkled with resinous dots. Black huckleberry, *G. baccata,* native to woodlands and swamps of N.E. United States and E. Canada, is a shrub growing 1 to 3 feet high, producing

edible black fruits. Bear huckleberry, *G. ursina,* native to woodlands of S.E. United States, is a slender shrub, less than a foot high, producing unpalatable reddish-black fruits. Dangleberry, *G. frondosa,* native to E. United States, is a low shrub producing dark-blue sweet fruits. Huckleberries are often cultivated in the U.S. for their foliage and fruit. Common market blueberries, which belong to the related genus *Vaccinium* (q.v.), are commonly but erroneously called huckleberries. Blueberry fruits contain many small seeds rather than ten large seeds as in huckleberry, and blueberry leaves lack the resinous dots found in huckleberry. The he-huckleberry, *Lyonia ligustrina,* native to E. United States, is another related species belonging to the Heath family.

HUDDERSFIELD, municipal, county, and parliamentary borough of the West Riding of Yorkshire, England, located on the Colne R., 16 miles S.W. of Leeds. It is served by several railroads and is connected by canal with the waterway system of Lancashire and Yorkshire. In the 11th century the borough was part of a manor acquired by the De Lacy family. It was incorporated in 1868 and made a county borough in 1888. Huddersfield attained importance with the introduction of the woolen trade in the 17th century, and is today the center of the fancy woolen goods industry of England, producing many types of woolens and worsteds. In addition, the borough contains iron foundries, machine shops, and factories making silk and cotton goods. Pop. (1953 est.) 127,200.

HUDSON, HENRY (?–1611?), English navigator, famous for four great voyages of discovery. Nothing is known of his life before 1607, the year in which he undertook his first expedition for the English Muscovy Company. Commanding a single ship, the *Hopewell,* Hudson touched the shores of Greenland and Spitsbergen, and sailed as far north as 80° 23' in an attempt to find a northeast passage to the Far East. During the following year he sailed again in the same ship under the auspices of the same company, and again attempted unsuccessfully to find a passage, this time by way of Novaya Zemlya. Upon his return the Muscovy Company withdrew their support, and Hudson turned to the Dutch East India Company for fresh funds and a ship to carry on his work. In their employ he sailed from Amsterdam on his third voyage in 1609, in the *Half Moon,* a vessel of about eighty tons, with a mixed Dutch and English crew of eighteen or twenty

Henry Hudson

men. He again began his explorations in Novaya Zemlya, intending to try a passage through the ice, but his crew became mutinous on account of the cold, and he headed west and south past Nova Scotia and down the American coast, in the belief that the Atlantic was separated from the Pacific only by a narrow isthmus. In September, 1609, he first entered New York Bay, and spent the following month exploring the Hudson River to a point about 150 m. from its mouth, at about the present site of the city of Albany. Before the end of the year Hudson and his men returned to England, where they and their ship were seized by the government, Hudson being commanded to serve only the country of his birth.

In 1610 Hudson set out on his final voyage under the patronage of a newly formed company of English gentlemen. In his new ship, the *Discovery,* he decided from the start to search for a northwest passage; he reached the Hudson Strait by the middle of the year, and passed into Hudson Bay beyond it, where he spent three months exploring the eastern islands and shores. By November his ship was frozen in, and a winter of extreme privation and cold led to dissension among the crew. A part of the crew mutinied in June, 1611, and put Hudson, his son, and seven others of the ship's company adrift in a small boat. A few survivors from among those on board reached England, where they were imprisoned, but the abandoned men were never seen again.

HUDSON, WILLIAM HENRY (1841–1922), British naturalist and author, born in Quilmes, Argentina, of American parents. Hudson spent his early years on the Argentinian pampas as a naturalist specializing in South American ornithology. In 1874 he settled in England, and in 1900 became a British citizen. His life was passed in poverty and obscurity until 1904, when his best-known work, the novel *Green Mansions,* was published. This romance of the South American wilderness is especially notable for its vivid descriptions and sensitive, poetic style, and is generally considered one of the finest English novels of the 20th century. Hudson also wrote *The Purple Land* (1885), *Argentine Ornithology* (1889), *British Birds* (1895), *Far Away and Long Ago* (1918), *The Book of a Naturalist* (1919), and *A Hind in Richmond Park* (1922).

HUDSON BAY, a large landlocked gulf or inland sea in N.E. Canada, consisting of an arm of the Arctic and Atlantic oceans, and extending from about lat. 51° N. to 64° N., or about 900 m., and from about long. 78° to 95° W., or about 600 m. Except for the shallower waters of its southern extremity, James Bay (q.v.), the average depth of the bay is about 70 fathoms, deepening at the inner mouth of Hudson Strait to about 100 fathoms. Hudson Bay as a whole is bounded by the Northwest Territories, Manitoba, Ontario, and Quebec (qq.v.).

Thirty rivers of considerable magnitude flow into Hudson and James bays, emptying a quantity of water so great that the water of the bay itself is brackish rather than salt. The most important of them is the Nelson River (q.v.), which drains Lake Winnipeg and a large number of inland tributaries; the next most important are the Churchill River, which has a deep though comparatively narrow mouth which can be entered by the largest ships at all tides, and the Severn River. Hudson Bay is navigable during the months from mid-June to October, and commercial interests have long attempted to extend this period of complete navigability. The center and western areas of the main bay are completely clear of rocks, shoals, and islands, and the entire region is singularly free from storms and fogs. Moreover, neither the bay nor Hudson Strait is entirely frozen over at any time of the year. On the other hand, both, particularly the strait, are beset by detached floes and bergs of ice, and the strait's outer mouth is surrounded by an ice-bearing ocean current extending over 100 m. out to sea. Another hazard to navigation is the unreliability or complete uselessness of the ordinary magnetic compass, due to the proximity of the entrance of the bay to the Magnetic Pole. New navigational aids, however, and the use of ice-breaking vessels as freighters, have been suggested for the exploitation of Hudson Bay as a water route for the grain of western Canada and the U.S. to the Atlantic Ocean, and the city of Churchill, with a railroad terminus and a potentially good harbor, already exists as a possible western port for this route.

The eastern shore of Hudson Bay is high and rocky, but all the other shores are low, and the land lying south and west of James Bay, except for some swamps and marshy areas, is suitable for dairy farming. The greater part of the region belongs geologically to the Laurentian system, with numerous rocky outcroppings of later formation in which iron and lead ores have been found. Caribou and musk ox inhabit the shores; whale, walrus, seal, and salmon abound in the waters of the bay; and such wild fowl as ducks, geese, loons, and ptarmigan are common. The Indians and Eskimos who inhabit the shores of Hudson Bay subsist chiefly by hunting. Neither the natural wealth of wild life nor the numerous stands of timber, including balsam, spruce, and poplar, which grow as far north as the northern end of James Bay, have been drawn upon by white men, except for the seasonal visits of American whalers. The fur trade of the Hudson's Bay Company (q.v.), however, less hampered by difficulties of transportation and long, severe winters, has been developed lucratively.

The earliest Europeans known to have entered Hudson Strait were John and Sebastian Cabot (qq.v.), in 1498, who were followed by several English explorers during the 16th century; Hudson Bay, however, was not explored until 1610, when Henry Hudson (q.v.), from whom the bay takes its name, made his way through the ice to the southern limits of James Bay.

HUDSONIA, genus of low, heathlike shrubs belonging to the Rockrose family, named after the English botanist William Hudson (1730?–93). The genus, which consists of three species, is native to dry situations in temperate regions of North America. The shrubs are covered with small, scalelike, downy leaves. The small, showy yellow flowers are borne on the upper parts of the branches and consist of two small and three large sepals, three or five regular petals, nine to thirty stamens, and a single pistil. The fruit is a one-celled pod. The genus comprises three species, which differ from one another in minor variations such as shape of leaves and length of flower stalks. *H. ericoides* grows on sandy, dry soil near the Atlantic coast from Newfoundland to Virginia; *H. tomentosa* grows in sandy regions near the Atlantic coast from Quebec to Maine, extending inland along the Great Lakes and Lake Champlain; *H. montana* grows in the mountains of North Carolina. Hudsonias may be grown from seed, but have a short life span and so are not often cultivated.

HUDSON RIVER, the principal river of New York State, located in the eastern part of the State. Its main sources are in the Adirondack Mountains (q.v.); it flows thence south to empty into New York Bay (q.v.), which is about 250 m. distant from the source in a straight line, or about 350 m. along the course of the river.

The headwaters of the Hudson are the outlets of 14 small lakes in Essex Co., high in the wildest part of the Adirondacks, one of which, Lake Tear-of-the-Clouds, is over 4300 ft. above sea level. The river falls rapidly in its upper waters, having a drop of 50 ft. at Glens Falls, the first sizable city on its course. At Cohoes, just above the city of Troy, it is joined by the Mohawk River, its principal tributary, which carries more water than the main stream itself. From Troy to the mouth of the Hudson the effect of tides are observable, with a mean range of rise and fall of 4.4 ft. at the Battery in New York City and of 3.3 ft. at Albany. The depression of the Hudson Valley floor, and the effects of tide water, make the Hudson navigable to Troy, about 150 m. from its mouth. As a tidal estuary, the so-called river has a volume of water far out of proportion to its drainage area, which is about 13,370 sq.m.

The Hudson has its main course within the Appalachian mountain (q.v.) system, flowing transversely through gaps in the Appalachian ridges rather than following the great longitudinal valleys. Accordingly its valley is in places very narrow, and its banks lined with high, steep hills and mountains, notable among which are the highlands below Newburgh, about 60 m. from New York, which are about 1600 ft. above sea level. The best-known peak in the highlands is Storm King, at 1530 ft. above sea level. Emerging from the highlands, the river widens in a broad expanse called Tappan Bay, 4½ m. wide and 13 m. long, and farther down, near the mouth, its west shore for about 18 m. is formed by a great dike of traprock, the Palisades (q.v.). The Catskill Mountains (q.v.) west of the Hudson approach to within 8 m. of the river.

Valuable shad and sturgeon fisheries are worked along the Hudson, and a certain amount of quarrying, particularly of traprock, is carried on along its shores. Its greatest commercial importance, however, is as a waterway and railroad trade route to the interior as far as the Great Lakes (via the Erie Canal, q.v.). The Hudson below Troy, a great waterway with a width for most of its length of from ½ to nearly 1½ miles, is one of the principal historical causes of the commercial supremacy of New York City. In its lower reaches, the river is used as an extension of the New York harbor (ocean-going vessels travel and are anchored along the river as far as Poughkeepsie, about 70 miles N. of New York).

Giovanni da Verrazano, who entered New York Bay in 1524, was the first European known to have seen the river, but it was first explored in 1609 by Henry Hudson (q.v.), from whom it takes its name. The valley was settled early in the history of the continent by the Dutch, and was of great commercial and military importance during the pre-Revolutionary period. In the highlands (see above), historical associations with the American Revolution (q.v.) are rich, especially in the region around West Point, 8 m. below Newburgh, where the U.S. Military Academy adjoins the ruins of Fort Putnam, built during the Revolution. Here too are located the great scenic and recreational features of the river, such as Bear Mountain, 44 miles N. of New York, where a State park has been established. In recent times the river has been improved for transportation by tunnels in the vicinity of New York City and by a number of bridges. Between Albany and New York City the Hudson is spanned by five bridges: the Alfred H. Smith bridge 10 m. below Albany; the Rip Van Winkle bridge 1 mile N. of Catskill; the Mid-Hudson bridge and the Poughkeepsie (railroad) bridge at Poughkeepsie; and the Bear Mountain bridge at Bear Mountain. For the topography of the mouth of the Hudson R., and for the bridges, tunnels, and docks in and around New York harbor, see NEW YORK CITY.

HUDSON RIVER SCHOOL OF PAINT-ING, the first independent group of landscape painters in America, founded in the early 19th century by Thomas Cole, Asher Brown Durand, and others. Deeply impressed by the romantic aspects of forests and mountains, they painted scenes in the Catskills and along the Hudson River, and developed an indigenous American landscape art. Their work combined realism and romanticism, and often displayed grand scenic effects and picturesque vistas rather than organic designs with social or human values. The school gave rise to a similar group of Western painters, chief among these being Frederick Edwin Church, Albert Bierstadt, and Thomas Moran. The Hudson River School had an important formative influence on the work of such American landscape masters as George Inness and Alexander Wyant.

HUDSON'S BAY COMPANY, an English corporation formed in 1670, when Charles II granted a charter to Prince Rupert (q.v.) and seventeen other noblemen and gentlemen which gave them a complete monopoly over trade in the region watered by streams flowing into Hudson Bay (q.v.). In this vast territory, which was to be known as Rupert's Land, their company also had the power to establish laws and impose penalties for their infraction, to erect forts, to maintain ships of war, and to make peace or war with the natives. The original capital of the company was about £110,000, a large capitalization for the period.

For almost a century their monopoly went unquestioned, though it was developed slowly. By 1749 the company had only four or five coastal forts and no more than 120 employees, and their annual trade, though immensely profitable, consisted only of the barter of three or four shiploads of coarse English goods for an approximately equal weight of furs and skins. In that year, an unsuccessful attempt was made in Parliament to revoke their charter on the grounds that its powers had not been used. After this period the company's development became more rapid. Conflicts with the French, which began with the company's birth, and had broken out into an open war settled in the company's favor in 1713, were finally resolved by the British conquest of Canada in 1763. This made the territories of the company accessible from the south as well as from the sea; trade increased immensely, and during the French wars from 1778 to 1783 the company was strong enough to bear a loss of £500,000.

A monopoly as profitable as this could not be long enjoyed. Private trappers and even rival companies soon entered the field, penetrating from the Great Lakes far up the Saskatchewan River toward the Rocky Mountains. In 1783 a group of these speculators formed the North West Fur Company of Montreal, and entered into fierce competition with the Hudson's Bay Company. During the following years the supply of fur-bearing animals threatened to become exhausted by the slaughter of animals during the breeding season; large groups of Indians were demoralized by bribery with goods and liquor; and both white and Indian settlements were inflamed to a point which at times reached open warfare. Eventually, in 1821, the two great companies were merged, with a combined territory extended by a license to the Arctic Ocean on the north and the Pacific Ocean on the west. In 1838 the Hudson's Bay Company again acquired the sole rights of trade in this area for a period of twenty-one years. At the expiration of the new license in 1859, however, the trade monopoly was abolished and trade in the region became open to any entrepreneur; but the company's claims of vested interests and property rights remained unsettled until 1869, when Rupert's Land was acquired by the Dominion of Canada in return for an indemnity of £300,000 and a land grant of 7,000,000 acres. The company retained its forts and trading posts, but gave up all its ancient monopolistic privileges.

Parts of the remnant of its once vast land empire were sold, and the company now holds only about 2,000,000 acres; the income from these sales were added to the company's assets for enterprises in hitherto untried fields. During World War I the Hudson's Bay Company operated a steamship line with over 300 vessels, and transported food and munitions for the French and Belgian governments. It built a chain of department stores in western Canada, the largest of which are in Winnipeg, Saskatoon, Calgary, Edmonton, Vancouver, and Victoria; the Beaver House, the company's warehouse in London, has become a center of the international fur trade. More recently the company's fur trading within Canada has been extended in a series of remote posts along the chain of the Aleutian Islands and toward Kamchatka and Siberia.

HUÉ, administrative center of Central Viet Nam (formerly Annam), Associated States of Indochina, on the Hué R., 8 miles E. of the China Sea and 60 m. by rail N.W. of the port of Tourane. For several hundred years prior to the establishment, in 1884, of a French protectorate over Annam, Hué was the capital of the Annamite empire, which included much

of the present-day Associated States of Indochina (see INDOCHINA, ASSOCIATED STATES OF). The former imperial residence is in the city. Beyond the city walls are the tombs of past emperors. Pop. (1950 est.) 25,000.

HUELVA, the name of a province of Spain and of its capital. The province borders on the Bay of Cádiz and is bounded on the w. by Portugal. The N. portion is mountainous, being traversed by the Sierra Morena range; the s. portion consists largely of lowlands. The Guadiana and Guadalquivir rivers, both of which are navigable, are the principal streams. Olives, grapes, cork, esparto grass, and fruit comprise the chief agricultural products of the province. Important industries are the manufacture of olive oil and wine; fishing; and the mining of copper, manganese, and iron. The famous Rio Tinto and Tharsis copper mines in the province have been worked since ancient times. Huelva, the capital and chief seaport, is situated on the Odiel R., 10 m. from the sea. It is served by several railroads. Fishing and fish processing are the leading industries. The city occupies the site of ancient Roman and Phenician settlements. Area of province, 3906 sq.m.; pop. (1950) 368,013. Pop. of city (1950) 63,648.

HUERTA, VICTORIANO (1854–1916), Mexican soldier and political figure, born in Colotlán, Jalisco, and educated at Chapultepec Military College. He served in the Mexican army and was promoted to the rank of brigadier general by President Porfirio Díaz in 1902. He remained on active service in the army during the administration of Francisco Madero (q.v.), but in February, 1913, while in command of the government forces sent to suppress an insurrection, turned against Madero, forced his resignation, and became provisional president of Mexico. The hostile attitude of the United States toward his regime, unpleasant incidents at Tampico and Veracruz involving the United States, and the rising pressure of his opponents finally caused Huerta to resign in July, 1914. He was in exile in Europe and the United States between 1914 and 1916, and was arrested twice in the United States for conspiring to incite a revolution in Mexico. He died in El Paso, Texas, while in custody of the U.S. government.

HUESCA, capital of the province of the same name, in N.E. Spain. The N. part of the province is crossed by the Pyrenees Mts., which reach their greatest height in Huesca at Aneto (11,168 ft. above sea level), in the Maladetta ridge. The s. portion of the prov-

Wide World Photo

Charles Evans Hughes

apply Doppler's principle (q.v.) to the detection and measurement of stellar velocities. He also demonstrated the presence of calcium in the sun. Huggins was president of the Royal Astronomical Society from 1876 to 1878 and of the Royal Society from 1900 to 1905. He wrote *An Atlas of Representative Stellar Spectra* (with his wife Margaret Murray, Lady Huggins, 1899).

HUGH CAPET or (Fr.) **HUGUES CAPET** (about 940–96), King of France, and founder of the Capetian dynasty, son of Hugh the Great, Count of Paris, whom he succeeded in 956. His lordship over many fiefs around Paris and Orléans made him the virtual ruler of France, and, when King Louis V, last of the Carolingian line, died without an heir in 987, Hugh's numerous vassals enabled him to win the election to the throne, defeating Charles, Duke of Lorraine. Charles and many other great nobles of the realm attempted to resist his authority but, through force of arms and by judicious purchasing of allegiance, as well as through the support of the Church, of which he was a devout member, Hugh established a measure of order within his kingdom. He had his son Robert, later known as Robert II or Robert the Pious, elected and crowned his successor in 988, thereby confirming the beginning of the Capetian dynasty. See CAPET.

HUGHES, CHARLES EVANS (1862–1948), American jurist and statesman, born in Glens Falls, N.Y., and educated at Brown University and the law school of Columbia University. In 1884 he was admitted to the New York bar and practiced law in New York City for the following twenty-two years, except for a period between 1891 and 1893 when he was professor of law at Cornell University. In 1905 Hughes served as counsel for special committees of the N.Y. State legislature investigating the gas companies of New York City and the financial practices of life-insurance companies in New York State; the latter investigation resulted in a complete reorganization of the laws governing life-insurance companies, established for Hughes a national reputation for fearless integrity, and became a model for subsequent inquiries of a similar nature.

In 1906, as the Republican candidate for the governorship of N.Y. State, Hughes defeated William Randolph Hearst. He was reelected in 1908, and during his tenure of office instituted many political reforms and eliminated a great part of the political corruption in both major parties. In 1910 he

ince is a plateau region. Among the principal rivers are the Cicca and the Aragon. In the mountain pastures cattle, sheep, and swine are raised. Grains, grapes, mulberries, and vegetables are produced in s. Huesca. The capital, which is situated 35 m. by rail N.N.E. of Zaragoza, was known by the Romans as *Osca* as early as 72 B.C. Sertorius, a Roman general, founded a school there in 77 B.C. In Huesca is a palace formerly used by the kings of Aragon, and a Gothic cathedral dating from 1400. Trade in agricultural produce, and the manufacture of cloth, leather, bricks, and pottery are the principal industries of the city. Area of province, 5849 sq.m.; pop. (1950) 236,232. Pop. of city (1940) 16,943.

HUGGINS, SIR WILLIAM (1824–1910), English astronomer, born in London, and educated at the City of London School and by private tutors. Having become interested in astronomy, in 1856 he built a private observatory in his London home. He was one of the first astronomers to apply the principles and techniques of spectroscopy to astronomical research, and in 1863 introduced the use of photography in recording the spectra of heavenly bodies. Huggins made important discoveries concerning the spectra of stars, comets, and planets. He determined the velocity of many stars, and was the first to resigned to become an associate justice of the U.S. Supreme Court, serving until 1916, when he was drafted by the Republican Party to run for the U.S. Presidency against Woodrow Wilson. Hughes lost the election by twenty-three electoral votes, most of his opposition coming from the Western States. During World War I President Wilson appointed Hughes head of the Draft Appeals Board of New York City and, later, chief of a special commission to investigate the national aircraft industry.

In 1921 President Warren G. Harding appointed Hughes U.S. secretary of state. During his four-year tenure of office Hughes convened the Naval Armament Conference in Washington, D.C., in 1921, and negotiated about fifty treaties and agreements with foreign powers, notably with Great Britain and Japan on military and commercial policies in the Far East, and an agreement with fifteen Latin American countries to provide a commission to arbitrate disputes which could not be settled by ordinary diplomatic means. At the beginning of President Calvin Coolidge's electoral term in 1925, Hughes returned to practice law in New York City. In 1926 Governor Alfred E. Smith appointed him chairman of a commission which reorganized the administration of the government of New York State. He served on the bench of the Permanent Court of International Justice at The Hague from 1928 to 1930, when he was appointed chief justice of the U.S.

Although Hughes was considered a conservative in politics, as chief justice he supported many liberal measures proposed by the New Deal administration of Franklin D. Roosevelt. He supported the second Agricultural Adjustment Act which went into effect in 1938, and wrote the five-to-four decisions of the Court upholding President Roosevelt's refusal to pay government obligations in gold, and approving the constitutionality of the Wagner Labor Relations Act. However, he administered several rebuffs to newly-created government agencies, notably the National Labor Relations Board, on the grounds that they were exceeding the authority granted to them and pre-empting the prerogatives of the judicial branch of the government. In 1941 he resigned from the bench and spent the last seven years of his life in retirement.

HUGHES, DAVID EDWARD (1831–1900), English-American inventor, born in London. He was brought to the United States when he was a boy, and was educated at Bardstown College, Ky. In 1856 he patented a type-print-ing telegraph which was superior to the machine patented in 1846 by the American inventor Royal Earl House (1814–95). The Hughes printing telegraph was adopted for use in many European countries and was sold in the United States to the American Telephone Co., which developed an instrument combining the best features of the machines of the two inventors. Hughes is also credited with the invention of the microphone in 1878 and the induction balance in 1879.

HUGHES, LANGSTON, full name JAMES LANGSTON HUGHES (1902–   ), American Negro writer, born in Joplin, Mo., and educated at Lincoln University, Pa. He worked as a seaman for several years, held various menial positions in several American cities, and also lived in Mexico, France, and Italy. In 1932–33 he spent a year of study in the Soviet Union, and in 1937, during the Spanish Civil War, was Madrid correspondent for a Baltimore periodical, the *Afro-American*. His poetical writings, which are notable for their disregard of classical forms, for their frequent use of jazz and Negro folk rhythms, and for their angry protest against social injustices, include *Weary Blues* (1926), *The Dream Keeper* (1932), *Shakespeare in Harlem* (1942), and *Fields of Wonder* (1947). He also wrote the novel *Not Without Laughter* (1930), the musical play *The Barrier* (1950), the short-story collections *The Ways of White Folks* (1934), *Simple Speaks His Mind* (1950), *Laughing to Keep from Crying* (1952), and *Simple Takes a Wife* (1953), and the biographical work *Famous American Negroes* (1954).

HUGHES, RUPERT (1872–   ), American writer, born in Lancaster, Mo., and educated at Adelbert College (now Western Reserve University) and at Yale University. He was for some years an assistant editor of the periodicals *Current Literature* and *The Criterion*. During World War I he was an infantry officer, rising to the rank of major in 1918. His writings cover a wide range of subjects. He was the author of *American Composers* (1900), *Love Affairs of Great Musicians* (1903), and the *Music Lovers' Cyclopedia* (1914). His biography *George Washington* (3 vols., 1926–30) is notable for its careful documentation; an unusual aspect of this biography is its studied omission of the many popular myths concerning Washington. His novels, which attained wide popularity, include *What Will People Say?* (1914), *Souls for Sale* (1922), *Ladies' Man* (1930), *The Man Without a Home* (1935), *City of Angels*

Pach Brothers

Rupert Hughes

(1941), and *The Giant Wakes* (1950). He was also the author of several plays and motion pictures.

HUGHES, THOMAS (1822–96), English jurist, reformer, and author, born in Uffington, Berkshire, and educated at Rugby School and Oxford University. He was called to the bar in 1848, became a queen's counsel in 1869, and was appointed a judge of the county court of Chester in 1882. In his youth he had become a follower of the Christian Socialist leader Frederick Denison Maurice (q.v.), whose movement he joined in 1848; see SOCIALISM. He helped to establish the Working Men's College, London, in 1854, and from 1872 to 1883 was its principal. During this time, from 1865 to 1874, he was a member of the House of Commons, and in 1879, while visiting the United States, he founded a co-operative community, at Rugby, Tenn., which later failed. His best-known work is *Tom Brown's School Days* (1857), a novel depicting life at Rugby School and intended by its author to bring about reform of the English school system. Among his other writings are a sequel to this work, *Tom Brown at Oxford* (1861), *Religio Laici* (1868), and *Life of Alfred the Great* (1869).

HUGH OF LINCOLN or **HUGH OF AVALON,** SAINT (about 1135–1200), English prelate, born in Avalon, Burgundy. His father, who was Lord of Avalon, renounced the world when Hugh was eight years old, and took his son with him to a monastery near Grenoble. In 1160 Hugh entered the Carthusian Order at the monastery of the Grande Chartreuse; there he rose to the office of procurator and first demonstrated his administrative ability. At the request of King Henry II, Hugh went, in about 1175, to England, where he founded the first Carthusian monastery in that country at Witham, Somersetshire. In 1186 he was appointed bishop of Lincoln, and during his administration of his see he proved a model of charity and benevolence, and a firm opponent of such injustices as the unfair taxation proposed by Richard I, Cœur de Lion, and the persecution of the Jews. He was responsible for building the cathedral of Lincoln, and on his death was buried there, his tomb soon becoming a place of pilgrimage. St. Hugh was canonized in 1220; his feast is celebrated on Nov. 17.

HUGLI RIVER. See HOOGHLY RIVER.

HUGO, VICTOR MARIE (1802–85), French author, born in Besançon, and educated at home and in Paris schools. He was a child prodigy, and before he was twenty years old received prizes for his poetry from the Académie Française. In his twenties he wrote a number of works in the anticlassical style for which he later became famous. These works include early novels, such as *Han d'Islande* (1823) and *Bug Jargal* (1824), and the poems *Odes et Ballades* (1826). His verse drama *Hernani* (1830) set the standard for the Romantic school which dominated French arts and letters for decades (see ROMANTICISM); in it he developed an imaginative but strained and unrealistic plot marked by highly sentimental situations and grandiloquent flights of oratory. The same combination of artificial plot and poetic language characterizes another verse drama, *Marion Delorme* (1830), and the prose dramas *Marie Tudor* (1833), *Ruy Blas* (1838), and *Les Burgaves* (1843). He also wrote the historical novel *Notre-Dame de Paris* (1831), set against a background of Paris in the time of Louis XI; the novel *Claude Gueux* (1834), an eloquent plea against capital punishment; and collections of poems, including *Les Rayons et les Ombres* (1840), which show the democratic sympathies that foreshadowed his later republican political activities.

Hugo's political views changed a number of times. A Bonapartist in his early youth, he afterward became a Royalist. In 1845, although he had again become a Bonapartist, he was created a peer of France by Louis Philippe. By 1848 he was a Socialist, and one of the revolutionary members of the Constitutional Assembly. In 1851 he participated in the unsuccessful insurrection against Louis Napoleon, and was obliged to flee to Belgium. Subsequently he moved to the island of Jersey, and then in 1855 took up residence on the island of Guernsey, where he remained in exile for fifteen years. While in exile he wrote the fiercely scurrilous verse *Napoléon le Petit* (1852), which was followed by the satiric poems *Les Châtiments* (1853) and the volume of lyric verse *Les Contemplations* (1856). Three years later the first volume of his epic poem *La Légende des Siècles* appeared. By 1862 Hugo had attained world-wide literary fame as a dramatist, poet, and novelist. That year his best-known novel *Les Misérables* (q.v.), was published in ten languages.

He returned to France in 1870 during the collapse of the Second Empire, and was elected to the National Assembly. Subsequently he wrote the most vigorous of his novels, *Quatre-vingt-treize* (1874), several volumes of poems, and the drama *Torquémada* (1882). In his last years he was acclaimed as one of the great men of France. He is buried in the Panthéon (q.v.).

Hugo's prolific writings gave the Romantic movement its greatest single impetus. His works set a standard for the rhetorical and poetic taste of at least three generations of French youth. Among his other important works are the poems *Chants du Crépuscule* (1835), *Les Voix Intérieures* (1837), *Chansons des Rues et des Bois* (1865), *L'Année Terrible* (1872), *L'Art d'Etre Grandpère* (1877), and *Les Quatre Vents de l'Esprit* (1881); the plays *Le Rois s'Amuse* (1832), *Lucrèce Borgia* (1833), and *Angelo, Tyran de Padoue* (1835); and the novels *Les Travailleurs de la Mer* (1866) and *L'Homme Qui Rit* (1869).

HUGO VAN DER GOES (d. 1482), Flemish painter of religious subjects, born in Goes (Zeeland). He painted chiefly at Ghent, where his name was first inscribed in the painter's guild in 1467. One of the most eminent painters of his period, he painted several versions of the Holy Family with the fervent attention to detail, delicate craftsmanship, and deep religious sentiment characteristic of Flemish painting at its peak of development. Among his celebrated works at Ghent was a wall-painting, depicting the story of Abigail, a copy of which survives at Prague. A large

tryptich "Nativity", now in the Uffizi gallery, Florence, was commissioned by Tommaso Portinari, agent at the port of Bruges for the Medici family, and was given by him to the Florentine hospital of Santa Maria Nuova in 1476. The work remained in the hospital chapel for 400 years, and was greatly admired by the Italian masters of the Renaissance. "The Holy Family" at the Royal Museum in Brussels is generally accepted as being his masterpiece.

HUGUENOTS, the name, of unknown origin, borne by the Protestants of France from about 1560 to 1629. Protestantism was introduced into France between 1520 and 1523, and its principles were accepted by many members of the nobility, the intellectual classes, and the middle classes. At first the new religion was protected by royalty, notably by Margaret, Queen of Navarre (see MARGARET OF NAVARRE), sister of Francis 1, King of France. Toward the end of his reign, however, Francis persecuted the French Protestants, and his successor Henry II followed his example. Nevertheless the French Protestants increased in number. At their first national synod or council (1559) fifteen churches were represented; at the next, held two years later, over two thousand churches sent representatives.

Victor Hugo

The rapid increase in the number of French Protestants excited the alarm and hatred of the French Roman Catholics. The religious hatred was exasperated by political rivalry between the house of Valois, then in possession of the French throne, and the house of Guise (qq.v.). Catherine de Médicis, who governed France in the name of her son Charles IX, allied herself at times with the Huguenots for political reasons, but generally sided against them. Religious intolerance and the political strife in which they became involved brought severe persecution upon the Huguenots in the reign of Charles IX and led to reprisals by them upon the Catholics. Finally open civil war broke out. Between 1562 and 1598 eight civil wars, interspersed with treaties of peace, and marked by bitter fighting and by assassinations and other acts of treachery, took place between French Catholics and Protestants.

The Huguenot leaders in the first ten years of the conflicts were Louis I de Bourbon, Prince de Condé (see CONDÉ) and Admiral Gaspard de Coligny (q.v.); later their leader was Henry of Navarre (see HENRY IV). The principal Catholic leaders were the Duc de Guise (Henri I de Lorraine) and Catherine de Médicis, and later Henry III (q.v.). Each side from time to time called on foreign help. The Huguenots obtained troops from England, Germany, and Switzerland, and the Catholics from Spain. The treaties that concluded the wars usually granted the Huguenots some measure of toleration, but always after the signing of a treaty the government's attempts to repudiate or ignore its terms led to a renewal of hostilities. The greatest act of treachery of the period took place in 1572. Two years previously Catherine and Charles IX had signed a treaty with the Huguenots granting them freedom of worship, and had remained on friendly terms with them, calling De Coligny to court, where he enjoyed great influence. Having lulled the Huguenots into a feeling of security, on St. Bartholomew's Day, August 24, 1572, the queen mother and the king caused thousands of them to be massacred (see MASSACRE OF ST. BARTHOLOMEW) in Paris and elsewhere in France. De Coligny was sought out and killed by the Duc de Guise himself.

The eighth civil war took place during the reign of Henry III, successor to Charles IX. The Huguenots, now led by Henry of Navarre, inflicted a crushing defeat upon the Catholics at Coutras, in 1587. Strife among the Catholics themselves, which resulted in the assassination of the Duc de Guise in 1588 and of Henry III in 1589, helped the Huguenot cause. With the death of Henry III the house of Valois became extinct, and Henry of Navarre, the first of the Bourbon line, became King of France as Henry IV. In order to avoid further civil strife, he conciliated the Catholics by becoming a Catholic (1593). In 1598 he issued the Edict of Nantes (see NANTES, EDICT OF), which gave the Huguenots almost complete religious freedom.

With the liberties they enjoyed in the reign of Henry IV the Huguenots became a strong political power in France. To break this power, which stood in the way of the absolutist type of government that Louis XIII and, particularly, Louis XIV wished to impose on France, both monarchs instigated new persecutions of the Huguenots, and new civil wars took place. Cardinal Richelieu broke the political power of the Huguenots by the capture in 1628, after a long siege, of their principal stronghold, La Rochelle; thereafter he sought to conciliate the Protestants. King Louis XIV, however, persecuted them mercilessly, and on October 18, 1685, he revoked the Edict of Nantes. Finding life in France intolerable under his persecutions and denial of religious liberty, hundreds of thousands of Huguenots fled to Switzerland, the Netherlands, England, Germany, and the English colonies in North America, including New York, Massachusetts, and South Carolina. The total emigration is believed to have been from four hundred thousand to one million, with about one million Protestants still remaining in France. Thousands of Protestants settled in the Cévennes mountain region of France, and became known as Camisards (q.v.); the attempt of Louis XIV's government to extirpate them resulted in the Camisard War (1702–05).

The enlightened and religiously skeptical spirit of the 18th century, however, was opposed to religious persecution, and during this time the French Protestants gradually regained many of their rights. Louis XV issued an edict in 1752 declaring marriages and baptisms by Protestant clergymen null and void, but under Louis XVI the edict was recalled, and after 1787, Protestant marriages were declared legal and other rights were also granted French Protestants. In 1801, by terms of a concordat between Napoleon and Pope Pius VII, Protestantism (Lutheran and Calvinistic), Judaism, and Catholicism were recognized as established religions entitled to

state support and subject to state control.
Several laws passed later in the 19th century
gave full religious freedom to all French sects,
including the Protestants; and in December,
1905, a law was passed which entirely separated church and state. During the 19th century and the first half of the 20th, French
Protestants, though comparatively few in
number, were an influential force in French
life. They played an important part in French
education, law, and finance, and in general
they took a liberal stand in regard to social
reform.

HULL. See KINGSTON UPON HULL.

HULL, capital of Hull County, Quebec,
Canada, located on the E. bank of the Ottawa
R., opposite the city of Ottawa, with which
it is linked by three bridges. It is a railway
junction and is connected with Ottawa and
Aylmer by electric railway. The city was first
settled in 1800 and was named for Hull, England. Hydroelectric power is generated at
Chaudiere Falls, on the Ottawa R., and is
used to operate many of the industrial establishments in the city, among which are sawmills, pulp and paper mills, meat-packing
plants, iron and steel foundries, and match,
clothing, and furniture factories. Pop. (1951)
43,483.

HULL, CORDELL (1871–   ), American
statesman, born in Overton (now Pickett)
Co., Tennessee, and educated at National
Normal University, Lebanon, Ohio, and at
the law school of Cumberland University. He
was a member of the Tennessee House of
Representatives from 1893 to 1897, and, after serving in the U.S. Army during the Spanish-American War, was district judge in Tennessee from 1903 to 1907. He served in the
U.S. House of Representatives from 1907 to
1921 and from 1923 until 1930. He was the
author of the Federal income-tax law of 1913,
and in 1916 he wrote the revision of that law
and sponsored Federal estate-tax legislation.
For eighteen years he was a member of the
Democratic Steering Committee of the House,
and from 1921 to 1924 was chairman of the
Democratic National Committee. In 1930
Hull was elected to the U.S. Senate, but resigned in 1933 when President Franklin D.
Roosevelt appointed him secretary of state.
In that office he did much to bring about re-
ciprocal trade, financial, and defense treaties
between the United States and other nations,
particularly those of Latin America. During
World War II he represented the United
States at meetings with the foreign ministers
of the U.S.S.R. and Great Britain. In 1944

Wide World Photo
Cordell Hull

he resigned from the cabinet because of failing health. The following year he was appointed senior advisor to the United States
delegation of the United Nations Conference
on International Organization, and was
awarded the Nobel Peace Prize. He wrote *The
Memoirs of Cordell Hull* (1948).

HULL, ISAAC (1773–1843), American naval
officer, born in Shelton, Conn. He became a
cabin boy on a merchant vessel at the age of
fourteen, and in 1798 entered the U.S. Navy
as a lieutenant. He served for several years
on the *Constitution*. Following the outbreak
of the War of 1812 he was placed in command of the *Constitution,* and on August 19,
1812, fought the celebrated engagement with
the British frigate *Guerrière*. Hull was raised
to the rank of commodore in 1823, and subsequently was in command of the Pacific squadron from 1824 to 1827, of the Washington
Navy Yard from 1829 to 1835, and of the
Mediterranean squadron from 1839 to 1841.

HULL HOUSE, an American social settlement, founded in 1889 in Chicago, Ill., by the
social reformer Jane Addams (q.v.) and her
associates. It was established primarily as a
welfare agency for needy families, and also
to combat juvenile delinquency by providing
recreational facilities for children living in
slum areas. It also sought to assist the foreign-
born, then a large proportion of the Chicago

population, to learn the English language and become American citizens. The settlement was originally housed in a single building; it later maintained thirteen buildings, and became one of the largest institutions of its kind in the United States. Its facilities include a day nursery, gymnasium, meeting and recreation rooms for youngsters and adults, arts-and-crafts workshops, classrooms for adult education, a music school, a theater for amateur dramatic performances, and a social-service center. Funds for the operation of Hull House are provided entirely by the voluntary contributions of private citizens and grants by other social-welfare agencies.

Since 1912 Hull House has operated a summer camp for children, called the Joseph T. Bowen Country Club, which is situated at Waukegan, Ill.

HUMAN BEING. See ANTHROPOLOGY; ARCHEOLOGY; MAN, ANCIENT; RACES OF MANKIND.

HUMANE ASSOCIATIONS. See CRUELTY TO ANIMALS; CRUELTY TO CHILDREN.

HUMANISM, the cultural movement which spread throughout western Europe in the 15th century, causing a break with the medieval traditions of Scholasticism (q.v.), and developing a general interest in the study of the Greek and Latin classics. It formed the first phase of the Renaissance (q.v.), and was itself marked by two divergent movements; one attempted to assimilate the classical learning into the existing Christian culture; the other endeavored to revive not only the art but also the pagan spirit of classical antiquity.

The movement started in Italy, where its precursors were Dante, Petrarch, and Boccaccio, who had done much to discover and preserve classical works. It was definitely established by the influx of Byzantine scholars who fled to Italy after the fall of Constantinople to the Turks in 1453. The discovery and collection of classical manuscripts became popular, especially among the higher clergy and nobility, and the invention of printing gave a further impetus to Humanism through the dissemination of editions of the classics. In Italy Humanism developed principally in the fields of literature and art; in central Europe, where it was introduced chiefly by Johann Reuchlin and Philip Melanchthon (qq.v.), the movement developed in the fields of theology and education, and led to the Reformation (q.v.).

One of the most influential scholars in the development of Humanism in France was the Dutch humanist Desiderius Erasmus, who also played an important part in introducing the movement into England. There it was definitely established at Oxford University by William Grocyn and Thomas Linacre, and at Cambridge University by Erasmus and by John Fisher. From the universities it spread throughout English society, and paved the way for the great Elizabethan development of literature and culture. See EDUCATION.

HUMBER (anc. *Abus*), estuary of the Trent and Ouse rivers, on the E. coast of England, and a boundary between the counties of York and Lincoln. It flows generally E. from the junction of the Trent and Ouse to the North Sea, a distance of about 37 miles. At its head the estuary is 1 m. in width; 8 m. above its mouth it widens to 8 m. A shallow bay, enclosed by a peninsula called Spurn Head, is located on the N. side of the mouth. Although navigation on parts of the Humber is made difficult by shoals, the river is an important shipping route, with the ports of Hull, Immingham, Grimsby, and Goole situated on its banks. In ancient times the Humber was a means of entrance to England for migrating peoples.

HUMBERT I (1844–1900), King of Italy, born in Turin. He entered the army with the rank of captain in 1858, and fought with conspicuous bravery in several battles of the wars against the Austrians for the unification of Italy; see ITALY: *History*. He succeeded to the throne upon the death of his father in 1878. A notable event of his relatively tranquil and popular reign was the signing by Italy, Austria-Hungary, and Germany, in 1882, of a military defense pact known as the Triple Alliance (q.v.). He also inaugurated a policy of colonial expansion by military force in Africa, but the defeat of the Italian army by the Ethiopians in the battle of Adowa in 1896 resulted in a decline in his popularity. Subsequently, he was assassinated by an anarchist at Monza.

HUMBOLDT, (FRIEDRICH HEINRICH) ALEXANDER, BARON VON (1769–1859), German naturalist, traveler, and statesman, born in Berlin, and educated privately with his elder brother Karl Wilhelm von Humboldt, and at the universities of Frankfort on the Oder, Berlin, and Göttingen, and the mining academy at Freiberg. His aptitude for science was demonstrated in his early years; during his residence as a student in Göttingen he made geological examinations in the Harz mountains and the Rhine valley which resulted in his first important work, a study of the basalts of the region, written in 1790. In the same year he traveled through Belgium, Holland, England, and France with Georg Forster, who exercised a strong influence on his career. His scientific work during his residence in Freiberg, which included investigations in chemistry, physics, and botany as well as mining, led to his appointment in 1792 to the post of superintendent of mines in the principalities of Bayreuth and Ansbach, and for the next three years he resided at Bayreuth, carrying on independent work, in the hours not claimed by official duties, on the nature of muscular and nervous energy.

In 1797 Humboldt spent three months in association with Johann von Goethe and Friedrich von Schiller, planning the great journey to Spanish-America with which his fame is now most closely associated. After two years in Europe, during which he continued his scientific studies, notably an investigation of the chemical composition of the atmosphere, Humboldt and his chief collaborator, the French naturalist Aimé Bonpland, left Spain in a frigate, the *Pizarro,* in 1799. They visited Tenerife for the ascent of the Peak, and made valuable observations there, as well as at sea during the voyage, which ended at Cumaná in Venezuela.

In Cumaná Humboldt studied the important meteor shower which occurred in November, 1799, and during the following year explored the entire region, crossing over to the upper waters of the Orinoco River, and establishing the connection between that stream and the upper Amazon River. In 1801 and 1802 his explorations were extended to Cuba, the basin of the Magdalena River, the Andes of Quito, where he made an ascent of Chimborazo, reaching an altitude of over 19,000 ft. above sea level, and finally Peru, where he devoted himself largely to electrical and astronomical research, and to studies of the cultivation of the cinchona plant and of the fertilizing properties of guano, the introduction of which into European agriculture is largely due to his writings. After a year in Mexico, spent largely in geographical explorations and the study of volcanic phenomena, and a short visit to the United States, Humboldt returned to Europe, landing at Bordeaux in August, 1804.

After a short trip to Italy for the investigation of magnetic declination, and an extended stay in Berlin during which he accompanied Prince Wilhelm of Prussia to France on a diplomatic mission in 1807, Humboldt obtained leave from his government to remain in Paris for the preparation and pub-

lication of an account of his travels. Here he settled in 1808, and with the co-operation of such men as Joseph Gay-Lussac and Georges Cuvier (qq.v.) he undertook the enormous task of organizing and analyzing the material he had accumulated. The thirty magnificent volumes he was able to produce, issued at irregular intervals until 1827, along with the great body of his other scientific writings, made Humboldt "the most famous man in Europe after Napoleon Bonaparte".

Frederick William III of Prussia granted him a court sinecure which required his occasional attendance at court and on diplomatic missions made by the monarch. In course of time, however, these obligations became more frequent, and in 1827 the king summoned him to reside at the court. He took up permanent residence in Berlin against his will, and attempted to carry on his investigations in new, uncongenial surroundings. One of his first studies in Berlin was on the nature of disturbances in the earth's magnetism for which he coined the term "magnetic storms"; his major work of this period was establishing international co-operation in the organization and publication of scientific work.

In 1829, under the patronage of the Russian government, Humboldt made his last voyage of scientific exploration, traveling through the Ural and Altai mountains, and traversing the Russian empire between the Neva and the Yenisei rivers; some of the fruits of this trip were the first accurate description of the geography and physical geography of central Asia, and the discovery of diamonds in the gold and platinum beds of the Urals. Upon his return to Berlin, Humboldt was forced to take a greater part in diplomatic activities; from 1830 to 1848 he was sent on frequent diplomatic journeys to Louis Philippe, whom he had known in France, and after the accession of Frederick William IV in 1840 Humboldt's high position at the Prussian court interfered more and more with his own work. He was able, however, to devote a certain amount of time to the writing of his *Kosmos,* which occupied him intermittently from the age of seventy-six until his death. This ambitious work, which had its origin in lectures delivered in Berlin from 1827 to 1828, was meant by Humboldt to be the great work of his life. Four volumes had been published by 1858, and a portion of the fifth was published posthumously in 1862. The *Kosmos* displayed his complete grasp of both the details and the generalizations of the sciences of his time, and is a product of the last period in

David Hume

the history of science in which a single scientist could hope to construct a complete description of the physical universe.

HUMBOLDT RIVER, the longest river of Nevada, rising in Elko Co., in the N.E. corner of the State, and flowing generally s.w. for a distance of about 375 m., emptying into Humboldt Lake, in Pershing and Churchill counties. It drains an area of about 8000 sq.m. The river is unnavigable, and its waters are subalkaline, evaporating rapidly from Humboldt Lake during dry seasons.

HUME, DAVID (1711–76), Scottish philosopher and historian, born in Edinburgh. He was educated at home and at the University of Edinburgh, where he matriculated at the age of twelve. His health was poor and, after a short period in a business house in Bristol, Hume went to live in France. From 1734 to 1737 he occupied himself intensively with the problems of speculative philosophy and, during this period, wrote his most important philosophical work, the *Treatise of Human Nature* (1739–40), which embodied the essence of his thinking. In spite of its importance, this work was ignored by the public and was, as Hume himself said, "dead-born". Following the publication of the *Treatise* Hume returned to his family estate in Berwickshire, where he turned his attention to the problems of ethics and political economy and wrote *Essays Moral and Political* (1741–42), which attained immediate success. Having failed to obtain an appointment to the faculty of the University of Edinburgh, he

became successively tutor to the lunatic marquis of Annandale and judge advocate to an English military expedition to France. His *Philisophical Essays* (afterward entitled *An Enquiry Concerning Human Understanding*) appeared in 1748. This work is in effect a condensation of the *Treatise*.

In 1751 Hume took up residence in Edinburgh. In the same year his *Political Discourses* was published, and in the following year, having again failed to obtain a university professorship, he received an appointment as librarian of the Advocates' Library in Edinburgh. During the twelve years of his stay in Edinburgh Hume worked chiefly on his five-volume *History of England,* which appeared at intervals from 1754 to 1762. In the years 1762 to 1765 Hume served as secretary of the British embassy in Paris. There he was lionized by French literary circles and formed a friendship with the French philosopher Jean Jacques Rousseau (q.v.). He brought Rousseau back with him to England, but the friendship dissolved in a quarrel. After serving in 1767–68 as undersecretary of state in London, Hume retired to Edinburgh, where he spent the rest of his life. His autobiography was published posthumously in 1777, and so was his *Dialogues Concerning Natural Religion* (1779). Hume had written the latter work in the early 1750's but had suppressed it because of its skepticism.

Hume's philosophical position is an extension of the ideas of John Locke and Bishop George Berkeley (qq.v.). Hume and Berkeley both differentiated between reason and sensation; however, Hume went farther, to endeavored to prove that reason and rational judgments have no actual existence but are merely habitual associations of distinct sensations or experiences. He rejected the entire mechanism of causation, maintaining that "reason can never show us the connexion of one object with another, tho' aided by experience, and the observation of their conjunction in all past instances. When the mind, therefore, passes from the idea or impression of one object to the idea or belief of another, it is not determined by reason, but by certain principles, which associate together the ideas of these objects and unite them in the imagination." Hume's skeptical approach denied the existence of both the spiritual substance postulated by Berkeley and the material substance in which Locke believed. Going farther, Hume denied the existence of the individual self, maintaining that since no man has a constant perception of himself as an entity, men "are nothing but a bundle or collection of different perceptions." According to Hume's philosophy, therefore, knowledge of matters of fact is impossible, although he admitted the existence of knowledge of the relationships of ideas, such as the relationships of numbers in mathematics.

In his ethical thinking, Hume states that the idea of right and wrong is not rational but arises from a regard for one's own happiness. The supreme moral good, according to his view, is benevolence, an unselfish regard for the general welfare of society, which Hume regarded as consistent with individual happiness.

As a historian Hume broke away from the traditional chronological account of wars and deeds of state and attempted to describe the economic and intellectual factors which played a part in his country's history. Although his history was for many years regarded as a classic, it suffered from his intense partisanship of Scotland and the Tory cause which led him into distortions and misstatements, particularly in the latter part of the work.

Hume's contributions to economic theory, which influenced Adam Smith (q.v.) and later economists, included his recognition of the essential difference between money and wealth and of the effect of social conditions on economics.

HUMIDITY, the moisture content of the atmosphere. The atmosphere always contains some moisture in the form of water vapor, the maximum amount depending on the temperature. The amount of vapor which will saturate the air increases with a rise in temperature: at 40° F. 1000 lbs. of moist air contains a maximum of 5 lbs. of water vapor; at 100° F. 1000 lbs. of moist air contains a maximum of 41 lbs. of water vapor. When the atmosphere is saturated with water, the evaporation of perspiration with its attendant cooling effect is impossible, thus accounting for the extreme discomfort encountered in hot, humid weather. Air-conditioning units therefore usually contain units for controlling moisture content as well as temperature of the air. See HEATING AND VENTILATION.

The weight of water vapor contained in a volume of air is known as the *absolute humidity,* and is often expressed in grains of water per cubic foot of moist air or in pounds of water per pound of dry air. *Relative humidity,* given in weather reports, is the ratio between the actual vapor content of the atmosphere and the vapor content of air at the same temperature saturated with water vapor. If the temperature of the atmosphere rises and there is no change in the vapor content of the atmosphere, the absolute humidity remains the same but the relative humidity is lowered. A fall in temperature increases the relative humidity, and if the *dew point,* the temperature at which the relative humidity is 100 percent, is reached, the water vapor deposits as liquid water on any surface, such as blades of grass or window panes; see DEW. Humidity is measured by means of a hygrometer (q.v.).

HUMMEL, JOHANN NEPOMUK (1778–1837), German pianist and composer, born in Pressburg. In 1785, in Vienna, where his father conducted a theater orchestra, his playing attracted the attention of the Austrian composer Wolfgang Amadeus Mozart, with whom he went to live and study for two years. His first public appearance was at a concert given by Mozart in 1787. Subsequently he gave recitals throughout Germany, Denmark, and Great Britain, returning to Vienna in 1793 to study. In 1804 he became Kapellmeister to Prince Miklos Esterházy (q.v.), and held similar posts at Stuttgart from 1816 to 1820 and later at Weimar. Hummel wrote over 125 compositions, including works for piano solo, piano concertos, chamber music, ballets, operas, and church music.

HUMMINGBIRD, HUMMER, COLIBRI, or FEATHERED GEM, common name of any of the small coraciiform New World birds constituting the family Trochilidae. The family contains the smallest of all birds, many species being under 3 in. in over-all length. The birds are known for their rapid flight; their narrow wings beat so quickly that they produce a hum; whence the common name. The birds

N.Y. Zoological Society
Ruby-throated hummingbird on its nest

are often seen hovering over flowers, the wings moving so rapidly to keep the birds aloft that the outlines of the bird are completely blurred to an observer; in many instances the bird is taken for a large moth. Hummingbirds have slender bills which vary in size and shape among different species according to the size and shape of the flowers from which the birds extract the insects, spiders, and nectar upon which they subsist. The tongue is long, hollow, and extensile, forked at the tip. The feathers of the bird are so delicately filamented that they diffract sunlight into many of its component colors and add artificial tinting to the hummingbird's natural pigments. The hummingbird builds a cup-shaped nest, sometimes as small as ¾ in. in diameter, on the branch of a tree, and camouflages it with lichen and small pieces of bark. Two white eggs, little more than ¼ in. in length, are laid by the female in a clutch. The hummingbird is an almost fearless animal and will attack even a hawk when that bird approaches its nest.

Over five hundred species of hummingbirds are known, occurring in every portion of the New World from Tierra del Fuego almost to the Arctic Circle. The only species in eastern U.S. is the ruby-throated hummingbird, *Archilochus colubris,* which is found from Labrador to E. Mexico and westward to central South Dakota. It is about 3¾ in. long. The adult male is metallic-green above; below, its throat is ruby-colored, its breast is white, and its abdomen is gray marked with green at the sides. The female is somewhat duller in general body color, and lacks the red throat patch. Another common hummingbird of the U.S. is the rufous hummingbird, *Selasphorus rufus,* found from Alaska to s. California. The bird is slightly more than 3½ in. in length. The adult male is rufous brown with a greenish-yellow sheen above, and white below. Its throat patch is red and greenish bronze. The female is greenish gold above with a brown rump; below, it is a grayish white with rufous sides. The calliope, *Stellula calliope,* is the smallest hummingbird found in the U.S., measuring slightly less than 3 in. in length. It is found in the mountainous regions of w. United States and Canada. The male is greenish bronze above and white below, with green sides. The upper portion of its bill is black. The female is yellowish green above and pale rufous below.

HUMMINGBIRD MOTH, common name for any of several hawk-moths (q.v.) which fly about during the daytime, and which resemble hummingbirds when hovering over flowers. The best-known American hummingbird moths belong to the genera *Hemaris* and *Amphion. Hemaris thysbe* is common in western U.S. It is about 1¼ in. long, and has a wing span of about 3 in. Each of its four wings has a large, colorless, central patch bordered with red. Its body is greenish, traversed on the abdomen by a broad band of red. *H. gracilis* is found in the E. coastal states; it differs from *H. thysbe* in the more pronounced green of its body color, and in having longitudinal red lines on its underside. *Amphion nessus* is about 1 in. long, and has a wing span of over 2 in. Its body is brown, traversed on the abdomen by a narrow band of yellow. Its wings are yellow and red.

HUMORS, normal fluids or semifluids of the body, such as blood, bile, or lymph. Ancient medical systems were based on the belief that all diseases result from disorders of the humors. Hippocrates (q.v.), a Greek physician of the 5th century B.C., was the first to propose a theory of diagnosis based on humors. He believed that the *temperament* (q.v.) of an individual, which determines predisposition to specific diseases, depends on the predominance in his body of one of four humors: yellow bile, blood, phlegm, and black bile. He identified each of these humors with one of the four elements (fire, air, water, and earth, respectively) which, he believed, compose the universe. Thus yellow bile was presumed to cause *choleric* temperament, characterized by quick and intense emotional behavior; blood was presumed to cause the *sanguine* temperament, characterized by quick and weak emotional behavior; phlegm was presumed to cause the *phlegmatic* temperament, characterized by slow and weak emotional behavior; and black bile was presumed to cause the *melancholic* temperament, characterized by slow and intense emotional behavior. Galen (q.v.), a Greek physician of the 2nd century A.D., believed that temperament and body disorders are caused by relative temperature and humidity, but used the framework of Hippocrates' theory; he substituted warmth and dryness for yellow bile, warmth and dampness for blood, coldness and dampness for phlegm, and coldness and dryness for black bile. Although physicians no longer ascribe disease and temperament to the influence of humors, the descriptive terms employed by Hippocrates are still in common use; since the Middle Ages choleric means easily angered, sanguine means hopeful, phlegmatic means calm, and melancholic means sad.

HUMPBACK. See HUNCHBACK.

HUMPBACK, common name for any whale-bone whale in the genus *Megaptera,* which is world-wide in distribution. Humpbacks are so called because of a hump, or prominence, on the forward portion of their backs. They reach a length of over sixty feet, and are black and white in color. Humpbacks have characteristically long flippers; the span from the tip of one flipper to the tip of the other measures almost one third of the body length. The oil and black whalebone of the hump-back are of little commercial value. The common Atlantic species of humpback is *Megaptera nodosa;* the common Pacific species, is *M. versabilis.*

HUMPBACKED SALMON. See DOG SALMON.

HUMPERDINCK, ENGELBERT (1854–1921), German composer, born in Siegburg, and edu-cated at the Cologne Conservatory. At the age of twenty-two he won a fellowship per-mitting him to continue his studies for two years at the Royal Music School in Munich. In 1879 he traveled to Italy on the proceeds of another grant; there he met and became a disciple of Richard Wagner (q.v.). He taught theory at the Conservatoire of Barcelona from 1885 to 1886, and was professor of music at the Hoch Conservatory in Frank-fort from 1890 to 1896. In 1900 he was elected to the Senate of the Royal Academy of Arts in Berlin, becoming its acting presi-dent in 1913. Humperdinck was well known for his operas, which include the popular *Hänsel und Gretel* (1893) and *Königskinder* (1910), and for his incidental music for plays, especially the plays of Shakespeare.

HUMPHREY, DUKE OF GLOUCESTER and EARL OF PEMBROKE (1391–1447), English no-bleman and patron of the arts, youngest son of King Henry IV. He was created Duke of Gloucester and Earl of Pembroke in 1414, soon after the accession of his brother as Henry V (q.v.). In 1415 Humphrey partici-pated in the invasion of France led by his brother, and was wounded at the battle of Agincourt. Three years later, during a second invasion of France, he commanded a force which captured Cherbourg. Humphrey served as Regent in 1420–21 during Henry's absence from England; and in 1422, upon the death of Henry, he claimed the title of Regent, but Parliament and the royal Council, desiring to limit his powers, granted him only the title and power of Protector, and only for the pe-riod of the absence of John of Lancaster (q.v.) from England. In the same year he

Engelbert Humperdinck

married Jacoba of Bavaria, heiress to the throne of Holland. Her claim was contested by the Duke of Burgundy in 1424, and Humphrey, after leading a brief campaign on her behalf, abandoned her to the Burgundian forces. The marriage was annulled in 1428.

In 1429 the Council, aroused against Hum-phrey's imprudent administration of the pro-tectorate, placed the youthful Henry VI (q.v.) upon the throne. Humphrey later re-established himself in popular esteem by de-manding war against the Duke of Burgundy, who opposed the claim of Henry to the French crown, and by launching an invasion of Bur-gundy's domain. His popularity began to wane in 1441, when his second wife, Eleanor Cob-ham, was condemned for allegedly practicing sorcery against the king. In 1447 Humphrey himself came under suspicion of plotting against the king's life; he was arrested and died while in custody. As a generous patron of scholarship and the arts, Humphrey was widely known as "the good Duke Humphrey". He was an avid collector of books, and en-riched the libraries of Oxford University with a large number of volumes. He donated sub-stantial sums for the construction of the Divinity School of the university, and par-ticularly for the furnishing of one of its rooms, which is called "Duke Humphrey's Library".

HUMPHREY, George Magoffin (1890–), American industrialist and government official, born in Cheboygan, Mich., and educated at the University of Michigan. He began to practice law in Saginaw, Mich., in 1912. In 1918 he was named general attorney for a steel-manufacturing firm in Cleveland, O. He was president of the company after 1929 and a director of various subsidiary and affiliated corporations. As one of the country's leading industrialists, Humphrey was appointed (1946) chairman of the business advisory council, U.S. Department of Commerce, and in 1948–49 he conducted a survey of German industry for the Economic Cooperation Administration. In January, 1953, he was appointed secretary of the treasury in the cabinet of President Dwight D. Eisenhower.

HUMUS, organic matter undergoing decomposition in the soil, and consisting of dead animal and plant material such as leaves, fruits, stems, insects and rodents, and manure. During early decomposition, some of the carbon, hydrogen, oxygen, and nitrogen are quickly passed off as water, carbon dioxide, methane, and ammonia, but the remaining constituents decompose slowly. The chemical composition of humus is variable, being dependent on the action of living soil organisms such as bacteria, protozoa, fungi, and pselaphid beetles, but usually contains varying amounts of apocrenic acid. Humus is a homogeneous, amorphous, dark-colored, and practically odorless material. The end products of the decomposition of humus are mineral salts.

Formation of humus is valuable as a means of converting plant nutrients from an unusable organic form to a usable mineral form. It also affects such important physical properties of the soil as structure, color, texture, and moisture-holding capacity; the formation of a granular structure favorable to the optimum development of crop plants, for example, depends on the humus content of the soil. In areas where cultivated plants are grown, humus is constantly being depleted from the soil by the succession of crops. Humus necessary to maintain the organic balance of the soil is added to cultivated land in the form of compost or manure, or by the process of green manuring. See SOILS AND SOIL MANAGEMENT.

HUN. See HUNS.

HUNAN, a province of central China. It comprises four river basins, which converge upon Lake Tunting in the N.E. portion of the province. The Si-kiang, the Tsze R., and the Yuen R. empty into the lake, and the Yangtze R. is fed by the lake. Hunan is extremely fertile, and in many areas two crops a year are produced. The principal crops are tea, rice, hemp, and tobacco. Coal, silver, gold, iron, copper, lead, tin, and zinc are mined in the province, and there are resources of timber. Changsha (q.v.) is the capital. Area, 79,516 sq.m.; pop. (1952 est.) 30,012,000.

HUNCHBACK, or HUMPBACK, the humped condition of the upper back resulting from an extreme curvature of the spine, or a person afflicted with this condition. This curvature may be either a *kyphosis,* an accentuation of the normal posterior curvature, or a combination of kyphosis and extreme lateral curvature (*scoliosis*) which is known as *kyphoscoliosis.* Scoliosis alone rarely creates a hunchback appearance. Kyphosis may be mild or severe. Its mild form is usually caused by poor posture (particularly in children) while the severe condition is the result of disease of the spine (especially Pott's disease, tuberculosis of the spine). Kyphoscoliosis can be acquired or congenital. As a result of the spinal deformity in hunchback, the ribs become contorted, compressing the internal organs and thrusting the collarbone and shoulder blades into distorted positions. Compensatory deformations take place in the hips and other parts of the body in its effort to maintain balance.

Treatment for hunchback is varied. A mild kyphosis can be corrected readily if diagnosed before the skeletal frame has completed its growth. Congenital deformities cannot be cured. The malformations of the vertebrae are embryological in origin and only a certain amount of the deformity can be minimized by surgery and local manipulation. Hunchback caused by spinal disease is also only slightly amenable to surgery and local treatment. Traction therapy, pads, and plaster-jacket supports are used in manipulative treatments. See SPINE.

Hunchbacks have been recorded as far back as Hippocrates and have usually been regarded with a mixture of suspicion and fear, as is aptly illustrated by Victor Hugo's well-known story of Quasimodo, the Hunchback of Notre Dame. Other hunchbacks, however, have mounted to success and renown. Among these are Henri Toulouse-Lautrec (1864–1901), the French painter, and Adam de le Halle (1238–88), known as Le Bossu d'Arras (the Hunchback of Arras), who wrote *Le Jeu de Robin et Marion,* the earliest French secular play with music.

HUNDRED YEARS' WAR, the name given to the series of armed conflicts, broken by a number of truces and treaties of peace, which were waged between England and France from 1337 to 1453. The fundamental cause of the war was the claim of the kings of England to the French throne; in particular Edward III (q.v.) of England maintained in 1337 that Philip VI (q.v.) of France, who actually ruled France at the time, was a usurper and that Edward was the rightful ruler. A contributing cause was the fear on the part of Edward that the French monarch, whose power over the feudal lords of France was strong, would deprive him of the Duchy of Guienne in France, which Edward held as a fief (see FEUDALISM) from Philip. Edward's animosity toward Philip was aggravated by the fact that France had helped Scotland in the wars waged by Edward II (q.v.) and Edward III against the Scottish kings for the throne of Scotland. An important economic cause of the Hundred Years' War was the rivalry between England and France for the trade of Flanders.

The war may be divided into two periods. The first part extended from 1337 to 1380. In 1338 Edward III declared himself king of France and invaded France from the north. Neither side won any decisive victory on land, but the English fleet defeated that of the French off Sluis in the Netherlands in 1340, and for many years thereafter had control of the English Channel. A three-year truce was signed between England and France in 1343, but in 1345 Edward again invaded France. On August 26, 1346, he led his army in a great victory over the French at Crécy (see CRÉCY, BATTLE OF), and in 1347 took the city of Calais after a siege. Another series of truces between 1347 and 1355 was followed by the capture of Bordeaux in 1355 by the English king's son, Edward the Black Prince (see EDWARD, known as *The Black Prince*); using Bordeaux as a base, the English raided and plundered most of southern France. On September 26, 1356, the English, led by the Black Prince, won their second victory of the war, at Poitiers (see POITIERS, BATTLE OF). In this battle the English captured the French king John II, who had succeeded Philip VI in 1350. In 1360 the Peace of Brétigny (see BRÉTIGNY, PEACE OF) ended this phase of the first period of the war; the terms of the treaty were generally favorable to England, which was left in possession of great areas of French territory. In 1369 Charles V of France, who had succeeded John II in 1364, renewed

the war. The French forces, under the leadership of the great general Bertrand Du Guesclin (see DU GUESCLIN), avoided pitched battles with the English and kept harrying them and cutting off their supplies. England fought under several disadvantages. It lost its best military leader by the death in 1376 of the Black Prince, and in 1377 Edward III himself died and was succeeded by his grandson, Richard II, who was a minor. The English war effort was so weakened by the loss of strong leadership that the guerilla tactics of Du Guesclin won back for France most of the territory ceded to England by the Treaty of Brétigny. The actual fighting in this first period of the war ended in 1386, but a truce was not signed until 1396.

The truce was intended to last for thirty years. In 1414, however, Henry V, then king of England, taking advantage of the civil war raging in France at the time between the houses of Burgundy and of Orléans for control of the regency which ruled the country for the intermittently insane King Charles VI, reasserted the claim of the English monarchy to the French throne. Henry V inaugurated the second period of the war by invading France in 1415. He captured Harfleur and defeated the French in the Battle of Agincourt (see AGINCOURT, BATTLE OF); then, in alliance with the house of Burgundy, he conquered all of France north of the Loire River, including Paris. On May 20, 1420, the Treaty of Troyes was signed by which Charles VI recognized Henry V as his heir and also as regent of France; Charles VI also declared his son Charles, the dauphin, to be illegitimate and repudiated him as his heir. The dauphin, however, refused to be bound by the treaty and continued to fight the English, who drove his forces across the Loire and then invaded the south of France.

In 1422 both Henry V and Charles VI died. On the death of his father, the dauphin proclaimed himself king of France, as Charles VII, but the English claimed the French throne for the infant Henry VI of England, whose affairs were being conducted by a regent, the Duke of Bedford. Charles VII was generally recognized as king of France south of the Loire R., and Henry VI as king of France north of the river. In the course of their invasion of the south of France, in 1428 the English laid siege to the last important stronghold of the French, the city of Orléans. The turning point of the entire Hundred Years' War came in 1429 when French forces under Joan of Arc (q.v.) raised the siege of Orléans, defeated the English in a number of battles, drove them north, and had Charles crowned king at Reims. Charles VII made his position as king of France stronger by making a separate peace with the Burgundians (Peace of Arras, 1435), the allies of the English up to this time, and the following year Charles took Paris from the English. From 1436 to 1449 was a period of military inaction; in the latter year the French vigorously attacked the English in Normandy and in Guienne, regaining Normandy in 1450 and Guienne in 1451. Fighting ceased completely in 1453, by which time the English held only Calais (q.v.) and a small adjoining district; they retained these possessions until 1558. No formal treaty was ever signed to end the war.

The Hundred Years' War caused the loss of thousands of lives on either side and also great devastation of lands and destruction of property in France. It had an important political and social result in France, helping to establish a strong monarchy and sense of nationalism and, by the virtual destruction of the nobility through losses in fighting, making possible the emergence in France of a strong middle class.

HUNGARIAN LANGUAGE, a member of the Ugric branch of the Finno-Ugric languages (q.v.), called *Magyar* by its speakers, and originally spoken on the eastern slopes of the Ural Mountains. It is now the language of the dominant people of Hungary, and is spoken by about 10,500,000 people, of whom about 500,000 are in the U.S.

By reason of its phonetic harmony, especially among vowels (see below), Hungarian is considered a musical language, particularly adapted to poetry and rhetoric. As a literary language it has the added advantages of being free of dialects and of displaying few differences of pronunciation in the various parts of the country. Moreover the vocabulary of the language, based upon an original stock of about 400 true Finno-Ugric words, has been built up for the most part upon Hungarian rather than foreign sources, in spite of the heterogeneity of the influences to which it has been exposed. Cultural contacts with alien peoples and the influence of foreign educators, administrators, and rulers have introduced a certain number of loan words, particularly from a group of unknown Eastern and Near-Eastern languages, from Turkish, from Latin and Old French, and from the modern languages of western Europe; but over eighty percent of the words of the current vocabulary

originated among speakers of Hungarian.

Like all languages of the Finno-Ugric group, Hungarian is agglutinative in structure. The basis of word formation is a group of monosyllabic roots, greatly enriched about the beginning of the Christian Era by the introduction of compound words and the use of suffixes. These suffixes are modified in obedience to a law of so-called vowel harmony, based upon the words in which agglutination occurs. The vowels are divided into three classes; open, close, and middle or neutral; if the final vowel of a root is open or close, the vowel of a suffix attached to that root must be of the same class. The pronunciation of consonants is similar to that of Latin, except for a group of sibilants and compound consonants peculiar to Hungarian. In transcription, however, though a Roman script introduced about 1000 A.D. is used, Hungarian differs widely from the Teutonic and Romance languages. Spelling is phonetic (that is, each letter invariably represents a single sound, and is clearly pronounced in both accented and unaccented words), but a number of consonant spellings are uniquely Hungarian. Examples of such spellings are *oz, dzs,* and *gy,* which are pronounced respectively as English *ts, j,* and *d.* Another source of difficulty for foreigners in acquiring facility in the language is a complex system of verb formation, by which verbs and derived verbs are modified by the addition of suffixes into eight distinct moods; moreover, as in many agglutinative languages, suffixes may also be added to one another to produce a great variety of mood combinations. The same process of word-building by agglutination is often applied in Hungarian to nouns and adjectives, resulting in a large number of bewilderingly complex compound words.

HUNGARIAN LITERATURE, the literature written in the Hungarian language from medieval times to the present. In medieval days Latin was the medium of expression of the cultured and ruling classes of Hungary. However, the beginnings of literature in the vernacular took place during this period, in the form of translations of legends and of books of the Bible. The earliest extant Hungarian literary work of importance is a funeral oration dating from about the beginning of the 13th century. From the middle of the 15th century to the second half of the 16th, the literature written in Hungarian consisted chiefly of translations from the Bible and of the lives and legends of the saints.

During the Reformation and the Renaissance (from about 1550 to the beginning of the 18th century) considerable activity took place in Hungarian literature. Outstanding among the poets who flourished during this time were Baron Bálint Balassa (1551–94), who wrote patriotic and religious poems and is particularly noted for his love poems; Sebastian Tinódi, who wrote historical chronicles in rhymed verse; Miklós Zrinyi (see ZRINYI), author of the volume of verse *The Siren of the Adriatic* (1651); and István Gyöngyösi (1620–1704), one of the principal early Hungarian poets, among whose works are the epic *Murányi Venus* (1664) and *Cupidó* (1695). During this period numerous works were written in Hungarian dealing with law and philology, and as polemics in religious controversy.

During the greater part of the 18th century the rulers of Hungary, the Hapsburgs (See HUNGARY: *History*), attempted to make Hungary part of a great Germanic empire. They encouraged the writing of books in German or Latin and suppressed the writing of books in Hungarian. The close of the century witnessed a violent reaction on the part of the Hungarian people against the political and literary policy of the Hapsburgs. Societies were formed for the cultivation of the Hungarian language, and a number of publications, among them the first newspaper in Hungarian, were founded. The 19th century witnessed a spirited development of the literature of the Hungarian people. Hungarian literature since the beginning of the 19th century may be divided into three periods: (1) from the beginning of the century through the unsuccessful revolution (1848–49) of the Hungarian people against their Austrian rulers; (2) from 1849 to 1867, when Hungary received a constitution making it a dual monarchy with Austria under the name of Austria-Hungary; and (3) from 1867 to the present. See separate articles on individual writers listed below whose names are not followed by birth and death dates.

The movement for a strongly nationalistic Hungarian literature received great impetus from Ferenc Kazinczy (1759–1831), who was instrumental in modernizing the Hungarian language. Among the important poets of the early part of this period were Mihály Csokonai Vitéz (1773–1805), among whose works are the philosophical poem *On the Immortality of the Soul* and the mock epic *Dorothy* (1804); and Sándor Kisfaludy, who wrote *Legends of the Olden Time in Hungary* (1807). Later eminent poets were Sándor

Petőfi, whose patriotic poems established him as the national poet of Hungary; and János Arany, author of many ballads and lyrics, and the epic *Toldi*, in twelve cantos, celebrating the exploits of a legendary Hungarian hero. The foundations of the Hungarian modern national drama were laid at this time by the work of Károly Kisfaludy, author of *The Tartars in Hungary* (1819) and other historical dramas, and also of tragedies and comedies of contemporary Hungarian life. The development of the drama continued with the work of Ede Szigligeti (1814–78), author of *The Deserter* (1843). The most noted fiction writers of the time were Baron Miklós von Jósika (1796–1865), who wrote the earliest Hungarian romantic historical novels; and József Eötvös, author of political novels. Interest in Hungarian folk songs and folk tales was advanced by the collections (1846–48) of folklore of János Erdélyi (1814–68).

The direct expression of Hungarian nationalistic aspirations was prohibited by Hungary's Austrian rulers after the failure of the 1848–49 revolution, and consequently lyric poetry, which had been the principal literary form used for such expression, was strictly censored. The novel and the drama, however, in which allusions to nationalistic ideas could be more covertly made than in lyric poetry, flourished during the period 1849–67. The principal Hungarian writers at this time were the novelist and dramatist Maurus Jókai, among whose works is *A Hungarian Nabob* (1854); and Károly Szász (1829–1905), author of plays, lyrics, and epics. In 1860 the Austrian authorities modified their restrictions on Hungarian poetry, and thereafter notable poetry was written by Imre Madách (1823–64), among whose works is the dramatic poem *The Tragedy of Man* (1861); and by Lajos Tolnai (1837–1902), whose works include *Ballads* (1861) and *Lyric Poems* (1865).

Among the significant Hungarian writers of the last three decades of the 19th century were the playwrights Gergely Csiky, noted principally for *The Proletariat*, and Stephen Toldy (1844–79), who wrote the satiric comedies *The Good Patriots* (1872) and *New Men* (1873); the poet János Vajda (1827–97), noted principally for his volume of lyric poems *From the Diary of Homeguard* (1869); and the novelists Kálmán Mikszáth (1847–1910), author of the humorous tales *St. Peter's Umbrella* (1895) and *A Ghost in Lublo* (1896), and Sándor Bródy (1863–1924), whose best-known work is *The Silver Goat*

(1898). Among the outstanding Hungarian writers of the 20th century are the novelist Zoltán Ambrus (1861–1933), author of *King Midas* (1906) and *Midgets and Giants* (1908); and the poet Enre Ady (1877–1919), who wrote the volumes of verse *Blood and Gold* (1907) and *Leading the Dead* (1918).

HUNGARIAN MUSIC, the national music of Hungary, based essentially upon the folk music of the natives of Hungary, the Magyars, and popularized throughout Europe since the 18th century through performances by Hungarian gypsies.

The earliest type of Hungarian music was performed by minstrels, who recited heroic poems to the accompaniment of a short lute, the koboz, which was the ancient national instrument. The Gregorian chant was introduced into Hungary in the 11th century, but the feeling for Hungarian folk music remained so strong that when the singing of hymns in the churches became general in the 14th and 15th centuries, the Hungarian language was used instead of Latin, and changes were made in the religious music of the time to make it more akin to the native Hungarian music.

From the 15th to the 18th century the Hungarian musical tradition was developed by gypsy musicians, primarily in a special style of instrumental dance music. The gypsy orchestras, led by a violin, performed compositions which consisted mainly of improvised variations on a melody, in a style marked by certain characteristic technical features. These were the so-called "gypsy scale" (a series of augmented seconds in the form of C, D, E♭, F♮, G, A♭, B, and C), the *alla zoppa* (literally "in a limping way") rhythm which accented the second beat in every measure, the use of ornate turns and embellishments of strongly Oriental character, and the tendency to make rubato stops and elongation of rhythms at the convenience of the performers. All of these traditions allowed the gypsy bands great freedom in playing any song, in much the same manner as a modern jazz band. The instruments used were generally those found in modern orchestras, with the addition of a cembalo, an oblong box with steel strings struck by two wooden hammers held by the performer. The best-known 18th-century dances of Hungary were the *verbunko,* a soldiers' dance with slow and fast sections, the *palotache,* a variety of the polonaise, and the *czardas,* named for an inn on the Puszta plain where it was first danced. The *czardas* has two parts: the slow *lassú* and the fast *friss.*

In the 18th century, German composers began using elements of this dance music in their works. Joseph Haydn used such music in his Trio No. 1 in G major, the *Gypsy Rondo,* and similar borrowings were made at a later date by Franz Schubert and Johannes Brahms. Franz Liszt (q.v.), who often composed in a Hungarian idiom, is sometimes considered a Hungarian composer, though modern scholars generally class his music with that of the German romantic composers; his *Hungarian Rhapsody No. 2* is an example of a *czardas.*

The first important Hungarian composer of modern times was Franz Erkel (1810–93), who composed the first opera with a Hungarian text, *Báthory Maria.* He was followed in more recent times by Ernö Dohnanyi (q.v.). The contemporary Hungarian composers Béla Bartók and Zoltán Kodály (qq.v.) have done valuable scholarly work in rediscovering both genuine gypsy forms and folk songs of Hungarian peasant origin, and have used this material in their creative work.

HUNGARY, a republic of central Europe, bounded on the N. by Czechoslovakia, on the N.E. by the Ukrainian Soviet Socialist Republic, on the E. by Romania, on the S. by Yugoslavia, and on the W. by Austria. Hungary is approximately oval in shape, with an extreme length from E. to W. of about 465 m. and a maximum width of about 75 m. The capital and largest city is Budapest (q.v.). Other leading cities are Szeged, Debrecen, Miskolc, Hódmezövásárhely, Kecskemét, Pécs, and Ujpest. Area, 35,912 sq.m.; pop. (1950 est.) 9,313,000.

Hungary is partly encircled by the Alps on the W. and by ranges of the Carpathian Mts. on the N. and on the E. The Danube R. (q.v.), which forms part of the N. boundary with Czechoslovakia, flows in a S. direction across the country into Yugoslavia, dividing Hungary into two general regions. A low, rolling plain, known as the Alfold or the Great Plain of Hungary, comprises the entire region E. of the Danube. Approximately in the center of the region W. of the Danube is located Lake Balaton (see BALATON, LAKE), the largest fresh-water lake in central Europe. Southeastward from the lake, extending to the Danube R. and to the Yugoslav border, is the plains region known as Transdanubia. North of the lake is the Bakony Forest, comprising a part of the Hungarian Mittelgebirg Mts. The range, a projection of the limestone formations of the Alps, extends in a N.E. direction, and contains the highest peaks in Hun-

Ewing Galloway

Budapest, situated on both sides of the Danube River, in Hungary

gary, reaching a maximum elevation of about 3300 ft. Northwest of the Mittelgebirg is the Kis-Alfold or Little Hungarian Plain. Besides the Danube R., other principal rivers of Hungary are the Raba in the N.W., the Kapos in the S.W., and the Tisza and its tributaries in the E.

Hungary possesses a continental climate, modified, however, by warm moist winds from the Mediterranean Sea. The annual range between maximum and minimum temperatures is generally less than 50° F. In S. Hungary the mean annual temperature is about 52° F. and the mean annual temperature in the N. part of the country is about 48° F. A long autumn season, a unique feature of the climate of Hungary, is favorable for agriculture. Maximum precipitation occurs in the N.W., where the annual fall is between 30 and 35 inches. The E. portion of Hungary is the most arid, annual precipitation sometimes amounting to less than 15 inches. May and June are the wettest months, but as a result of the influence of the Mediterranean Sea, fairly heavy rains occur during October in the S.W. part of the country.

Hungary is primarily an agricultural country, and its fertile plains are among the most productive agricultural areas in Europe. A distinctive feature of the rural economy of Hungary prior to the establishment of the

republic early in 1946 was the large number of big estates. In the years immediately following 1945, fundamental land reforms were instituted, with the distribution of arable lands among individual farmers and later among collectives. By 1953 collectives and state farms comprised nearly 25 percent of the arable acreage. The leading crops produced in a recent year were corn, 2,862,000 tons; wheat, 2,040,000 tons; sugar beets, 1,240,000 tons; potatoes, 1,224,000 tons; rye, 790,000 tons; and barley, 640,000 tons. Other important crops are grapes, apricots, apples, cherries, and market produce. The wines produced in the Tokay region are internationally famous. In a recent year there were about 569,000 horses, 1,700,000 cattle, 650,000 sheep, and 4,500,000 hogs on Hungarian farms. Large numbers of goats and poultry also are raised.

Hungary has small deposits of a variety of minerals, including manganese, lignite, silver, copper, mercury, nickel, lead, sulfur, soda, saltpeter, alum, vitriol, iron, coal, and petroleum. The bauxite reserves are among the largest in the world.

The manufacturing industries of Hungary are largely dependent upon the agricultural and mineral production of the country. The principal industries are flour milling, brewing, canning, distilling, sugar refining, and the manufacture of hemp products, iron and steel, hardware, machinery, cotton, woolen, and linen goods, and electrical equipment. By 1948 all enterprises having over 100 employees were nationalized, as well as certain special industries with fewer workers. The following year nationalization was extended to include all enterprises which had more than 10 employees or were financed by foreign capital. The number employed in industry recently was estimated at 989,000.

The fisheries and the forests of Hungary also figure prominently in the domestic economy. The important fisheries of the country are those of Lake Balaton, the Danube R., and the Tisza R. Large catches of pike, carp, sheatfish, perch, shad, and other varieties of fish are harvested annually. The forests of Hungary, consisting chiefly of beech, oak, and pine, cover about 2,682,300 acres.

The Danube R. is the major artery of the Hungarian transportation system. With its navigable affluents, the Danube provides low-cost transit for a large portion of the domestic freight and passenger traffic. The river also figures significantly in the foreign trade of the country, affording ready access to the markets of central and s.e. Europe and to the Black Sea. In a recent year, Hungarian inland-water carriers numbered over 500 vessels of nearly 120,000 gross tons. The railway system of Hungary was extensively damaged during World War II. Over 7100 m. of main-track lines were in operation in a recent year. The Hungarian highway system comprises about 16,000 m. of roads.

The population of Hungary consists principally of Magyars, a branch of the Finno-Ugric linguistic stock. Hungarian and German are the principal languages of Hungary (see FINNO-UGRIC LANGUAGE). Approximately 66% of the Hungarian churchgoers are communicants of the Roman Catholic Church. The other leading religious groups of Hungary are, in the order of number of adherents, members of the Reformed Church, all Protestant denominations, and Jews.

The public-school system of Hungary consists of institutions of higher learning, intermediate schools, and general schools. The last-named category, which was introduced in 1945, includes the former elementary, primary, and lower secondary schools. Attendance at general schools is compulsory for all children between the ages of six and fourteen. By the terms of legislation that went into effect on June 16, 1948, almost all parochial schools were nationalized. The institutions of higher education consist of technical schools, normal schools, and universities, which offer courses in agriculture, forestry, engineering, mining, metallurgy, theology, law, medicine, and the liberal and fine arts. In a recent year the enrollment of these institutions was about 45,000. The University of Budapest is the country's leading university.

The republic of Hungary, proclaimed by the National Assembly on Feb. 1, 1946, is governed according to the provisions of the Constitution of 1949. By the terms of this document, executive power is vested in a council of ministers, or cabinet, headed by a prime minister. The highest organ of the State is the unicameral National Assembly, consisting of 400 deputies elected for a four-year term. The Assembly elects a 21-member presidium which meets between legislative sessions. Justice is administered through a system of county courts, and by various higher courts. The county courts try cases involving minor civil and petty offenses. More important civil and criminal cases are heard by courts of appeal, of which there are five. Appeals from the lower courts are heard by the supreme court, the court of highest resort in all civil and criminal matters.

History. The region comprising contemporary Hungary was part of the ancient Roman provinces of Dacia and Pannonia (qq.v.). Situated on the periphery of the Empire, these provinces were among the first to fall to the Germanic tribes that began to overrun the Roman dominions in the closing years of the 2nd century A.D. The Germanic tribes were later driven from the region by the Huns (q.v.). After the death of the great Hunnish chieftain Attila (q.v.), the Germans reoccupied the area, but were again expelled, in the 5th century, by the Avars, an Asiatic people. With the decline of the Avars' power during the 8th century, the Moravians, a Slavic tribe, seized the N. and E. portions of the region and, between 791 and 797, the Frankish emperor Charlemagne (q.v.) added the remainder to his domains (see MORAVIA). The next conquest of the region occurred when, in 895 or 896, the Magyars, a tribe of uncertain racial origin, seized control of former Pannonia. Under the leadership of their semilegendary chieftain Árpád (q.v.), the invaders conquered Moravia, raided the Italian peninsula, and made incursions into Germany. The Magyars ranged over central Europe for more than half a century after the death (907) of Árpád, and in 955 devastated Burgundy. Later in 955 they were defeated by the Holy Roman emperor Otto I on the Lech River. After this defeat, the Magyars maintained friendlier relations with the Holy Roman Empire (q.v.), with the result that Christianity and Western culture began to penetrate Hungary. The Hungarian ruler Géza was converted to Christianity in 975. His son Stephen I (q.v.), the founder of the Árpád dynasty, received formal recognition as King of Hungary when, in the year 1001, Pope Sylvester II granted him the title of "Apostolic Majesty," an appellation retained by the Hungarian kings for more than nine centuries.

With Stephen, who was later (1087) canonized, a new era began for Hungary. Christianity became the official religion, paganism was suppressed, royal authority was centralized, and the country was divided into counties for administrative purposes. No attempt was made, however, to ease the lot of the non-Magyar sections of the population. Treated as subject races, they were forced to shoulder a disproportionate burden of toil and taxation. This aspect of Hungarian civilization endured for many centuries. After Stephen's death a pagan reaction developed, and his immediate successors had to contend also against barbarian and German invasions. Ladislas I the Saint (1077–95), renowned for his wise legislation and for great personal valor, arranged an alliance with Pope Gregory VII during the Investiture (q.v.) conflict. Thus strengthened, Hungary again became a powerful kingdom. Stephen subjugated Croatia (see CROATIA AND SLAVONIA), Bosnia (q.v.), and part of Transylvania, and his successor Koloman (1095–1114) gained possession of part of Dalmatia (q.v.).

Royal authority in Hungary declined during the 12th century, chiefly because of internal strife instigated by the Byzantine emperor Manuel I Comnenus. Seizing control of the Hungarian throne, he bestowed huge grants of the crown lands on partisans among the native nobility, thereby providing substantial foundations for the development of feudalism. The Byzantine influence disappeared after the death (1180) of Manuel, but the barons retained their privileged status. King Andrew II, who ascended the throne in 1205, attempted to re-establish a centralized regime. In 1222 he issued the Golden Bull, sometimes called the Hungarian Magna Charta, which extended various rights, including tax exemptions, to the nobility. Although the decree gained some adherents among the weaker barons, it failed to reduce the power of the great landowners.

During the reign (1235–70) of Andrew's successor Béla IV, Hungary was overrun by Mongol invaders. Most of the Mongols withdrew from the country in 1241, but subsequent wars, notably with Austria, and further royal concessions to the barons accelerated the disintegration of the kingdom. Civil war raged in Hungary from 1301 to 1308, the year of the death of Andrew III, the last Árpád king. Charles Robert of Anjou, who secured election as sovereign of Hungary in the same year, restored order, imposed limitations on the barons, and generally consolidated the realm. During his reign, which ended in 1342, Charles also made a number of territorial acquisitions, including Bosnia and part of Serbia. Through his marriage to the sister of Casimir III of Poland, he insured the succession of his son Louis to the Polish crown.

The reign of Louis I lasted until 1382. By virtue of his Polish inheritance, obtained in 1370, and of wars of conquest against Venice, Hungary became one of the largest realms of Europe. Louis instituted numerous administrative reforms, further curbed the power of the feudal lords, and promoted the development of commerce, science, and industry. In the closing years of his reign, the Turks, advancing steadily northward into the Balkan peninsula, established their suzerainty in several of Hungary's southern buffer provinces, regions traditionally hostile to Hungarian rule. Sigismund (q.v.), who was elected king in 1387, organized a crusade against the Turks, but was overwhelmingly defeated in 1396. Additional disasters followed in quick succession, including defeats by the Venetians and a costly struggle with the Hussites (q.v.). As Holy Roman emperor, a post to which he was elevated in 1411, Sigismund relentlessly persecuted the Hungarian and Bohemian followers of John Huss (q.v.).

Hungary was again menaced by the Turks during the reign of Sigismund's son-in-law and successor Albert II, a Hapsburg (q.v.) and the duke of Austria. A bitter contest for the throne developed after Albert's death, in 1439, and Hungary was saved from extinction chiefly through the capable military leadership of John Hunyadi (q.v.). Hunyadi, still regarded as the national hero of Hungary, climaxed his career by breaking (1456) the Turkish siege of Belgrade.

Hunyadi's son Matthias Corvinus (q.v.) was elected king, in 1458, in the face of strong opposition from partisans of the Holy Roman emperor Frederick III (q.v.). The new monarch, probably the most able and enlightened ruler of his time, inaugurated various administrative reforms, created a standing army, and promoted the commercial and cultural development of the nation. A brilliant militarist, he inflicted a number of serious defeats on the Turks and, after a prolonged war (1468–78), added Bohemia to his realm. Other territorial acquisitions, including Moravia, Silesia, and Lusatia, made Hungary the strongest kingdom of central Europe.

After the death of Matthias in 1490, the feudal barons regained their former status. In consequence, Hungary was soon engulfed in factional strife, including a peasant rebellion. The general political chaos became intensified during the first two decades of the 16th century, rendering the nation incapable of effective defense against its foreign foes. In August, 1521, a Turkish army under Suleiman I (q.v.) captured Belgrade and Sabac, the chief strongholds of the kingdom in the south. Hungary was spared further attacks by the Turks for five years after this catastrophe, but on August 29, 1526, Suleiman crushed the Hungarian army at Mohács, where King Louis II and more than 20,000 of his men perished. Following the capture (September 10) of Buda, Suleiman withdrew from Hungary.

For more than 150 years after the defeat at Mohács, Hungary was the scene of almost continuous sanguinary strife. The leading participants in the wars of this period were the Hapsburgs, who seized control of the western portion of the defunct kingdom, the Turks, who established their suzerainty in the central region, and important groupings of the native nobility, chiefly that of Transylvania. In the course of the three-cornered struggle for hegemony in Hungary, Transylvania became the center of the Magyar movement against Turkish and Austrian (Hapsburg) domination. The Magyars had abandoned the Church during the Protestant Reformation, thereby aggravating the enmity of the Hapsburgs. After the middle of the 16th century and the beginning of the Counter Reformation, the strife between the Protestant Magyars and the Catholic Hapsburgs became increasingly violent. In the so-called Long War (1593–1606), the Magyars confronted a coalition that included both the Holy Roman emperor and the sultan of Turkey. The Holy Roman emperor Rudolf II triumphed in the first phase of the conflict, and the Magyars were subjected to savage reprisals. In 1604 the Transylvanian Magyars, led by István

Bocskay, rebelled against their persecutors. The insurgents inflicted a series of defeats on the Imperial armies, forcing Rudolf to sue for peace. Concluded in June, 1606, the agreement granted the Magyars of Transylvania political and religious autonomy, additional territory, and other concessions.

The Hungarian nationalist movement, firmly based in Transylvania, struck repeatedly at the Hapsburgs during the next half century. Imperial involvement in the Thirty Years' War (1618–48) created favorable conditions for these onslaughts, which were led at first by Gabriel Bethlen (q.v.), Prince of Transylvania. George Rákóczy, who succeeded Bethlen in 1631, resumed the fight against Hapsburg domination of w. Hungary. In alliance with the Swedes and French, he invaded Austrian territory in 1644. Ferdinand III, the Holy Roman emperor, was forced to meet many of Rákóczy's demands, including the extension of full freedom of religion to all Hungarians under Hapsburg rule. In the decade following the accession to power of George Rákóczy II, an inept ruler, the Turks, who had not been active since the Long War, extended their spheres of influence into Transylvania, gradually reducing it, in effect, to provincial status. Meanwhile, the Jesuits had made remarkable progress in the Hapsburg section of Hungary, winning large sectors of the population back into the Roman Catholic Church. Under the influence of the Church, these Hungarians abandoned the nationalist fight against Hapsburg overlordship. Political reaction ensued as a natural consequence. Increasingly repressive measures were adopted against Protestants. These persecutions provoked a new revolutionary uprising in the Hungarian dominions of the Hapsburgs. Led by Count Imre Thököly, the rebels won a series of victories over the forces of the Holy Roman emperor Leopold I. Thököly obtained, in 1682, the military support of the Turks, and on July 14, 1683, a Turkish army laid siege to Vienna. The siege was broken on September 12 by an army of Poles and Germans commanded by John II Sobieski and Charles of Lorraine. Hostilities continued for more than fifteen years, with the Imperial forces winning a decisive victory over the Turks at Zenta in 1697. The collapse of Thököly's insurgent armies swiftly followed. Besides taking severe reprisals against the rebel leaders, Leopold I forced the Hungarian diet to declare the crown of Hungary forever hereditary in the house of Hapsburg. By the provisions of the Treaty of Karlowitz (1699), the

Eva Besnyö, Max Pohly, from Black Star

SCENES IN HUNGARY. *Top: Peasant woman performing her chores in the farmyard.*
Bottom: A street in the Taban quarter of Budapest.

Turks retained only the Hungarian Banat (q.v.), a region they lost nineteen years later. The Treaty of Karlowitz also secured Transylvania to the Hapsburgs.

In 1703 Francis Rákóczy, taking advantage of Austrian involvement in the War of the Spanish Succession, incited a new uprising against Austrian rule. Rákóczy, who received substantial help from the French, organized a provisional government and held the Austrians at bay until 1708, when he met disastrous defeat at Trenčin. Rebel resistance continued until, in April, 1711, the Holy Roman emperor Charles VI offered satsifactory peace terms. These terms provided for a general amnesty, religious freedom, and various political concessions.

Relations between the Hapsburgs and their Hungarian subjects were generally tranquil for more than a century after the termination of the rebellion of 1703. Queen Maria Theresa (q.v.), who reigned from 1740 to 1780, pursued a genuinely liberal policy in Hungary, extending the educational system, improving the lot of the serfs, and otherwise contributing to national betterment. Throughout the tumultuous period following the outbreak (1789) of the French Revolution, the overwhelming majority of the Hungarian population remained loyal to Austria. The antiabsolutist doctrines of the Jacobins found numerous adherents among the Magyar nationalists, however. Their propaganda led inevitably to a resurgence of Hungarian nationalism, beginning about 1815. Among other things, this development resulted in the creation of a Liberal Party, which launched a vigorous campaign for constitutional government and other reforms. The Liberal movement, headed by such men as Count István Széchenyi, József Eötvös, Ferencz Deák, Lajos Kossuth (qq.v.), and Lajos Batthyányi, was accompanied by remarkable activity in the field of literature (see HUNGARIAN LITERATURE). Overcoming repressive moves by the government, the Liberals secured the passage of a number of progressive bills, including a measure that made commoners eligible for public office and another that curtailed certain feudal restrictions on the peasantry.

The progressive political groupings of Hungary won a decisive victory in the diet election of 1847, but the government refused to recognize this mandate from the voters. On March 13 of the following year, a revolutionary uprising in Vienna forced the downfall of the Austrian government and the flight abroad of its reactionary leader Prince Klem-

ens Metternich (q.v.). The Austrian emperor Ferdinand I shortly yielded to Hungarian nationalist demands and authorized the formation of a Hungarian ministry, with Prince Lajos Batthyány as premier. By the terms of legislation enacted later in March, the ministry severed practically all ties with Austria. Extreme Magyar nationalism, expressed in part by a decree making Hungarian the official language of the state, rapidly alienated the Slavic section of the population. Under the guidance of Count Josip Jelačić od Bužima, a Croatian general, political leader, and supporter of the empire, the Slavic movement against Magyar domination soon flared, in southern Hungary (Croatia), into open insurrection. The Walachians (q.v.) of Transylvania also revolted. Taking advantage of the dissension and turmoil within the country, Emperor Ferdinand, on October 2, appointed Jelačić commander of the royalist forces in Hungary and proclaimed martial law. The revolutionary government at Vienna fell on November 1, leaving the Austrian royalists free to deal with Hungary. Between December 1848, when Francis Joseph I succeeded Ferdinand, and April, 1849, when the Hungarian diet proclaimed establishment of a republic, the revolutionary forces inflicted successive defeats on the Austrian armies.

Emperor Francis Joseph succeeded, in May, in arranging a military alliance with the czar of Russia. Austrian and Russian arms were uniformly successful against the outnumbered Hungarians, who surrendered in August, 1849. On August 13, 1849, still a day of national mourning in Hungary, Batthyány and thirteen other revolutionary leaders were executed. This and other severe reprisals inaugurated a period of despotic Austrian rule extending over more than a decade. After the Austrian defeat (1859) in the Italian War of Liberation, the imperial regime suffered a succession of diplomatic and military reverses. Emperor Francis Joseph was consequently obliged to adopt a conciliatory attitude toward his Hungarian subjects. Magyar nationalism, ably guided by Ferencz Deák, gradually re-emerged as an important force in Hungary. In 1865, the imperial government sanctioned the draft of a new constitution for the Magyar nation. Before this document could be completed, Prussia defeated Austria in the Seven Weeks' War, a debacle that vastly strengthened the position of the Hungarians. By the provisions of the compromise constitution, as finally adopted in March, 1867, Austria and Hungary became dual monarch-

Ewing Galloway

Farmers near Mesökövesd, Hungary, placing ears of corn in the farmyard to dry

ies, under the one king. The constitution granted Hungary full sovereignty in the conduct of internal affairs and parity with Austria in the conduct of national defense, foreign affairs, and certain other matters. On June 8, 1867, Francis Joseph was crowned king of Hungary. The dualist arrangement between Austria and Hungary endured until the defeat of the Central Powers in World War I. (For data relative to the joint monarchies during this period, see AUSTRIA-HUNGARY; FRANCIS JOSEPH I; WORLD WAR I.)

Hungary entered World War I (q.v.) on the side of Austria, largely because of fears in leading Hungarian circles that a Russian victory would alienate the loyalty of the Slavic minority. As the conflict continued, war losses, food shortages, and other privations engendered profound dissatisfaction among the Hungarian people. The death of Emperor Francis Joseph on November 21, 1916, and the succession of Archduke Charles as Charles IV of Hungary weakened the ties between Hungary and Austria. Friction between the new sovereign and the Hungarian premier István Tisza (q.v.) culminated in the latter's resignation, in May, 1917. Internal unrest increased steadily thereafter, and on Oc-

tober 25, Count Mihály Károlyi (q.v.), who had assumed the leadership of the peace movement, established a national council, which intensified the struggle for general suffrage, dissolution of the parliament, and the conclusion of peace with the Allies. The empire was officially dissolved on November 11, 1918, and five days later the national council proclaimed the Hungarian People's Republic, with Károlyi as its first president.

Social and political unrest attained revolutionary proportions in Hungary during the winter of 1918–19, and the extreme left grouping of the Social Democratic Party won increasing support among the industrial working class. This grouping emerged as the Communist Party of Hungary. Under the leadership of Béla Kun (q.v.), an advocate of policies similar to those of the Russian Bolsheviks, the Communists amalgamated with the Social Democrats and, forcing Károlyi to surrender power, established the Soviet Republic of Hungary. The new government which came into being on March 21, 1919, confiscated all industrial and commercial enterprises as communal property. Banks were expropriated and all bourgeois newspapers were banned. Many rebellious elements were summarily executed. Meanwhile, the Czechs had invaded Hungary from the N. and the Romanians from the S. Unable to cope with foreign intervention and confronted by growing counterrevolution among the peasantry, the Soviet government resigned on August 1, 1919. Kun and his chief associates fled into Austria. Budapest was occupied on August 4 by the Romanians, who retained effective control of the nation until their withdrawal, on November 14.

Under Allied supervision, an interim government, representative of the various political parties of Hungary, was established on November 25, 1919. This government was dominated by Admiral Miklos Horthy, a former Austro-Hungarian naval officer who had organized a counterrevolutionary army and government during the period of Communist rule. Horthy immediately instituted severe reprisals against leftists and liberal political groupings. On Allied insistence general elections for a national assembly were held early in 1920. The national assembly officially dissolved all Hungarian affiliations with Austria, proclaimed the country a monarchy, and named Horthy as regent. On June 4, 1920, the Hungarian government accepted the Treaty of Trianon (see TRIANON, TREATY OF), which imposed the peace conditions of the Allied powers. Under the provisions of this document, Hungary was deprived of about two thirds of its territory and half of its population. Territorial cessions included Transylvania to Romania, Croatia to Yugoslavia, and the Slovakian provinces to Czechoslovakia. In 1921 King Charles returned to Hungary from exile on two occasions and demanded his restoration to the throne. The king's demands were rejected by Horthy, who retained his dictatorial hold on the Hungarian government for more than two decades thereafter.

Under the guidance of Count Stephen Bethlen (q.v.), who was appointed premier by Horthy in 1921, Hungary achieved a measure of political stability internally and in its foreign relations. The economic condition of the country grew worse during the decade he held office, however. This circumstance, progressively aggravated by reparations payments and the beginnings (1929–30) of the world economic crisis, and the widespread desire for revenge inspired by the humiliating terms of the Trianon treaty, provided incentive for resurgent Hungarian nationalism. Strong demand arose for revision of the Trianon document and for the enthronement of

Archduke Otto, son of King Charles. The period following Bethlen's resignation (August, 1931) was marked by a sharp increase in nationalist activity and influence. After Horthy's appointment, in September, 1932, of Gyula von Gombos (q.v.) as premier, Hungarian nationalism assumed a fascist orientation, characterized by the suppression of political opposition, persecution of the Jews, an aggressive foreign policy toward neighboring democracies, and rapprochement with the totalitarian regimes of Italy and the Third Reich. The German occupation of Austria, in March, 1938, resulted in even closer relations between Hitler Germany and Hungary. As an immediate consequence, the anti-Semitic policies of the Hungarian government were extended. Close collaboration with the Third Reich brought substantial rewards when, following the partition of Czechoslovakia, Germany agreed to the allocation of part of Slovakia and all of Ruthenia to Hungary. The Hungarian government subsequently withdrew from the League of Nations and became (January, 1939) a signatory, with Germany, Italy, and Japan, of the Anti-Comintern Pact.

On the outbreak of World War II, the government of Hungary officially proclaimed neutrality, but its subsequent actions indicated complete sympathy with Axis objectives. Nationalist demands for the return of Transylvania were partially satisfied on August 30, 1940, when Italy and Germany awarded Hungary the N. portion of the Romanian province. In April, 1921, the Hungarian regime, taking advantage of the German attack on Yugoslavia, ordered its troops into the territory awarded to the last-named nation by the Treaty of Trianon. On June 27, 1941, Hungary declared war on the Soviet Union, and on the following December 13, on the United States. The Hungarian army suffered heavy losses on the Russian front, and in August, 1943, the government directed peace overtures to the Allied powers, asking that Hungary be allowed to withdraw from the conflict at an opportune moment without the sacrifice of territorial gains. These and later overtures of a similar nature were rejected. In March, 1944, German troops occupied the country, and, with Horthy's consent, installed a puppet regime. This regime immediately embarked on a campaign of terror against all dissidents and against the Jews, several hundred thousand of whom were either put to death or deported. The Soviet armies invaded Hungary on October 7, and eight days later Horthy, who had meanwhile

Ewing Galloway

Pump, driven by a horse, is used for irrigating fields on farm near Budapest, Hungary

captured control of the government, announced the successful conclusion of armistice negotiations at Moscow. Horthy was immediately placed under arrest by the German military, which installed a government led by the head of the Hungarian Fascist party (Arrow Cross).

On December 26, shortly after the formation in Russian-held territory of a provisional government with General Béla Miklosz as premier, Soviet troops invested Budapest. The city, almost totally destroyed in the siege, fell on February 13, 1945. Meanwhile, on January 20, representatives of the provisional government signed the armistice terms of the Allied nations. Among other items, these terms provided for the restoration of the Hungarian boundaries of 1938, for Allied rule of the country through an Allied Control Commission, and for reparations in the value of $300,000,000. The provisional government instituted large-scale land reforms in March, 1945, confiscating all of the huge feudal and ecclesiastical holdings. In the campaign preceding the election of a national assembly, the re-established Communist Party, one of the most influential in Hungary, made a vigorous attempt to win majority status. However, the elections, held on November 4, were won by the Small Landholders' Party, led by Baron Zoltan Tildy. On February 1, 1946, at the session which resulted in the proclamation of the Republic, Tildy was elect-

ed president. A coalition cabinet was formed, with Ferenc Nagy (q.v.), a prominent member of the Small Landholders' Party, as premier and Matthias Rakosi, the general secretary of the Hungarian Communist Party, as vice premier.

For many months after the creation of the Hungarian Republic, the nation was on the verge of bankruptcy. Lack of foodstuffs, inflated prices, the damaged transport system, and other economic dislocations severely impeded national recovery. Because of the burgeoning diplomatic struggle, popularly known as the "cold war", between the Soviet Union and the United States, Hungarian hopes for an early peace treaty were frustrated. The "Big-Four" powers (France, Great Britain, the U.S., and the U.S.S.R.), after deliberations extending throughout most of 1946, finally reached agreement in December, 1946, on peace terms for all the former German satellite nations, including Hungary. By the provisions of the treaty, which became effective on September 15, 1947, Hungarian requests for lenient conditions were ignored; the armistice terms with respect to frontiers and reparations were confirmed.

American-Soviet antagonisms were sharply reflected in the sphere of Hungarian politics. Soviet military occupation, which continued until effectuation of the peace treaty, and Communist control of the Hungarian police establishment created insuperable obstacles for Hungarian non-Communists and partisans of the Western democracies. Grouped largely in the Small Landholders' Party, opponents of the sovietization of Hungary shortly collided with Soviet authority and with the rival Communist Party. As early as June, 1946, the Soviet military command had demanded the suppression of anti-Communist propaganda within the Roman Catholic Church, and had taken other steps hostile to Catholicism. A number of leaders of the Landholders' Party were charged, in January, 1947, with conspiracy to overthrow the Republic and placed under arrest. Additional arrests followed, and on May 29, Premier Nagy, then on vacation in Switzerland, submitted his resignation by telephone. Nagy and other prominent political leaders were subsequently accused of participation in the alleged anti-Republican conspiracy. Great Britain and the United States were charged with complicity in the plot. The Hungarian government also launched a purge of army officers and men suspected of disloyalty to the Communist-dominated regime. On July 25, 1947, the national assembly was dissolved. The new parliamentary elections, held on August 31, gave a plurality (100) of the seats to the Communist Party. A combined total of 195 seats was won by the Landholders', Socialist, and People's Democratic parties, all members of the government coalition. Responsible British and American officials declared that a million anti-Communist voters had been disfranchised prior to the election.

The Communist and Socialist parties of Hungary merged as the Hungarian Workers' Party on June 12, 1948. On June 16, after a prolonged and bitter controversy between the government and Jozsef Cardinal Mindszenty (q.v.), head of the Roman Catholic Church in Hungary, the Catholic schools were nationalized by an act of the national assembly. All Catholic members of the assembly who voted for the measure were excommunicated from the Church on June 24. Relations between the government and the leaders of the Church deteriorated steadily in the ensuing period, particularly after the arrest (July 1) of hundreds of priests and nuns because of their opposition to the national school program. The struggle between Church and state was climaxed, on December 27, 1948, by the arrest of Cardinal Mindszenty, an outspoken foe of Communism, his secretary, and twelve alleged accomplices on a variety of charges, including espionage, black-market dealings in currency, and treason.

Cardinal Mindszenty and the other accused were brought to trial on February 3, 1949. The proceedings were marked by several sensational developments, notably the prelate's admission that he was "guilty in principle and detail of most of the accusations made". On February 8 he was found guilty of treason and sentenced to life imprisonment. The verdicts were condemned throughout the democratic world by clerical, lay, and government spokesmen, many of whom charged that the confession had been extorted by means of drugs or torture. On February 9 U.S. Secretary of State Dean Acheson characterized the trial as "a conscienceless attack upon religious and personal freedom".

A new Hungarian legislative body, called the National Assembly, was elected on May 15. The election resembled a plebiscite, with the "Peoples' Front", composed of the major parties, submitting a common list of candidates. On August 10 the National Assembly adopted a new constitution. This document proclaimed the "Hungarian Peoples' Republic", described as a state of workers and peasants.

Hungarian-American relations were further embittered by the arrest (November, 1949) of Robert Vogeler, an American businessman, on charges of espionage and sabotage. Failing to secure his release, the U.S. government forbade (December 20) American citizens to travel in Hungary; a few weeks later Hungary was ordered to close its consulates in New York City and Cleveland. Vogeler was released in April, 1951, under the terms of a "ransom" agreement which included provisions for the reopening of the Hungarian consulates and for ending the ban on American travel.

Relations between the United States and Hungary almost reached the breaking point when the crew of a U.S. Air Force plane, forced down on Nov. 19 by Soviet aircraft in Hungarian territory, was held for trial on charges of "espionage". The U.S. State Department paid a $123,000 fine to secure the release (Dec. 28) of the fliers. In retaliation, the U.S. government again closed the Hungarian consulates in New York and Cleveland and banned travel by American nationals in Hungary.

During 1951 the industrial goals of the Five-Year Plan were revised upward, and the government increased its efforts to bring more women into industry. On Aug. 14, 1952 Matthias Rakosi succeeded Istvan Dobi as prime minister. Dobi was made president of the republic. The dual emphasis on industrialization and the collectivization of agriculture continued during 1952, which was a disastrous year for crops. Famine was averted by heavy imports of food.

In October, 1952, Yugoslavia accused Hungary of provoking border incidents. Four Hungarians, convicted of spying for Yugoslavia, were sentenced to death on Nov. 17. The Yugoslav chargé d'affaires was expelled from Hungary shortly thereafter.

In April, 1953, the government nationalized housing and land, providing a legal basis for its use of evictions and mass deportations as weapons against politically "unreliable" persons. A new all-communist parliament was elected on May 17. On July 4 the veteran communist leader Imre Nagy became prime minister. Characterizing the anticommunist uprisings in East Berlin during the month of June as a "sign" pointing to the need for change, Nagy announced (July 4) a "softer" government program, including less emphasis on industrialization, restoration of the land to the farmers, and tolerance of private enterprise and religion. On July 26 the government granted amnesty to thousands of nonpolitical prisoners and authorized farm collectives to dissolve. In the arena of foreign affairs the new "line" resulted in improved relations with Yugoslavia.

Lt. Gen. Gabor Peter, who as chief of the security police had prepared the charges against Cardinal Mindszenty in 1948, was convicted of antistate crimes in March, 1954, and sentenced to life imprisonment. Unsubstantiated reports were widely circulated late in 1954 that Cardinal Mindszenty had been released.

HUNGER. See FAMINE; FASTING.

HUNG WU. See CHU YÜAN-CHANG.

HUNS, a nomadic Asiatic people, probably of Turkish, Tataric, or Ugrian stock, who spread from the Caspian steppes to make repeated incursions upon the Roman Empire culminating in a series of wars under Attila (q.v.), the most renowned of its leaders, which brought the Roman Empires of both the East and the West to the verge of destruction. At the height of their power the Huns absorbed a number of different racial strains in their armies, and assimilated the characteristics of the populations of their environment, so that in Europe they gradually lost their distinct Asiatic character; but even in their pre-European period they were highly variable in their physical characteristics, and of no certain ethnic or linguistic identity.

All accounts, however, agree in describing them as an aggressive nomadic people of great vigor and comparatively low cultural development, who had developed much skill in the techniques of contemporary warfare, particularly in military horsemanship.

Before the beginning of their recorded European history, the Huns overran the Chinese Empire about 200 B.C., and forced the Emperor Kao-ti to capitulation. Their power in the East was weakened during the following century, and eventually they separated into two distinct camps, one of which, amounting to about 50,000 families, went southward, while most of the remainder, after attempting to maintain themselves on the Caspian steppes, went west and northwest in search of new homes. Of those that went northwest, a large number settled for a time on the banks of the Volga R.; then, under a leader called Balamir, or Balamber, they advanced into the territories of the Alani (q.v.), a powerful people dwelling between the Volga and the Don rivers, and in a battle fought on the banks of the Don completely routed the Alani army and added most of the survivors to their own numbers.

With this event, which occurred in the second half of the 4th century A.D., the history of the Huns in Europe may be said to begin. Their next conquest was over the country of the Ostrogoths, whose retreat they followed to occupy territories abandoned by the Ostrogoths and Visigoths (see GOTHS) as far west as the Danube R. A few years later the Goths revolted against Roman authority, and the Huns crossed the Danube to join them in hostilities against the Eastern Roman Empire. In the wars that immediately followed, the Huns did not play a conspicuous part, but early in the following century they seem to have been joined by fresh hordes, and by 432 A.D., during the reign of the Roman Emperor Theodosius the Younger, they had increased so considerably in power that the Hunnish king, Roas, or Rugilas, was receiving an annual tribute from Rome equivalent to about $70,000 in modern money.

Roas died in 434, and was succeeded by his nephews Attila and Bleda. After the latter's death about 444, Attila extended the Hunnish dominions westward to Gaul and Italy; for the history of the Huns during this period, see ATTILA. After Attila's death in 454, however, the power of the Huns was broken and they ceased to exist as an important factor in European history; many took service in the Roman armies, while oth-

Leigh Hunt (from a drawing)

ers joined fresh hordes of invaders from the north and east, aiding them in their repeated attacks upon the Empire.

HUNSAKER, JEROME CLARKE (1886–   ), American aeronautical engineer, born in Creston, Ia., and educated at the U.S. Naval Academy at Annapolis and at Massachusetts Institute of Technology. He served in the U.S. Navy from 1909 to 1926, advancing to the rank of commander, and was in charge of aircraft design for the Navy Department in Washington, D.C., from 1916 to 1923. He designed the airship (q.v.) *Shenandoah,* and the flying boat NC-4, the first aircraft to fly across the Atlantic Ocean. In 1933, after holding executive positions with Bell Telephone Laboratories and the Goodyear-Zeppelin Corporation, Hunsaker became head of the departments of mechanical and aeronautical engineering at M.I.T. He was elected chairman of the National Advisory Committee for Aeronautics in 1941.

HUNT, HELEN. See JACKSON, HELEN HUNT.

HUNT, HOLMAN, in full WILLIAM HOLMAN (1827–1910), English painter, born in London. "Hark", the first picture he exhibited at the Royal Academy, in 1846, attracted widespread attention. In 1849 he joined the brotherhood of English painters known as the Pre-Raphaelites (q.v.), which included, among others, Dante Gabriel Rossetti and John Everett Millais. He became a fervent disciple of this art movement, which believed in the expression of lofty sentiments in art. In 1854 he visited Egypt and Syria and later painted pictures in Jerusalem, where he became in-terested in the history of the Scriptures. His works, principally moral allegories, include "The Light of the World", an allegorical presentation of Christ knocking at the door of the human soul, and "The Shadow of Death" (both in the Manchester Art Gallery), and "The Triumph of the Innocents" (Birmingham Art Gallery). He wrote *Pre-Raphaelitism and the Pre-Raphaelite Brotherhood* (1905).

HUNT, LEIGH, in full JAMES HENRY LEIGH HUNT (1784–1859), English essayist and poet, born in Southgate, Middlesex, and educated at Christ's Hospital, London. Soon after he left school he began to write verse and to contribute articles to newspapers. In 1808 he began editing a liberal newspaper, the *Examiner,* owned by his brother; he continued his association with it as editor and contributor for thirteen years. In 1813, an article published in the *Examiner* describing the Prince Regent of England as "a fat Adonis of fifty" led to the conviction of Hunt and his brother for libel. They were sentenced to imprisonment for two years and were fined £500. In 1821, after leaving the *Examiner,* Hunt founded a liberal newspaper in Italy in collaboration with the poets Lord Byron and Percy Shelley. In 1825 Hunt returned to England, where he spent the rest of his life and was often in financial difficulties. His last years were made easier, in part, by a government pension granted him in 1847.

Hunt wrote many volumes of criticism and literary anecdote; he was noted for his generous, discerning approach to the work of new poets and writers, typified by his early recognition of the poetic genius of John Keats (q.v.). His essays are imaginative and graceful; his works in this field include *Imagination and Fancy* (1844), *Wit and Humor* (1846), *Men, Women, and Books* (1847), *A Book for a Corner* (2 vols., 1849), and *Table Talk* (1851). His narrative poem *Story of Rimini* (1816) is regarded by literary historians as the precursor of the poetry of the romantic school in England (see ENGLISH LITERATURE: *The Nineteenth Century*); his shorter narrative poem *Abou ben Adhem* is perhaps his best known composition in this field. Among Hunt's other poetic works are *Foliage* (1818), *Hero and Leander* (1819), *Captain Sword and Captain Pen* (1835), and a collection of narrative poems *Stories in Verse* (1855). He was also the author of a play *A Legend of Florence* (1840), and *Autobiography* (3 vols., 1850).

HUNT, RICHARD MORRIS (1827–95), American architect, born in Brattleboro, Vt.

He studied architecture at the École des Beaux-Arts in Paris, and became the leading exponent in the United States of the conservative Beaux-Arts tradition in architecture, which emphasized dignity, symmetry, and the use of ornamental detail taken from historical styles. His work was much in demand at the end of the 19th century when many huge private houses were being built in the United States; these were characterized by imposing effects in imitation of Renaissance architecture, especially the early Renaissance châteaux of France. With the passing of the period of palatial homes, many of his buildings were torn down; still standing are the Vanderbilt residence at Biltmore, North Carolina, and several houses, including "The Breakers", at the fashionable summer resort of Newport, R.I. His public buildings include the Capitol extension, Washington, D.C.; the Yorktown Monument, Va.; and the Fogg Museum, Cambridge, Mass. He helped to found the Institute of Architects, of which he served a term as president.

HUNT, WILLIAM MORRIS (1824–79), American landscape and portrait painter, born in Brattleboro, Vt., and educated at Harvard College. He studied painting with Thomas Couture in Paris, where he also met and was influenced by the painter Jean François Millet. In 1855 he returned to the United States and opened an art school in Boston. He introduced the open-air style of the Barbizon School (q.v.), and was also instrumental in establishing the vogue, still followed by many American painters, of studying art in Paris. Hunt became a fashionable portrait painter, his sitters including Lemuel Shaw, chief justice of the Massachusetts Supreme Court, and Mrs. Charles Francis Adams. His importance to American painting, however, lay in his application of new French methods to landscape painting. Examples of his landscape work are "Peasant Girl at Barbizon" (Boston Museum of Fine Arts) and "Bathers" (Metropolitan Museum of Art, New York City).

HUNTER, JOHN (1728–93), British anatomist and surgeon, born in Long Calderwood, Scotland. His early education was meager and he worked as apprentice to a cabinetmaker, but in 1748 he undertook the study of anatomy under the tuition of his brother William (1718–83). He then studied under several famous surgeons, and finally matriculated at Oxford University. After 1763 he practiced surgery in London, becoming surgeon at St. George's Hospital in 1768, surgeon extraordinary to the king in 1776, and surgeon general to the army in 1793.

Hunter was a tireless student of comparative anatomy and physiology, and insisted that surgery be taught as a science with its basis in anatomy and physiology. His research covered a wide field of subjects, among which were the function of the lymphatic system, the repair of tendons, the development of collateral circulation, the surgical treatment of aneurysm, transplantation and regeneration of tissue, venereal disease, and diseases of the teeth. His surgical technique was the most skillful and advanced in England.

Hunter collected and studied animals from all over the world. At the time of his death his museum contained over ten thousand specimens and preparations useful in the study of anatomy, physiology, and pathology. His collection was purchased by the government after his death and presented to the Royal College of Surgeons. Hunter was elected a Fellow of the Royal Society in 1767. Among his many writings are *A Treatise on the Natural History of the Human Teeth* (1771), *A Treatise on the Venereal Disease* (1786), *Observations on Certain Parts of the Animal Economy* (1786), and *A Treatise on the Blood, Inflammation and Gunshot Wounds* (1794).

HUNTER COLLEGE OF THE CITY OF NEW YORK, a municipal college of liberal arts and sciences, founded in 1869 under the name Female Normal and High School as a training school for women teachers. It was renamed the Normal College of the City of New York in 1870, and received its present name in 1914 in honor of the first president of the college, Thomas Hunter (1831–1914). In addition to academic courses leading to baccalaureate and master's degrees, Hunter College offers specialized courses in journalism, business administration, and social work, and premedical courses. Graduate courses, and evening, extension, and summer sessions were instituted between 1916 and 1921. Admission is open only to residents of New York City; matriculated undergraduates are not required to pay tuition fees. The college is supported by public funds, and is governed by the New York City Board of Higher Education. It is housed in two separate establishments, comprising four buildings erected in 1931 in the borough of The Bronx, and a sixteen-story building erected in 1940 in the borough of Manhattan. Men have been admitted as undergraduates in the Bronx division since 1951. In the fall of 1953 the total

The Cape hunting dog

number of students enrolled was 12,241, of whom 1900 were men; members of the faculty numbered 722.

HUNTER'S MOON. See HARVEST MOON.

HUNTING DOG, common name for either of two mammals, the dhole (see DOG), which is an Indian wild dog, and the Cape hunting dog, *Lycaon pictus,* which is an African animal closely related to the true dogs.

The Cape hunting dog, or hyena dog, is an aberrant species, distinguished from the typical canine by having four toes on each foot. It reaches a length of about five feet, and stands as high as a greyhound. The head is broad and flat, and has a short muzzle, massive teeth, and large upstanding ears, so that the beast somewhat resembles a hyena. The fur is short, thick, and smooth; the tail is long and wolflike. The general color is spotted yellowish gray. The Cape hunting dogs inhabit the open parts of Africa south of the Sahara desert. They travel in packs, hunting large antelope, and killing domesticated cattle and sheep. The animals can be trained to be friendly to man, but cannot be completely domesticated; natives of the Kalahari plateau utilize semidomesticated Cape hunting dogs in the chase.

HUNTINGDON, HENRY HASTINGS, 3rd EARL OF. See HASTINGS, family.

HUNTINGDON, SELINA, COUNTESS OF. See HASTINGS, family.

HUNTINGDONSHIRE or HUNTINGDON, or HUNTS, county of E. central England. Pre-Roman and Roman remains have been found there. During the 6th century it was occupied by an East Anglian tribe and in the 9th and early 10th centuries it was an important center of the Danes; it was recovered for the English by Edward the Elder about 921. The present-day boundaries of the county have changed little since the Domesday Survey in the 11th century. The Ouse and the None are the principal rivers of Huntingdonshire. The terrain of the county is generally undulating and suitable for cultivation and grazing, which are the chief occupations. Brewing, malting and the manufacture of paper and parchment are among the other industries. The capital is Huntingdon (pop., 1951 prelim., 5,282). The principal towns are Old Fletton (pop., 1951 prelim., 8955), Ramsey (5772), and St. Ives (3077). Area, 366 sq.m.; pop. (1951 prelim.) 69,273.

HUNTING LEOPARD, or HUNTING CAT. See CHEETAH.

HUNTINGTON, county seat of Cabell Co., W.Va., situated on the Ohio R., near the mouth of the Guyandot R., 50 miles w. of Charleston. It is served by two railroads, by air lines, and by river barges. The city is the manufacturing and commercial center of an area producing large quantities of oil and natural gas, and is an important river terminal for coal shipments from the nearby bituminous fields. Among the products produced by the numerous industrial establishments in the city are monel metal, nickel and nickel alloys, steel rails and switches, railway cars, thermos bottles, stoves, lenses, glass specialties, furniture, paints, dyestuffs, oxygen, and garments. Huntington also contains railroad repair shops, foundries, machine shops, and breweries. In addition, it is a market for the agricultural products of the surrounding area, chiefly apples and tobacco. The city is the site of the West Virginia Industrial Home for Colored Girls, West Virginia Colored Orphans Home, West Virginia Home for Aged and Infirm Colored Men and Women, a U.S. Veterans Hospital, Huntington State Hospital for mental disorders, and Marshall College. Huntington was laid out in 1869 as the w. terminus for the Chesapeake and Ohio Railroad. It was incorporated as a city in 1871 and named in honor of Collis P. Huntington, then president of the railroad. Pop. (1950) 86,353.

HUNTINGTON, ANNA HYATT (1876–   ), American sculptor, born in Cambridge, Mass. A pupil of the American sculptors Hermon Atkins MacNeil and Gutzon Borglum, she first became known through her small bronzes of animals, of which examples are to be found in the Metropolitan Museum of Art, New York City, in other American museums, in the Edinburgh Museum, Scotland, and in the Luxembourg, Paris. Among her larger sculptures are the colossal "Lions" (Dayton, Ohio), a life-size equestrian statue of Joan of Arc

(Riverside Park, New York City), statues of El Cid (New York City; Seville, Spain; and Buenos Aires, Argentina), and a bust of Louis Agassiz (Hall of Fame for Great Americans, New York University, New York City).

HUNTINGTON, ELLSWORTH (1876–1947), American geographer, explorer, and author, born in Galesburg, Ill., and educated at Beloit College and at Harvard and Yale universities. From 1897 to 1901 he was on the teaching staff of Euphrates College in Turkey, and in the latter year he explored the canyons of the Euphrates River. He accompanied the Pumpelly expedition to Russian Turkestan from 1903 to 1904, and the Barrett expedition to Chinese Turkestan from 1905 to 1906. In the following year Huntington began to teach at Yale University, where he became a research associate in geography with the rank of professor in 1917, and remained until his retirement as professor emeritus in 1945. Huntington's teaching career was interrupted by an expedition to Asia Minor in 1909, a series of climatic investigations in the U.S., Mexico, and Central America as a research associate of the Carnegie Institute of Washington from 1910 to 1913, and service in military intelligence with the rank of captain during World War I.

Huntington was an authority on the relations between environment and heredity among large masses of people, and did particularly important, though as yet controversial, work on the effects of climate upon culture and large-scale migrations. His writings include *The Pulse of Asia* (1907), *Civilization and Climate* (1915), *World Power and Evolution* (1919), *The Character of Races* (1924), *The Pulse of Progress* (1926), *The Human Habitat* (1927), and *Mainsprings of Civilization* (1945).

HUNTINGTON, SAMUEL (1731–96), American Revolutionary leader, born in Windham, Conn. In his youth he devoted his leisure hours to the study of law, and later became a successful attorney in Norwich, Conn. He was elected to the Connecticut Assembly in 1764, became king's attorney in 1765, an associate justice of the Connecticut Supreme Court in 1774, and a member of the Governor's Council in 1775. Notwithstanding his long and loyal service to the British crown, he supported the colonists in their struggle against Great Britain. He was elected a delegate to the Continental Congress in 1776, was one of the signers of the Declaration of Independence, and in 1779 was chosen president of the Congress, in which he served until

1783. He became chief justice of Connecticut in 1784; elected governor of the State in 1786, he was re-elected annually until his death.

HUNTLY, EARLS OF. See GORDON, family.

HUNYADI, HUNYADY, or HUNIADES, JÁNOS or JOHN (about 1387–1456), soldier and national hero of Hungary. He first served under King Sigismund, taking part in the Hussite Wars (q.v.) and in action against the Turks (1437). During the reign of King Albert II, Sigismund's successor, János became known as a brilliant soldier. When, after Albert's death, the nobles of Hungary elected King Ladislas III of Poland to the Hungarian throne, János supported the new king against the Turks who threatened to overwhelm Hungary. János defeated the Turks in several battles during 1441–43. In a new war which Ladislas launched in 1444 in the hope of driving the Turks from Europe, János joined forces with the king, but both were overwhelmingly defeated at Varna in 1444, and Ladislas was killed. Ladislas V, Albert's son, became king, and János was appointed regent, serving from 1446 until 1452. Historians regard his greatest achievements as the destruction of the Turkish fleet in the Danube River in 1456 and his concomitant success against the Turkish army of Mohammed II in raising the siege of Belgrade. See HUNGARY: *History.*

HUNZAS, one of the Dard peoples of N. India, speaking the Dardic language Burishki. All Hunzas belong to a single caste, known as the Yeshkun. They are organized in the petty states of Hunza and Nagar in the Hunza Valley; their situation high in a recess in the mountains has made them one of the most isolated peoples of Dardistan (q.v.).

HUPA, an American Indian tribe of the Athapascan linguistic stock, originally occupying a number of small villages along the Trinity River in the Hoopa Valley of N.W. California, and now gathered in a U.S. government reservation in the same region. Until 1848 the tribe was completely isolated; in the next few years the Hoopa Valley was overrun during the gold rush and the Hupa were driven from their homes; subsequent resettlement and the securing to them of the reservation in 1864 did not wholly succeed in re-establishing the patterns of their primitive life, but intensive ethnological study of the culture has made it one of the best known, and shown it to be one of the most advanced, of the Pacific coast division of the Athapascan family. In recent times the population of the tribe has become stabilized at approximately 600 persons.

Hupa culture, similar to that of the Yurok and Karok tribes (qq.v.), is the southernmost example of the Indian cultures of the Pacific Northwest, though it lacks certain characteristic features of the northern tribes, such as secret societies, masks, totem poles, and potlatch ceremonies. Like the tribes of the Northwest, the Hupa base many of their customs (such as marriage by purchase) and social distinctions (such as the assumption of chieftainship) upon wealth; an aristocracy of the wealthy in earlier days commanded the services of its debtors as slaves. Wealth was acquired through the ownership of fishing sites and oak groves, and by hunting deer, elk, panthers, and other big game, and fishing salmon and sturgeon in the Trinity River; it was reckoned in dentalium-shell and woodpecker-scalp currencies and in hides. Vegetable foods used by the Hupa include a variety of wild seeds and nuts, particularly the acorn, and tobacco is cultivated. The art of the tribe consists chiefly in rich basketry, clothing and skin ornaments, and a body of nonreligious, wealth-displaying dances accompanied by the recitation of narrative and magical formulas.

HUPEH, province of central China, situated in the Yangtze R. valley. The region is mountainous in the N., and level in the central and the S. portions. The Yangtze R. and its tributary the Han cross the center of the great plain, making it extremely fertile. Adjacent to the Yangtze are numerous lakes, serving as reservoirs for the flood waters of the river. The principal crops of Hupeh are rice, cotton, and legumes. Wuchang (q.v.) is the capital, and Hankow (q.v.) is the most important commercial city of the province. Area 71,796 sq.m.; pop. (1952 est.) 21,470,000.

HURDY-GURDY, a medieval musical instrument resembling a lute or viol. It is sometimes confused in popular usage with the hand organ or barrel organ (q.v.). The strings of a true hurdy-gurdy are vibrated by a rotating, rosined wheel acting as a bow and turned by a crank. Several strings are constant in pitch and provide a bass drone; the others (usually two in number) are tuned in unison and are strung along a finger board to which is attached a keyboard mechanism. This mechanism, operated by the hand not engaged in turning the crank, lengthens or shortens the strings, thereby effecting changes in pitch. The hurdy-gurdy was popular from the 10th to the 12th century, and again in the 18th century.

HURLEY, PATRICK JAY (1883–   ), American soldier and diplomat, born in the Choctaw Nation Indian Territory (now Oklahoma), and educated at the Indian University (now Bacone College), at the National University Law School, and at George Washington University. He was attorney for the Choctaw Nation from 1912 to 1917, and after America's entry into World War I he served as a U.S. Army officer in France. During the 1920's he was active in the Republican Party, and from 1929 to 1933 he was secretary of war in the cabinet of President Herbert Hoover. He again attained prominence during World War II, in January, 1942, when he was recalled to active military duty, promoted to the rank of brigadier general, and assigned to the Far East Theater of Operations. Late in 1942 and throughout 1943 he acted as personal representative of President Franklin D. Roosevelt in the Soviet Union and in a number of countries in the Near and Far East. He was promoted to the rank of major general in 1944, and after serving for some months as a personal Presidential envoy in China, was appointed U.S. ambassador to that country. There, he attempted to bring about an end to the civil war between the government of Chiang Kai-shek and the communists (see CHINA: *History*); he resigned in November, 1945, and returned to the United States. He was the unsuccessful Republican candidate for the office of U.S. senator from New Mexico in 1948 and 1952.

HURONIAN, system of sedimentary rock strata deposited during the Algonkian (Proterozoic) era in North America. The system is exposed in an area north and west of Lake Huron, and indicates the existence of an inland sea at the time of deposition. Huronian strata reach a thickness of as much as 15,000 to 20,000 feet, and are divided by unconformities into three distinct series: Upper Huronian (Animikean), Middle Huronian, and Lower Huronian. The strata consist predominantly of arkoses, quartzites, and sandstones, and contain smaller deposits of limestones and fine shales. Glacial striations and grooves found in lower Middle Huronian strata are evidence of the earliest Ice Age known to geologists. Iron carbonate beds which produce about 80 percent of iron mined in the Lake Superior region are outcrops of Huronian beds which have been oxidized and concentrated into massive deposits by percolating subsurface water. The Huronian system was succeeded by the Keweenawan (q.v.) series. See GEOLOGY, SYSTEMATIC.

HURON, LAKE, the second largest of the Great Lakes of North America, located on the northern border of the U.S. between Lake Superior on the N.W. and Lake Erie on the S.W. It is connected with both of these lakes and with Lake Michigan on the W., and is bounded on the W. by Michigan and on the N., E., and S. by Ontario, Canada. The total area of Lake Huron is about 23,200 sq.m., of which about 9100 sq.m. are in the U.S. The greatest length of the main body of the lake is 235 m., and its average width about 70 m.; a large arm to the east known as Georgian Bay, extending far into Ontario, is 125 m. long and 60 m. at its maximum width.

The surface of the lake, with occasional fluctuations due to winds, variations in barometric pressure, and seasonal cycles of water supply, is about 581 ft. above sea level. The mean depth of the water is about 250 ft., and the maximum depth about 750 ft. The waters of the lake are transparent and pure and abound in fish, of which the whitefish is commercially the most important. Though the main body of water is clear, the lake contains about three thousand islands, grouped mainly in the N. and nearly all belonging to Canada, the largest of which is Grand Manitoulin.

Navigation on Lake Huron is impossible for large vessels during parts of winter and spring because of the violent storms to which the lake, like all the Great Lakes, is subject. The period of safe navigation extends from the first half of April to the middle of December in the north and to the end of December in the south. There are many good harbors, most of them on the Canadian side; the only U.S. ports with sufficient depth to handle large vessels are Rockport and Calcite, Mich., which have been built up by trade and shipping in limestone. Harbor Beach, Mich. (pop. in 1950, 2349), about 60 miles w. of the St. Clair River, has a breakwater with a sheltered area within it of about 650 acres. Other ports in Michigan are Alpena, Cheboygan, Bay City, and Port Huron. The Canadian ports include Goderich, Collingwood, Kincardine, Midland, and Blind River. Large quantities of iron and copper ore, grain, coal, and limestone are transported on the lake.

For a description of the geological features of Lake Huron and the shipping on the lake, see GREAT LAKES.

HURONS (an unkempt person or ruffian, from Fr. *hure,* "a disheveled head of hair"), originally, a confederation of four Iroquoian tribes living in the region between lakes Huron, Erie, and Ontario. At the beginning of the 17th century, when the first French settlers and missionaries arrived in this region, the Hurons were at the height of their power, with their main concentration in about twenty-five villages near the Georgian Bay of Lake Huron, and a population which has been variously estimated at from 10,000 to 30,000. Their numbers, however, were greatly reduced about 1625 by smallpox and other epidemics. The French missionaries began to establish Jesuit missions among them about this time, and made many converts and brought a measure of stability to the communities in which they worked.

The Huron confederacy consisted entirely of Indians of the Iroquoian family (q.v.), and the culture of the tribes was similar to that of the Iroquois (q.v.), but the Iroquois and the Hurons were bitter hereditary enemies, and in the years between 1648 and 1650 Iroquoian invasions decimated the tribes and drove them westward, where they first attempted to settle with a closely related tribe, the Tionontati, and then, in company with this tribe, continued their westward migration which eventually ended around the present site of Detroit, Mich. By the time they were formally admitted to the friendship of the Iroquois in 1723, the Hurons were a small, comparatively diffuse group. The most important descendants of the members of the confederacy, organized in the Wyandot (q.v.) tribe, acquired a certain prominence in the Ohio country. The remaining Huron survivors are now found at Jeune Lorette, near Quebec, at Sandwich, Ontario, and at the Wyandotte reservation, Oklahoma.

HURRICANE, name applied to migratory, tropical cyclones (q.v.) which originate over oceans in certain regions near the equator, and particularly to those arising in the West Indian reigon, including the Caribbean Sea and the Gulf of Mexico. Cyclones of the hurricane type which arise in the western Pacific are known as typhoons.

Most hurricanes originate within the doldrums, a narrow equatorial belt characterized by intermittent calms, light variable breezes, and frequent squalls, and lying between the northeast and southeast trade winds. As the doldrums of the Atlantic are situated largely to the north of the equator, hurricanes do not occur in the South Atlantic Ocean. The Pacific doldrums extend north and south of the equator; consequently hurricanes occur in the South Pacific and North Pacific oceans.

Hurricanes consist of high-velocity winds

Harper Bros.

Fannie Hurst

blowing circularly around a low-pressure center, known as the eye of the storm. The low-pressure center developes when the warm, saturated air prevalent in the doldrums is underrun and forced upward by denser, cooler air. From the edge of the storm toward its center, the atmospheric pressure drops sharply and the wind velocity rises. The winds attain maixmum force close to the point of lowest pressure (about 28.5 in.). In a fully developed hurricane the winds exceed 75 m.p.h. and may attain velocities as high as 150 m.p.h. The diameter of the area affected by winds of destructive force may be over 150 mi. Gale winds prevail over a larger area, the diameter of which averages 300 mi. Within the eye of the storm, which averages about 15 mi. in diameter, the winds cease abruptly, the storm clouds lift, and the seas are exceptionally violent and confused.

Hurricanes generally move in a path resembling the curve of a parabola (q.v.). In the northern hemisphere the storms usually travel first in a northwesterly direction and in the higher latitudes turn toward the northeast. In the southern hemisphere the usual path of the hurricane is initially to the southwest and subsequently to the southeast. Hurricanes travel at varying rates of progression. In the lower latitudes the rate ranges from 5 to 20 m.p.h. and in the higher latitudes it may increase to as much as 50 m.p.h. Those areas in which the hurricane winds blow in the same direction as the general movement of the storm are subjected to the hurricane's maximum destructive violence. Three severe hurricanes caused extensive damage in N.E. North America in the late summer and early fall of 1954. Thereafter U.S. metereologists intensified their studies of the nature and behavior of these storms. See also METEOROLOGY.

HURST, FANNIE (1889–   ), American short-story writer and novelist, born in Hamilton, Ohio, and educated at Washington University, St. Louis, Mo. She was a school teacher for a time and then took up writing as a career in New York City; she contributed short stories to leading American magazines and gradually became one of the most popular American authors of her time. Her short stories and novels dealt with varied subjects, including the life of the poor and the middle class in New York City, the modern woman and her problems, and the life of actors and musicians. Among her volumes of short stories are *Just Around the Corner* (1914), *Gaslight Sonatas* (1918), *Humoresque* (1919), and *Procession* (1929). Her novels include *Star Dust* (1921), *Lummox* (1923), *Five and Ten* (1929), *Back Street* (1930), *Great Laughter* (1936), *Hallelujah* (1944), *Hands of Veronica* (1947), and *Anywoman* (1950). Her stories have been translated into many languages and have formed the basis for many motion pictures.

HURSTMONCEUX CASTLE. See GREENWICH OBSERVATORY.

HUSBAND AND WIFE, in law, the relationship between two persons, established by the marriage contract and resulting in the creation of rights and obligations of the spouses between themselves and in relation to others.

In the United States today the legal status of husband and wife varies among the forty-eight States; it ranges from the early common-law status in which husband and wife are a single legal entity, to that established by modern statutes in which husband and wife are separate entities. As a general rule in the United States, the personal rights of the husband over the wife are now very limited. He has no right of chastisement, as under the early common law. The husband is the legal head of the family and the domicile (q.v.) established by him must be followed by the wife. He has the duty to support his wife and family. The husband is liable for the debts of the wife contracted for food, clothing, and other necessaries unless the wife abandons the husband without just cause. A husband who abandons his wife or children may be arrested and punished for nonsupport. A husband is not liable for the torts or crimes of his wife. In cases of personal injuries to a wife caused by a third person the wife has a cause of action for injuries to her person and the husband has a cause of action for loss of services of his wife. In cases involving ownership of property and negotiation of contracts the wife is generally considered as if she were single. In most States a wife is as competent as her husband to make a testamentary disposition of property. However, in some States the rights of dower (q.v.) and curtsy still exist. In legal proceedings husband and wife are generally permitted to testify against each other, except in criminal actions, or when such testimony will disclose a confidential communication arising out of the marital relationship. See DIVORCE; MARRIAGE; SEPARATION.

HUSS, JOHN, or (Czech) JAN HUS (1369?–1415), Bohemian religious reformer, born in Husinec, near Budweis, and educated at the University of Prague. He became lecturer in theology at the university in 1398; in 1401 he was ordained a priest, and in 1402 became rector of the university. He came under the influence of the doctrines of John Wycliffe, whose *Trialogus* he translated (1403) into the Bohemian language. In 1408 the subject matter of some of his sermons was made grounds of complaint to the archbishop, and Huss was forbidden to exercise his priestly functions in the diocese. In this connection Pope Alexander V issued a bull condemning the teachings of Wycliffe and ordering his books burned; the bull also forbade preaching in any but parish, collegiate, and monastery churches. Huss was excommunicated in 1410 for teaching Wycliffe's doctrines. Popular riots broke out in the city, and Huss, backed by the popular will, continued to preach, even after the city was laid under interdict in 1412. By the next year, however, many of his influential supporters had fallen away, and Huss fled from Prague, finding refuge in the castles of several friendly noblemen. During this time he wrote his principal work, *De Ecclesia.* In 1414 Huss was summoned to appear before a general council at Constance, being guaranteed safe conduct by the Emperor Sigismund. He was imprisoned, however, and was tried for heresy. Called upon to recant and pledge himself not to advocate or teach his doctrines (see HUSSITES), Huss refused categorically. He was condemned and burned at the stake. This act of the council gave rise to the Hussite Wars (q.v.).

HUSSEIN (1935–   ), King of Jordan from 1952, son of Talal I, educated at Harrow School, England. The Jordanian parliament deposed his father, the victim of a serious mental disease, on Aug. 11, 1952, and proclaimed Hussein king the same day. During the remainder of his minority a regency council exercised his prerogatives. Hussein formally ascended the throne on May 2, 1953, his eighteenth birthday.

HUSSEIN KAMIL or **KEMAL** (1850?–1917), Sultan of Egypt, the son of the khedive of Egypt Ismail Pasha (q.v.), born in Cairo, and educated in local schools and in Paris. After 1883 he held a number of important governmental posts and became a close associate of the British colonial administrators in Egypt, especially of Lord Horatio Kitchener. Hussein was elevated to the sultanate by the British upon the outbreak of World War I, to replace his nephew, the khedive Abbas Hilmi II, following an attempt by the latter to make Egypt an ally of Turkey and the Central Powers. Hussein rendered substantial military aid to the British in the defense of the Suez Canal against the Turks and also in the Gallipoli and Dardanelles Campaign (q.v.) of 1915–16. See EGYPT: *History.*

HUSSITES, members of a Christian sect which, composed of the followers of John Huss, arose in the early 15th century. The preaching of Huss was largely concerned with church reform, rather than theological doctrines, in which he followed John Wycliffe. After the death of Huss the movement assumed a revolutionary character (see HUSSITE WARS). Almost from its inception, it was split into two factions: the Calixtines (q.v.), who favored *Utraquism,* or Communion in Both Kinds (q.v.); and the more radical Taborites, who rejected most of the doctrines and practices of the Church, except the sacraments of Baptism and the Lord's Supper, and favored a democratic and puritanical organization and apostolic communism. The doctrines acceptable to both parties were formulated in the demands of the Articles of Prague, as follows:

"1. The word of God shall be preached . . . freely and in an orderly manner by the priests of the Lord . . .

"2. The sacrament of the most Holy Eucharist shall be freely administered in the two kinds, that is bread and wine . . .

University of Chicago
Robert Hutchins

"3. The secular power over riches and worldly goods which the clergy possesses . . . shall be taken and withdrawn from it . . .

"4. All mortal sins, and in particular all public and other disorders . . . shall in every rank of life be duly and judiciously prohibited and destroyed by those whose office it is."

HUSSITE WARS, a series of conflicts within the Holy Roman Empire, lasting from 1415 to 1436. The condemnation to death of John Huss (q.v.) by the Council of Constance, while Huss was under a guarantee of safe conduct by the Holy Roman emperor Sigismund, resulted in the identification of the religious revolt of his followers with Bohemian nationalism. Honoring Huss as a martyr, about 450 Bohemian noblemen formed a league, defying the decrees of the bishops and the pope. King Wenceslaus of Bohemia, brother of the emperor, granted them the use of many churches. After the death of Wenceslaus in 1419, the majority of the members of the league refused to recognize the right of the emperor to rule as king of Bohemia.

In 1420 a crusade was proclaimed against Bohemia by Pope Martin V. The proclamation had the effect of uniting the nation under Jan Zizka (q.v.), who defeated the forces repeatedly sent against the Hussites by the emperor and the pope. On the death of Zizka in 1424, Andrew Procop (called Procop the Great) assumed command of the Hussite forces; he defeated the three crusades of 1426, 1427, and 1431, and raided neighboring German territories. In 1434 the dissentions between the Calixtines and the Taborites (see HUSSITES) broke into open civil war; the Taborites were defeated at the battle of Lipan, and were almost annihilated. The moderate Calixtines accepted a compromise offered by the Council of Basel, and in 1436 signed the *Compactata of Prague,* winning the right to retain the churches they held, the right to preaching in the Bohemian language, and to Communion in Both Kinds (q.v.).

HUTCHESON, FRANCIS (1694–1746), Scottish philosopher, born in County Down, Ireland, and educated at the University of Glasgow. After a short period of preaching as a minister of the Presbyterian church, he opened a private academy in Dublin in 1719, where he wrote the works upon which his reputation is based, notably *Inquiry Concerning Moral Good and Evil* (1725), *Essay on the Nature and Conduct of the Passions and Affections* (1728), and *Illustrations upon the Moral Sense* (1728). In 1729 he returned to Glasgow to assume the post of professor of moral philosophy at the unversity, and there remained until his death.

Though Hutcheson made contributions to the fields of logic, esthetics, and mental philosophy which are historically interesting as links between the thought of the English philosopher John Locke (q.v.) and that of the Scottish school, his main importance rests upon his ethical system. His system is, to a large extent, similar to that of the 3rd Earl of Shaftesbury (q.v.), but has the advantages of being more complete, coherent, and clearly illustrated. Hutcheson postulated a "moral sense" which operated as a judge of the good, and a principle of conduct called by him "calm benevolence", as opposed to simple self-interest. In this respect he was the forerunner of the English utilitarians (see UTILITARIANISM), even anticipating their use of the phrase "the greatest happiness for the greatest number". Hutcheson's last major work, *System of Moral Philosophy,* was published posthumously in 1755. See ETHICS.

HUTCHINS, ROBERT MAYNARD (1899–), American educator and author, born in Brooklyn, N.Y., and educated at Oberlin College and Yale University. He was lecturer at the Yale Law School from 1925 to 1927, and in the ensuing two years was successively acting dean and dean. During this time, in association with Milton Charles Winternitz (1885–   ), dean of the Yale Medical School, he established at Yale the Institute of Human Relations, for the study of the social sciences. Hutchins was president of the University of Chicago from 1929 to 1945, and chancellor until 1951. He introduced a number of administrative reforms at that institution, eliminating required courses as a condition for graduation, the use of grades, and the recording of class attendance. From 1951 to 1954 he was an associate director of the Ford Foundation. After 1954 he was president of the Fund for the Republic, a research organization in the field of civil liberties.

As a leading advocate of the doctrine of intellectualism (q.v.), Hutchins asserted that the cultivation of the intellect should be the true aim of education. He opposed the disproportionate emphasis allegedly placed by American universities on practical, scientific, and technical studies; and he urged intensive study of the great writings of the past, and of formal grammar, logic, rhetoric, and mathematics as the proper means of producing a genuinely well-educated citizenry. His writings include, besides numerous magazine articles, *No Friendly Voice* (1936), *The Higher Learning in America* (1936), *Education for Freedom* (1943), and *The University of Utopia* (1953).

HUTCHINSON, county seat of Reno Co., Kans., situated on the Arkansas R., 50 miles N.W. of Wichita. It is served by three railroads, and is the fourth-largest city in the State, and a leading market for hard wheat. The city is the center and shipping point of an area producing also livestock, poultry, dairy products, lumber, and salt. Beneath the surface of the city and the surrounding area lie beds of salt 400 ft. thick. Among the industrial establishments in Hutchinson are creameries, grain elevators, meat-packing plants, flour mills, salt-evaporating plants, oil refineries, and factories manufacturing soda ash and strawboard. The city is the site of the State Industrial Reformatory and of the annual Kansas State Fair. Hutchinson was founded in 1871 and incorporated as a city in 1872. Pop. (1950) 33,524.

HUTCHINSON, ANNE (1591–1643), American religious reformer, born in Alford, England. She married William Hutchinson in 1612, and emigrated with him to Boston, Mass., in 1634. At meetings which she organized among Boston women, which were later attended by many of the leaders of the community, she preached a doctrine of salvation through intuitive apprehension of grace rather than by works, attacking the rigid moral and legal codes of the New England Puritans. In 1637 she was tried by the General Court of Massachusetts on the charge of "traducing the ministers", and was banished from the Massachusetts colony. She moved with her husband and family to Aquidneck (now in Rhode Island), and after the death of her husband in 1642, she settled near the present site of Pelham Bay, N.Y. In the following year she and all the members of her family, except one daughter, were killed in an Indian massacre.

HUTCHINSON, THOMAS (1711–80), American colonial governor, born in Boston, Mass., and educated at Harvard College. After holding a number of minor posts in the Massachusetts colony, he was appointed lieutenant governor in 1758, and chief justice of the Superior Court in 1761. In 1765, when the Stamp Act (q.v.) was passed by the English Parliament, he regarded it as unwise and urged its repeal, but nevertheless insisted that it be enforced. As a result of his attitude the Boston populace became incensed against him and sacked his home, destroying a num-

Sculpture of Anne Hutchinson and daughter

Harper Bros.

Aldous Huxley

ber of valuable historical documents. He was acting as governor of the colony in 1770 when the Boston Massacre (q.v.) occurred, and he was afterward compelled by a deputation of citizens headed by Samuel Adams, to order the removal of the British troops from the city. In 1771 he became governor; three years later popular resentment against his continued support of the British regime rose to such a pitch that he asked for and obtained a leave of absence. He spent the rest of his life in England, where he acted as adviser on American affairs to George III and the British cabinet. His writings include *A Brief Statement on the Claim of the Colonies* (1764), and *History of the Province of Massachusetts Bay* (vol. 1, 1764; vol. 2, 1767; vol. 3 published posthumously, 1828).

HUTTEN, ULRICH VON (1488–1523), German reformer, author, and soldier, born near Fulda, Prussia. In early life he was sent to the Benedictine monastery at Fulda, but he became an opponent of the teachings of the Church and in 1505 fled from the monastery. After studying at a number of German and Italian universities, and serving briefly in the army of the Holy Roman emperor Maximilian I, he secured the patronage of the elector of Mainz in 1514. In the following year, when his uncle, Hans von Hutten, was murdered at the instigation of Duke Ul-

rich of Württemberg, Hutten launched a campaign of literary invective against the duke which made him famous throughout the empire. Maximilian I proclaimed him poet laureate in 1517. Two years later Hutten participated in the campaign launched by the Swabian League of German cities against Duke Ulrich. During this campaign Hutten became a close friend of the soldier and reformer Franz von Sickingen; in association with Sickingen he later became an outstanding advocate of German patriotism and of the sovereignty of the emperor with regard both to the papacy and the nobility. He also was an ardent supporter of the Protestant reformer Martin Luther (q.v.), whose doctrines he defended in a series of works. These activities eventually alienated his patron, and Hutten spent the last years of his life in poverty. He was the chief author of the second part of the satirical *Epistolæ Obscurorum Virorum* (q.v.). His other writings include *Ars Versificandi* (1511); a series of polemics against Duke Ulrich, notably *Ciceronian Orations* and *Letters* (both 1519); and *Vadismus* (1520).

HUTTON, JAMES (1726–97), Scottish geologist, born in Edinburgh. Hutton was educated as a doctor in Edinburgh and Paris, but turned from this profession to the study and practice of agriculture. He farmed successfully in Berwickshire until 1768, when he retired to Edinburgh to devote himself to scientific research. He made contributions in a number of fields of physical science, including meteorology and the study of heat, light, and the nature of matter, but his most important work was the systematization of his geological observations and those of earlier geologists and the statement of a uniform theory of the nature of geological processes. In 1785 Hutton communicated his theory in a paper to the Royal Society of Edinburgh, and enlarged it in his *Theory of the Earth, with Proofs and Illustrations* (1795).

Hutton was the first exponent of the doctrine of uniformitarianism, which holds that all rocks and natural features of the earth's surface were created by the erosional and land-building forces that are still at work. In this he differed from almost all earlier geologists, who explained the structure of rocks and of the earth's crust as being partly or wholly due to cataclysmic action at the time of the creation of the world. Hutton showed that certain rocks had been formed by sediments on the sea bottom which had been subjected to great pressure, that others had been formed by volcanic action, and that earlier rocks had frequently been distorted and changed in structure by volcanic action and movements of the earth's crust. He also stated that all rocks are subject to decay through weathering and must ultimately return to the floor of the sea in the form of sediment. With certain modifications, Hutton's theories are those of present-day geologists, and he is usually regarded as the creator of modern geological science. Hutton's own treatise on geology was an obscure and difficult work and did not obtain recognition until after his death. In 1802 the Scottish mathematician John Playfair (1748–1819) published *Illustrations of the Huttonian Theory of the Earth* which summarized and illustrated Hutton's thesis, and Hutton's beliefs soon won general acceptance. Hutton also wrote a *Theory of Rain* (1784) and *Dissertations on Different Subjects in Natural Philosophy* (1792).

HUXLEY, ALDOUS LEONARD (1894–   ), English novelist, essayist, and critic, grandson of Thomas Henry Huxley (q.v.), born in Godalming, Surrey, and educated at Eton College and Oxford University. In 1919–20 he worked on the staff of the magazine *Athenæum* in London, writing musical, dramatic, and art criticism. He worked also in 1920–21 as dramatic critic on the literary periodical the *Westminster Gazette*. In 1937 he emigrated to the United States. His first novel *Crome Yellow* (1921) was followed, among others, by *Antic Hay* (1923), dealing with the effect of skepticism on life; *Those Barren Leaves* (1925); *Point Counter Point* (1928), perhaps his most widely-discussed piece of fiction; *Brave New World* (1932); *Eyeless in Gaza* (1936); and *After Many a Summer Dies the Swan* (1940). Among Huxley's other works are the volumes of essays *On the Margin* (1923), *Jesting Pilate* (1926), *Proper Studies* (1927), *Music at Night* (1931), and *The Olive Tree* (1937); the volumes of poems *The Burning Wheel* (1916), *Leda* (1920), *Arabia Infelix* (1929), and *The Cicadas* (1936); and the volumes of short stories *Little Mexican and Other Stories* (1924), *Two or Three Graces* (1926), and *Brief Candles* (1930). Huxley is also the author of *Grey Eminence* (1941), a study of the relations between politics and mystical religion, written in the form of a biography of Father Joseph, coadjutor of the French ecclesiastic Cardinal Richelieu; *The Art of Seeing* (1942); *Perennial Philosophy* (1945); *Science, Liberty and Peace* (1946); *Ape*

and Essence (1948); *The Devils of Loudun* (1952); and *The Doors of Perception* (1954).

HUXLEY, JULIAN SORELL (1887–   ), British biologist and author, born in London, and educated at Balliol College, Oxford. He was the grandson of Thomas Henry Huxley and brother of Aldous Huxley. From 1913 to 1916 he was assistant professor of zoology at Rice Institute, Houston, Texas. During World War I he served at Allied General Headquarters in Italy. He was a Fellow of New College, Oxford, from 1919 to 1925, and professor of zoology at King's College, London, from 1925 to 1927. He was professor of physiology at the Royal Institution from 1926 to 1939, and secretary of the Zoological Society of London from 1935 to 1942. In 1946 he was appointed executive secretary of the Preparatory Commission of the United Nations Educational, Scientific, and Cultural Organization (UNESCO). He served (1947–48) as director-general of UNESCO. Huxley made extensive use of writing and film production as means for popularizing science. He was particularly interested in problems of evolution and growth. His writings include *Essays of a Biologist* (1923), *Essays in Popular Science* (1926), *Bird-watching and Bird Behavior* (1930), *Problems of Relative Growth* (1932), *Scientific Research and Social Needs* (1934), *The Living Thoughts of Darwin* (1939), *The New Systematics* (1940), *Evolution: The Modern Synthesis* (1943), *Evolution and Ethics* (1947), *Heredity, East and West* (1949), *Evolution in Action* (1953), and *From an Antique Land* (1954).

HUXLEY, THOMAS HENRY (1825–95), English biologist, born in Ealing, Middlesex, and educated in medicine at Charing Cross Hospital, London. He graduated and was admitted to the Royal College of Surgeons in 1845. The following year he entered the Royal Navy as assistant surgeon of H.M.S. *Rattlesnake*. During his tour of duty in Australasian waters, which lasted until 1850, Huxley became thoroughly familiar with the surface animals of tropical seas. His observations on the Medusa family of jellyfish led to the formulation of the zoological class, Hydrozoa, and to the realization that the two germ layers found in members of the class are homologous with the two germ layers which arise in the early embryological stages of higher animals. Returning to England in 1850, Huxley was made a Fellow of the Royal Society. The Royal Navy retained him as a nominal assistant surgeon until 1853; Huxley used this time to write several scientific papers, including an authoritative work on the morphology of cephalopod molluscs. Huxley became professor of natural history and paleontology at the Royal School of Mines in 1854. He accompanied the Irish physicist John Tyndall (q.v.) on an expedition to the Alps, where they studied glaciation.

When Charles Darwin published *The Origin of Species,* in 1859, Huxley became the foremost supporter in England of Darwin's theories. Huxley's popular lectures on organic evolution, which he gave at various times from 1860 until the time of his death, were an important factor in the acceptance of the theory of evolution, both by laymen and scientists. His speeches and writings were characterized by acute perception and unusual lucidity of expression. His chief writings include *Zoological Evidences as to Man's Place in Nature* (1863), *Lay Sermons* (1870), *Manual of the Comparative Anatomy of Vertebrated Animals* (1871), *Science and Culture* (1881), and *Evolution and Ethics* (1893).

HUYGENS or **HUYGHENS,** CHRISTIAN (1629–95), Dutch astronomer, mathematician, and physicist, born in The Hague, son of Constantijn Huygens (q.v.), and educated at the University of Leiden. In 1655 he developed a new method of grinding and polishing lenses, and constructed a telescope using his improved lenses. The increased resolution obtained with this telescope enabled him to detect a satellite of Saturn and the gap between the rings of Saturn. He devised an achromatic negative eyepiece (q.v.), still known as the Huygenian eyepiece, and a micrometer (q.v.) for use in telescopes.

In 1656, needing an accurate clock for measuring time in his astronomical work, he used the pendulum to regulate the movement of clocks, thereby constructing the first accurate timepiece. In *Horologium Oscillatorium* (1673) he presented a theoretical discussion of the dynamics of the oscillations of the pendulum. He determined the true relation between the length of a pendulum and the period of its oscillation and developed theorems on centrifugal force in circular motion which were of assistance to Isaac Newton (q.v.) in formulating the law of gravitation.

The work for which Huygens is best known is his development of the wave theory of light in opposition to the corpuscular theory of Newton. He formulated the principle, known as Huygens' principle, according to which the surface constituting a wave front may be determined. See LIGHT; OPTICS. His

research in optics and his experiments with polarization of light were recorded in *Traité de la Lumière* (1678).

HUYGENS, CONSTANTIJN (1596–1687), Dutch poet and statesman, father of Christian Huygens (q.v.), born in The Hague. A successful diplomat, he also exerted an important influence on Dutch literature. Between 1658 and 1672 Huygens wrote numerous poems, all of which appeared in an edition of his collected works in twenty-seven volumes under the title *Korenbloemen* ("Cornflowers").

HUYSMANS, CORNELIS (1648–1727), Dutch landscape and religious painter, born in Antwerp. He studied at Brussels under Jacques d'Arthois, a highly popular landscape painter of the day. In 1682 he settled at Mechlin, where he remained the rest of his life except for a period at Antwerp from 1702 to 1716. His landscapes were rustic in character, often portraying figures and cattle and a profusion of plant forms in the foreground. Extreme fidelity of drawing, pleasingly grouped compositions, and a skillful rendering of foliage characterize his work. He often painted the figures for the landscapes of other painters, and backgrounds for their historical pictures. One of his most notable works is "The Disciples at Emmaus" in the Church of Notre Dame at Mechlin. There are pictures by him in the museums of Antwerp, Berlin, Kassel, and Dresden, and in the Louvre, Paris, and the Tate Gallery, London.

HUYSMANS, JORIS KARL, real name CHARLES MARIE GEORGES HUYSMANS (1848–1907), French novelist, born in Paris. He was a minor official in the French Ministry of the Interior at Paris from 1866 to 1898. Early in life he abandoned the Roman Catholic religion, in which he had been reared, but later was reconverted to Catholicism. His literary career comprised two periods. In the first (1876–84), he followed the principles of the naturalistic school (see NATURALISM), as set forth by their most eminent French practitioner, the novelist Émile Zola (q.v.). Huysmans' important novels during this period include *Marthe, Histoire d'une Fille* (1876), *Les Sœurs Vatard* (1879), *En Ménage* (1881), *À Vau-l'Eau* (1882), and *En Rade* (not published until 1887, during the second period). From 1884 Huysmans was concerned no longer with the faithful depiction of sordid aspects of life, but with a search of art and religion for spiritual values. His novels of this period include *À Rebours* (1884), in which the hero vainly seeks spiritual salvation in art and literature; *Là-Bas* (1891); and four novels based on his reconversion to Catholicism, *En Route* (1895), *La Cathédrale* (1898), *L'Oblat* (1903), and *Les Foules de Lourdes* (1925). The first of these novels was the cause of many conversions to the Catholic faith. Huysmans' style is distinguished for its color, complexity, irony, and use of crude and forceful epithets. He had a two-fold influence on the life of his time; on the one hand, through his novel *À Rebours*, he encouraged a love for the artificial and decadent in art; and on the other, in his Catholic tetralogy, he revealed for many people a source of spiritual happiness through religion.

HWANG HO or **YELLOW RIVER,** a river of northern China, the second largest in the country, with a total length of approximately 2700 m. The Hwang Ho rises in a series of springs and lakes in the mountainous area north of the Tibetan plateau and south of the Gobi desert. From its source the river flows first eastward through tremendous gorges and then turns northeast at the city of Lanchow in Kansu province, whence it flows for many hundreds of miles through the Ordos, an easterly extension of the Gobi. Turning eastward, the river flows due east for about 200 miles. The Hwang Ho then turns its course due south and flows swiftly through a young valley cut in loess deposits between Shensi and Shansi provinces. In this portion of its course the river picks up and carries in suspension a large burden of yellow silt, which gives the river its characteristic yellow color. The load of sediment is augmented by the loess carried into the main stream by a number of tributaries including the Fen Ho and the Wei Ho. The Wei Ho enters the Hwang Ho in the central portion of Shensi, and the river then flows east across the northern portion of Honan to the plains of north China.

At the city of Kaifeng the river enters the plains and changes from a torrent to a meandering stream with a broad channel enclosed by man-made dikes. The dikes have been built over a period of centuries to control the river and prevent floods, but have actually had the opposite effect. Because of the large amount of sediment carried by the stream, the Hwang Ho has silted up the bottom of its bed and its level has risen, necessitating the construction of higher and higher dikes. (Had the dikes not been built, the silt would have been deposited in the flood plain outside the river bed; see FLOODS, CONTROL OF). As a result, in many portions of its lower course the river is as much as 70 ft. above the surrounding plain, and when the river level rises, disastrous floods occur. The deforestation of the mountains in the upper part of the river's course has increased the run-off and increased the flood heights. The floods of the Hwang Ho have been so frequent and so devastating that the river is often called "China's Sorrow". The worst flood in the river's history and probably the worst flood the world has ever known occurred when the Hwang Ho overran its banks in 1931. Between July and November 34,000 sq.m. of land were completely flooded and a further 8000 sq.m. partially flooded. The floods swept over villages and fields, making approximately 80,000,000 people homeless. About 1,000,000 died in the flood itself and in the famines and epidemics which followed.

The Hwang Ho has during its history altered its lower course a number of times. For several centuries before 1852 it emptied into the Yellow Sea south of the highlands of Shantung. In that year, however, the river changed its course hundreds of miles northward and now flows into the Gulf of Pohai, north of the highlands.

HYACINTH, a mineral. See ZIRCON.

HYACINTH, common name of plants of the genus *Hyacinthus*, belonging to the Lily family. The genus is native to the Old World, and one of its species is cultivated as a garden or house plant in temperate and tropical climates all over the world. Hyacinth is a bulbous plant with long, sword-shaped leaves. The flowers, which are produced on long spikes, have three petal-like sepals, three petals, six stamens, and a three-celled pistil. The fruit is a loculicidal capsule.

The cultivated hyacinth, *H. orientalis,* is commonly called the Dutch hyacinth, and one of its varieties, *H. orientalis* var. *albulus,* is called the Roman hyacinth. The cultivated hyacinth is native to Greece and Asia Minor, but horticultural varieties have been so extensively modified by breeders that they bear little resemblance to the wild original. All cultivated hyacinth varieties are fragrant. The color of hyacinth flowers ranges from white through yellow, red, blue, and purple. Single-flowered Dutch hyacinths have dense, erect spikes; double-flowered forms have loose, drooping spikes. Roman hyacinths produce several loosely flowered, graceful spikes from each bulb. Hyacinths are always grown from bulbs; most bulbs of Dutch hyacinth are produced in the Netherlands, and bulbs of Roman hyacinths in Italy and s. France.

Dutch hyacinths may be grown outdoors in all parts of the U.S., but Roman hyacinths can be grown only indoors except in the southern States. Both varieties flower in early spring.

HYACINTHE, PÈRE. See LOYSON, CHARLES.

HYACINTHUS, in Greek mythology, a beautiful youth, son of Amyclas, ruler of Amyclæ, in Laconia. Hyacinthus, beloved by both Apollo, god of the sun, and Zephyrus, god of the west wind, reciprocated the affection of Apollo. As the sun god was teaching his favorite to throw quoits, Zephyrus, consumed by jealousy, blew upon the quoit which Apollo had thrown, causing it to deviate from its course and strike Hyacinthus in the head, thereby killing him. From the blood of the slain youth Apollo caused a flower to spring up, each petal inscribed with an exclamation of lament (Gr. *Ai,* "alas"). The flower of the myth does not correspond to that familiarly known as hyacinth; the ancient flower was possibly a small iris with markings bearing a recognizable resemblance to the Greek word *Ai.* The death of Hyacinthus was commemorated at Amyclæ by a great festival, the *Hyacinthia,* held for three days each spring.

HYATT, ANNA VAUGHN. See HUNTINGTON, ANNA HYATT.

HYATT, JOHN WESLEY. See CELLULOID; PLASTICS.

HYBRID, offspring of parents belonging to different varieties, subspecies, species, genera or families; more loosely, offspring of parents unlike in any hereditary trait or traits. Hybrids may occur under natural conditions or may be produced artificially by insuring the meeting of sex cells from organisms of unlike types. Successful production of hybrids depends on the closeness of relationship between the two parents. Two parent organisms which differ only in a pigment trait, such as flower color or fur color, will always produce a normal hybrid under normal circumstances. Animals belonging to different species, however, usually produce sterile hybrids. The mule, for example, is the sterile offspring of a mating between a mare and a male ass. Offspring of crosses between two plant species are also usually sterile, but reproduction of such hybrids may be accomplished by use of cuttings, grafting, or layering (qq.v.) without requiring further sexual reproduction. Many sterile hybrid plants can be made fertile by treatment with colchicine (q.v.). A few sterile hybrids have been obtained from crosses between plants belonging to different genera, such as a hybrid between cabbage and radish.

Although hybridization in nature is extensive, most reproduction takes place between parents belonging to the same species. Natural hybridization between closely related organisms is restricted by several factors, including (1) difference in season in which breeding normally takes place; (2) difference in type of breeding place chosen by closely related organisms; (3) psychological barriers, such as reactions of repugnance to the odor of another species; and (4) mechanical barriers, such as possession of copulatory organs which cannot be brought together.

Hybridization has been successfully employed in agriculture for many centuries, but the scientific laws followed by hybrid organisms were not discovered until the end of the 19th century. Practically all aspects of hybridization can now be explained by discoveries in the science of heredity. See BREEDING; HEREDITY; PLANT BREEDING.

HYDE, DOUGLAS (1860–1949), Irish statesman and scholar, born in Frenchpark, County Roscommon, and educated at Trinity College, Dublin. He joined the Irish nationalist movement in his youth, and in 1893 was one of the founders of the Gaelic League (q.v.), an organization for the propagation of Irish culture. He was president of the League until 1915. From 1909 to 1932 he was professor of modern Irish language and literature at the National University of Ireland, Dublin. As a leader in the movement to preserve and stimulate interest in Irish culture, Hyde succeeded in making the study of the Irish language compulsory in the public schools. He was elected to the Irish senate in 1925. In 1938 he was elected president of Ireland and served until 1945. He wrote in both English and Irish; among his works are *Love Songs of Connacht* (1894), *A Literary History of Ireland* (1899), *Ubhla den Chraoibh* (1900), *Legends of Saints and Sinners from the Irish* (1915), *An Leath-rann* (1922), and *Mise Agus an Connradh* (1938).

HYDE, EDWARD, 1st EARL OF CLARENDON (1609–74), English statesman and historian, born in Dinton, Wiltshire, and educated at Magdalen Hall, Oxford University. Hyde entered the Middle Temple to study law in 1625, but devoted most of his time to literary friendships and studies; Ben Jonson, Edward Waller, and Lord Falkland were among his friends at this time. He was admitted to the bar in 1633, and his social connections helped him to win a successful practice. In the spring of 1640 he became a member of the Short Parliament, and later in the year was elected to the Long Parliament. In Parliament, Hyde at first supported the Popular party, but his staunch allegiance to the Church of England and the Old Constitution led him to turn gradually to the Royalist party, which he joined openly in June 1642. Hyde's legal advice and the political manifestoes he wrote for King Charles I won half the nation to the support of the Royalist cause, but his efforts to win the king to moderation were overcome by the advice of more intransigently conservative courtiers and politicians, and the First Civil War (see GREAT REBELLION) broke out in the summer of the same year.

Parliament expelled Hyde from the House of Commons in August, 1642, and he followed King Charles throughout the war, continually attempting conciliation with the Parliamentary party. He was knighted and made a member of the privy council in February, 1645, and in March was appointed chancellor of the exchequer. Hyde's policies were less and less supported by the king, until, in 1646, he was sent to Jersey as one of the guardians of Prince Charles (later King Charles II). Hyde continued to remain in exile in various Continental countries, mostly in France, throughout the Parliamentary regime, and at this time began his famous historical work, *History of the Rebellion.*

At the time of the Restoration of the British monarchy, in 1660, Hyde was instrumental in ensuring that the change in government was a true reflection of the people's will, through parliamentary action, and not a mere coup d'état accomplished by force. Charles II immediately made Hyde chancellor of the exchequer, but he resigned the office to become speaker of the House of Lords. In 1660 he was made Baron Hyde of Hindon, and in 1661 was created Viscount Cornbury and Earl of Clarendon. Hyde was the virtual head of the British government from the beginning of the Restoration until 1667. During this period he enforced a repressive religious policy, enacting during his regime the group of measures against religious freedom known as the Clarendon Code, which included the Act of Uniformity, the Corporation Act, the Conventicle Act, and the Five-Mile Act. He encouraged an enlightened and moderate policy toward Ireland and supported the development of the American colonies, becoming one of the lords proprietors of the colony of Carolina. His foreign policy was weak, de-

pending on subsidies from the French crown; he was responsible for the outbreak of the Second Dutch War (see DUTCH WARS), in 1664, and was greatly blamed by the people for its unfortunate outcome. In a period of almost universal corruption in office, Hyde retained his personal integrity, but he fell a victim to court intrigues and the unpopularity of his foreign and religious policies, and was banished to France in 1667.

Hyde spent the rest of his life in exile in France, and was denied permission to see his children and to correspond with anyone in Great Britain. His last six years were devoted to completing his historical works, which are renowned for a series of contemporary portraits and for the grand style in which they are written. The works include the *History of the Rebellion* (first printed in 1702–04 from a copy, and in 1826 from the original manuscript), *History of the Rebellion and Civil War in Ireland* (1719), and an autobiography, *Life of Edward, Earl of Clarendon* (3 vols., 1759). He also wrote, during this period, a volume of *Contemplations on the Psalms* and several moral essays.

Hyde's daughter ANNE (1637–71) was secretly married to James II of Great Britain in 1660, when he was still Duke of York, and two of the children of this union, Mary and Anne, were later queens of Great Britain.

HYDE PARK, an enclosure of 364 acres in London, England, about $2\frac{1}{4}$ miles w. of St. Paul's Cathedral. It derives its name from Hyde Manor, which belonged to the abbey of Westminster. It became famous as the scene of duels, deer hunts, and horse races. King Charles II laid out drives and promenades which became and have remained gathering places for fashionable London society. The park also serves as the place of large popular meetings. Its prominent features are Rotten Row, the Ladies' Mile, the Serpentine, the Marble Arch, the statue of Lord Byron, and Westmacott's colossal statue of Achilles, erected in honor of the Duke of Wellington and cast from cannon captured at Waterloo.

HYDERABAD, state of the Union of India, located in the central portion of the Deccan. Most of Hyderabad is fertile plateau land. It is watered by the Godavari, Wardha, and Kistna rivers and their tributaries, by irrigation canals, and by artificial lakes. Agriculture is the principal occupation, and rice, wheat, cotton, tobacco, oilseeds, fruits, millet, and vegetables are raised. Lac, lumber, gums, and oils are obtained from the forests of the state. Coal, copper, gold, iron, and diamonds are among the mineral deposits, which, however, are little exploited. The weaving of cotton and the milling of flour are the chief manufacturing industries.

Much of the area now covered by the state of Hyderabad was conquered by the Mogul (q.v.) dynasty and made a part of their empire by 1687. In 1713 a Turkoman general of the Mogul empire, Mir Kamruddin Ali Khan, also known as Asaf Jah, was appointed subahdar, or viceroy, of the Mogul territories in the Deccan, with the title of Nizam-ul-Mulk. He eventually became independent of the Mogul court, creating for himself the state of Hyderabad in the Deccan and establishing his capital in the city of Hyderabad (q.v.). In 1724 Nizam-ul-Mulk founded the ruling dynasty of Hyderabad nizams. During the 18th and 19th centuries the Hyderabad rulers co-operated with the British in several Indian wars, and during the Indian Mutiny (q.v.) of 1857 they supported the British against the Indian rebels. The state experienced continuous financial difficulties until 1902, when Berar, a territory connected with Hyderabad, was leased to the British, establishing a regular source of income. At that time also a British adviser was appointed to supervise financial reform. By 1947 Hyderabad had become the wealthiest and most important native state in India. When, in that year, India was granted freedom by Great Britain and partitioned into the states of Pakistan (q.v.) and the Union of India (see INDIA, UNION OF), Hyderabad remained an independent unit.

Although the Nizam, Nawab Mir Sir Osman Ali Khan was himself a Moslem, 88 percent of the population, at the time of partition, was Hindu. In 1947–48 the Hindu Union attempted, first by negotiation with the Nizam and later by economic blockade of the state, to induce Hyderabad to join the Union of India. On August 10, 1948, a White Paper was issued by the Union of India declaring it impossible for Hyderabad, completely surrounded by the dominions of the Union, to remain independent, and demanding that feudalism be abolished within the state. Meanwhile, rioting between the Hindus and Moslems had broken out in the Hyderabad city of Secunderabad, and on September 10 the Union of India served notice that its troops would invade Hyderabad if the Nizam would not allow the Union to quell disorder in Secunderabad. Because the demand was rejected by the Nizam, Indian troops entered Hyderabad on September 13. After four days of fighting,

they captured Secunderabad and on the fifth day occupied the capital. The Nizam thereupon surrendered to the Hindus and Hyderabad joined the Union of India. Area, 82,313 sq.m.; pop. (1951) 18,655,108.

HYDERABAD or **HAIDARABAD,** capital of the state of Hyderabad and of the district of the same name, Union of India, located on the Musi River, 5½ miles s.w. of Secunderabad and about 400 m. by rail s.e. of Bombay. It is one of the most populous cities in the Union of India. Hyderabad was founded in 1589 by Mohammed Kuli, a Kutb Shahi king of Golconda. The Char Minar, or Four Minarets, a building constructed in 1591 as a Moslem college and now used as a warehouse, stands in the center of the city, at the intersection of two roads, which pass through its archways. A cathedral mosque, the Jumma Musjid, is a replica of the Kaaba of Mecca. Several palaces built by various of the Hyderabad rulers, a hospital, bazaars, Osmania University, and the Nizam college, an affiliate of Madras University, are also in the city. Hyderabad is encircled by a wall completed by the first Nizam ruler in the 18th century. Near the city are two large artificial lakes which are used as reservoirs.

Five days after the Union of India forces invaded the princely state of Hyderabad in September, 1948, the city of Hyderabad was captured. It became the capital of the state when Hyderabad subsequently entered the Union of India. The city is a center of trade; the manufacture of cotton and silk textiles and of cement are its principal industries. Pop. (1951) 1,085,722. Area of district, 4476 sq.m.; pop. (1951) 1,511,336.

HYDERABAD or **HAIDARABAD,** a city of Sind, Pakistan, situated on the Indus R., about 100 m. by rail N.E. of Karachi. Its fort, formerly the provincial arsenal, stands on the site of ancient Nirun. The modern city was founded in 1768, and from that date until 1843 it was the capital of Sind. Hyderabad contains a number of outstanding educational institutions, including a medical school and a technical school. Cotton ginning and milling, rice and oilseed milling, and the manufacture of embroidered work, lacquered goods, and pottery are the principal industries. Pop. (1951) 229,000.

HYDRA, technical name for a genus of small hydrozoan coelenterate, fresh-water animals, 1/10 in. to 1 in. in length, which are among the simplest in structure of all the multicellular animals, and which consequently are often studied in elementary biology courses. A hydra is a hollow, cylindrical animal, closed at one end, which is known as the *foot,* and opening at the other into the *mouth,* which is surrounded by six to ten tentacles. It moves either by gliding on the foot, after the fashion of a snail, or by somersaulting.

The body of a hydra is made up of two layers of cells, an outside layer, or *ectoderm,* and an inside layer, or *endoderm,* separated by a thin layer of secreted jelly. An animal of this structure is known as a simple polyp. Both layers of the hydra's cells contain contractile fibers, forerunners of the muscles in higher animals, which relax to allow the animal to expand, and which are used in locomotion. *Interstitial cells,* scattered cells found among the ectodermal and endodermal cells, give rise to a network of nerve threads running over the entire body, and to several testes and ovaries on each animal. Each ovary contains a single egg and each testis contains several sperms. The eggs develop within the body wall of the parent hydra; the embryos then rupture through the body wall and grow, like buds on a plant, into full-sized adults still attached to the parent. Several such buds may be growing from a hydra at one time; eventually they leave the parent and become independent individuals, attaching themselves by their sticky feet to a floating leaf or twig.

In order to capture minute forms of life and to defend itself from larger animals, the hydra is equipped with poison-containing structures in the ectodermal layer called stinging cells, or *nematocysts.* Small animals paralyzed by the stinging cells are forced into the mouth by the tentacles and then transported to the body cavity where they are either taken into a single cell by pseudopodia or digested by secretions from all the endodermal cells. Hydras are remarkable for their powers of regeneration. When a hydra is cut into fairly large pieces, each piece develops into a complete individual; small pieces of a hydra, when placed in contact with each other, grow together to form a complete individual.

Two species of hydra are common in ponds of the U.S., *Hydra fusca,* a brownish-gray species, and *H. viridis,* a green species. The green color of *H. viridis* is due to an alga of the genus *Chloerella* which lives symbiotically within the body cells of the hydra, and which is passed on to the hydra's young after entering the sex cells.

HYDRA, an astronomical constellation of great length. It is located almost entirely within the southern hemisphere of the heavens, south of Cancer, Sextans, Corvus, and

Hydrangea macrophylla

Virgo, and at its northern extremity it crosses the celestial equator between Sextans and Canis Minor. Hydra is sometimes called the Water Monster; representations of it on ancient star maps give it the figure of a serpent. Its most prominent star is Alphard.

HYDRANGEA, scientific name of a genus of shrubs and woody vines, and common name of the family, the Hydrangeaceae, to which the genus belongs. The Hydrangea family also includes mock orange (q.v.), and several smaller genera.

Plants of the genus *Hydrangea* are native to Asia and the New World. The flowers are borne in compound cymes. Outermost flowers of a cyme consist merely of a colored, membranaceous calyx, but flowers from the center of a cluster have an eight to ten-ribbed, tubular calyx, four or five ovate petals, eight to ten slender stamens, and a two-celled pistil. The fruit of the hydrangea is a many-seeded capsule.

The wild hydrangea of E. United States, *H. arborescens,* is an erect shrub which grows as tall as 10 feet. It bears white flowers in round clusters. Two other white-flowered species, *H. cinerea* and *H. radiata,* are smaller, spreading shrubs which grow as high as 6 feet. The American species are cultivated in gardens to some extent, but the showier hydrangeas are cultivated Asiatic species. *H. macrophylla* has broad, thick, shining leaves, and produces white, blue, or pink flowers in round or flat clusters. The species grows as tall as 12 feet under favorable climatic and soil conditions. Blue and pink flowers may be produced by the same shrub; acid soil produces blue hydrangeas and alkaline soil produces pink hydrangeas, due to the reaction of flower pigments called anthocyanins (q.v.). *H. paniculata* is a taller, hardier shrub, sometimes assuming the form of a small tree, which bears white flowers in long panicles. *H. Petiolaris* is a climbing, white-flowered species, producing aerial rootlets which enable it to cling to walls or tree trunks.

Hydrangeas are usually grown from cuttings or layers, which are planted in pots until a root system is established. They grow best in rich, moist soil under a wide range of light conditions. The rose chafer, *Cetonia aurata,* and the tarnished plant bug, *Lygus pratensis,* often attack hydrangeas. The shrubs are also susceptible to leaf spot, but this disease seldom causes serious damage.

HYDRAULIC PRESS. See HYDROMECHANICS.

HYDRAULIC RAM, a device for pumping water to a height above the source of supply by means of the momentum of the water itself flowing downward under the influence of gravity. The ram consists of a supply pipe, a waste valve, a pressure chamber, and an outlet pipe. The machine operates continuously and automatically and employs no power except that supplied by the water itself.

Water flowing downward from the source through the supply pipe escapes through the waste valve until it has built up sufficient momentum to close this valve. When the valve is closed, the pressure in the pipe rises sufficiently to open the check valve, allowing water to flow into the pressure chamber and the outlet pipe. The weight of water in the pressure chamber and the outlet pipe, plus the pressure of air trapped at the top of the pressure chamber, forces the check valve to close. Then the air pressure in the chamber raises the water in the outlet pipe until the weight of water in the pipe balances the pressure. In the meantime the pressure in the supply pipe has been relieved and the cycle repeats itself.

The hydraulic ram was introduced by the French inventor Joseph Michel de Montgolfier in 1796. The device is sometimes used for pumping domestic and farm water supplies where water is plentiful. It has also been employed as a source of compressed air in engineering works.

HYDRAULICS. See HYDROMECHANICS.

HYDRIODIC ACID. See HYDROCHLORIC ACID.

HYDROBROMIC ACID. See BROMINE; HYDROCHLORIC ACID.

HYDROCARBONS, a family of organic compounds, composed entirely of carbon and hydrogen. They are the simplest of organic compounds in structure and composition, and may be considered the parent substances from which all other organic compounds are derived. The hydrocarbons are conveniently classified into two major groups, aliphatic and cyclic. In aliphatic compounds containing more than one carbon atom, the carbon atoms are attached to each other to form an open chain; the chain may be either straight or branched. In cyclic compounds the carbon atoms form a closed ring. See CHEMISTRY, ORGANIC. The two major groups are subdivided according to chemical behavior into saturated and unsaturated compounds.

Aliphatic Hydrocarbons. The saturated aliphatic hydrocarbons form a homologous series called the paraffin (Lat. *parum affinis,* "little affinity") series or the methane series. The composition of each of the members of the series corresponds to the formula C_nH_{2n+2}, where n is the number of carbon atoms in the molecule. Among the members of the series are methane, CH_4; ethane, C_2H_6; butane, C_4H_{10}; and octane, C_8H_{18}. All the members of the series are chemically stable; i.e., they do not react readily at ordinary temperatures with such reagents as acids, alkalies, or oxidizers. The first four members of the series are gases at ordinary temperature and pressure; intermediate members are liquids; and the heavier members are semisolids or solids. Petroleum (q.v.) contains a great variety of saturated hydrocarbons, and petroleum products, such as gasoline, kerosene, heavy fuel oil, lubricating oils, petroleum jelly, and paraffin, consist principally of mixtures of paraffin hydrocarbons ranging from the lighter liquid members to solid members.

The unsaturated aliphatic hydrocarbons include the ethylene or olefin series, the diolefin series, and the acetylene series. The olefin series is made up of chain hydrocarbons in which there is a double bond between two carbon atoms. The general formula for the series is C_nH_{2n} where n is the number of carbon atoms. As in the paraffin series, the lower members are gases, intermediate compounds are liquids, and the higher members of the series are solids. The olefin series compounds are more active chemically and less stable than the saturated compounds. They easily react with substances such as halogens, adding atoms at the double bonds. They are not found to any extent in natural products, but are produced in the destructive distillation of complex natural substances, such as coal, and are formed in large amounts in petroleum refining, particularly in the "cracking" process. The first member of the series is ethylene.

The diolefins contain two double bonds between pairs of carbon atoms in the molecule. They are related to the complex hydrocarbons in natural rubber and are important in the manufacture of synthetic rubber and plastics; important members of this series are isoprene and butadiene.

The members of the acetylene series contain a triple bond between a pair of carbon atoms in the molecule. They are very active chemically and are not found free in nature. They form a series analagous to the ethylene series. The first and most important member of the series is acetylene.

Cyclic Hydrocarbons. Saturated hydrocarbons containing molecules arranged in a closed ring are the naphthenic hydrocarbons. Each member consists of a closed ring of carbon atoms, with two hydrogen atoms attached to each carbon atom. The first member of the series is cyclopropane $(CH_2)_3$. The naphthenes are important constituents of crude petroleums found in Russia, Oklahoma, Texas, and California.

The most important group of cyclic compounds are the unsaturated aromatic hydrocarbons, consisting of liquid and solid hydrocarbons of which anthracene, benzene, phenanthrene, naphthalene, and toluene are important members. See AROMATIC COMPOUNDS.

Terpene hydrocarbons are naturally occurring substances, generally having the empirical formula $C_{10}H_{16}$, found in many volatile oils obtained by the distillation of plants. They include both open-chain and cyclic compounds, camphor and pinene being among the important cyclic terpenes.

HYDROCHLORIC ACID, or MURIATIC ACID, aqueous solution of hydrogen chloride. Hydrogen chloride, HCl, formed by the direct union of hydrogen and chlorine (qq.v.), is a colorless gas, heavier than air, with a penetrating, suffocating odor; its b.p. is —85° C. (—121° F.). It is extremely soluble in water, one volume of water at 0° C. (32° F.) absorbing 507 volumes of hydrogen chloride (to form hydrochloric acid) at atmospheric pressure, and much more at higher pressures. The commercial form of hydrochloric acid, prepared by the action of concentrated sulfuric acid on sodium chloride, contains about 35.4 percent hydrogen chloride, has a specific gravity of 1.18, and is usually colored yellow by

the presence of impurities such as iron.

Hydrochloric acid dissociates readily in water and is one of the most active acids. It reacts with bases, salts, and metals to form chlorides. All the chlorides are soluble in water with the exception of silver chloride, mercurous chloride, cuprous chloride, thallous chloride and lead chloride, the last named being soluble only in hot water. The most important and abundant salt of hydrochloric acid is sodium chloride or salt (q.v.).

Hydrochloric acid is used in large quantities in the preparation of chlorides and for cleaning metals. It is used in many industrial processes, such as the preparation of corn syrup and glucose (q.v.) from cornstarch and the manufacture of rayon and mercerized cotton. It is an extremely important reagent in the chemical laboratory. A small amount of hydrochloric acid occurs in the gastric juice of man, and plays an important part in the digestive processes.

Fluorine, bromine, and iodine (qq.v.), which with chlorine and astatine form the halogen family (see HALOGENS), also react with hydrogen to form hydrogen fluoride, hydrogen bromide, and hydrogen iodide, respectively. The hydrogen compounds dissolve in water to form hydrofluoric, hydrobromic, and hydriodic acids, respectively.

Hydrobromic Acid, HBr, the water solution of hydrogen bromide, a colorless gas with a penetrating odor, b.p. —67° C. (—88.6° F.), is formed by the direct union of hydrogen and bromine in the presence of a catalyst, such as platinum, or by brominating phosphorus to form phosphorus tribromide, which decomposes in water to form phosphorous acid and hydrobromic acid. Hydrobromic acid, like hydrochloric acid, is a strong acid. It reacts with metals, salts, and bases to form bromides (q.v.).

Hydriodic Acid, HI, the water solution of hydrogen iodide, a colorless gas with a penetrating odor, b.p. —34° C. (—29° F.), is formed in the same manner as hydrobromic acid. Hydriodic acid is less stable than any of the other acids described above. It decomposes readily into iodine and hydrogen, and is often used as a reducing agent in chemical reactions.

HYDROCORTISONE. See CORTISONE; SUPRARENAL GLAND.

HYDROCYANIC ACID, or PRUSSIC ACID, HCN, an extremely poisonous, colorless liquid with a characteristic bitter-almond odor, m.p. —14° C. (6.8° F.), b.p. 26° C. (78.8° F.). It is a very weak, volatile acid, miscible with water in all proportions, which polymerizes readily unless it is free of all impurities. Hydrocyanic acid has a dielectric (q.v.) constant of about 96, which is higher even than that of water, and has consequently been used in studying the dissociation of electrolytes. It is industrially used as a fumigant and exterminator. It was originally prepared from Prussian blue (see IRON), from which the secondary name is derived, but is now prepared by the action of acid on a cyanide salt, such as sodium cyanide.

Hydrocyanic acid exists in two isomeric forms, HCN and HNC; see ISOMER. Although the latter form has not been isolated in the free state it forms salts called isocyanides. The abundant form of the acid, HCN, forms salts known as cyanides, all of which are poisonous. The cyanides, particularly sodium and potassium cyanide, are of industrial importance. Sodium cyanide is prepared by treating sodamide with coke or by fusing calcium cyanamide with coke and sodium chloride. Steel is often casehardened by immersion in a bath of fused sodium cyanide; see IRON, METALLURGY OF. Gold and silver are extracted from their ores by treatment with cyanides. The cyanides form complex ions with gold and silver, forming such compounds as sodium auricyanide and sodium argenticyanide, solutions of which are used in electroplating gold and silver.

HYDRODYNAMICS. See HYDROMECHANICS.

HYDROELECTRIC. See DAMS; DYNAMO-ELECTRIC MACHINERY; WATER POWER.

HYDROFLUORIC ACID. See FLUORINE; HYDROCHLORIC ACID.

HYDROFLUOSILICIC ACID. See FLUORINE.

HYDROGEN (Gr. "water former"), the lightest of all the elements, with atomic number 1, atomic weight 1.0081, symbol H. It was confused with other gases until Henry Cavendish (q.v.) demonstrated in 1766 that it was evolved by the action of sulfuric acid on metals and also showed at a later date that it was an independent substance that combined with oxygen to form water. Joseph Priestley (q.v.) named the gas "inflammable air" in 1781, and Antoine Laurent Lavoisier (q.v.) renamed it "hydrogen"; see CHEMISTRY: *History*.

Free hydrogen is found only in very small traces in the atmosphere, but solar and stellar spectra show that it occurs in the sun and other stars. In combination with other elements it is very widely distributed on the earth. Its most important and abundant compound is water, H_2O. It is a component of all the constituents of living matter as well as of many minerals. It forms an essential part of all hydrocarbons (q.v.) and a vast variety of other organic substances. All acids contain hydrogen; the distinguishing characteristic of an acid is its dissociation, upon going into solution, to yield hydrogen ions.

At ordinary temperatures hydrogen is a colorless, tasteless, odorless gas, with a density about 7/100 that of air. It is highly inflammable. Like most gaseous elements it is diatomic (its molecules contain two atoms), but it dissociates into free atoms at high temperatures. Hydrogen has a lower boiling point, $-252.7°$ C. ($-422.9°$ F.), and melting point, $-259.1°$ C. ($-434.4°$ F.), than any other substance except helium (q.v.). Liquid hydrogen, first obtained by Sir James Dewar (see CRYOGENICS) in 1898, is colorless (light blue in thick layers) and has a specific gravity of 0.079. When allowed to evaporate rapidly under reduced pressure it freezes into a colorless solid.

Hydrogen is a mixture of two allotropic forms, orthohydrogen and parahydrogen, ordinary hydrogen containing about three fourths of the ortho form and one fourth of the para form. The melting point and boiling point of the two forms differ slightly from those of ordinary hydrogen. Practically pure parahydrogen is obtained by adsorbing ordinary hydrogen on charcoal at about $-225°$ C. ($-373°$ F.).

Hydrogen is known to exist in three isotopic forms; see ISOTOPE. The nucleus of each atom of ordinary hydrogen is composed of one proton. Deuterium (q.v.), present in ordinary hydrogen to the extent of 0.02%, contains one proton and one neutron in the nucleus of each atom and has an atomic mass of two. Tritium (q.v.), an unstable, radioactive isotope, contains one proton and two neutrons in the nucleus of each atom, and has an atomic mass of three. See HYDROGEN BOMB.

Hydrogen reacts chemically with many nonmetals. It combines with nitrogen in the presence of a catalyst to form ammonia (see NITROGEN FIXATION), with sulfur to form hydrogen sulfide, with chlorine to form hydrogen chloride, and with oxygen to form water. The reaction of oxygen and hydrogen takes place at room temperature only in the presence of a catalyst such as finely divided platinum. When hydrogen is mixed with air or oxygen and ignited, the mixture explodes. Hydrogen also combines with some metals, such as sodium and lithium, to form hydrides. It acts as a reducing agent on metallic oxides, such as copper oxide, removing the oxygen and leaving the metal in a free state. It reacts with unsaturated organic compounds to form corresponding saturated compounds.

Hydrogen is prepared in the laboratory by the action of dilute acid on metals, such as zinc, and by the electrolysis of water. Large quantities of the gas are produced industrially from various fuel gases. Hydrogen is separated from water gas, natural gas, and coal gas (see GAS) either by liquefaction of the other components of the gas or by catalytic conversion of the carbon monoxide to carbon dioxide, which is easily removed.

In many electrolysis reactions (see ELECTROCHEMISTRY) hydrogen is an important by-product. Enormous quantities of hydrogen are used in the manufacture of ammonia and in the synthesis of methyl alcohol. It is one of the important combustible constituents of fuel (q.v.). The hydrogenation (q.v.) of oils to produce edible fats, of coal to form synthetic petroleum, and of petroleum oils to enrich the gasoline fraction, requires large amounts of hydrogen.

The lightest in weight of all gases, hydrogen has been used for the inflation of balloons and dirigibles. However, it ignites very easily, a small spark causing it to burn, and several dirigibles, including the *Hindenburg,* have been destroyed by hydrogen fires. Helium, which has 92% of the lifting power of hydrogen and is not inflammable, is used whenever possible.

Hydrogen is also used in high-temperature torches for cutting, melting, and welding metals; see ATOMIC HYDROGEN FLAME.

HYDROGENATION, chemical reaction involving the combination of hydrogen with unsaturated organic compounds; see HYDROCARBONS. When an unsaturated compound, such as ethylene (C_2H_4), is treated with hydrogen at a suitable temperature and in the presence of a catalyst, such as finely divided nickel, platinum, or palladium, the double bond between the carbon atoms is broken and a hydrogen atom attaches itself to each carbon atom; in the case of ethylene, ethane (C_2H_6) is formed. This reaction also takes place with more complicated molecules, yielding a great variety of "synthetic" products which are of importance in the laboratory and for industrial purposes.

The hydrogenation reaction is applied on a large industrial scale to a number of processes, the most important of which in the United States is the hydrogenation of vegetable oils to produce edible fats. Oils are esters of fatty acids (q.v.) containing one or more double-bond linkages between carbon atoms; solid fats are saturated compounds. To convert the oils, which often have an unpleasant taste and odor, to fats with odor and taste sufficiently innocuous so that they can be used for cooking purposes, the oils are hydrogenated. The reaction is performed at a temperature of about 200° C. (392° F.) in the presence of finely divided nickel, and under a pressure of three to four atmospheres of hydrogen. Nearly 600,000 tons of refined cottonseed oil, which was formerly a waste product, are produced annually in the United States. A large portion of this oil is converted to edible shortening. Low-grade oils, such as fish oils, are hydrogenated and used for the manufacture of soap and wax.

The hydrogenation process is also applied in the production of synthetic gasoline. The Bergius process, originated in Germany, and used on a large scale in many parts of the world where petroleum resources are low, utilizes coal and coal tar as a starting material. The coal, mixed with a heavy oil, is ground to a fine paste and heated with hydrogen, under pressure, in the presence of a catalyst composed of metallic sulfides. The resulting oil is further hydrogenated, and a third hydrogenation yields gasoline. One ton of coal yields about 200 gallons of gasoline.

The Fischer-Tropsch process is a method for synthesizing gasoline from water gas; see GAS. Water gas, which consists of carbon monoxide and hydrogen, is transformed into saturated hydrocarbons by passing it over suitable catalysts, such as iron and nickel, at a temperature of about 200° C. (392° F.) at ordinary pressure. Fractionation of the product yields gasoline, the antiknock properties of which are improved by further treatment.

For the hydrogenation of low-grade petroleum to produce high-quality gasoline, see GASOLINE.

HYDROGEN BOMB, superatomic war weapon of vast explosive power resulting from the nuclear fusion of heavy hydrogen isotopes (q.v.). Because nuclear fusion can occur only at extremely high temperatures (over 50,000,-000° C.), the fusion process is known as a thermonuclear reaction. Unlike the fission process employed in uranium and plutonium bombs, whereby the energy is released through the splitting of heavier elements into lighter ones, the fusion process in hydrogen bombs liberates energy by the merging of lighter atoms to form heavier ones. Fusion bombs are composed basically of a main charge of light elements, such as hydrogen, and of a "fuze", or igniting device, which provides the initial high temperatures required to set off the thermonuclear reaction. Such high temperatures may be obtained, for example, by the explosion of a plutonium fission device, which will ignite the main charge. See ATOMIC ENERGY AND ATOMIC BOMB.

In a fusion bomb utilizing hydrogen as its fusionable material, the hydrogen isotopes deuterium and tritium (qq.v.) are subjected to extremely high temperatures. The deuterium nucleus (1 neutron and 1 proton) is combined by thermonuclear reaction with the tritium nucleus (2 neutrons and 1 proton). The fusion of these nuclei forms a helium nucleus (2 neutrons and 2 protons), and liberates the extra neutron from the tritium nucleus. The resulting loss of mass is converted into energy in accordance with the equation $E = mc^2$ (energy is equal to mass times the velocity of light squared) ; see RELATIVITY.

The first successful hydrogen device was exploded by the United States in November, 1952, at Eniwetok Atoll in the Pacific Ocean. According to authoritative reports, deuterium and tritium were used as its main charge and a plutonium fission device was employed as the detonator. It was subsequently revealed that the blast had a destructive power equivalent to 5 million tons of TNT.

In 1953 the Soviet Union announced the successful test of a hydrogen bomb. This claim was substantiated by the U.S. Atomic Energy Commission, which reported that it had evidence of a Soviet explosion similar to those in American tests.

Additional U.S. fusion bombs were detonated on March 1, March 26, and April 6, 1954. The blasts were reported to be many times more powerful than the explosion of the first U.S. hydrogen device. It was further announced that, unlike the first, which could not be "delivered", these were transportable as practical weapons of war. The force of the device which was exploded on March 1, 1954, tremendously exceeded the calculated estimate, indicating that a different type of fusion bomb had been developed.

The new fusion bombs contained, according to current speculations, other light elements in addition to hydrogen. Many authorities presumed that the fusionable material was a compound of lithium and hydrogen, probably lithium-6 deuteride. Other improvements may have included the addition of tritium and deuterium in the fission device which sets off the explosion; such improved "fuzes" are called fusion-boosted detonators.

The destructive potential of the hydrogen bomb derives from the fact that its size (i.e., the amount of fusionable material which may be subjected to the thermonuclear reaction) is unlimited by any theoretical consideration. This is in contrast to the fission bomb which is limited in size (i.e., the amount of fissionable material subject to the chain reaction) by a certain critical mass. The significance of this can be fully realized in light of the generally accepted estimate that a hydrogen bomb has more than 10 times the destructive power of a fission bomb of equal weight. It was reported that the explosion of March 1, 1954, was 750 times more devastating than the atomic bomb exploded at Hiroshima in 1945, during World War II. According to scientific reports, the hydrogen bomb can be made many times more radioactive than those used in recent tests by encasing the bomb in a shell of cobalt.

HYDROGRAPHY. See MAP; SURVEYING.

HYDROLYSIS, a type of chemical decomposition involving water as a reactant. In a hydrolysis reaction of a salt, water dissociates into hydrogen and hydroxyl ions (q.v.), which combine with the ions of the other substance. Sodium acetate combines with water to form sodium hyroxide and acetic acid; magnesium chloride combines with water to form magnesium hydroxide and hydrochloric acid. The hydrolysis of a salt, such as sodium carbonate (washing soda), formed by the reaction of a strong base and a weak acid, yields an alkaline solution because of the presence of an excess of hydroxyl ions in solution. The hydrolysis of a salt, such as ammonium chloride (sal ammoniac), formed by the reaction of a strong acid and a weak base, yields an acid solution because of the excess of hydrogen ions in solution. See ACID.

Hydrolysis reactions which break down complicated molecules into simpler ones are fundamental in many of the life processes of animals and plants. Carbohydrates and complex sugars are decomposed by the action of water into simple sugars; proteins yield amino acids (q.v.) ; and fats and oils yield glycerin and fatty acids upon hydrolysis. These reactions, important to the digestive processes, are catalyzed by enzymes (q.v.).

HYDROMECHANICS, the branch of the science of physics which deals with the laws governing fluids in rest and in motion. In general the term may be applied to the properties of any fluid, liquid or gaseous, but is usually limited to the study of incompressible (or almost incompressible) liquids such as water rather than to compressible gases. Hydromechanics is commonly subdivided into three fields: *hydrostatics* which deals with pressure and equilibrium in liquids at rest; *hydrodynamics* (sometimes called *hydrokinetics*), which deals with liquids in motion; and *hydraulics,* which deals with the practical and engineering applications of hydrodynamics and hydrostatics.

Hydrostatics. The fundamental characteristic of a body of liquid standing at rest is that the pressure exerted on any particle of the liquid is uniform from all directions. If these pressures were unequal, the particle would move in the direction of least pressure. It follows that the pressure exerted by a liquid against the walls of a containing vessel of any shape is perpendicular to the walls at every point of their inner surfaces, for if the pressure were not exerted in a perpendicular direction, the liquid would move along the walls of the vessel. Furthermore, the top surface of liquid in an open vessel arranges itself in a surface perpendicularly to the only force acting on it, the force of gravity, and is, therefore, usually horizontal. When other forces besides gravity act on an open vessel containing a liquid, the form of the free surface of the liquid is such that each portion of the surface is perpendicular to the resultant of the forces acting on it. If a glass of water is spun rapidly on its vertical axis, its upper surface will take the form of a parabola, representing the combined effect of centrifugal force and the force of gravity. This property of forming a parabola during rotation has been applied to the formation of parabolic telescope mirrors by the rotation of a shallow pan of mercury.

The pressure at any point in an open vessel of liquid subjected to no force other than the force of gravity is proportional to the depth of the liquid at that point. At equal depths in the same liquid the pressure is always equal, no matter what the shape of the container. Thus the pressure at the bottom of a one-inch pipe 50 ft. high, filled with water, is the same as the pressure on a lake bottom at a depth of 50 ft. Similarly if a pipe 100 ft. long is slanted so that the top is only 50 ft. above the bottom, the same pressure will exist on the bottom of the pipe, although this point is at a much greater distance from the water level, meas-

Hydraulic Press Manufacturing Co.

Hydraulic press for stamping metal parts, an application of principles of hydromechanics

ured along the diagonal path of the pipe.

In the study of hydrostatics certain quantities are constantly referred to and are necessary for the calculation of even simple problems. The pressure of water at a depth of 1 ft. is equal to 0.433 lb. per sq. in., and a pressure of 1 lb. per sq. in. corresponds to a water depth of 2.31 ft. (These figures are for fresh water; the corresponding figures for salt water are approximately 0.446 lb. per sq. in. at 1 foot and 2.24 ft. per lb.) The pressure of mercury at a depth of 1 meter or 100 centimeters is equal to 1360 grams per sq. cm. The pressure of air at the surface of the earth under standard conditions is conventionally taken to be 14.7 lb. per sq. in., which is equivalent to the pressure of 760 mm. (or 29.92 in.) of mercury or 32.5 ft. of water.

The principles given above have been combined into a law which was first stated by the French scientist Blaise Pascal (q.v.) and is called *Pascal's law.* This law is usually formulated: pressure applied to an enclosed fluid is transmitted equally in all directions to all parts of the enclosing vessel. This principle has extremely important practical applications; see under *Hydraulics,* below.

The final basic principle of hydrostatics is the principle of displacement, attributed to the Greek philosopher Archimedes about

250 B.C. This principle states that if any body is placed in a liquid, the liquid will push upward on the body with a force equal to the weight of the liquid which the body displaces. This is the principle that lies behind buoyancy and explains why a heavily laden steel ship will float in water, although both the steel hull and the cargo are of themselves heavier than water. The ship's hull is so designed that it displaces a volume of water weighing more than the hull and the cargo combined and hence the water exerts a net upward thrust on the ship. Under different conditions of loading, the amount of water displaced by the submerged portion of a ship's hull always weighs precisely the same as the total weight of the ship and its cargo. Archimedes' principle also provides a means of determining the density of an object even though the object is so irregular in shape that its volume cannot be measured by any ordinary means. If the object is weighed in air and then weighed again while suspended in water, the difference in the weights will be the weight of a volume of water equal to the volume of the object; the density of the object (its weight divided by its volume) can at once be determined. Archimedes is said to have discovered the displacement principle while trying to find a way to determine whether the metal of a gold crown belonging to his patron had been debased by alloying with silver. By developing this method of finding density he was able to discover whether any of the silver (which is less dense than gold) had been added to the ornament. In precise weighings in chemical laboratories it is necessary to consider the effect of the relative displacements of air of the objects weighed and the weights used to balance them, and to correct the observed weight to allow for this factor.

Hydrodynamics. The simple laws of hydrostatic pressure are considerably modified for liquids that are in motion. If an ideal fluid —one that is incompressible and has no viscosity (q.v.)—is made to flow through an ideally smooth pipe, the motion of flow follows a definite set of imaginary lines called flow lines or streamlines which represent lines which are at all times parallel to the direction of flow. By shaping the surfaces over which the fluid flows to conform with the streamlines, smooth flow is obtained. In practice no liquid or gas behaves as a perfect fluid, and the study of fluid flow is complicated by compressibility and viscosity, and even more by the presence of *turbulence* (local eddies or variations of speed within the main flow) and of friction between the fluid and any surface over which it flows. The effects of turbulence and friction are extremely complex and calculations of turbulent flow are usually empirical or "rule of thumb" in nature rather than based on exact physical laws. True streamline flow, which occurs only in very narrow tubes, at very low speeds of flow, or with very viscous fluids, is subject to exact mathematical analysis.

In the field of hydrodynamics one basic principle does exist. This principle, called Bernoulli's principle (q.v.) after its discoverer the Swiss mathematician Daniel Bernoulli, describes in mathematical terms the phenomenon observed when fluid changes its rate of flow, as when a fluid flowing steadily through a pipe is made to pass through a section of pipe of smaller diameter than the main body of the pipe. For the same amount of fluid to flow through the constriction, its speed must be greater than the speed of flow in the main section of the pipe. The fluid gains this increment of velocity at the expense of loss in pressure, so that the pressure is greater upstream or downstream from the constriction then in the constriction. Thus the pressure exerted by a fluid in motion changes inversely with the speed of flow. This principle is of first importance not only in the field of hydrodynamics but also in aerodynamics, since it is the basic principle on which an airfoil (see FLIGHT, THEORY OF) operates. Many types of instruments for measuring the rate of flow of liquids and gases are constructed to operate in accordance with this principle.

(In strict terms Bernoulli's law states that the sum of the kinetic energy due to velocity and the potential energy due to pressure and to elevation at one point in a flowing stream is equal to the sum of the same energies at another point in the stream minus the loss due to friction between those points.)

Most of the other laws of hydrodynamics are special cases of Bernoulli's law. Among them is Torricelli's law, which states that the speed of a liquid issuing from a hole or orifice in a system containing a liquid is equal to the speed of a body falling freely from a height equal to the height of the surface of the liquid above the orifice.

For discussion of aerodynamics (the hydrodynamics of gases) see PNEUMATICS.

Hydraulics. The engineering science of hydraulics includes all the practical applications of hydrostatics and hydrodynamics and deals with such problems as the determination of the effects of friction on the flow of liquids through pipes; the design of turbines, dams, and other engineering structures for the control and utilization of liquids (usually water); and the design of nozzles, jets, meters, and valves used as parts of such structures. One of the most important fields of hydraulics is the design of hydraulic machinery. If a liquid is enclosed between two movable pistons, one of which has an area of 1 sq. in. and the other an area of 10 sq. in., a force of 1 pound on the smaller piston will result in a total force of 10 pounds on the larger piston, since the pressure is applied over an area ten times as great. The mechanical advantage obtained by hydraulic pressure is used for a variety of purposes. A comparatively light pressure on the pedal of a hydraulic brake system in an automobile results in a heavy pressure on the brake shoes. The control surfaces of large airplanes are operated by hydraulic booster systems. Hydraulic jacks and lifts are used for raising cars in filling stations and in construction work. In industry hydraulic presses are employed in the shaping and stamping of metal and for testing materials under high pressures. In special hydraulic presses, pressures as high as 7,000,000 lbs. per sq. in. have been attained. Hydraulic presses are sometimes called hydrostatic presses, or Bramah presses after their inventor Joseph Bramah.

HYDROPHILIDAE. See WATER SCAVENGER BEETLE.

HYDROPHIS. See SEA SNAKE.

HYDROPHOBIA or **RABIES,** an acute central nervous system infection by a specific virus which enters the body through the bite of an animal suffering from the disease. All warm-blooded animals are susceptible, but the disease is most common in dogs, cats, horses, cattle, foxes, wolves, coyotes, and skunks. Over 90 percent of the cases in man are caused by the bite of an infected dog.

The length of the incubation period of the disease varies among the different species of animals; in the dog it is very short. In man, the length of the incubation period depends upon the site and extent of the bite; bites in the head region, close to the brain, cause an earlier appearance of symptoms than bites about the legs; and deep bites produce symptoms more rapidly than superficial wounds. The incubation period in man varies from three weeks to a year, with an average of about six weeks.

Course in Man. At the end of the incubation period, the site of the wound, which had apparently healed quickly, becomes irritated and painful, and the tissues about the site may become numb. Depression and anxiety are common, often due in part to worry about being bitten and contracting hydrophobia. In cases of people bitten by noninfected animals such anxiety may lead to a hysterical condition in which the individual demonstrates most of the symptoms and passes through most of the stages associated with true hydrophobia. This *premonitory stage* lasts for about two days. In the next stage, the patient becomes irritable and hypersensitive; the general mental attitude is one of terror, intensified by difficult breathing and swallowing and a feeling of strangulation, caused by spasmodic contractions of the diaphragm and larynx. The patient is extremely thirsty but goes into convulsions when water is presented or even mentioned, whence the common name of the disease (Gr. *hydor,* "water"; *phobos,* "fear"). The intense excitation of the individual often produces a demented rage. Vomiting, pallor, and fever of about 102°F. (39°C.) are common during this stage. A thick, viscid secretion of mucus collects in the mouth and throat, and in an effort to get rid of the secretion without swallowing (swallowing is extremely painful during this stage), the individual expectorates frequently or attempts to cough. The cough is hoarse and somewhat resembles the bark of a dog. This *stage of excitement* lasts from one to four days; then the *terminal* or *paralytic stage,* which usually lasts no more than several hours, supervenes. The convulsions and spasms cease; paralysis and unconsciousness ensue; and the person dies. When once the premonitory stage is entered, the disease is invariably fatal; during the early stages of the incubation period hydrophobia can usually be checked.

Course in the Dog. In the dog rabies takes two forms, *furious* or *irritable rabies,* and *dumb* or *paralytic rabies.* The stages of furious rabies are similar to those through which an infected human passes; during the stage of excitement the so-called "mad dog" usually runs amuck, biting and snapping at any living thing in its path. Others of the lower animals in this stage behave somewhat similarly. Hooved animals bite and lash out with their legs, and birds attack with their beaks. In dumb rabies, which is not as common as furious rabies, the stage of excitement is of very short duration or is absent, and the paralytic stage sets in early in the disease, first attacking the muscles of the jaws and larynx. The lower jaw of the dog drops, and the animal is incapable of biting or of making a sound. This form of rabies is more difficult to recognize than furious rabies, and humans sometimes expose themselves to the disease by reaching into the throat of a dog so affected to explore for possible obstructions.

History and Treatment. Hydrophobia is described in medical writings dating from 300 B.C., but the method of transmission was not recognized until 1804. From 1804 to 1884 efforts to stop the disease after a person had been bitten by a rabid animal were confined to crude, painful cauterization of the wound or amputation of the bitten part, and were rarely successful.

Louis Pasteur (q.v.) developed a preventive vaccine against hydrophobia in 1884; modifications of Pasteur's methods are still used in rabies therapy today. Pasteur found that the rabies virus is present in the spinal cord and brain, as well as in the saliva, of infected animals, and that by injecting nerve material from such animals into similar or different species he could develop a controlled vaccine; he found that the strength of the virus could be decreased in various ways, one of which was by drying it in air.

The Pasteur Institute for the treatment of hydrophobia was established in Paris in 1888; since then similar institutes have been opened throughout the world. The Pasteur treatment has reduced mortality from hydrophobia in humans to less than one half of one percent. This treatment consists of immediate cauterization of the bite wound with nitric acid, followed during the next three weeks by continual administration of successively stronger doses of the preventive vaccine.

Until recently the Pasteur treatment has been attended by the slight danger of a paralytic reaction; for this reason, the treatment was usually postponed when the animal responsible for the bite was available for observation, and not given if the animal did not prove to be "mad". In 1949 the U.S. Bureau of Health prepared a vaccine from which the paralytic factor is eliminated, making the Pasteur treatment completely harmless. Inoculation of humans against hydrophobia usually confers immunity for about one to two years.

Control of Hydrophobia. Since dogs are the chief spreaders of rabies, control of the disease is directed at wiping it out among these animals. Strict muzzling rules are in effect in many nations, and stray dogs are regularly destroyed. England has a quarantine law barring the entrance of dogs unless they have previously been under observation for half a year. In many States of the U.S., yearly preventive inoculation of all dogs is required.

HYDROPHYTES, term applied to plants which grow in water or moist soil, or under very moist atmospheric conditions, as distinguished from mesophytes and xerophytes (qq.v.). Hydrophytes comprise a large part of the plant kingdom, including all algae and many families of fungi, mosses, liverworts, ferns, and seed plants. They grow in oceans, lakes, rivers, streams, swamps, wet meadows, and wet forests. Hydrophytes are adapted to meet the low oxygen content of watery environments. The smallest hydrophytes, such as lower algae, never develop more than a single layer of cells; such a unicellular layer can absorb sufficient oxygen through its surface for normal respiration. Larger plants having several layers of cells cannot present enough surface to absorb sufficient oxygen through the water; these plants are adapted to floating by various mechanisms, such as air-bladders or superficial hairs which retain small quantities of air, making the plants buoyant. Leaves of floating plants usually have very thin surface layers which permit easy absorption of oxygen; see LEAF.

Hydrophytes which live on relatively dry ground under very moist atmospheric conditions are called *hygrophytes*. Most of the vegetation of tropical rain forests is hygrophytic, having thick leaves protected with heavy layers of cuticle. Inner layers of the leaves are adapted to hold large quantities of water.

HYDROPONICS, term applied to cultivation of plants in nutrient solutions without use of soil. Soilless growing of cultivated plants began in the 1930's as an outgrowth of the culture techniques used by plant physiologists in plant nutrition experiments. Successful methods of soilless growth, developed since that time, differ in particulars but have two common features: (1) nutrients are supplied in liquid solutions; (2) plants are supported by porous material, such as

Mechanix Illustrated

Hydroponics: plants growing without soil, supported in gravel, are fed a solution of calcium nitrate, magnesium, and ammonium and potassium phosphates.

peat, sand, gravel, or glass wool, which acts as a "wick" in relaying the nutrient solution from its source to the roots of the plants.

Green plants manufacture their own organic food, using carbon dioxide and oxygen as raw materials; see PHOTOSYNTHESIS. The nutrients usually supplied to plants by soil are almost entirely mineral salts. Plant physiologists have discovered that plants require carbon, hydrogen, oxygen, nitrogen, phosphorus, potassium, magnesium, sulfur, calcium, iron, manganese, boron, zinc, copper, and probably molybdenum. Carbon, hydrogen and oxygen are obtained in large quantities from water and air, but the remaining elements are ordinarily supplied as salts by the soil. The relative amount of each of these elements required for normal growth is different in each plant, but all plants require relatively large percentages of nitrogen, phosphorus, potassium, magnesium, sulfur, and calcium. Iron, manganese, boron, zinc, copper, and molybdenum are supplied in minute quantities, and are called micronutrients or trace elements (q.v.). The specific salts used to supply these elements may be varied at the discretion of the grower; a typical solution of primary minerals is composed of distilled water containing potassium nitrate, KNO_3, calcium nitrate, $Ca(NO_3)_2$, potassium acid phosphate, KH_2PO_4, and magnesium sulfate, $MgSO_4$. In solution, the salts dissociate into ions (q.v.); potassium nitrate, for example, is available to plants as the ions K^+ and NO_3^-. A solution of micronutrient salts is added to the solution of primary elements to complete the nutrient solution. A small amount of fungicide is usually added to prevent growth of mold.

Several culture techniques are in use among growers and experimenters. The most practical method for commercial use is the *subirrigation method* in which plants are grown in trays filled with gravel, cinders, or other coarse materials, and periodically flooded with nutrient solution. The solution is allowed to drain off after each flooding, and may be re-used as long as sufficient minerals remain in it. The *water-culture method* is widely used for botanical experimentation. A common type of water culture consists of glazed porcelain jars filled with solution; the plants are placed in beds of glass wool or similar material which are supported at the surface of the solution. Roots of the plants penetrate the beds and remain in the solution. The least exact method, commonly called the *"slop" method,* is the easiest to operate. Course, clean sand is used in place of soil, and nutrient solution is poured on the sand in approximately equal amounts at regular intervals. A refinement of this practice is the *drip method,* in which a steady, slow feed of nutrient is maintained. Excess nutrient solution is allowed to drain off in both slop and drip methods.

Hydroponic culture methods are being used successfully to produce plants out of season in greenhouses, and to produce plants in areas where either the soil or climate is not suitable for the crop grown. During World War II, for example, several U.S. Army units successfully produced vegetables hydroponically at various overseas bases. Growers have discovered that unknown potentialities of plants can be realized through growth in nutrient solutions. Orchids, for example, grow well at the normal low nutritional level, but hydroponic methods can be used to increase both total growth and number of blooms produced. Rhododendrons in hydroponic culture have been grown from the seed stage to flowering in two and a half years instead of the usual five years.

HYDROQUINONE. See DIHYDROXYBENZENE.

HYDROSTATICS. See HYDROMECHANICS.

HYDROTHORAX. See DROPSY.

HYDROTROPISM. See TROPISM.

HYDROZOA, a class of coelenterates of which most species show alternation of generations (q.v.). One generation is colonial, and is known as a *hydroid* because of the resemblance of its members to *Hydra* (q.v.), which is the simplest of all hydrazoans. The other generation, known as a *hydromedusa,* is a free-swimming, sexual individual which produces either eggs or sperm; the familiar jellyfish is a typical hydromedusa. Each fertilized egg of a hydromedusa develops into a ciliated larva, known as a *planula,* from which the hydroid develops. The hydroid, in turn, gives rise to the hydromedusae by budding.

Hydrozoans differ in their conformance to the typical alternation of generations. Hydrida, the order to which *Hydra* belongs, never has free-swimming forms. Siphonophora, the order containing the Portuguese man-of-war (q.v.), has a short-lived hydromedusa, the larvae of which develop into medusalike organisms from which the colony arises; the individual members of a siphonophoran colony are extremely specialized, and

the polyps specializing in defense produce a poison so strong that it can kill a human being. Trachylina, another order, has a short-lived polyp stage (in some species no polyp stage has yet been observed), and spends most of its life as a free-swimming hydromedusa.

Hydrozoa contains seven orders, one of which, that containing the graptolites (q.v.), is presently extinct, and three of which have already been mentioned above. Campanulariae, or Leptomedusae, is characterized by a horny layer covering the individual members of its colony stage, and shows a well-differentiated alternation of generations. Hydractinia, which lives on the shell of the hermit crab (q.v.) is a well-known genus in this order. Anthomedusae differs from Campanulariae in having the horny covering only over the tissue connecting the polyps of a hydroid, but not on the polyps themselves. *Tubularia indivisa* is a common American species; *Bougainvillea fructuosa* is a common English species. Hydrocorallinae contains a number of interesting forms which secrete a large, hard, calcareous exoskeleton and often form corals (q.v.). *Millepora* is the best-known genus of this order.

HYENA, common name for any of three species of large, carnivorous, Old World mammals constituting the family Hyaenidae. The animals somewhat resemble wolves but are more massive, reaching a length of over 5 ft., and a weight of over 250 lbs. Their heads are large, with long, pointed ears. They have strong jaws, jaw muscles, and teeth, and so can crush thick bones. Their backs are covered with long, stiff hair extending from the neck to the base of the tail. Their forelegs are longer than their hind legs; each foot has four toes, each of which bears a nonretractile claw. Hyenas are solitary, nocturnal animals; they are known for their cowardice, preferring to eat meat already killed by other animals, and killing their own prey only when sharply driven by hunger. Hyenas are occasionally domesticated to serve as scavengers.

The hyena with the widest distribution is the striped hyena, *Hyaena striata,* found from N. Africa through s.w. Asia to India. This species is ashy brown in color and is striped transversely with dark brown. The spotted or laughing hyena, or tiger wolf, *H. crocuta,* is found in all parts of Africa s. of Ethiopia. Its coat is brownish yellow marked with round, dark brown spots. It is noted for its cry which resembles the laugh-

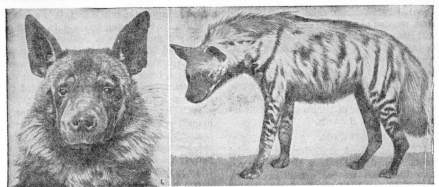

Left: The brown hyena. Right: Museum specimen of a striped hyena.

ter of a demented human being. The brown hyena, or strand wolf, *H. brunnea,* is found in s. Africa. It is brownish gray in general body color and has dark brown stripes on its legs. This species is often found along the shores of streams, and is fond of crabs and dead fish.

Fossil remains of hyenas which lived during the Pliocene epoch have been found in England, Germany, and France. The remains have been identified as being those of animals nearly identical with the striped hyena.

A marsupial of Tasmania, the thylacine (q.v.), is sometimes called a hyena.

HYENA DOG. See HUNTING DOG.

HYETOGRAPHY. See RAIN.

HYGROMETER, any of various types of instruments used to measure atmospheric humidity (q.v.). A simple form of hygrometer, used in the home and in offices, utilizes the change in length in organic fibers brought about by the absorption of moisture. A single blond human hair is often used. The fiber tends to shrink in damp air, and the apparatus is so arranged that the change in length of the fiber moves a pointer across a dial, which is calibrated to give *percent relative humidity.* This type of hygrometer gives only an approximate indication of humidity and is not used for accurate, quantitative determinations.

The instrument most commonly used in laboratories to measure relative humidity is the psychrometer or wet-and-dry-bulb thermometer. Two similar thermometers are mounted side by side; one has its bulb exposed to the atmosphere (the dry bulb) and the bulb of the other (the wet bulb) is wrapped in a suitable material, such as muslin, which is immersed in water and serves as a wick. The wet bulb is cooled by evaporation of the water, the amount of evaporation and consequent cooling of the thermometer depending on the humidity of the atmosphere (the dryer the atmosphere, the more rapidly the water evaporates). A table accompanying the instrument gives the relative humidity in terms of the readings of the wet-bulb and dry-bulb thermometers.

The dew-point hygrometer measures relative humidity by means of the dew point. A small amount of ether is placed in a highly polished, thin, metallic cup, and the evaporation of the ether (accelerated by blowing air through it) lowers the temperature of the cup. When the dew point of the surrounding air is reached a film of moisture suddenly appears upon the surface of the cup. The temperature is read by means of a thermometer, and a table accompanying the instrument gives the relative humidity in terms of the atmospheric and dew-point temperatures.

HYGROPHYTES. See HYDROPHYTES.

HYKSOS, in ancient Egypt, the kings of the XVth and XVIth dynasties, reigning from 1680 to 1580 B.C. The name has been interpreted by Egyptologists as meaning "shepherd kings" and, less commonly, "foreign kings." Sweeping south into Egypt, probably from Palestine and Syria, they and their nomadic followers captured Memphis and exacted tribute from the rest of the country. They established a stronghold at Avaris on the northeastern border of the Nile delta, but left the territory above Memphis under the rule of tributary princes of the old nobility. These vassals started the revolt which finally drove out the foreign dynasty. The only detailed ancient account of the Hyksos is in a passage cited by Josephus (q.v.). Direct evidence from inscriptions and from remains of sculpture and pottery shows that they adapted themselves to Egyptian customs and took Egyptian names. They introduced the horse into Egypt, and maintained tribute or trade relations with the Minoans and the Babylonians. No remarkable buildings of the Hyksos kings have survived; only traces of temple restorations remain, mainly at Bubastis.

HYLA. See TREE FROG.

HYLAS, in Greek mythology, a beautiful youth favored by the hero Hercules (q.v.), who took him on the expedition of the Argonauts (q.v.) in search of the Golden Fleece. When they stopped on the coast of Mysia in Asia Minor, Hylas was drawn by the nymphs into the spring from which he was drawing water. Hercules abandoned the expedition in order to seek Hylas, and threatened to destroy the country if the youth were not found. The inhabitants began to search, and forever after, on a certain day each year, ranged through the mountains crying out for Hylas. They were also compelled by Hercules to make sacrifices to Hylas at the spring wherein the latter disappeared.

HYLOBATES. See GIBBON.

HYMANS, PAUL (1865–1941), Belgian statesman, born in Brussels. He studied law at the University of Brussels, and from 1898 to 1914 was professor of comparative parliamentary history at that institution. He was ambassador to Great Britain from 1915 to 1917, became minister for foreign affairs in 1918, and after World War I represented Belgium at the Paris Peace Conference of 1919. He was a signatory of the Versailles Treaty ending World War I, and drafted part of the Covenant of the League of Nations. He was appointed Belgian delegate to the League in 1920, and was elected the first president of the Assembly of the League later that year. In 1924-26, from 1927 to 1934, and in 1935-36, he again served in the Belgian government as minister for foreign affairs. He was the author of *Portraits, Essais, et Discours* (1914) and *Pages Libérales* (1936).

HYMENOPHYLLACEAE, or FILMY FERNS, family of ferns belonging to the order Filicales, which have delicate leaves composed of a single layer of cells. The family is almost entirely tropical and includes over two hundred species. The typical genus, *Hymenophyllum,* is an entirely tropical plant, which is often epiphytic. Another large genus, *Trichomanes,* is represented in the U.S. by

T. boschianum, the bristle fern. It is a small, creeping plant, bearing leaves 4 to 8 inches long, and grows on wet sandstone cliffs in S.E. United States. A genus of fossil ferns of the Carboniferous period, called *Hymenophyllites,* bears a close external resemblance to *Hymenophyllum,* and may be related to the filmy ferns. See FERN.

HYMENOPTERA (Gr. *hymen,* "membrane"; *pteron,* "wing"), an order of insects containing over 70,000 species, including the ant, bee, bumblebee, chalcid fly, digger wasp, hornet, ichneumon fly, sawfly, and wasp (qq.v.), and the gall wasp (see GALL). The insects of this order are more specialized and show a higher degree of comparative intelligence than any other insects.

All hymenopterans have mouth parts adapted for biting; many species have them further adapted for sucking and absorbing surface juices; others have them also prolonged in order to enable the insect to draw nectar from deep flowers; and certain species, such as the bees, are able to use their mouth parts as tools for the handling of wax. Hymenopterans typically show six abdominal segments in the female and seven in the male; an additional abdominal segment in each sex is completely fused to the thorax, and is popularly considered part of the thorax. Between the thoracic abdominal segment and the posterior segments, the body of all hymenopterans except sawflies narrows into a "waist." Hymenopterans either have four membranous wings or are wingless; the forewings are larger than the hind wings and in flight are joined to the hind wings by means of small hooklets. The ovipositor (egg-laying organ) of female hymenopterans may be adapted for drilling, sawing, or stinging. Hymenopteran larvae are usually legless; those of the horntail and sawfly have thoracic and abdominal legs. Young hymenopterans go through a complete metamorphosis.

Many hymenopterans, especially ants, live in well-integrated colonies, the individual members of which are morphologically differentiated for the performance of a specialized function (see INSECT: *Social Insects*). The social structure of hymenopterans is higher, or more similar to the human social structure, than that of any of the other invertebrates.

Hymenopterans vary in their feeding habits; some are plant eaters, others carnivores, while still others feed on nectar and manufactured honey. The gall wasps are the most destructive to cultivated plants. The larvae of plant-eating species, such as ichneumon and chalcid flies, are carnivorous; they are parasites, and destroy many harmful insects. Honeybees are the most important of the nectar feeders; the honey (q.v.) they manufacture is put to many uses by man. One hymenopteran is very important in the cultivation of figs.

HYMETTUS, a mountain in Greece, 5 miles S.E. of Athens. It is 3370 ft. above sea level. In ancient times it was famous for the honey found on its slopes, and for its blue-gray marble used for building and sculpture in classic Athens.

HYMN, a musical composition, usually meant to be sung by a chorus or congregation of people, in praise or adoration of a deity. The earliest known hymns are two Greek compositions of about 150 B.C., dedicated to Apollo. In the first years of the Christian era any song in praise of God, including settings of passages from the Bible, was called a hymn. By the 2nd century A.D., however, the term was restricted to newly-written sacred poems set to music, and a popular collection of paraphrases of the Biblical psalms, prepared for the Gnostics (q.v.) and called the *Gnostic Psalter* (2nd century A.D.), marks the beginning of hymn writing, or hymnody, in Christian times. The success of this work led the Syrian monk, St. Ephrem of Edessa (306-73), to write Christian hymns with the purpose of establishing Christian orthodoxy; he has since been regarded by historians as the father of Christian hymnody. His work was carried on in Constantinople by St. Chrysostom (q.v.).

The most important development of the hymn during the Middle Ages was the use of plain song as accompaniment, beginning approximately in the 11th century. Such arrangements differ from those of Gregorian chant (q.v.) in that the plain song observes no fixed metrical scheme, but follows exactly the words of the hymn. In later centuries, with the growth of polyphony (see HARMONY), many melodies taken from plainsong hymns were used as the bases of masses and motets.

The earliest hymns in English were translations from Latin; with the 17th century original Lutheran hymns in German became the predominating influence upon English and American hymnodists. The earliest book of original English hymns, *Hymns and Songs of the Church* (1623), with music by Orlando Gibbons, met with little success, but during the 18th century many new hymn books appeared, and hymns became established as part of the regular service of the Anglican Church. In America, simultaneously with the popularity of the English hymn books in England, new hymns were composed as early as the middle of the 18th century. The earliest known American hymnodists were William Billings (1746–1800) and Lowell Mason (1792–1872). In the 19th century thousands of hymns were written by English and American hymnodists, and many official hymn books were compiled for various church denominations; among those still used at the present time are *Church Hymns* (1852), *The Hymns Ancient and Modern* (1861), and *The Hymnal Companion to the Book of Common Prayer*.

Hymnals, or collections of hymns, and communal singing occupy a prominent place in the service of almost every religion and religious denomination of modern times.

HYNDMAN, HENRY MAYERS (1842–1921), founder of the modern British socialist movement, born in London, and educated at Cambridge University. In 1871 he visited France, where he studied and was profoundly impressed by the revolutionary uprising which took place in Paris (see COMMUNE OF 1871). During the economic depression of the 1870's he became an increasingly vehement critic of British capitalism and, after reading a portion of the writings of the communist leader Karl Marx, adopted certain of the revolutionary doctrines expounded by Marx. In 1881 Hyndman founded in England the Democratic Federation (later the Social Democratic Federation), as an instrument for revolutionary propaganda. Its membership never exceeded 10,000. Nevertheless, under Hyndman's leadership, the Federation attained wide influence in British politics. Hyndman, however, was never able to win a seat in Parliament. In 1911 the Federation became the British Socialist Party; three years later, when the other leaders of the party declared themselves opposed to British participation in World War I, Hyndman, who, in the meantime, had become an ardent nationalist, withdrew from the party. In 1916 he organized the National Socialist Party, a group which never attained substantial size or influence, and which disappeared soon afterward. Among his writings are *The Historical Basis of Socialism in England* (1883), *The Economics of Socialism* (1896), *A Record of an Adventurous Life* (1911), and *The Evolution of Revolution* (1920).

HYOSCYAMUS. See HENBANE.

HYPATIA (370?-415 A.D.), Greek philosopher, born in Alexandria, Egypt, daughter of the mathematician Theon. She assisted her father in his writings, and succeeded him as lecturer on mathematics and Greek philosophy. Her intellectual gifts and her beauty attracted students from foreign countries; and her judgment was so respected that the city magistrates of Alexandria consulted her on important cases. In about 400 A.D. she was the undisputed leader of the Neoplatonic school of philosophy at Alexandria (see NEOPLATONISM). She was the author of commentaries on ancient astronomical and mathematical works. Because of her association with Orestes, the pagan prefect of Alexandria who opposed the persecution of the Jews and other non-Christians initiated by Bishop Cyril (see CYRIL, SAINT), Hypatia was murdered by a mob of Christians and her body was burned. She is the heroine of the historical romance *Hypatia* (1853) by the English novelist Charles Kingsley.

HYPERICACEAE. See ST.-JOHN'S-WORT.

HYPERMNESTRA. See DANAÜS.

HYPEROPIA, farsightedness. See SIGHT, DEFECTS OF; EYEGLASSES.

HYPNOTISM, a general term applied to the study and inducing of a condition of artificial sleep called *hypnosis,* characterized by close outward resemblances to normal sleep and somnambulism.

Hypnotism, in various forms, has been practiced since ancient times. Modern techniques of hypnotism are in the main based upon a condition of rapport between the hypnotist and the subject, during which hypnosis is induced by the concentration of the subject's attention upon an object or light held close to the subject's eyes, by oral suggestion, and by mild, monotonously repeated sensory stimulation, such as stroking the limbs or face. To be readily hypnotized, a person must be highly susceptible to external influence and suggestion. Suggestibility permits the hypnotist to induce the early stages of hypnotic sleep (sometimes called *lethargic hypnosis*), characterized by languor and drowsiness; suggestibility is also the major characteristic of the most advanced stages (sometimes called *cataleptic* or *somnambulistic hypnosis*), which resembles a trance. Under deep hypnosis, the subject may be made to simulate physical phenomena such as anesthesia, blindness, and paralysis, and psychological phenomena such as hallucination, all at the suggestion of the hypnotist. Suggestions made by the hypnotist to the subject at this time may be extended to include acts to be performed after the hypnotic trance has been broken; this device is known as *posthypnotic suggestion.* A subject under the influence of hypnosis or posthypnotic suggestion cannot be induced to commit an offense or crime which violates his ethical principles or convictions, though the relaxation of inhibitions operative in his normal state may permit the carrying out of arbitrary and even irrational instructions.

The exaggerated state of passive attention and obedience induced in a hypnotized subject has long been a source of both the abuse and constructive development of hypnotism. Charlatans have at different periods in history made use of the technique, and the power exhibited by extremely susceptible or frequently hypnotized persons of spontaneously inducing or dropping off into hypnotic sleep (a phenomenon which is known as *self-hypnosis* or *autosuggestion*), has been exploited in religion by ascetics and in therapy by such men as the French mental healer, Émile Coué (q.v.). On the other hand, many modern psychologists beginning with Pierre Janet (q.v.) and including Sigmund Freud (q.v.) have used hypnotism experimentally in investigations of the constitution of the mind; and the possibilities of hypnotism as both a diagnostic aid and a source of curative posthypnotic suggestion therapy by such men as the French mental therapists, and a neo-Freudian school of psychoanalysts using a group of hypnotic techniques known collectively as *hypnoanalysis.* In recent therapeutic and diagnostic work narcotic drugs known as hypnotics are frequently employed to initiate or hasten hypnosis. Compare MESMER, FRIEDERICH ANTON; MESMERISM.

HYPOBLAST. See EMBRYOLOGY: *Germ Layers.*

HYPOCAUST. See BATH: *Roman.*

HYPOCHLOROUS ACID, an acid, formula HCLO, which acts as an oxidizer and bleaching agent. The bleaching property of chlorine (q.v.) is due to its reaction with water to form hypochlorous acid; hydrochloric acid is also formed in this reaction. Hypochlorous acid is unstable and is generally used in the form of its salts, hypochlorites. Sodium hypochlorite, made by reacting sodium hydroxide and chlorine water, is a popular bleaching agent and sterilizer used in the household. See BLEACHING POWDER.

HYPOCHONDRIA or **HYPOCHONDRI-ASIS,** a morbid condition characterized by an increase in sensitivity to changes in the internal organs, by simulation of the symptoms of any of several diseases, and in its advanced stages by anxiety and melancholia. A person suffering from this condition, called a hypochondriac, is frequently convinced that he is suffering from some specific and grave disease. In pathological and psychiatric terms, hypochondriasis may be more precisely defined as any illness or symptom referred by a patient to some part, organ, or organic symptom when no physical or causal relation can be found between the complaint and an actual functional or structural disorder. A predisposing physical cause of hypochondriasis may exist in a congenitally high sensitivity to sensations and changes in the internal organs; in psychiatry and abnormal psychology, however, it is treated solely as a symptom of any of several mental illnesses, such as neurasthenia, involutional melancholia, and dementia praecox. See PSYCHOLOGY, ABNORMAL.

HYRACOIDEA, an order of mammals. See HYRAX.

HYRAX, ROCK RABBIT, or CONY, common name for any of the curious Old World mammals in the order Hyracoidea (Gr. *hyrax,* "shrew mouse"), which, in external appearance, resemble large rabbits, and, in internal anatomy, resemble both horses and elephants. They are timid animals which feed on vegetation. Hyraxes have thick, pointed heads with short, rounded ears, and short, thick necks. Their yellowish-gray or brown bodies are squat and furry; their tails are rudimentary; their legs are short and thin. The feet, which are equipped with rough pads for climbing, are hoofed; each forefoot has five toes, and each hind foot has four. One toe on each foot is much reduced in size.

HYRCANUS. See MACCABEES.

HYSSOP, common name of small perennial herbs of the genus *Hyssopus,* belonging to the Mint family. The common hyssop, *H. officinalis,* is native to Europe. It became naturalized in the United States, where it has escaped from gardens. It is a small plant, growing about 2 feet high, having narrow, woody stems, and elliptical, aromatic leaves. The small flowers, borne on clustered spikes, have a five-toothed, tubular calyx, five-lobed, asymmetrical corolla, two stamens, and a single pistil. The fruit is a smooth nutlet.

Hyrax (Procavia capensis) of South Africa

Wild hyssop flowers are bluish purple, but cultivated varieties may have bluish purple, red, or white flowers. The aromatic oil, called oil of hyssop, contained in its leaves is used in the manufacture of liqueurs. The leaves, formerly used as a medicinal herb, were administered as tea to persons with pulmonary and catarrhal disorders.

The hyssop mentioned in the Bible was probably a related mint called thyme (q.v.). The common name "giant hyssop" is often applied to mints of the genus *Agastache,* which are taller plants, 3 to 5 feet high, bearing hyssoplike flowers. The hedge hyssop is a member of the Figwort family, unrelated to hyssop; see GRATIOLA.

HYSTASPES. See DARIUS.

HYSTERESIS. See MAGNETISM.

HYSTERIA, in psychopathology, a form of psychoneurosis usually characterized by physiologically or organically inexplicable disturbances or failures in the control of any of several bodily functions. This basic set of physical symptoms is now generally known as *conversion hysteria.* Another, somewhat more unusual behavioral disorder characterized chiefly by mental symptoms occurs in a few hysterical patients; it is marked by deep and prolonged dissociated states, and in its extreme stage is called *dissociated personality.*

Conversion Hysteria. Conversion hysteria is displayed to some extent in normal behavior. Normal people often have headaches or pains with no recognizable organic basis; these symptoms are essentially hysterical in nature, and may properly be classed as hysteria. In extreme cases, when difficult or insoluble emotional problems of adjustment are "converted" by neurotic individuals into physical symptoms, physical disturbances of the gravest kind involving almost any organ or function of the body may result. Such symptoms most often take the form of anesthesia, particularly of the skin, blindness, deafness, motor paralysis, and tremors. Other disturbances of function center about the throat and gastrointestinal system, and range from nausea and compulsive vomiting to the *globus hystericus,* a choking sensation as from a lump in the throat which is often considered one of the truest indicators of hysteria. Another class of conversion symptoms simulate and are often mistaken for the symptoms of epilepsy.

Dissociated Personality. Mental and emotional disturbances may also be hysterical. In their mildest form, these disturbances are exhibited in nervousness and excitability, exaggerated or uncontrolled emotion, egoism, and a tendency toward fantasy. More extreme symptoms are sleepwalking, hallucinations, amnesia, and a variety of delirious and trance states. At this extreme stage, the dissociation of a part of the content of the mind takes place, with the dissociated portion acting in substantial independence from the usual or "main" personality. When trance and amnesic states become exaggerated and systematic, the phenomenon known as double personality (q.v.) or multiple personality may occur. In this condition two or more personalities coexist in the individual, each of which is sufficiently integrated and developed to lead a unified and co-ordinated personal life. Although hysterics in whom dissociation has occurred may retain conscious control of their personalities during dissociated states, the shifts from one personality to another are involuntary and uncontrollable, and the secondary personalities may become powerful enough to exercise complete dominance under certain conditions.

The Study and Treatment of Hysteria. Hysteria has been for centuries an object of clinical investigation, psychological speculation, and popular curiosity. As early as Hippocrates (q.v.), who gave the disorder its name, hysterical states were described; it was thought to be peculiar to women, and

to be the result of spasms of the uterus or womb. By the end of the 17th century, the occurrence of hysteria among men had been observed, and its broad range of symptoms had been described. Scientific study and treatment was obviated, however, by the attribution of extreme hysterical phenomena to demonic possession or to witchcraft. Though the next two centuries witnessed an increasing insight into hysterical manifestations, hysteria became one of the most common sources of incorrect medical diagnosis and unnecessary surgery.

Physicians eventually learned to recognize hysterical conditions, but a modern and systematic description of hysteria was not made until the 1880's when the French neurologist Jean Martin Charcot and his students showed that hysterical symptoms could be induced and dispelled by suggestion. Subsequently Pierre Janet (q.v.) formulated the first description of hysteria as a purely psychological disorder, and made the first scientific study of dissociation. The most important single revolution in the whole concept of hysteria was made by Sigmund Freud (q.v.); in Freud's developed theory, hysterical symptoms are the results of conflicts between the conscious mind and some unsuccessfully repressed "wish" which is incompatible with the social or ethical standards of the individual. Such wishes are not inactive, and reappear in symbolic or disguised forms such as the conversion phenomena which are the major physical signs of hysteria.

In the light of this explanation of hysterical phenomena, modern treatment is based on some form of psychotherapy. The hysteric is recognized as a poorly organized, unstable personality, and his treatment is not complete until the psychic cause of his neurosis has been unearthed. Immediate relief may be obtained in some cases by persuasion, suggestion, or hypnotism. See Psychology, Abnormal.

HYSTRIX. See Porcupine.

the ninth letter and third vowel in the alphabets of western Europe. It was called *iota* by the Greeks from its Semitic name, *yodh*. The word *yodh* meant "hand", and was named after the form of the character in the Egyptian hieratic alphabet, which bore some resemblance to a hand with the thumb held apart from the fingers. The Phenician alphabet was derived from the Egyptian, and gave rise in turn to that of early Greece, in which the form of the letter was angular, resembling that of the English letter Z. An intermediate S-like form was succeeded in the 7th century B.C. by a vertical stroke, the form used in the Roman alphabet. It has since varied less in form than any other letter. The main stages in the development of the upper-case or capital I may be given as: Roman | , < Early Greek ⟨ or ⟨ , < Phenician ⟨ , < hieratic Egyptian ⟨ . The dot over the lower-case or minuscle *i* first came into use in the 11th century A.D. It was originally an accent, *í*, and was employed only to distinguish *ii* from *u,* or to mark the *i* in the combinations *iu* and *ui.*

In many European languages, such as Italian, and in some English words, such as *machine* and *police,* the sound of the letter is that of the Latin long *ī* (usually called long ē in English). The sound commonly called long ī in English, as in *ice, fine,* and the sound of the letter itself, is really a diphthong made by premature opening of the lengthened vowel (long ē) under stress accent, and is a phonetic change dating from the period of Middle English. The most common sound of the letter in English is that heard in *bit, dip,* and *sit,* and was taken over unchanged from the Latin short *i;* it is represented by a variety of other spellings, such as *y* in *cymbal, u* in *busy, o* in *women, ei* in *forfeit, ie* in *sieve, ui* in *guilt,* and *ia* in *carriage.*

As an abbreviation, the capital I is used for personal names beginning with I, such as *Isabella* and *Isaac,* for an incisor tooth (in dental formulas), for a variety of titles such as Imperator and Imperatrix, and occasionally for the states of Idaho and Iowa. The lower-case i is used as an abbreviation in chemistry for inactive, as in *i*-camphor, or for insoluble.

As a symbol, the capital I is used in chemistry for iodine in all languages except German, and in logic for the particular affirmative proposition (some A is B). In either upper or lower case the I (or i) is used as the Roman numeral one. Repeated once or twice, it indicates respectively two or three units (for example, III equals 3). Before higher numerals, such as V, X, or L, it indicates the subtraction of one unit (for example, IX equals 9); and after higher numerals it indicates the addition of one unit, or more if repeated (for example, XII equals 12). The lower-case i is used in mathematics as the symbol for the imaginary quantity $\sqrt{-1}$ (see IMAGINARY NUMBER). The letter, usually in the form of a qualifying noun, also denotes an object having the form of a capital I, as in the terms *I beam* and *I frame.*

IBADAN, a city of Oyo Province, the Western Provinces, Nigeria, British West Africa, situated 123 m. by rail N.E. of Lagos. The city, the largest in population in Nigeria, is surrounded by mud walls; most of the dwellings are thatch-roofed mud huts. Farming and the making of handicraft articles are the principal occupations of the inhabitants. Native officials administer the government under the guidance of a British official. Pop. (1953 est.) 459,000.

IBAGUÉ, capital of Tolima Department, Colombia, situated about 60 miles w. of Bogotá. Because of its location on the road over the Quindio mountain pass into the fertile Cauca Valley, it is an important commercial center. In the vicinity of Ibagué tobacco, rice, sugar cane, and cacao are raised. An important occupation of the townspeople is the extraction of sulfur and silver from nearby deposits. Pop. (1950 est.) 94,000.

IBÁÑEZ, VICENTE BLASCO (1867–1928), Spanish antimonarchist and novelist, born in Valencia. He joined the republican movement in his youth and soon became editor of the antimonarchist newspaper *El Pueblo*. His career as a novelist began with the publication of *Arroz y Tartana* (1894), the first of a series of works realistically and vividly depicting life in the Valencia region. This novel, like many of his subsequent writings, attracted little attention in Spain. In 1889, to avoid arrest for his political activities, he fled to France. He resumed his attacks on the government after his return and in 1895 again sought refuge abroad. Back in Spain the following year, he was arrested and sentenced to two years at hard labor. Ibáñez served eight consecutive terms as a Republican Party deputy in the Cortes between 1898 and 1907. In 1909 he retired from politics; the following year he went to South America. Returning to Spain in 1914, he became an ardent supporter of the Allied cause in World War I. In 1923, after the seizure of power in Spain by Gen. Primo de Rivera, he escaped to France.

Ibáñez achieved his first important literary success with *La Barraca* (1898), a novel exposing agrarian evils and social injustice in the Valencia countryside. His other works in the regional genre include *Entre Naranhos* (1902; Eng. trans. *The Torrent*, 1920); *Cañas y Barro* (1902; Eng. trans. *Reeds and Mud*, 1928); *La Catedral* (1903; Eng. trans. *The Shadow of the Cathedral*, 1909); and *Sangre y Arena* (1908; Eng. trans. *Blood and Sand*, 1913). In the view of many critics *Cañas y*

Barro is his masterpiece. With the publication of *Los Cuatro Jinetes del Apocalipsis* (1916; Eng. trans. *The Four Horsemen of the Apocalypse*, 1918), a work which brought him international recognition, Ibáñez introduced a series of novels dealing with broad philosophical and cultural themes. Among others in the series are *Mare Nostrum* (1918; Eng. trans. *Our Sea*, 1920); *El Papa del Mar* (1926; Eng. trans. *The Pope of the Sea*, 1927); and *Á los Pies de Venus* (1926; Eng. trans. *The Borgias; or, At the Feet of Venus*, 1930).

IBERIA, ancient name for both Spain and the Georgian Soviet Socialist Republic, U.S.S.R.

IBERIAN LANGUAGE. See GEORGIAN.

IBERIANS, an ancient people of the Spanish peninsula, who originally lived in the region around the Iberus (now Ebro) River. The oldest historical records of the Iberians were made by early Greek navigators; in later classical times they were known to the Greeks and Romans as a large group of separate Spanish tribes related in race and speaking any of several similar languages. Modern archeological and anthropological study has resulted in the application of the term "Iberian" to primitive neolithic and bronze-age men whose remains and relics are found in ancient graves, grottoes, and refuse heaps throughout western Europe. Members of the race thus defined are small in stature and have ovoid or ellipsoid crania; they resemble the peoples of ancient Italy, Greece, Asia Minor, Egypt, Ethiopia, and north Africa, and are found today among the Basques and throughout the Iberian Peninsula. The northern limits of settlement are less easy to trace, but the Iberians have been identified with such northern peoples as the Welsh, the Picts, and other groups. Thus the term "Iberian" is somewhat misleading for so widespread a race; many ethnologists have suggested alternate names, of which the most popular are "Mediterranean" and "Eur-African."

Knowledge of the ancient Iberians of the Spanish Peninsula has been gained in the main from studies of their coins and of the Basque language (q.v.), which is the only surviving representative of their ancient languages. The majority of the coins are inscribed in an alphabet similar to the alphabets of western Greece, but a few characters occur from an older, indigenous script. This Iberian alphabet was also used in a few extant inscriptions; it has been translated through the occurrence of known place names on coins or inscriptions found in places bearing these names. Moreover, the authentication of some Basque place names by their appearance on these coins has enabled linguistic scientists to link Basque with other non-Indo-European languages of the western Mediterranean and the Atlantic seaboard of Europe. The most prominent of these students, Karl Wilhelm von Humboldt, claimed to have identified on linguistic evidence alone a great primitive Iberian people, speaking an unknown language which was the parent of Basque, and inhabiting, before their expulsion or absorption, Sicily, Sardinia, Corsica, southern France, and the British Isles. See also MAN, ANCIENT.

IBERT, JACQUES (1890-   ), French composer, born in Paris, and educated at the Paris Conservatory. In 1919 he won the Prix de Rome, and in 1937 was appointed director of the French Academy in Rome, the institution which selects the recipients of this award. Ibert was an ingenious and witty composer, revealing in his style the influence of Claude Debussy and Maurice Ravel (qq.v.). He wrote works for the ballet, cinema, chamber groups, voice, and orchestra; his best known composition is the orchestral suite, *Escales* (1922).

IBERUS. See EBRO.

IBERVILLE, PIERRE LEMOYNE SIEUR D' (1661-1706), French-Canadian explorer and naval officer, born in Montreal, Canada. Appointed a midshipman in the French navy at the age of 14, he was sent to France and served there until 1679, when he returned to Canada. From 1686 to 1697 he led successive land and sea expeditions against stations of the Hudson's Bay Company in an effort to dislodge British power in Canada. In the latter year, after a victory over a superior British naval force, he captured Fort Nelson, thereby destroying the single remaining post of the Hudson's Bay Company in Canada. Commissioned to find and colonize the mouth of the Mississippi River, he sailed from France in 1698, reached the Gulf of Mexico, and established French power in Louisiana by founding colonies at what are now Biloxi, Miss., and Mobile, Ala. The renewal of hostilities between France and England interrupted his colonizing efforts. He was made a captain in the French navy in 1702. After assuming command of the West Indian fleet in 1706, he sailed for the West Indies, where he died from an attack of fever.

IBEX, common name for any of several

The Alpine ibex

species of large, wild, Old World goats characterized by long, backward-curved horns in the males. The horns have projecting knobs or shelves running across their forward surfaces. Ibexes stand about 3 ft. high at the shoulder, and are generally brown above with white rumps and underparts. They show remarkable agility and power in leaping about in the high mountain ranges where they live.

Ibexes are easily tamed. The bezoar goat (see GOAT), one of the ibexes, is believed to be the ancestor of the domestic goat. The Alpine ibex, or bouquetin, *Capra ibex,* was once common in the Alps, but has been hunted almost to extinction; it is now extant only on a preserve on the Italian side of Monte Rosa. The largest ibex, *C. sibirica,* which stands about 3⅓ ft. high at the shoulder, and which has horns almost 55 in. long, lives in central Asia in the Altai and Himalaya ranges. The jaal goat, or beden, *C. nubiana,* has slenderer horns than most of the other ibexes, and is found in Ethiopia, Egypt, and Arabia.

IBIS, common name for any of about thirty species of long-legged, long-necked wading birds in the Stork order, constituting with the spoonbills the family Threskiornithidae. Ibis are characterized by long, heavy, downcurving bills grooved above from base to tip. The birds average two feet in length, and have short tails. They live in large flocks

Ibis of Argentina (Phimosus infuscatus)

and feed on fish, shellfish, frogs, toads, and small reptiles. Unlike the closely related herons (q.v.), ibis fly with their necks straight and their heads held forward. They breed in marshes in warm regions throughout the world, and build their nests, which are about one foot in diameter, in weeds or bushes. The female lays three to five eggs, whitish or greenish, spotted with darker hues.

The Egyptian ibis, *Threskiornis aethiopica,* common in the Nile basin, was the sacred ibis of ancient times, depicted in the sculpture and painting of Egypt. This bird is white in general body color, with black head and neck and black tail feathers.

The white ibis, *Guara alba,* a white species with a scarlet face, is found from lower California and South Carolina s. into South America. The white-faced glossy ibis, *Plegadis guarauna,* so-called because a circle of white feathers surrounds the base of its bill, is a glossy reddish-brown species of western U.S., found from California and Kansas s. to South America. The scarlet ibis *G. rubra,* which occasionally is found in southern U.S., is common in South America, and is noted for its beautiful plumage, tinted with various shades of red.

The name wood ibis is given to various Old World species of ibis, and to an unrelated bird of the Stork family.

IBN EZRA, or ABENEZRA (1092-1167), in full, ABRAHAM BEN MEÏR IBN EZRA, Spanish scholar and author, born in Toledo, Spain. As a young man he became widely known as a poet and thinker. Shortly before 1140 he left Spain to travel and teach, spending more than twenty-five years in northern Africa, England, France, and Italy. The last years of his life were spent in Rome.

Ibn Ezra was the greatest scholar of medieval Spain; he was a master of numerous languages, including Hebrew, Arabic, and Aramaic. His most important works are scriptural commentaries, many of which are commonly included in Hebrew editions of the Old Testament. His attempt in these commentaries to derive the basic sense of the text by applying grammatical principles was criticised by the Talmudists; see TALMUD. He was the author of numerous books on mathematics, astronomy, philosophy, medicine, and astrology. Ibn Ezra was also an outstanding poet, and served as the inspiration for Robert Browning's poem, *Rabbi Ben Ezra.* His other writings include *Yōsōd Mēra* (1158), which explains the reasons for the Biblical commandments; *Isaiah; Miscellany of Hebrew Literature;* and *Diwan.*

IBN-KHALDUN, or (Ar.) 'ABD-AL-RAHMAN IBN-KHALDUN (1332-1406), Arab historian, born in Tunis. He was appointed to the religious office of grand cadi of Cairo in 1384, and later held a number of posts in the Egyptian government. As the author of the *Universal History,* the earliest work to embody an examination of the influence of physical environment, food supply, and similar factors on the development of states and empires, Ibn-Khaldun is regarded by many scholars as the founder of modern sociology. The work comprised three major sections: a preface, embodying a scholarly thesis on the philosophy of history; a history of the Arabs, principally those of Spain; and a history of the Berber tribes and Mohammedan dynasties of North Africa.

IBN-SAUD. See ABDUL-AZIZ IBN-SAUD.

IBO, a large Negro tribe consisting of a group of 33 subtribes living around the delta of the Niger River in Southern Nigeria. Their number is estimated at about 4,000,000. The majority are settled in independent towns or villages governed by a head chief and a group of local chiefs. Extended family groups, within which marriage is usually forbidden, inhabit a single district in a village, and reckon descent and authority patrilineally. Authority within the tribe is also assumed by membership in an age class, and secret societies based on these age classes control much of the Ibo ceremonies and rituals. The Ibo were at one time frequently raided by American slave traders; members of the tribe brought to the U.S. were known as Eboe.

IBRAHIM PASHA (1789-1848), Egyptian soldier, born in Kavalla, Macedonia, the son, or the adopted son, of Mehemet Ali (q.v.), the pasha of Egypt. He was placed in command of the Egyptian troops in Arabia in 1816, and after a campaign lasting two years subjugated the Wahabi tribesmen. In 1824 he was dispatched by his father to aid the sultan of Turkey in quelling a rebellion in Greece. He defeated the regular Greek troops, and when the Greeks launched a guerrilla campaign against him, he retaliated by devastating the country and deporting great numbers of the inhabitants to Egypt, where they were held as slaves. When the English, French, and Russian governments intervened diplomatically, Ibrahim was forced to withdraw from Greece in 1828. Three years later he launched an invasion of Syria, then under Turkish rule, defeated the Turkish armies in a series of battles, and in 1833 became governor of Syria. Turkey renewed the conflict in 1838, and Ibrahim again routed the Turkish forces. However, England and Austria, which wished to maintain the integrity of the Turkish empire, intervened with military forces and compelled Ibrahim to withdraw to Egypt in 1841. In 1848, when his father was senile, Ibrahim became viceroy of Egypt.

IBSEN, HENRIK (1828-1906), the greatest of Norwegian dramatists, born in Skien. He studied the sciences at a school in his native town, was assistant to a druggist in the town of Grimstad, and, beginning in 1850, studied medicine in Christiania (now Oslo). His first drama was the tragedy in blank verse *Catalina* (published in 1850 under the pseudonym of "Brynjolf Bjarme"). The successful production of his play *The Warrior's Mound* in Christiania in 1851 made him decide to give up the study of medicine and to pursue the career of dramatist. He wrote political satires for the weekly journal *Andhrimner,* which he also helped edit; was stage manager, from 1851 to 1857, of the theater established in Bergen by the noted violinist Ole Bull to encourage the Norwegian drama; became nationally famous through the production in 1856 of his historical drama *The Feast at Solhaug;* and from 1857 to 1862 was director of the Norwegian Theater at Christiania. This organization produced two of his most important early plays: *The

Warriors at Helgoland (1858), the first Norwegian national drama written in a realistic vein; and *Love's Comedy* (1862), in which love is destroyed by the social conventions attending courtship and marriage. *Love's Comedy* was the forerunner of the later group of plays, dealing with social and psychological themes, by which Ibsen is best known internationally. From 1863 to 1891 Ibsen lived outside of Norway, chiefly in Germany. Before his plays became well known he subsisted on a traveling scholarship and then an annual pension, both granted by the Storting, the Norwegian parliament. After 1891 he lived in Christiania.

Two themes formed the basis for all the plays he wrote from 1866 to the end of his writing career in 1900: the importance of the individual and the need for a society which would give the individual the fullest opportunity for self-development; and the evils caused in life by the denial of love. In the dramatic poem *Brand* (1866) Ibsen maintained the duty of the individual to be true to his best characteristics, and in the dramatic poem *Peer Gynt* (1867) he demonstrated the tragic final degeneration of an individual who lacks moral fiber and seeks to escape responsibility through dreaming and idle distraction. *The League of Youth* (1869),

Henrik Ibsen

a prose satire on Norwegian politics, shows the comic confusion caused by an attempt to take leadership on the part of a young man much like Peer Gynt in character. Beginning in 1877 Ibsen wrote the series of prose plays which made him world-famous. *The Pillars of Society* (1877) is a drama of a businessman who gives up love for wealth and social power; *A Doll's House* (1879) is a protest against marriage that is not based on love and on respect of the individual; *Ghosts* (1881) deals with the transmission of a diseased body and mind to the offspring of a morally unsound marriage; *An Enemy of the People* (1882) attacks social hypocrisy as exemplified by people who refuse to acknowledge the truth when it is not personally convenient to do so; *The Wild Duck* (1884) shows the reverse of this idea, namely, that a merely superficial grasp of a social truth even by people eager to accept it leads to tragic consequences. The rest of Ibsen's plays, which deal with various aspects of the individual's struggle with himself, with other individuals, and with society as a whole, and with the tragedy resulting from the denial of love, are *Rosmersholm* (1886), *The Lady from the Sea* (1888), *Hedda Gabler* (1890), *The Master Builder* (1892), *Little Eyolf* (1894), *John Gabriel Borkman* (1896), and *When We Dead Awaken* (1900).

The plays of Ibsen dealing with social and psychological themes aroused virulent criticism in Norway and then throughout Europe. His realistic depiction of the evils of modern society shocked those who were accustomed to the drama as mere entertainment and not as serious commentary on life, and his plays were declared immoral, cynical, and unduly pessimistic. However, critics such as William Archer and George Bernard Shaw (qq.v.) in England and Georg Brandes in Denmark championed Ibsen and the serious drama of ideas for which he stood, and in time Ibsen's plays were accepted everywhere as sincere and highly moral criticisms of society. They have been translated into most European languages and also into Japanese, and have exerted an immense influence on world drama.

IBYCUS (6th cent. B.C.), Greek lyric poet, born in Rhegium. He lived the life of a wandering minstrel and passed some time at the court of Polycrates, Tyrant of Samos. He is supposed to have been killed by robbers, near Corinth. When dying, Ibycus called on a flock of cranes to avenge his death; later one of the robbers, in a theater at Corinth, betrayed himself and his accomplices by crying "Behold the avengers of Ibycus!" when cranes flew overhead. Ibycus wrote seven books of poetry, most of them erotic. Only fragments are extant.

ICA. See PUTUMAYO.

ICARIANS, members of a 19th-century communistic society founded in the United States by the French social reformer Étienne Cabet (q.v.). Under the influence of the English utopian socialist Robert Owen, and inspired by *Utopia* by the English statesman Sir Thomas More (qq.v.), Cabet wrote a famous work, *Voyage en Icarie* (1840). In it he outlined his theories of social reform, including compulsory work for all members of society, progressive taxation, pensions for the aged, and equal distribution of the products of labor. In his plan, the government would have the sole right to engage in trade, and would be the supervisor of education and work. Seeking to put the ideal republic he envisaged into practice, Cabet raised money with the support of disciples throughout Europe, and bought a tract of land on the Red River, Texas, where he established a colony in 1848. In 1849 the colony was moved to the former Mormon town of Nauvoo, Ill. A period of prosperity ensued, but internal dissensions arose at Nauvoo, and in 1856 Cabet led a part of the community to Cheltenham, Iowa. In 1881 a few of the Iowa Icarians moved to California, but the movement was by that time in decline, and the last Icarian community was disbanded in 1895.

ICARUS. See DAEDALUS.

ICE, water in the solid state. Ice is colorless and transparent and crystallizes in the hexagonal system. The melting point of ice is 0°C. (32°F.), and the freezing point of pure water is usually said to be the same temperature, although experiments have shown that it is impossible to freeze water at temperatures as high as 0°C. unless the water is in contact with ice. Sea water freezes at a temperature several degrees lower than the freezing point of pure water.

One important property of ice is that it expands upon freezing and at 0°C. has a density of 0.9168 as compared to a density of 0.9998 for water at the same temperature; as a result ice floats in water. Another important effect of the expansion of ice on freezing is the geological effect. Water that enters minute cracks of rocks on the earth's surface creates an enormous pressure when it freezes, and splits or breaks the rocks. Thus the action of ice plays a great part in erosion (q.v.).

Because ice expands on freezing, an increase of pressure tends to change ice into water and, therefore, lowers the melting point of ice. For ordinary increases of pressure this effect is not very marked, and at a pressure 100 times the normal atmospheric pressure the melting point of ice is only about 1°C. less than at normal pressure. However at higher pressures several allotropic modifications of ice are formed which are designated Ice II, Ice III, Ice V, and Ice VI (ordinary ice is called Ice I). These allotropes are denser than water and their melting points *rise* with increased pressure. At about 6000 atmospheres (88,200 pounds per sq. in.) the melting point is again 0°C. (32°F.), and at a pressure of 20,000 atmospheres (294,000 pounds per sq. in.) the melting point rises to about 70° C. (158° F.).

When the temperature of the surface of an open body of water is reduced toward the freezing point, the surface water becomes denser as it cools, and therefore sinks, being replaced at the surface by warmer water from beneath. Eventually, because of this circulation, the entire body of water reaches a uniform temperature of 4.0°C. (39.2°F.), at which point water has its maximum density; if the water is cooled further, its density again decreases and finally ice is formed on the surface. Bodies of water freeze from the top down rather than from the bottom up because of these density differences. In rivers, however, ice is sometimes formed beneath the surface. On cold winter nights the surface of a swiftly-flowing stream may become cooled well below 0°C. because of its contact with the air. Such "undercooled" water, mixing with the warmer layers beneath, produces a spongy mass of ice crystals known as *frazil*, which floats downstream. Sometimes masses of frazil lodging under surface ice in quieter water may dam a stream and cause floods. Another form of below-surface ice is *anchor ice,* which is formed around rocks on stream beds. During cold nights enough heat may be radiated from the rocks so that they become sufficiently cool to freeze the water flowing around them. When the rocks are warmed by the sun in the daytime, masses of the anchor ice may gradually become detached and rise to the surface of the stream. See SNOW.

Icebergs. Whenever glaciers or ice sheets (see GLACIER) reach the sea, the movement of the glacier or sheet eventually pushes the end of the sheet into water which is deeper than the thickness of the glacier ice. When this condition occurs, portions of the end of the glacier break off and form floating masses known as *icebergs* or *bergs.* Icebergs are often of enormous size and may reach a height of 300 to 500 ft. above the surface of the sea. About 90 percent of the mass of an iceberg is beneath the surface, so that the visible portion of the berg is only a small part of the total. Icebergs are common in both the arctic and antarctic regions and are often carried into lower latitudes by sea currents, particularly in the North Atlantic. North Atlantic icebergs all come from the Great Greenland ice sheet and have been observed as far as 2000 m. from their origin. Because bergs represent a hazard to shipping, the U.S. Coast Guard maintains an Ice Patrol which reports the presence of bergs, and destroys by means of explosives and shell-fire bergs which have drifted into the shipping lanes.

ICE AGE. See QUATERNARY PERIOD.

ICEBERG. See ICE.

ICEBOAT, a framework or boatlike structure propelled over ice by sails and traveling on runners. Modern iceboats have several important features in common, including a central *hull* portion consisting of a fuselage or sometimes merely a plank, a *runner plank* extending at right angles to the hull and bearing two runners at its ends, and a third runner serving as a rudder and placed either forward or aft. Iceboating originated in ancient times in the Scandinavian countries, where primitive iceboats were used for haulage and transport. These boats probably consisted of sleds with sails attached or of skis with superstructures of platforms, masts, and sails. The earliest American models appeared on the Hudson River in the Poughkeepsie district about 1790; they traveled on double runners supporting a simple platform.

Iceboating as a sport originated on the Shrewsbury River in New Jersey, in about 1840. There the structure of the boats first assumed their standard modern form, with three runners in the form of a triangle. This design spread to other parts of the country, but the Shrewsbury River iceboaters continually improved it, and they retained leadership in the sport throughout the second half of the 19th century. About 1890 a group

Wide World Photo

Iceboats on the Shrewsbury River at Red Bank, New Jersey

of enthusiasts following the sport on the lakes of Wisconsin began to develop faster boats characterized by streamlining and light materials. They used the lightest woods consistent with minimum structural strength, and substituted aluminum for heavier metals. The hulls were redesigned as long, slim, airplanelike fuselages. The pilot and passengers sat in deep cockpits rather than on an exposed plank, and the rudder was placed in the bow rather than in the stern. The runners, too, were modified, having straight bottoms rather than the rockers of the older models. The Wisconsin innovations made the iceboats of the first decade of the 20th century the fastest conveyances then known to man; after their introduction the sport reached its peak in the U.S., and large, expensive, high-speed models were built in great numbers. The largest class for racing carried more than 750 sq.ft. of sail, and other classes, with maxima of 750, 450, 350, and 175 sq.ft. were entered in the more important racing meets. Since about 1935 manufacturers have been building smaller, cheaper boats, known by popular nicknames or trade names such as "Frostbites" and "Scooters", which often compare favorably in speed with larger models. The latest development in the field, a jet-propelled iceboat introduced on Lake

Hopatcong, N.J., in the winter of 1946-47, is said to be capable of a speed of 250 miles per hour, though no official records have yet been set by boats of this design.

Iceboats equipped with sails attain their maximum speed when sailing crosswind or partly into the wind; under such circumstances iceboats can travel several times as fast as the wind which is driving them. The official speed record for U.S. iceboats is 143 miles an hour, but some have traveled as fast as 160 miles an hour in unrecorded or unofficial "flights".

ICEBREAKER, a vessel designed to make or keep open a navigable passage through ice. It is equipped with a heavy, usually overhanging bow, and armored sides; the effectiveness of the sides in breaking up the ice is sometimes increased by a heavy gyroscope mounted within the ship to make it roll artificially. Icebreakers shatter the portion of the ice sheet directly ahead of them either by ramming or by running up onto the ice at their bows and breaking it with their weight; they are heavily built to withstand the shocks involved in these processes. The main use of such vessels has been in clearing channels during the winter in bodies of water such as the Great Lakes and the Baltic Sea, but in recent years they have been increasingly used in arctic and antarctic exploration.

ICE CREAM, a popular frozen food made of milk, cream, sugar, and flavoring. Ice cream was first made in Italy in the 17th century and appeared in the U.S. in the early 18th century. Ice cream manufacture, as an industry, began in America in 1851.

Early methods of manufacture, which are still sometimes used in home production of ice cream, consisted of placing the ingredients in a metal container, surrounded by a freezing mixture of ice and coarse salt, and mixing them until they were smooth. In modern plants the basic ingredients, plus gelatin, used as a *stabilizer* to give the product a smooth consistency, are poured into a tank in which they are mixed and pasteurized; they are then homogenized, to break up particles of butterfat, and cooled; the mixture is then piped to a freezing tank where it is beaten until smooth, and where nuts or fruits are sometimes added. The ice cream emerges from the freezing tank partially frozen, and is packed into containers which are stored in a refrigerated room until hard. During World War II, dehydrated ice cream was prepared for shipment overseas.

French ice cream is ice cream enriched with egg yolks; *parfait* and *mousse* are ice cream preparations which have not been beaten during the freezing process; *biscuit glacé* is ice cream to which rum or other alcoholic beverages have been added; *biscuit Tortoni* is a rich ice cream sprinkled with powdered almonds or macaroons; and *spumone* is a mousselike ice cream to which fruits and nuts have been added.

IÇEL, or ICHILI, il of s. Turkey, bordering on the Mediterranean Sea. The region comprising the present-day il was part of ancient Cilicia (q.v.). The capital and chief town, known as Mersin or Içel, is situated at the mouth of the Gök R., which drains into the Mediterranean Sea. Area, 3800 sq.m.; pop. (1950 prelim.) 317,853. Pop. of town (1950) 37,508.

ICELAND (Icelandic *Ísland;* Dan. *Island*), insular republic, consisting of the island of the same name and a number of small offlying islands, and bounded on the N. by the Arctic Ocean, on the E. by the Norwegian Sea, on the s. by the North Atlantic Ocean, and on the w. by Denmark Strait. The northernmost and southernmost limits of the island are demarcated by lat. 66°33' N. and 63°24' N. respectively, and it extends from long. 13°31' W. to long. 24°30' W., a distance of about 290 m.

Greenland, the nearest land mass, is about 155 miles N.W. of Iceland; Norway, the nearest part of the European mainland, is about 570 m. to the E. Scotland lies about 500 m. to the S.E.

The capital of Iceland and its only important town is Reykjavík (q.v.). Other towns, with their populations in 1951, are Akureyri (7263), Hafnarfjördur (5152), Vestmannaeyjar (3747), Siglufjördur (2980), and Isafjördur (2779). Area of Iceland, including peripheral islands, 39,709 sq.m.; pop. (1951 est.) 146,540.

Physical Features. In shape the island is generally elliptical, but the coast line, with a total length of about 3700 m., is deeply indented, especially in the w. and N. Important embayments on the w. coast are Faxa Bay and Breidi Fjord. Projecting northwestward between the latter and Húna Bay, one of the major indentations on the N. coast, is an irregularly formed peninsula fringed by precipitous cliffs. The peninsular coast line is over 30 percent of the total for the island. Volcanic in origin, Iceland consists predominantly of uninhabitable lava tablelands with mountainous outcroppings; lowlands, situated mainly in the s., occupy about 25 percent of the total area. The bulk of the Icelandic population is concentrated in these regions.

Elevations in the uplands average between 2000 and 3000 ft. Öraefajökul (6420 ft.), in the S.E., is the highest summit. Nearly 15 percent of the surface of the island is covered by snowfields and glaciers. Vatnajökull (or Klofajökull), a snowfield in the S.E., has an area of about 3300 sq.m. There are more than 120 glaciers on the island. Numerous small lakes and rivers characterize the hydrography of Iceland.

Iceland is remarkable for the number of its volcanoes, craters, and thermal springs, and for the frequency of its earthquakes. More than 100 extinct and quiescent volcanoes, including at least 25 which have erupted within historic times, are situated on the island. Noteworthy among the volcanoes are Mt. Hecla (4447 ft.), known to have erupted on 19 occasions up to 1947, Mt. Askja (3376 ft.), with a crater 34 sq.m. in area, Mt. Katla, which last erupted in 1860, and Laki, with about 100 separate craters. Vast lava fields, among them a field 1700 sq.m. in area, have been created by these and other volcanoes, and many eruptions have caused widespread devastation. In 1783, when the only known eruption of Laki occurred, molten lava, volcanic ashes and

American Scandinavian Review

Buildings in Reykjavik, the capital of Iceland

gasses, and torrential floods resulting from melting ice and snow ruined large tracts of arable land, destroyed about 80 percent of the livestock on the island, and created conditions leading to the death of more than 9000 persons.

Thermal springs are the most common phenomenon in Iceland. Particularly numerous in the volcanic areas, the springs occur as geysers, boiling mud lakes, and in various other forms. Great Geyser, generally regarded as the most spectacular, erupts at irregular intervals (usually from 5 to 36 hours), ejecting a column of boiling water between 80 and 150 ft. in height. Many homes and industrial establishments in Reykjavík are heated by water piped from nearby geysers.

Climate. Iceland has a relatively mild and equable climate, despite its proximity to the Arctic Regions. Due to oceanic influences, notably the Gulf Stream, climatic conditions are moderate in all sections of the island. The mean annual temperature at Reykjavík is 39.4° F., with a range from 34.2° F. in January to 51.6° F. in July. In the N.W., N., and E. coastal regions, subject to the effects of polar currents and drifting ice, temperatures are generally lower. Wind storms of considerable violence are characteristic during the winter season. Annual precipitation ranges from about 50 inches in the lowlands to about 79 inches in the interior.

Flora and Fauna. The vegetation of Iceland is of the Arctic-European type. Grass and heather are abundant along the southern coast, and afford pasturage for sheep and other livestock. Extensive forests probably existed on the island in prehistoric times, but present-day trees are relatively scarce; the principal species are beech, willow, birch, and mountain ash, which seldom attain a height exceeding 30 feet. Billberries and crowberries are the only kinds of fruit which grow on the island. The fox is probably the only quadruped indigenous to the island. Reindeer were introduced about 1770; rodents were brought in on ships. Neither reptiles nor batrachians (frogs and toads) are found. About 100 species of birds inhabit the island; many of these species are aquatic, among them the whistling swan and several kinds of duck. The eider duck is valued for its down. Whales and seals are plentiful along the coasts of Iceland, and there are almost seventy species of fish, notably the cod and the herring. Salmon and trout abound in the inland waters.

Industry and Production. About 30 percent of Iceland's population is engaged in agriculture; less than 1 percent of the land area is under cultivation. The principal crops are hay, turnips, and potatoes. Livestock raising is a major occupation. In a recent year the livestock herds included about 42,300 horses, 44,500 cattle, and 415,500 sheep. The fishing industry of Iceland gives employment to about 16 percent of the people. In a recent year the catch totaled over 370,000 long tons. Iceland's fisheries, regularly visited by the fishing fleets of Norway, Great Britain, and France, are the world's chief source of cod, and are also rich in herring, halibut, and plaice (a species of European flounder). Fish curing and canning and the production of cod-liver oil, woolen textiles, eiderdown comforters and pillows, fishing nets, paint, and soap are among the principal manufacturing industries. Most of these industries are small-scale enterprises employing approximately

21 percent of the total population.

Commerce. The imports of Iceland, valued in a recent year at about 922,069,000 krónur (16.26 kr.=$1.00), come principally from the United States, Great Britain, the Netherlands West Indies, and Denmark, and include machinery, automotive vehicles, gasoline, coal, timber and wooden articles, textiles, metals, hardware, paper, and cereals. Exports, valued at about 726,608,000 krónur, are absorbed chiefly by Great Britain, the United States, the Netherlands, and Italy, and include ice-packed fresh fish, salt fish, spiced herring, herring oil, cod-liver oil, herring guano (pulverized herring used for fertilizer), fresh and salted mutton, sheepskin, and wool.

Communications. Iceland has about 4500 m. of highways, but no railroads. In recent years automobiles have largely supplanted the traditional horse cart. Coastal steamers maintain regular sailings around the shores of the island, putting in at almost every port. The merchant marine consists of over 140 vessels of 100 or more gross tons. Air services link Reykjavík with other points on the island, and also connect Iceland with countries abroad.

Education and Religion. Illiteracy is virtually nonexistent. Education is compulsory for all children between the ages of seven and fifteen. In a recent year there were 213 elementary schools, with 15,115 enrolled pupils; 55 secondary schools, with 4575 pupils; and 60 technical and other schools, with about 5160 pupils. Mobile schools travel through the thinly populated portions of the island where no regular educational facilities are available. The University of Reykjavík, established in 1911, has departments of medicine, philosophy, theology, and law. The majority of the population of Iceland are communicants of the state-supported Evangelical Lutheran Church, but absolute freedom of worship is guaranteed to all religious denominations.

Government. Iceland is governed according to the provisions of the constitution of 1920, as amended in 1934 and 1941. At the head of the government is the president, elected for a term of four years by popular suffrage. Executive power is exercised under the president by a six-member cabinet, including a prime minister. Parliament, called the *Althing,* has an aggregate of 52 members, and is divided into two houses, the upper house having 17 members, the lower house 35. Administratively, the island is organized into sixteen provinces, each province subdivided into one or two municipal districts. The sixteen provinces are governed by a like number of ex-

ecutive deputies. Independent of the provinces, but constituting administrative districts co-ordinate with them, are thirteen urban municipalities. Men and women who have passed their twenty-first birthday are entitled to vote.

History. Iceland was not visited by Europeans, as far as is known, until the end of the 8th century A.D., when a number of Culdees, or Celtic monks, landed on the island. About 850 it was discovered, or rediscovered, by Norse explorers, one of whom gave the island its present name. Soon thereafter Norsemen began to arrive in large numbers, partly in consequence of the despotism of Harold I of Norway. Many natives of Ireland were among the early settlers. Political units consisting of free landowners and closely resembling the clan were developed during the initial period of colonization, and permanent settlements were established, including Reykjavík. About 930 the various clans, in an effort to centralize authority on the island, drafted the document known in history as the *Constitution of Ulfjot,* establishing a rough political framework and providing for a yearly assembly, the Althing. Constitutional modifications were soon introduced, specifically the *Reforms of Thord Gellir,* which divided Iceland into four districts and set up the so-called quarter court at the head of each district; and the *Innovations of Skapti the Law-Speaker,* which established a fifth court as the supreme tribunal for criminal cases. Freedom and a measure of justice were guaranteed under the basic law provided by these documents, and despite certain internal weaknesses, such as failure to curb the power of the clan chieftains, the Icelandic republic endured for more than three centuries. During this period, often identified as the golden age of national history, Icelandic mariners and heroes performed many of the legendary exploits recounted in the sagas of Icelandic literature (q.v.).

Christianity was introduced into Iceland by Norwegian missionaries about 1100. The Church effected numerous reforms and, for a time, stabilized political relations among the clans. In the 13th century a number of chieftains challenged the power of the ecclesiastical authorities, precipitating civil war. At length, in 1262, the opposing factions appealed to the Norwegian king Haakon IV, who prevailed upon Iceland to unite itself to Norway. In violation of the treaty consummating the union, the Norwegian government imposed severe restrictions on Icelandic political and commercial activity, initiating a protracted period of social and economic stagnation. Recurring natural catastrophes, particularly destructive volcanic eruptions and epidemics of bubonic plague, brought the nation to the brink of ruin.

With the accession (1380) of Olaf II, King of Denmark, to the Norwegian throne, Iceland was placed under Danish sovereignty. The Danish monarchs perpetuated the restrictive policies of their Norwegian predecessors. In 1540 Christian III of Denmark introduced the Reformation (q.v.) into Iceland, and the Protestant faith quickly spread throughout the island. During the 18th century, famine, smallpox, sheep disease, and destructive volcanic eruptions in 1765 and 1783 took a great toll of life and property. Iceland was captured by Great Britain during the Napoleonic Wars, but was returned to Denmark again by the Treaty of Vienna in 1815.

The Icelandic people, taking advantage of the opportunities afforded by the declining power of absolutism in Europe, conducted a vigorous struggle for political reforms during the 19th century. Under the leadership of the scholar and statesman Jón Sigurdsson (1811–79), the Icelanders obtained (1874) from Denmark a constitution granting limited home rule. The nation won complete domestic autonomy in 1903. By the terms of the Icelandic-Danish Act of Union (1918), Iceland became a sovereign kingdom under the crown of Denmark.

Before the outbreak of World War II in 1939, the German air ministry vainly sought permission to establish bases in Iceland, ostensibly for an air service between the island and Germany. Following the German occupation of Denmark on April 9, 1940, Iceland established direct diplomatic relations with the United States and Great Britain. A month later British troops occupied the island. The British government declared that the action had been taken to forestall a possible German invasion of Iceland, and guaranteed that there would be no interference with local administration, but the Icelandic government formally protested against the British occupation. Early in 1941 German airplanes attacked the British airfield near Reykjavík. German air attacks were likewise directed against shipping in Icelandic waters.

On May 16, 1941, the Althing adopted four constitutional amendments designed to effect Iceland's complete separation from Denmark. Danish officials were assured, however, that action on the matter would be postponed until the end of the war. The political leader Sveinn Björnsson, a former ambassador to Denmark, was elected regent.

On July 7, 1941, U.S. President Franklin Delano Roosevelt announced that in accordance with an agreement with the premier of Iceland, U.S. naval units were supplementing, and would eventually supplant, British forces in the defense of the island. U.S. forces arrived in Iceland on the same day. On July 10 the Althing voted approval of the "agreement between the Government and the President of the United States for American military protection of Iceland while the present war lasts". The U.S. Navy began the construction of installations at Reykjavík later in the year; for the duration of the war the port served as an American naval base.

In February, 1944, the Althing by a unanimous vote adopted a resolution terminating the Icelandic-Danish Act of Union. The resolution was approved by an overwhelming majority in a plebiscite held in May. Iceland was formally proclaimed a republic on June 17, and the Althing elected Regent Björnsson president for a one-year term. During a visit to the capital of the United States later in the year President Björnsson, commenting on rumors that the U.S. government might seek to establish peacetime military bases in Iceland after the war, declared that his country was unalterably opposed to such an arrangement.

In the absence of opposition candidates for the presidency, the Althing cancelled (March, 1945) the presidential election planned for May and elected Björnsson for the regular four-year term beginning in June. During 1945 reports were widely circulated that the United States had begun to negotiate for a long-term lease of the military and naval bases on the island. The reports engendered uneasiness in Icelandic political circles, especially among groups under communist influence. In April, 1946, the government revealed that American proposals regarding the bases had been rejected. Soon thereafter Iceland concluded with the Soviet Union a highly favorable trade treaty, under the terms of which the U.S.S.R. agreed to purchase a major portion of the fish catch. On September 19 the United States submitted a note to Iceland formally proposing that all American troops be withdrawn from the island within six months; and that U.S. airfields be transferred to the Icelandic government, with the proviso, however, that a particular airport be made available for use by aircraft (both civil and military) operated by or on behalf of the United States in connection with the fulfilment of U.S. obligations in occupied Germany. The Icelandic government accepted these proposals despite the vigorous opposition of its two communist members. Communist-organized street demonstrations in Reykjavík and a twenty-four-hour general strike by the membership of the Reykjavík Trade Union Council failed to alter the government's decision. The evacuation of the remaining U.S. military personnel began in October.

The General Assembly of the United Nations approved the U.N. membership application of Iceland on November 9, 1946, making the island republic the fifty-third member of the world organization. In July, 1948, Iceland formally adhered to the European Recovery Program (q.v.), primarily an American-financed plan for the economic rehabilitation of western Europe. The country shortly thereafter received a $2.3 million loan under the program for the development of the fishing industry. Despite violent communist opposition the Althing approved (March 30, 1949) the North Atlantic Treaty (q.v.), an alliance designed to discourage Soviet aggression in Europe. President Björnsson was re-elected without opposition in June.

As part of its obligations under the North Atlantic Treaty, Iceland signed (May 5, 1951) an agreement with the United States authorizing American military forces to garrison bases on the island. A small contingent of United States troops arrived in Reykjavík on May 7.

President Björnsson died on Jan. 25, 1952. In a special election, held on June 29, the Social Democratic leader Asgeir Asgeirsson (1894–) was chosen to succeed him. The presidential election was the first to be based on the direct ballot since Iceland became a republic. Meanwhile, the Icelandic government, following the example of Norway, extended the limit of its territorial waters from 3 miles to 4 miles. This action led to a sharp dispute with Great Britain, long active in the rich Icelandic fisheries. Great Britain filed a formal protest with Iceland on May 2. On May 15 the Icelandic government rejected the protest, whereupon Great Britain indicated it would place the issue before the International Court of Justice. During 1952 the most pressing domestic economic problem was the high cost of living, which rose more than 50 percent within a two-year period. British fish-interests, resentful over the exclusion of their

American Scandinavian Review
Fisherman of Reydarfjörthur, Iceland

vessels from Icelandic waters, imposed a virtual embargo in 1953 on imports of fish from Iceland, aggravating the fisheries dispute and causing a further deterioration of the republic's economy. Charging the embargo had official sanction, the Icelandic government refused in November to submit the dispute to the International Court.

ICELANDIC LITERATURE, the literature created by the inhabitants of Iceland from about the 9th century A.D. to the present time. Because the original inhabitants of Iceland were chiefly Norwegians, who colonized the country in the 9th century (see ICELAND: *History*), Icelandic literature, the only Scandinavian literature which flourished in medieval times, is sometimes referred to as Old Norse Literature. Icelandic literature is divided into three principal periods: (1) Classical, (2) Post-Classical, and (3) Modern.

THE CLASSICAL PERIOD (from about the 9th to about the 14th century). The form of literature for which Iceland is most famous, the saga (q.v.), originated during the classical period; sagas were tales of legendary or historical Icelandic heroes or heroines, and were composed in prose by bards or scalds (see SCALD or SKALD) for recitation at feasts, entertainments, and other gatherings. These tales were first written down between 1140 and 1220; none of the manuscripts dating from that time is extant, and present knowledge of the Icelandic sagas derives from the 14th-century collections of manuscripts which were the result of much editing, revising, and amplifying of the original manuscripts. The authors of the sagas are unknown. It is believed that about one hundred and twenty sagas were written in the 14th century; out of this number about forty are extant. They include the *Egla Saga* (870-980), the tale of the heroic poet Egil, one of the early settlers in Iceland; the *Laxdaela Saga* (910-1026), which treats of the romantic life of the heroine Gudrun; the *Nial Saga* (970-1014), considered the best of Icelandic sagas, a complex account of the life and good deeds of Nial, a benevolent lawyer; and the *Gretti Saga* (1010-31), which tells of the career of a famous Icelandic outlaw. The central characters of the above-mentioned sagas are either legendary or flourished in periods of history prior to the time of writing. In the 13th century the saga form was used for a new purpose, that of writing the biographies of contemporary personages. This new type of saga, although less epic in style than the original examples, was, however, similarly characterized by simplicity, realism, and a strictly objective point of view on the part of the writer, who allowed none of his own emotions to appear in the narrative. The best of the biographical type of saga are the *Islendinga Saga*, covering events of the years 1202 to 1262, and the *Thorgils Saga*, narrating events of 1252 to 1261; these sagas, both by Lawman Sturla (about 1214-84), tell of the lives of noted Icelanders of the 13th century and give a vivid account of the current civil wars in Iceland.

The classical period of Icelandic literature is also noted for two additional forms of writing, the edda (q.v.) and historical works. The term *edda* is applied to each of two famous collections of Icelandic literature: the *Poetic Edda* or *Elder Edda* (9th to 12th century), a collection of thirty lays or poems by anonymous writers; and the *Prose Edda* or *Younger Edda* (13th century), an account of Norse mythology (see SCANDINAVIAN MYTHOLOGY) and also a guide to poetic composition by the historian and poet Snorri Sturluson (see SNORRI). The greatest Icelandic writer of history was Ari Thorgilsson (1067-1148); his best-known work is *Book of Kings*, which tells the story of the kings of Norway from the legendary period of their first dynasty, the Ynglings, to 1066, the date of the death of King Harald Haardraade (see NORWAY: *History*). An important historical work of the 13th century, based in part on that of Thorgilsson, is the *Heimskringla* (q.v.) by Snorri Sturluson.

THE POST-CLASSICAL PERIOD (from about the 14th to the 19th century). This period was chiefly one of accomplishment in translation, and in compilation and collection of manuscripts. The 14th century was marked by the copying and collecting of works previously written. In the 16th century a number of notable Icelandic translations of the Bible were made by Protestant theologians. Among these translations were that of Odd Gottskalksson (d.1556), published in Denmark in 1540, and that of Bishop Gudbrand, published in Iceland in 1584 and based in part on the work by Gottskalksson; Gudbrand's Bible served as a model for every Icelandic version of the Bible until 1826. Highly popular in Iceland until the 19th century was the *Postil-Book,* a collection of sermons and other theological material, by Bishop John Vidalin (1666-1720). In the 17th century a number of collections of Icelandic folk tales, fairy tales, proverbs, and other folk literature were made by various Icelandic scholars, laying the foundation for the important collection of folk literature contained in *Popular Legends of Iceland* (1862-64) by the Icelandic antiquary Jón Árnason (1819–88). In the late 17th and early 18th century the noted Icelandic philologist and antiquary Árni Magnússon (1663–1730) collected all the obtainable manuscripts of the Icelandic literature of the classical period. This collection, which required over forty years to complete, has been in the University of Copenhagen since about 1730 and has been invaluable to students of Icelandic literature.

MODERN PERIOD (19th century to the present). The chief characteristic of the Icelandic literature dating from the beginning of the 19th century is its nationalistic spirit. The modern period is also the first since the classical in which a genuine creative spirit is manifest in Icelandic writing. The following are chronological lists of representative Icelandic writers of the modern period, together with characteristic works. Where dates are not conjoined to an author's name, further information will be found in a separate article under his name.

Poets: Jónas Hallgrimsson, the principal lyric poet of Iceland, whose poems, all contained in the single volume *Ljóðmæli og Onnur Rit,* inaugurated the use in modern Icelandic literature of the Icelandic language purged of outworn figures of speech and foreign words; Grímur Thomsen (1820-96), among whose works are Ljóðmæli ("Poems", 1880) and Ljóðmæli Nýtt og Gamalt ("Poems Old and New", 1906); Benedikt S. Gröndal (1826-1907), author of Kvæðabók ("Poems", 1900), the satire Heljarsloðarorusta (1859, a burlesque of the battle of Solferino), and the autobiography Dægradvöl (1923); Steingrímur Thorsteinsson (1831-1913), among whose works are volumes of poems published in 1881, 1893, and 1910, and translations into Icelandic of poems of Goethe, Schiller, and Byron; Matthías Jochumsson (1835-1920), poet laureate of Iceland (1900-20), whose complete poetic works were posthumously published in 1936; Stephan G. Stephansson (1854-1927), who lived with Icelandic colonists in the United States and Canada and wrote poems in Icelandic on life and nature in both America and Iceland, such as Andvökur ("Wakeful Nights", 6 vols., 1909-38); Einar Benediktsson (1864-1940), one of the greatest of modern Icelandic poets, among whose works are Hafblik ("Smooth Seas", 1906) and Hvammar ("Hollows", 1930); Stefán frá Hvítadal (1887-1933), among whose works are the volume of lyrics Söngvarförumannsinns ("The Songs of the Wanderer", 1918); Davíð Stéfánsson (1895-), author of six volumes of poetry (1919-36); Jón Magnússon (1896-1944), among whose works is Bláskógar ("Blue Forests", 1925); Jón Helgason (1899-), whose works include Úr Landsuðri ("From the Southeast", 1939); and Tómas Guðmundsson (1901-), author of Fagra Veröld ("Fair World", 1933) and other works.

Playwrights: Matthiás Jochumsson (1835-1920), author of two noted plays, Útilegumennirnir ("The Outlaws", 1864), and Jón Arason (1900); Indriði Einarsson (1851-1939), a popular writer of romantic and realistic dramas; Jóhann Sigurjónsson (1880-1919), who attained world fame with Bjærg-Ejvind og hans Hustru (1911, written in Danish; Icelandic title Fjalla-Eyvindur, "Eyvind of the Hills"); and Davíð Stéfánsson (1895-), among whose plays is Vopn Guðanna ("The Weapons of the Gods", 1943).

Novelists and Short-Story Writers: Jón Thordarson Thóroddsen, generally considered the greatest of modern Icelandic novelists, author of Piltur og Stúlka ("Lad and Lass", 1850) and Mathur og Kona ("Man and Wife", published posthumously, 1876); Porsteinn Erlingsson (1858-1914), among whose works is the volume of animal stories Mál-

leysingjar ("The Dumb Ones", 1928); Jóhann Magnús Bjarnason (1867-1945), author of adventure stories, who, like the poet Stephansson, lived in Canada; Jón Trausti (1873-1918), among whose works are the volume of stories Sögur frá Skaftáreldi ("Stories from the Eruption of Skafta", 2 vols., 1912-13) and the novel Bessi Gamli ("Old Bessi", 1918); Gunnar Gunnarsson (1889-), among whose writings are the novels Livets Strand ("The Shore of Life", 1915) and Heiðaharmur ("The Heath Laments", 1940); G.G. Hagalín (1898-), author of the novels Kristrún í Hamravik (1933) and Sturla í Vogum (2 vols., 1938); Kristmann Guðmundsson (1902-), author of the novels Morgunn Lífsins ("Morning of Life", 1932) and Jordens Barn ("Children of Earth", 1934); and Halldór Kiljan Laxness (1902-), novelist of social protest, whose novels include Undir Helgahnúk ("Under the Holy Mountain", 1924) and Ljós Heimsins ("The Light of the World", 4 vols., 1937-40).

Essayists and Writers of Other Types of Prose Literature: Sigurður Nordal (1886-), author of Íslenzk Menning ("Icelandic Culture", Vol. 1, 1942); and þorbergur þorðarson (1889-), author of the essays written from the Socialist point of view Bréf til Láru ("Letter to Laura", 1924).

ICELAND MOSS, common name of an erect, mosslike, foliaceous lichen, Cetraria islandica, which grows in mountainous and low rocky regions of Iceland, Norway, Great Britain, and Ireland. Iceland moss ranges from light brown to pale gray in color. It grows from 3 to 4 inches tall, with tubular branches tipped with fringed lobes. The plant contains about 70 percent of an amorphous starch called lichenin. Iceland moss is used as food by Icelanders and Laplanders; a bitter principle which the plant contains is removed by steeping in order to make it palatable. Small quantities of the plant are used in sizing paper and in dressing the warp in weaving.

ICELAND SPAR, a colorless, transparent variety of calcite (q.v.). It exhibits the property of double refraction to such a strong degree that it is used in optical instruments for obtaining polarized light, particularly in the form of the Nicol prism (q.v.). The chief source of the mineral in the past has been Iceland, but with the depletion of deposits in Iceland the greatest supply of the mineral now comes from South Africa.

ICENI. See BOADICEA.

ICE PLANT, common name of a hardy annual herb, *Mesembryanthemum crystallinum,* belonging to the Carpetweed family. It is native to warm, dry climates all over the world. The ice plant is a fleshy, spreading plant, having leaves covered with large, shining vesicles which have the appearance of ice. The inconspicuous flowers bear many slender, pinkish-white petals. The plant grows well in rocky or sandy situations and is extensively cultivated in rock gardens. When grown on alkaline ground, the plant removes soda, potash, and other alkaline salts from the soil, which may then be used for cultivation. The plant was formerly often burned to produce an impure variety of soda ash called *barilla.* Several other members of the same genus are also called ice plants. The Hottentot's-fig, *M. edule,* is a South African plant which bears edible fruits, and is used as a sand binder on the coast of s. California. The beach apple, sea fig, or fig marigold, *M. aequilaterale,* is a small plant with thick, triangular leaves, which is native to the coast of California.

ICHNEUMON. See MONGOOSE.

ICHNEUMON FLY (Gr. *ichneumon,* "the tracker"), common name for any of several thousand species of parasitic hymenopterus insects constituting the superfamily Ichneumonoidea. Ichneumon flies are world-wide in distribution, and are economically important because their larvae feed on and destroy insects injurious to man, especially moths. The larvae also feed on many harmless and some helpful insects, including other species of valuable ichneumon flies; the last-named parasites are themselves sometimes parasitized by still other species. The adult female ichneumon fly, which feeds on plant sap, lays her eggs beneath the skin of an insect larva, or on the larva or egg. Many species have long, sharp ovipositors (egg-laying organs) with which they pierce earth or wood to place their eggs near a burrowing insect, which they locate by smell. The larvae consume the host; occasionally they

Female ichneumon fly, about 2 inches long

allow it to live long enough to spin a cocoon, and then kill it and pupate within its cocoon.

The largest family of ichneumon flies is Ichneumonidae, in which the first abdominal segment is large and rounded. *Ophion macrurum,* a common American species, is about one inch long. See PARASITE.

ICHNOLOGY. See PALEONTOLOGY.

ICKES, HAROLD LE CLAIRE (1874–1952), American lawyer, government official, and journalist, born in Frankstown Township, Pa., and educated at the University of Chicago. After working for some years as a reporter for several Chicago newspapers, he began to practice law in Chicago in 1907. He later participated in a number of campaigns for the election of reform candidates to positions in the municipal government of Chicago, and in 1912 he played a leading role in the formation of the Progressive Party (q.v.), organized by Theodore Roosevelt as a dissident offshoot of the Republican Party. In 1916 Ickes was the campaign manager of the Republican Presidential candidate Charles Evans Hughes. After the entry of the United States into World War I in 1917, Ickes joined the staff of the Young Men's Christian Association in France. Throughout the 1920's, Ickes was one of the most active members of the Republican Party, acquiring a wide reputation as an exponent of liberal reform. In 1933 he became secretary of the interior in the New Deal (q.v.) cabinet of President Franklin D. Roosevelt, who made him administrator of public works in July of the same year. In that capacity Ickes was responsible for the disbursement of $3,300,000,000 appropriated by Congress for the construction of public works, in order to alleviate the effects of the depression.

Throughout the 1930's Ickes continued to serve as one of Roosevelt's chief assistants in the effectuation of the President's social-reform program. In 1941, shortly before the entry of the United States into World War II, he was appointed to the key posts of petroleum administrator and solid-fuels administrator. After Roosevelt's death in 1945, Ickes' disapproval of the policies initiated by President Harry S. Truman caused him to resign in 1946 from his positions in the government. Later in that year he began to write a daily newspaper column, comprising chiefly political analysis and commentary, which appeared in newspapers in many of the largest cities of the United States. Among the books written by Ickes are *The New Democracy* (1934), *Back to Work* (1935), *America's House of Lords* (1939), *The Third Term Bugaboo* (1940), and *Autobiography of a Curmudgeon* (1943). The first volume of his *Secret Diary* was published posthumously in 1953.

ICONOCLASM (Gr. *eikon*, "image"; *klæin*, "to break"), name given to any movement against the religious use of images, but especially to that which disturbed the Eastern Church in the 8th and 9th centuries. In 726 the Byzantine emperor Leo III, known as the Isurian, issued an edict forbidding his people to venerate sacred images, and shortly thereafter issued another edict ordering the destruction of the images. The pope and the patriarch of Constantinople declared the veneration of images to be in conformance with the doctrines and practices of the church, and excommunicated the emperor. The controversy raged with great bitterness until the Empress Irene accepted the condemnation of the Iconoclasts by the Council at Nicæa in 787. The controversy was revived under Nicephorus, Irene's successor, and was finally settled under the Empress Theodora in 842, when the veneration of images was restored.

ICONOSCOPE. See TELEVISION.

ICTERUS. See JAUNDICE.

ICTINUS (5th century B.C.), Greek architect. He designed the Parthenon in association with Callicrates. The temple of Apollo Epicurius at Bassæ, near Phigalia, and the Telesterion çt Eleusis (see ELEUSINIAN MYSTERIES) are also ascribed to him.

ID, in psychoanalytic theory, one of the three basic elements of personality, the others being the *ego* and the *superego* (qq.v.). The id is the major portion of the mind which in common usage is called the "unconscious", and to which psychoanalysts have ascribed a specialized content and a group of specialized functions. According to them, the id is the source of the dynamic and instinctual content of mental life, including such drives as urges, wishes, and affective motives. In strict Freudian theory (as distinct from a number of neo-Freudian variations and developments), the energy behind such drives is known as the *libido* (q.v.), a generalized force, basically sexual in nature, through which the sexual and psychosexual nature of the individual finds expression in the mind. The drives resident in the id, which are often socially unacceptable or mutually contradictory, are usually the starting point for mechanisms of inhibition and repression;

Harold Ickes

disguised or distorted, they are the basis for much of the content of dreams, and for many of the conflicts both of everyday life and of the neurotic or psychotic personality. See PSYCHOANALYSIS; PSYCHOLOGY, ABNORMAL.

IDA, a mountain range of ancient Phrygia in Asia Minor, now known by its Turkish name, Kaz-Dagh. The highest peak (5750 ft.) of the southern part of the range was called Mt. Gargarus; at its northern base was situated the city of Troy. The range is famous in mythology as the place where Ganymede was carried off to Olympus by the eagle of Zeus; where Paris judged the beauty of the three goddesses Hera, Athena, and Aphrodite; and where the Olympian gods stood to watch the battles of the Trojan War on the plain below.

IDAHO, one of the Mountain States of the United States, bounded on the N. by Canada, on the E. by Montana and Wyoming, on the S. by Utah and Nevada, and on the W. by Oregon and Washington. It ranks as the twelfth State of the Union in area, the forty-third (1950) in population, and the thirtieth in order of admission after the 13 original States, having been admitted as a State on July 3, 1890. The State capital and largest city is Boise (q.v.); Pocatello, Idaho Falls, Twin Falls, Nampa, Lewiston, and Coeur d'Alene (qq.v.) are the next-largest cities in descending order of population. Idaho has an extreme length of about 490 m. from N. to S. and a maximum width of about 300 m. The area of the State is 83,557 sq.m., including 749 sq.m. of inland water surface. Pop. (1950) 588,637.

One of the most mountainous States of the Union, Idaho has an average elevation of about 5000 ft. The main chain of the Rocky Mts. traverses almost the entire length of eastern Idaho, and various subsidiary ranges and spurs of the chain project across the N. central part of the State to its western boundary. Among the principal ranges of the Rockies in E. Idaho are the Bitterroot Mts., with a maximum elevation (Mt. Ajax) of 10,900 ft. and numerous summits over 8000 ft., and the Cabinet Mts., with a maximum elevation of about 9000 ft. A section of the Continental Divide, the crest of the main chain of the Rockies, demarcates part of the Montana-Idaho boundary. Important subsidiary ranges of the Rockies in Idaho include the Lemhi Range, with elevations up to 11,324 ft.; Lost River Range, in which is

situated Borah Peak (12,655 ft.), the highest point in the State; and the Salmon River Mts., containing elevations up to 10,328 ft. Several lesser uplifts are situated in the extreme S. portion of Idaho. Lying between and to the N. of these uplifts is the Snake R. plain, an upland plateau stretching across the State in a crescent-shaped belt 50 to 75 m. wide and 350 m. in length along its medial line. The elevation of this plain increases from 2114 ft. above sea level on the W. to 4959 ft. on the E. Geologically, it consists principally of lava outpoured in great horizontal sheets in the Tertiary period, of lake and stream sedimentation, and of aeolian deposits. The plain was formerly arid sagebrush land but extensive irrigation projects have transformed it into the most productive agricultural area of the State.

The Snake R. (q.v.) traverses the plain in box canyons in the E. part of the State and in built-up flood plains in the W. In addition to the Snake R., which empties into the Columbia R., the Boise, Payette, Salmon, and Clearwater rivers drain the center of the State; the Kootenai, Pend Oreille, and Spokane drain the N. part of the State; and the Bear R. drains the S. part of the State. In the

Idaho State Chamber of Commerce

Shoshone Falls on the Snake River, near the city of Twin Falls in southern Idaho

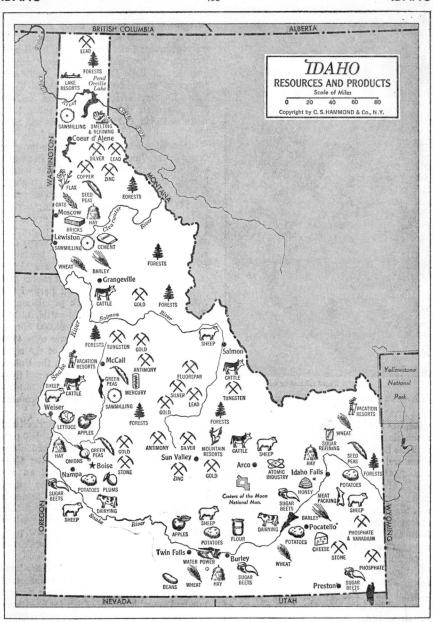

N. are numerous lakes, notably Lake Pend Oreille, largest fresh-water lake wholly within the State, and Coeur d'Alene and Priest lakes. In the center of the State are the Payette lakes, and in the S.E., extending across the Utah boundary, Bear Lake.

Pronounced aridity and sharp diurnal and seasonal variations of temperature are characteristic of climatic conditions in the State. In the N. portion oceanic influences, particularly moist air masses drifting eastward from the Pacific Ocean, have a moderating influence on extremes of heat and cold, and the chinook, a downward-moving, warm, dry

Idaho State Chamber of Commerce

Scene in mountains near Ketchum, Idaho

wind, has a similar effect on conditions in the mountains. The average annual temperature at Boise is 51° F.; average annual daily maximum and minimum temperatures are 62.8° F. and 39.4° F. During January, the coldest month of the year in Idaho, temperatures at Boise average −28° F.; temperatures for August, the hottest month, average 112° F. The average annual rainfall in the vicinity of Boise totals about 13 inches; annual snowfall averages somewhat over 24 inches.

Agriculture is the most important industry of Idaho. In 1950 farms in the State numbered nearly 40,300, with a total area of about 13,225,000 acres and an aggregate value in excess of $905,495,000. About 70 percent of the farms, occupying over 2,135,000 acres, are under irrigation. The principal region dependent on irrigation for crop production is the Snake R. plain, one of the most fertile areas in the State. Among major irrigation facilities in this region are Anderson Ranch Dam (456 ft. high) and Reservoir, on the South

Fork of the Boise R., in Elmore County; Arrowrock Dam (350 ft. high) and Reservoir, on the Boise R., between Boise and Elmore counties; Falls Dam (94 ft. high) and Reservoir, on the Snake R., in Power County; and Salmon Falls Dam (220 ft. high) and Reservoir, on Salmon Falls Creek, in Twin Falls County. Irrigation projects include 5100 diversion dams, 360 reservoirs, 1370 wells, and over 15,750 m. of canals and pipe lines.

Idaho is one of the chief potato-growing States in the Union, ranking second in annual yield after Maine; in 1953 the Idaho potato harvest totaled about 41,440,000 bushels. Other leading crops, with production estimates for 1953 are wheat, 42,828,000 bu.; barley, 10,112,000 bu.; oats, 7,392,000 bu.; dry beans, 135,000 tons; hay, 2,588,000 tons.; corn, 2,484,000 bu.; sugar beets, 1,350,000 tons; and apples, 1,554,000 bu. Extensive tracts of semiarid farm land in the State are highly suitable for grazing, and livestock raising and dairying comprise an important part of the rural economy. The livestock population in 1953 included about 1,227,000 cattle, 1,030,000 sheep, 143,000 swine, and 68,000 horses. In a recent year the wool clip was over 4700 tons, a total making Idaho one of the eight ranking wool-producing States in the Union. Cash receipts from the sale of crops and livestock in 1952 amounted to nearly $376,342,000; farm income from Federal government subsidies was about $4,584,000.

Lumbering is the principal nonagricultural industry of Idaho. Forests cover about 40 percent of the total area of the State, and Idaho ranks second among the States (after California) in national-forest acreage, an aggregate of over 21,500,000 acres. The largest stand of virgin pine in the United States is situated in Idaho; other species of timber trees indigenous to the State include western red cedar, western white pine, yellow pine, larch, white fir, Douglas fir, and Engelmann spruce.

Sawmilling, veneer milling, and other lumber enterprises comprise the most important manufacturing industry. There are several hundred sawmills, one of which (at Lewiston) is the largest in the world. Beet-sugar refining, meat packing, flour milling, the canning and drying of fruits and vegetables, and the manufacture of malt liquors, brick and hollow tile, concrete products, metal castings, machinery, and mattresses and bedsprings are other leading industries.

(continued in next volume)